ייִדיש אויסגאַבעס און פֿאָרשונג

Jiddistik Edition & Forschung
Yiddish Editions & Research

Herausgegeben von Efrat Gal-Ed,
Roland Gruschka und Simon Neuberg

Band 8

Socialist *Yiddishlands*

Language Politics and Transnational Entanglements between 1941 and 1991

Edited by
Miriam Chorley-Schulz and Alexander Walther

d|u|p

Yidish: oysgabes un forshung
Jiddistik: Edition & Forschung
Yiddish: Editions & Research

Herausgegeben von Efrat Gal-Ed, Roland Gruschka und Simon Neuberg

Band 8

Socialist Yiddishlands
Language Politics and Transnational Entanglements between 1941 and 1991

This publication is supported by

First Edition

d|u|p düsseldorf university press is an imprint of Walter de Gruyter GmbH

Library of Congress Control Number: 2023935920
Bibliographic information published by the Deutsche Nationalbibliothek
The Deutsche Nationalbibliothek lists this publication in the Deutsche Nationalbibliografie; detailed bibliographic data are available on the Internet at http://dnb.dnb.de.

ISBN 978-3-11-076386-7
e-ISBN (PDF) 978-3-11-076409-3
ISSN (Print) 2702-9425
ISSN (Online) 2702-9433

Cover design, typography, typesetting: Efrat Gal-Ed
Printing and binding: Memminger MedienCentrum AG
Main fonts: Adobe Garamond, Hadassah EF
Paper: 80 g / m2 Salzer EOS

Printed in Germany

To David Shneer, z"l

Content

Gregg Drinkwater

To David Shneer, z"l

A Dedication

David Shneer – my husband of nearly 27 years – died prematurely at age 48 in November 2020. In addition to the incalculable loss to me, his family, and his friends, his death created a hole in the scholarly and cultural landscapes of Yiddish studies, Soviet and post-Soviet studies, Jewish studies, Jewish history, Jewish culture, Holocaust studies, cultural history, and other overlapping fields of scholarship around the world. At the time of his death, David was the Louis P. Singer Chair of Jewish History and Professor of History, Jewish Studies, and Religious Studies at the University of Colorado, Boulder, where he was instrumental in building the university's program in Jewish Studies into a nationally and internationally renowned center of research, teaching, and Jewish culture. In what follows, I am not offering a eulogy or a reflection on my life with David. Such stories are for more intimate and personal contexts and forums. Rather, as a scholar of Jewish history myself, I will focus on David's scholarly work and its links to the theme of this volume: Yiddish and transnational culture(s) in the 20th century in Eastern Europe, the Soviet Union, and beyond.

A key theme in much of David's research, what I would argue was a through line in much of his scholarship over at least two and a half decades, was thinking about how historical actors create culture within political, social, and cultural universes shaped by state power and politics. In other words, how do state power and state politics influence cultural production and vice versa? More specifically, he often thought about the ways in which culture makers and communities are shaped by state power, but also more significantly, reversing the equation, thinking about how cultural producers themselves demonstrated agency by shaping and reshaping state power, often in unexpected ways. In this dialectical relationship, the cultural producers David studied sometimes created culture that transformed or exceeded the capacity of the state to control or manage it. In the bulk of his work, he focused this analytical lens on the overlapping and interlinked worlds of Soviet and post-Soviet Jews, Yiddish culture, and European Jewish life (with forays into the world-making potential of queer Jews and those Jews who reject notions of diaspora and exile, instead fostering local and global communities and cultures of resistance).

He began this work with his first monograph, *Yiddish and the Creation of Soviet Jewish Culture, 1918–1930* (Cambridge University Press, 2004), a finalist for the 2005 National Jewish Book Award and a revision of his doctoral dissertation at UC Berkeley. The dissertation had been produced under the guidance of Reginald Zelnik, David Biale, Chana Kronfeld, Naomi Seidman, and Yuri Slezkine (and while at Berkeley, in addition to this dissertation committee of leading scholars in the field, David had the opportunity to work with or learn from a number of other notable scholars of Soviet studies, Yiddish studies, Jewish studies, and Russian history, including Robert Alter, George Breslauer, Bluma Goldstein, Ken Jowitt, Eli Katz, Martin Malia, the Nobel laureate Czesław Miłosz, Nicholas Riasanovsky, and many others).

In *Yiddish and the Creation of Soviet Jewish Culture*, David critically engaged with the extant scholarship on Soviet Jewish history, much of which had been written through a Cold War lens that primarily supported what had been until then the dominant narrative about Jewish life and culture in the Soviet Union, namely: that Jews and Jewish cultural producers were members of an embattled community severely constrained by Soviet oppression of Jews and Soviet state antisemitism. Despite the boom in scholarship on Soviet Jewish life in the 1990s, nearly all the studies then emerging at the time still framed Soviet Jewish history through a lens of tragedy, as a series of failed experiments. From this perspective, Soviet Jewish cultural producers and Jewish activists involved in building the Soviet state and its vast array of social and cultural institutions were naïve historical actors who didn't realize the very horrible and tragic end that would come to many of them and their work.

David, instead, tried to avoid backshadowing the deaths of Jewish cultural producers, and thus directly or indirectly diminishing the cultural vibrancy of Soviet Yiddish culture. Rather than starting at the end and looking back from the vantage point of their deaths (many at the hands of the state), the purges, the legacies of the Holocaust, and the other horrible events that marked the darkest moments of Soviet Jewish culture and Soviet Jewish life, he wanted to go back to the energetic and dynamic moments in the 1920s when they were actually making Soviet Jewish culture while often enthusiastically contributing to building the Soviet state. While not denying the tragic events of later decades, David refused to center the "death" of the cultural project of this early generation of Soviet Jewish cultural producers. Instead, he wrote about the choices members of the Soviet Yiddish intelligentsia made in the 1920s when they were thrust into positions of state power. In one of the most dynamic flowerings of Yiddish culture in history, these Yiddish-speaking actors, writers, scholars, artists, and activists were building Jewish publishing houses, Jewish schools, Yiddish theaters, and remaking modern Jewish culture through a Soviet lens.

From this deep dive into Yiddish culture and the 1920s, David then went on to produce his next monograph, titled *Through Soviet Jewish Eyes: Photography, War and the Holocaust* (Rutgers University Press, 2010). Winner of the Jordan Schnitzer Prize of the Association for Jewish Studies and a finalist for the 2011 National Jewish Book Award, this book emerged from a chance encounter at a Moscow gallery in 2002. David and I had wandered into the gallery of the Union of Art Photographers on a whim, finding there an exhibit of Soviet photography of World War II. Reading the names of the photographers, David couldn't help but notice that the majority were Jewish. He dared to ask the curator and gallery manager, Maria Zhotikova, if the bulk of the work on the walls was, indeed, by Jewish photographers. Zhotikova, the granddaughter of Arkady Shaykhet (one of the most famous Soviet – and Jewish – photographers), responded "of course," adding that 50-60 percent of Soviet war photographers were Jewish. At that moment, David had his next book project.

In *Through Soviet Jewish Eyes*, David explored Soviet Holocaust photography and the Jewish photographers who took wartime pictures for the Russian- and Yiddish-language press. David examined why so many photojournalists in the Soviet Union were Jewish, and what role their Jewishness played in their work during World War II. In relation to Soviet Yiddish culture, in this work, David asked how the war was narrated within the Soviet Yiddish press and in Soviet Jewish contexts, comparing that to how the war was understood within the Russian-language press. And as he had done with his first book, David asked how these photographers were constrained by state power and the wartime needs of the Soviet Union, but also how they contributed to shaping Soviet narratives about the war, the Holocaust, Nazi atrocities, and liberation. Many of the wartime photographs by Soviet Jewish photographers became icons of the war and of the Holocaust in the Soviet Union, shaping memory of the war and of the Holocaust in the Soviet context for generations.

As part of his work on this book, David continued to move beyond the traditional and narrow domain of the scholar – the printed word – by creating and co-curating a traveling exhibit of Soviet Jewish photography from World War II that began in Denver and went to cities across the country. David had already co-curated two other exhibits of Soviet photography, his first focused on the photographs of photojournalist Mark Markov-Grinberg and the famed Soviet writer Ilya Ilf (exhibited in Denver in 2004) and another centered on the photography of Semyon Fridlyand (exhibited in Denver in 2008).

The exhibit that grew out of *Through Soviet Jewish Eyes* notably included a 2015 show at the Illinois Holocaust Museum in Chicago, for which David helped produce interpretative panels for the exhibit in both Russian and English, the first such bilingual exhibit at the museum. This wasn't David's first foray into cultural outreach among Russian speakers in the U.S. In Denver, for example, David spoke several times at the annual September commemoration at Denver's Babi Yar Memorial Park, offering his remarks bilingually, alternating between Russian and English, offering a more inclusive program for Colorado's significant population of post-Soviet immigrants. In 2008, David served as scholar-in-residence for an immersive study tour of historical Jewish Spain for young Russian-speaking Jews from both the US and Europe, created by the Genesis Philanthropy Group. He also regularly served as a consultant or speaker for US-based and global agencies serving Russian-speaking Jewish communities.

In addition to his monographs, David, who in graduate school worked part-time as the director of children's education at San Francisco's LGBTQ synagogue, Congregation Sha'ar Zahav, helped produce books exploring queer Jewish life, including the groundbreaking edited volume *Queer Jews* (co-edited with Caryn Aviv, Routledge, 2002), *Torah Queeries: Weekly Commentaries on the Hebrew Bible* (co-edited with me and Joshua Lesser, NYU Press, 2009), and a co-authored book with Caryn Aviv, *New Jews: The End of the Jewish Diaspora* (NYU Press, 2005). In that last volume, which sparked conversation and debate throughout the Jewish world, the authors explored forms of Jewish culture that resisted the idea of diaspora, arguing for a new model of global Jewish culture in which Jews are at home wherever they are.

Although this book wasn't engaged with Yiddish studies, its core argument was grounded in the Yiddishist and Bundist conception of *doikayt*, the idea that Jews should be grounded in their "here-ness," where they are settled, that they should create Jewish life and Jewish culture rooted in local contexts, while maintaining universalist and global ties. *Doikayt* rejects the idea that Jews need to understand themselves in relation to some mythologized Jewish center from which Jews and Jewish culture exist in exile, incomplete and longing for return.

In 2011, as a Yiddishist, David, along with Joseph Sherman, Gennady Estraikh, and Jordan Finkin co-edited a study of one of Eastern Europe's most famous Yiddish writers, titled *A Captive of the Dawn: The Life and Work of Peretz Markish, 1895–1952* (Legenda, Oxford, 2011). Also as a Yiddishist, David co-edited with Rob Adler-Peckerar a Festschrift in celebration of Chana Kronfeld, published as "The Berkeley School of Jewish Literature" in a special issue of the *Journal of Jewish Identities* (2014, Vol. 10, no. 1). David taught for several summers at the Yiddish Book Center in Massachusetts as academic director of the Steiner Summer Yiddish Program, helping foster a new generation of Yiddish studies scholars and inculcating a love of Yiddish language and culture among a diverse range of students. David also collaborated for many years with Rob Adler-Peckerar as director of research at *Yiddishkayt*, the Los Angeles-based organization Adler-Peckerar founded to promote the celebration and study of Yiddish culture and of the cultures of the borderlands of Eastern Europe. Through the biannual Helix Fellowship, David and Rob took small cohorts of artists, activists, educators, and scholars on immersive trips through the heartland of historic Yiddish culture in Belarus, Ukraine, and Lithuania.

A few months before David's death, his last book appeared: *Grief: The Biography of a Holocaust Photograph* (Oxford University Press, 2020). This book tells the story of a single image titled "Grief," an iconic photograph by the Soviet Jewish photographer Dmitry Baltermants, taken in the killing fields of Kerch in the Crimean Peninsula in January 1942. Soviet forces had just successfully retaken Kerch, liberating the town from the Nazis. A few miles from the center of Kerch, they discovered atrocities the Nazis had conducted in that area, including trenches filled with thousands of bodies. Building on *Through Soviet Jewish Eyes*, the book examines this single Holocaust liberation photograph and the life of Baltermants, one of the most celebrated photographers of the Soviet Union. The photo became the earliest published Holocaust liberation photograph, and in the book, David traces how the photographer, along with curators, collectors, editors, and historians, used the photograph to mediate Soviet memories of World War II and the Holocaust throughout the Cold War and into the post-Cold War decades.

David's last public lecture was at Yad Vashem in Israel in late 2019, months before the onset of the Covid-19 pandemic. He explained the story of *Grief*, tracing the photograph's origins in the brutality of war and murder, through its use in publications and exhibitions worldwide, and finally on to the walls of the Museum of Modern Art in New York and into the collections of museums and private collectors globally. In addition to demonstrating the ways the photograph contributed to producing particular Soviet memories and understandings of World War II, David explained how in the postwar decades, the art world displayed, valued, commercialized, and sold "Grief," contributing to the photo becoming among the most well-known images of the 20th century, and an art-market commodity.

At the time of his death, David was hard at work on his latest project, *Art is My Weapon: The Radical Musical Life of Lin Jaldati*, a book-length study of the life of Lin Jaldati, a Dutch-born Jewish cabaret singer, Yiddishist, and Holocaust survivor who moved to East Berlin after the war to help build the new socialist state and to promote antifascist art and culture through the lens of Yiddish culture and song.[1] In this book, David sought to tell how the performances of antifascist Yiddish music by Lin Jaldati and her non-Jewish communist husband, Eberhard Rebling, built bridges across Cold War divides and animated the memory of World War II, Jewish life in Europe, and the Holocaust from the 1940s until the late 1980s. David's work on Jaldati and Rebling shows how the two of them also simultaneously helped build community in East Berlin, East Germany, and throughout Europe and the world, while envisioning a future grounded in peace and an antifascist, universalist politics. Jaldati's life and legacy spanned the key decades of the 20th century, bridging prewar Yiddish culture, World War II and the Holocaust, and the Cold War decades until the moments before the Berlin Wall fell. Histories of Jewish culture, and especially of Yiddish culture in East Germany, have largely been ignored by scholars. David's work on Jaldati stands as a crucial corrective to this gap, born of the simplistic presumption that Yiddish

1 See Jalda Rebling's contribution and the interview with her in this volume.

and Jewish culture was either non-existent in East Germany, or at best on the margin of the margins. Jaldati's life as the "Yiddish diva" of the communist world (as David liked to call her), as an important and well-known figure in East German culture, and as one of the key public bearers of Holocaust memory for the East German state and society (with Jaldati regularly appearing at Holocaust commemoration events with leaders of the East German state, for example) proves that overlooking figures like Jaldati distorts the historical record.

David's work on the *Art is My Weapon* project sought to expand the historical record to show the capacity of Jaldati's Yiddish performances to animate memory by commemorating the past, creating community in the present, and envisioning a peaceful future. For this project, David also turned to his background as an amateur singer in choirs and performance groups and joined forces with his dear friend, the radical Jewish musician, composer, and performer Jewlia Eisenberg, who sadly passed away in March 2021. David and Jewlia created a cabaret show for *Art is My Weapon*, a multimedia performance that tells the story of Lin Jaldati's life through Yiddish song and images. David and Jewlia took this program all over the world (with performances in London, Los Angeles, Philadelphia, New York City, and elsewhere) and had plans in spring 2020 to take it to Prague and other cities in Europe. But Covid-19 caused them to cancel, and sadly, their deaths but months apart ended the musical element of the project. I am, though, working with colleagues and friends to bring David's half-complete manuscript on Jaldati to completion.

As with *Through Soviet Jewish Eyes*, this project was the daughter of serendipity. David learned of Jaldati's story through meeting her daughter, the Berlin-based musician and Cantor Jalda Rebling. I had made the *shidduch*, having first met Jalda and her wife, the artist Anna Adam, in Colorado at Ohalah, an annual gathering of clergy, artists, and communal leaders affiliated with the Jewish Renewal community (Jalda was ordained as a cantor through Jewish Renewal). Shortly after we met, Jalda and Anna invited us to a Shabbat dinner at Anna's studio while David and I were in Berlin for one of David's research trips. Over dinner, Jalda told the story of her family and her mother, including that her mother was among the last to see Anne Frank alive. David made the decision then and there that this was going to be his next book project. In addition to several scholarly and popular press articles on Jaldati, David published a very small book version of his research in 2015, in German, as *Lin Jaldati: Trümmerfrau der Seele* (Hentrich & Hentrich, 2015).

In addition to the book-length projects David worked on as an author, co-author and co-editor, he wrote dozens of scholarly articles appearing in such journals as the *American Historical Review*, *Shofar*, *Slavic Review*, *Humanity*, *AJS Perspectives*, *Prooftexts*, the *Leo Baeck Institute Year Book*, and in such edited volumes as *Laughter After: Humor after the Holocaust* (Wayne State University Press, 2020), *Jewish Music in Germany after the Holocaust* (Oxford University Press, 2014), *Getting the Picture: The History and Visual Culture of the News* (Bloomsburg, 2015), *Jews and Muslims in the Tsarist Empire and the Soviet Union* (Vandenhoeck & Ruprecht, 2015), and *The Oxford Handbook of the Jewish Diaspora* (Oxford University Press, 2021).

He served for over six years as co-editor, with the University of Toronto's Anna Shternshis, of the journal *East European Jewish Affairs* and was a frequent contributor to non-academic publications covering Jewish arts, culture, and politics. He gave invited talks to scholars and community groups on every continent except Antarctica.

In a memorial post for David created by the Digital Yiddish Theater Project, Michael Berkowitz of University College, London, wrote: "In terms of quality, heft, and impact on the field, David's scholarship did more to bridge the traditional disciplinary boundaries, and to enhance modern Jewish history from the perspective of interdisciplinarity, than that of any other historian of Jewish studies of his generation."[2] Berkowitz went on to note that *Yiddish and the Creation of Soviet Jewish Culture* "attained the status of a classic after only a few years," and "helped shape an entire field."

Producers of Yiddish culture today continue to ground their work in a deep appreciation for the historical context of Yiddish as a world-making language for European Jews, while simultaneously offering a vision of a different future informed by the radical potential of generations of Yiddishists. David's talks, performances, teaching, and writing for the popular press contributed to maintaining the vibrancy of contemporary Yiddish culture. And his scholarly work contributed to laying the foundations in the Yiddish studies field generally and for much of the work in this volume specifically.

2 "The DYTP Remembers David Shneer," by Joel Berkowitz, Sonia Gollance, Nick Underwood, Michael Berkowitz, and Jeffrey Veidlinger, Digital Yiddish Theater Project, December 10, 2020, https://web.uwm.edu/yiddish-stage/the-dytp-remembers-david-shneer.

Acknowledgements

This collection of articles is by and large an outcome of the workshop 'Hidden in Plain Sight: Yiddish in the Socialist Bloc and its Transnationality, 1941–1991' held virtually as part of the Global Education Outreach Program of Warsaw's POLIN Museum of the History of Polish Jewry from 22 to 24 November 2021. The program was made possible thanks to Taube Philanthropies, the William, K. Bowes, Jr. Foundation, and the Association of the Jewish Historical Institute of Poland. We are deeply grateful to a number of individuals and institutions that made the organization of the conference and the publication of this edited volume possible despite the obstacles the Covid-19 pandemic posed: the POLIN Museum of the History of Polish Jewry, the Arthur and Barbara Mokin Fund for Holocaust Studies at the University of Oregon, the Anne Tanenbaum Centre of Jewish Studies at the University of Toronto, the Imre Kertész Kolleg and the chair of Eastern European history at the Schiller-Universität in Jena, the Taube Department of Jewish Studies at the University of Wrocław, the European Association of Jewish Studies, the Deutsch-Polnische Wissenschaftsstiftung, the Szloma-Albam-Stiftung, and the Anton-Betz-Stiftung der Rheinischen Post e.V. We would also like to thank our publisher dup/de Gruyter – particularly Dr. Anne Sokoll who was in support of the project from the start; the editorial team of the series *Yiddish Studies: Editions & Research*, Prof. Dr. Efrat Gal-Ed for her inexhaustible knowledge and for being reachable night and day for any question we had, as well as Prof. Dr. Roland Gruschka for his editorial work and help in making this book a reality; finally, special thanks to the copy editor Jasmine Chorley-Schulz for meticulous work with complex, multilingual texts.

Note on Spelling and Transliteration

Following the *Yiddish Editions & Research* series stylesheet, quotes and cited literature are first given in the original language, be it Yiddish, Russian, Polish, Romanian or German, followed by an English translation. Yiddish transliterations of single words are given in italics and follow the rules of the ייִדישער וויסנשאַפֿטלעכער אינסטיטוט [*Yidisher visnshaftlekher institut*, Institute for Jewish Research, YIVO], such as *khurbn* [חורבן, the Nazi genocide of Jews], except in few cases of well-known words which are commonly used in English texts and cultures in a different spelling, such as *chutzpah* instead of *khutspe*. Other than with Soviet Yiddish sources, we have standardized Yiddish texts and citations according to the modern standard Yiddish orthography rules provided by the YIVO, as well. Spellings of Soviet Yiddish texts have been retained so as to underline that standardization projects of Yiddish were similarly marked by the Cold War and an East-West-divide, as the introduction elaborates.

Transliterations of place names are necessarily political and have been increasingly contested in the past years, especially since the beginning of Russia's war against Ukraine. Particularly in the Eastern European regions this volume primarily focuses on, place names are as manifold as languages spoken. In this volume, we follow academic common practices. For place names of capitals and bigger cities we use the well-established and accepted English spelling, such as Warsaw, Moscow, Vilna. Other cases are more complicated. A city located in today's Western Ukraine, for instance, has been named Львів [Lviv, Ukrainian], Львов [Lvov, Russian], Lwów [Polish], Lemberg [German], or לעמבעריק [*Lemberik*, Yiddish] throughout the centuries. Given the long history of changing borders and belongings, we have decided to use the city names (other than of capitals) in the language officially spoken today. Hence, the above-mentioned city will appear as Lviv. In a few instances, different spellings are explicitly given in the texts to underline the change of borders the cities were subjected to, to highlight the geographical and political surroundings in the biographies of those persons mentioned and/or the historical context in which a certain text was produced. People's names follow the same rules. For authors with established or official English names and/or transliterations, we use those: thus, שלום־עליכם will appear as Sholem Aleichem rather than Sholem-Aleykhem. In lesser-known cases, the names will be given according to the YIVO-transliteration rules: פּרץ מאַרקיש will appear as Perets Markish rather than Peretz Markish.

Abbreviations

AdK	Akademie der Künste	Academy of Arts, Berlin
AK	Armia Krajowa	Home Army
AMIA	Asociación Mutual Israelita Argentina	Israelite Argentine Mutual Association
APWr	Archiwum Państwowe we Wrocławiu	State Archives in Wrocław
BArch	Bundesarchiv	German Federal Archive
CJCS	צענטראַלע ייִדישע קולטור־געזעלשאַפֿט	Central Jewish Cultural Society
CKŻP	צענטראַלער קאָמיטעט פֿון די ייִדן אין פּוילן [Centralny Komitet Żydów w Polsce]	Central Committee of the Jews in Poland
CUPJA	צענטראַל־פֿאַרבאַנד פֿון פּוילישע ייִדן אין אַרגענטינע	Central Union of Polish Jews in Argentina
DAIA	Delegación de Asociaciones Israelitas Argentinas	Delegation of Israelite Argentine Associations
DP	Displaced Persons	
DRC	המרכז לחקר התפוצות ע״ש גולדשטיין־גורן	Goldstein-Goren Diaspora Research Center, Tel Aviv University
FDJ	Freie Deutsche Jugend	Free German Youth
FL	פֿעדעראַציע פֿון לאַנדסמאַנשאַפֿטן	Federation of *landsmanshaftn*
GARF	Государственный архив Российской Федерации	State Archive of the Russian Federation
GDR	Deutsche Demokratische Republik	German Democratic Republic
GEOP	Global Education Outreach Program	
GITIS	Российский институт театрального искусства	Russian Institute of Theater Arts
GOSET	Московский Государственный Еврейский Театр	Moscow State Jewish Theater
GTA	Yehuda Gabay Theater Archive	
HAD SBU	Галузевий державний архів Служби безпеки України	Sectoral State Archive of the Security Service of Ukraine
HIAS	American Hebrew Immigrant Aid Society	

ICDPA	המרכז הישראלי לתיעוד אמנויות הבמה	The Israeli Center for the Documentation of the Performing Arts
JAFC	ייִדישער אנטיפאשיסטישער קאָמיטעט	Jewish Antifascist Committee
JDC	American Jewish Joint Distribution Committee	
JLC	Jewish Labor Committee, New York	
NKVD	Народный комиссариат внутренних дел	People's Commissariat for Internal Affairs
NCFRS	נאַציאָנאַל־ראַט פֿון די פֿאַרבאַנדן	National Council of Former Residents' Societies
OCA	Organización Central de Ayuda	Central Relief Organization
OIA	Organización Israelita Argentina	Argentine Israelite Organization
PCA	Partido Comunista Argentino	Argentine Communist Party
POW	Prisoner of war	
PPR	Polska Partia Robotnicza	Polish Workers' Party
PPS	Polska Partia Socjalistyczna	Polish Socialist Party
PTŻ	Państwowy Teatr Żydowski	Polish State Yiddish Theater
PZPR	Polska Zjednoczona Partia Robotnicza	Polish United Workers' Party
RGALI	Российский государственный архив литературы и искусства	Russian State Archive of Literature and Art
RGASPI	Российский государственный архив социально-политической истории	Russian State Archive of Socio-Political History
ROLIT	Робітник літератури	Worker of Literature
SFRWVA	לאַנדסלײַט־פֿאַריין פֿון וואַרשע און אומגעגענט אין אַרגענטינע	Society of Former Residents of Warsaw and Its Vicinity in Argentina
TES	Teatrul Evreiesc de Stat	Jewish State Theater
TCKŻP	Tymczasowy Centralny Komitet Żydów w Polsce	Temporary Central Committee of the Jews in Poland
TsDAGO	Центральний державний архів громадських об'єднань України	Central State Archives of Public Organizations of Ukraine
TLA	NYU Taminent Library Archives	
UNESCO	United Nations Educational, Scientific and Cultural Organization	
USSR	Союз Советских Социалистических Республик	Union of Soviet Socialist Republics
USC VHA	University of Southern California, Shoah Foundation Institute for Visual History and Education	

USW	Союз советских писателей	Union of Soviet Writers
VUSPP	Всеукраїнська спілка пролетарських письменників	All-Ukrainian Association of Proletarian Writers
VVN	Vereinigung der Verfolgten des Naziregimes	Association of Those Persecuted by the Nazi Regime
WKŻ	Wojewódzki Komitet Żydów	Provincial Committee of Jews
YIFT	ייִדישער פֿאָלקס־טעאַטער	Jewish Popular Theater
YIVO	ייִדישער וויסנשאַפֿטלעכער אינסטיטוט	Institute for Jewish Research
YKUF	ייִדישער קולטור־פֿאַרבאַנד	Jewish Cultural Association
YKGF	ייִדישער קולטור־געזעלשאַפֿטלעכער פֿאַרבאַנד פֿון די ייִדן אין פּוילן [Towarzystwo Społeczno-Kulturalne Żydów w Polsce]	Socio-Cultural Society of Jews in Poland
ŻIH	Żydowski Instytut Historyczny	Jewish Historical Institute
ŻOB	Żydowska Organizacja Bojowa	Jewish Combat Organization
ŻZW	Żydowski Związek Wojskowy	Jewish Military Union

Miriam Chorley-Schulz

From Yiddishland to Yiddishlands

An Introduction

"Where else if not among Jews," Arn Vergelis (1918–1999) noted in a letter in 1971, "should a sort of literature be widespread that reports about journeys across borders and countries!"[1] [בא ווײַ נאָך, אויב ניט בא די ייִדן דארף זיַין ברייט פארשפרייט דער מין ליטעראטור, וועלכער דערציילט וועגן רײַזעס איבער קאנטן און לענדער!] Vergelis, a Soviet Yiddish communist poet-cum-globetrotter, made his mark on travel literature in a Cold War world – a world marked by curtains, walls, borders, and new nation-states. His widely overlooked epistle travelogues are an incredibly illuminating entry point for the edited volume at hand, which endeavors to showcase new approaches to the study of Yiddish in the socialist bloc and its global entanglements.

Apart from being a poet of disputed talent and ambivalent repute, Vergelis crowned his career in 1961 with the editorship of סאָוועטיש היימלאַנד [*Sovetish heymland*, Soviet Homeland] – staying in this position for the remaining thirty years of the periodical's and the Soviet Union's existence.[2] A crucial component of being the figurehead of the only official and globally distributed post-Stalinist Soviet literary and political journal in the Yiddish language were trips abroad between 1963 and 1991. On his many voyages, including to the United States, Poland, Uruguay, and Monaco, Vergelis repeatedly turned to the genre of letter-writing.[3] With an aura of intimacy: that was his way to bring readers along on his *international* adventures that for most of them were exotic and out of reach. Today, they can help in rethinking the complex politics of Yiddish during the long Cold War and illuminate the Yiddish

I would like to thank Dr. Alexander Walther, Prof. Dr. Roland Gruschka, Jasmine Chorley-Schulz, and the participants of the "Eye on Work" workshop at the University of Oregon for their invaluable feedback that improved the present chapter invaluably. All mistakes and flaws are mine.

1 Vergelis 1976, 320. All translations will be mine. Soviet Yiddish orthography is reproduced; non-Soviet Yiddish sources are standardized according to the YIVO rules.

2 For overviews of the (primarily negative) representation of Vergelis during the Cold War, see Kupovetsky 2007; Estraikh 2008, 65–82; Estraikh 2018; Estraikh 2020.

3 For a collection of the letters in translation, see Vergelis 1972.

world's reconfigurations in the second half of the 20th century into interconnected, but often competing cultural spaces in East and West.

Cold War Yiddishlands – Towards a Reconceptualization

'Yiddishland' refers to a transnational cultural entity linked through diverse and dynamic local intellectual, literary, cultural, and political practices in Yiddish. As a world unto itself, linked by Yiddish but connected to and overlapping with many other languages, this entity was reshuffled and reconceptualized by wars and genocides, revolution and decolonization in the 20th century. One reconceptualization of 'Yiddishland' can be gleaned at in Arn Vergelis' aforementioned letter, penned in Geneva in 1971:

> בא ייִדן אין זייער צעשפּרייטקייַט וועט איר געפינען אלע פארבן פון דער הויט, אלע מא־
> נירן צו ריידן, אלע געריכטן צו עסן, אלע מינים בגאָדים, אלע לעשוינעס [...]. ס׳איז א פאקט,
> אז ייִדן אין פארשיידענע לענדער שטייען אונטער פארשיידענע פענער, זינגען פארשיידענע
> הימנען. מיט עטלעכע טעג צוריק האָב איך אין זשענעווער ,פּאלאץ פון די נאציעס׳, איידער
> עס האָט זיך דאָרט אָנגעהויבן מייַן פּרעסע־קאָנפערענץ, געהערט, ווי עס האָבן געשמועסט
> צווישן זיך צוויי ייִדן – זשורנאליסטן. איינער האָט געזאָגט: ,מיר – זאמביער׳, דער צווייטער
> האָט געענטפערט: ,מיר – נייַ־זעלאנדער׳. ס׳האָט געפעלט, אז איך, אין מייַן ריי, זאָל זאָגן:
> ,מיר – רוסן׳... [4]

> Among Jews in their global dispersion, you will find all colors of skin, all manners and ways to speak, all kinds of food, all kinds of clothes, all languages [...]. It is a fact that Jews in different countries stand underneath different flags, sing different national anthems. A few days ago in Geneva's Palais des Nations, right before my press conference started, I overheard how two Jews talked to each other – they were journalists. One of them said:
>
> "We – Zambians," to which the second replied: "We – New Zealanders." The only thing that was missing was for me, at my turn, to say: "We – Russians..."

At first glance, Vergelis' 1971 reflections seem to invoke ideas of Yiddishland's "polyterritoriality" that were raised as early as 1922 by such figures as the New York-based Yiddish literary critic and public intellectual Shmuel Charney[5] (1883–1955) in the pages of New York's oldest Yiddish socialist monthly די צוקונפֿט [*Di tsukunft*, The Future]:

4 Vergelis 1976, 320.

5 I use Shmuel Charney's family name rather than his more established pen name. In that, I

> אין דער אמתן זײַנען מיר אין איינעם מיט אונדזער שפּראַך און ליטעראַטור און אונדזער גאַנצן גײַסטיקן פֿאַרמעגן – פּאָליטעריטאָריאַל, ד.ה. מיר שוועבן ניט אין דער לופֿטן, מיר זײַנען ניט אָפּגעריסן פֿון באָדן, נאָר פֿאַרקערט, מיר ציִען די חיונה פֿון פֿאַרשיידענע באָדנס, געפֿינען זיך אונטער דעם אײַנפֿלוס פֿון פֿאַרשיידענע קלימאַטן, פֿאַרשיידענע סבֿיבֿות. זייערע אַלגעמיינס ווירקונגען באַגעגענען זיך, קומען זיך צונויף, שטויסן זיך צוזאַמען אָדער באַהעפֿטן זיך אין אונדזער אַלגעמיין נאַציאָנאַלן שאַפֿן.[6]
>
> In truth we are, along with our language and our literature and our entire intellectual capability *polyterritorial*, that is, we are not hovering in the air, we are not deracinated from the ground; on the contrary, we are in fact nourished from different soils, are under the sway of different climates, various habitats. The overall effects of all of these meet each other, coalesce, clash or unite within our common national work.

Repudiating the antisemitic tropes of the 'Wandering Jew' or לופֿטמענטש [*luftmentsh*, man of air] or the very validity of any 'Jewish Question' with the same stroke, both Charney and Vergelis 'indigenize'[7] Yiddish speakers in the localities in which they live and connect them rhizomatically across borders and continents. We may deduce that such conceptualizations of Yiddishland are closer to an ancient Greek sense of διασπορά [diaspora] which, while emerging from a word meaning 'scattering,' by and large positively encapsulates the *creation of home* rather than a *lack* or *absence* of a home(land).[8] It echoes in fact the mantra of the אַלגעמיינער ייִדישער אַרבעטער־בונד אין ליטע, פּוילן און רוסלאַנד [*Algemeyner yidisher arbeter-bund in Lite, Poyln un Rusland*, General Jewish Labor Bund in Lithuania, Poland and Russia, short: Bund] that דאָרטן, ווו מיר לעבן, דאָרט איז אונדזער לאַנד! [There, where we live, is our country]: Yiddishlands according to this are one interconnected space without a hierarchy or center.

It would be wrong, however, to suggest that there was no development

follow Eli Bromberg's recent intervention in problematizing Shmuel Charney's pen name ניגער [transliterated as 'Niger' and 'Nigger'], a racial slur that historically functioned as the American Yiddish equivalent to the n-word, and its usage and reproduction in academic scholarship. See: Bromberg 2019.

6 Charney [Niger] 1922, 308, cited in Gal-Ed 2021, 143.

7 I use this term mindful of the fact that Yiddish speakers, even if marginalized and fleeing from oppression and persecution, may themselves become structurally implicated in settler colonialism, depending on where they live, and that they need to be analyzed as such. This exceeds the purpose of the chapter at hand. Max Kaiser has masterfully explored the case of Australia and may serve as a guide for future studies, see Kaiser 2022. For the global application of Bundist דאָיִקייט [*doikayt*, hereness], even in settler-colonial contexts, see Wolff 2020.

8 Boyarin 2023, 29.

between the 1922 and 1971 conceptualizations of that 'land' called Yiddish. As Efrat Gal-Ed has shown, ideas about this specific *res publica literarum* that was envisioned to bond Yiddish speakers together globally underwent continuous revisions in concert with the shifting status of Yiddish and the ever-changing material and existential conditions its speakers found themselves in during the interwar period,[9] the Second World War, and Cold War. Arguably, this process continues today.[10]

Whereas in 1922 Charney predicted an ultimate synthesis, פֿאַראייניקונג [*fareynikung*, unification] of the different אָרטיקע קרעפֿטן [*ortike kreftn*, local energies],[11] after 1945 Yiddishland had been irrecoverably remapped and internally disintegrated – with new centers and peripheries in both the West and East as they were reconfigured. With the majority of its speakers lost in what Yiddish speakers (mostly) refer to as חורבן [*khurbn*, literally destruction, in this case the Nazi genocide of Jews], questions of belongings and anxieties about cultural cohesion changed for the traumatized remnant, too: was a unification between East and West Yiddishlands even desired anymore? Now Yiddishland spanned not only continents but Worlds – First, Second, and Third. Fractured by the geographical-cum-ideological bloc borders of the Cold War, the chapters in this volume demonstrate that Yiddishland's 'polyterritoriality,' the multitudes it had always contained, figured as more distinct, locally demarcated Yiddishlands that both cross-fertilized *and* competed against each other for ideological supremacy in a world that was gradually decolonizing and globalizing.

Importantly, these *lands* had to position themselves vis-à-vis Israel/Palestine. It is no accident that Vergelis mentions Jews hailing from New Zealand and the Republic of Zambia: the first a Pacific settler colonial country that had gained sovereign status and Commonwealth membership in 1947; the second a south-central African country that emerged from British colonialism in 1964, was ruled by Kenneth Kaunda's socialist United National Independence Party until 1991, and established diplomatic relations with the Soviet Union upon gaining independence.[12] They present two diverging ciphers for the break-up of the British Empire and successes of decolonial movements

9 Gal-Ed 2021.

10 For contemporary reconceptualizations of Yiddishland and diaspora nationalism more generally, see e.g. Aviv and Shneer 2005, Boyarin 2023.

11 Charney [Niger] 1922, 308, cited in Gal-Ed 2021, 143.

12 See ft. 7.

after 1945[13] and hint at a potential alternative globalization with Jews in the front seat and acting in solidarity with the colonized and oppressed. Tellingly, however, Vergelis does not mention, at least not there, the elephant in the room, Israel/Palestine, itself. It remains a specter that haunts the gradual post-1945 dismantlement of British imperialism and reconfiguration as much as it weighed on (socialist) Yiddishlands.

Instead, Vergelis charts a vision of Jewishness and Yiddish that is – in deliberate contradistinction to the ideology of Zionism – both locally distinct and globally connected, socialist and internationalist and by that definition not containable in a ethno-state or reducible to social constructs like 'race.' He, in other words, maps the inherent contradictions of proletarian internationalism, first spelled out in the *Communist Manifesto* itself, onto Cold War Yiddishlands – Vergelis urges Yiddishlands to "consent not to be a single being"[14] and not to flatten the differences but to embrace the revolutionary potentials of its inherent multiplicity and diversity.

This vision outward can be refracted back into the Soviet Union itself. Indeed, under Vergelis' leadership, *Sovetish heymland* in its thirty years of existence became a forum for ethnically, culturally, and socially diverse and heterogeneous Jewish and non-Jewish voices (of other Soviet national minorities, Arab Palestinians, Israeli communists, etc.), all miraculously made to speak Yiddish, from within and outside the Soviet Union. A close examination of the journal alone calls the bluff to the discursive construct of "Soviet Jewry," misconstrued as one homogenous unit. But it may stand in for a more nuanced understanding of socialist Yiddishlands per se: Soviet Yiddish diversified socialism from within by injecting Yiddish into predominantly non-Yiddish environments and stretching this environment's dominant norms and normativities; and it diversified Jewishness by injecting socialism into outer realms where dogmatic anti-communism was increasingly the norm. Charney's "polyterritoriality" had undergone a revolution.

This volume explores exactly these *diverse* Yiddish cultural activities

13 For new studies of socialist internationalism in the Cold War and Third World solidarity, see e.g. Djagalov 2020, Maasri, Bergin and Burke 2022, Parrott and Atwood Lawrence 2022.

14 These ideas, in my interpretation, echo thoughts of radical Black thought that are not part of the afro-pessimist school. The citation ("*consent à n'être plus un seul*") is a passing remark by Édouard Glissant in his *L'Intention poétique*, who thought through the history, present, and future of the similarly scattered archipelago of the Caribbean and the Black diaspora. It was taken up and developed further most famously by Moten 2017, 16.

stretching from the Soviet Union to the German Democratic Republic [GDR], from Romania to Poland, and from there to England, Israel/Palestine, Argentina – coalescing and cross-fertilizing, competing or outwardly fighting against each other as alluded to in the 1971 letter from Geneva. Much like Vergelis, the chapters of this volume present promising new directions in researching localized cultures of the transnationally connected Yiddishlands from the vantage point of the 'Second World' and from there crossing into the 'First' and 'Third Worlds.' In that, this volume contributes to the growing body of scholarship on Jewish life and Yiddish cultures in state-socialist countries which illuminate the broader histories of these societies as a whole.[15] They show that what is generally perceived of as one pervasively repressive "Soviet model" successfully colonizing Eastern Europe was in fact a rather diverse political, social, cultural, and economic organism, changing over time, made up of very different social orders, actors, and manifestations of state-socialism, including vis-à-vis local Yiddish speakers.[16]

By showcasing Yiddishland's transnationalism, this volume also aims to intervene into the study of the Cold War writ large by queering bloc binaries. In this way we aim to challenge what we know, or thought we knew, about this conflict that was never really cold – fueled by the wars and brutal regime changes devastating the Global South – and how it shaped the second half of the 20th century.[17] We do so by way of new methods, sources, and concepts and in the realm of what is commonly relegated to the socio-cultural periphery: Yiddish culture and politics transgressing national, geopolitical, and ideological boundaries. Yiddishland is therefore, we argue, a fruitful place for the writing of a new "comparative socio-cultural history of the Cold War."[18] As the chapters in this volume show, the peripheral socialist Yiddishlands with their inherent trans-socialist and cross-bloc entanglements and manifestations can be central in re-periodizing and remapping the Cold War (Jewish) world, rethinking Cold War narratives about and constructs of Jewishness in socialist countries, and de-essentializing Jewishness altogether in the course of it.

15 Important forerunners have been: Čapková and Kijek 2022, Grözinger and Ruta 2008, Sherman 2004.

16 This has also been proven persuasively in the recent edited volume by Čapková and Kijek 2022.

17 Mikkonen, Scott-Smith, and Parkkinen 2019.

18 Major and Mitter 2003.

The Heavy Burden of Cold War Narratives – Alive and Well

As recently as 2022, the editors of another volume, *Jewish Life under Communism*,[19] have raised the alarm about how much the Cold War still dictates (scholarly) thinking and writing about this topic. The lacuna of scholarship into Vergelis' himself whose travelogues and reflections have received little attention even within the otherwise pathbreaking, pioneering field of the new revisionist school of Soviet Yiddish studies (and even in their available English translations) is representative of this Cold War myopia. Take his letter from Geneva of 1971, penned right in the middle of the Brezhnev era (1964–1985). For a long time, scholarship under-theorized this era as the 'period of stagnation' understood to have heralded the (in this reading predestined) Soviet collapse. The hegemonic "assumption that the period as a whole was characterized by rampant cynicism and decline of faith in the socialist creed," this scholarship suggests,[20] could not account for figures like *Sovetish heymland's* Vergelis, who did remain committed to communism, was not blind to the challenges the Soviet system faced and searched for solutions in Yiddish, across Yiddishland, and the rest of the globe. While no other Soviet minority is arguably as well-studied as the Jewish one and no other Jewish community in the socialist bloc as well-researched as the Soviet one, Soviet Yiddish studies is only beginning to systematically investigate the effects of the Cold War in the making of Soviet Yiddish cultures and subjectivities after Stalin's death in 1953. The vast majority of studies, that is to say, focus on the time before 1953. We may now start to think in more nuanced and dynamic ways about Soviet Yiddish in the anything-but-stagnant 1970s and beyond.

Soviet Yiddish studies is part of a broader trend in the study of the Soviet Union that, starting around the turn of the millennium, has spearheaded novel approaches to Soviet cultural, social, and economic life and successfully addressed and corrected many of the historical interpretations produced during the Cold War about Soviet Jewry. As early as 2004, David Shneer, to whom this volume is dedicated and in many respects indebted, set out to break with the hegemonic Western narrative mode which presented the whole story as tragedy: they had read Soviet Yiddish history *backwards* from the purges of the Jewish intelligentsia starting in the late 1940s as the unavoidable teleol-

19 Čapková and Kijek 2022, 1.

20 Fainberg and Kalinovsky 2016, vii.

ogy of a brutal romance between Jewishness and communism that ended irrevocably in 1952–53. It was in August 1952 that the main representatives of Soviet Yiddish literature Dovid Bergelson (1884–1952), Perets Markish (1895–1952), Itsik Fefer (1900–1952), Dovid Hofshteyn (1889–1952), and Leyb Kvitko (1890–1952) were murdered.[21] This new school has re-equipped Yiddish cultural actors with agency,[22] revealed bottom-up participation in the construction of Soviet Jewish popular culture,[23] and refocused Soviet Yiddish literary studies,[24] including responses to the *khurbn*.[25] Where the 'Cold War school' offered little more than dichotomous thinking in zero-sum narratives of death and oppression, resistance or collaboration,[26] these later studies have shown that Jewishness, and specifically a form of cultural-secular *Yidishkayt*, and Soviet-ness are not at all mutually exclusive. They paved the way for queering endeavors such as the present volume.[27]

However, Cold War narratives are deeply rooted in Western imaginaries of the socialist bloc, and have been resilient, at times even within this new school of Soviet Yiddish studies. One way this manifests is by way of periodization: despite important exceptions that touch on Soviet *Yiddish* after Stalin's death,[28] most interpretations of Soviet Yiddish culture beyond narratives of oppression and persecution end in 1952 at the latest. This chosen endpoint has awarded Stalin with an uncomfortable posthumous victory by affirming that this important Jewish emancipatory tradition had indeed been killed institutionally and culturally *past recovery*.[29] While the chapters in this

21 Shneer 2004.

22 See e.g. Veidlinger 2000, Estraikh 1999.

23 See e.g. Shternshis 2006, Bemporad 2013.

24 Murav 2011, Murav 2019, Krutikov 2011, Krutikov 2019.

25 See, for example, the collection of articles on specific Soviet Yiddish writers, such as Dovid Bergelson, Perets Markish, Der Nister as part of Oxford's Leganda Series in Yiddish Studies, further Murav and Estraikh 2014.

26 See, e.g., Schwarz 1988, Pinkus 1988, Gitelman 1988, for a most recent revisiting of the very common left to right 'conversion' of American Jewish intellectuals (especially of the New York guild), who more often than not produced exactly these zero-sum narratives post-conversion, see Sinkoff 2020.

27 See e.g. Estraikh 2005.

28 Estraikh 2008, Murav 2011, Krutikov 2014, Shternshis 2017, Zeltser 2018, Shneer 2020, [Chorley-]Schulz 2021a, Estraikh 2023. The NYU Shvidler Project of Soviet Jewry is in the process of working on a comprehensive history of Soviet Jewry extending to the Cold War period.

29 This is a natural outcome of the heavy focus on exactly those literary elite figures that were killed in the purges, see, e.g., Mantovan 2012, fns. 19 and 20.

volume both build on this important scholarship and extend it to the Cold War period, the consequences of this lopsided historiographical record that bracketed out the Cold War period itself, can be illustrated in the figure of Arn Vergelis – for not only have his writings by and large been overlooked or dismissed, we are indeed still stuck with a specific ideological picture of him and the political project he represented.

Vergelis was, to borrow Gennady Estraikh's words, "a big fish in the small pond"[30] of post-Stalinist Soviet Yiddish publishing, and his own itinerant Cold Warrior career was steeped in contradictions. At home, his career holds interesting dimensions for rethinking Yiddish within a clearly heterogeneous Soviet state that was not only multiethnic but also, I suggest, internally diverse in regards to the communist visions that were practiced. Vergelis' comparative unimportance and limited amount of power in the realm of *high politics*, for instance, are poignantly captured by the surprise with which General Secretary Leonid Brezhnev (1906–1982) and other members of the Politburo reacted, in 1973, to the 'news' that the Soviet Writers' Union had been issuing a monthly Yiddish journal edited by a *certain* Arn Vergelis for twelve years.[31] Acting outside of the limelight of the authorities afforded Vergelis (and other cultural activists) a somewhat autonomous space "occupied with" his own matters – i.e. building a communist Yiddish culture – as he himself noted in an interview in September 1994 with the privilege of hindsight:

> You, like others, will in the future evaluate what I did or did not do in the course of my life. But one does not have to see everything as either black or white. Keep in mind that I acted under specific conditions, at a specific time and place. […] What is true is that I was and remain a committed Communist. However, I also was and remain a Jew who has felt the pain of his people. I defended them and devotedly served our *mameloshn* [sic] I did what others could not do or did not want to do. […] As for the authorities, they were occupied with their matters and I – with mine.[32]

More work needs to follow that investigates the, however limited, complicated autonomous workings of Soviet Yiddish culture and its post-Stalinist

30 Estraikh 2020, 112.

31 Morozov 1999, 174.

32 Cited from an interview that Mark Kupovetsky conducted with Arn Vergelis in 1994, see Kupovetsky 2007, 41–42.

project of socialism that were clearly out of sight of this 'police state' and the present volume starts to think in this direction.

Abroad, in contrast, the *Sovetish heymland* editor's imagined power in the realm of Soviet policies vis-à-vis its Jewish population was artificially inflated to the point that Vergelis himself became the face behind these policies and the very target of the Soviet Jewry movement's human rights campaigns.[33] By way of his travels, in other words, he started to play a crucial and polarizing role on the Jewish margins of the Cold War fought out in the theater of Jewish culture: from boycotts to curated welcoming ceremonies, the reception history of this Soviet Yiddish cultural activist in the countries he visited upon invitation allows a contemporary scholar to chart a map of ideological alliances and fault lines of Jewish political actors *outside* the Soviet Union. These non-Soviet Jewish actors trafficked in Soviet Jewish affairs by way of Vergelis, we can now understand, as one avenue of political (re)positioning in their respective societal and political surroundings. As I have argued elsewhere, claims that Vergelis 'betrayed' an alleged 'Jewish essence' or transgressed 'Jewishness' altogether by putting himself in the service of the Soviet project, perhaps most famously popularized by Elie Wiesel,[34] were structured by Western Jewish Cold War anxieties in an age of 'religious' anti-communism. During the 1977 World Conference for Yiddish and Yiddish Culture, for instance, which established the day of Stalin's murder of the Soviet Yiddish intelligentsia (12 August 1952) as a global day of mourning, Vergelis was demonized as a "Soviet Gauleiter" with "bloody NKVD hands" who allegedly informed on the murdered Yiddish literati.[35] Some presented his editorial tenure at *Sovetish heymland* as having been achieved by usurping the murdered; the magazine's participation in an anti-Zionist campaign was the nail in the coffin for an already-vilified cultural project on the international stage. The same anxieties simultaneously constructed Vergelis' imagined opposite and victim – the 'organically anti-communist' Soviet Jew in need of Western rescue.[36]

This short outline with the heavy focus on the Soviet Yiddish milieu owes to the fact that similarly revolutionary scholarship on Jewish experiences in

33 This is best summarized in Estraikh 2020.

34 Elie Wiesel would go so far to say: "He [Vergelis], I believe, is an enemy of the Jewish people and should be treated as such." See: Abrahamson 1985, 234.

35 Liptzin 1973, 111; Anonymous 1977, 192; further Estraikh 2020.

36 [Chorley-]Schulz 2021b.

other socialist countries is, for the most part,[37] still sorely lacking despite promising examples of local studies without specifically Jewish foci.[38] Revealing the deep legacies of the Cold War, most studies on Jews in East Central Europe, first among them Poland,[39] craft either teleological narratives of demise where waves of persecution are followed by waves of emigration with little attention to Jewish agency,[40] or conspiratorial (nationalistic and, even if unconsciously, antisemitic) narratives about an alleged overrepresentation of Jews in states' apparatus, othering Jews as the villains behind communist 'colonization' of 'non-Jewish nations.'[41] *Socialist Yiddishlands* breaks with these paradigms in several ways.

Shift in Imagination

Revisiting socialist Yiddishlands builds upon and within a broader renaissance since the financial crisis in 2008 of exploring alternatives to a capitalism well on the way to destroying the planet. There has been a renewed interest in socialism, Marxism, and working-class history in their many global varieties, including a critical reappraisal of the Soviet and state-socialist experiments, and *Socialist Yiddishlands* was conceived as part of this new direction.[42] Part of this renaissance is the attempt to tell much more complicated stories about the histories of socialism in different state-formations, that is by *not ignoring its failures* but indeed thinking through and with them. These studies depart from simplistic liberal and anarchist narratives in relation to the Russian Revolution and its aftermath that have ultimately left us with nothing to scrutinize: socialist projects went wrong, they claim, because they were rotten from the start. Rather, newer studies pose the question of *how* these perhaps most ambitious attempts at human emancipation – i.e., to overcome capitalism

37 Promising exceptions are, e.g. Auerbach 2013, Niether 2015, Nalewajko-Kulikov 2020, Walther 2022.

38 Kenney 1995, Fidelis 2010, Bren 2010, Lebow 2013, Horváth 2017, Koch 2023.

39 Čapková and Kijek 2022, 2.

40 See, e.g., Dobroszycki 1994, Shlomi 2001, Gross 2006, Tokarska-Bakir 2012, Zaremba 2022, Cichopek-Gajraj 2014, Tokarska-Bakir 2018, Krzyżanowski 2020. For cases other than Poland, see Bankier 2005, Ofer 2012.

41 For examples, see Paczkowski 2001, Chodakiewicz 2003, Śpiewak 2012. For good analyses of the myth of "Judeo-Bolshevism," see Hanebrink 2018.

42 Mark and Betts 2022, Mark, Kalinovsky and Marung 2020, Djagalov 2020, Tyerman 2022, Wilder 2022.

itself – ended up building societies that failed so terribly in practice. The challenge is therefore to engage these tragedies in nuanced ways through new questions, methodologies, and sources.[43]

One way in which *Socialist Yiddishlands* departs from most previous scholarship is by situating Yiddish speakers as active members of state-socialist societies who shaped and were shaped by the societies in which they lived. They were part of building these societies, including through Yiddish language and culture, in complicated, at times contradictory, ways. The shift in imagination that we are suggesting is one that investigates Jewish life not *under* communism, as if buried by an avalanche and necessarily desperate to escape for the air of capitalism,[44] but Jewish life in its diverse expressions dialectically shaping and transforming these social projects from *within* – for some earnestly, for some inadvertently or cynically, for some against their will.

Examples in this volume abound: the reproduction of Arn Vergelis' travel report to Poland with a new English translation and an introduction and comprehensive commentary prepared by Miriam Chorley-Schulz and Binyamin Hunyadi introduces a figure in shaping and bridging socialist Yiddishlands who has been up until now deemed too politically corrupt to take his writings seriously. The extensive conversation with Jalda Rebling introduces another actor in another socialist setting. Daughter of the trailblazing Yiddish singer Lin Jaldati (1912–1988), the latter a star in the GDR and from there the socialist globe,[45] and the former an important Jewish cultural figure in her own right, Rebling provides crucial insights into Yiddish culture in the GDR from the vantage point of an established cultural activist that was (and is) a critic of the failures of many 20th century state socialist experiments but *not* of socialism as a political project. Rebling also challenges simplistic accounts of the non-existence of Jewish identities in East Germany or construing them as always already victims and dissidents by virtue of an essentialist Jewish identity. She instead urges us to acknowledge and understand the new

43 "A strategic vision of a renewed left, informed by Marxism, would benefit from incorporating some practices identified with anarchism — such as more systematic democratic processes and the fostering of communities evidencing genuine concern for their members' cultural and material needs. The scarcity of these communitarian practices in Communist countries and Communist parties outside of the socialist bloc contributed to their failure in the 20th century." Meyer 2018, 360.

44 See Miriam Chorley-Schulz' paper on this motif of Jewish studies and its racial-essentialist dangers: [Chorley-]Schulz 2021b.

45 Shneer 2022.

forms of secular, socialist Jewish self-consciousness that emerged amidst state socialist projects and how they informed cultural activities and (global) social networks in turn.

In her chapter, Agniezska Żółkiewska narrates an institutional history of Polish Jewish culture within communism after 1945, adding to existing scholarship on the postwar institutionalization,[46] with a specific focus on the importance of Yiddish in the building of these institutions. She paints an ambivalent picture of a Polish Jewish community increasingly scattered across the globe: in many respects, Polish Yiddishland did not differ significantly from its global outgrowths in outlook and cultural activity, specifically regarding the realm of *khurbn-forshung* [destruction research],[47] despite the efforts to streamline postwar Polish Jewish culture along political lines.

Gennady Estraikh reconstructs the rise and fall and rise again of Rive Balyasne (1910 – 1980), a Soviet Yiddish writer who was part of the Soviet Yiddish intelligentsia throughout its tumultuous history. She remained a communist of some sort even after being persecuted by Stalin which demands of us to rethink the continuities in change of Jewish commitments to communism from 1917 to 1991. Estraikh thereby opens up potential future inquiries – importantly from a woman's perspective, still an unfortunate rarity.

Binyamin Hunyadi revisits the relatively unknown case of postwar Romanian Yiddish literature through the life and work of Volf Tambur (1916 – 1995), in some sense Vergelis' Romanian equivalent. Tambur's life and career sheds a light on Romanian Yiddish culture, its positioning within Romanian socialist visions of past, present, and future that were very different and, in fact, deliberately opposing Soviet (Yiddish) ideas and cultural manifestations.

Transnational Integrative Scholarship

While many of the following chapters are populated by cultural elites, they simultaneously break down the binaries of top-down and bottom-up divisions through what has been elsewhere termed "integrated" scholarship. First conceptualized in the field of Holocaust studies,[48] integrative scholarship

46 Aleksiun 2002, Berendt 2006, Grabski 2015.

47 For a discussion of the privileging of the term *khurbn* over Holocaust or Shoah see below in this introduction.

48 This notion was first coined and employed by Saul Friedländer in his magnum opus *Nazi Germany and the Jews* (1997 – 2007) and has since spread across the field.

is inherently interdisciplinary and aims to combine and critically approach sources from different provenances in order to craft a much more nuanced account of the subject at hand by taking into account the abundance of available perspectives and interpretations, combining perspectives from above and below, from the center and the margin, not "strictly from without the event, but also from within."[49] The different sources employed to advance the interdisciplinary integrative research in this volume demonstrates the complexity of the making of socialist Yiddishlands in their local and global contexts. Given the transnationality of Yiddishland itself, the archives consulted are spread throughout the world as well.

Kamil Kijek, for instance, relies on a transnational archive of literary, journalistic, archival, and oral history sources. He paints a remapped, politically diverse Polish Yiddishland in the immediate postwar period with new centers and peripheries built by Jewish survivors. They, for the most part, attempted to build a new Poland with varied visions of Jewish and human emancipation, created new social networks, and produced diverse Yiddish cultures.

Part of this transnationalization[50] of integrative scholarship is to consider in what way the Cold War shaped Yiddishlands outside of the socialist core and critically engage with the sources at hand from the whole political spectrum. Malena Chinski shows through critical engagement with diverse sources how Argentine Yiddishland cannot be thought anymore without situating it both in its local, national, and transnational contexts amidst the geopolitics of the Cold War. Gennady Estraikh consults previously sealed state files from Ukrainian archives, literary sources, and interviews in his biographical reconstruction, and Corina Petrescu follows the Bucharest Jewish State Theater in their international travels by similarly consulting international archives from Romania to Israel to Germany, using interviews and interpreting diverse genres of sources as textual remnants.

Socialist Yiddishlands, importantly, also included source material in translation itself in order to escape the Orientalist pitfall of speaking *about* rather than *with* the East: the aforementioned conversation with Jalda Rebling as well as Vergelis' travel report with annotations is further accompanied by the very first translation of an interview with Sholem Rubinger (?–1988), trans-

49 Bartov 2022, 65.

50 Also advocated for and applied in Čapková and Kijek 2022, 3.

lator and editor-in-chief of Romanian Yiddish radio for twenty-five years, first published in the Romanian Yiddish journal בוקאַרעשטער שריפֿטן [*Bukareshter shriftn*, Bucharest Writings] in 1983. The importance of oral history for the study of socialist Yiddishlands is further evinced by Katharina Friedla's contribution. By tracing the role of Yiddish in the lives of Jewish refugees in the Soviet Union in several different oral history archives around the globe, she gives voice to those who have so far been muted. They tell complicated, often painful, stories about the question of belonging to Yiddishland, whose borders were strictly policed, between 1939 and 1945, a time when a feeling of belonging was perhaps most pressing.

Finally, and against narratives of death and demise, the continued presence and underestimated importance of Yiddish in the postwar period must be traced in the nebulous shapes and forms it took. Alexander Walther, in this vein, revisits the so far overlooked cases of translations from Yiddish into German in the GDR as one avenue to spur discussions about the Nazi genocide of Jews and more firmly integrate the memory of what we call *khurbn* into the broader antifascist memory culture.

Reclaiming *Khurbn*

Socialist Yiddishlands privileges the term *khurbn* over the much more established terms Holocaust and Shoah to refer to the Nazi genocide of Jews. This is, firstly, an overdue gesture to return and retrieve a term Yiddish-speaking victims and survivors themselves predominantly (but not exclusively) used in a volume committed to *Yiddish* cultures.[51]

Khurbn is formed from the three-letter root ח-ר-ב [waste, desolate] and is etymologically connected to the proto-semitic *xarb* or Hebrew חֶרֶב [*kherev*, sword]. The term itself is used in post-biblical sources to describe specifically the destruction of the First and Second Temple in Jerusalem, which in their own rights reshaped Jewish life from the ground up. Cognates also made it into the Bible or later texts fanning out the diverse meanings produced from this root in Hebrew. *Khurbn* entered Yiddish exactly through its dynamic Hebraic component. It was used in Yiddish over centuries to refer to the destruction of the Temples as well as to document other destructions of

[51] Previous studies have re-introduced the term, see Sneh 2017, Pollin-Galay 2018, [Chorley-] Schulz 2019.

countries, cities, and buildings, ruinations and devastations small and big. In the 20th century alone *khurbn* was used to capture the havoc of the First World War as well as to refer to the massive pogroms during the Russian Civil War before Yiddish speakers also applied the term to different stages of the gradual obliteration of Jewish (and non-Jewish) life perpetrated during the Second World War.

Secondly, we understand the reclaiming of *khurbn* as an important *conceptual* intervention: 'Holocaust' or 'Shoah,' 'Genocide' or 'Auschwitz,' 'Endlösung' or 'khurbn' are *by no means* neutral or apolitical synonyms. Naming encapsulates specific historical, political, cultural moments; it is always already an interpretation. Naming is political. The complicated and fraught histories of the term Holocaust and Shoah as hegemonic designator *solely* for the organized mass murder of Jews by Nazi Germany – erasing the persecution and mass murder of millions of other 'undesirables' in the course of it – are well recorded.[52] שואה [*Shoah*, calamity, destruction], like *khurbn*, is also a biblical term, but, as opposed to the latter, was not incorporated into Yiddish. Shoah denotes an unforeseen individual or collective, often *divinely punitive*, disaster of cosmic proportions. While the term became the designator for the Nazi genocide of Jews in Israel/Palestine already by the late 1940s (and later elsewhere, such as France), Holocaust, though derived from the Septuagint translation of עֹלָה [*olah*', "that which goes up (in smoke)," i.e. burnt offering to God], was in fact widely used until the 1960s in the English language to denote 'destruction' and 'war' generally. It was only with the somewhat belated rise of a Western memory culture that pronounced the Nazi genocide of Jews singular and incomparable, gave it metaphysical import, and lifted it outside of longer histories of imperialism and genocide that 'holocaust' became 'the Holocaust.' While there is no space here for a thorough elaboration, the 'victory' of these terms point us to distinct historical conjunctures: on the one hand, scholars have shown that Shoah deliberately replaced the much more common, traditional Hebrew and, especially important for this volume, Yiddish term '*khurbn*' shortly after the founding of Israel as part of its ideological 'negation of the diaspora'[53] and related sup-

[52] There have been several studies on the genealogy of the term 'Holocaust' and 'Shoah' as well as calls for a more ethical usage of language and terminologies in Holocaust studies. As far as I know, a thorough analysis of the Yiddish alternate lexicon of persecution has not taken place, though. See, e.g., Petrie 2000, Ofer 1996, Michman 2003, Marrus 1987, Young 1988, Utz 2016, Blurton 2014.

[53] Ofer 1996.

pression of the Yiddish language.[54] On the other hand, the gradual process from 'holocaust' to 'Holocaust' maps on to the initially resistant and then full embrace of Holocaust memory in the West, so imbricated in the cultural Cold War itself and strategically positioned against the alternative memory cultures of the East.[55] Finally, Holocaust is not a term commonly used in Yiddish – in the East or West.

It is no coincidence that scholars of socialist Yiddishlands are used to stumbling over studies that claim that "the term 'Holocaust' is completely unknown in the Soviet literature. [...] It is only recently [i.e. shortly before 1997] that 'Holocaust,' transliterated from English, has appeared."[56] While factual, the interpretations are often misleading: this lexical lack has been taken to reveal a much deeper "Memory Hole"[57] of Cold War Eastern Europe regarding the events of the *khurbn*, presumed completely and successfully suppressed by the allegedly antithetical forces of antifascist memory. This idea has shaped a slew of scholarship that 'unearths' Holocaust memory in the Soviet Union and socialist Eastern Europe *despite* antifascism.[58] Only recently has the premise of these studies – an *a priori* conception of Holocaust Memory (good) as ontologically irreconcilable with antifascism (bad) – been called into question: the burgeoning field of new antifascist studies demonstrates that antifascism and *khurbn*-memory are not always already mutually exclusive – they rather work pursuant to different philosophies, histories, vocabularies, and are therefore not easily recognizable or assimilable to the Western memory regime.[59] Rather than this imposition of exterior terminologies onto the research subjects, we suggest a return to the terminologies our subjects actually used and proceed with the analysis from there: first among them *khurbn*.[60] In this we follow such eminent scholars of Jewish studies

54 Chaver 2004, Rojanski 2020.

55 [Chorley-]Schulz 2021a.

56 See Gitelman 1997, 18–19; Gitelman 2005, 102.

57 Korey 1983.

58 Bohus 2015, Bohus, Hallama and Stach 2022, Esbenshade 2019, Stach 2017, Hallama and Stach 2015, Walther 2022.

59 Murav and Estraikh suggest this also for Soviet Yiddish culture and its responses to fascism in the early 1940s in their introduction, see Estraikh and Murav 2014, 7–8; further [Chorley-]Schulz 2021a; Kaiser 2022; for particularly incisive summary and case study showing the interventions of new antifascism studies, see Kékesi and Zombory 2022; further see e.g. García, Yusta, Tabet and Clímaco 2016; Seidman 2018; Braskén and Copsey, Featherstone 2020; Kaiser 2022; Wegewitz 2023.

60 Terms such as уничтожение [annihilation] or катастрофа [catastrophe] had in fact been in use

as Daniel Boyarin who has argued in a different, yet surprisingly relevant context that "[u]tilizing terms [...] to delineate the concept worlds of people who had no such concepts, or words, is a practice of self-defeat – pure or not. We will never find the other as long as we persist in reducing the unknown to the known."[61] Alexander Walther's, Malena Chinski's, Alexandra Polyan's chapters on the GDR, Zionist and socialist Argentina, and the Soviet Union and Britain respectively point to the intrinsically contentious natures of *khurbn*-memory in interconnected Cold War Yiddishlands as does Arn Verglis' travel report detailing his 1964 visit to Auschwitz and Treblinka first published in the pages of *Sovetish heymland* in 1965. It showcases him as a practitioner of *khurbn*-memory in his own right – even if not immediately legible to the Western-trained Holocaust scholar.

Part of this return to the term *khurbn* includes an attempt at understanding the historical sediments that shape the meaning of this term over its centuries-long use in many local contexts. It necessitates, in other words, a similarly critical *Begriffsgeschichte* that already exists for the terms 'Holocaust' and 'Shoah.' These *Begriffsgeschichten* have shown for 'Holocaust' that we *cannot* draw a straight line from the Septuagint to the post-1945 use. This would only obfuscate the century-long *secular* recycling of the term in English and other languages and assert that the word still carries the identical ancient religious/sacrificial overtones. *Khurbn*, too, has a religious genesis and once denoted the destructions of the First and Second Temple in Jerusalem. But the complicated, allusive, and very productive nature of לשון־קודש [*loshn-koydesh*, sacred language, Hebrew component] in Yiddish similarly prohibits any presumption of *stasis* – implying that this component simply and always works in the realm of the sacral. While Yiddish speakers (primarily outside of socialist Yiddishlands) did start to use the term דריטער חורבן[62] [*driter khurbn*, third destruction] stringing the Nazi genocide in its immensity to the two destructions of the Temples, it would be wrong to necessarily and only understand *khurbn* in strictly theological terms, all the more so in cultural realms like the Soviet Union or postwar Eastern Europe that were by and large secular, secularizing, and antifascist. Alexandra Polyan, talking about Perets Markish's (1895–1952) dramatic oeuvre and its potentially too gener-

in Russian discussions of the Nazi destruction of Jews and deserve further analysis. קאַטאַסטראָפֿע [catastrophe] is used in Soviet Yiddish, as well.

61 Boyarin 2018, 24, 8.

62 See, e.g., Varshavski 1952, Ravitch 1966, Belek 1971.

ous 'borrowing' from an English Yiddish playwright, and Malena Chinski, analyzing contentious celebrations of the Warsaw Ghetto Uprising in Perón's Argentina of the immediate postwar period, demonstrate how contested the *khurbn* and its meaning was for building a world in its wake. Words are sites of struggle pointing us to historically contingent mechanisms of power and hegemony. While we are still in need of a systematic analysis of the term – its genealogy, differing uses, connotations, and reinterpretations over time – we want to suggest a more protean reading of *khurbn* in diasporic and localized, secular and antifascist fashion. Many (though not all) Yiddish speakers, while naturally affected most by the Nazi's specific attack on Jewish life, did reject ethno-reductionist readings of the *khurboynes* of the Second World War, and understand Jewish and non-Jewish suffering as part of an apocalypse that threatened humanity and its sustaining world. The destruction under fascism to them was a watershed moment of Jewish *and* world history with subsequent cultural transformations of indeterminate proportions. Rather than a lachrymose Judeo-pessimist reading of Jewish history, their "never again" conjured up different uses of ח-ר-ב, such as: "Nations [גוֹי, *goy*] shall not take up / Sword [חֶרֶב] against nation [אֶל-גּוֹי]; They shall never again know war" (Isa 2:4). But to understand *khurbn* (and "goy"[63]) in these terms presupposes a groundedness in a common, interdependent humanity and a situating of the Nazi genocide of Jews in longer histories of imperialism, colonialism, and racism; it entails exactly the conceptual interventions the chapters in this volume suggest: politically, transnationally, and in terms of non-periodization.

Khurboynes, whether ancient or modern, can hardly be captured in bracketed periods: they describe the process of brutal destruction itself, of migration, and (re)constituting transformed remnants of the past in the present. Past, present, and future bleed into one another – undermining the idea of complete and final rupture: Kamil Kijek demonstrates how Polish Jewish political life in many respects resumed after the war where it had left off in 1939.

63 Adi Ophir and Ishay Rosen-Zvi have masterfully demonstrated that the binary division of humanity into "goyim" and Jews is the outcome of a long conceptual transformation. Of relevance to this chapter, Ophir and Rosen-Zvi begin their erudite analysis exactly with the Book of Isaiah to showcase the later metamorphosis of "goy," which is a comparatively uncharged word in Biblical Hebrew, simply meaning "nation" and encompassing Jews as such (specifically in Isa 40:17), into a signifier of the ontological difference of the "gentile" or non-Jew in rabbinic literature (specifically t. Ber. 6:18). I'm invoking here the Biblical meaning that encompasses an understanding of human interconnectedness and interdependence without erasing Jewish difference. See: Ophir and Rosen-Zvi 2018; also Boyarin 2023, 7–8, 17.

Katharina Friedla and Alexandra Polyan make us question whether the Second World War indeed ended as early as 1945 and whether the (inter-Jewish) conflicts we associate with the Cold War commenced earlier than 1946. They suggest that these histories interlace and are not easily or neatly separable. Alexander Walther traces the history of German translations from Yiddish in order to better understand the significance of the reappearance of this genre in the GDR. Gennady Estraikh and Binyamin Hunyadi, finally, break open long-standing parameters of periodization altogether by reconstructing the micro-histories of one entire life as a window to the bigger historical and social picture. Jalda Rebling journeys through different periods, while Arn Vergelis time-travels to the streets of prewar Warsaw after confronting the *khurbn* in Treblinka and Auschwitz in 1964. While we accompany the Bucharest Jewish State Theater across geographical frontiers and political boundaries in Corina Petrescu's chapter, Sholem Rubinger, finally, narrates how Romanian Yiddish radio waves diffracted and communicated across borders – geographically in that they reached Yiddish-speakers in all of Romania and beyond, temporally in that they produced a socialist Romanian Yiddish canon of old and new Yiddish works, ideologically in that they crossed the Iron Curtain, and ethnically in that they registered with non-Jews around the globe as well.

Together these chapters chart new, complicated narratives – extending Yiddish histories in socialist countries beyond teleological diagnoses of inevitable demise; challenging 'accepted' and essentializing notions of Jewishness; and transgressing previously set boundaries of periodization and national histories. The editors of the volume hope that it gives food for thought for more research into *socialist Yiddishlands*, diversifying ideas of Jewishness, and reconsidering their implications for the darkening present.

Bibliography

Abrahamson, Irving, ed., 1985: *Against Silence: The Voice and Vision of Elie Wiesel.* New York, NY: Holocaust Library.

Aleksiun, Natalia, 2002: *Dokąd dalej? Ruch syjonistyczny w Polsce (1944–1950).* Warsaw: Trio.

Amar, Tarik, 2015: *The Paradox of Ukrainian Lviv: A Borderland City between Stalinists, Nazis, and Nationalists*. Ithaca, NY: Cornell University Press.

Anonymous, 1977 אַנאָנים, 1977: נאָך דער וועלט־קאָנפֿערענץ פֿאַר ייִדיש און ייִדישע קולטור. אין: **בײַ זיך** (תּל־אָבֿיבֿ) 8: 192.

Auerbach, Karen, 2013: *The House at Ujazdowskie 16: Jewish Families in Warsaw after the Holocaust.* Bloomington, Ind.: Indiana University Press.

Aviv, Caryn, and David Shneer, 2005: *New Jews: The End of the Jewish Diaspora.* New York, NY: New York University Press.

Bankier, David, ed., 2005: *The Jews Are Coming Back: The Return of the Jews to Their Countries after WWII.* Jerusalem: Yad Vashem.

Bartov, Omer, 2022: Between Integrated and First-Person History: Writing the Holocaust from Within. In: *The Journal of Holocaust Research* 37 (1): 65–71.

Belek, Yankev, 1971 בעלעק, יעקבֿ: דער נבֿיא פֿון דריטן חורבן. תּל־אַבֿיבֿ: י. ל. פּרץ פֿאַרלאַג.

Bemporad, Elissa, 2013: *Becoming Soviet Jews: The Bolshevik Experiment in Minsk.* Bloomington, Ind.: Indiana University Press.

Berendt, Grzegorz, 2006: *Życie żydowskie w Polsce w latach 1950–1956: Z dziejów Towarzystwa Społeczno-Kulturalnego Żydów w Polsce.* Gdańsk: Wydawnictwo Uniwersytetu Gdańskiego.

Blurton, Heather, 2014: 'The History of an Incorrect Term': Agamben, Etymology and the Medieval History of the Holocaust. In: *postmedieval: a journal of medieval cultural studies* 5: 336–345.

Bohus, Kata, 2015: Not a Jewish Question? The Holocaust in Hungary in the Press and Propaganda of the K.d.r. regime during the Trial of Adolf Eichmann. In: *Hungarian Historical Review* 4 (3): 737–772.

Bohus, Kata, Peter Hallama, and Stephan Stach, eds., 2022: *Growing in the Shadow of Antifascism: Remembering the Holocaust in State-Socialist Eastern Europe.* Vienna: Central European University Press.

Boyarin, Daniel, 2018: *Judaism: The Genealogy of a Modern Notion.* New Brunswick, NJ: Rutgers University Press.

Boyarin, Daniel, 2023: *The No-State Solution. A Jewish Manifesto.* New Haven, Conn.: Yale University Press.

Braskén, Kasper, Nigel Copsey and David Featherstone, eds., 2020: *Anti-Fascism in a Global Perspective: Transnational Networks, Exile Communities, and Radical Internationalism.* London: Routledge.

Bren, Paulina, 2010: *The Greengrocer and His TV: The Culture of Communism after the 1968 Prague Spring.* Ithaca, NY: Cornell University Press.

Bromberg, Eli, 2019: We need to talk about Shmuel Charney. In: *In Geveb. A Journal of Yiddish Studies*, <https://ingeveb.org/articles/we-need-to-talk-about-shmuel-charney>, April 12, 2024.

Čapková, Katerina, and Kamil Kijek, eds., 2022: *Jewish Life under Communism: New Perspective.* New Brunswick, NJ: Rutgers University Press.

Charney [Niger], Shmuel, 1922 ניגער, שמועל: די געגענט־פֿראַגע אין דער ייִדישער ליטעראַטור. אַן ענפֿער בעל־מחשבֿותן. אין: **די צוקונפֿט** 27 (ניו־יאָרק), 5טער מײַ: 325–329.

Chaver, Yael, 2004: *What must be forgotten: The Survival of Yiddish in Zionist Palestine.* Syracuse, NY: Syracuse University Press.

CHODAKIEWICZ, Marek Jan, 2003: *After the Holocaust: Polish-Jewish Conflict in the Wake of World War II.* Boulder, Co.: East European Monographs.

[CHORLEY-]SCHULZ, Miriam, 2019: 'Gornisht oyser verter?': Khurbn-shprakh as a Mirror of the Dynamics of Violence in German-Occupied Eastern Europe. In: Gaëlle Fisher and Caroline Mezger, eds., *The Holocaust in the Borderlands: Interethnic Relations and the Dynamics of Violence in Occupied Eastern Europe.* Göttingen: Wallstein Verlag, 185–207.

[CHORLEY-]SCHULZ, Miriam, 2021a: *Keyner iz nit fargesn. Soviet Yiddish Antifascism and the Holocaust.* PhD Dissertation. Columbia University.

[CHORLEY-]SCHULZ, Miriam, 2021b: 'The Deepest Self Denies the Face': Polish Jewish Intellectuals and the Birth of the 'Soviet Marrano.' In: Katharina Friedla and Markus Nesselrodt, eds., *Polish Jews in the Soviet Union (1939–1959): History and Memory of Deportation, Exile, and Survival.* Boston, Mass.: Academic Studies Press, 143–174.

CICHOPEK-GAJRAJ, Anna, 2014: *Beyond Violence: Jewish Survivors in Poland and Slovakia, 1944–48.* Cambridge: Cambridge University Press.

DJAGALOV, Rossen, 2020: *From Internationalism to Postcolonialism: Literature and Cinema between the Second and the Third Worlds.* Montreal: McGill-Queen's University Press.

DOBROSZYCKI, Lucjan, 1994: *Survivors of the Holocaust in Poland: A Portrait Based on Jewish Community Records, 1944–1947.* Armonk, NY: M. E. Sharpe.

ESBENSHADE, Richard S., 2019: 'Anti-fascist literature' as Holocaust Literature? The Holocaust in the Hungarian Socialist Literary Marketplace, 1956-1970. In: *Polin: Studies in Polish Jewry* 31: 409–426.

ESTRAIKH, Gennady, 1999: *Soviet Yiddish: Language Planning and Linguistic Development.* New York, NY: Clarendon Press.

ESTRAIKH, Gennady, 2005: *In Harness: Yiddish Writers' Romance with Communism.* Syracuse, NY: Syracuse University Press.

ESTRAIKH, Gennady, 2008: *Yiddish in the Cold War.* Leeds: Legenda.

ESTRAIKH, Gennady, 2018: Эстрайх, Геннадий: Одиночество еврейского редактора. К 100-летию со дня рождения Арона Вергелиса. В: Народ книги в мире книг, <http://narodknigi.ru/journals/133/odinochestvo_evreyskogo_redaktora/>, August 16, 2023.

ESTRAIKH, Gennady, 2020: Creating a Cold War Boogeyman: Aron Vergelis's Political Career. In: *Jewish Social Studies* 25 (3): 103–129.

ESTRAIKH, Gennady, 2023: *The History of Birobidzhan: Building a Soviet Jewish Homeland in Siberia.* New York, NY: Bloomsbury.

FAINBERG, Dina, and Artemy M. KALINVOSKY, 2016: Introduction. Stagnation and Its Discontents: The Creation of a Political and Historical Paradigm. In: Dina Fainberg and Artemy M. Kalinvosky, eds., *Reconsidering Stagnation in the Brezhnev Era : Ideology and Exchange.* Lanham, Md.: Lexington Books/Fortress Academic, vii–xxii.

Fidelis, Malgorzata, 2010: *Women, Communism, and Industrialization in Postwar Poland.* New York, NY: Cambridge University Press.

Fitzpatrick, Sheila, 2000: *Everyday Stalinism: Ordinary Life in Extraordinary Times, Soviet Russia in the 1930s.* Oxford: Oxford University Press.

Gal-Ed, Efrat, 2021: Yiddishland: A Promise of Belonging. In: *Journal of Modern Jewish Studies* 2 (2): 141–169.

García, Hugo, Mercedes Yusta, Xavier Tabet, and Cristina Clímaco, 2016: *Rethinking Antifascism: History, Memory and Politics, 1922 to the Present.* Oxford: Berghahn.

Gitelman, Zvi, 1988: *A Century of Ambivalence: The Jews of Russia and the Soviet Union, 1881 to the Present.* New York, NY: Schocken Books.

Gitelman, Zvi, ed., 1997: *Bitter Legacy: Confronting the Holocaust in the USSR.* Bloomington, Ind.: Indiana University Press.

Gitelman, Zvi, 2005: Internationalism, Patriotism, and Disillusion: Soviet Jewish Veterans remember World War II and the Holocaust. In: *The Holocaust in the Soviet Union.* Symposium Presentations at the United States Holocaust Memorial Museum, Center for Advanced Holocaust Studies, 95–126.

Grabski, August, 2015: *Centralny Komitet Żydów w Polsce (1944–1950): Historia polityczna.* Warsaw: Żydowski Instytut Historyczny.

Gross, Jan T., 2006: *Fear: Anti-Semitism in Poland after Auschwitz: An Essay in Historical Interpretation.* Princeton, NJ: Princeton University Press.

Grözinger, Elvira, and Magdalena Ruta, 2008: *Under the Red Banner: Yiddish Culture in the Communist Countries in the Postwar Era.* Wiesbaden: Harrassowitz.

Hallama, Peter, and Stephan Stach, 2015: *Gegengeschichte: Zweiter Weltkrieg und Holocaust im ostmitteleuropäischen Dissens.* Leipzig: Leipziger Universitätsverlag.

Hanebrink, Paul, 2018: *A Specter Haunting Europe: The Myth of Judeo-Bolshevism.* Cambridge, MA: Harvard University Press.

Hellbeck, Jochen, 2009: *Revolution on my Mind: Writing a Diary under Stalin.* Cambridge, Mass.: Harvard University Press.

Horváth, Sándor, 2017: *Stalinism Reloaded: Everyday Life in Stalin-City, Hungary.* Bloomington, Ind.: Indiana University Press.

Ives, Peter, 2017: *Gramsci's Politics of Language: Engaging the Bakhtin Circle and the Frankfurt School.* Toronto: University of Toronto Press.

Kaiser, Max, 2022: *Jewish Antifascism and the False Promise of Settler Colonialism.* Cham: Palgrave Macmillan.

Kékesi, Zoltán, and Máté Zombory, 2022: Antifascist memory revisited: Hungarian historical exhibitions in Oświęcim and Paris, 1965. In: *Memory Studies* 15 (5): 1087–1104.

Kenney, Padraic, 1995: *Rebuilding Poland: Workers and Communists, 1945–1950.* Ithaca, NY: Cornell University Press.

Koch, Anna, 2023: *Home after Fascism. Italian and German Jews after the Holocaust.* Bloomington, Ind.: Indiana University Press.

Korey, William, 1983: In History's 'Memory Hole': The Soviet Treatment of the Holocaust. In: Randolph L. Braham, ed., *Contemporary Views on the Holocaust.* Boston, Mass.: Nijhoff Publishing, 145–157.

Kotkin, Stephen, 1995: *Magnetic Mountain: Stalinism as a Civilization.* Berkeley, Calif.: University of California Press.

Krutikov, Mikhail, 2011: *From Kabbalah to Class Struggle: Expressionism, Marxism, and Yiddish Literature in the Life and Work of Meir Wiener.* Stanford, Calif.: Stanford University Press.

Krutikov, Mikhail, 2014: In Search of a Soviet Yiddishland: The Poetics of Absence in Shmuel Gordon's Travelogue. In: *Aschkenas* 24 (1): 129–143.

Krutikov, Mikhail, 2019: *Der Nister's Soviet Years: Soviet Yiddish Writer as Witness to the People.* Bloomington, Ind.: Indiana University Press.

Krzyżanowski, Łukasz, 2020: *Ghost Citizens. Jewish Return to a Postwar City.* Cambridge, Mass.: Harvard University Press.

Kupovetsky, Mark, 2007: Aron Vergelis: Survivor of the Destruction of Soviet Yiddish Culture, 1949–1953. In: *Jews in Russia and Eastern Europe* 58: 40–94.

Lebow, Katherine, 2013: *Unfinished Utopia: Nowa Huta, Stalinism and Polish Society, 1944–1956.* Ithaca, NY: Cornell University Press.

Liptzin, Sol, 1973: Vergelis, Aron. In: *Encyclopedia Judaica,* 2nd ed., 16 (Jerusalem), 111.

Maasri, Zeina, Cathy Bergin, and Francesca Burke, 2022: *Transnational Solidarity: Anticolonialism in the Global Sixties.* Manchester: Manchester University Press.

Major, Patrick, and Rana Mitter, 2003: East is East and West is West? Towards a Comparative Socio-Cultural History of the Cold War. In: *Cold War History* 4 (1): 1–22.

Mantovan, Daniela, ed., 2012: *Yiddish Poets and the Soviet Union, 1917–1948.* Heidelberg: Universitätsverlag Winter.

Mark, James, and Paul Betts, eds., 2022: *Socialism goes Global: The Soviet Union and Eastern Europe in the Age of Decolonization.* Oxford: Oxford University Press.

Mark, James, Artemy M. Kalinovsky, and Steffi Marung, eds., 2020: *Alternative Globalizations: Eastern Europe and the Postcolonial World.* Bloomington, Mass.: Indiana University Press.

Marrus, Michael R., 1987: *The Holocaust in History.* Hanover, NH: University Press of New England.

Meyer, Gerald, 2018. Marxism and Anarchism: Their Contradictions. In: *Science & Society* (New York. 1936) 82 (3): 360–385.

Michman, Dan, 2003: *Holocaust Historiography. A Jewish Perspective: Conceptualizations, Terminology, Approaches and Fundamental Issues.* London: Vallentine Mitchell.

Mikkonen, Simo, Giles Scott-Smith, and Jari Parkkinen, eds., 2019: *Entangled East and West. Cultural Diplomacy and Artistic Interaction during the Cold War.* Berlin, Boston: De Gruyter Oldenbourg.

Morozov, Boris, ed., 1999: *Documents on Soviet Jewish Emigration.* London: Frank Cass.

Moten, Fred, 2017: *Black and Blur.* Durham, NC: Duke University Press.

Murav, Harriet, 2011: *Music from a Speeding Train: Jewish Literature in Post-Revolutionary Russia.* Stanford, Calif.: Stanford University Press.

Murav, Harriet, 2019: *David Bergelson's Strange New World: Untimeliness and Futurity.* Bloomington, Ind.: Indiana University Press.

Murav, Harriet, and Gennady Estraikh, 2014: *Soviet Jews in World War II: Fighting, Witnessing, Remembering.* Boston, Mass.: Academic Studies Press.

Nalewajko-Kulikov, Joanna, 2020: *A Citizen of Yiddishland: Dovid Sfard and the Jewish Communist Milieu in Poland*, trans. Paul Glasser. Berlin: Peter Lang.

Niether, Hendrik, 2015: *Leipziger Juden und die DDR: Eine Existenzerfahrung im Kalten Krieg.* Göttingen: Vandenhoeck & Ruprecht.

Ofer, Dalia, 1996: Linguistic Conceptualization of the Holocaust in Palestine and Israel, 1942–53. In: *Journal of Contemporary History* 31 (3): 567–595.

Ofer, Dalia, et al., eds., 2012: *Holocaust Survivors: Resettlement, Memories, Identities.* New York, NY: Berghahn Books.

Ophir, Adi, and Ishay Rosen-Zvi, 2018. *Goy: Israel's Multiple Others and the Birth of the Gentile.* Oxford: Oxford University Press.

Paczkowski, Andrzej, 2001: Żydzi w UB–próba weryfikacji stereotypu. In: Tomasz Szarota, ed., *Komunizm. Ideologia, system, ludzie.* Warsaw: Neriton, Instytut Historii, 192–204.

Parrott, R. Joseph, and Mark Atwood Lawrence, eds., 2022: *The Tricontinental Revolution: Third World Radicalism and the Cold War.* Cambridge: Cambridge University Press.

Petrie, Jon, 2000: The Secular Word Holocaust: Scholarly Myths, History, and 20th Century Meanings. In: *Journal of Genocide Research* 2 (1): 31–63.

Pinkus, Benjamin, 1988: *The Jews in the Soviet Union: The History of a National Minority.* Cambridge: Cambridge University Press.

Pollin-Galay, Hannah, 2018: *Ecologies of Witnessing: Language, Place and Holocaust Testimony.* New Haven, Conn.: Yale University Press.

Ravitch, Melech, 1966 ראַוויטש, מלך: **דאָס אַמאָליקע ייִדישע וואַרשע ביז דער שוועל פֿון דריטן חורבן**. מאָנטרעאַל: פֿאַרבאַנד פֿון וואַרשעווער ייִדן

Rojanski, Rachel, 2020: *Yiddish in Israel: A History.* Bloomington, Ind.: Indiana University Press.

Sapir, Edward, 1929: The Status of Linguistics as a Science. In: *Language* 5 (4): 207–214.

Schwarz, Solomon M., 1988: *The Jews in the Soviet Union.* Syracuse, NY: Syracuse University Press, 1988.

Seidman, Michael, 2018: *Transatlantic Antifascisms: From the Spanish Civil War to the End of World War II.* Cambridge: Cambridge University Press.

Sherman, Joseph, ed., 2004: *Yiddish after the Holocaust.* Oxford: Boulevard Books.

Shlomi, Hana, 2001 שלומי, חנה: **אסופת מחקרים לתולדות שארית־הפליטה היהודית בפולין, 1944–1950**. תל־אביב: המרכז לחקר תולדות היהודים בפולין ומורשתם, המכון לחקר התפוצות, אוניברסיטת תל־אביב.

Shneer, David, 2004: *Yiddish and the Creation of Soviet Jewish Culture.* Cambridge: Cambridge University Press.

Shneer, David, 2020: *Grief: The Biography of a Holocaust Photograph.* Oxford: Oxford University Press.

Shneer, David, 2022: An Alternative World: Jews in the German Democratic Republic, Their Transnational Networks, and a Global Jewish Communist Community. In: Čapková, Katerina, and Kamil Kijek, eds., 2022: *Jewish Lives under Communism: New Perspectives.* New Brunswick, NJ: Rutgers University Press, 153–173.

Shternshis, Anna, 2006: *Soviet and Kosher: Jewish Popular Culture in the Soviet Union, 1923–1939.* Bloomington, Ind.: Indiana University Press.

Shternshis, Anna, 2017: *When Sonia met Boris: An Oral History of Jewish Life under Stalin.* New York, NY: Oxford University Press.

Sinkoff, Nancy, 2020: *From Left to Right: Lucy S. Dawidowicz, the New York Intellectuals, and the Politics of Jewish History.* Detroit, Mich.: Wayne State University Press.

Sneh, Perla, 2017: Khurbn Yiddish: An Absent Absence. In: Wendy Lower and Lauren Faulkner Rossi, eds., *Lessons and Legacies XII: New Directions in Holocaust Research and Education.* Evanston, Ill.: Northwestern University Press, 215–231.

Śpiewak, Paweł, 2012: *Żydokomuna: interpretacje historyczne.* Warsaw: Czerwone i Czarne.

Stach, Stephan, 2017: 'Duch czasu wycisnął jednak na tej pracy swe piętno': Historia Zagłady w badaniach Żydowskiego Instytutu Historycznego w okresie stalinowskim. In: *Zagłada Żydów: studia i materiały* 13: 138–159.

Tokarska-Bakir, Joanna, 2012: *Okrzyki pogromowe: Szkice z antropologii historycznej Polski lat 1939–1946.* Wołowiec: Wydawnictwo Czarne.

Tokarska-Bakir, Joanna, 2018: *Pod klątwą: Społeczny portret pogromu kieleckiego,* vol. I–II. Warsaw: Czarna Owca.

Tyerman, Edward, 2022: *Internationalist Aesthetics: China and Early Soviet Culture.* New York, NY: Columbia University Press.

Utz, Raphael, 2016: Die Sprache der Shoah: Verschleierung – Pragmatismus – Euphemismus. In: Jörg Ganzenmüller and Raphael Utz, eds., *Orte der Shoah in Polen, Gedenkstätten zwischen Mahnmal und Museum.* Cologne: Böhlau Verlag, 25–48.

VARSHAVSKI, Dov, 1952 וואַרשאַווסקי, דובֿ: **מגילת איכה פֿון דריטן חורבן. צום צענטן יאָר־צייט פֿון די מיליאָנען ייִדישע קדושים**. שיקאַגאָ: שיקאַגער צײַטשריפֿט.

VEIDLINGER, Jeffrey, 2000: *The Moscow State Yiddish Theater: Jewish Culture on the Soviet Stage*. Bloomington, Ind.: Indiana University Press.

VERGELIS, Arn, 1972: *Letters from Europe (January–March 1971)*. Moscow: Novosti Press Agency Publishing House.

VERGELIS, Arn, 1976 ווערגעליס, ארן: **רײַזעס**. מאָסקווע: פֿארלאג סאָוועטסקי פּיסאטעל.

WALTHER, Alexander: *Die Shoah und die DDR. Aneignungen und Initiativen im Antifaschismus.* Dissertation. Friedrich-Schiller-Universität Jena.

WEGEWITZ, Markus, 2023: *Antifaschistische Kultur. Nico Rost und der lange Kampf gegen den Nationalsozialismus 1919–1965*. Göttingen: Wallstein.

WILDER, Gary, 2022: *Concrete Utopianism: The Politics of Temporality and Solidarity*. New York, NY: Fordham University Press.

WOLFF, Frank, 2020. *Yiddish Revolutionaries in Migration. The Transnational History of the Jewish Labour Bund*. Chicago, Ill.: Haymarket Books.

YOUNG, James E., 1988: *Writing and Rewriting the Holocaust: Narrative and the Consequences of Interpretation*. Bloomington, Ind.: Indiana University Press.

YURCHAK, Alexei, 2005: *Everything Was Forever, until It Was No More: The Last Soviet Generation*. Princeton, NJ: Princeton University Press.

ZAREMBA, Marcin, 2022: *Entangled in Fear. Everyday Terror in Poland, 1944–1947*. Bloomington, Ind.: Indiana University Press.

ZELTSER, Arkadi, 2018: *Unwelcome Memory. Holocaust Monuments in the Soviet Union*. Jerusalem: Yad Vashem.

Katharina Friedla

“*Bist a yid?* Can’t you speak to me in Yiddish?”[1]

Yiddish as a Marker of Identity among Polish Jews in the Soviet Union

Despite the growing body of scholarly works on Polish Jewish experiences in the Soviet Union during the Second World War,[2] this field still leaves many issues to be explored. Among these is the meaning and role the Yiddish language and culture played in the context of wartime displacement and refugeedom.[3]

Polish Jewish refugees, deportees, and evacuees[4] in the Soviet hinterland formed an extremely heterogeneous group: it included people who were strongly assimilated into the Polish culture, others less so; many were secular, others devoutly religious; there were those with left-wing sympathies and others who were politically conservative or indifferent; alongside students of prewar rabbinical schools, there were members of the intelligentsia, workers, and craftsmen; the majority were multilingual of some kind, for some Yiddish was their second language, others had very little knowledge of Polish and spoke mainly Yiddish. During the Second World War they found themselves in the multi-ethnic and multilingual surroundings of the Soviet state. In this “Tower of Babel”[5] many continued to speak מאַמע־לשון [*mame-loshn,* mother tongue, term of endearment used for Yiddish]; others adapted to their new surroundings, using Yiddish occasionally and learning Russian.

Rather than tread the beaten tracks of historiography concerning the involvement of refugees belonging to a Polish Jewish intelligentsia in creating Soviet Yiddish culture,[6] this paper sheds light on the ways in which ‘ordi-

1 Braitberg 2000, 40.

2 Edele, Fitzpatrick and Grossmann 2017, Nesselrodt 2019, Adler 2020, Zessin-Jurek and Friedla 2020, Nesselrodt and Friedla 2021.

3 On the refugeedom of Polish Jews in the Soviet Union see e.g., Seri-Levi 2019.

4 In this paper I will refer to all of them as refugees. Due to the fact that after the German invasion of the Soviet Union and signing the Polish-Soviet agreement in the summer of 1941, Polish citizens were granted “amnesty.” Most of them opted to migrate southwards and found refuge in Soviet Central Asia.

5 Blattberg Blumstein 2003, 35.

6 Estraikh 2016, Levin 1995, Nalewajko-Kulikov 2009.

nary' refugees made sense of their belonging and created communities in the context of their exile in the expanses of the Soviet Union. I will focus on just one aspect of this experience, namely the question of how the Yiddish language was used as a marker of ethnic identification. Although these refugees represented a diverse cross section of Polish Jewish society, with different backgrounds and language skills, I will show with the help of ego documents, mainly interviews with and testimonies of Polish Jewish 'exile survivors,' that Yiddish played an important role as a signifier of a shared identity. This might come as a surprise given that the Yiddish language, both in the former Second Polish Republic and the former Soviet Union, is generally seen as having lost its importance in daily communication and cultural production due to the increasing Polonization and Russification after the First World War. Especially those Polish and Soviet Jews who came of age in the interwar period went to Polish, Russian, Ukrainian, and Belorussian schools. For the majority of them, Polish or Russian respectively were the languages of education, culture, and professional life.[7] In this chapter, I will demonstrate that Yiddish regained immense power in the wake of the Second World War, was not only used as a communication tool but, furthermore, has shaped and influenced the relationship between Polish and Ashkenazi Soviet Jews.[8]

For refugees, having long and painful journeys behind them, accompanied by traumatic and harsh experiences and isolated in an unfamiliar environment, even a quick word in Yiddish, testimonies indicate, was of great importance. It evoked positive emotions and memories of secure and happy prewar existence in the home country, and empowered refugees to assert themselves in a strange and often unfriendly environment. Described by Eliyana Adler as a "secret code,"[9] the question ביסט אַ ייִד? [*Bist a yid?* Are you a Jew?] uttered in Yiddish was regularly used to reveal oneself as Jewish[10] publicly to both Polish and Ashkenazi Soviet Jews.

7 Estraikh 2008, 73.

8 In this chapter, I use the term "Ashkenazi Soviet Jews" to underline the difference between this group and non-Ashkenazi Jews, e.g., Bukharan Jews, living in the Central Asian Soviet republics such as Uzbekistan, Kyrgyzstan, and Kazakhstan. Polish Jewish refugees also encountered the Bukharan Jews, especially after the "amnesty" in the Summer of 1941, when the vast majority of Polish Jews left places of their imprisonment in the North and rushed southward to the Central Asian Soviet republics.

9 Adler 2016.

10 Also the Hebrew word עמך [*amkho*; your / our nation] was used to reveal Jewish identity.

Polish Jewish refugees survived the Second World War in a number of distinct locations in the USSR. Therefore, in this paper I will concentrate on the brief time they spent in the formerly Polish territories annexed by the Soviet Union, their deportation and time spent in special settlements or labor camps in Siberia and Kazakhstan, and their time of refuge in the Soviet Central Asian republics following their "amnesty"[11] in late 1941. During this period, Polish Jews interacted with each other and with different ethnic groups in each of the Soviet areas. Along the way they also had to learn to navigate and to deal with the Soviet realities they found themselves in. Finally, I will discuss the relationship between Ashkenazi Soviet Jews and Polish Jewish refugees.

War and Flight Migration: Place Changes, Sound Changes

The German-Soviet occupation of Poland and the Soviet Union's annexation of large swaths of prewar Polish territory in the fall of 1939 increased the Soviet Union's Jewish population by 1.6 million people (including the Polish Jewish refugees from the German occupied zone).[12] Many refugees described their first impression after arriving in the newly annexed territories. In these parts of the former Second Polish Republic, they were confronted with more conservative and religious Jewish communities. Joseph Ceder from Łódź, who fled in December 1939 to Białystok, recounted:

> From Bialystok [sic] I proceeded to Grodno [sic]. There were all kinds of people who fled the German occupation. In these parts of Poland people were more religious than in Lodz [sic]. Many spoke Litvak Yiddish which I hardly understood.[13]

Despite the initial difficulties, Ceder gradually got used to the dialectical differences and was able to communicate well. Moshe Prywes, another

[11] The word amnesty was used in the Polish-Soviet agreement, signed in July 1941, which made provision for the release of Polish 'enemy aliens' from Soviet special settlements, forced labor camps, and prisons. Yet, the Polish government in exile stressed that Polish citizens on Soviet territory were held captive for no legitimate reason, which is why most historians reject the term. From the Soviet standpoint, the imprisonment of those who were in special settlements and other forced labor camps was legal.

[12] Edele, Warlik 2017, 102.

[13] Interview with Joseph Ceder, May 12, 1996, Far Rockaway (New York), University of Southern California, Shoah Foundation Institute for Visual History and Education (USC VHA), 28343, tape 3.

refugee, who had studied medicine and graduated from the University of Warsaw in 1939, found refuge in several small villages between Rivne and Kovel together with his friends. He writes: "The population of these places was heavily Jewish. Among ourselves, we all conversed in Yiddish."[14]

Many former Polish Jewish refugees remember their encounters with Red Army soldiers or Soviet officials serving in the annexed territories with whom they also conversed in Yiddish.[15] Zev Katz describes the moment when he first met a Soviet officer: "Suddenly he opened up in Yiddish – *'Ir zayt Yidn? Ikh bin fun Odess!'* A short, friendly exchange followed between the overwhelmed local Jews and this Yiddish-speaking Soviet cavalry officer."[16] The older generation of Polish Jews, in particular, was often impressed to hear a Soviet officer or official speaking Yiddish. And what surprised them most was the presence of Jewish officers in the Army, in contrast to the prewar Polish Army, where Jewish officers were hard to be found.

Among the refugees, however, there were also assimilated and acculturated Polish Jewish families, as well as young people socialized in the Second Polish Republic and educated in Polish schools. They usually had either limited or no knowledge of Yiddish at all and were generally estranged from any Yiddish culture – not to mention Soviet Yiddish culture. Nevertheless, as Rabbi Shimen Huberband stated "some of the representatives of the younger generation benefitted to a certain extent from the widespread proliferation of opportunities for Yiddish culture in the Soviet annexed territories."[17] What Huberman alludes to is the rather unique Soviet state support of Yiddish since 1918 – through newspapers, theater, cultural events, and schools – transforming the language into "the only legitimate medium for Ashkenazi Jewish – national in form and socialist in content – cultural expression"[18] in the Soviet sphere. While most Soviet Yiddish-speakers like their non-Soviet counterparts would eventually assimilate linguistically into majority languages, in this

14 Prywes 1996, 86.

15 Interview with Yakov Shepetinsky, March 9, 2008, Tel Aviv, IS085, Blavatnik Archive.

16 Katz 2004, 19.

17 Account of Salomea L., From the other side (obtained from a migrant). Second notebook. Recorded by Rabbi Shimon Huberband, on the situation of the Jewish population at the territories under Soviet occupation and the first weeks of the German occupation in Białystok and Lwów. In: Żbikowski 2018, 102.

18 Estraikh 2008, 65.

case Russian, at the event of the Second World War Polish Jewish refugees encountered many Soviet Jews who were products of Yiddish state schools and spoke the language at home.

In early 1942, Huberband, who was a member of the Oyneg Shabes Archive project in the Warsaw Ghetto, recorded a testimony by 24-year-old Salomea L. A mathematics student at Warsaw University before the war with no knowledge of Yiddish from home, Salomea fled the Polish capital to Soviet occupied Białystok in October 1939. In her testimony she described the first weeks and months of life in Białystok under the Soviet occupation where she learned to speak Yiddish, to write a little, and became acquainted with the literature.[19]

Jakub Bukowski, another Polish Jewish refugee, crossed the new German-Soviet border with his two older brothers and like Salomea L., he also arrived in Białystok and found shelter in one of the local synagogues as hundreds of other refugees. The city was overcrowded with newcomers and, on the streets, one heard mainly Yiddish. Bukowski describes how his older brother, who spoke Yiddish fluently, was tasked to get crucial information on what to do next.[20] Soon the Bukowski brothers opted for work outside the former Polish areas and were sent to Nizhny Tagil in Sverdlovsk Oblast, on the boundary between Asia and Europe.

Scholarship into (flight) migration generally foregrounds the importance of pre-existing networks, extended families and friends in facilitating a more or less successful first escape and smooth arrival at the destination. This is true for Polish Jewish refugees from Nazi persecution who arrived in newly Soviet-occupied territories as well. As can be gleaned from the examples cited above, knowledge of Yiddish was a crucial ingredient as well. Language skills are always of significant importance in refugee movements and adaptation to the new place, though, during this particular refugee odyssey, the role of Yiddish can be seen in a multidimensional way. On the one hand, it was a widely spoken language in Soviet-occupied territories. On the other, it played an essential role in Soviet (Jewish) ideology. Last but not least, it was targeted for destruction by Nazi Germany.

19 Żbikowski 2018, 102.

20 Bukowski 2002, 53.

Soviet "Towers of Babel"

Polish Jewish refugees and non-Jewish Poles were among the first to experience the Soviet population transfer policy: in 1940 – deemed 'enemy aliens' of the Soviet state – they were deported to distant Eastern parts of the USSR. The incarceration of foreign nationals of enemy countries is certainly not unique to the Soviet case – France, Great Britain, Canada, the United States, etc., implemented similar policies at the same time – but the high proportion of Jewish refugees among the deportees in June 1940 meant that many so-called спецпоселения [*spetsposeleniya*, special settlements][21] consisted almost exclusively of Jewish prisoners. Henry Borenstein was deported to a 'special settlement' in Asino (near Tomsk) with his family where, according to his memoir, Yiddish was the primary language of the majority of refugees.[22] His father, who was fluent in Yiddish and Russian, served as a translator.[23]

There were also cases when refugees who found themselves among an overwhelmingly Yiddish-speaking group either learned or 'refreshed' their language familiarity. Henry Galler, born in 1923 in Jarosław, grew up in a Polish-speaking environment, but being deported with his parents from Soviet-occupied Tarnopol to a special settlement near Omsk, he "learned Yiddish in the camp in Siberia because most of the inmates were Yiddish speakers."[24] Aleksander Ziemny, born 1924, originally from Kraków, describes a similar phenomenon about the situation in a Soviet forced labor camp in Ural: "In exile with me were Jews from Sosnowiec, Będzin, but also Jews from Bukowina, German Jews, from various different places. They often talked to each other in Yiddish and, in that way, I refreshed the language."[25]

In many 'special settlements' Polish Jewish refugees were imprisoned with other ethnic groups. Some eyewitnesses recall these places as "Towers of Ba-

21 The civilian deportees were sent to 'special settlements' under the supervision of the Народный комиссариат внутренних дел [*Narodnyi komissariat vnutrennikh del*, People's Commissariat for Internal Affairs, NKVD], while POWs, as well as convicted criminals or political prisoners (on mostly false charges), were sent to the Gulag.

22 Borenstein 2012, 41. See also Interview with Roman Litman, 22 February 1997, Lublin (Poland), USC VHA, 28343, tape 2; Interview with Marek Bojm, 12 September 1996, Kraków (Poland), USC VHA, 20508, tape 2; Interview with Rivka Agron, 11 November 1996, Jerusalem (Israel), USC VHA, 22887, tape 3.

23 Borenstein 2012, 41.

24 Interview with Henry Galler, 8 September 1995, Toronto, USC VHA, 6574, tape 2.

25 Interview with Aleksander Ziemny, May 2004, Warsaw (Poland), Centropa, Central Europe Center for Research and Documentation.

bel" where many people and languages intermixed. Felix Flicker, deported with his family in April 1940 to a village near Pavlodar (northern Kazakhstan), states in his oral testimony that "between us we spoke Yiddish, with Polish friends we were together with, we spoke Polish, and we learned Russian."[26] As opposed to Flicker's seemingly neat division of language use, some witnesses recount more complicated, if not conflictual, encounters between different strata of Polish Jewish refugees. Janina Brajtburg ended up in a 'special settlement' in Mari ASSR with her parents. Janina, who grew up in an assimilated family in Warsaw, remembers a group of religious Jews from Poland, mainly Yiddish speakers. The group of assimilated, secular refugees occupied separate barracks, and as Brajtburg testified "Te dwie grupy nie były ze sobą powiązane" [these two groups did not associate with one another].[27] Furthermore, conflicts related to language, political affiliation, social class, and cultural codes occurred.[28]

Powers Reversed: From German to Yiddish

Among the Polish Jewish deportees there were Jews who had been either born and socialized in Germany or resided there for a long time. Due to the insecure economic situation, antisemitism, and pogroms most of them or their parents fled Poland during or shortly after the First World War and settled in Germany. In March 1938, the Sejm amended a law in order to revoke Polish citizenship after October 30 from Jews with Polish passports who had lived outside the country for an extended period of time, seeking to bar them from entry in the wake of the anti-Jewish policies in Germany and post-"Anschluss" Austria and the migration they predicted would follow. The German government used this as a pretense to force approximately 17,000 German-socialized Jews with Polish passports onto trains and transported them to the German-Polish border during the last week of October 1938 where they were refused entry. Most refugees found themselves in the no-man's-land of the border town and ad hoc refugee camp of Zbąszyń for several months until they were allowed to move to other parts of Poland.

26 Interview with Felix Flicker, 9 June 1997, Melbourne, USC VHA, 32399, tape 3.

27 Brajtburg 2016, 102.

28 Interview with Maria Dawidowicz, 14 April 1997, Bielsko Biała (Poland), USC VHA, 33034, tape 3.

Paris-based Herschel Grynszpan shot the German diplomat Ernst vom Rath in the German embassy in Paris on 7 November 1938 protesting the forced displacement and plight of his family members who were among the deportees. The German Ministry of Propaganda lost no time and used Grynszpan's act of political outcry and personal self-defense as an excuse to terrorize the Jewish population in the November pogroms on November 9 and 10, 1938. These events led many of the victims of the so-called *Polenaktion* [Poland Action] to escape to the Eastern parts of Poland by the outbreak of the Second World War roughly a year later, which were at that time under Soviet occupation. From there many of them were then deported into the interior of the Soviet Union. Among these deportees were many young people and children who were raised in Germany and the German language. During their short stay in Poland, many of them quickly learned Yiddish to navigate the new social reality. Later on, after being deported to the 'special settlements' in the distant parts of the Soviet Union, one of the first obstacles the newcomers faced was another barrier. Ten-year-old Joseph Rosenbaum, originally from Cologne, landed in one of the 'special settlements' in Altaisky Kray. This is how he described his experiences:

> In our settlement there were Polish Jews and Catholic Poles. I spoke there only Yiddish. […] I learned the language during my brief stay in Poland. Well, it still was not perfect and I used a lot of German words. […] There were also Polish kids, I spoke Yiddish, but they knew: this is the German, this is the Yekke,[29] they called me so. So, I had to go by my own because the kids didn't want me there.[30]

In numerous testimonies most of these survivors attest that their experience of exclusion from the Polish Jewish community was extremely painful. Often in the 'special settlements' Polish Jewish deportees reacted negatively to Jews from Germany, and made sure they felt it. Even if Rosenbaum was already able to communicate in Yiddish, he was stigmatized as German, rendered an 'enemy alien' of a different kind, and excluded from the Polish

[29] Jews of German-speaking origin. This term was usually in use in the British Mandate of Palestine at that time, and it is rather unlikely that this expression was in use in the distant parts of the Soviet Union. However, Polish Jews surely were familiar with the term, not least through the Polish Jewish Zionist press.

[30] Interview with Joseph Rosenbaum, 10 February 1994, San Francisco (California), United States Holocaust Memorial Museum, 1999.A.0122.235, RG-50.477.0235, tape 1.

Jewish children's community. What Rosenbaum's testimony suggests is, in a first step, the pervasiveness of the 'monolingual paradigm' (Yasemin Yildiz) that renders one's *first* language synonymous with *national* belonging and, in a second step, that German, the 'enemy-language' of Nazi Germany, could not count as a Jewish language among Polish Jewish refugees any longer. The harsh experiences of German-socialized Jews with Polish passports in Soviet exile not only point to the significant differences and conflicts between the eastern and western European Jewish worlds but indicate that despite their shared fate of being persecuted as Jews, they were incapable of creating a community based on Jewish-identification.

The experience of refuge in Soviet Russia clearly points to the thorny issues of national and cultural identity. German-speaker Norbert Fluss was born in 1922 to a Polish Jewish family in Berlin. He was first expelled to Poland in October 1938 and then deported by the NKVD from Lviv to a 'special settlement' in the Mari Republic after the outbreak of the war. In 1944, Fluss was conscripted into the Polish Armed Forces in the USSR, the so-called Berling Army.[31] In his testimony, he reiterates what Rosenbaum's account suggested in that his experiences in the Soviet Union were marked by constant questions of belonging:

> It was so difficult for me... In Lviv I have learned Yiddish. But Yiddish native speakers immediately recognized that my first language was German. Later on, in the Berling Army, outside of service I chatted with some Jewish soldiers in Yiddish, of course they noticed I am a German. Officially I couldn't say I was German, because we were fighting the Germans, so I always said I was Polish and have studied in Germany, so I knew the German language so good. But my problem was that my Yiddish and Polish were not that good as my German...[32]

In general, the German-speaking refugees found themselves in a more disadvantaged position than Jews from Poland, who spoke Yiddish, Polish or Russian. The social and cultural background of German-speaking Polish Jews very often complicated their existence as refugees in the USSR. Undoubtedly,

31 In May 1943, Stalin sanctioned the creation of a communist-controlled military force headed by a prewar-Polish officer, Colonel Zygmunt Berling. In the autumn of that year, its units fought in the Battle of Lenino, later took part in fighting in Ukraine and the liberation of Polish lands from German occupation, and some of its units were even part of the liberation of Berlin.

32 Interview with Norbert Fluss, 10 July 2011, New York, Authors Archive.

most of them identified as Jews, in a sense of ethnicity and religion, while technically being culturally German with Polish citizenship.

Soviet-Polish Encounters in Yiddish

As Eliyana Adler has demonstrated in her recent monograph on Polish Jewish refugees in the Soviet Union, the microcosm of Jewish refugees "in general constituted their primary social world – even those, from different regions, generations, and backgrounds, shared certain fundamental commonalities and were most comfortable with one another."[33] The war conditions also led to an unprecedented number of encounters between Soviet and Polish Jews. Whereas the majority of Polish Jews had originally been deported to isolated camps and kolkhozes where they were far more likely to meet Kazakhs, Karelians, Uzbeks than Jews, the "amnesty" for Polish citizens announced in the summer of 1941 and evacuation to Central Asian Soviet Republics changed this situation tremendously. Meanwhile, millions of Soviet citizens were on the move, relocated by the state as part of organized evacuations from the Western territories or escaping the Nazi onslaught eastward on their own. The result was an influx of far more people than resources could support. But there was also an opportunity for social interactions previously unimaginable.

Thus, roughly twenty years after the 'separation' wrought by the October Revolution of 1917 and the creation of the Second Polish Republic in the aftermath of the First World War, Soviet and Polish Jews had the opportunity to live side-by-side and to speak with one another to a far greater degree than before. As reported in numerous testimonies by Polish Jews, the Soviet Jews played an important role as helpers, supporters, and mediators even though contacts between Polish Jewish refugees and Soviet Jews were seldom long-term. Usually, the two groups met each other sporadically, sometimes only once, and had casual exchanges – often in the common language Yiddish. The spectrum of everyday contact zones included the workplace, the bazaar or Red Army service. Many Polish Jews reported that the question asked in Yiddish *"Bist a yid?"* opened many doors that would otherwise have remained closed to them. Shlomo Leser for example, redeemed his food stamps in a small shop in Osh, Kyrgyzstan. One day the Jewish salesman asked him: *"A*

33 Adler 2020, 168.

yid?," and then gave him preferential treatment.[34] David Brandspiegel and his family breathed a huge sigh of relief when the officer who caught them sleeping in the forest and took them originally for draft dodgers began to speak Yiddish. In their own language they were able to explain the circumstances of their plight and elicit pity and help.[35] Morris Gruda during his flight after German invasion in June 1941, arriving in Kiev wondered where to go next. On the street he met a man:

> He asked in a very nice Yiddish 'are you Jewish?' Understandably, I was happy to hear the question, and I told him in Yiddish where I came from. He told me that he had lost his wife not long ago and he lived alone in a large house; then he invited me to stay with him as long as I wanted.[36]

The connecting factor of this tentative conversation with Soviet Jews was the shared language of Yiddish. Polish Jews were generally moved when they could communicate with Soviet Jews in *mame-loshn*. Even a word in Yiddish, mentioned in passing, was of great importance in this perpetual state of uncertainty. Recognizing the Jews within the people around them helped many refugees to feel slightly less alienated. Moreover, Soviet Jews often played important roles in familiarizing Polish Jews with the Soviet system.[37] Beside this, these accounts emphasize, retrospectively, Soviet Jews' curiosity about Jewish life and culture and their yearning for a stronger connection with their Jewish identity. It seems that the shared language of Yiddish as well as Jewish identity brought Soviet and Polish Jews together.

And yet, as Natalie Belsky has demonstrated, there remained significant differences between the evacuees and the refugees.[38] In testimonies and memories of Soviet Jews there are relatively few references to interactions with Polish Jews.[39] Belsky also points out that Polish Jews are described in stereotypical terms and often remain nameless, and seem in these narratives to function as a symbolic "Other" against which the Soviet Jews define them-

34 Leser 2004, 2–3; Leser 2010, 4.

35 Brandspiegel 1998, 141.

36 Gruda 2006, 129–130; Interview with Morris Gruda, 22 April 1996, Toronto, USC VHA, 14395, Tape 2.

37 Taube 2007, 53–54; Shternfeld 1999, 180; Goldkorn 1998, 230–237.

38 Belsky 2017, 175f.

39 See e.g., United States Holocaust Memorial Museum Archives, RG 31.053; Judaica Institute, Kiev, Ukraine; Blavatnik Archive; Centropa Archive.

selves.[40] Nevertheless, these important sources can tell us a great deal about the encounters between these two groups and furthermore give a glimpse into the amorphous issue of identity. Above all, the presented ego documents validate that Yiddish created some sense of shared national and cultural community between Ashkenazi Soviet and Polish Jews as much as the sudden influx of Polish Jews into the war-torn Soviet Union allowed some Soviet Jews to reconnect with Judaism and other forms of Jewishness.[41]

The linguistic kinship of some, on the one hand, was accompanied by difficult, painful encounters between German-speaking Jews and Polish Jewish refugees as well as between the religious Yiddish-speaking and assimilated Polish-speaking refugees, on the other. Language, in other words, possessed enormous potential for intra-Jewish conflicts, which governed the relationship between the various sections of Polish Jewish refugees, particularly concerning German speakers. The lack of Yiddish language skills or speaking Yiddish with a German accent often led to exclusion from refugee communities. At the same time, among fluent Yiddish-speakers, the language could serve as a powerful and multidimensional tool. It undoubtedly helped refugees to communicate amongst each other, build communities in an unfamiliar country, and navigate a complex new reality.

Bibliography

Adler, Eliyana R., 2020: *Survival on the Margins: Polish Jewish Refugees in the Wartime Soviet Union*. Cambridge, Mass.: Harvard University Press.

Adler, Eliyana R., 2016: Lecture: *Polish Jewish Refugees in Central Asia during the Shoah*, Conference: The Jewish Refugee Problem During the Shoah (1933–1945) Reconsidered, The International Institute for Holocaust Research, Yad Vashem, Jerusalem, December 2016.

Belsky, Natalie, 2017: Fraught Friendships: Soviet Jews and Polish Jews on the Soviet Home Front. In: Mark Edele, Sheila Fitzpatrick, and Atina Grossmann, eds., *Shelter from the Holocaust. Rethinking Jewish Survival in the Soviet Union*, Detroit. Mich.: Wayne State University Press, 161–184.

Belsky, Natalie, 2021: Contested Memories: Soviet and Polish Jewish Refugees and Evacuees Recount Their Experience on the Soviet Home Front. In: Markus Nesselrodt, and Katharina Friedla, eds., *Polish Jews in the Soviet Union (1939–1959): History and Memory of Deportation, Exile and Survival.* Boston, Mass.: Academic Studies Press, 200–213.

40 Belsky 2021, 212f.

41 Friedla 2021, 108.

Blattberg Blumstein, Rita, 2003: *Like Leaves in the Wind*. London, Portland, Oreg.: Vallentine Mitchell.

Borenstein, Henry H., 2012: *From Leszno-Street, Warsaw, Poland (1924) to Delray Beach, Florida, USA (2012). Autobiography*. United States: Henry H. Borenstein.

Braitberg, Gregor Chaim, 2000: *A Wartime Odyssey. A Memoir*. St. Louis, Miss.: Gregor Chaim Braitberg.

Brajtburg, Janina, 2016: *Świece pamięci*. Montreal: Polish-Jewish Heritage Foundation of Canada.

Brandspiegel, David, 1998 ברנדשפיגל, דוד: **הישרדות: סיפור חייהם של היהודים בברית־המועצות בזמן מלחמת העולם השניה**. תל אביב: פרוינד.

Bukowski, Jakub, 2002: *Opowieść o życiu*. Warsaw: Żydowski Instytut Historyczny.

Edele, Mark, Sheila Fitzpatrick, and Atina Grossmann, eds., 2017: *Shelter from the Holocaust. Rethinking Jewish Survival in the Soviet Union*. Detroit, Mich.: Wayne State University Press.

Edele, Mark, and Wanda Warlik, 2017: Saved by Stalin? Trajectories and Numbers of Polish Jews in the Soviet Second World War. In: Mark Edele, Sheila Fitzpatrick, and Atina Grossmann, eds., *Shelter from the Holocaust. Rethinking Jewish Survival in the Soviet Union*. Detroit, Mich.: Wayne State University Press, 95–131.

Estraikh, Gennady, 2016: The Missing Years: Yiddish Writers in Soviet Bialystok, 1939–1941. In: *East European Jewish Affairs* 46 (2): 176–191.

Estraikh, Gennady, 2008: From Yiddish to Russian: A Story of Linguistic and Cultural Appropriation. In: *Studia Hebraica* 8: 62–71.

Friedla, Katharina, 2021: "When the Shabbat Became Sunday": Religious and Social Life of Polish Jews in the USSR during World War II. In: Mikhaela Gligor, ed., *Memories of Terror. Essays on Recent Histories*. Frankfurt am Main: CEEOLPRESS, 79–124.

Goldkorn, Yosef, 1998 גאָלדקאָרן, יוסף: **נע־ונד איבער די שליאַכן פֿון רוסלאַנד**. תל־אבֿיבֿ: ה. לייוויק־פֿאַרלאַג.

Gruda, Morris, 2006: *Tricks of Fate. Escape, Survival and Rescue, 1939–1945*, ed. and trans. from Yiddish by Adam Fuerstenberg. Oakville: Mosaic Press.

Katz, Zev, 2004: *From the Gestapo to the Gulags. One Jewish Life*. London, Portland, Oreg.: Vallentine Mitchell.

Leser, Shlomo, 2004: *Poems and Sketches Reminiscing the War-times in the* USSR. Haifa: unpublished manuscript, Part 1 & 2.

Leser, Shlomo, 2010: *The Jewish World War II Refugees from Poland in Uzbekistan, Kazakhstan and Tajikistan in 1941–1946 – a concise overview*. Haifa: unpublished manuscript.

Levin, Dov, 1995: *The Lesser of Two Evils. Eastern European Jewry under Soviet Rule, 1939–1941*. Philadelphia, Penn.: Jewish Publication Society.

Nalewajko-Kulikov, Joanna, 2009: *Obywatel Jidyszlandu. Rzecz o komunistach żydowskich w Polsce*. Warsaw: Neriton.

Nesselrodt, Markus, 2019: *Dem Holocaust entkommen. Polnische Juden in der Sowjetunion (1939–1946)*. Berlin: De Gruyter Oldenbourg.

Nesselrodt, Markus, and Katharina Friedla, eds., 2021: *Polish Jews in the Soviet Union (1939–1959). History and Memory of Deportation, Exile and Survival*. Boston, Mass.: Academic Studies Press.

Prywes, Moshe, 1996: *Prisoner of Hope. Moshe Prywes As Told to Haim Chertok*. Waltham, Mass.: Brandeis University Press.

Redlich, Shimon, 1971: The Jews in the Soviet Annexed Territories 1939–41. In: *Soviet Jewish Affairs* 1 (1): 81–90.

Shternfeld, Shaul, 1999 שטרנפלד, שאול: **חלום בין גדרות**. תל אביב: חלונות.

Shternshis, Anna, 2001: Passover in the Soviet Union, 1917–41. In: *East European Jewish Affairs* 31 (1): 61–76.

Taube, Herman, 2007: *Surviving Despair: A Story about Perseverance*. Bloomington, Ind.: AuthorHouse.

Zessin-Jurek, Lidia, and Katharina Friedla, eds., 2020: *Syberiada Żydów polskich. Losy uchodźców z Zagłady*. Warsaw: Żydowski Instytut Historyczny.

Żbikowski, Andrzej, ed., 2018: *Accounts from the Borderlands, 1939–1941*. Warsaw: Żydowski Instytut Historyczny.

Kamil Kijek

Yiddish Spaces and Daily Culture in Early Post-*Khurbn* Poland

A Preliminary Analysis

There is no doubt that the חורבן [*khurbn,* destruction, Shoah, Holocaust] killed not only people but also almost eradicated Yiddish culture in Poland along with them.[1] Yiddish schools, publishing houses, synagogues, and other social spaces of daily life disappeared. Another byproduct of the destruction under Nazi occupation was the dislocation of around 300,000 Polish Jews. Whether they survived in the Soviet Union, in camps in Poland or Germany, in the woods, in hiding or on so-called Aryan papers, almost none of them could return to the places that they were living in before 1939. Returning to their old homes and social milieus was impossible.[2]

Yet, the *khurbn* did *not* spell the end of the Yiddish language and culture in Poland. Indeed, I argue, even the total demise of Yiddish in Poland *after* 1945 was far from inevitable. Against the standard teleological narrative of Polish and Jewish historiography, there were a number of possible futures of Yiddish culture in postwar Poland within the state-socialist socio-political system. Although going through deep crisis and ultimately arriving at a post-vernacular stage, the 'spaces of Yiddish' in the late 1940s were operative and at times even flourishing. These spaces of Yiddish challenge scholarship's dominant teleological visions of post-1945 Polish Jewish history that purport a linear, inevitable demise of both the Jewish community and Yiddish culture under socialism.

While far from being exhaustive, this chapter illuminates three dimen-

1 Research for this article was done in the framework of the Polish National Science Center (NCN), Grant Nr.: 2018/31/B/HS3/00228 ("The last Polish shtetl? The Jewish community of Dzierzoniow, Jewish World, Cold War and Communism (1945–1950)").

A note on Yiddish spelling and transcription: citations from Yiddish sources were given in Hebrew script in YIVO's Modern Standard Yiddish. I have used the YIVO transliteration for Yiddish expressions/names/organizations and the Congress Library Transliteration System for Hebrew terms/names respectively in the body of the text.

I'd like to thank the editors Miriam Chorley-Schulz and Alexander Walther for their helpful feedback on this chapter.

2 For general overviews of history of Polish Jewish community after the *khurbn* see: Cichopek-Gajraj 2014; Adelson 1993, 387–477; Dobroszycki 1994; Kichelewski 2021.

sions of Yiddish life in Poland in the late 1940s – institutional-political, sociological, and geographical – with a focus on the two less researched latter aspects. After a short review of the well-researched institutional rebirth of Yiddish life in early postwar Poland, I will analyze the little known daily workings of the Yiddish language in specific social and geographical spaces. Showing how in particular contexts and localities Yiddish was spoken, read, and heard will allow me to demonstrate the so far unacknowledged cultural force of Yiddish in Poland in the immediate postwar period. Its later demise had political but also sociological causes comparable to those that also affected Yiddish cultures on the other side of the Iron Curtain.

Institutions and Politics of Yiddish in Early Postwar Poland

The initially named Tymczasowy Centralny Komitet Żydów w Polsce [Temporary Central Committee of the Jews in Poland, TCKŻP], later renamed צענטראַלער קאָמיטעט פֿון די ייִדן אין פּוילן [*Tsentraler komitet fun di yidn in Poyln*, Centralny Komitet Żydów w Polsce; Central Committee of the Jews in Poland, CKŻP] became the leading Polish Jewish institution from September 1944 until its liquidation in 1950.[3] Formed out of a cross-ideological coalition of all secular Jewish political parties in Poland, center and left-wing Zionists, Communists, and Bundists, CKŻP's mission was to rehabilitate the Polish Jewish community physically, economically, and psychologically and, most crucially, to rebuild Jewish culture in Poland, with Yiddish at its center.[4]

Despite the dominance of Zionist affinities on the *yidishe gas* [Jewish street] and, numerically, on the boards in both CKŻP headquarters and its regional branches, representatives from the Jewish faction of the communist Polska Partia Robotnicza [Polish Workers' Party] played a leading role in the institution. Its cultural politics mainly followed the program of נוסח־פּוילן [*nusekh Poyln*, Polish Style], a Jewish communist program of (re-)building progressive, secular, and socialist Jewish culture in Poland through the Yiddish language and in interaction with Jewish communities, both within and beyond the socialist bloc.[5]

3 For more on this topic see Agnieszka Żółkiewska's chapter in this volume.

4 Grabski, 2015. For information on the formation of TCKŻP and CKŻP see: Ibid., 18–22; Shlomi 2001, 31–54.

5 Nalewajko-Kulikov 2009, 173, 181–182, 187–190 (English translation of this book: Nalewajko-Kulikov 2020); Grabski, Rusiniak 2008, 53–64.

Under the leadership of CKŻP and with the financial support of Polish government and, especially, of the American Jewish Joint Distribution Committee [JDC] and various other Jewish institutions from the West, the Polish Jewish community was able to reconstruct many institutional features of prewar Yiddish cultural life: press, book publishing, theater companies as well as Yiddish cinema.[6] Alongside this impressive cultural rebuilding, historical scholarship reemerged as one important avenue of postwar Polish Yiddish culture with a particular focus on the documentation and studying of the *khurbn* itself.[7]

Probably most crucial to secure a future for all those cultural institutions was Jewish school education in the Yiddish language. The obstacles it faced in the early postwar period, however, reveal the inherent limitations of a full-blown postwar rebirth of Yiddish. As of July 1945, CKŻP decided to open Jewish schools with Yiddish as the main language of instruction alongside Polish and, to a lesser extent, Hebrew.[8] Despite lacking Yiddish teaching materials and qualified teachers due in part to ongoing emigration, Jewish schools grew in subsequent years. In June 1946, CKŻP was overseeing twenty-five Jewish schools with 2,900 pupils. Even after Polish Jews emigrated en masse in the wake of the infamous Kielce pogrom on 4 July 1946, enrollment numbers remained stable with 3,200 students.[9] By 1948, thirty-five CKŻP "Yiddish schools" still counted around 3,000 pupils.[10] Minor competitors of CKŻP Yiddish schools were ten Hebrew schools by 1947 run by the Zionist movement with approximately 600 pupils as well as thirty-six *khadorim* [traditional private Jewish primary schools] and *talmud-toyres* [supplementary community-run Jewish education] with a total of 1,100 pupils that were operated by the orthodox community.[11]

While the numbers suggest that Yiddish indeed dominated formal Jewish education, the situation appeared much more complicated in practice. Indeed, faced with the reality that many Jewish children, who survived in

6 Koźmińska-Frejlak 2012, 211–230; Nalewajko-Kulikov 2007, 257–278; Bergman 2017, 170–171; Ruta 2017; Nalewajko-Kulikov, Ruta 2012, 284–293; Gross 2002, 117–140; Kałużna 2015, 34–133; Turkov-Grudberg 1952, 135–176; Egit 1947, 72–73.

7 Aleksiun 2008, 74–97; Jockusch 2012, 5–6, 88–120; Stach 2008, 401–416.

8 Datner 2016, 254–256. Yiddish language and culture was a crucial element of children's rehabilitation, "psychological" and "national" recovery also in CKŻP orphanages, Zahra 2011, 103–104.

9 Adelson 1993, 464.

10 Wiener Library Archives in London, Microfilm collection, Reel 190 II.22C, clipping from *Congress Bulletin*, April 1948 [no exact date or page number given].

11 Cała, Datner 1997, 222–224.

hiding or in the Soviet Union, did not know Yiddish to begin with and combined with the undeniable necessity of knowing the Polish language in a majoritarian Polish-speaking society, CKŻP schools soon realized that they had to shelve the original plan of instructing primarily in Yiddish. According to the report of the Lower Silesian Jewish Committee from May 1946, 144 hours of teaching in Yiddish were matched by the exact same number of hours in Polish in its eight schools.[12] In reality, the latter was in fact dominating. According to Anselm Reis (1886–1984), a Zionist activist who had played an important role in the interwar תרבות [*Tarbut*, Culture], a secular, Hebrew-language school system, and visited Poland in early 1947, the majority of Jewish children at the time "were far remote [sic] from our national Jewish life. They knew many languages, Russian, Polish, Ukrainian, Uzbec, Tatar, Kirgisian[13] but very few could speak or understood Yiddish."[14] This pessimistic assessment of a potential rebirth of Yiddish among Jewish children, was shared even by Salo Fishgrund (1893–1971), the head of the postwar Polish אַלגעמיינער ייִדישער אַרבעטער־בונד [*Algemeyner yidisher arbeter-bund*, General Jewish Labor Bund, short: Bund] – a diaspora-nationalist, socialist party with a strong Yiddishist outlook and the fiercest anti-Zionist stance among all Jewish political parties in postwar Poland. In his report of 1946 for the New York Jewish Labor Committee [JLC], an organizational supporter of rebuilding Jewish life in Poland, Fishgrund stressed that most of the 5,000 Jewish child survivors in Poland (and not in the Soviet interior), having mostly survived with Christian religious institutions or families, did not know Yiddish either.[15]

Pre-*Khurbn* Centers in Ruins: Obstacles of Yiddish Futures

While the example of Yiddish school education suggests that the political and institutional development of Yiddish culture grew on rather shaky social and sociological grounds, it by no means tells the entire story of the (im-)

12 Archiwum Państwowe we Wrocławiu [APWr], 415 Wojewódzki Komitet Żydów [WKŻ], Folder 5, k. 62.

13 Uzbek, Tatar, Kirgisian owing to the fact that the majority were born or survived the *khurbn* in Soviet Central Asia.

14 YIVO Archives, RG 116 Poland 3, Folder 11, clipping from *Congress Weekly*, 7th of March 1947, 65.

15 Taminent Library Archives [TLA], Jewish Labour Committee Records [JLC], Part 1, WAG 25.001, Box 35, Folder 10, Salo Fishgrund *Yidishe kinder shulen in Poyln* (no date given), p. 1–3.

possibilities of a rebirth of Yiddish in postwar Poland. An expression of the profound transnational character of postwar Yiddishland(s), a host of Jewish visitors to Poland assessed the future of Yiddish in formerly bustling Polish Jewish centers as grim despite the institutional rebuilding efforts outlined above: the combination of Nazi destruction, simmering postwar antisemitism, and waves of Jewish emigration could hardly suggest otherwise.

Particularly Warsaw, the once-Yiddish metropolis now in ruin, shocked even the most enthusiastic, such as American Yiddish communist Peysekh Novick (1891–1989), and put the rebirth of Yiddish blatantly in question. Generally enthusiastic about the building of socialism in the Polish People's Republic and its potential for a revived Yiddish culture, he was stunned by the ruins of Warsaw and level of its destruction.[16] But nothing could compare to what he saw in the former ghetto:

> איך קום נאָר־וואָס פֿון דער ,געטאָ׳ – דאָרט ווו ס׳איז אַמאָל געווען וואַרשע, די ייִדי־שע וואַרשע. [...] האָב איך געבלאָנקעט איבער די בערגלעך צעהאַקטע, צעשטויבטע ציגל, אַרויפֿגעשטעלט זיך אויף אַ העכער בערגל און געקוקט אַרום, ווי ווייַט, ווייַל עס איז פֿון דער אַמאָליקער ייִדישער וואַרשע ניטאָ קיין איין הויז.[17]
>
> I just came from the 'ghetto' – there where once was Warsaw, the Jewish Warsaw. […] So I wandered across hills of broken, pulverized bricks, and I stood atop a hill and I looked around, so far, since there is not one house standing from the former Jewish Warsaw.

Mordechai Tsanin (1906–2009), a Yiddish journalist who visited Poland in 1946 from British Mandate Palestine, painted a similar spectral landscape. "One big pile of rubble," the rebuilding of "Polish" Warsaw is juxtaposed to "Jewish" Warsaw which remains in ruins and has only the cemetery [בית־החיים, *beys hakhayim,* literally 'House of the Living'] as the only 'living' space left. His pessimism about Polish Yiddish futures took a downward turn on Yom Kippur during a visit to Warsaw's only remaining synagogue at Twarda street. He speaks of hundreds of Jews outside the synagogue hiding their identity, with false names, in military uniforms or ministerial positions, wearing crosses around their necks and crying as they listened to *Kol Nidre* [vow recited at the beginning of Yom Kippur evening service].[18] Khayim Shoshkes (1891–1958), another

16 Novick 1948, 60.

17 Ibid., 74–75.

18 Tsanin 2018, 39–40, 43, 45–47, 49–55, 57–63.

traveler from the United States who used to be an important interwar Polish Jewish social activist, classified many Warsaw Jews as מאָדערן־טאָג מאַראַנאָס [*modern-tog maranos,* modern day marranos]. Just like their Sephardic predecessors in the wake of the Spanish Inquisition, he alleged that they were simply too afraid to reveal their Jewish identity in the postwar atmosphere of heavy antisemitism. It led to the situation in which

> באַהאַלטן זיך די גאָלדשטיינס, פֿינקלשטיינס און ראָזענבלומס אונטער פֿרעמדע נע־מען, וועלכע שמעקן מיט עכט־פּוילישקייט: זיי רופֿן זיך פּעטראָווסקי, זאַוואַדסקי, צאַצ־קאָווסקי, מיטן צולייג פֿון יאַן, סטעפֿאַן און מאַריאַן.[19]
>
> The Goldsteins, Finkelsteins, and Rozenblums hide behind alien surnames, which reek of proper ethnic-Polishness: they call themselves Piotrowski, Zawadzki, Cackowski, and add Jan, Stefan and Marian.

Many of these people wore crosses on their necks. Emblematic of this broader phenomenon was Rokhl Elboym, widow of a friend of Shoshkes' and granddaughter of Menachem Mendel Morgensztern, the esteemed Hasidic *rebbe* of Kock. When Shoshkes met her, she was almost unrecognizable to him. Having dyed her hair blond, she ran a large book store under the Polonized surname 'Karnowska' in order to disguise her Jewish heritage from her Polish co-workers. Her son, too, was renamed Jerzy and wore a medallion with a Christian saint up until the fateful meeting with Shoshkes. 8-year-old Jerzy was told he was Jewish and taken to synagogue to say *Kaddish* [Jewish mourner's prayer] for the perished family-members.[20]

A host of travel reports by Yiddish Westerners suggest that the situation was by and large not better in most small towns and *shtetlekh* in Central Poland with a large prewar Jewish population.[21] These were now, as Shoshkes tellingly entitled one of his travelogue's chapters, שטעטלעך אָן ייִדן [*shtetlekh on yidn, shtetlekh* without Jews]. It was simply too dangerous for Jews to live in and commute between them.[22] Bialystok-born Yankev Pat (1890–1966), an important figure of the Polish Bund and upon emigration to the Unit-

19 Shoshkes 1946, 24.

20 Ibid. 1946, 19–29. He described many other situations of this kind, ibid., 53–58, 75–78, 82–86.

21 Novick 1948, 59–75; Wohl 1947, 15–21, 47–52; Shulshteyn 1949, 20–31, 49–79; Schneiderman 1947, 38–47.

22 Shoshkes 1946, 110–120.

ed States in 1937 the chairman and executive director of JLC in New York, accompanied his *landsman* Shoshkes on his *shtetl*-tour through Central Poland and generally agreed: but few anxious *khurbn*-survivors were scattered in uncannily Jew-less towns amidst viral antisemitism.[23] Having journeyed through dozens of former *shtetlekh* across the Polish People's Republic, the aforementioned Mordechai Tsanin concluded that the *khurbn* had rendered these spaces cemeteries of Jewish life.[24]

If the *khurbn* and widespread antisemitism were not enough, the resultant large-scale emigration additionally hampered the possibility for a sustained growth of a postwar Polish Yiddish culture. Between 1945 and early 1947 alone (when the anti-Jewish violence and illegal emigration came to a halt), between 120,000 and 150,000 Jewish Poles left Poland – with many of those who remained ready to leave as soon as the political situation took another downward turn.[25] Among the émigrés were many Yiddish writers and cultural activists.[26] Emigration, in other words, not only depleted the consumers of rebuilt Yiddish institutional infrastructure but also the producers.

The social process often imprecisely dubbed 'assimilation' had a hand in this, too. Ranging from 'passing' as a non-Jewish Pole to adopting Polish as one's primary language, these processes that began long before the Second World War accelerated after 1945 when the socialist restructuring of the state opened up previous prohibited professional avenues to Polish Jews, including state careers. The newly-emerging Polish elite of Jewish descent avoided Yiddish publicly and certainly did not pass it on to their children.[27] The impressive reconstruction of institutional Yiddish life then saw a decline of Yiddish speakers and cultural consumers, particularly in Warsaw and former centers of Polish Jewish life. However, if we take seriously that the war-cum-*khurbn* did indeed change everything, this great catastrophe also remapped Polish Yiddishland. While Western visitors found only death, destruction, and hostility in the centers of prewar Jewish Poland, they could find Yiddish cultural reawakening in unfamiliar peripheries.

23 Pat 1946, 85–91.

24 Tsanin 2018. The same situation was reported by American Yiddish press, see: Dorfzon 1945, 1; Lerner 1945, 6; Anonymous 1945, 2; Bader 1945, 7; Kersht 1946, 6; Schneiderman 1946, 2.

25 Stankowski 2010, 110; Kichelewski 2021, 77–78, 82.

26 Cohen 2008, 151–164.

27 For a study of the few Warsaw Jewish families of this kind see Auerbach 2013.

The New Map of Postwar Polish Yiddishland

An anonymous JDC report written most probably in the summer of 1947 in fact juxtaposed Warsaw's 'new marranos' with the other half of the Polish Jewish population that now lived in Poland's newly acquired, former German territory stripped of much of the ethnically German population, mainly in Lower Silesia.[28] This community was first initiated by a few thousand Polish *khurbn*-survivors freed from local concentration camps and grew exponentially in the first half of 1946, when most of the around 140,000 Polish Jewish repatriates from the Soviet Union were directed to this area. Concentrated in few towns, thousands of Jews made up a high percentage of the overall population and worked in Jewish cooperatives and Jewish cultural institutions.[29] Unlike Warsaw and former *shtetlekh* marked by a double alienation from non-Jewish neighbors and from their Jewish heritage,[30] in cities such as Łódź (the second largest Polish city in Central Poland at the time with the largest postwar Jewish population (20,000)),[31] and especially in former German territories, in Szczecin, Wrocław, Dzierżoniów, and Wałbrzych, Jews lived collectively in their thousands and organized around dense networks of various political, social, and cultural institutions.

While living in the United States and writing for New York Yiddish מאָרגן־זשורנאַל [*Morgn-zhurnal*, Morning Journal], Shmuel Leyb Schneiderman (1906–1996), the renowned interwar Polish Jewish journalist, provides a highly ambivalent picture of the situation in Łódź in the summer of 1946 in the wake of the Kielce pogrom and amidst the concomitant migration panic. As thousands of local Jews made anxious plans to leave Poland, out of the 2,100 Jews working in the state textile factories of Łódź, most concealed their identity due to the strong antisemitic atmosphere. At the same time, Łódź was home to dense, organized and protected Jewish spaces. The strongest and most visible was the Jewish religious community (acting separately from the secular local Jewish Committee) located at Zachodnia street. According to Schneiderman, this part of Łódź was a "fortress of orthodox Jewry" where

28 For the genesis and early years of the Polish Jewish community in postwar Lower Silesia, Szaynok 2000; Cichopek 2014, 181, 184–187, 190–197, 203, 206.

29 YIVO Archives, RG 116 Poland 3, Folder 2, manuscript "Fun nokh di milkhome," unpaginated.

30 For a microhistorical study of this kind of situation in one of the towns in Central Poland, Radom, see Krzyzanowski 2020.

31 For the history of Jewish community in postwar Łódź, Redlich 2010.

religious Jews spoke Yiddish and gathered in the buildings of the Jewish Religious Congregation, its courtyard or its *mikve* [ritual bath house]. Boys with *peyes* [sidelocks] frequented the *kheyder* on its premises so that "for a moment one could think that is in a courtyard of prewar Nalewki [a Jewish neighborhood of Warsaw] or in a some small Galician town."[32] Two *yeshives* and synagogues were filled with men studying. The building also accommodated a branch of the orthodox political party, אגודת ישראל [*Agudes Yisroel*, Union of Israel], and a tailor's workshop that employed more than seventy Jewish girls. Women and men met with relatives, exchanged or traded goods, lived their traditional life – and talked proud and loud mostly in Yiddish. As Schneiderman wrote: "I looked at these Jews with beards of all shapes […]. I looked into their eyes, which showed less fear than the eyes of the beardless Jews who lived in Łódź under 'Aryan' names. I was deeply moved by the vitality of these people, by the faith and fearlessness which emanated from their emaciated faces."[33] Similar to this orthodox community, a different Jewish milieu in Łódź was committed to life in Poland and to rebuilding its Yiddish culture: members of the many Jewish cooperatives operating in the city.

Khayim Shoshkes seconded Schneiderman's Łódź impressions. On the one hand, he encountered 'new marranos,' on the other, he met Jewish soldiers of the Polish Army, who were proudly Jewish and active in one of many local Zionist camps, participating in *hakhshara* [so-called pioneer training] and preparing themselves for departure to Palestine. In front of a hotel that hosted members of the Anglo-American Committee,[34] he also encountered thousands of Polish Jews – Zionists, Bundists, Communists – united and loudly protesting in favor of opening Palestine for Jewish emigration and creating a Jewish state. Bundists, Communists, and members of Jewish cooperatives in Łódź were committed to rebuilding Jewish life in Poland, their own 'Yiddishland,' and they were active around the local Jewish Committee.[35]

Łódź was by no means unique. Lower Silesia was full of remarkable 'spac-

32 Schneiderman 1947, 159.

33 Ibid., 161.

34 The Anglo-American Committee of enquiry regarding the problems of European Jewry and Palestine was assembled by the US and British governments in January of 1946. Its goal was to assess both the situation of Jewish refugees in post-*khurbn* Europe and the socio-political situation in Palestine, to which massive Jewish migration was banned due to the decision of British Mandate authorities and Arab opposition towards it. In March 1946 three members of the Anglo-American Committee visited Poland to assess the situation of Polish Jewry.

35 Shoshkes 1946, 140, 143–156.

es of Yiddish' where the Eastern European Jewish vernacular was the dominant language and a stable, natural element of its social landscape. Yankev Pat (1890–1966), active in the prewar Polish Bund and leading member of JLC in New York, described his visit to one of the towns in the area in March of 1946 as follows:

> איך בין געווען אַזוי איבעראַשט, ווי איך וואָלט אַרײַנגעפֿאַלן אין אַן אַנדער פּלאַנעט. [...] דער מאַרק־פּלאַץ איז גרויס, קײַלעכדיק און גאַנץ, ייִדן גייען, שטייען אין געזעמלעך, לויפֿן פֿאַרנומען אַהין און צוריק. [...] איך זע דאָס צום ערשטן מאָל אין פּוילן. אַ ייִדישער שילד מיט גרויסע ייִדישע בוכשטאַבן, באַלויכטן מיט עלעקטרישע לאָמפּן – „קולטור־הויז“. דאָס איז אוממעגלעך צו זען אין וואַרשע, אין לאָדזש, אין ביאַליסטאָק, אין קראָקע, אין טשענסטאָכאָוו, אין קאַטאָוויץ. דאָס איז מעגלעך אין ריכבאַך. „דאָ ווערט אַ ייִדישע שטאָט“ – זאָגט מיר דער ייִדישער אַקטיאָר פֿון דער געוועזענער ווילנער טרופּע, שׂמחה נאַטאַן [...].[36]
>
> I was so surprised as if arriving on a different planet [...] The market square is big, round and intact, full of Jews standing in groups, busily running around [...] It's the first time I see such a thing in [postwar] Poland: a large signboard in Yiddish, written in big Hebrew letters and illuminated by an electric lamp – 'house of culture'. This is not possible in Warsaw, Łódź, Białystok, Kraków, Częstochowa or Katowice – it is possible in Rychbach [Dzierżoniów]. 'A Jewish town is in the making' – I am told by actor of the former Vilne Troupe, Simkhe Natan [...].

The president of the World and American Federations of Polish Jews, Joseph Tenenbaum (1887–1961), described the same town, Dzierżoniów, as "the Polish-Jewish settlement, with a Jewish majority, Jewish officials, Jewish militia and a Jewish life charged with vigor and activity. [...] I was struck by the sound of Yiddish everywhere, Yiddish posters, large streamers in Yiddish calling for May Day celebrations, Yiddish theater bills, and in the Silesian Hotel Polonia where I was lodged, a dance was given that night to Yiddish music and songs. I have even heard some of the non-Jewish Poles massacre their tongues with an atrocious Polish accent as if in the recognition that Yiddish was the official language of the 'Jewish town'."[37]

To the aforementioned Shmuel Leyb Schneiderman the Jewish presence in Lower Silesia was the "light in the darkest darkness."[38] Pat, Tenenbaum, Schneiderman, and others also pointed to the considerable continuations

[36] Pat 1946, 211–212. Additions by K. K.

[37] Tenenbaum 1948, 253.

[38] Schneiderman 1947, 232, 242.

of pre-1939 Eastern European Yiddish culture in this uncanny post-German space: hundreds of Jews from Vilna, Grodno (today's Hrodna), and Warsaw, joined their *landsmanshaftn* [hometown societies of Jewish emigrants] active in Lower Silesia and established cooperatives, libraries, houses of culture, newspapers, literary evenings, schools, party locals, soup kitchens, *kibbutzim* [Zionist communes training their members for emigration and life in Palestine], and synagogues using their pre-*khurbn* networks.[39]

Clearly, intimacy and a sense of safety was crucial for the formation of these Yiddish spaces. Jews needed to be in large, tight communities. Besides Dzierżoniów, there were only a few places in Lower Silesia that provided such spaces – most importantly its regional capital, Wrocław, where thousands of Polish Jews were repatriated from the Soviet Union. Włodkowica street became the home to the regional Jewish Committee, a religious congregation (running synagogue, *shul* and *mikve*), kibbutzim and offices of Zionist organizations.[40] Dzierżoniów's neighboring towns Bielawa and Pieszyce, as well as the important industrial and coal mining centers Wałbrzych and Legnica (home to Red Army headquarters) had significant Jewish populations, too. In June 1947, the פֿאָרווערטס [*Forverts*, Jewish Daily Forward] column on Lower Silesia confirmed that the region's Jewish residents were generally not obsessed with emigration but rather focused on building a stable, 'normal' life in Poland.[41] Even Zionist organizations, hardly interested in rebuilding Jewish life in the diaspora, had to concur.[42] A delegate of the Rescue Committee of Jewish Agency of Palestine, for instance, reported that "Reichenbach [Dzierżoniów] is a little Jewish town. Its population consists of 11,000 Jews, 8,000 to 9,000 Germans and 3,000 to 5,000 Poles. For the first time since my arrival in Poland, I met there Jews who spoke Yiddish in the streets, just as in good old days..."[43]

This dense Jewish social and institutional ecosystem was conducive to Yiddish cultural production *and* consumption. The elites of Polish Jewish politics and culture, living mainly in Warsaw and concentrated in the CKŻP,

39 Ibid., 153–183, 229–242; Pat 1946, 195–196, 211–218; Wohl 1947, 22, 50–51, 53–56; Tenenbaum 1947, 253–259; Novick 1948, 106–125, 142–143; Shulshteyn 1949, 78–83, 94–101.

40 Novick 1948, 111–115.

41 Forverts, 12 June 1947, 2.

42 See for example: Yad Yaari Archives, 1–2 Ha-Shomer Ha-Tzair be-Polin achrei milchemet ha-dam ha-shniya (HShHTzbP), 51 (1), letter from Ha-Shomer ha-Tzair Central Command in Poland to the Ha-Shomer ha-Tzair Central Command in Kibbutz Marhavia, 05.10.1946.

43 Loḥamei Ha-Getaot Archives, 04236–4, "The Rescue Committee of Jewish Agency of Palestine Bulletin", September 1946, 6.

Kiosk at Włodkowica street in Wrocław, 1947, Archive of the Tadeusz Taube Department of Jewish Studies of the University of Wrocław.

were well aware of the fact that the bulk of consumers of Yiddish culture lived on the Lower Silesian periphery far away from the capital. Most Warsaw- or Łódź-produced Yiddish newspapers and books were sent there. The October 1946 statistics of Dzierżoniów county's *powiat* [Jewish Committee] alone recorded 800 attendees of literary evenings, 2,400 of plays and 1,600 of concerts.[44] In that very October, Dzierżoniów hosted a series of literary evenings with the most renowned Polish Yiddish writers, such as Leyb Olitski (1895–1975), Chaim Grade (1910–1982), Avrom Zak (1891–1980), and Shmerke Katsherginsky (1908–1954), as well as Yiddish concerts by, among others, Judith Berg (1905–1992), one of the stars of pre- and postwar Yiddish culture. Two months later, the local Yiddish cultural development experienced another boost when the First Lower Silesian Congress of Yiddish Culture took place in Wrocław – funded by the Polish government and the JDC and encompassing 106 different cultural events with a total of 25,000 participants organized all over the region; twenty exhibitions of Jewish visual

44 APWr, 415 WKŻ, 9, k. 42, 51.

artists had drawn 22,000 spectators.[45] 400 delegates arriving from all over Poland attended the congress itself and were joined by two thousand local Jews who came to listen to the discussions. The participants received greetings and letters of support from the ייִדישער אנטיפאשיסטישער קאָמיטעט [*Yidisher antifashistisher komitet*, Jewish Antifascist Committee] in Moscow, undersigned by Shloyme Mikhoels (1890–1948) and Itsik Fefer (1900–1952), but also from the YIVO in New York and its director, Max Weinreich (1894–1969), in addition to the Polish government and the JDC.[46] The recognition was mutual: the Congress declared the deep cultural connection of Lower Silesian Jews with their brethren in the Soviet Union, Palestine, and the United States and concluded that

> אויף די רויִנען פֿון דער אַמאָל וואַקסנדיקער ייִדישער מאַסן־קולטור, וואָס איז געפּלעגט און געפֿורמט געוואָרן דורך דעם גרויסן פּרץ, דורך שלום אַשן און ווײַסנבערגן, דורך טויזנטער און טויזנטער ייִדישע פֿאָלקס־אינטעליגענטן [...] זענען מיר, די לעבנגעבליבענע געקומען, כּדי ווײַטער צו שמידן די גאָלדענע קייט פֿון דער ייִדישער מאַסן־קולטור אויף דער פּוילישער ערד.
>
> On the ruins of the once flourishing Yiddish mass culture, which was fostered and shaped by greats such as [Y. L.] Peretz, Sholem Ash and [Itshe Meyer] Weissenberg, by thousands of the Yiddish peoples' intelligentsia (...) we, the survivors, came here in order to continue forging the golden chain of Yiddish mass culture on Polish soil.[47]

By 1947, Lower Silesian Yiddish culture stood on firm grounds and continued to grow. By March 1947, 72,000 Jews living in thirty-eight localities had at their disposal nineteen Yiddish drama circles, five choirs, two orchestras, nineteen libraries, twenty kindergartens, two children's homes, and twenty-two schools. Between January and March 1947 alone, the Jewish Peoples University provided forty lectures on Jewish history and culture in various places of Lower Silesia.[48] In August, eight public meetings welcomed 1,760 participants to honor *khurbn*-victim and Yiddish poet Mordkhe Ge-

45 YIVO Archives, RG 116 Poland 3, Folder 97, Yiddish proclamation regarding the First Congress of Jewish Culture in Lower Silesia.

46 YIVO Archives, RG 116 Poland 3, Folder 102, materials of the First Congress of Jewish Culture in Lower Silesia, unpaginated.

47 Egit 1947, 73–78 (quotation is from page 75).

48 YIVO Archives, RG 116 Poland 3, Folder 1, clipping from "Poland of Today", vol. 2, no.3, March 1947, 17.

birtig (1877–1942), 250 participants to honor Yiddish literary icon Sholem Aleichem (Sholem Rabinovitsh; 1859–1916), and 500 participants to honor Spanish Civil War hero Yitskhok Naftali Botwin (1905–1925).[49] Two thousand people attended seventeen historical and political lectures in twelve different towns and a further 220 joined three lectures organized by the Jewish People's University. The Lower Silesian Yiddish theater entertained 2,930 spectators in seven performances, while amateur Lower Silesian Yiddish drama circles staged eleven performances in front of 2,420 people.[50] Overall, what these numbers amount to is a year of immense cultural activity: the Lower Silesian Jewish Committees organized 262 public gatherings with 74,912 participants in addition to the uncounted numbers of Yiddish events organized outside this institutional framework by the Zionist and Orthodox movements; they further organized 238 lectures for 25,017 audience members; the Jewish People's University offered 196 classes for 18,471 students; the Lower Silesian Yiddish theater staged 115 plays for 58,755 spectators; the amateur theaters performed 189 plays for an audience of 44,068. Lower Silesian Jewish schools, run in part in Yiddish, counted more than 2,000 pupils.[51] The local community had ten *kultur-hayzer* [houses of culture] at their disposal, some of them equipped with theater stages which were used by sixty-four Yiddish drama circles active in the area.[52] The content of school curricula, plays, lectures, workshops, and all other events was progressive, left-leaning, and pluralistic.

Further information about the vitality of Yiddish in Lower Silesia can be derived from available library statistics. As of September 1947, the Regional Jewish Committee operated twenty-nine Jewish libraries in the area with a collection of 9,900 books.[53] Additionally, each larger Zionist or Bundist party cell, kibbutz, or religious congregation had their own library, partly comprised of Yiddish books. In October 1947, 2,109 people borrowed a total of 1,645 books in Polish and 1,025 in Yiddish (and only seventeen in Hebrew

49 Yitskhok Naftali Botwin was a Polish Jewish communist and labor activist who was executed by a firing squad in 1925 for the murder of a Polish secret police agent and informer on the Communist Party; the international brigade Naftali Botwin Company was named in his honor during the Spanish Civil War.

50 APWr, 415 WKŻ, 5, k. 128.

51 YIVO Archives A, RG 116 Poland 3, Folder 99, „Barikht iber der tetikayt fun der kultur un kunst-gezelshaft in Niedershlezye farn yor 1947," unpaginated; APWr, 415 WKŻ DS, k. 130.

52 Egit 1947, 72

53 APWr, 415 WKŻ, 5, k. 129.

and 151 in other languages) from Lower Silesian Jewish Committee libraries.[54] While there is no doubt that Polish increasingly gained in importance also in Yiddish Lower Silesia, as late as 1947 Yiddish culture was strong and stable, functioning simultaneous to and cross-fertilizing with Polish language culture of Polish Jews.

On the thirty-third *yortsayt* [anniversary of the death] of Yiddish classic writer Yitskhok-Leybush Peretz (1852–1915), April 1948 was pronounced the "month of Yiddish culture" and 8,000 people joined events in thirty-five Lower Silesian towns.[55] April was surpassed by the cultural activities in June and August, when there were fourteen appearances of Polish Jewish star Ida Kamińska's (1899–1980) theater troupe in places such as Wrocław, Wałbrzych, Dzierżoniów, and Pieszyce averaging 500-person audiences.[56]

In the specific social space of Jewish Lower Silesia, so-called new mass Jewish politics[57] created a favorable socio-cultural context for numerous political gatherings that were attended by tens, hundreds, or thousands of people. Be it May Day parades, public demonstrations pertaining to events in Palestine, *khurbn* commemorative events or the special event of the second anniversary of the "Jewish settlement of Lower Silesia" in June 1947 – thousands of Jews took part, bringing with them banners and chants in Yiddish.[58] The major center of such events was Łódź. But Lower Silesian towns with Jewish populations of twenty to forty percent were hubs for mass Jewish politics in the second half of the 1940s, as well. It was here that the Jewish political movements active in Poland organized most of their youth camps that attracted young Jews from all across the country. A case in point is צוקונפֿט [*Tsukunft*, Future], the Bundist youth movement, and its summer camp of 1946, organized in Kamionki in the Lower Silesian Owl mountains and welcoming 120 campers. The camp was framed around the idea of the "children's republic"[59]

54 YIVO Archives, RG 116 Poland 3, Folder 100, October 1947 report of "Kultur un kunst-gezelshaft in Niedershlezye," unpaginated.

55 YIVO Archives, RG 116 Poland 3, Folder 97, report "Yiddish-kultur-khoydesh in Niedershlezye".

56 YIVO Archives, RG 116 Poland 3, Folder 99, August 1948 report of 'Kultur un kunst-gezelshaft in Niedershlezye", unpaginated.

57 Mendelsohn 1993.

58 See for example: APWr, 415 WKŻ, 9, k. 108; Loḥamei Ha-Getaot Archives, 24961, clipping on November 1947 commemoration of victims of Lower Silesian concentration camps.

59 For Bundist models of children's and youth education see Jacobs 2009; Kozłowska 2014, 49–62.

Members of *Ha-shōmēr ha-ẓāʿīr*, children from a Jewish orphanage, Archive of the Tadeusz Taube Department of Jewish Studies of the University of Wrocław.

which resumed interwar Bundist traditions of introducing self-government to childcare institutions supervised by the party. It was operating entirely in Yiddish under the Bundist red banner and party slogans aiming firstly to commemorate the *khurbn*, secondly to pass on a Bundist ethos, and thirdly to inculcate the Jewish youth with socialist Yiddish culture.[60]

While the commitment to Yiddish was inherent to the Bund, even its Zionist rivals created venues for everyday Yiddish culture and used the language in their educational material. Like all other major Jewish political movements in Poland, Zionists considered the ongoing 'assimilation' of many Polish Jews problematic. Speaking Polish was acceptable as long as simultaneous knowledge in Jewish languages – preferably Hebrew, of course –, culture, and tradition existed too. In 1947, surprisingly, even the most fervently Hebraist השומר הצעיר [*Ha-shōmēr ha-ẓāʿīr*, The Young Guard] summer camp in Lower Silesian Rościszów had a lot of Yiddish content. While prioritizing the Hebrew language and inculcating summer campers with Zionist ideology and mythology around ארץ־ישׂראל [*'Ereẓ Yiśrā'ēl*, Land of Israel] as well as שלילת הגלות [*shĕlīlat ha-gālūt*, negation of the diaspora], the camp's daily education-

60 Anonymous 1946, 8.

Members of the party פועלי ציון שמאל [*Pōaley ziyyōn śmōl*, Poale Zion Left] and Jewish farmers during the 1947 May Day demonstration in Dzierżoniów, Archive of the Tadeusz Taube Department of Jewish Studies of the University of Wrocław.

al activities included readings from the Yiddish classics, such as the works of Sholem Aleichem, Mendele Moykher-Sforim [penname of Sholem-Yankev Abramovitsh] (1836–1917) or Sholem Ash (1880–1957) in the name of "the fight against assimilation."[61] Daily calls were conducted not in Hebrew or Polish, but in Yiddish. This resembles the situation in *Ha-shōmēr ha-ẓāʿīr* pioneer training camps all over Poland.[62]

Transnationalism

Another dimension of Jewish life in which the Yiddish language was of paramount importance was postwar Jewish transnationalism. Since its beginnings, almost all members of the Jewish community in Lower Silesia

61 Yad Yaari Archives, 1–2 HShHTzbP, 57 (3), various reports from moshavot Bogrim and Maapalim in Rościszów, July and August 1947, unpaginated.

62 See for example "La Negev," handwritten newspaper of kibbutz "Loḥamei Getaot" from Gdańsk in northern Poland. As hardly any of its members could read Hebrew well, it was bilingual, with some articles in Polish but the majority of them in Yiddish, Yad Yaari Archives, 1–2 HShHTzbP, 48 (7), various issues of "La Negev" newspaper, unpaginated.

looked for family members or friends abroad, usually on the other side of the so-called Iron Curtain – in the United States, South America, Palestine, or Western Europe. Yiddish was the *lingua franca* of communication with US branches of dozens of *landsmanshaftn* active in Lower Silesia.[63] For example, in the spring of 1946, just one Warsaw *landsmanshaft* in Lower Silesia had 3,000 members.[64] The New York פֿאַראייניקטער גראָדנער רעליף [*Fareynikter Grodner Relif*, United Grodner Relief] regularly sent financial help to its sister organization in the area and helped individual Jews of prewar Grodno now living in western Poland.[65] The same is true for individual correspondences of Polish Jews with Western organizations helping to contact their family members, receiving packages with material or financial help or acquiring emigration visas.[66] Lower Silesia welcomed Jewish journalists, reporters, writers, political or social activists, singers, and actors from abroad. Organized by the JLC, famous Yiddish actress Molly Picon (1898–1992) visited Poland and other European countries with her husband Jacob Kalich (1891–1975) in 1946.[67] Picon gave concerts in Warsaw, Łódź, and at a Jewish orphanage in Helenówek before heading to Lower Silesia, where she performed for massive Jewish audiences in Wałbrzych and Dzierżoniów.[68] An additional important resource of transnational cultural support for Polish Jewry by western Jewish organizations were thousands of Yiddish books sent monthly to all Jewish communities in Poland, but especially to Łódź and Lower Silesia. This diverse mix mirrored the incredible political and cultural plurality of Yiddish culture at the time transgressing the communist *nusekh Poyln* version.[69]

The transnational nature of postwar Polish Yiddishland combined with

63 APWr 415 WKŻ, 9, k. 115; TLA, WAG 25.001, Box 35 – Folders 17–18, 21, 24, Box 36 – Folder correspondence regarding landsmanshaftn activities in Poland, 1946–1947.

64 Wohl 1947, 55.

65 TLA, WAG 25.001, Box 35 – Folders 16, various JLC letters informing about help of *Fareynikter Grodner Relif* sent to Poland.

66 TLA, WAG 25.001, Box 35 – Folders 6, 10, 11–21, 24, 25, Box 36 – Folders 1–5, WAG 25.002, Box 92 – Folder 36, Box 93 – Folder 1, various JLC correspondence with Jews from Poland, 1946–1948.

67 Smolyar 1982, 67; TLA, WAG.025.001, Box 17 – Folder 2, JLC letter to Swiss consul in New York, 07 March 1946; JLC letter to Molly Picon and Jacob Kalich, 30 April 1946, customs certificate granted by JLC to Picon and Kalich and signed by Jacob Pat, 03 May 1946.

68 Picon, Grillo 1980, 112–117.

69 See for example: TLA, WAG 25.001 – Jewish Labour Committee Records Part I, Box 35 – Folders 20–25: unpaginated lists of book packages sent by JLC to Poland between February and July 1947.

the political and ideological pluralism of the Jewish public spaces growing on the fertile soil of their social intimacy meant not only 'starting life anew,' but in many respects resuming old paths. In 1946, meditating on his trip to Lower Silesia, מאָרגן־פֿרײַהייט [*Morgn-frayhayt*, Morning Freedom] longtime editor Peysakh Novick recognized אַ שטיק ייִדיש לעבן פֿון דעם אַלטן פּוילן, אַ געזונט לעבן, איז אין נידערשלעזיע אויפֿגעשטאַנען תּחית־המתים [a piece of Jewish life from the old Poland, the healthy life, is now resurrected in Lower Silesia].[70] Comparable to a Yiddish melting pot, Moyshe Shulshteyn (1911 – 1981) observed that the regions

> באַשטייען אויס ייִדן פֿון אַלע עקן פּוילן. עס קרייצן זיך דאָ פֿאַרשיידענע מנהגים, קאָלאָ־ריט און שטייגער פֿון פֿאַרשיידענע געגנטן. עס באַגעגענען זיך דיאַלעקטן און אויסשפּראַכן. [...] דורך אַלע אויסשפּראַכן און דיאַלעקטן קען מען לײַכט דערקענען אַ שטיקעלע ווילנע, אַ שטיקעלע טשענסטאָכאָוו, אַ שטיקעלע קאָלאָמיי און אַ שטיקעלע לובלין. עס טרעפֿן זיך לאַנדסלײַט מיט לאַנדסלײַט, מען דערציילט זיך מיט באַדויערן זכרונות פֿון פֿאַריתומטקייט און עלנט און פֿרייד פֿון ווידערזען און פֿון פֿאָלקס־באַהעפֿטונג.
>
> consist of Jews from all corners of Poland. Different customs, colors, and ways of life from different regions cross here. Dialects and pronunciation bump into each other. [...] From the pronunciations and dialects it is easy to detect a bit of Vilna, a bit of Tchenstochov, a bit of Kolomiya and a bit of Lublin. *Landslayt* meet *landslayt* and they regretfully tell each other stories of being orphaned and in distress, of joy about the seeing each other again and reunion.[71]

So, what about the alleged unavoidable, linear demise of Yiddish in Poland? And, more importantly, how did contemporaries assess the situation themselves in 1947 – in the post-Kielce so-called year of stabilization? To the chagrin of Yitzhak Grünbaum (1879 – 1970), the world leader of General Zionism, member of the board of Jewish Agency, and future first Interior Minister of the state of Israel, who visited Poland in the spring of 1947, the majority of Polish Jews behaved as if וועז עס האָבן אין פּוילן געלעבט דרײַ מיליאָן ייִדן [Poland was still inhabited by 3 million Jews][72] and could still imagine their future in Polish Yiddishland. Believing that all Jews should strive for life in a future state of Israel, Grünbaum communicated to the *Morgn-zhurnal*

70 Novick 1947, 111.

71 Shulshteyn 1949, 82 – 83.

72 Klinov 1947, 5.

readership that this attitude of Łódź and Lower Silesian Jews was synonymous with national treason. In the timeframe between the war's end and the 'year of stabilization,' what Shulshteyn, and many other – markedly non- or even anti-communist – Western contemporaries observed was that despite the destruction under Nazi occupation, the Kielce pogrom, and postwar Jewish mass migration, against all grim expectations, Jewish culture was partly reborn in Poland, and its new center was located in an exotic, post-German space. One of the core elements of this rebirth was Yiddish. Here, the Jewish numerical dominance, social and institutional cohesiveness, socio-cultural and political pluralism, state-support, and vast transnational connections made this possible. It changed dramatically only with the radicalization of communist regime in Poland and its 'Stalinization' in the years 1948–1950.[73]

Limitations of Yiddish Rebirth and Evolution of its Role in the Life of Polish Jews

As much as I have argued against a teleologically tragic reading of postwar Polish Jewish/Yiddish history, I simultaneously warn of a simplistic celebratory prediction of a continuous Yiddish rebirth and growth if it was not for Poland's 'Stalinization.' Despite the immense cultural productivity, postwar Polish Yiddish culture faced deep structural and, in many regards, insurmountable problems. While Jewish children often did not know the language, Yiddish schools, as much as Jewish orphanages, lacked textbooks and qualified teachers to remedy the situation. And as much as the conditions in Lower Silesia were conducive to Yiddish cultural growth, the new map of Polish Yiddishland was inherently flawed. The Polish Yiddish cultural establishment was concentrated mainly in Warsaw, while Yiddish cultural consumers were living on the Western periphery with few Yiddish intellectuals of their own to draw on. This was a substantial problem of Yiddish life in late 1940s Poland that was exacerbated further by interconnected rise of linguistic acculturation to Polish – a socio-cultural process that long preceded the *khurbn* but was accelerated in the postwar years due to trauma and fear, on the one hand, and previously unknown opportunities of social mobility, on the other.

These findings are corroborated, to a certain degree, by the work of Irena

73 Grabski 2015, 192–252; Szaynok 2007, 165–177.

Hurwic-Nowakowska (1912–2006), who between 1947 and 1950 as part of her dissertation research at the Warsaw University Institute of Sociology interviewed 817 people and gathered 6,000 survey questionnaires from Jewish respondents in Warsaw, Łódź, and Dzierżoniów. Nowakowska, too, saw the geographical division between the former centers and Lower Silesia where "I found a Jewish community with indigenous folklore and culture."[74] While, according to her data, it was only in Dzierżoniów that Yiddish was used both in private and public life, still only fifteen percent of the interviewees in Dzierżoniów declared Yiddish their primary language (surmounting Warsaw with a mere 0.4 percent and Łódź with 6.5 percent). The survey presented still different results: fifty-five percent of respondents from Dzierżoniów declared Yiddish their primary language, an additional sixteen percent declared equal use of Polish and Yiddish, and yet her research clearly pointed to an ongoing decline of daily usage of Yiddish as the main language of Polish Jews.[75] It was the social and communal infrastructure in Lower Silesia that kept it afloat. And this infrastructure was crumbling in 1949 and 1950, when 28,000 Polish Jews, half of them from Lower Silesia, decided to leave for the newly formed state of Israel.[76]

Yet, even after 1950, Yiddish culture and its presence in the daily lives of Polish Jews did not disappear completely, even among the younger generation. Although this fascinating problem still awaits further research, some important implications can be drawn from oral histories among postwar Polish Jews.[77] Insights into the Polish Jewish 1950s and 1960s were offered to me in three interviews that I have conducted with former and current Jewish inhabitants of Dzierżoniów, born between 1935 and 1941. Two left Poland with their families in 1957, one stayed in Dzierżoniów until today.

They all went to various Jewish educational institutions (along with Polish ones) in the late 1940s, spoke Yiddish at home with their parents, and while two of them were raised in communist homes, they were nevertheless exposed to elements of Jewish religiosity. Even in the 1950s, while leaving Dzierżoniów, all three not only knew Yiddish and spoke it with elders, but peppered their conversations with Yiddish idioms or singular words. It was

74 Hurwic-Nowakowska 1986, 10.

75 Ibid., 15–16, 88–89, table 4 (at the end of the book).

76 Stola 2010, 53–63.

77 There are thousands of interviews recorded by USC Shoah Foundation, Yale University Fortunoff archives, and many other institutions narrating not only *khurbn* experience but also Jewish life in post-*khurbn* Poland, including its Jewish centers such as Łódź and Lower Silesian towns.

their *mame-loshn* and it continued to play a role in the various manifestations of their Jewishness. This role surely changed but never disappeared entirely.[78]

My interviews, in a sense, normalize the postwar Polish Yiddish experience: Yiddish in Poland in the late 1940s and 1950s underwent the process described by Jeffrey Shandler for the American context as "post-vernacularization."[79] Like in all the other centers of the postwar Jewish world, Yiddish gradually lost its vernacular nature, that is, being a language mainly spoken, written and read by Jews. However, Yiddish remained significant performatively and semiotically in Jewish identity formations as diaspora Jewishness transformed itself through urbanization and professionalization, from nationhood to peoplehood. As in the United States or other places, Yiddish as a Jewish vernacular of daily life outside of orthodox circles would have endured in Poland as long as there would have been coherent community structures as well as economic opportunities that provided a safe space for expressing Jewishness in a more traditional, prewar register. This somewhat natural process was accelerated by the political developments in socialist Poland: first, 'Stalinization' (1948–1950), impoverishing Jewish plurality, interrupting its transnationality, and spurring further migration; second, Stalinism (1950–1956), not unlike what was happening simultaneously in the Soviet Union, putting Jewish communities under constant threat and suspicion regarding their ties to the non-communist West;[80] third, the so-called Thaw (1957–1960) of political liberalization bringing a wave of antisemitism and further migration;[81] and, finally, the 1968 antisemitic campaign drawing the final curtain of Jewish life in socialist Poland by coercing the majority of remaining Polish Jews to migrate elsewhere.[82]

Conclusion

The post-vernacularity of Yiddish in socialist Poland should not overshadow the vernacular status of Yiddish in the early postwar period. Future research should investigate the role of Yiddish in various sociological contexts

78 Interview with Frieda Pertman, 20–21 February 2009, Baltimore; Interview with Shlomo Ponczak, 16 February 2009, Baltimore; Interview with Bela Flajs, 8 September 2008, Dzierżoniów.

79 Shandler 2008, 1–5, 19–26, 183–202.

80 Szaynok 2007, 206–244, 259–282; Berendt 2008.

81 Machcewicz 1993, 216–233; Kichelewski 2021, 139–161; Stola 2010, 129–140.

82 Stola 2000, Plocker 2022.

and in the lives of ordinary Jews beyond the already well-developed research into Yiddish institutions in the Polish People's Republic. How did Yiddish usage interact with Polish and Hebrew, for instance? This and other questions need to be answered, as I tried to show in this chapter, with an attention to the material spaces in which these linguistic interactions and interconnected political and cultural expressions took place. In early postwar Poland, ripe with antisemitism, trauma and fear, what would nowadays be called cultural and material 'safe spaces' *mattered* – whether at home, in a small Lower Silesian town with a large percentage of Jews, or the protected few blocks of 'Jewish neighborhoods' in cities like Łódź or Wrocław.

The study of Yiddish in early postwar Poland is also necessarily connected with the political culture of the time. Until 1948–1949, Poland was not yet fully 'Stalinized' and the spaces of Yiddish not fully subjugated to party or state control. Yiddish communist and socialist discourses existed alongside Zionist and orthodox ones, the latter of which also partly using Yiddish, producing various, pluralistic cultural identities. This relative plurality of the years 1945 to 1948 was also tied to the inherent transnationality of Polish Jewry of those years performed through close personal and institutional connections to the West and within the socialist bloc and expressed at least partially in Yiddish.

As I have tried to demonstrate, Yiddish culture in the first years of postwar Poland had far transcended the narrow margins of the official state ideology of *nusekh Poyln*. If the pluralism of Jewish life had been retained and socially dense and cohesive Jewish communities had continued to operate in Poland after 1948, I speculate that Yiddish would have continued to play various, interesting post-vernacular roles – comparable to the role it played and plays in the United States and some other parts of the world today. For this to have happened, it would have needed free movement of people, ideas, and money sustaining pluralism of cultural and political life. This was foreclosed by specific political decisions at the end of 1940s, but these and later developments should not overshadow events and processes that took place earlier and which still await much multidisciplinary research.

Bibliography

Archival Sources

Archiwum Państwowe we Wrocławiu, 415 Wojewódzki Komitet Żydów, Folder 5, k. 62.

Archiwum Państwowe we Wrocławiu, 415 Wojewódzki Komitet Żydów, Folder 5, k. 128.

Archiwum Państwowe we Wrocławiu, 415 Wojewódzki Komitet Żydów, Folder 5, k. 129.

Archiwum Państwowe we Wrocławiu, 415 Wojewódzki Komitet Żydow, Folder 9, k. 42.

Archiwum Państwowe we Wrocławiu, 415 Wojewódzki Komitet Żydów, Folder 9, k. 108.

Archiwum Państwowe we Wrocławiu, 415 Wojewódzki Komitet Żydowski na Dolnym Śląsku, k. 130.

Archiwum Państwowe we Wrocławiu, 415 Wojewódzki Komitet Żydów, 9, k. 115.

Loḥamei Ha-Getaot Archives, 04236–4, "The Rescue Committee of Jewish Agency of Palestine Bulletin", September 1946.

Loḥamei Ha-Getaot Archives, 24961, clipping on November 1947 commemoration of victims of Lower Silesian concentration camps.

NYU Taminent Library Archives, Jewish Labour Committee Records (JLC), Part 1, WAG 25.001, Box 35 – Folder 10, Salo Fishgrund *Yidishe kinder shulen in Poyln* (no date given).

NYU Taminent Library Archives, WAG.025.001, Box 17 – Folder 2, JLC letter to Swiss consul in New York, 07.03.1946; JLC letter to Molly Picon and Jacob Kalich, 30.04.1946, customs certificate granted by JLC to Picon and Kalich and signed by Jacob Pat, 03.05.1946.

NYU Taminent Library Archives, WAG 25.001, Box 35 – Folders 6, 10, 11–21, 24, 25.

NYU Taminent Library Archives, WAG 25.001, Box 35 – Folders 16, various JLC letters informing about help of *Fareynikter Grodner Relif* send to Poland.

NYU Taminent Library Archives, WAG 25.001, Box 35 – Folders 17–18, 21, 24, Box 36 – Folder correspondence regarding *landsmanshaftn* activities in Poland, 1946–1947.

NYU Taminent Library Archives, WAG 25.001 – Jewish Labour Committee Records Part I, Box 35 – Folders 20–25: unpaginated lists of book packages send by Jewish Labour Committee to Poland between February and July 1947.

NYU Taminent Library Archives, WAG 25.001, Box 36 – Folders 1–5.

NYU Taminent Library Archives, WAG 25.001, WAG 25.002, Box 92 – Folder 36, various JLC correspondence with Jews from Poland, 1946–1948.

NYU Taminent Library Archives, WAG 25.001, WAG 25.002, Box 93 – Folder 1, various JLC correspondence with Jews from Poland, 1946–1948.

Wiener Library Archives in London, Microfilm collection, Reel 190 II.22C, clipping from *Congress Bulletin*, April 1948 [no exact date or page number given].
Yad Yaari Archives, 1–2 Ha-Shomer Ha-Tzair be-Polin achrei milchemet ha-dam ha-shniya, 51 (1), letter from Ha-Shomer ha-Tzair Central Command in Poland to the Ha-Shomer ha-Tzair Central Command in Kibbutz Marhavia, 05 October 1946.
Yad Yaari Archives, 1–2 Ha-Shomer Ha-Tzair be-Polin achrei milchemet ha-dam ha-shniya, 48 (7), various issues of "La Negev" newspaper, unpaginated.
Yad Yaari Archives, 1–2 Ha-Shomer Ha-Tzair be-Polin achrei milchemet ha-dam ha-shniya, 57 (3), various reports from moshavot Bogrim and Ma'apalim in Rościszów, July and August 1947, unpaginated.
YIVO Archives, RG 116 Poland 3, Folder 1, clipping from "Poland of Today", vol. 2, no.3 , March 1947, 17.
YIVO Archives, RG 116 Poland 3, Folder 2, manuscript "Fun nokh di milkhome," unpaginated.
YIVO Archives, RG 116 Poland 3, Folder 11, clipping from *Congress Weekly*, 7 March 1947, 65.
YIVO Archives, RG 116 Poland 3, Folder 97, Yiddish proclamation regarding the First Congress of Jewish Culture in Lower Silesia.
YIVO Archives, RG 116 Poland 3, Folder 97, report "Yiddish-kultur-khoydesh in Nidershlezye".
YIVO Archives A, RG 116 Poland 3, Folder 99, „Barikht iber der tetikayt fun der kultur un kunst-gezelshaft in Nidershlezye farn yor 1947", unpaginated.
YIVO Archives, RG 116 Poland 3, Folder 99, August 1948 report of 'Kultur un kunst-gezelshaft in Nidershlezye", unpaginated.
YIVO Archives, RG 116 Poland 3, Folder 100, October 1947 report of 'Kultur un kunst-gezelshaft in Nidershlezye," unpaginated.
YIVO Archives, RG 116 Poland 3, Folder 102, materials of the First Congress of Jewish Culture in Lower Silesia, unpaginated.

Sources

Aleksiun, Natalia, 2008: The Central Jewish Historical Commission in Poland 1944–1947. In: *Polin* 20: 74–97.
Anonymous, 1945 אַנאָנים: בריף פֿון גראַטעוועטע אִידען פֿון לעמבערג, וואלאטשיק, יאַנאָוו־פּאָדאָלסקי, גלובאקע. אין: **פֿאָרווערטס** (ניו־יאָרק), 20סטער סעפּטעמבער, ז׳ 2.
Anonymous, 1946 אַנאָנים: אונטער בלויע הימלען. פֿון צענטראַלן זומער־לאַגער. אין: **יוגנט וועקער** (וואַרשע) 1, ז׳ 8.
Auerbach, Karen, 2013: *The House at Ujazdowskie 16: Jewish Families in Warsaw after the Holocaust*. Bloomington, Ind.: Indiana University Press.
Adelson, Józef, 1993: W Polsce zwanej Ludową. In: Jerzy Tomaszewski, ed. *Najnowsze dzieje Żydów w Polsce w zarysie (do 1950 roku)*. Warsaw: PWN, 387–477.

Bader, Gershom, 1945 באַדער, גרשם: וואָס גאַליציע איז געווען און וואָס זי איז איצט. אין: **מאָרגען־זשורנאַל** (ניו־יאָרק), 7טער אָקטאָבער, ז׳ 7.

Berendt, Grzegorz, 2008: *Życie żydowskie w Polsce w latach 1950–1956: z dziejów Towarzystwa Społeczno-Kulturalnego Żydów w Polsce*. Gdańsk: Wydawnictwo Uniwersytetu Gdańskiego.

Bergman, Eleonora, 2017: Yiddish in Poland after 1945. In: Gennady Estraikh and Mikhail Krutikov, eds., *Yiddish and the Left*. London: Legenda, 167–177.

Cała, Alina, and Helena Datner, eds., 1997: *Dzieje Żydów w Polsce, 1944–1968*. Warsaw: ŻIH.

Cichopek-Gajraj, Anna, 2014: *Beyond Violence. Jewish Survivors in Poland and Slovakia, 1944–1948*. Cambridge: Cambridge University Press.

Cohen, Nathan, 2008: Motives for the Emigration of Yiddish Writers from Poland (1945–1948)". In: Elvira Grözinger and Magdalena Ruta, eds., *Under the Red Banner. Yiddish Culture in the Communist Countries in the Postwar Era*. Wiesbaden: Harrassowitz, 151–164.

Datner, Helena, 2016: *Po Zagładzie. Społeczna historia żydowskich domów dziecka, szkół, kół studentów w dokumentach Centralnego Komitetu Żydów w Polsce*. Warsaw: ŻIH.

Dobroszycki, Lucjan, 1994: *Survivors of the Holocaust in Poland: A Portrait Based on Jewish Community Records, 1944–1947*. New York, NY: M. E Sharpe, Armonk.

Dorfzon, Sh.Y., 1945 דאָרפֿזאָן, ש.י.: לאָדזער אידען זיינען מקבר אין נײַן קברים אכציג ספר־תורה׳ס, וועלכע די נאציס האָבען געשענדעט. אין: **מאָרגען־זשורנאַל** (ניו־יאָרק), 8טער יולי, ז׳ 1.

Egit, Yankev, 1947 עגיט, יעקבֿ: **צו אַ נײַ לעבן (צוויי יאָר יִדישער ישובֿ אין נידערשלעזיע)**. ווראָצלאַוו: נידערשלעזיע.

Grabski, August, and Martyna Rusiniak, 2008: Żydowscy komuniści po Holokauście wobec języków polskiego żydostwa. In: Magdalena Ruta, ed., *Nusech Pojln. Studia z dziejów kultury jidysz w powojennej Polsce*. Budapest-Kraków: Austeria.

Grabski, August, 2015: *Centralny Komitet Żydów w Polsce (1944–1950). Historia polityczna*. Warsaw: ŻIH, 2015.

Gross, Natan, 2002: *Film żydowski w Polsc*e. Translated by Anna Ćwiakowska. Kraków: Fundacja Dziedzictwo.

Hurwic-Nowakowska, Irena, 1986: *A Social Analysis of Postwar Polish Jewry*. Translated by Jerzy Michałowicz. Jerusalem: Zalman Shazar.

Izraeli, Shloyme, 1947 איזראַעלי, שלמה: די 80 טויזענט אִידען אין פּוילען – וואָס זיי טוען, ווי זיי לעבען אין: **פֿאָרווערטס** (ניו־יאָרק), 12טער יוני, ז׳ 2.

Jacobs, Jack, 2009: *Bundist Counterculture in Interwar Poland*. Syracuse, NY Syracuse University Press.

Jockusch, Laura, 2012: *Collect and Record! Jewish Historical Documentation in Early Postwar Europe*. New York, NY: Oxford University Press.

Kałużna, Anna, 2015: *Teatr żydowski na Dolnym Śląsku, 1945–1968*. Doctoral dissertation, University of Wrocław.

Kersht, Y. M., 1946; קערשט, י. מ.: בריף פֿון חרובֿ־געוואָרענע אידישע שטעט און שטעטלאַך. אין: **פֿאָרווערטס** (ניו־יאָרק), 14טער מאַרץ, ז׳ 6.

Kichelewski, Audrey, 2021: *Ocalali. Żydzi polscy po Zagładzie*. Translated by Katarzyna Marczewska, Natalia Krasicka. Warsaw: ŻIH.

Klinov, Y., 1947 קלינאָוו, י.: דער גורם וואָס יצחק גרינבוים גיט אָפּ פֿון הײַנטיגען פּוילען. אין: **מאָרגען־זשורנאַל** (ניו־יאָרק), 2טער אַפּריל, ז׳ 5.

Kozłowska, Magdalena, 2014: "In Sunshine and Joy"? The Story of Medem Sanatorium in Miedzeszyn. In: *East European Politics and Societies and Cultures* 28:1: 49–62.

Koźmińska-Frejlak, Ewa, 2012: Powojenna prasa żydowska w języku polskim (1944–1950). In: Joanna Nalewajko-Kulikov, ed., *Studia z dziejów trójjęzycznej prasy żydowskiej na ziemiach polskich (XIX – XX w.)*. Warsaw: PAN.

Krzyzanowski, Łukasz, 2020: *Ghost Citizens: Jewish Return to a Postwar City*. Translated by Madeline G. Levine. Cambridge, Mass.: Harvard University Press.

Lerner, H., 1945 לערנער, ה.: ווי אזוי ס׳זעהט אויס די איצטיגע וואַרשע. אין: **מאָרגען־זשורנאַל** (ניו־יאָרק), 8טער יולי, ז׳ 6.

Machcewicz, Paweł, 1993: *Polski rok 1956*. Warsaw: Mówią Wieki.

Mendelsohn, Ezra, 1993: *On Modern Jewish Politics*. New York, NY: Oxford University Press.

Nalewajko-Kulikov, Joanna, 2007: 'Syjonistyczna z lekkim zabarwieniem PPR-owskim'. 'Dos Naje Leben' (1945–1950) – gazeta Centralnego Komitetu Żydów w Polsce. In: August Grabski, ed., *Żydzi a lewica: zbiór studiów historycznych*. Warsaw: ŻIH.

Nalewajko-Kulikov, Joanna, 2009: *Obywatel Jidyszlandu: rzecz o żydowskich komunistach w Polsce*. Warsaw: Neriton, 2009.

Nalewajko-Kulikov, Joanna, and Magdalena Ruta, 2012: Kultura jidysz po II wojnie światowej. In: Feliks Tych, Monika Adamczyk Garbowska, eds., *Następstwa Zagłady Żydów: Polska 1944–2010*. Lublin: UMCS, ŻIH, 284–304.

Novick, Peysakh, 1948 נאָוויק, פּסח: **אייראָפּע – צווישן מלחמה און שלום. רײַזע־בילדער. באַטראַכטונגען**. ניו־יאָרק: איקוף־פֿאַרלאַג.

Pat, Yankev, 1946 פּאַט, יעקבֿ: **אַש און פֿײַער. איבער די חורבֿות פֿון פּוילן**. ניו־יאָרק: צענטראַלע יידישע קולטור־אָרגאַניזאַציע.

Picon, Molly, and Jean B. Grillo, 1980: *Molly! An Autobiography by Molly Picon*. New York, NY: Simon and Schuster.

Plocker, Anat, 2022: *The Expulsion of Jews from Communist Poland. Memory Wars and Homeland Anxieties*. Bloomington, Ind.: Indiana University Press.

Redlich, Shimon, 2010: *Life in Transit. Jews in postwar Lodz, 1945–1950*. Boston, Mass.: Academic Studies Press.

Ruta, Magdalena, 2017: *Without Jews?: Yiddish Literature in the People's Republic of Poland on the Holocaust, Poland and Communism*. Kraków: Jagiellonian University Press.

Schneiderman, Sh. L., 1946 שניידערמאַן, ש. ל.: פּאָגראָמען אין פּוילען ערב וואלען; בונד פיהרער ניימאן ערמאָרדעט. אין: **מאָרגען־זשורנאַל** (ניו־יאָרק), 30סטער יוני, ז׳ 2.

Schneiderman, Samuel Leyb, 1947: *Between Fear and Hope*. Translated by Norbert Guterman. New York, NY: Arco Publishing.

Shandler, Jeffrey, 2008: *Adventures in Yiddishland: postvernacular language and culture*. Berkeley, Calif.: University of California Press.

Shlomi, Hana, 2001 שלומי, חנה: **אסופת מאמרים לתולדות שארית הפליטה היהודית בפולין. 1944–1950**. תל אביב: אוניברסיטת תל-אביב.

Shoshkes, Khayim, 1946 שאָשקעס, חיים: **פּוילן – 1946. אײַנדרוקן פֿון אַ רײַזע**. בוענאָס־אײַרעס: צענטראַל־פֿאַרבאַנד פֿון פּוילישע ייִדן אין אַרגענטינע.

Shulshteyn, Moyshe, 1949 שולשטיין, משה: **צווישן רוּינען און רושטאָוואַניעס (פֿון אַ רײַזע אין פּוילן)**. פּאַריז: ייִדישע פֿאָלקס־ביבליאָטעק.

Smolyar, Hersh, 1982 סמאָליאַר, הערש: **אויף דער לעצטער פּאָזיציע מיט דער לעצטער האָפֿענונג**. תל־אביב: פֿאַרלאַג י. ל. פּרץ.

Stach, Stephan, 2008: Geschichtsschreibung und politische Vereinnahmungen: Das Jüdische Historische Institut in Warschau 1947–1968. In: *Simon Dubnow Institute Yearbook* 7: 401–431.

Stankowski, Albert, 2010: Nowe spojrzenie na statystyki dotyczące emigracji Żydów z Polski po 1944 roku. In: Grzegorz Berendt, August Grabski and Albert Stankowski: *Studia z dziejów Żydów w Polsce po 1945*. Warsaw: ŻIH, 103–151.

Stola, Dariusz, 2000: *Kampania antysyjonistyczna w Polsce 1967–1968*. Warsaw: Instytut Studiów Politycznych Polskiej Akademii Nauk.

Stola, Dariusz, 2010: *Kraj bez wyjścia? Migracje z Polski 1949–1989*. Warszawa: Instytut Pamięci Narodowej.

Szaynok, Bożena, 2000: *Ludność żydowska na Dolnym Śląsku 1945–1950*. Wrocław: Wydawnictwo Uniwersytetu Wrocławskiego.

Szaynok, Bożena, 2007: *Z historią i Moskwą w tle. Polska a Izrael 1944–1968*. Warszawa: Instytut Pamięci Narodowej.

Tenenbaum, Joseph, 1948: *In Search of a Lost People*. New York, NY: Beechhurst Press.

Tsanin, Mordechai, 2018: *Przez ruiny i zgliszcza. Podróż po stu zgładzonych gminach żydowskich w Polsce*. Translated by Monika Adamczyk-Garbowska. Warsaw: ŻIH.

Turkov-Grudberg, Yitskhok, 1952 טורקאָוו־גרודבערג, יצחק: **ייִדיש טעאַטער אין פּוילן**. וואַרשע: ייִדיש־בוך.

Wohl, Samuel Leo, 1947 וואָהל, סעמיועל: **מײַן רײַזע קיין וואַרשע**. ניו־יאָרק: [self-published].

Zahra, Tara, 2011: *The Lost Children. Resurrecting Europe's Families after World War II*. Cambridge, Mass.: Harvard University Press.

Alexandra Polyan

Khurbn-Plays with No Nazis in Them:
Shmuel-Yankev Harendorf and Perets Markish on the King of Lampedusa

On 13 June 1943, the British newspaper *News Chronicle* published an article titled "London Tailor's Cutter Is Now 'King of Lampedusa'." It recounted an episode from 12 June 1943, when Sydney Cohen, a 22-year-old British Army pilot, navigator Peter Tait, and gunner Les Wright were on their way to their British military base in Malta. As they were about to reach their destination, the plane went off course and, short in fuel, was forced to land on the tiny island of Lampedusa. For the Italian garrison on the island, it was the first face-to-face encounter with an Allied soldier. There was no source of drinking water on Lampedusa, and Italy's Prime Minister and "Duce" Benito Mussolini (1883–1945) permitted the military personnel (numbered about 4,000 men) to surrender if threatened. According to the report, the Italian officers invited Cohen, Tait, and Wright to their headquarters and handed Cohen a note of surrender, allowed his crew to refuel and take off.[1] *News Chronicle's* account,[2] however, was not completely accurate. Indeed, the significance of this incident has been greatly exaggerated by British propaganda. It omitted the massive, prolonged bombardment of the island and portrayed the event as if a single British soldier had forced the surrender of an entire garrison of over 4,000 soldiers. For the Italian defenders of the garrison to mistake Cohen's emergency landing for the beginning of a ground operation

This research work was conducted as part of the project *The Short Life of Soviet Yiddish Literature* (Dubnow Institute – University of Regensburg – Zentrum für Literatur- und Kulturforschung), and I am grateful to my academic supervisors and colleagues Prof. Sabine Koller, Prof. Yfaat Weiss, Dr. Matthias Schwartz, Dr. Brett Winestock, and Dr. Jakob Stürmann, as well as to Prof. Ber Kotlerman for discussing this paper with me. I owe special thanks to my editor Larisa Privalskaya and to the editors of this volume, Dr. Miriam Chorley-Schulz and Alexander Walther.

1 Harendorf 1955, 212.

2 The version of the events outlined above can still be found in non-academic publications: <http://www.jtrails.org.uk/trails/brackley/articles/c-1167/sydney-cohen-the-king-of-lampedusa-and-brackley/> January 18, 2021, <https://www.thejc.com/news/world/tailor-s-cutter-who-became-king-of-lampedusa-1.66766> January 18, 2021, https://theaviationgeekclub.com/the-king-of-lampedusa-the-day-4300-italian-soldiers-surrendered-to-a-raf-swordfish-pilot/" January 18, 2021, etc.

was neither reckless, nor cowardly, but rather understandable. It did not occur to them that the whole thing might have been a mere coincidence.[3]

Ironically, this odd incident was a turning point in the military confrontation between the British and the Nazis in the Mediterranean: it proved to be the Allies' first local victory over the Axis powers. Sure enough, the Jewish press pored over this episode with great delight: not only were the Axis troops defeated, with a sizable military division surrendering to a single British soldier, but the latter was a Jew after all and one from a poor family from London's Whitechapel district at that!

Five months later, the first work of fiction devoted to the events was written by Samuel (Shmuel Yankev) Harendorf (English: Charendorf) (1900–1969), the London correspondent of the Yiddish magazine מאָרגן [*Morgn*, Morning]. In the Fall of 1943, he wrote the comedy דער קעניג פֿון לאַמפּעדוזע [*Der kenig fun Lampeduze*, The King of Lampedusa][4] that premiered at London's Yiddish Grand Palais Theater on 31 December 1943[5] and ran for a total of 200 performances over six months – more than any other Yiddish play in London's history.[6]

Several years later, after the Second World War had ended, Moscow-based author Perets Markish (1895–1952) wrote a play bearing the same title. It was about to become a part of the repertoire of the Московский Государственный Еврейский Театр [*Moskovskiy Gosudarstvenny Evreyskiy Teatr*, Moscow State Jewish Theater, GOSET]. Two attempts to stage it were undertaken: the first one, by Shloyme Mikhoels (1890–1948), the famous Soviet Jewish actor, the artistic director of GOSET, in 1947, and the second one, after his assassination, in 1948. Each time the Russian translation of the play (made by Mikhail Shambadal) was submitted for consideration to Главрепертком

3 Hiscock 2001, Nieuwint 2015.

4 In 2003, it was published in English translation by Heather Valencia (Harendorf 2003). Harendorf's papers are preserved in the YIVO Archive. In 2017, Katie Power discovered among them five original pieces of music written for the play: an overture, two songs, and two finales: see <https://arts-uni-southampton.org.uk/2019/08/28/rediscovering-the-king-of-lampedusa-an-evening-of-performance-and-talks-with-the-parkes-institute/>, July 24, 2021. The composer's name is Phil Bernstein (Harendorf 1955, 221). For a biography of Harendorf, see his obituary by Joseph Fraenkel (Fraenkel 1969). I would like to thank Dov-Ber Kerler for bringing Harendorf's memoirs and Fraenkel's article to my attention, and Katie Power for kindly sharing her findings with me and letting me read Valencia's edition, which is now a bibliographic rarity.

5 Harendorf 1955, 221.

6 <https://jewishmuseum.org.uk/50-objects/ylc-3/>, June 29, 2021.

[*Glavrepertkom*, Central Commission for Approval of Performers' Repertoire at the Ministry of Education of the Russian Soviet Federal Socialist Republic].[7] The play was, however, never approved for staging.

This chapter explores *The King of Lampedusa* – in its two versions. An extraordinary expression of Eastern European Jewish transnationality, this Yiddish play is devoted to events near Malta, was written in Britain, staged in Palestine and Argentina – while the war still raged – and then served as a "source of inspiration" for a play of the same name written in the USSR.

In analyzing and comparing two Yiddish plays, created in dissimilar contexts but sharing a name and some storylines, I highlight the differences between them. Focusing on Markish's play, I show how the plot taken from a British Yiddish play was adapted to constantly changing ideological guidelines of the postwar Soviet Yiddish theater: How much "Jewishness" could be brought to the stage? Could Jewish ideological movements, i.e. Zionism, be referred to in a play? How could the חורבן [*khurbn*, destruction, Holocaust] be referenced?

Shmuel-Yankev Harendorf's *The King of Lampedusa*

The play's protagonist is Sam Kagan – a fictionalized Sydney Cohen – and the action takes place unsurprisingly in Lampedusa and Whitechapel, London, where his father keeps a shabby tailor shop.[8] In Act One, Sam is away from home, and his beloved Lily and his parents in Whitechapel have not heard from him in a long time. Then one day, out of the blue, excited crowds start greeting them in the street: congratulations abound. Everybody is telling them the news about Sam, and begging their favors and protection. Lily's well-off parents, who used to object to her marrying Sam, are now pleased with the prospect. On top of a luxurious dowry for their daughter, they offer the groom's parents an expensive house in a fancy London neighborhood.

The second act of the play is set in the Throne Hall of the royal palace in Lampedusa. Enter an aide to the new "king," Sam Kagan. On behalf of

7 The first one is available at the archive of the Goldstein-Goren Diaspora Research Center at Tel Aviv University [DRC], P-20, 92; the other one is preserved at Российский государственный архив литературы и искусства [Russian State Archive of Literature and Art, RGALI] F. 656. Op. 5. D. 5153. Unfortunately, no Yiddish copy of Markish's *Der kenig fun Lampeduze* has survived to this day. My special thanks goes to Ms. Anat Shimoni, the archivist of the DRC, for her generous help.

8 The real Sydney Cohen lost his parents as a child, see: Alt Miller 2019.

His Majesty, the “royal family” is invited to visit Lampedusa, the land of milk and honey, free of antisemitism. All of Sam’s relatives, as well as Lily, arrive in Lampedusa and proceed to the “king’s” palace, where the “king” awaits them to announce his political agenda. The palace’s interior features the Ten Commandments Tablets, the Star of David, and the words of the Torah rendering this achievement of Jewish political sovereignty a fulfillment of biblical prophecy: שום תשים עליך מלך [...] מקרב אחיך תשים עליך מלך [You may indeed set a king over you […] from among your brothers you shall set a king over you.[9]

> סעם: [...] אָט דאָס האָב איך מיר געשטעלט פֿאַר מײַן ערשטן ציל, צו שאַפֿן אַ ייִדישע אַרמיי [...] מײַן פֿעסטער ווילן איז, צו זאַמלען די כּוחות פֿון אונדזער יוגנט אונטער דער ייִדישער פֿאָן. איך זע שוין, ווי עס קומט דער טאָג, ווען עס וועט מקוים ווערן די נבֿואה: „והיה ביום ההוא יתּקע בשופר גדול ובאו האובדים בארץ אשור והנדחים בארץ מצרים“ און אַלע צעזייטע און צעשפּרייטע וועלן זיך פֿאַראייניקן צו איין גרויס און מעכטיק ייִדיש פֿאָלק.[10]
>
> Sam: […] This is what I have set for myself as my first task, to create a Jewish army […] I am absolutely determined to gather the strength of our young people under the Jewish flag. I see the day coming when the prophecy will come true: “And it shall come to pass in that day, that the great trumpet shall be blown, and they shall come which were ready to perish in the land of Assyria, and the outcasts in the land of Egypt,”[11] and all the scattered and dispersed people will unite as one great and mighty Jewish nation.[12]

Sam’s ambitions go even further: he will not only reestablish communal institutions, including secular ones, but also restore Jewish religious life:

> סעם: מײַן פּראָגראַם איז אײַנצופֿלאַנצן אַ ייִדיש לעבן און צו דעם צוועק מוזן געגרינ־דעט ווערן קהילות, עס מוז געשאַפֿן ווערן אַ נעץ פֿון שולן און ישיבֿות, אוניווערסיטעטן און סינאַגאָגעס, וועלכע זאָלן אָפּשפּיגלען דעם גלאַנץ פֿון אונדזער רומרײַכן בית־המדרש. איך וועל אויפֿבויען אַ ייִדיש לאַנד לויט דער טראַדיציע פֿון אונדזער תּורה און לויטן פּרינציפּ פֿון אמת, יושר און גערעכטיקייט. איך וועל ווידער אויפֿלעבן די טראַדיציע פֿון אונדזער סנהדרין – דעם ערשטן פּאַרלאַמענט אין דער מענטשלעכער געשיכטע, – אויפֿסנײַ אַכטונג צו געבן, אַז אונדזערע ייִדישע געזעצן, די גערעכטסטע און מענטשלעכסטע, זאָלן ווערן אָפּ־געהיטן פֿון אַלע און פֿאַר אַלע.[13]

9 Deut. 17:15.

10 Harendorf 2003, 59. A note on Yiddish spelling and transliteration: Yiddish spelling is standardized according to the YIVO rules, except for citations from Soviet Yiddish sources which are reproduced according to the Soviet spelling. Transliteration follows YIVO.

11 Isa 27:13.

12 Harendorf 2003, lvii.

13 Ibid., 51–53.

> Sam: My program is to make Jewish life take root here and to this end we have to create community organizations: a network of schools and yeshivas, universities and synagogues, which will reflect the glory of our famous temple. I will build up a Jewish state according to the tradition of our Torah and following the principles of truth, fairness, and justice. I will revive the tradition of our Sanhedrin – the first parliament in human history – in order to ensure anew that our Jewish laws, which are the most just and humane in existence, should be kept by all and for all.[14]

Thus, Sam's program mainly concerns Jews: it is their job to carry it out, not anybody else's. Jews have to fight and toil for their own future, bringing closer the moment when the Jewish people can enjoy the benefits of having their own state. Harendorf also touches upon the internal political struggle among Jews. Among his characters there are two Reform rabbis: hard-headed anti-Zionists, "dressed like priests, with top hats." They petition the King of Lampedusa not to create a Jewish army, for it may exacerbate antisemitism. Sam patiently explains that with their own state and army the Jews will be infinitely better protected. Before tearing their petition to pieces, he proclaims:[15]

> נו, זאָגט מיר, וועלכעס לאַנד האָט ברייט געעפֿנט זײַנע טויערן פֿאַר דעם געפּלאָגטן פֿאָלק? אָט דערפֿאַר דאַרפֿן מיר ייִדן האָבן אַן אייגן לאַנד און אַן אייגענע אַרמיי. איר הערט, רעפֿאָרם־ראַבײַס?! מיר מוזן געבן אַ היים פֿאַר די מיליאָנען היימלאָזע ברידער און שוועסטער. גענוג געוואַרט, נאָך אַ צוויי־טויזנט יאָריקן גלות מוזן מיר האָבן אַן אייגענע היים און אָט דאָס איז מײַן ענטפֿער![16]

> Tell me which country has opened its doors wide for our persecuted people? Thus we Jews must have our own land and our own army. You hear me, Reform rabbis? We must give a home to the millions of our homeless brothers and sisters. We have waited long enough. After an exile which has lasted two thousand years, we must have our homeland and so this is my answer![17]

The third act returns to Whitechapel and indeed to the realities of wartime life. The fuss around Sam has already died down and the Lampedusa of Act Two turned out to be merely a dream. At last, Sam appears: he got a

14 Ibid., liii.

15 Later on Harendorf wrote that he was a staunch opponent of Jewish assimilationism (Harendorf 1955, 219).

16 Harendorf 2003, 63.

17 Ibid., lix.

well-deserved leave. He refutes the rumors about his kinghood, proposes to Lily, and speaks about the anticipated victory over Nazism.

In his memoirs, Harendorf elaborates on Lampedusa as a Jewish messianic dream: in 1943, when the Nazi extermination machine was in full swing, British Jews perceived the island incident as the beginning of גאולה [*geule,* salvation]. The popular imagination likened the Jewish king Sydney Cohen to King Solomon and saw his faraway land of Lampedusa as a temporary solution to the problem of Jewish exile.[18] "In those bitter days and months, when Hitler's world war was raging on all fronts, my play carried out its task of enhancing the confidence of the Jews. The content of the play appealed to the Jewish audience, giving them courage not to despair and awakening their national consciousness," wrote Harendorf.[19]

The play was conceived as a musical. Employing a fashionable modern genre, Harendorf at the same time incorporates a traditional East European Jewish genre – פורים־שפיל [*purimshpil,* Purim performance], which also combines prosaic text and songs. Conforming to the canon, *The King of Lampedusa* opens with a prologue that lays out the play's plot. Harendorf makes further use of a comical device typical of Yiddish *shund*-theater – word mangling, mostly of loanwords and proper names. Sam's father, for one, continuously fails to pronounce 'Lampedusa' and renders it as לסוסתי [*Lesusosi*, 'to my horse'], אסתר־תענית [*Ester-tones*, 'the Fast of Esther'], or לאַמטידערייִנעם [*Lamtidereynem*, a non-word].[20] He mocks Ribbentrop, Germany's foreign minister, calling him גריוונטאָפּ [*Grivntop*, 'a pot of cracklings'].[21] Sam's mother, in turn, confuses the words אימפּערייטאָר [*impereytor,* emperor] and אָפּערייטאָר [*opereytor*, operator].[22] Some of Harendorf's characters are almost spoofs of those created by Mendele Moykher Sforim and Sholem Aleichem. Sam's father, just like טבֿיה דער מילכיקער [*Tevye der milkhiker*, Tevye the Dairyman], is a layman who loves to quote the Bible and imitate Hebrew

18 Harendorf 1955, 215–216.

19 Ibid., 229.

20 Harendorf 2003, 17, 19.

21 Ibid., 55.

22 Ibid., 43. The playwright also pays tribute to his great contemporary, the poet Itzik Manger, who in 1936 wrote מגילה־לידער [*Megile-lider*, Songs of the Megilah], a *purimshpil* stylization about current events in Europe. One of Manger's characters, a young socialist apprentice tailor, called Fastriguse, mimics the Aramaic names from the Book of Esther and is reminiscent of the Ukrainian verb стригти [to cut, shear]. The King's aide in Harendorf's play is called Parshanduse – also a quasi-Aramaic name, derived from פּרשן [a commentator].

words and phrases. Kagans' neighbors generously share their preposterous political forecasts with others, just like the devotees of the prayer house in Teterevke in Mendele's מסעות בנימין השלישי [*Masoes Benyomen hashlishi*, The Travels of Benjamin III].

Sam and Lily are juxtaposed with the older generation. In the dream scene, Sam explains to his mother that becoming a king is neither about infinite wealth, nor a license to be cruel to others. "It's your outfit that is new now… Well, and a much higher level of responsibility."[23] In another scene, Sam's bride informs him that she, being "a Jewish girl," decided to volunteer for the Auxiliary Territorial Service:[24] "for the land where I was born and grew up in freedom."[25] Sam's parents, on the other hand, have always been trying hard to stay away from anything related to the war and avoid any involvement with the state, which they perceive as a potential threat.

The play was attended by the complete spectrum of British society – from British writers and politicians to Jewish soldiers on leave as well as the common Yiddish-speaking Londoners.[26] The play's extraordinary popularity attracted even the attention of the Nazi propaganda apparatus. Harendorf recalled that he was 'honored' with a piece of criticism from Lord Haw-Haw (William Joyce) – member of Oswald Mosley's British Union of Fascists and the famous Nazi propaganda broadcaster from Germany to Britain.[27] The play crossed political and linguistic borders even during the war. It was also adapted for English radio and aired on the BBC on 17 May 1944. Three months later, it was shown for the first time in Buenos Aires.[28] It was translated into Hebrew and staged at the Tel Aviv-based תאטרון המטאטא [*Tēaṭěrōn ha-maṭaṭē*, Matate Theater], premiering on 15 November 1944 in Rishon leZion. On 30 November 1944, while on leave, the real Sydney Cohen visited Palestine by invitation and watched the play performed in Haifa.

23 Ibid., 49.

24 The women's branch of the British Army (1938 – 1949).

25 Ibid., 51, lii.

26 Harendorf 1955, 225.

27 Ibid., 223. William Joyce was born in 1906 in America. Raised in Ireland, he moved to England in his adolescence and became an entrepreneur. In 1932, he joined the British Union of Fascists, and eventually was put in charge of the propaganda there. In 1939, he went to Nazi Germany and became the host of the radio show *Germany Calling*, specifically targeting British audiences. In 1945, he was arrested by the British troops, tried as a war criminal, and sentenced to death. In 1946, he was hung in one of London's prisons.

28 Ibid., 228.

Perets Markish's *The King of Lampedusa*

In 1946–1947, when Perets Markish was finishing the first draft of his play *The King of Lampedusa*, the war was over and the world had changed dramatically with the onset of the Cold War. Yesterday's allies (Britain and the USA on the one hand, and the USSR on the other hand) were now political enemies, competing for influence in Germany and the Middle East.[29]

Markish's protagonist, Dave Globus, along with co-pilot Jack and radioman Charles, land on Lampedusa and occupy it. Inaccurately, Markish's play portrays Lampedusa as controlled only by German troops rather than by both Germans and Italians. On the island, Dave encounters two concentration camps: one for Jews and the other for Soviet prisoners of war. He liberates one of them himself and assists in liberating the other.

The next three scenes are set in London where Dave's parents work at their tailor shop on a tuxedo for Lord Greyford, a fictional antisemite and anti-communist. A long-awaited letter arrives from their older son Nathan – a British soldier in Palestine. He relates his admiration for the Soviets who "pound" the Nazis and his outrage over the brutality of the imperialist British administration towards the Jews. Rumor has it that Nathan is facing court martial for whipping two British officers, one of whom happens to be Lord Greyford's son, known to be particularly cruel to the Jewish population. Worried about the consequences of Nathan's actions, the Globus family learns about their son Dave's coronation as King of Lampedusa. Enter Lord Greyford to try on his tuxedo. Enraged about what happened in Palestine, he swears that all Jews in England will have to pay for his son's humiliation.

The fifth scene takes us to Lampedusa. Dave's radioman receives a message from Britain: his commanders intend to bring Globus to justice for the unauthorized action of liberating the Soviet prisoners of war. Together with Fyodor, a former Soviet inmate, Dave escapes to the USSR on a primitive wooden boat – a happy ending in the eyes of his family.

The main message of Markish's *The King of Lampedusa*, like the message of Harendorf's play, has little to do with the historical events of the war. Both authors speculate about the postwar political situation in Europe. With Germany defeated, Markish paints Britain, at the time still the imperial force in Palestine, as the worst enemy of the USSR, the world proletariat, and particularly the Jews.

29 For more details, see: Chubarian and Westad 2021, 376–394.

Markish juxtaposes Britain with the idealized USSR represented by Russian soldierly ethics in combat. Dave warns his crew against looting: "Слыхал, как русские солдаты отдают свой паек детям, когда освобождают село или город?" [Haven't you heard? Russian soldiers give their food rations to the children of the villages and towns they liberate!][30] After the liberation, Fyodor, the aforementioned prisoner of war, distributes the food rations miraculously found in his backpack among all those in need.[31] He also uses his bayonet to stab a wild boar that attacks one of the British crew members and grills it to feed people.[32] His moral character and patriotism convinces Dave Globus to become a Soviet citizen.

The play tells us that the most dangerous country for the Jews is Mandate Palestine. While the East London Globuses and their friends only anticipate outbursts of antisemitism, antisemitic violence is felt day and night from the Mandate administration. Nathan Globus writes to his parents: "Здесь, в Палестине ... Льется кровь... Еврейская кровь... Английские жандармы уничтожают целые селения... до тла." [Here, in Palestine ... blood is being shed... Jewish blood... The British gendarmes destroy whole settlements... to the ground.][33] His mother wonders: "Я хотела бы только знать, с кем англичане воюют в Палестине? Ведь там, кажется, немцев нет?" [I would be keen to know who the English are fighting in Palestine? It doesn't look like there are any Germans there, does it?][34] In Markish's 1947 draft, Nathan accuses the British of complicity with the Nazis: "Английские жандармы с собаками гонятся за малыми детьми, которые бегут из немецких лагерей" [The British gendarmes use dogs to chase the children that flee German camps].[35]

30 RGALI F. 656. Op. 5. D. 5153. L. 12.

31 Ibid., 16.

32 Ibid., 73.

33 Ibid., 24.

34 Ibid., 25.

35 DRC, P-20, 92. P. 22. In his criticism of Britain and its mandate policy, Markish was not necessarily wrong. Trying to avoid riots from the Arab population, the British administration in Palestine refused to create "the Jewish national home in Palestine," promised by the Balfour Declaration. Apart from hampering Jewish immigration, the British authorities sought to limit the territory populated by Jews: they hindered Jewish land ownership and harshly persecuted the Jewish resistance movement. There were also fascists in Britain: in the late 1940s, neo-fascist organizations, such as the Union Movement party and the British League of Ex-Servicemen, were legal and active.

Two drafts of Markish's *The King of Lampedusa*

As already mentioned, two drafts of the play survive to this day, one preserved in Tel Aviv and the other in Moscow. When was the first draft written and what inspired it? Markish must have written the play after May 1945, since Nazi Germany was clearly defeated.

The play deals, first of all, with Soviet-British relations. After the Second World War, the Allies were no longer united. Nine days after Churchill gave the Fulton speech launching the Cold War, in an interview to *Правда* [*Pravda*, Truth], Stalin compared Churchill to Hitler, accusing the former of being the latter's disciple and a proponent of the English "racial theory […] called upon to decide the destinies of the entire world" and of standing "in the position of a firebrand of war."[36] In his play, Markish deploys a similar rhetoric: the British Empire is the new Nazi Germany. Following Hitler's footsteps, British imperialism implements Nazi-like racial policies across the world. It is not impossible that this aspect of the play was intended as lip service to Stalin, which shifts the date at least to the spring of 1946.

The play was not staged in 1947 and, unfortunately, we do not know why. On 12 January 1948, Mikhoels was assassinated by order of the authorities. His murder marked the beginning of the repression of Soviet Jewish culture and organizations, resulting in the liquidation of the ייִדישער אנטיפאשיסטישער קאָמיטעט [*Yidisher antifashistisher komitet*, Jewish Antifascist Committee, JAFC] and its outlets, including the אייניקייַט [*Eynikayt*, Unification], its official newspaper, in November 1948, the shutdown of GOSET in November 1949 and culminating in the JAFC trial: leading members of the Committee were arrested, accused of treason and "bourgeois Jewish nationalism", and executed on 12 August 1952.[37]

On 23 March 1948 still, six months before its closure, *Eynikayt* published an announcement about the upcoming premiere of *The King of Lampedusa*, which, as already mentioned, never came to pass. Since *Eynikayt* only adver-

36 Stalin 1946. For the Soviet reaction to Churchill's Fulton speech, see: Chubarian and Westad 2021, 390–391; Pechatnov 1998, 92. About 1946 as the year of a dire crisis in the Soviet-British relations see also: Naumov 1994, 327.

37 For the liquidation of the JAFC and the anti-Jewish campaigns, see Redlich 2013, 121–143, 451–470; Kostyrchenko 1994; Kostyrchenko 2005, 8–11, 138–386. For the JAFC trial, see Naumov 1994; Redlich 2013, 145–158; Estraikh 2018, 143–145; Shneer 2011 a, 209–218.

tised GOSET's newly approved plays,[38] one of the most likely reasons for such inconsistency should be sought in the interim developments in and around the Middle East. The newly declared state of Israel (May 1948) enjoyed the support of the Soviet regime for a short while. But already in October 1948 things changed to the opposite.[39] The official propaganda claimed that Soviet Jews did not need their own state outside of the Soviet realm – their home, freed from antisemitism.

It is quite possible that Markish had to revise his play to fit the new agenda, and the two drafts differ quite significantly. He removed everything that could be construed as allusions to Israel as the only Jewish national home and turned against Britain even harder than before. In the second draft, Dave's father is attacked in London, his head bashed. A dialogue between Mr. Globus and his neighbor, Mr. Chowl, reads:

> М-р Глобус: Вы хотите знать, как я себя чувствую, мистер Чаул? Как все евреи чувствуют себя в Лондоне! Как положено чувствовать себя еврею, которому разбили на улице голову! Так, вероятно, чувствовали себя евреи в Германии!
>
> М-р Чаул: Да, мистер Глобус... Фашизм пока что изжарили только в русских котлах... А у нас, видать, надо будет для него лишь начинать клепать котлы... И подложить под них огонь...[40]

> Mr. Globus: "You would like to know how I feel, Mr. Chowl, wouldn't you? Just like any other Jew in London! Just like a Jew whose head has been bashed is supposed to feel! Just how the Jews in Germany must have felt!"
>
> Mr. Chowl: "Yes, Mr. Globus… Fascism has been burned up only in Russian caldrons… And here it looks like we are yet to begin welding those caldrons… And to make a fire under them…"

Britain is also criticized for supporting the Arabs in Palestine: the second draft was most likely written, when the Soviet authorities still sympathized with the Zionist project in Palestine.[41] But by December 1948, when the play

[38] One more play rehearsed in those days but never performed was the famous *Prints Reubeyni* by Dovid Bergelson. For more details, see Novershtern 2003, 313.

[39] For Golda Meir's role in the change of the official Soviet position, see Kostyrchenko 2005, 387–399.

[40] RGALI, F. 656. Op. 5. D. 5153. L. 89–90.

[41] As Gennady Estraikh claims, for some time in the mid 1940s, "Soviet Yiddish literati were allowed to write about Palestine without concentration on harmfulness of Zionism." Estraikh 2008, 13.

was discussed by the Writers Union (see below), the situation had changed and the play was rejected.

Plagiarism Scandal

In September 1948, a letter[42] signed by Sh. Y. Dorfson (a pseudonym of Harendorf's) arrived at the editorial office of the *Eynikayt* accusing Markish of plagiarism:

> אין די מאָסקווער „אייניקייַט“ (אָרגאַנ פונעמ ייִדישנ אנטיפאשיסטישנ קאָמיטעט אינ סאָוועטנפארבאנד) איז דעמ 23סטנ מערצ, 1948 דערשינענ א מודעה, אז דער מאָס־קווער ייִדישער מעלוכע־טעאטער גרייט צו די אויפפירונג פונ מייַנ פּיעסע „דער קעניג פונ לאמפּעדוסע“ [!] אונ צו מייַנ גרויסער איבערראשונג – פיגורירט ניט אלס מחבר דער שרייַבער פונ די שורות, נאָר פּרצ מארקיש...
>
> On 23 March 1948, Moscow-based Eynikayt (the organ of the Jewish Antifascist Committee of the Soviet Union) printed an announcement that GOSET was about to put on my play The King of Lampedusa, and – to my utter surprise – it's not the writer of these lines who was indicated as the author, but Perets Markish…[43]

According to Harendorf, he had met Mikhoels and Fefer in London in 1943. It was then that the Soviet authorities commissioned Mikhoels, the chairman of JAFC at that time, and Fefer, a Soviet Yiddish poet and the vice-chairman of JAFC, to travel to North and Middle America to raise support for the Red Army primarily from local Jews and Jewish organizations. In October-November 1943, on their way back to the USSR, they stopped in London. By that time, Harendorf had already completed his *The King of Lampedusa* and read it out to Mikhoels and Fefer. Mikhoels was fascinated and expressed his desire to stage it. Harendorf was flattered and excited about the prospect of taking the play to international stages and especially to have it staged by the famous Mikhoels. The latter, however, presented him with two conditions: first, delete the 'Zionist-mystical' (Mikhoels' wording) tone, and second, move the key action from Lampedusa to the Soviet Jewish Au-

42 The letter, retyped by an *Eynikayt* secretary, became part of the JAFC collection in the Государственный архив Российской Федерации [State Archive of the Russian Federation, GARF] and was also published in the London Yiddish magazine לשון און לעבן [*Loshn un lebn*, Language and Life].

43 It is quite likely that Harendorf saw the ad in *Eynikayt*: the paper was mainly circulated in the West.

tonomous Oblast with its capital in Birobidzhan. Both requirements appear to have been of a purely pragmatic rather than artistic nature: for Mikhoels, eliminating Zionist references would increase the probability of clearing the play with Soviet censorship. By the same token, the only Jewish center with a chance of approval would be the one (more or less) pre-approved by the state. And as of 1943, it was Birobidzhan. Harendorf declined the proposition. Two months later, in February 1944 Mikhoels followed up, saying that he was willing to take the play 'as is.' What might explain his about-face?

On 12 February 1944, Mikhoels, Fefer, and JAFC-secretary Shakhno Epshteyn had an audience with Vyacheslav Molotov, Soviet Minister of Foreign Affairs. They presented their project to create a Jewish national home in Crimea (which was still under Nazi occupation at that point). Molotov suggested that the petitioners address the authorities with a formal letter. On 15 February, Mikhoels, Fefer, and Solomon Lozovsky, the Deputy People's Commissar for Foreign Affairs and a JAFC member, sent Stalin the so-called Crimean letter, in which they criticized Birobidzhan and asked the authorities to create the "Jewish Soviet Socialistic Republic" in Crimea.[44] Stalin dismissed the plan. Notably, no consequences followed – at least not immediately.[45] As Shimon Redlich claims, "the possibility of a Jewish republic in the Crimea had been discussed quite openly in Moscow in the spring of 1944."[46] Maybe in February 1944 Mikhoels hoped that if it was allowed to talk to the authorities about any other Jewish settlement project than Birobidzhan, it would also be allowed to stage a play set someplace else. Unfortunately, we don't know if Mikhoels attempted to stage Harendorf's play.

Upon receiving Mikhoels' 1944 letter, Harendorf sent him the script, but never heard back: his letters went unanswered, and his fee remained unpaid. Yet, since the play, after all, was not staged, Harendorf was fine with letting the whole thing go and not pressing any charges. It all changed when he saw

44 A week later (on February, 21), they sent the same letter to Molotov. See: Kostyrchenko 2003; GARF. F. 8114. Op. 1. D. 792. L. 32–36; Российский государственный архив социально-политической истории [Russian State Archive of Socio-Political History, RGASPI] F. 17. Op. 125. D. 246. L. 169–172. For the Russian original, see Kostyrchenko 2005, 44–48; and https://document.wikireading.ru/honqwhrg6h; for the English translation, see Redlich 2013, 264–267. For more on the "Crimean letter", see: Ibid., 459; Novershtern 2003, 312; Estraikh 2008, 7, 26; Estraikh 2018, 142; Fitzpatrick 2017, 145f.

45 It was later used as a piece of evidence at the JAFC trial.

46 Redlich 2013, 470, n, 61. See also Ibid., 267–270. On Markish's role in discussing the Crimean plans, see Ibid., 458.

the ad for the upcoming performance of his very own play with Perets Markish's name on it.

> עס איז מעגלעך, אַז מיכאָעלס האָט, באַם בעסטן ווילן, ניט געקאָנט אופֿפֿירן מײַן פּיעסע לויט אונדזער אָפּמאַך, און דער מאַנוסקריפּט איז פֿאַרבליבן אינעם אַרכיוו פֿונעם מאָסקווער ייִדישן מעלוכע־טעאַטער, ביז פּערעץ מאַרקיש האָט זיך איבער די פּיעסע „מרחם" געווען און די טעמע פֿאַרוואָנדן פֿאַר זיך.[47]
>
> It is possible that Mikhoels, as much as he wanted to stage my play as agreed, failed to do so. Then the manuscript was kept in the archive of Moscow Yiddish State Theater till Markish "took pity" on it and utilized it for himself…

Harendorf had not read Markish's play, so he was not able to assess if it had been indeed plagiarized. But the fact that Markish used the same title understandably seemed to be all the evidence that he needed. He contacted GOSET and demanded that the title be changed. He received no reply, but his demand seems to have been fulfilled: a later issue of *Eynikayt* announced the upcoming premiere of the play דאָקטאָר לאַמפּעדוזע [*Doktor Lampeduze*, Doctor Lampedusa]. We cannot know for sure, though, if it was a follow-up on Harendorf's letter or a mere misprint. Harendorf was not satisfied: if anything, GOSET seemed to have tacitly acknowledged his suspicion that Markish had indeed plagiarized and tried to avoid a scandal. Harendorf contacted GOSET demanding to be listed as the play's author and Markish as its editor.

The letter was forwarded to the Writers' Union. The State Archive of the Russian Federation owns a copy, with hand-written note by Arn Vergelis (Chairman of the Yiddish Section of the Union), "Получил для рассмотрения (нрзб) на бюро еврейских писателей при ССП СССР" [Received at the Bureau of Jewish Writers for consideration at the (next meeting of the) Soviet Writers' Union]. Unfortunately, the minutes of the meeting have not been preserved, so we cannot confirm that it actually took place.

On 2 October 1948, *Eynikayt* published GOSET's reaction to Harendorf's letter. By then Mikhoels had already been killed, so the letter was signed by his successors: the art director Benjamin Zuskin and the managing director Grigory Fishman. Both denied (most probably under pressure) any previous contact with Harendorf or any familiarity with his play. In fact, they didn't

47 GARF F. R-8114. Op. 1. D. 510. L. 279.

even address him directly. Theirs was more of an open letter to *Eynikayt*'s editor Grigory Zhits:

כאַשעווער כאַווער רעדאַקטאָר!

אינעמ זשורנאַל „לאָשנ אונ לעבנ“, וואָס דערשײַנט אינ לאָנדאָנ, איז פאַרעפנטלעכט אַנ אָנקלאָגע פונ אײנעמ ש.י. דאָרפזאָנ, אַז פּ. מאַרקיש האָט, קלוימערשט, פּלאַגיִאַטיש צוגעײגנט די טעמע פונ זײַנ, דאָרפזאָנס, פּיעסע וועגנ לאַמפּעדוזע, וועלכע דער מאָסקווער ייִדישער מעלוכע־טעאַטער אפ ש. מיכאָעלסעס נאָמענ האָט זיכ, קלוימערשט, אײַנגעשאַפט בא אימ.

דערלויבט אונדז צו מעלדנ דורכ אײַער צײַטונג, אַז דער מאָסקווער ייִדישער מלוכע־טעאַטער איז קײנמאָל ניט אַרײַנגעטראָטנ אינ אונטערהאַנדלונגענ מיט דעמ דאָזיקנ אָנקלאָגער, ווײסט ביכלאַל ניט, ווער איז דער ש.י. דאָרפזאָנ און קײנ שומ פּיעסע קײנמאָל בא אימ ניט באַשטעלט. די אָנקלאָגע איז, ווײַזט אויס, אויסגערעכנט אפ טרויעריקער פּאָפּוליאַריטעט פאַר אימ, – אויב ניט פונ אַ דראַמאַטורגיש ווערק, איז לעכאָלאַפּאָכעס פונ אַ געמײנהײַט.

וואָס שײַעכ דעמ נאָמענ פונ פּערעצ מאַרקישעס קאָמעדיע, איז ער קײנמאָל ניט געענדערט געוואָרנ. פּונקט ווי עס זײַנענ ניט געענדערט דער נאָמענ פונעמ אינדזל און די ראָל פונעמ העלד.[48]

Dear Comrade Editor!

London-based magazine *Loshn un lebn* published a complaint of a certain Sh.Y. Dorfson. He claims that P. Markish has plagiarized a work of his, [namely] a play about Lampedusa that the Moscow State Jewish Theater under the auspices of Sh. Mikhoels' had allegedly procured from him.

Let us declare via your newspaper that the Moscow State Jewish Theater has never entered into any dealings with this complainant, never had a slightest idea who this Sh. Y. Dorfson was, and never commissioned any plays from him. The complaint seems to be meant towards getting bad publicity – that is if not for the playwright's merits, then at least for his malice.

As for the name of Perets Markish's comedy, it was never changed. Neither was the name of the island or the nature of the main character.

In the December issue of *Loshn un leben*, Harendorf replied. He referred to a number of *Eynikayt* issues, as well as YKUF's New York-based magazine ייִדישע קולטור [*Yidishe kultur*, Yiddish Culture] and Paris-based magazine אויפֿסנײַ [*Oyfsnay*, Anew], to prove that Markish did change the title of his play into *Doktor Lampeduze*.[49]

48 Fishman and Zuskin 1948, 4.

49 Harendorf 1948, 56f. I am grateful to Amanda Miriem-Khaye Seigel of NYPL for locating this document for me.

Did Markish plagiarize?

It is highly likely that Markish was familiar with Harendorf's text. We can assume that after the end of the Second World War Harendorf's play could not be staged in the USSR because it was written by a contemporary British author, and Harendorf's Zionist story was no longer acceptable. Therefore, we can infer that Mikhoels commissioned an alternative version from Markish. So, did Markish represent another author's work of art as his own? In addition to the shared title and historical event, there is no doubt that certain plot-lines, motifs, and characters resemble each other. But a couple of contextual circumstances should be factored in.

Soviet adaptations of Western books were not rare, especially in children's literature: for instance, Aleksey Tolstoy's *Буратино* [Buratino] was a retelling of Carlo Collodi's *Pinocchio*; Korney Chukovsky's *Айболит* [Aybolit] was based on Hugh Lofting's *Doctor Dolittle*; Lasar Lagin's *Старик Хоттабыч* [The Old Genie Hottabych] was inspired by F. Anstey's (Thomas Anstey Guthrie) *The Brass Bottle*; and Alexander Volkov's *Волшебник изумрудного города* [The Wizard of the Emerald City] was an adaptation of L. Frank Baum's *The Wonderful Wizard of Oz*.[50] In the case of *The King of Lampedusa*, despite sharing the title, the plays' plots and ideological messages are not even remotely similar: Harendorf's protagonist dreams to create a Jewish army, to establish a Jewish state, and to restore Jewish life. By contrast, Markish's protagonist holds Soviet values, strives to become a Soviet citizen, and escapes to the USSR.

Multiple motifs in Markish's play suggest that it was conceived as a Soviet response to Harendorf's play. Harendorf tells a distinctly Zionist story where Jews can only be safe and happy in their own state, ideally in Palestine. In Markish's telling, the only place where Jews can enjoy safety and civil rights is the USSR. For Harendorf, being a patriotic British yet Zionist Jew implies loyalty towards Great Britain – as Lily puts it, "the land where I was born and grew up in freedom"[51] – and eventually a Jewish state. For Markish, a progressive Jew should have no loyalty to their homeland (of course, unless his homeland is the USSR). Joining the Soviet people – that's what any Jew should aspire to. According to the wartime and postwar Stalinist ideology,

50 For Soviet adaptations and their originals, see Kaloh Vid 2013, Drews-Sylla 2013, Veligorsky 2022, Mitrokhina 1996–1997, Haber 2017.

51 Harendorf 2003, lii.

scholarship suggests, once accepted into the "family of Soviet nations," Jews (or any other people, for that matter) will have to content themselves with being "younger brothers" and eternally grateful to their "older brother" – the Russian people.[52] This is why Markish did not highlight the theme of Jewish heroism. At the Soviet Writers' Union about to decide the fate of his play, he highlighted the value to the secondary Russian character, rather than to any of the more central, more Jewish, characters:

> Что здесь ценное? Федор. Абсолютно верно, что я без Федора не могу сделать пьесы. Потому что мне во всем мире, где бы я ни находился, нужна Россия. Мне кажется, что всем людям, где бы ни находились, нужна Россия, сознание, что есть Россия. ... Я хотел еще раз показать, что точно так же, как Россия спасла Англию, так он спасает английских офицеров, т.е. процесс спасения Россией мира продолжается в маленькой капле, как он развивался в больших планах.
>
> What is the most valuable thing here? Fyodor. It is absolutely true that without Fyodor I'd have no play. Because wherever I am in the world, I need Russia. I think that everyone, wherever they are, needs Russia, needs to be sure that Russia exists… I wanted to show once more that just as Russia rescued England, so he [Fyodor] rescues English officers, i.e. the process of Russia's saving the world develops on a little plane, just as it unfolded on macrolevels.

By contrast, Harendorf admires "Jewish young people who are fighting in the ranks of all the free nations," shedding their "blood for the sake of freedom."

Both plays omit any direct references to Nazi soldiers specifically or to Nazism generally.[53] The reasons for such an omission are, however, rather different. Harendorf, writing his play in 1943, focused on the desired Jewish redemption and not on Jewish suffering. For Markish, the reasons for writing a *khurbn* play with no German Nazis in it are similarly political. At the time he was writing it, the political landscape had changed. Just like for the USSR, the most vicious enemy of the Jews in his play needed to be *not* the Nazis, but the British.

52 See for example, Veidlinger 2000, 233, 235. For more on Russian nationalism of the wartime and postwar Soviet bureaucracy, see Zeltser 2014.

53 For the strategy of expressing existential fear by elimination of the enemy, who "remains unidentified and acts as an impersonal agent of evil," see Krutikov 2023.

Noteworthy are some of the episodes and motifs clearly resembling Harendorf's play that were featured in the earlier version of Markish's piece but omitted later: visitors coming to Dave's parents' house (neighbors, reporters, salesmen, etc.); Globuses' neighbors' plan to go to Lampedusa to seek some favors from the King; jokes about the word Lampedusa; the question of what language is spoken on Lampedusa; and a comic device of amateur political judgements given by the protagonist's father and his friends and neighbors. It very well may be that Markish decided to get rid of most of such 'coincidences' in his 1948 rewrite in order to avoid charges of plagiarism.

"There Are Too Many Jews in This Play, Aren't There?" The Writers' Union discusses Markish's play

When the Second World War began, it had taken a while for the Yiddish press to figure out how to cover current events: Was it allowed to cite the number of victims? To publish survivors' testimonies? To talk about Nazi atrocities in detail? To write about Jewish resistance?[54] Some guidelines were formed, and after the war they became a basis for a new standard of writing about the *khurbn*. The writers had to focus on heroic deeds, and, as Gennady Estraikh notes, "Jewish heroism had to be balanced against non-Jewish heroism."[55] Between the assassination of Mikhoels in 1948 and Stalin's death in 1953, depicting Jews as heroes fighting by themselves for their own people was classified as "bourgeois Jewish nationalism."[56]

Right after the war, when Mikhoels was still alive, Markish tried to probe the new boundaries. His play דער אופשטאנד אינ געטאָ [*Der ufshtand in geto*, The Ghetto Uprising][57] (its Russian version bore the name Беловежская пуща [Białowieża Forest]) was one of the first attempts to address the topic of the *khurbn* on stage.[58] The play is devoted to the uprising in the Vilna

54 Kerler 2003.

55 Estraikh 2014, 86, see also Estraikh 2008, 101.

56 Kotlerman 2008, 129. For Markish's depictions of Jews fighting for themselves, and for his being accused of nationalism for that, see Redlich 2013, 210, 292, 302, 414, 417–421; Estraikh 2017; Shneer 2011a, 211f; 2011b, 150–152; Murav 2011, 113f.

57 Its copy in RGALI is dated 1946, however, Kotlerman 2008 suggests that 1945 might be more accurate.

58 For earlier attempts (Markish's אנ אויג פאר אנ אויג [*An oyg far an oyg*, An Eye for an Eye] (1942), Dovid Bergelson's כ'וועל לעבנ [*Kh'vel lebn*, I will live] (1943), Yekhezkl Dobrushin's א ווונדערלעכע געשיכטע [*A vunderlekhe geshikhte*, Marvelous History] (1944), Moyshe Pinchevski's איכ לעב [*Ikh*

Ghetto and ends with a grand battle scene, where all the main characters are killed. Like many other plays of his, *The Ghetto Uprising* shows a generational gap: the young fight uncompromisingly, whereas the old cave in without even trying to save themselves, let alone other Jews. The Jewish youth is thus portrayed as lionhearted heirs of their biblical ancestors, such as Moses or Samson, while the older generation voluntarily rejects the Jewish tradition of self-defense.[59] Additionally, the ghetto uprising could not have happened, if not for a non-Jewish, ethnically Russian character – the Soviet Communist Party instructor Andrey Semibrat. He joins the rebels in the ghetto and becomes their leading force, symbolizing the "leadership and guidance" of the Party.[60]

The King of Lampedusa was therefore Markish's second play about the *khurbn* written after the war. As already mentioned, in the fall of 1948, the play had still not been staged, and due to the events in the Middle East, the play had to be rewritten. Besides being sent to Glavrepertkom, the new Russian translation (of 1948) was also submitted for approval to the Writers' Union.[61] According to the minutes, the meeting at the Union took place on 6 December 1948.[62] According to the jury at the Writers' Union, this time he failed to create an adequate, internationalist balance between different ethnicities. Thus said Ivan Chicherov, a literary critic:

> Еврейская тема для нас приемлема тогда, когда она звучит интернационалистически, а не тогда, когда звучит националистически. Что я этим хочу сказать? Я хочу сказать, что в «Беловежской пуще» еврейское ощущение мира и борьбы звучало более интернационалистически, чем звучит в этой пьесе.[63]

> We can allow writing about the Jews, but only if it translates the international agenda, not a nationalistic one. What do I mean by that? I mean that in Białowieża Forest [The Ghetto Uprising], the Jewish take on peace and struggle was more internationalist, than in this play.

leb, I live] (1945), Zalman-Shneer Okun's פריילעכס [*Freylekhs*, Merry dance] (1945) et. al.); see Veidlinger 2000, 239–241, 246–249. Markish's play *An oyg far an oyg* is also discussed at length in: Polyan 2021.

59 See also: Shneer 2011a, 194; Shneer, 2011b, 146f; Veidlinger 2011, 168–196.

60 Kotlerman 2008, 128.

61 Since the submitted text was in Russian, it was discussed not by the Yiddish Section, but by a special commission in charge of the Russian-language theater repertoire.

62 RGALI, F. 631. Op. 38. D. 176.

63 Ibid., 17.

Markish was required to depict a heroic Russian character: that is why his Dave Globus does not liberate Fyodor, and only befriends him after he has already been liberated. It is unfathomable that a Soviet soldier would be rescued by British Jews, so in the play Globus and his crew liberate just one concentration camp, the Jewish one. At the very beginning of the discussion at the Writers Union, Soviet playwright and prose writer Khrisanf Khersonsky complained that Fyodor was too simplistic and unconvincing – unlike Markish's Jewish characters.[64] Chicherov seconded this opinion.[65] The critics at the Union were careful to meet all unspoken censorship requirements. They had to make sure that class struggle in the play received a proper representation. They also advised that Markish show a broader social vista, encompassing British workers and their struggle against capitalists. Chicherov said:

> Мне кажется, не слишком ли много евреев в пьесе? Ведь этот самый портной Глобус живет не в еврейском квартале, он живет в английском квартале. Его соседи англичане. И вот, чтобы показать, что существует единый классовый фронт, кого-то из этих жильцов сделать англичанами, это выявит более социально-политический фон пьесы в самой Англии.[66]

> There are too many Jews in this play, aren't there? Look, this tailor – Globus: he doesn't live in a Jewish neighborhood, but in an English one, right? His neighbors are Englishmen. Then to show that there is a united class battlefront, [you have to] make some of these neighbors English. This will expose the social and political background of this play in England proper.

Novelist Alexander Avdeyenko recommended that Markish incorporate some assimilated Jews, to remind his audience that the Soviet Union was the only true Jewish homeland. Other remarks engaged with shortcomings and logical flaws found in the play. Abram Plavnik argued that all characters have to be plausible and expressed his disappointment with Markish's Lord who was too far from believable.[67] Soviet Yiddish writer Zalman Vendrov wondered why a British Lord would become a customer of a poor tailor with a ramshackle workshop in Whitechapel? Others pointed out that British soldiers were ordinary, working-class people, but that they were painted as despicable, greedy creatures in the play. To still others, the punishment that

64 Ibid., 4.
65 Ibid., 18.
66 Ibid., 19.
67 Ibid., 12.

Dave Globus receives for liberating the concentration camps sounded inaccurate since British martial laws did not criminalize such deeds. Occasionally, someone would forget the current political agenda and let it slip that, back in 1943, Great Britain and the USSR were allies. Others were more circumspect and made sure to mention British and American imperialism as a worthy motif for Markish's play.[68]

Markish promised to follow all recommendations and make his play shorter and denser. He, however, disagreed with the jury on one significant point: he refused to acknowledge that his play was "nationalistic" and that the Jewish theme should only be explored from the positions of "internationalism."[69] Less than two months later Perets Markish was arrested and charged with Jewish nationalism. His play has never been staged. In GARF, an abstract of Harendorf's letter is preserved, written in Russian in 1952: it was likely used in preparations for the JAFC trial.

Conclusion

It is almost certain that Markish read Harendorf's *The King of Lampedusa* before creating his play of the same name. In both plays, the *khurbn* becomes a topic relevant to addressing contemporary political issues. The two *Kings* overlap at many points, but the differences are more significant.

The story of *The King of Lampedusa* crosses many borders from Malta to England, from England to Palestine, Latin America, and the Soviet Union. It also crossed ideological barriers. Harendorf's wartime play conveys a distinct Zionist message: Jews are in danger, and in order to survive they need a state of their own. To make it happen, they have to fight to secure their nation's future. By contrast, Markish's postwar play postulates that the only place the Jews can call home is the USSR. Capitalist Europe is described as a place where fascism was yet to be defeated. Markish's Jews never fight alone: they are led to the battlefield by Russian comrades. This case study contributes to our understanding of the Soviet Yiddish culture's surprising openness to contemporary Western influences. It also shows the role Yiddish enjoyed in the postwar Stalinist Soviet Union: a vehicle in the ideological struggle and a medium of transnational communication.

68 Ibid., 22.

69 Ibid., 29.

Bibliography

Archival Sources

Государственный архив Российской Федерации [The State Archive of the Russian Federation, GARF]:

GARF F. R-8114. Op. 1. D. 510. – Articles by Eynikayt writers in Yiddish. D – David et. al. (undated).

Российский государственный архив литературы и искусства [Russian State Archive of Literature and Art, RGALI]:

RGALI F. 631. Op. 38. D. 176 – Minutes of the Commission for Discussion P. Markish's Play *Korol' Lampeduzy* [The King of Lampedusa] (06.12.1948).

RGALI F. 656. Op. 5. D. 5153 – Markish P. D. *Korol' Lampeduzy* [The King of Lampedusa]. A play in 3 acts, 6 episodes. Performance in GOSET permitted after being censored. Translation by Shambadal M.A. (1948).

Российский государственный архив социально-политической истории [Russian State Archive of Socio-Political History, RGASPI] F. 17. Op. 125. D. 246. L. 169–172.

The Goldstein-Goren Diaspora Research Center [DRC], Tel Aviv University:

DRC P-20. 92 – Markish P. D. *Korol' Lampeduzy* [The King of Lampedusa]. A play in 3 acts, (1947).

Published Sources and Secondary Literature

Alt Miller, Yvette, 2019: The Jewish "King" of Lampedusa, Aish.com <https://www.aish.com/jw/s/The-Jewish-King-of-Lampedusa.html>, December 7, 2020.

Chubarian, Alexander, and Odd Arne Westad, eds., 2021: *Советско-британские отношения в 1943 – 1953 гг. Документы и материалы. Под ред. А.О. Чубарьяна и О.А. Вестада.* Москва: Аспект Пресс.

Drews-Sylla, Gesine, 2013: Wie Doctor Dolittle zu Doktor Ajbolit und was aus ihnen wurde. Geschichte einer kulturellen Übersetzung. In: Schamma Schahadat, Renata Makarska and Claudia Dathe, eds., *Zwischentexte. Literarisches Übersetzen in Theorie und Praxis*. Berlin: Frank & Timme, 215–235.

Estraikh, Gennady, 2008: *Yiddish in the Cold War*. Oxford: Legenda.

Estraikh, Gennady, 2014: Jews and Cossacks: A Symbiosis in Literature and Life. In: Harriet Murav and Gennady Estraikh, eds., *Soviet Jews in World War II: Fighting, Witnessing, Remembering*. Boston, Mass.: Academic Studies Press, 85–103.

Estraikh, Gennady, 2017: Эстрайх, Геннадий: (Интер)национализм в творчестве Переца Маркиша. О роли литературоведческого интерфейса в еврейской литературе» In: *Советская иудаика: история, проблематика, персоналии. Под. ред. М. Куповецкого.* Москва: Гешарим / Мосты культуры, 136 – 156.

Estraikh, Gennady, 2018: The Life, Death, and Afterlife of the Jewish Anti-Fascist Committee. In: *East European Jewish Affairs* 48 (2), 139 – 148.

Fishman, Grigory, and Benjamin Zuskin, 1948 פֿישמאַן, גריגאָרי און בנימין זוסקין: א בריוו אין רעדאַקציע. אין: **איינִיקייַט** (מאָסקווע) 119 (680), 2טער אָקטאָבער 1948: ז' 4.

Fitzpatrick, Sheila, 2017: Annexation, Evacuation and Antisemitism in the Soviet Union, 1939 – 46. In: Mark Edele, Sheila Fitzpatrick and Atina Grossmann, eds., *Shelter from the Holocaust: Rethinking Jewish Survival in the Soviet Union*. Detroit, Mich.: Wayne State University Press, 133 – 160.

Fraenkel, Yosef, 1969: Samuel Jacob Harendorf (Dorfson) – Author of The King of Lampedusa. In: *The Detroit Jewish News* (Detroit) 1 August 1969, 15.

Haber, Erika, 2017: *Oz behind the Iron Curtain: Aleksandr Volkov and His Magic Land Series*. Jackson, Miss: University Press of Mississippi.

Harendorf, Sh. Y., 1955 האַרענדאָרף, ש. י.: טעאַטער קאַראַוואַנען: **מעשׂה׳לעך און עפּיזאָדן פֿון מייַנע וואַנדערונגען מיט ייִדיש טעאַטער**. לאָנדאָן: פּרייַנט פֿון ייִדיש לשון.

Harendorf, Sh. Y., 1948 האַרענדאָרף, ש. י.: אַ תּשובֿה אויף אַ "הייליקן" אמת! אין: **לשון און לעבן**. חודש־זשורנאַל פֿאַר ליטעראַטור, טעאַטער, קונסט און קולטור (לאָנדאָן) יאָר 9, 107: 12, דעצעמבער 1948: זז' 56 – 57.

Harendorf, Sh. Y., 2003: *The King of Lampedusa: a Musical Comedy in Three Acts with Prologue.* Translated by Heather Valencia. London: Jewish Music Institute International Forum for Yiddish Culture.

Hiscock, John, 2001: Hollywood hails King Syd. The bizarre tale of an RAF pilot whose crash-landing led to the surrender of an entire island is finally to be filmed. In: *The Telegraph,* 28 December 2001, https://www.telegraph.co.uk/culture/4727143/Hollywood-hails-King-Syd.html, December 7, 2020.

Kaloh Vid, Natalia, 2013: Translation of Children's Literature in the Soviet Union: How Pinocchio Got a Golden Key. In: *International Research in Children's Literature* 6 (1): 90 – 103.

Kerler, Dov Ber, 2003: The Soviet Yiddish Press: During the War, 1942 – 1945. In: Robert Moses Shapiro, ed., *Why Didn't the Press Shout?: American & International Journalism During the Holocaust*. Jersey City, NJ: Yeshiva University, 221 – 250.

Kostyrchenko, Gennady, 1994: Костырченко, Геннадий: *В плену у красного фараона. Политические преследования евреев в последнее сталинское десятилетие*. Москва: Международные отношения, 1994.

Kostyrchenko, Gennady, 2003: Костырченко, Геннадий : «Дело Михоэлса»: Новый взгляд. In: *Лехаим* 11 (139), <https://lechaim.ru/arhiv/139/kostyr.htm>, May 20, 2022.

Kostyrchenko, Gennady, 2005: *Государственный антисемитизм в СССР. От начала до кульминации. 1938–1945. Под ред. Г.В. Костырченко*. Москва: МФД, Материк.

Kotlerman, Ber B., 2008 קוטלרמן, בר ב.: מחזותיו של פרץ מרקיש: הליכה על כחול דק בין ,יהודי׳ ל,סובייטי׳. בתוך: **ביקורת ופרשנות** 41: 111 – 129.

Krutikov, Mikhail, 2023: Between Horror and Jubilation: The Sublime in Leyb Kvitko's Poetics. In: Harriet Murav, Gennady Estraikh and Myroslav Shkandrij, eds., *Building Modern Jewish Culture. The Yiddish* Kultur-Lige. Oxford: Legenda, 78 – 94.

Mitrokhina, Xenia, 1996 – 97: The Land of Oz in the Land of Soviets. In: *Children's Literature Association Quarterly* 21 (4): 183 – 188.

Murav, Harriet, 2011: *Music from a Speeding Train: Jewish Literature in Post-Revolution Russia.* Stanford, Calif.: Stanford University Press.

Naumov, Vladimir, 1994: *Неправедный суд. Последний сталинский расстрел. Под ред. В.П. Наумова.* Москва: Наука.

Nieuwint, Joris, 2015: In 1943 a British pilot made an emergency landing on the Italian island of Lampedusa, only to have it surrender to him, in: *War history online*, <https://www.warhistoryonline.com/war-articles/british-pilot-emergency-landing-lampedusa-surrender.html>, December 7, 2020.

Novershtern, Avraham, 2003 נוברשטרן, אברהם: **קסם הדמדומים: אפוקליפסה ומשיחיות בספרות יידיש**. ירושלים : הוצאת ספרים על שם י״ל מאגנס.

Pechatnov, Vladimir, 1998: Печатнов, Владимир: Фултонская речь Черчилля. In: *Источник* 1, 88 – 99.

Polyan, Alexandra, 2021: Полян, Александра. Перец Маркиш о Холокосте в 1942 и 1947 годах In: *Тирош. Труды по иудаике, славистике, ориенталистике*: 148 – 170.

Redlich, Shimon, 2013: *War, Holocaust and Stalinism. A Documented Study of the Jewish Anti-Fascist Committee in the USSR*. London, New York, NY: Routledge.

Shneer, David, 2011a: *Through Soviet Jewish Eyes: Photography, War, and the Holocaust.* New Brunswick, NJ: Rutgers University Press.

Shneer, David, 2011b: Rivers of Blood: Peretz Markish, the Holocaust, and Jewish Vengeance. In: Joseph Sherman, Gennady Estraikh, Jordan Finkin, David Shneer, eds., *A Captive of the Dawn. The Life and Work of Peretz Markish (1895 – 1952)*. Oxford: Legenda, 139 – 156.

Stalin, Iosif, 1946: Интервью И. В. Сталина с корреспондентом Правды относительно речи Г. Черчилля. In: *Правда*, March 14, 1946, 1. Russian original: <https://history.wikireading.ru/253144>, May 27, 2021. English translation: <https://alphahistory.com/coldwar/stalin-responds-iron-curtain-speech-1946/>, May 27, 2021.

Veidlinger, Jeffrey, 2000: *The Moscow State Jewish Theater: Jewish Culture on the Soviet Stage*. Bloomington, Ind.: Indiana University Press.

Veidlinger, Jeffrey, 2011: The Pen and the Sword: The Wartime Plays of Peretz Markish. In: Joseph Sherman, Gennady Estraikh, Jordan Finkin, David Shneer, eds., *A Captive of the Dawn. The Life and Work of Peretz Markish (1895 – 1952)*. Oxford: MHRA, Legenda, 157 – 171.

Veligorsky, Georgy, 2022: Велигорский, Георгий: Разные лики Старика Хоттабыча: жанровые «приключения» сюжета («Медный кувшин» Ф. Энсти, «Старик Хоттабыч» Л. Лагина, «Медный кувшин Старика Хоттабыча» С. Кладо, к/ф «}{отт@бь)ч» П. Точилина). In: *Филологический вестник*, 1 (60): 252–264.
Zeltser, Arkady, 2014: How the Jewish Intelligentsia Created the Jewishness of the Jewish Hero: The Soviet Yiddish Press. In: Harriet Murav and Gennady Estraikh, eds., *Soviet Jews in World War II: Fighting, Witnessing, Remembering*. Boston, Mass.: Academic Studies Press, 104–128.

Agnieszka Żółkiewska

Of Broken Pasts, Presents, Futures

The Short Life of Yiddish Cultural (Re)Construction in Poland 1945–1950

"It is really unbelievable," wrote Yiddish philologist and חורבן [*khurbn*, destruction, Holocaust] historian Nakhmen Blumental (1902–1983) about the immediate postwar period.

> ס׳איז ממש נישט צו גלויבן מיט וואָס פֿאַר אַן אימפּעט די רעשטלעך פֿונעם פּוילישן ייִדנ־
> טום האָבן זיך גענומען צו רעסטאַווררירן זייער נאַציאָנאַל לעבן, ס׳האָט זיך ווי אויסגעוויזן,
> אַז דאָ קומט צום אויסדרוק דער אינסטינקטיווער כּוח פֿון פֿאָלק, ממשיך צו זײַן די גאָלדענע
> קייט, וואָס דער שׂונא האָט געוואָלט מיט אַן אומגלויבלעכער אַכזריותדיקייט איבערהאַקן;
> און דאָס קליינע הײַפֿל לעבנגעבליבענע האָט זיך באַמיט מיט אַלע כּוחות אויפֿשטעלן צוריק
> דאָס, וואָס דער שׂונא האָט באַוויזן צו פֿאַרניכטן, און דאָס מיט מער פּראַכט ווי אַמאָל.[1]
>
> It is really unbelievable with what energy the remnants of Polish Jewry started to rebuild their national life, it seemed that the instinctive strength of the nation was expressed here, the continuation of the golden chain, which the enemy wanted to break with incredible cruelty – this small handful of survivors tried with all their might to restore what the enemy decided to destroy, and with more flair than before.

Through archival data, press materials, and memories, this chapter reconstructs how Yiddish culture came into shape during the first five postwar years in the newly formed Polish People's Republic. It was a turbulent period for Jews living in Poland, for so many burdensome political, cultural, and socio-demographic changes happened in such a short time.

The pillars of postwar Yiddish culture were three organizations, reactivated shortly after the end of the Second World War by the צענטראַלער קאָמיטעט פֿון די ייִדן אין פּוילן [*Tsentraler komitet fun di yidn in Poyln*; Centralny Komitet

The basis for this chapter are the findings from the source monograph, compiled and published by myself in Polish, see: Żółkiewska 2017.

1 Blumental 1952, 594. I use YIVO's Modern Standard Yiddish for reproducing Yiddish sources throughout this chapter. For transliteration, I follow YIVO's rules as well.

Żydów w Polsce; Central Committee of the Jews in Poland, CKŻP], the פֿאַראיין פֿון ייִדישע ליטעראַטן און זשורנאַליסטן אין פּוילן [*Fareyn fun yidishe literatn un zhurnalistn in Poyln*, Jewish Writers and Journalists Union in Poland],[2] the פֿאַראיין פֿון ייִדישע קינסטלער [*Fareyn fun yidishe kinstler*, Jewish Artists' Union], and the געזעלשאַפֿט צו פֿאַרשפּרייטן ייִדישע קונסט [*Gezelshaft tsu farshpreytn yidishe kunst*, Jewish Society of Fine Arts Promotion].[3]

The war changed and complicated these organizations' internal structures. They still consisted mainly of Yiddish-speaking cultural activists: writers, journalists, actors, and fine artists. Most of them survived the *khurbn* in the Soviet Union; others in ghettos and camps in German-occupied Poland; some in hiding.[4] However, a substantial number of Polish-speaking cultural activists, of which some were very involved in Polish culture as well, started to enter the organizations.[5] Together, they formed a broken substitute for the former multilingual Jewish intelligentsia, horribly devastated and decimated by the war.

All these artists were united by the awareness of their common fate and the need to rebuild the devastated cultural infrastructure. Thanks to the equal rights granted to Jews, some of them believed, at least initially, that in liberated postwar Poland they would be able to start a new life, and that the new system of the so-called people's democracy would be the best guarantee of this. They believed that the re-emergent antisemitism, which had the Kielce pogrom in 1946 as its tragic climax, was the product of forces opposing this

2 On the postwar Association of Jewish Writers and Journalists, see: Cohen 2004, 15–36; Cohen 2008, 231–146; Grabski and Rusiniak 2008, 51–64; Grabski 2004; Nalewajko-Kulikov 2009; Ruta 2008, 247–276; Żółkiewska 2017, 62–87.

3 On the postwar Jewish Society of Fine Arts Promotion, see Sandel 1947, 14; Sandel 1950, 19f; Podhoritszr-Zaykin 1947, 9; Podhorizer-Sandel 1973, 111–119; Podhorizer-Sandel 1974, 37–50; Podhorizer-Sandel and Mórawski 1980, 61–75; Piątkowska 2008, 67–99; Piątkowska 2004, 197–204; Piątkowska 2010, 339–358; Żółkiewska 2017, 95–107.

4 Yiddish cultural activists who survived in Poland under German occupation include: Rokhl Oyerbakh (in the Warsaw ghetto and on the non-Jewish side in Warsaw), Yehuda Elberg (in the ghetto and on the non-Jewish side in Warsaw), Ruven Feldshuh (in the Warsaw ghetto and on the non-Jewish side in Radzymin), Grisha vel Grzegorz Jaszunski (in the Vilna ghetto, later partisan), Yehoshua Shlayen (in the Lviv ghetto and the Janów camp, on the non-Jewish side of Lviv), Shaye [Yeshayahu] Shpigl (in the Łódź ghetto, Auschwitz, and other camps in Germany), Leyb Rokhman (in the Warsaw ghetto, on the non-Jewish side in Kałuszyn), Dovid Hofnung (in the ghetto and on the non-Jewish side in Katowice), Yonas Turkov, and Diana Blumenfeld (the Warsaw ghetto and the non-Jewish side in Warsaw).

5 The members of the Association of Jewish Writers and Journalists became writers and journalists, who in the prewar period had published mostly in Polish-Jewish press (namely Horacy Safrin, Maksymilian Taukhner, Noe Grüss, Adolf Berman, Michał Hofman, Stefan Gelbart) as well as writers with strong ties to the Polish literary milieu (Izabela Czajka-Stachowicz, Michał Maksymilian Borwicz).

system, soldiers of the Armia Krajowa [Home Army] and the Narodowe Siły Zbrojne [National Armed Forces], who supported the Polish government in exile. As a rule, Yiddish cultural activists assumed that a systemic change was for the better, towards stability and security.[6]

Those great hopes and expectations of rebuilding Jewish life after the war vanished very quickly. In the course of five years, the postwar Polish Yiddish intelligentsia grew disillusioned: along with the simmering antisemitism came the realities of a Stalinized version of socialism. Before the 'great disillusionment,' however, efforts were made to revive Yiddish culture, literature, and art in the form reminiscent of the prewar years.

New life

The postwar revival of Yiddish culture occurred under extremely difficult conditions. All organizations and institutions were created from scratch, without any surviving administrative and institutional infrastructure: without buildings, financial resources, and people.[7] The war had completely changed Jewish cultural life, not only in terms of infrastructural destruction but also through geopolitical changes. Until 1939, Jewish cultural life was concentrated in a few of the largest Jewish communities, located mainly in central and eastern Poland. As a result of shifting borders, two important cultural centers – Vilna and Lviv – changed hands from Poland to Soviet Lithuania and Ukraine respectively as did numerous smaller centers in the Eastern borderlands. Thus, the prewar culture of 'small homelands' created by local Jewish communities disappeared from the map of Jewish Poland.

Likewise, within the territory of postwar Poland, there were significant changes and movements. Ruined Warsaw, where the most important Jewish institutions, organizations, and publishing houses had been located before the war, had ceased to function as a center until the end of the 1940s, when it again became a Jewish social and cultural center. In the intervening years, it was replaced first by Lublin, the first unofficial capital of liberated Poland, and then Łódź.[8]

6 Polish Committee of National Liberation 1944; Zomershteyn 1945 1, 2; Mirski 1945 1, 3; Mirski 1945, 17, 4; Tauchner 1946, 8, 1; Zak 1947, 92 and 14; Zak 1968, 105f; Olejnik 2003.

7 On the losses of the Jewish cultural heritage in Poland, see Ayzenbakh 1946, 42, 3; Szner 1947, 3, 4; Podhorizer-Sandel 1973, 2f; 232–237; Sandel 1953, 2, 93.

8 Olejnik 2006.

Another change resulting from the new geopolitical situation was the concentration and flourishing of Jewish cultural life in Lower Silesia, former German territory.[9] In this region upon liberation and forced migration of the German population, thousands of Jewish repatriates, displaced persons, and voluntary settlers, including former prisoners of concentration camps, began to form the largest Jewish population in Poland.[10] By the end of 1946, there were six larger and twenty-five smaller community centers with reading spaces, eight libraries, ten drama clubs, four choirs, and five orchestras. For a short period of time, the Lower Silesian town Rychbach, today's Dzierżoniów, became the largest Jewish settlement in that area, counting 12,000 inhabitants,[11] and was soon called "Polish Jerusalem."[12]

Patronage over Yiddish culture had also changed. Before the war, it was deprived of the effective support from state and regional governments. Institutions had to rely on their own resources and support from private patrons and donors. After the war, patronage of Jewish culture was assumed by the צענטראַלער קאָמיטעט פֿון פּוילישע ייִדן [*Tsentraler komitet fun poylishe yidn*, Central Committee of Polish Jews], later renamed the CKŻP – a body established in Lublin on 29 November 1944 tasked to officially represent Jews within the country and abroad.[13]

In fact, the CKŻP initially played a less prominent role than it had set out to do. It was a distributor of aid arriving from foreign Jewish organizations, among which the largest donor was the American Jewish Joint Distribution Committee.[14] Out of the monthly allocated 109 million Polish złoty, 80 million was allocated by the CKŻP to the needs of various Jewish institutions and centers in Poland. The unit of the Committee that dealt directly with matters of the creative intelligentsia was the Department of Culture and Propaganda. It supported poets, writers, artists, and painters in order to make "ułatwiając im otrzymanie odpowiedniej pracy oraz udzielając pomocy finansowej przy urządzaniu się po powrocie do Polski" [it easier for them to obtain a suitable job and financial assistance in settling after returning to Poland].[15]

9 See Kamil Kijek's chapter in the present volume.

10 Lisek 2008, 12.

11 Szaynok 2007, 27.

12 Ibid., 26.

13 Central Committee of Jews in Poland 1946a, 2.

14 Beyn 1947, 13.

15 Central Committee of Polish Jews 1947, 11.

Many of the surviving artists found employment in the extensive structures of the aforementioned department. The CKŻP was also in charge of publishing houses (Publishing Office) and the press bodies of the committee (Press Office).[16] Some of the Yiddish cultural activists found employment with the Central Jewish Historical Commission established in 1944.

The reconstruction of Jewish cultural life would not have been possible had it not been for the favorable attitude of the new Polish authorities, which granted Jews, then the only officially recognized national minority in Poland, the right to pursue a free cultural policy within their own cultural institutions. Yiddish cultural producers, marginalized before the war, obtained the same rights as Polish cultural producers. Equality and the financial support of the Polish state allowed for developmental opportunities that Yiddish had never had before. Since the whole country was in the process of reconstruction, subsidies from the Polish government were small in the first years after the war. This changed in the early 1950s, when the state took over almost all costs related to cultural activities of Jews in Poland, alongside the nationalization of some Jewish institutions and closing of others.

The postwar promotion of Yiddish culture was instrumental in its relatively quick revival, despite the enormous losses in people and institutions during the war. Already in 1944, the Association of Jewish Writers and Journalists was reestablished at the CKŻP in liberated Lublin.[17] In July 1946, the Jewish Artists' Union resumed its activities, bringing together theater actors, and in October, the Jewish Society of Fine Arts Promotion, where painters and sculptors congregated. Initially, these institutions were de facto self-help organizations. Their activities geared towards supporting the surviving Yiddish cultural producers, many of whom were destitute.

Pre-Stalinization

All Yiddish cultural organizations in Poland, reactivated immediately after the war, resumed the traditions and ideological agendas of their prewar equivalents.[18] Pluralism was a special feature of the first two years after liber-

16 Central Committee of Polish Jews 1946b, 1.

17 Cohen 2004, 16.

18 Ibid., 20.

ation.[19] A "collective Pesach seder"[20] for instance, held at the Jewish Writers and Journalists' Union in Łódź, encapsulated the plurality of the Jewish artistic and literary world at the time. During these celebrations, which followed a strictly religious rite, people of different political views – both from the left and the right, namely Zionists, Bundists, and communists – celebrated at the same table.

It was clearly a transitional period in which all efforts on the Jewish and Polish side were focused on rebuilding life, broadly understood. At that time, as Maria Hirszowicz notes, the introduction of Stalinism in its Polish variant was "still distant, yet not ubiquitous, still limited, yet not omnipotent, still delegating, yet not disrupting grassroots initiatives."[21] The situation changed dramatically in 1947, when the entire country began to be structurally Stalinized. And a small group of Yiddish culture activists, who identified as communists, actively participated in it.

In Yiddish, ideological opponents referred to Jewish communists of the old days as *frume komunistn* [pious communists] or *koshere komunistn* [kosher communists] probably to emphasize their alleged ardent, quasi-religious party commitment.[22] Before the war, they were persecuted for illegal political activities: they were in hiding or imprisoned. During the war, however, most of these party veterans survived in the Soviet Union. Among them were teachers, social and cultural activists, journalists, and writers, including Binem Heller (1908–1998), Bernard (Ber) Mark (1908–1966), Michał Mirski (born Moyshe Hersh Tabatshnik, 1902–1994), Hadasa Rubin (1912–2003), Dovid Sfard (1905–1981), Hersh Smolyar (1905–1993), and Szymon Zachariasz (1900–1970).[23] Their faith in communism was fueled by the dream of a new, just world that would guarantee Jews a better life and the right to

19 It is hard to determine whether it indeed was a period of relative pluralism or rather an illusory, Moscow-controlled liberalization of the socio-cultural life in Poland from the very start. Key members of the Centralny Komitet Polskiej Zjednoczonej Partii Robotniczej [Central Committee of the Polish United Workers' Party], such as Edward Ochab, were of the opinion that Stalinist control was significant from the very start, and that it is illogical to divide the postwar period into phases (see Torańska Teresa 2004, 55). Most scholars do think, however, that Stalinization didn't come to pass immediately and the turning point marking its beginning was the period between the years 1947–1948, see e.g. Hirszowicz 2001, 84.

20 Zak 1968, 207.

21 Ibid., 87.

22 Schatz 1991; Schatz 2007, 27–49.

23 Zachariasz 1950.

develop their own secular culture in Yiddish. Within this group, especially among less dogmatic activists, there had always been a tension between internationalism and Jewish nationalism.[24] They never questioned their origin, and never assimilated fully to Polish-ness. Throughout their lives they felt as "Yiddish citizens,"[25] emotionally attached to the Yiddish language and culture which they were born into and grew up in.

In the first years after the war, Jewish Communists were a minority in Jewish politics. They remained in the shadows of other parties, the strongest of which were Zionist. Various factors may have contributed to the initial weakness of this grouping: August Grabski, for one, points to a small membership base, lack of leaders enjoying the trust of the party and the Jewish community, antisemitism, and the unstable position of the Communist Party itself in Poland right after the war.[26]

The weak political position of these Jewish Communists must have had an impact on the, initially rather moderate, course of their policies.[27] They were also possibly simply realistic and pragmatic about what was most important in this first period. They worked towards compromises and cooperation with other political groups in the implementation of general, immediate goals, such as providing medical care, financial assistance, and physical safety to Jews in Poland.[28]

Jewish Communists, in this initial period, approached the issue of Jewish culture in an equally liberal way. They had not yet attempted to influence the general direction of its development. Indeed, the first, quite general, demands for change appeared in the press, but they were announced without a sense of pressure, with full respect for the entire cultural heritage of Polish Jews.

24 Sfard 1984, 175.

25 Coined by Joanna Nalewajko-Kulikov, see Nalewajko-Kulikov 2009, 8.

26 Grabski 2004, 193f.

27 To prevent staff shortages in the Jewish Faction of the Polish Workers' Party, Soviet authorities brought in special reinforcements from Moscow. Yonas Turkov mentions that from the list of writers, artists, and journalists, which the CKŻP had submitted to the Polish authorities, asking for help in accelerating their arrival from the Soviet Union, the names Broderson, Finkelshteyn, and Grosman were deleted and replaced by names of party members with little involvement in cultural work – among them Khaskiel Kameraz, for instance, an old Bolshevik from Vilna, long-time university lecturer, and famously sentenced to seven years in prison in a 1937 Moscow trial. He was sent from Moscow directly to Poland to organize the party in 1945. He later claimed the task was assigned to him against his will, having little to no connections to Poland or Polish language skills. He was sent to the CKŻP, where he took charge of the Productization Division. See Turkov 1959, 90f and 198f.

28 Ibid., 194.

Moreover, they recognized this heritage, at least initially, as the foundation of the new, postwar Jewish culture in Poland.[29] They recognized Yiddish as the fundamental cultural influence.[30] Because of this, they called for educating Jewish children in this language and opposed assimilation.[31] Their goal was to develop a Jewish national culture – a Polish *Yiddishland* – based on cultural particularity of the Jewish population and socialist principles.[32] Many of them initially believed that the cultural and national autonomy granted to Jews could be maintained within the new political realities.[33]

Incubation Phase of Stalinization

The Polish Workers' Party took charge of Yiddish culture, and in turn of socio-political life of Polish Jews, with the formation of the צענטראַלע ייִדישע קולטור־געזעלשאַפֿט [*Tsentrale yidishe kultur-gezelshaft*, Central Jewish Cultural Society; CJCS] at the beginning of November 1947, originally named צענטראַלע ייִדישע געזעלשאַפֿט פֿאַר קולטור און קונסט [*Tsentrale yidishe gezelshaft far kultur un kunst,* Central Jewish Society for Culture and Art].[34] It was not created entirely from scratch. Its origin was the Jewish Society of Culture and Art in Lower Silesia, operating from the end of 1946.[35] The CJCS aimed to build a new, much more politicized cultural landscape for Jewish society in Poland, based on the implementation of party ideology through literature, art, and culture.

The new organization was characterized by a complex, multi-leveled organizational structure, mimicking the general administrative structure of the CKŻP. The headquarters of the Main Board was located in Łódź and the forty-nine branches were located mostly in cities of Upper and Lower Silesia.[36] CJCS branches were the equivalent of a dense network of Polish cultural and

29 Mirski 1946, 7.

30 Sfard 1946, 5.

31 Grabski, Rusiniak 2008, 51–64.

32 Mark 1947, 4.

33 Mark 1946, 3; this was an attempt to resume the cultural project of Yiddishland that had been developed in Warsaw in 1926, cf. Gal-Ed 2021.

34 Both names of this organization, that is the Central Jewish Cultural Society and the Central Jewish Society of Culture and Art, were used interchangeably.

35 Anonymous 1947a, 10; Jewish Press Agency, 1947c, 1f.

36 Zachariasz 1948a, 100; Central Jewish Cultural Society 1949c, 6; Central Jewish Cultural Society 1949d.

educational institutions established throughout the country. By 1950, nearly 20,000 of them had been built.[37] The latter, as noted by Wita Szulc, were seemingly self-governing cultural organizations, but in fact were tasked to "transmit" the party's policy into the whole of society.[38] The CJCS played a similar role. It was an organization headed by self-identified Jewish Communists, subordinated to Poland's ruling party and its doctrine operating "on the basis of a Marxist-Leninist worldview."[39] Its politicization was reflected in the composition of its central and local leadership, in which the key positions of chairman and secretary were filled mainly by members of the Polish Workers' Party.

The CJCS budget amounted to 40 million złoty per year and was financed mainly through funds of foreign organizations, primarily the American Jewish Joint Distribution Committee, but also from contributions paid by members and occasionally events were organized with the financial support of local city boards.[40]

As for members, there were no admission criteria. According to the statute, any Polish citizen could be a member.[41] Recruitment was conducted mainly in workers' and craftsmen's cooperatives as well as in vocational schools operated by provincial committees of the CKŻP. Attempts were made to attract independent professionals, members of the religious congregation, and various Jewish institutions and associations. Recruitment reached record highs in 1948 (10,500 new members) and again in 1949 (12,000 new members). Yet not everyone joined voluntarily. In fact, the preserved documentation suggests that the recruitment process also involved administrative coercion as well as intrusive agitation and propaganda.[42]

The mass recruitment policy was primarily aimed at organizational and political uniformity of the entire Jewish community. The most important element was political education akin to what had happened in the Soviet Yiddish sphere in the 1920s and 1930s. Jewish Communists joined under the influence of the resolutions of the April plenum of the Central Committee of

37 Szulc 2009, 13.

38 Ibid., 16.

39 Central Jewish Cultural Society 1949a.

40 Ibid., 2.

41 Central Jewish Cultural Society 1948b.

42 Central Jewish Cultural Society 1949d.

the Polish United Workers' Party in 1947, which ordered the education of the entire nation in the spirit of the party's ideology. To achieve this goal, in Jewish cooperatives, local CJCS authorities selected commissions and appointed full-time activist-educators, responsible for all cultural and educational work.

Political education was carried out mainly by methods tested in the Soviet Union, organizing large mass events in a properly selected socialist realist aesthetic. The program of these events included a repertoire in accordance with the line of the Communist Party and did not differ significantly from that of analogous Polish institutions. Each year, anniversaries of the October Revolution, the creation of the Soviet Army, the death of Vladimir Lenin, and Polish-Soviet friendship were commemorated, and from 1948 the anniversary of the unification of Polish Workers' parties, as well as Labor Day and Women's Day.[43]

It was symptomatic that strictly Jewish celebrations, like the official ceremonies in honor of the classics of Yiddish literature,[44] occupied a modest or even marginal place in this Party repertoire. The only exception were the celebrations of subsequent anniversaries of the Warsaw Ghetto Uprising, as in the new state of Israel, albeit in a different political register.[45]

Likewise, the subject of the lectures organized in the society's branches did not differ significantly from the party canon. Following the methods used in the Soviet Union, CJCS departments conducted, among others, 'press readings' and 'film collectors,' talks on political topics illustrated with examples from newspapers or film.[46]

Courses conducted by the CJCS in Jewish cooperatives, boarding houses, and social organizations played an important role in spreading the content consistent with the party's guidelines. Educational programs included the study of Marxism and the history of the workers' movement in Poland, the purpose of which was to develop a new intelligentsia in an accelerated manner, a politically aware and dedicated party cadre.[47]

43 Jewish Press Agency 1945a, 4; Association of Jewish Writers and Journalists 1947c, 26.

44 Association of Jewish Writers and Journalists 1947d, 27; Ruta 2009, 26–29.

45 On this, see Kobylarz 2009; Leociak 2000, 29–49; Piątkowska 2004, 197–204. On the role of the Warsaw Ghetto Uprising in different, competing Jewish political movements and narratives, see Malena Chinski's chapter in the present volume.

46 Central Jewish Cultural Society 1949b.

47 Zachariasz 1948b.

All cultural and educational organizations and institutions were gathered, without exception, under the management of the CJCS. Centralization affected even such small and, as it might seem, insignificant institutions, such as choirs and orchestras. To draw as many members as possible into the orbit of the new organization, small choirs at cooperatives were liquidated, and their members were incorporated into the society's central choirs. All these activities resulted in the elimination from public life of independent educational and cultural organizations led by other parties, including the greatest political rival of Jewish communism: Zionism.

During the first year of its existence, the CJCS established a network of branches throughout Poland. In addition, an impressive forty-three community centers, nineteen Houses of Culture and people's clubs, thirty-eight libraries, seventeen drama clubs, six choirs, and six orchestras were established. There were folk universities and evening courses in Polish language and literature.[48] The latter were part of the nationwide action to combat illiteracy, as well as the national policy of the Polish authorities, which aimed at creating an ethnically homogeneous state. In the Jewish context, attempts were made to achieve this goal not only by the universal teaching of the Polish language and Polish literature, but also of Jewish history in Poland. Articles published in the Yiddish press referred to figures, at times semi-legendary, such as Abraham Prochownik and Berek Joselewicz, emphasizing their importance for common Polish-Jewish history.[49] Much space was devoted to the classics of Polish literature, especially Polish national poets Adam Mickiewicz and Juliusz Słowacki[50] with an emphasis on the former's friendship and defense of oppressed and persecuted nations, especially of Jews. The CJCS also organized Yiddish language courses, but without meeting broad interest. "Czyniliśmy wiele starań, aby prowadzić kurs języka żydowskiego, lecz w żaden sposób nam się nie udało" [We made a lot of efforts to conduct a Yiddish language course, but we did not succeed in any way], reported the branch management in Otwock, "chętnych znalazło się tylko 2 osoby" [there were only two people interested].[51]

The CJCS reached its peak in 1949 with a total of forty-nine branches, thirty community centers, twenty houses of culture, forty-seven libraries and artistic groups, and 16,000 registered members. These figures suggest that

48 Central Jewish Cultural Society 1947b.

49 Zonshayn 1947.

50 Mark 1949, Turkov 1949, Słowacki 1949, Lastik 1950.

51 Central Jewish Cultural Society 1949c.

the center was successful in implementing what was expected of it. It was only a partial success, however – organizationally, not socially. The preserved documentation points to resistance and lack of interest in the activities of the CJCS not only on the part of the Jewish population generally, but also by activists of this organization themselves – mostly people who had been coerced or accidentally incorporated into its structures. Contrary to expectations, the creation of new cadres went forth very slowly and with great hesitation. A younger generation showed little interest in the project. The older, prewar intelligentsia reacted in a similar way.[52] It should be noted that such hesitation was detectable across the spectrum of ordinary members and those who held managerial positions.[53]

Jewish artists were also under the ideological supervision of the Society in a separate division: the Artists' Section.[54] The section organized several collective exhibitions – the first of which took place as early as 11 April 1947 in the Gong Theater in Łódź followed by several others.[55] The works presented were considered proof that "plastycy zrozumieli zadania stojące przed nimi jako twórcami sztuki ludowej i dla ludu" [the artists understood the tasks facing them as creators of folk art for the people].[56]

For the sake of stimulating a local visual arts community, a decision was made in mid-June of 1948 to send two groups of representatives to Lower Silesia to give lectures and talks.[57] First works attempting to follow the new socialist realism began to appear. They dealt mainly with the subject of Jewish 'productization,' as exemplified by the paintings אַ ייִדישער פּויער פֿון נידערשלעזיע [*A yidisher poyer fun Nidershlezye*, A Jewish Peasant from Lower Silesia] by Henryk Hechtkopf, אין הוטע [*In hute*, In the Steelworks] by Shmuel Vaynshtok, and דער וועבער ישׂראל [*Der veber Yisroel*, The Weaver Yisroel] by Dorota Szenfeld. This corresponded to ideological expectations: the 'New Jew' was to overcome capitalist class structures and embrace the task of a full-fledged builder of socialism – "przodownika pracy z fabryki, kopalni, roli i spółdzielni [...] wypełniającego ponad 300% normy produkcyjnej" [a

52 Ibid.

53 Central Jewish Cultural Society 1947c.

54 Jewish Press Agency 1948, 1f.

55 Anonymous 1948b, 9.

56 Central Jewish Cultural Society 1947a.

57 Anonymous 1948d, 8; Hechtkopf 1948, 9.

labor leader from a factory, a mine, a farm, and a cooperative [...] fulfilling over 300% of the production norm].[58]

In addition to visual artists, the CJCS also took on the supervision of Jewish writers. They were tasked to form *literarishe brigades* [literary brigades] and, too, visited the Jewish communities in Lower and Upper Silesia.[59] Visits to schools, dormitories, workplaces, and cooperatives were a regular feature of this type of itinerary. In the years 1947 and 1948, in accordance with the guidelines of the Ministry of Culture and Art, "akcja terenowa" [area operations] or "akcją zaznajomienia literatów ze środowiskiem robotniczo-chłopskim" [operations acquainting writers with the working-peasant environment] applied to all artists in the country.[60] Yet, also in the literary milieu, pervasive control was hardly achieved. The impatience of the authorities resulted in increased disciplining of Yiddish writers. At a meeting of Jewish activists of the Polish Workers' Party, organized in August 1948, Szymon Zachariasz stated:

> Mnie się wydaje, że uporczywe trzymanie się przez naszych literatów tematki gettowej, okupacyjnej, zagłady, uporczywe pisanie tylko o tyma, co było w przeszłości – nie jest czynnikiem umacniania socjalizmu w środowisku żydowskim
>
> It seems to me that our writers' persistent adherence to the subject of the ghetto, occupation, extermination, and persistent writing only about what was in the past, is not a strengthening factor of socialism in the Jewish community.[61]

In addition, they were accused of "detaching from the masses" and a "pretty-bourgeois mentality."[62]

The Jewish establishment also took charge of organizing Jewish actors. During a conference on Yiddish theater in Poland on 14 February 1947 at the CKŻP,[63] the participants approved the creation of the Theater Council. The council was to represent the interests of Jewish actors in Poland externally,

58 Zachariasz 1948a.

59 Association of Jewish Writers and Journalists 1948e.

60 Ashendorf 1947, 4; Anonymous 1947e, 28; Anonymous 1948e, 10.

61 Zachariasz 1947, 45–46.

62 Ibid.

63 Jewish Press Agency 1947a, 1f; Association of Jewish Writers and Journalists 1947a, 15f.

but it was quickly transformed by the CJCS into an administrative body meant to micromanage Yiddish theaters. It operated in this form until its nationalization in 1950. As in other cultural spheres, the political pressure exerted on the actors did not immediately bring about the desired result. The repertoire from the prewar era continued to dominate.[64]

Things turned more dogmatic when, in August 1949, the Komisja Repertuarowa [Repertoire Committee] was established. It was composed of Yiddish actress Ida Kamińska (1899 – 1980), Yiddish writer Dovid Sfard, and Yiddish actor Yitskhok Turkov-Grudberg (1906 – 1970). The establishment of the committee was explained by the shortage of an appropriate repertoire on the Jewish scene; there was a shortage of new arts to meet the current political needs.[65] As in the case of Polish theater, the repertoire's shortcomings were supplemented with translations of Soviet plays from Russian, but even when selecting them, great caution was exercised. In dubious cases, Moscow was consulted directly.[66] Indeed, the repertoire problem could not be fully resolved, ending up with a mix of approved Russian and Polish language plays newly translated into Yiddish as well as classic Yiddish plays.

Tipping Point

A congress of the CJCS organized in October 1949 in Wrocław was a turning point in postwar Polish Jewish history. Carried out under the slogan: "Kultura żydowska w służbie ludu — w służbie socjalizmu!" [Jewish culture in the service of the people – in the service of socialism!],[67] Polish Jewish cultural life transitioned from the incubation phase of Stalinization into its Stalinist era.

Similar conventions took place simultaneously across Poland, organized in various artistic environments. Their goal was to publicly mark the adoption of the principles of socialist realism, which was tantamount to subordinating all artistic creativity to the needs of the party.

While earlier, communist activists embraced the motto of creating a culture that was "national in form and socialist in content," during the Wrocław convention, it was rendered a sign of dangerous political eclecticism. The

64 Ibid., 6.

65 Central Committee of Jews in Poland 1949a, 34.

66 Ibid., 32.

67 Central Jewish Cultural Society 1950b.

radical aim now was to free themselves from all Zionist and nationalist features spelling an end to the Polish Jewish cultural and political pluralism of the interwar period.

The effects of the Stalinization of Yiddish culture could not be fully felt until the end of the 1940s; it was in 1949 that the possibility of free writing and open exchange of ideas was over. Dogmatists appeared, vigilantly demanding 'socialist realist righteousness.' The Jewish press, reduced to just a few journals, became a propaganda instrument. In 1950, the journals דאָס נײַע לעבן [*Dos naye lebn*, The New Life], פֿאָלקס־שטימע [*Folks-shtime*, People's Voice], נידערשלעזיע [*Nidershlezye*, Lower Silesia] merged into: פֿאָלקס־שטימע [*Folks-shtime*].[68] A similar merger was carried out in the Polish-language press. In 1950, *Nowa Kultura* [New Culture] was created by merging *Odrodzenie* [Rebirth] and *Kuźnica* [Hammer Mill];[69] it was supposed to popularize the party line.

Political control over the commemoration of *khurbn*-victims was also increasingly exercised, limiting it to the celebration of the Warsaw Ghetto Uprising. All historians, without exception, were under pressure to apply Marxist methodology.[70] More and more frequently, facts related to the catastrophic past were either concealed or distorted.[71]

Stalinization meant rapid changes and Jewish and non-Jewish organizations in Poland were affected. Like ethnically Polish organizations, Polish Jewish ones lost their trade union character. "Jewish writers," Avraham Zak recalls, יִדישע שרײַבער זײַנען געוואָרן האָזן און אין שרײַבער־פֿאַראיין איז געוואָרן שיטערער [became [hunted] rabbits and the ranks in the (Jewish) Writers' Union thinned out].[72]

In the spring of 1949, coinciding with the Soviet anti-Jewish purges of late Stalinism that were underway to virtually destroy institutional Soviet Yiddish culture, the CKŻP, now under control of the Jewish section of the Polish Workers' Party, proceeded to dissolve organizations that had been re-established after the war, focusing specifically on Yiddish culture. In agreement with the Jewish Artists' Union, for instance, it was decided that the organi-

68 Zachariasz 1950.

69 Słomkowska 1979, 273.

70 Eisenbach 1950, 6.

71 For examples, see Tauchner 1948, 4; Person and Żółkiewska 2022, 21–37.

72 Zak 1968, 45.

zation would be disbanded, and its members – actors, musicians, designers, and technicians – would join the new, nationwide Union of Culture and Art Workers.[73] It was also decided that both the Wrocław and Łódź theater groups would be merged and transformed into one nationalized institution, implemented a year later.[74] The Jewish Society of Fine Arts Promotion was disbanded in December 1949;[75] its collections moved to the Jewish Historical Institute in Warsaw, which had replaced the Central Jewish Historical Commission.[76]

In 1949, the closing down of the Jewish Writers and Journalists Union in Poland began.[77] Its members were to join the Związek Literatów Polskich [Polish Writers' Union].[78] Rather than understanding the eradication of this organization as an attack on the plurality and autonomy of the Jewish intelligentsia, the establishment presented it as the long-awaited act of cultural symbiosis of Poles and Jews.[79]

Cold War Chasms: A New Diaspora – New Transnationalism

Between 1949 and 1951, due to the rapidly deteriorating political atmosphere at the time, 30,000 people left Poland.[80] The top-down attempt to transform the prewar creators of Yiddish culture into functionaries of the new regime seemingly ended in failure. Reasons for leaving Poland varied; first among them among Jews was certainly the reinvigorated antisemitism that found its most extreme expression in pogroms in Kielce and Kraków.[81] To a greater or lesser degree, though, people left out of disillusionment or rejection with postwar Poland's political trajectory. And this was not limited to Jews alone. A host of representatives of the non-Jewish Polish intellectual elite left Poland at that time for the same reasons. Yet the Jewish establish-

73 Central Committee of Jews in Poland 1949b and 1949c.

74 Ibid.

75 Ibid.

76 On the Central Jewish Historical Commission and the early years of the Jewish Historical Institute, see Aleksiun 2007, 74–97; Jokusch 2007, 441–473; Stach 2008, 401–431. On the situation under Stalinism, see Stach 2010, 273–287; Szurek 2003, 51–82.

77 Jewish Press Agency 1949a, 1f.

78 Polish Writers' Union 1949, 1f; Association of Jewish Writers and Journalists 1949, 10.

79 Association of Jewish Writers and Journalists 1950, 8.

80 On emigration, see Pisarski 1997, 71–73.

81 On this nexus, see Kamil Kijek's chapter in this volume.

ment did everything in their power to prevent Yiddish cultural activists from emigrating, especially those deemed "valuable."[82]

The incipient Cold War weakened the once deep ties in literary Yiddishland, creating a new map of more separate Yiddishlands. The changes occurring both in Poland and in the entire socialist bloc had a stifling effect on contacts with the transnational diaspora. Contacts with colleagues across the Iron Curtain, if not entirely severed, went dormant for many years.

The exodus at the end of the 1940s led to the final disintegration and dispersal of the Polish Yiddish-speaking intelligentsia who had survived the war. For many people, hopes for a revival of the largest and most dynamic Jewish community in the prewar world were buried.

The establishment of the state of Israel in 1948 undoubtedly facilitated the exodus from Poland but did not determine its direction. Emigrating Yiddish-speakers from Poland settled in centers of vibrant Jewish / Yiddish life such as France, Argentina, the United States, Canada, South Africa, and Australia. Israel mainly attracted writers and artists with Zionist views or sympathies, and while they were probably the majority, not all chose this destination. One reason was undoubtedly the country's very own repressive policy towards the Yiddish language.[83] With these new migration movements, the Jewish diaspora reconfigured itself and with it new transnational Yiddish cultures emerged.[84] The latter quickly evolved from a living culture into a culture of memory, specifically *khurbn*-memory.[85] Indeed, for all the quarrels and ideological differences as well as the aspired ideological rigidity, the Jewish intelligentsia that remained in Poland differed little from that of the Polish Jewish intellectual émigré circles. In fact, they overlapped in many ways, most importantly regarding the commemoration and study of the *khurbn*.[86]

Remnants in the Polish People's Republic – Conclusion

Only a small group of artists previously associated with Jewish artistic and cultural organizations at the CKŻP decided to stay in Poland. Jewish artists, who joined the Polish Artists' Union after the war, quickly merged into

82 Central Committee of Jews in Poland 1949, 24.

83 Ofner 1947, 11; Jewish Press Agency 1949c; Jewish Press Agency 1949d.

84 Schwarz 2015, 118–121.

85 Ibid.

86 Ruta 2012, 409f.

the Polish artistic community. For those who wrote in Yiddish, the situation became much more precarious. After the dissolution of the Jewish Writers and Journalists Union in 1949, they came under the umbrella of the Związek Literatów Polskich.[87] As part of this organization, they created a club of a dozen or so people, named the Klub Pisarzy Żydowskich [Jewish Writers' Club], probably to emphasize their cultural distinctiveness.[88] But from the very beginning, just like in other parts of the world, the main problem of the small Polish Yiddish sphere was the inability to foster a new generation. Gradually, but inevitably, it began to dissolve – additionally weakened by successive waves of emigration.[89] For some, hopes for a communist utopia in Poland that would honor Polish Jewish culture ended in 1956, when Khrushchev's secret speech and news coverage in *Folks-shtime* and the פֿאָרווערטס [*Forverts*, Jewish Daily Forward] revealed the attempted destruction of Yiddish culture in the USSR; for others, disillusionment set in with the Polish antisemitic campaigns starting in March 1968.[90]

After a relatively short period of growth during the years 1944–1950, postwar Yiddish culture never regained its former vitality. A few more Yiddish journals were published, ייִדיש־בוך [*Yidish-bukh*, Yiddish Book] publishing house printed books in Yiddish, and theater plays in Yiddish were staged. But Jewish institutions operated under the constant threat of being accused of 'national deviation.' Also, as could be witnessed in other national contexts, such as the United States, accelerated linguistic[91] and cultural[92] assimilation into Polish majority culture limited the evolution of postwar Polish Yiddish culture to such an extent that it has also been compared, in retrospect, to the equally curious situation in the Jewish autonomous region in the Soviet Union – Birobidzhan: "życie dość suchotnicze, bez ekspresji, bez wchłaniania nowych elementów" [life quite consumptive, without expression, without absorbing new elements].[93]

87 Polish Writers' Union 1949, 6.

88 Berendt 2006, 31–238; Jewish Historical Institute 1954; Jewish Historical Institute 1956, 6.

89 On emigration, see Ruta 2012, 408; Cohen 2008, 231–146.

90 Ibid.

91 At the turn of 1954 and 1955, Yiddish ceased to be the language of instruction in Jewish schools, and after their closure in 1968, it almost completely disappeared from Jewish life, see further Mieczkowski 1998, 36; Pęziński 2014, 195–222.

92 Schatz 2007, 45f.

93 For Jakub Berman's quote, see Torańska 2004, 240.

For those who left, the 'golden chain' of Yiddish culture mythically invoked to signify the continuity between the past, present, and future of generations of Polish Jews that the Nazi genocide had brutally broken now seemed irreparable. Nakhmen Blumental, only a few years after the enthusiasm and hope he expressed about the rebuilding of Polish Yiddish life cited at the beginning of this chapter, concluded upon his departure from Poland, און עס טוט וויי – פֿאַרלוירענע פֿאַרגאַנגענהייט, וואָס איז איבערגעהאַקט געוואָרן אָן איבערצולאָזן נאָך זיך נאָכוווּקס, די צוקונפֿט, ווײַל וואָס וואָס, די פֿאַרגאַנגענהייט וועט זיך שוין נישט אומקערן... [and still, it hurts – the lost past, which was forsaken without leaving a future behind, because what has passed will never return…]. [94]

Bibliography

Anonymus, 1947: Z działalności Żyd[owskiego] Tow[arzystwa] Krzewienia Sztuk Pięknych. In: *Opinia* (Łódź) 26, 22 October: 13.

Anonymous, 1947a: Konferencja działaczy kultury żyd[owskiej] na D[olnym] Śląsku. In: *Nowe Życie* (Wrocław) 10, 1 January: 2 and 5.

Anonymous, 1948b: Otwarcie I-szej Wystawy żydowskich artystów plastyków w Łodzi. In: *Opinia* (Łódź) 28, 25 January: 9.

Aleksiun, Natalia, 2007: The Central Jewish Historical Commission in Poland, 1944–1947. In: *Polin* 20: 74–97.

Ashendorf, Yisroel, 1947 אַשענדאָרף, ישׂראל: אונדזער ליטעראַרישער טורנײ איבער נידער־שלעזיע. אין: **דאָס נײַע לעבן** (לאָדזש) 53, דעם 21סטן יולי: 4.

Association of Jewish Writers and Journalists, 1947a ייִדישע ליטעראַטן און זשורנאַליסטן אין פּוילן: קאָנפֿערענץ וועגן ייִדישן טעאַטער. אין: **ייִדישע שריפֿטן** (לאָדזש) 4, מאַרץ: 15–16.

Association of Jewish Writers and Journalists, 1947b ייִדישע ליטעראַטן און זשורנאַליסטן אין פּוילן: בריגאַדע פֿון ייִדישע שרײַבער אין נידער־שלעזיע. אין: **ייִדישע שריפֿטן** (לאָדזש) 28, יוני־יולי: 7–8.

Association of Jewish Writers and Journalists, 1947c ייִדישע ליטעראַטן און זשורנאַליסטן אין פּוילן: אַקאַדעמיע געווידמעט דער סאָוועטישער ליטעראַטור. אין: **ייִדישע שריפֿטן** (לאָדזש) 10, דעצעמבער: 26.

Association of Jewish Writers and Journalists, 1947d ייִדישע ליטעראַטן און זשורנאַליסטן אין פּוילן: מענדעלע־פֿײַערונגען אײַנגעאָרדנט דורך דער צענטראַלער קולטור און קונסט־געזעלשאַפֿט. אין: **ייִדישע שריפֿטן** (לאָדזש) 10, דעצעמבער: 27.

Association of Jewish Writers and Journalists, 1948d ייִדישע ליטעראַטן און זשורנאַליסטן אין פּוילן: פֿון ייִדישן פּלאַסטיקער־פֿאַריין. אין: **ייִדישע שריפֿטן** (לאָדזש) 6, יוני: 8.

94 Blumental 1952, 598.

Association of Jewish Writers and Journalists, 1948e ייִדישע ליטעראַטן און זשור־נאַליסטן אין פּוילן: טורנײ פֿון ייִדישע שרײַבער. אין: **ייִדישע שריפֿטן** (לאָדזש) 5, מײַ: 10

Association of Jewish Writers and Journalists, 1949 ייִדישע ליטעראַטן און זשורנאַליסטן אין פּוילן: פֿערטע אַלגעמיינע פֿאַרזאַמלונג פֿון ייִדישן ליטעראַטן־פֿאַריין אין פּוילן. אין: **ייִדישע שריפֿטן** (וואַרשע) 6, יוני: 10

Association of Jewish Writers and Journalists, 1950 ייִדישע ליטעראַטן און זשורנאַליסטן אין פּוילן: אַלגעמיינע פֿאַרזאַמלונג פֿון ייִדישע שרײַבער. אין: **ייִדישע שריפֿטן** (וואַרשע) 6, יוני: 8.

Ayzenbakh, Arn, 1946 אײַזענבאַך, אהרן: וועגן דער רעווינדיקאַציע פֿון אונדזערע קולטור־אוצרות. אין: **דאָס נײַע לעבן** (לאָדזש) 42, דעם 18טן נאָוועמבער: 3

Berendt, Grzegorz, 2004: Michała Mirskiego rozrachunek z Polską Ludową. In: Niepodległość. Warsaw: 284–314.

Berendt, Grzegorz, 2006: Życie żydowskie w Polsce w latach 1950–1956: z dziejów Towarzystwa Społeczno-Kulturalnego Żydów w Polsce. Gdańsk: Uniwersytet Gdański.

Beyn, Leyb, 1947 ביין, לייב: אַמעריקן דזשוינט דיסטריביושן קאָמיטי (״דזשוינט״). די גרעסטע ייִדישע הילפֿס־אָרגאַניזאַציע. אין: **דאָס נײַע לעבן** (לאָדזש) 92, יובילײ אויסגאַבע [אומדאַטירט]: 13.

Blumental, Nakhman, 1952 בלומענטאַל, נחמן: לובלין נאָך דער צווייטער וועלט־מלחמה. אין: **פֿאַריזער קאָמיטעט פֿאַר שאַפֿן אַ מאָנאָגראַפֿיע וועגן ייִדישן ישובֿ אין לובלין, דאָס בוך פֿון לובלין: זכרונות, גבֿית־עדות און מאַטעריאַלן איבערן לעבן, קאַמף און מאַרטירערטום פֿון לובלינער ייִדישן ישובֿ.** פּאַריז: 593–598

Boruchowicz, Maksymilian, 1946: Doniosłość powstania. In: *Zew Młodych* (Łódź) 3, April-May: 12.

Central Committee of Jews in Poland, 1946a צענטראַלער קאָמיטעט פֿון די ייִדן אין פּוילן: Statut Centralnego Komitetu Żydów w Polsce [Statute of the Central Committee of the Jews in Poland]. Archiwum Żydowskiego Instytutu Historycznego /303/I/1.

Central Committee of Jews in Poland, 1946b צענטראַלער קאָמיטעט פֿון די ייִדן אין פּוילן: Structure of the Department of Culture and Propaganda. Archiwum Żydowskiego Instytutu Historycznego/303/XIII/1.

Central Committee of Jews in Poland, 1947: Zarys działalności Centralnego Komitetu Żydów w Polsce. Za okres od 1 stycznia do 30 czerwca 1946. Warsaw.

Central Committee of Jews in Poland, 1949a צענטראַלער קאָמיטעט פֿון די ייִדן אין פּוילן: Protocol no. 21 by the Central Committee of Jews in Poland, 13 April. Archiwum Żydowskiego Instytutu Historycznego/303/I/32.

Central Committee of Jews in Poland, 1949b צענטראַלער קאָמיטעט פֿון די ייִדן אין פּוילן: Protocol no. 25 by the Central Committee of Jews in Poland, 16 May. Archiwum Żydowskiego Instytutu Historycznego/303/I/32.

Central Committee of Jews in Poland, 1949c: Protocol no. 42, 25 August: 34. Archiwum Żydowskiego Instytutu Historycznego/303/I/33.

Central Jewish Cultural Society, 1947a צענטראַלע ייִדישע קולטור-געזעלשאַפֿט: Życie kulturalne w Polsce. Archiwum Żydowskiego Instytutu Historycznego/369/5.

Central Jewish Cultural Society, 1947b צענטראַלע ייִדישע קולטור-געזעלשאַפֿט: Annual report by the CJCS in Poland. Archiwum Żydowskiego Instytutu Historycznego/369/6.

Central Jewish Cultural Society, 1947c צענטראַלע ייִדישע קולטור-געזעלשאַפֿט: Annual report of the CJCS in Świdnica. Archiwum Żydowskiego Instytutu Historycznego/369/92.

Central Jewish Cultural Society 1948a צענטראַלע ייִדישע קולטור-געזעלשאַפֿט: Adresy CŻTK w Polsce. Archiwum Żydowskiego Instytutu Historycznego/369/2.

Central Jewish Cultural Society, 1948b צענטראַלע ייִדישע קולטור-געזעלשאַפֿט: Statut CŻTK w Polsce. Archiwum Żydowskiego Intytutu Historycznego/369/1.

Central Jewish Cultural Society, 1949a צענטראַלע ייִדישע קולטור-געזעלשאַפֿט: Raport CŻTK w Warszawie, 4 February: 168. Archiwum Żydowskiego Instytutu Historycznego /369/21.

Central Jewish Cultural Society, 1949b צענטראַלע ייִדישע קולטור-געזעלשאַפֿט: Raport CŻTK w Otwocku, 27 June. Archiwum Żydowskiego Instytutu Historycznego/369/85.

Central Jewish Cultural Society 1949c צענטראַלע ייִדישע קולטור-געזעלשאַפֿט. Raport CŻTK w Polsce, Warsaw, 25 August: 6. Archiwum Żydowskiego Instytutu Historycznego/369/6.

Central Jewish Cultural Society 1949d צענטראַלע ייִדישע קולטור-געזעלשאַפֿט: Sprawozdanie CŻTK w Polsce (Kraków), 19 September: 1. Archiwum Żydowskiego Instytutu Historycznego/369/81.

Central Jewish Cultural Society, 1950 צענטראַלע ייִדישע קולטור-געזעלשאַפֿט: Żydowskie Towarzystwo Kultury w Polsce: Zjazd Krajowy: Wrocław, 14–16 października 1949 roku. Wrocław: Żydowskie Tow[arzystwo] Kultury.

Cohen, Nathan, 2004: The Renewed Association of Yiddish Writers and Journalists in Poland, 1945–1948. In: Joseph Sherman, ed., *Yiddish after the Holocaust*. Oxford: Boulevard, 15–36.

Cohen, Nathan, 2008: Przyczyny emigracji pisarzy jidysz z Polski (1945–1948). In: Magdalena Ruta, ed., *Nusech Pojln: studia z dziejów kultury jidysz w powojennej Polsce*. Kraków-Budapest a.o.: Austeria.

Egit, Jakub, 1947: O nową kulturą kulturę żydowską (z przemówienia na konferencji działaczy kultury żydowskiej). In: *Nowe Życie* (Wrocław) 10, 1 January: 3.

Eisenbach, Artur, 1950: Podziemne Archiwum Historyczne. In: *Biuletyn Żydowskiego Instytutu Historycznego przy C[entralny] K[omitet] Żydów w Polsce* (Warsaw) 1, March 1950: 5–6.

EISENBACH, Artur, 1986: W dwudziestą rocznicę śmierci profesora Bernarda Marka. In: *BŻIH* (Warsaw) 1–2, January-June 1986: 201–204.

GAL-ED, Efrat, 2021: Yiddishland: A Promise of Belonging. In: *Journal of Modern Jewish Studies* 2 (2): 141–169.

GRABSKI, August, 2004: *Działalność komunistów wśród Żydów w Polsce (1944–1949)*. Warsaw: Trio.

GRABSKI, August, and Martyna RUSINIAK, 2008: Żydowscy komuniści po holokauście wobec języków polskiego Żydostwa. In: Magdalena Ruta, ed., *Nusech Pojln: studia z dziejów kultury jidysz w powojennej Polsce*. Kraków-Budapest a.o.: Austeria, 51–64.

HECHTKOPF, Khaim, 1948 העכטקאָף, חיים: אויף נייַע יסודות. אין: **יידישע שריפֿטן** (לאָדזש) 9, נאָוועמבער: 9.

HIRSZOWICZ, Maria, 2001: *Pułapki zaangażowania: intelektualiści w służbie komunistów*. Warsaw: Scholar.

JEWISH HISTORICAL INSTITUTE, 1954: Letter by Bernard Mark to the Management of the Polish Writers' Union, 12 April. Archiwum Żydowskiego Instytutu Historycznego/310/336/74.

JEWISH HISTORICAL INSTITUTE, 1956: 6, Sytuacja ludności żydowskiej w Polsce Ludowej (informacja dla Ambasady PRL w Londynie [State of the Jews in the Polish People's Republic (Memo for the Polish Embassy in London)]. Archiwum Żydowskiego Intytutu Historycznego/310/336.

JEWISH PRESS AGENCY, 1945: Akademia ku czci październikowej rewolucji w Warszawie [The celebaration in honor of the October Revolution. In: *Biuletyn ŻAP* (Łódź) 103, 22 November: 4.

JEWISH PRESS AGENCY, 1947a: Konferencja w sprawie teatru żydowskiego w Polsce w C.K.Ż.P. w Polsce. In: *Biuletyn ŻAP* (Łódź) 14, 17 February: 1–2.

JEWISH PRESS AGENCY, 1947b: Ogólnokrajowa organizacja działaczy kultury i sztuki. In: *Biuletyn ŻAP* (Łódź) 69: 2.

JEWISH PRESS AGENCY, 1947c: Rezolucja. Krajowa Narada Działaczy Kultury Żydowskiej. In: *Biuletyn ŻAP* (Łódź) 116: 1–2.

JEWISH PRESS AGENCY, 1948: Otwarcie pierwszej zbiorowej wystawy artystów plastyków. In: *Biuletyn ŻAP* (Łódź) 4, 12 January: 1–2.

JEWISH PRESS AGENCY, 1949a: Walne zebranie Związku Literatów Żydowskich w Polsce. In: *Biuletyn ŻAP* (Warsaw) 44, 24 May: 1–2.

JEWISH PRESS AGENCY, 1949c: Teatr żydowski zakazany w Izraelu. In: *Biuletyn ŻAP* (Łódż) 47, 1 June: 9.

JEWISH PRESS AGENCY, 1949d: Związek Literatów w Tel-Avivie uprawia dyskryminację wobec pisarzy żydowskich. In: *Biuletyn ŻAP* (Warsaw) 73, 14 September: 8.

JOKUSCH, Laura, 2007: Khurbn-Forshung. In: *Simon-Dubnow-Institute Yearbook VI*: 441–73.

Kobylarz, Renata, 2009: *Walka o pamięć. Polityczne aspekty obchodów rocznicy powstania w getcie warszawskim 1944–1989*. Warsaw: Instytut Pamięci Narodowej.

Lastik, Shloyme, 1950 לאַסטיק, שלומה: עליזאַ אָזשעשקאָ (צום 40סטן יאָרטאָג נאָך איר טויט). אין: **ייִדישע שריפֿטן** (וואַרשע) 6, יוני: 2.

Leociak, Jacek, 2000: Zraniona pamięć. (Rocznice powstania w getcie warszawskim w prasie polskiej 1944–1989). In: Alina Brodzka-Wald and Dorota Krawczyńska and Jacek Leociak, eds., *Literatura polska wobec Zagłady*. Warsaw: Żydowski Instytut Historyczny Instytut Naukowo-Badawczy, 29–49.

Lisek, Joanna, 2008: Jidiszer Jiszew in Niderszlezje. Żydowskie osiedle na Dolnym Śląsku. In: *Słowo Żydowskie* (Warsaw) 9–10, April 2008: 12.

Mark, Ber [Bernard], 1946 מאַרק, בער: פּראָבלעמען פֿון ייִדישן לעבן אין פּוילן. אין: **דאָס נײַע לעבן** (לאָדזש) 41, דעם 15טן נאָוועמבער: 3.

Mark, Ber [Bernard], 1947: O współpracy literatury żydowskiej i polskiej. In: *Mosty* (Łódż) 73, 4 November 1947: 4.

Mark, Ber [Bernard], 1949 מאַרק, בער: אַדאַם מיצקיעוויטש – דער פֿרײַנט און טריבון פֿון אונטערדריקטע פֿעלקער. אין: **ייִדישע שריפֿטן** (וואַרשע) 1, יאַנואַר 1949: 1–2.

Mirski, Mikhal [Michał], 1945 מירסקי, מיכאַל: דער גורל פֿון ייִדישן פֿאָלק איז פֿאַרבונדן מיטן גורל פֿון דער דעמאָקראַטיע. אין: **דאָס נײַע לעבן** (לאָדזש) 17, 28 סעפּטעמבער: 4.

Mirski, Mikhal [Michał], 1945 מירסקי, מיכאַל: פֿאַר אַ נײַ לעבן. אין: **דאָס נײַע לעבן** (לאָדזש) 1, 3. : 10 אַפּריל 1945.

Mirski, Mikhal [Michał], 1946 מירסקי, מיכאַל: די יסודות פֿון אונדזער קולטור־שאַפֿונג. אין: **ייִדישע שריפֿטן** (לאָדזש) 2, דעצעמבער 1946: 6–7.

Nalewajko-Kulikov, Joanna, 2008: Trzy kolory: szary: szkic do portretu Bernarda Marka. In: *Zagłada Żydów*. Studia i materiały. Warsaw: Centrum Badań nad Zagładą, 4, 263–284.

Nalewajko-Kulikov, Joanna, 2009: *Obywatel Jidyszlandu. Rzecz o komunistach w Polsce*. Warsaw: Neriton.

Ofner, A., 1947 אָפֿנער, אַ.: ייִדיש פֿאָרדערט רעכט בײַ ייִדן (אַ בריוו פֿון פּאַלעסטינע). אין: **פֿאָלקס־צײַטונג** (וואַרשע) 18–19, נאָוועמבער 1947: 11.

Olejnik, Leszek, 2003: *Polityka narodowościowa Polski w latach 1944–1960*. Łódż: The University of Łódź.

Olejnik, Leszek, 2006: Łódź jako centrum społeczności żydowskiej w Polsce (1945–1949). In: Paweł Samuś and Wiesława Pusia, eds., *Fenomen getta łódzkiego 1940–1944*. Łódż: The University of Łódź, 54–69.

Person, Katarzyna, and Agnieszka Żółkiewska, 2022: Edition of Documents from the Ringelblum Archive (the Underground Archive of the Warsaw Ghetto) in Stalinist Poland. In: Bohus, Kata Hallama, Peter Stach, Stephan, eds., *Growing in the Shadow of Antifascism: Remembering the Holocaust in State-Socialist Eastern Europe*. Budapest-Vienna-New York: Central European University Press, 21–37.

Piątkowska, Renata, 2004: Konkursy na plakat rozpisane z okazji 4. i 5. rocznicy powstania w getcie warszawskim. In: *Kwartalnik Historii Żydów* 2: 197–204.

Piątkowska, Renata, 2008: Żydowskie Towarzystwo Krzewienia Sztuk Pięknych (Jidisze gezelszaft cu farszprojtn kunst) – Próba kontynuowania żydowskiego życia artystycznego w latach 1946–1949. In: Magdalena Ruta, ed., *Nusech Pojln. Studia z dziejów kultury jidysz w powojennej Polsce*. Kraków-Budapest a.o.: Austeria, 67–99.

Piątkowska, Renata, 2010: Żydowskie życie artystyczne po Zagładzie. In: Feliks Tych and Monika Adamczyk-Garbowska, eds., *Następstwa zagłady Żydów. Polska 1944–2010*. Lublin: Uniwersytet Marii Curie-Skłodowskiej and Żydowski Instytut Historyczny im. Emanuela Ringelbluma, 339–358.

Pisarski, Maciej: Emigracja Żydów z Polski w latach 1945–1951. In: Jerzy Tomaszewski, ed., *Studia z dziejów i kultury Żydów w Polsce po roku 1945*. Warsaw: Uniwersytet Warszawski Centrum Badania i Nauczania Dziejów i Kultury Żydów w Polsce im. Mordechaja Anielewicza, and Wydawnictwo Trio, 71–83.

Podhoritser-Zaykin [Podhorizer-Sandel], Ernestine, 1947 פּאָדהאָריצער־זײַקין, ערנעסטינע: אַ יאָר טעטיקייט פֿון ייִדישער געזעלשאַפֿט צו פֿאַרשפּרייטן קונסט. אין: **דאָס נײַע לעבן** (לאָדזש) 81, 21 נאָוועמבער 1947: 9.

Podhorizer-Sandel, Ernestyna, 1973: Wspomnienie o Józefie Sandlu (w 10 rocznicę śmierci). In: *Biuletyn Żydowskiego Instytutu Historycznego* (Warsaw) 1, January–March 1973: 111–119.

Podhorizer-Sandel, Ernestyna, 1973: Zniszczenie zabytków kultury i sztuki żydowskiej w Warszawie. In: *BŻIH* (Warsaw) 2–3, April–September 1973: 231–237.

Podhorizer-Sandel, Ernestyna, 1974: Żydowskie Towarzystwo Krzewienia Sztuk Pięknych. In: *Biuletyn Żydowskiego Instytutu Historycznego* (Warsaw) 3, July–September 1974: 37–50.

Podhorizer-Sandel, Ernestyna, and Karol Mórawski, 1980: Z działalności Muzeum Żydowskiego Instytutu w Polsce. In: *Trzydzieści pięć lat działalności Żydowskiego Instytutu Historycznego w Polsce Ludowej*. Warsaw: P[aństwowe] W[ydwanictwo] N[aukowe], 61–75.

Polish Committee of National Liberation, 1944: *Polski Komitet Wyzwolenia Narodowego: Manifest Polskiego Komitetu Narodowego Wyzwolenia*. Chelm-Moscow: 22 July.

Polish Writers' Union, 1949: Protocol no. 18, Warsaw, 13 December: 6. Archiwum Związku Literatów Polskich/11.664.

Ruta, Magdalena, 2008: Tematy literatury jidysz w Polsce lat 1945–1949. Rekonesans Badawczy. In: Magdalena Ruta, ed., *Nusech Pojln: studia z dziejów kultury jidysz w powojennej Polsce*. Kraków-Budapest a.o.: Austeria, 247–276.

Ruta, Magdalena, 2009: Z dziejów recepcji literatury jidysz. Szolem Alejchem czytany w przedmarcowej Polsce. In: *Słowo Żydowskie* (Warsaw) 11: 26–29.

Ruta, Magdalena, 2012: *Bez Żydów? Literatura jidysz w PRL o Zagładzie, Polsce i komunizmie*. Kraków-Budapest: a.o.: Austeria.

Sandel, Józef, 1947 סאַנדעל, יוסף: ייִדישע פּלאַסטישע קונסט. אין: **דאָס נײַע לעבן** (לאָדזש) 92., יובילײ־אויסגאַבע 1947 [אומדאַטירט]: 14

Sandel, Józef, 1950: O projektowanym historycznym leksykonie plastyków żydowskich w Polsce. In: *Biuletyn Żydowskiego Instytutu Historycznego* (Warsaw) 2, November: 19–20.

Sandel, Józef, 1953: Żydowska sztuka kultowa. In: *Straty wojenne zbiorów polskich w dziedzinie rzemiosła artystycznego*. Warsaw: Centralny Zarząd Muzeów.

Schatz, Jaff, 1991: *The Generation: The Rise and Fall of the Jewish Communists of Poland*. Berkeley, Calif.: University of California Press.

Schatz, Jaff, 2007: Komuniści w "sektorze żydowskim": tożsamość, etos i struktura instytucjonalna, translated by Magdalena Ruta. In: Magdalena Ruta, ed., *Nusech Pojln. Studia z dziejów kultury jidysz w powojennej Polsce*. Kraków-Budapest a.o.: Austeria, 27–49.

Schwarz, Jan, 2015: Preface and acknowledgments. In: Jan Schwarz, *Survivors and Exiles. Yiddish Culture after the Holocaust*. Detroit, Mich.: Wayne State University Press.

Sfard, Dovid, 1946 ספֿאַרד, דוד: לאָמיר געבן אַ טיקן דעם ייִדישן וואָרט. אין: **דאָס נײַע לעבן** (לאָדזש) 43, דעם 5טן נאָוועמבער 1946: 21

Sfard, Dovid, 1984 ספֿאַרד, דוד: פּראָפּ׳ ב. מאַרק. אין: **מיט זיך און מיט אַנדערע: אויטאָ־ביאָגראַפֿיע און ליטעראַרישע עסייען.** ירושלים: ירושלימער אַלמאַנאַך, 375–379

Słowacki, Juliusz, 1949 סלאָוואַצקי, יוליוש: צו דער מוטער (פֿראַגמענט פֿון בריוו), איבערגעזעצט פֿון ישעיהו שפּיגל. אין: **ייִדישע שריפֿטן** (וואַרשע) 5, מײַ 1949: 2

Słomkowska, Alina, 1979: *Prasa w PRL: szkice historyczne*. Warsaw: Państwowe Wydawnictwo Naukowe.

Stach, Stephan, 2008: Geschichtsschreibung und politische Vereinnahmung: Das Jüdische Historische Institut in Warschau, 1947–1968. In: *Simon-Dubnow-Institute Yearbook VII*, 401–431.

Stach, Stephan, 2010: Walka klas w getcie? Badania nad Zagładą prowadzone w ŻIH w Warszawie w okresie stalinowskim. In: Krzysztof Pilarczyk, ed., *Żydzi i judaizm we współczesnych badaniach polskich*. Kraków: Polska Akademia Umiejętności, vol. 5, 273–87.

Szaynok, Bożena, 2007: Żydzi w Dzierżoniowie (1945–1950). In: Sebastian Ligarski and Tomasz Przerwa, eds., *Dzierżoniów — wiek miniony. Materiały pokonferencyjne*. Wrocław: Instytut Pamięci Narodowej, 26–34.

Szner, Henryk, 1947: Nasze straty (w przededniu zawarcia traktatu pokojowego z Niemcami). In: *Nasze Słowo* (Łódż) 3, 18 February: 4.

Szulc, Wita, 2009: *Kultura dla mas Polski Ludowej: wizje ideologów, twórców i publicystów z lat 1944–1956*. Wrocław: Oficyna Wydawnicza Atut – Wrocławskie Wydawnictwo Oświatowe, 13.

Szurek, Jean Charles, 2003: Être témoin sous le stalinisme: Les premieres années de l'Institut Historique Juif de Varsovie. In: Delphine Bechtel, ed., et al., *Écriture de l'histoire et identité juive L'Europe ashkénaze XIXe–XXe siècle*. Paris: Les Belles Lettres, 51–82.

Tauchner, Maksymilian, 1946: Przed werdyktem Narodu. In: *Opinia* (Łódź) 8, 30 November: 1.

Tauchner, Maksymilian, 1948: Cieniom najdroższym… In: *Opinia* (Łódź) 33, 19 April: 4.

Tomaszewski, Jan, 1996: Żydowski Instytut Historyczny w polskiej historiografii. In: *Żydowski Instytut Historyczny 50 lat działalności. Materiały z konferencji jubileuszowej*. Warsaw: Żydowski Instytut Historyczny w Warszawie, 15–30.

Torańska, Teresa, 2004: *Oni*. Warsaw: Iskry.

Turkov-Grudberg, Yitskhok, 1947: Turkow, Izaak: Teatr i koła dramatyczne. In: *Nowe Życie* (Wrocław) 10, 1 January 1947: 4.

Turkov-Grudberg, Yitskhok, 1949 טורקאָוו, יצחק: דער דיכטער פֿון פּוילנס פּײַן און האָפֿענונג (הונדערט יאָר נאָכן טויט פֿון יוליוש סלאָוואַצקי). אין: **ייִדישע שריפֿטן** (וואַרשע) 5, מײַ 1949: 2.

Turkov, Yonas, 1959 טורקאָוו, יאָנאַס: **נאָך דער באַפֿרײַונג: זכרונות**. בוענאָס־אײַרעס: צענטראַל־פֿאַרבאַנד פֿון פּוילישע ייִדן אין אַרגענטינע.

Zachariasz, Szymon, 1947: Raport o działalności żydowskich partii [Report of the Jewish Party's Activity] 31 October and 1 November. Archiwum Akt Nowych/1354/476/20: 45–46.

Zachariasz, Szymon, 1948a זאַכאַריאַש, שימאָן: **צום צענטראַלן קאָמיטעט פֿון פּפּר בײַם צענטראַלן ייִדישן קאָמיטעט אין וואַרשע**. Archiwum Akt Nowych/1354/476/22: 100.

Zachariasz, Szymon, 1948b: Protokół PPR [Protocol by PPR], 5–6 August. Archiwum Akt Nowych/1354/476/20.

Zachariasz, Szymon, 1950: Notatka o prasie żydowskiej w Polsce [Memo on the Jewish Press in Poland], 1 February. Archiwum Akt Nowych/1354/476/21.

Zak, Avrom, 1947 זאַק, אבֿרהם: דער באַנײַטער ליטעראַטן־פֿאַראײן. אין: **דאָס נײַע לעבן** (לאָדזש) 92, יובֿילײ־אויסגאַבע 1947 [אומדאַטירט]: 14.

Zak, Avrom, 1968 זאַק, אבֿרהם: **געווען אַ ייִדיש פּוילן: עסייען און דערמאָנונגען**. בוענאָס־אײַרעס: פֿאַרבאַנד פֿון שארית־הפּליטה אין אַרגענטינע.

Zomershteyn, Emil, 1945 זאָמערשטיין, עמיל: מיר ווילן – און וועלן לעבן. אין: **דאָס נײַע לעבן** (לאָדזש) אַפּריל: 2.

Żółkiewska, Agnieszka, 2017: *Zerwana przeszłość. Powojenne środowisko żydowskiej inteligencji twórczej. Pomoc materialna i organizacyjna ze strony CKŻP*. Warsaw: Żydowski Instytut Historyczny im. Emanuela Ringelbluma.

Zonshayn, Yankev, 1947 זאָנשײַן, יעקבֿ: פּיִאַסט און אבֿרהם פּראָכאָווניק. אין: **דאָס נײַע לעבן** (לאָדזש) 40, דעם 30סטן מײַ: 5.

Malena Chinski

Meanings and Lessons of the Warsaw Ghetto Uprising

Memory Struggles Among Polish Jews in Buenos Aires, 1944–1955

On the occasion of the sixth anniversary of the Warsaw Ghetto Uprising, Krakówian survivor scholar Joseph Wulf (1912–1974), then residing in Paris, warned against the rising tendency to mythologize the events of April-May 1943 within the Jewish world:

> זינט דער באַפֿרייַונג מערקט זיך עפּעס אַ מאָדנע באַוועגונג פֿון מוסיף זייַן פֿאַרשידענע
> פּרטי־פּרטים אַרום דעם אויפֿשטאַנד פֿון געטאָ אין וואַרשע. אַ סך פֿון די מאַטעריאַלן האָבן
> נישט קיין שום יסוד און קיין שום מקור. מען איז מוסיף נישט קיין פֿאַקטן, נאָר אויסגעטראַכ־
> טע מעשׂיות. אַזוי אַרום ווערן מיר נישט רייַכער נאָר אָרעמער. און צום סוף ווערט דאָס בילד
> אַזוי ווייַט מטושטש, אַז עס איז פּשוט שווער זיך פֿאַנאַנדערצוקלייַבן און פֿאַרשטיין וואָס עס
> איז באמת פֿאָרגעקומען אויפֿן שטח פֿון וואַרשעווער געטאָ פֿאַרן און נאָכן 19 אַפּריל 1943.[1]

> Since Liberation we have noticed an odd impulse to collect diverse painstaking details regarding the revolt in the Warsaw Ghetto. Many of these materials have no basis and no sources. What is collected is not facts, but invented stories. This does not enrich but rather impoverishes us [our knowledge]. And in the end, the resulting picture is so vague that we are unable to orient ourselves and understand what really happened in the area of the Warsaw Ghetto before and after April 19, 1943.

Wulf's statement highlights the extent to which the episode of Jewish armed resistance in the Warsaw Ghetto[2] had become a subject of worship

This article is an updated version of a chapter of my doctoral dissertation (Chinski 2017, 199–252), funded by the Consejo Nacional de Investigaciones Científicas y Técnicas (CONICET) in Argentina. I would like to express my gratitude to the editors of this volume, Miriam Chorley-Schulz and Alexander Walther, and to the book series' editor, Roland Gruschka, for their contributions to this chapter. I would also like to thank Alan Astro, Constance Pâris de Bollardière, Simon Perego, Florencia Osuna, and Raanan Rein, for their valuable comments and bibliographic orientation.

1 Wulf 1949, 5. All translations have been done by the author of this paper, unless otherwise indicated. Hebrew-script quotations from Yiddish have been rendered in YIVO standard orthography.

2 Interwar Warsaw was the city with the second largest Jewish population worldwide after New York. According to the Nazi-ordered census of late September 1939, some 360,000 Jews lived there (Gutman 1982, 18). The Nazis officially established the Warsaw ghetto in October 1940. Regarding the establishment of the Warsaw Ghetto, see Gutman 1982, 48–61.

and political instrumentalization globally already by the end of the 1940s.[3] Historical documentation was undertaken and memoirs by surviving Ghetto fighters were published. Moreover, Jewish armed resistance was the subject of a great variety of cultural productions including theater pieces, radio broadcasts, and fiction inspired by the Uprising in its early aftermath.[4]

The poignant asymmetry between the opposing forces, Nazi occupiers vs the surviving remnant of the ghetto prisoner population, had contributed to the construction of the Warsaw Ghetto Uprising as the paradigmatic act of heroism during the Second World War. It is estimated that the underground organizations that came together to create the Żydowska Organizacja Bojowa [Jewish Combat Organization, ŻOB] included more than 500 fighters in total,[5] while almost the entire remaining ghetto population barricaded themselves in hiding places and bunkers; this "network of cells and tunnels resembled a subterranean Jewish city."[6] The supply of a small amount of weapons was possible thanks to the ŻOB's contacts with the Polish underground movement Armia Krajowa [Home Army, AK].[7] Thousands of people held out for almost a month in the hiding places while fighters carried out sporadic attacks against the Nazis up until the Ghetto was reduced to rubble.

3 Even though there were attempts at armed resistance in approximately one hundred ghettos during the Nazi occupation of Europe, this phenomenon remained marginal in quantitative terms (Bauer 2002, 137). The case of the Warsaw Ghetto was exceptional, due to the fact that the population did massively support the fighters. Two circumstances help to explain this: first, the Warsaw Ghetto inhabitants were well aware of the existence of the Treblinka extermination camp as the final destination for deportations; second, the fighters had become the new *de facto* authority in the ghetto, after having subjugated the *Judenrat* and individual collaborators. On the Warsaw Ghetto Uprising, see Gutman 1982 and 1994.

4 On the overall postwar significance of the Warsaw Ghetto Uprising, see Patt 2021, 1–4. On cultural artifacts inspired by the revolt in the Warsaw Ghetto, see Baskind 2019. An example of historical documentation can be consulted in Chinski 2021, 199–200. On the first testimonies by ghetto fighters, see Patt 2021, 305–346. New research on the Warsaw Ghetto Uprising was presented at the international conference "Looking at the Ghetto… The Warsaw Ghetto Uprising: Eighty Years in Retrospect," Leibniz Institute for Jewish History and Culture – Simon Dubnow, Leipzig, 17–19 April 2023. See conference program: https://www.dubnow.de/fileadmin/user_upload/PDF/Veranstaltungen/Konferenzen/Program_Uprising_web.pdf, June 15, 2023.

5 Gutman 1982, 348. On the establishment of the ŻOB, see Gutman 1982, 236–243. For a recent reassessment regarding the collective character of the ŻOB leadership, see Dreifuss 2017. In addition to the 500 fighters affiliated to the ŻOB, approximately 250 fighters in the ranks of the Żydowski Związek Wojskowy [Jewish Military Union, ŻZW] took part in the Uprising (Gutman 1982, 365). On the founding of the ŻZW, see Gutman 1982, 293–297.

6 Gutman 1982, 354. On the building of bunkers in the Warsaw Ghetto, see Gutman 1982, 351–353.

7 On this, see Gutman 1982, 307–344.

Impressed by this example of armed resistance under unprecedented extreme conditions, Jewish organizations throughout the world soon established annual commemorations of the Warsaw Ghetto Uprising. Specific practices of memory of the Uprising have only recently been addressed by scholars.[8] My article focuses on commemoration undertaken by Polish Jews in Buenos Aires in the context of the Cold War, when memory entrepreneurs[9] were increasingly divided politically over the meanings and lessons to be drawn from the Warsaw Ghetto Uprising.

The period under study begins with the first ceremony devoted to the Warsaw Ghetto Uprising (1944), and runs throughout the two consecutive Peronist mandates (1946–1955), in order to assess the impact of both international and national politics within the realm of Jewish commemoration between 1944 and 1955. Juan Domingo Perón (1895–1974) implemented a Cold War policy deemed by himself the "Third Position," which sought to maintain Argentina's independence from the United States and the Soviet Union. Argentina pursued diplomatic and commercial relations with both world powers; however, Perón affirmed that in case of a war, Argentina would align itself with the United States.[10]

This case study aims at contributing to the growing body of scholarly literature about the political influences on, as well as cultural and intellectual local manifestations of, the Cold War in Latin America.[11] In particular, I examine to what extent the early Cold War affected and transformed Latin American immigrant communities.[12] I will concentrate on two sectors of Polish Jewish לאַנדסמאַנשאַפֿטן [*landsmanshaftn*][13] that organized memorial ceremonies devoted to the Warsaw Ghetto Uprising in Buenos Aires:[14] one Zionist and one communist.

8 On the case of commemoration of the Warsaw Ghetto Uprising in Paris, see Perego 2020, 186–192. On annual commemorations organized by *khurbn*-survivors [Holocaust survivors] in New York, see Slucki 2019.

9 Jelin 2002, 48, n. 2.

10 Sheinin 2006, 96–100. On the relations between the United States and Perón, see also Rapoport and Spiguel 2009.

11 Albuquerque Fuschini 2011, Calandra and Franco 2012, Petra 2022, Rupprecht 2015, Zourek 2014.

12 On a different case study following this approach, see Galván 2017.

13 Jewish immigrant societies of voluntary affiliation, composed of former residents of the same town or city.

14 Unlike the commemorative calendar of other Jewish communities around the world, which

The Cold War deepened the chasm between communists and Zionists, not only in respect to their understanding of the contemporary geopolitical map, but also, and not unconnected, in their interpretation of what they deemed to be the 'true' meaning of the Warsaw Ghetto Uprising.[15] Crucial questions were at stake a few years after the annihilation of one third of the world's Jewish population: What was the safest place for the reconstruction of Jewish life? What political project was worth investing in? How should one position oneself and prevent another Jewish catastrophe? As internal political confrontation grew, the scope of the memorial ceremonies also grew in an effort by both sides to recruit support from other Jewish institutions beyond the realm of immigrant societies. This resulted in the gradual formation of two opposing memorial blocs or coalitions.

The Jews in Buenos Aires in the Turmoil of Argentine Politics, 1944–1955

The national census carried out in 1947, which introduced a question regarding religious affiliation, estimated an Argentine Jewish population of 249,326.[16] Demographers Schmelz and Della Pergola have readjusted this number to 285,800, considering that many Jews refused for various reasons to declare their religious affiliation (while others simply did not consider themselves as adhering to any religion).[17] As of that same year, 75 to 80 percent of the Jewish population resided in the city of Buenos Aires.[18]

Even though the early history of the Argentine Jewish community (before 1890) is linked to a small migrant group of Jews from France, Italy, England, and Germany, most of those who settled in the country after 1890 came from Eastern Europe, mainly the Russian Empire, independent Poland (since 1918) and, to a lesser extent, Romania.[19] Eastern European Jews made up between

included a variety of dates of remembrance, in the case of Argentina, the commemoration of the persecution and extermination of European Jews focused almost exclusively on the events of the Warsaw Ghetto Uprising. (See, for instance, the rich commemorative calendar of the Jews in France in Perego 2020, 62–64).

15 Bundists organized separate annual ceremonies in remembrance of the Warsaw Ghetto Uprising (Laubstein 1997, 197). It has not yet been possible to study these commemorations, due to the lack of sources.

16 Rein 2001, 26f.

17 Figure cited in Rein 2001, 27.

18 Sofer 1982, 4.

19 For a general history of Jewish immigration to Argentina, see Avni 1983.

80 and 85 percent of the foreign-born Jewish population in the interwar period in Buenos Aires amounting to some 55,000 Polish Jews emigrating to Argentina between 1919 and 1939 according to Marta Kowalska.[20]

Jews coming from Eastern Europe, and especially from Poland, established strong transnational relations with historical Eastern European Jewish centers, and this influenced the process of identity construction within the Yiddish-speaking diaspora in Buenos Aires.[21] As Leonardo Senkman has noted:

> A pesar de las diferencias ideológicas y políticas entre ellos [los judíos polacos], compartían una común matriz nacional judía idishista, y se resistían en Argentina a abandonar la concepción de autonomía cultural que gozaban las minorías en Polonia.[22]

> Despite the ideological and political differences between them [Polish Jews], they shared a common Yiddishist national matrix, and were reluctant in Argentina to abandon the idea of cultural autonomy enjoyed by minorities in Poland.

Transnational relations continued among Yiddish-speaking Jews throughout the globe in the aftermath of the חורבן [*khurbn*, destruction, Holocaust]; moreover, Yiddish would remain a spoken language in Argentina for a few decades.[23] According to the sources consulted for this research,[24] Yiddish was the vernacular language of most of the participants in the ceremonies I analyze, including the organizers, speakers, performing artists, and the audiences.

This study of commemoration among Polish Jews in Buenos Aires begins by focusing on the first anniversary of the Warsaw Ghetto Uprising in the context of a military dictatorship. On 4 June 1943, Generals Arturo Rawson and Pedro Pablo Ramírez carried out a military coup in Argentina.[25] This

20 Mirelman 1988, 16 and Kowalska 1989, 259. For other estimations, see Kałczewiak 2019, 6–9, and Porada 2022, 235 and 244.

21 Senkman 2007a, 423. On transnational relations developed by Polish Jews in Argentina in the interwar period, see Kałczewiak 2019.

22 Senkman 2007, 424. Transnationalist culture has been particularly studied for the case of Bundist Jews in Buenos Aires, see Wolff 2013.

23 Chinski and Astro 2018, 1–3.

24 The information and speeches concerning memorial ceremonies were drawn from reviews published in the daily and weekly Yiddish press of Buenos Aires.

25 This 'National Revolution' was led by General Arturo Rawson, who had to resign due to internal army pressures; General Pedro Pablo Ramírez, former Minister of War, took his place; he would govern the country for the next seven months until March 1944, when he was replaced by Edelmiro Farrell (1944–1946).

year marked the end of a period popularly known in Argentine history as 'the infamous decade' (1932–1943), characterized by significant political corruption, fervent Catholic nationalism, and antisemitism.[26] In continuity with this preceding period, the new power aimed at establishing a 'national-Catholic regime': Catholicism was a means of providing the military rulers with ideological legitimacy.[27] Restriction of freedoms and repression characterized the period following the military coup. The new regime maintained the policy of Argentine neutrality in the Second World War up until January 1944.[28]

Even though the life of Argentinian Jews in the 'infamous decade' cannot be reduced to their status as victims of antisemitism, the phenomenon reached such visibility that it led to the creation of institutions conceived specifically to combat antisemitism, all the more forcefully in a context of daily press reports on Nazism in Europe.[29] For instance, the umbrella organization Delegación de Asociaciones Israelitas Argentinas [Delegation of Israelite Argentine Associations, DAIA] was established in 1935 – a political entity that would play an increasingly important role with respect to commemoration.[30]

The rise of Perón to the presidency in June 1946 meant a transformation of the relations between the state and its Jewish population. Although there were incidents of state antisemitism during Perón's government (1946–1955) – for example, in the area of immigration selection[31] – generally speaking Perón fought antisemitism and promoted policies of integration of Jews, as well as other marginalized groups.[32] However, dissident sectors were heavily

26 Lvovich 2003, 293–371, 302–307, 313.

27 Rouquié 1982, 37.

28 This policy was maintained by four presidents between 1939 and 1944, and enjoyed public support. In January 1944 Argentina broke off diplomatic relations with the Axis, and in March 1945 signed the Pan-American Agreement and declared war. With this gesture, the United States recognized the military government, but pressed for the expulsion of Nazi agents and German interests on Argentine territory. De facto president Edelmiro Farrell had to call a general election on February 1946, in which Perón was elected, see Rein 2001, 33–39.

29 State antisemitism took the form of refusal to allow Jewish refugees to enter the country. On Argentine immigration policies regarding Jews seeking to escape Nazi persecution, see Senkman 1991.

30 Public protests were organized in Buenos Aires in response to Jewish persecution in Germany since 1933. These initiatives resulted in the founding of the DAIA. On the DAIA, see Schenkolewski-Kroll 1991.

31 Senkman 2007b, 1–7.

32 Rein 2001, 98. However, mistrust of Perón by Jewish public opinion remained persistent because of the support Perón had received from violent antisemitic nationalist groups during and after the presidential campaign. Once elected, Perón took distance from such groups (Rein 2001, 62–67).

persecuted, especially communist groups with many Jewish members among them.[33] These internal policies against communism, and an ideological positioning vis-à-vis antisemitism in the USSR, as we will see, influenced the evolution of Jewish commemoration in Argentina directly.

Polish Jews in Buenos Aires Commemorate the Warsaw Ghetto Uprising: From Plurality to Unity, 1944–1948

The commemoration of the Warsaw Ghetto Uprising was initiated by two associations of Polish Jews in Buenos Aires. One of them was a federation of associations, the צענטראַל־פֿאַרבאַנד פֿון פּוילישע ייִדן אין אַרגענטינע [*Tsentral-farband fun poylishe yidn in Argentine*, Central Union of Polish Jews in Argentina, CUPJA], bringing together a number of Zionist-oriented Polish Jewish *landsmanshaftn*. In the 1930s, it became the largest Polish Jewish association in the country, with 2,000 members, a credit union, its own journal, a cultural center and a library.[34] The other group was a single *landsmanshaft*, the לאַנדסלײַט־פֿאַריין פֿון וואַרשע און אומגעגענט אין אַרגענטינע [*Landslayt-fareyn fun Varshe un umgegent in Argentine*, Society of Former Residents of Warsaw and Its Vicinity in Argentina, SFRWVA]. Founded in 1945 to organize aid for survivors in Poland, it had a membership of 1,000.[35] This society was affiliated to the Argentine branch of the ייִדישער קולטור־פֿאַרבאַנד [*Yidisher kultur-farband*, Jewish Cultural Federation, YKUF],[36] a federation bringing together a number of educational, social, and cultural institutions of Jews sympathetic to communism or affiliated with the Communist Party, who referred to themselves as 'progressive.'[37]

From 1944 to 1946, only one annual commemoration of the Warsaw Ghetto Uprising took place, organized by either one or the other of the aforementioned immigrant societies; in 1947, each organized its own commem-

33 This topic will be discussed in the last section of this paper.

34 Rollansky 1998a, 127. Its origins date back to 1916, when it was founded under the name of פּוילישער פֿאַרבאַנד [*Poylisher farband*, Polish Jewish Union].

35 Anonymous 1955c, v.

36 Spelled 'ICUF' in Argentina. On the foundation of the YKUF in 1937 in Paris, see Estraikh 2020.

37 See a list of Argentine Jewish institutions affiliated to the local branch of the YKUF in Visacovsky 2015, 267–269. However, YKUF-affiliated *landsmanshaftn* are not listed. On 'progressive' Jews in the Americas, see Visacovsky 2022.

oration on dates close to 19 April but not on the same date.[38] Despite being two institutions whose positions on Jewish politics were antagonistic, the CUPJA (Zionists) and the SFRWVA (communists) did not differ substantially in the way they chose to commemorate the Warsaw Ghetto Uprising.[39] These early ceremonies had a common morphology, characterized by a fusion of registers:[40] discursive, liturgical, and artistic elements were deployed within a scenic arrangement, in which candles were frequently lit as a symbol of mourning, as well as flags and banners with memorial inscriptions. The spaces allocated for these ceremonies were secular venues such as theaters and community halls (with the exception of the very first anniversary, when the ceremony was held in a synagogue). The meaning attributed to the Uprising by both institutions was still similar as well. Speakers usually claimed that the Ghetto heroes had not let themselves be 'slaughtered like sheep' – an extension of heroism to all the 'martyrs' that had its origins in a pamphlet of the Vilna Ghetto's Jewish partisan organization, active from December 1941 until its insurrection in September 1943 that was brutally squashed with the 'liquidation' of the Ghetto.[41] However, two interrelated topics that would later become the subject of bitter debate between the two associations were already present in this early stage: the relation to postwar Communist-ruled Poland, on the one hand, and the representation of the attitudes of non-Jewish Poles during the Warsaw Ghetto Uprising, on the other.

Only in communist events, a bond of friendship with Poland was constantly made explicit. In both 1946 and 1947, the SFRWVA included two prominent non-Jewish Polish speakers in their ceremonies, the editor of the weekly *Polska Wizwolona* [Liberated Poland][42] and the new Polish minister (a

38 Tsentral-farband fun poylishe yidn in Argentine 1945, 5; Anonymous 1945, 4; Anonymous 1946, 4; Anonymous 1947a, 4; Anonymous 1947b, 4.

39 One aspect that differentiated the events was the stable presence of one female participant among the speakers in the case of the communist events (1946 and 1947), while speakers were always exclusively male in Zionist events. Women were prominent generally through the Women's Organization in the YKUF culture, and in Soviet Jewish culture more broadly (Visacovsky 2015, 159–164). YKUF newspapers regularly highlighted the role of women in the resistance against Nazism and published stories about the Uprising written by women. Accordingly, female heroes were enhanced in Soviet Yiddish literature since the 1940s, operating as an allegory for the "unprecedented struggle of the Jewish people as a whole," in the sense that "the seemingly weak will at the end have the upper hand in this struggle between good and evil" ([Chorley-]Schulz 2019, 207).

40 On the morphology of remembrance ceremonies, see Perego 2017.

41 On its later re-signification as an expression of contempt toward the victims, see Zertal 2010, 59.

42 This Argentine Polish periodical, which defined itself as a 'periódico democrático polaco'

post equivalent to that of ambassador) in Argentina respectively.[43] When one of the Polish guests predicted in April 1946 that Poland would be free of antisemitism,[44] he could not have known that three months later the infamous Kielce pogrom would break out, where a mob of Polish soldiers, policemen, and civilians murdered more than forty Jews following medieval-style 'blood libel accusations.'[45] This did not change the tune at YKUF's 1947 event. One activist reduced the pogrom to 'Polish fascists;' another reiterated that Poland was the only country, ווּ ס׳הערשט די ברייטסטע טאָלעראַנץ פֿאַר אַלע גלויבנס און ראַסן, ווּ די ייִדן [...] ווערן גשטיצט פֿון דער רעגירונג צו אַנטוויקלען זייער קולטור און זיך שאַפֿן אַ נײַ פּראָדוקטיוו לעבן [where the broadest tolerance of all creeds and races reigns, and where Jews […] receive support from the government to develop their culture and to create a new productive life for themselves].[46]

That same year, at the Zionist ceremony in contrast, the renowned journalist and president of the CUPJA, Mark Turkow (1904–1983), spoke for the first time of the Ghetto Uprising's 'meaning,' outlining ideas that echoed Zionist ideology. Turkow, who was a eminent figure within the world of Yiddish letters as the editor of the memorial book collection דאָס פּוילישע ייִדנטום [*Dos poylishe yidntum*, The Polish Jewry] since 1946,[47] criticized the indifference of the world, and especially די אומפֿאַרשטענדלעכע גלײַכגילטיקייט פֿון פּוילישן פֿאָלק, וואָס האָט זיך אין געוויסע מאָמענטן דערנענטערט צו די טויערן פֿון געטאָ און צוגעקוקט מיט אַ שמייכל פֿון צופֿרידנקייט די גרענעצלאָזע ייִדישע לײַדן [the incomprehensible indifference of the Polish people, who at certain moments approached the gates of the Ghetto and looked with a satisfied smile at the boundless

[democratic Polish periodical], was consulted at the Biblioteca Polaca Ignacio Domeyko in Buenos Aires. Edited by Martin Raduj (of whom no biographical information is available), this was the only non-Jewish periodical that annually recalled the struggle of the Jews in the Warsaw Ghetto on the date of the anniversary of the Uprising throughout the period of publication (1945–1950), and it regularly reproduced literary texts concerning Polish Jews.

43 Newspaper reports do not specify whether speeches in Polish were translated into Yiddish. We may assume, however that the Polish language was understood by many members of the audience.

44 Anonymous 1946, 4.

45 On the Kielce pogrom, see Gross 2007. On *khurbn*-survivors in postwar Poland more broadly, see Kichelewski 2018.

46 Anonymous 1947a, 4.

47 Mark Turkow was born in 1904 in Warsaw, was Jewish religiously educated, and worked as a translator and journalist in Poland. He visited Argentina for the first time in 1937 and settled in Buenos Aires permanently two years later. During the early postwar years, he was president of the Central Union of Polish Jews in Argentina and director of the Hebrew Immigrant Aid Society [HIAS] for Latin America. He also edited the book series *Biblioteca popular judía*. On Turkow, see Weinstein and Toker 2004, 186f. On *Dos poylishe yidntum*, see Chinski 2011 and Schwarz 2008.

Jewish sufferings].[48] He concluded that מיר געפֿינען זיך אין אַ שטענדיקן מלחמה־צושטאַנד, און דאָס איז געווען דער זין פֿון וואַרשעווער אויפֿשטאַנד [We find ourselves in a situation of permanent war, and that was the meaning of the Warsaw [Ghetto] Uprising].[49]

At this stage of the incipient Cold War, all their ideological differences did not prevent the two Polish Jewish associations from coming together in a joint ceremony of broader scope in Buenos Aires on the occasion of the fifth anniversary of the Uprising. Two non-immigrant Jewish institutions joined in organizing the 1948 ceremony:[50] the DAIA, by then a well-established representative body of all Argentine Jews before the government with explicit Zionist leanings, and the Organización Central de Ayuda [Central Relief Organization, OCA], formed in 1947 with the aim of bringing together competing postwar relief campaigns.[51]

On 18 April 1948, the audience numbered around 15,000 at the Luna Park stadium in downtown Buenos Aires,[52] outnumbering previous events by up to 3,000. Celebrated by all Jewish organizations in Buenos Aires, the 1948 memorial event was particularly important due to both the coming unveiling of sculptor Nathan Rapoport's monument in Warsaw honoring the Ghetto Uprising and the unfolding situation in Palestine on the eve of the proclamation of the state of Israel.[53] Expressions of solidarity with survivors of the *khurbn* in Poland were matched by speeches of support for the Jewish fight in Palestine against the British Mandate. At the Luna Park, Warsaw and Jerusalem were evoked as two symbolic poles of Jewish heroism. The event included an envoy from the Jewish settlement in Palestine among the speakers as well as Polish officials.

This convergence between Zionists and communists in Buenos Aires reflected a particular conjuncture: the crucial Soviet support for the imminent foundation of the state of Israel.[54] At that point, the Jewish fight for national

48 Anonymous 1947b, 4.

49 Ibid.

50 Anonymous 1948, 4.

51 Senkman 2007, 9.

52 Anonymous 1948, 4.

53 On Rapoport's trajectory, the history of the monument and its characteristics, see Young 1993, 155–184.

54 The USSR provided not only diplomatic support to the creation of the state of Israel, but also military support through the indirect provision of arms and men (Rucker 2008, 374–376). On the

self-determination in Palestine did not necessarily contradict socialist hopes in this fight but was deemed part of the ongoing anti-imperialist struggle of the oppressed and colonized generally.[55] DAIA and CUPJA representatives for their part greeted the Polish officials present in the audience[56] and kept the questioning of whether the Ghetto fighters had received 'enough help' from the Polish population brief and imprecise.[57] The artistic program also reflected Zionist spirit, particularly in form of the collective singing of התקוה [*Ha-tiqwāh*, The Hope], Israel's future national anthem. The ceremony culminated in the symbolic unveiling of a small model of Nathan Rapoport's monument placed center-stage followed by the recital of a letter by the צענטראַלער קאָמיטעט פֿון די ייִדן אין פּוילן [*Tsentraler komitet fun di yidn in Poyln*, Central Committee of Jews in Poland] in support of new Jewish life. It was the first and last time for Zionist and communist organizations in Argentina to jointly remember the Warsaw Ghetto Uprising.

The Formation of Two Memorial Blocs, 1949–1952

Things changed in 1949. Building upon the symbolism of the large event of 1948, the sixth anniversary of the Uprising saw one communist event. While Zionist commemoration was limited to a mere statement of remembrance by the DAIA,[58] the SFRWVA organized a memorial event with representatives from the state of Israel and from the Polish embassy.[59] From now on, SFRWVA events would be supported by the YKUF-affiliated פֿעדעראַציע פֿון לאַנדסמאַנשאַפֿטן [*Federatsye fun landsmanshaftn*, Federation of *landsmanshaftn*, FL][60] – a 1945-founded communist federation of Polish-Jewish *landsmanshaftn* competing for membership with the Zionist CUPJA in Buenos Aires.[61] A year later, both Zionists and communists held parallel events on the same date: organized by the YKUF-affiliated institutions, on the one hand;

heterogeneous Soviet motivations for this support, see Lotersztain 2014, 128.

55 For enthusiastic reporting about the fighting in YKUF daily דער וועג [*Der veg*, The Path], see Lotersztain 2014, 138.

56 Anonymous 1948, 4.

57 Ibid.

58 Anonymous 1949b, 4; Anonymous 1949c, not paginated.

59 Anonymous 1949a, 4.

60 Ibid.; on FL, see Zonabend 1952, 2.

61 Rollansky 1988b, 70f.

and the CUPJA in cooperation with the new more pronouncedly anti-communist Zionist נאַציאָנאַל־ראַט פֿון די פֿאַרבאַנדן [*Natsyonal-rat fun di farbandn*, National Council of Former Residents' Societies, NCFRS], on the other.[62] FL's involvement in the former and the new Zionist formation in the latter is indicative of the incipient formation of two memorial blocs resulting from the political divisions that were beginning to run more deeply through the Jewish immigrant associations since late 1948.

Political tensions within Buenos Aires' Jewish community had been mounting in the previous two years in the wake of growing antisemitism in the Soviet Union. By the end of 1948 the ייִדישער אַנטיפֿאַשיסטישער קאָמיטעט [*Yidisher antifashistisher komitet*, Jewish Antifascist Committee; JAFC] had been dissolved and its leading officials arrested, and all Yiddish publishing houses and cultural institutions in the Soviet Union had been closed. From then on, an attempted destruction of Yiddish culture in the USSR included the systematic arrest of hundreds of Jewish cultural figures, who were sent to forced labor camps on charges of 'bourgeois nationalism' and treason against the Soviet Union. The Stalinist anti-Jewish purges were accompanied by antisemitic campaigns against 'rootless cosmopolitanism' and climaxed in the arrest and later execution of famed Jewish writers, among them Itsik Fefer (1900–1952), Dovid Bergelson (1884–1952), Leyb Kvitko (1890–1952) and Perets Markish (1895–1952), all of whom were committed communists.[63] Though the real extent of the purges would only come to light in 1956, Jewish communities worldwide, including the Argentine Zionist faction, began protesting the apparent attack on Soviet Jewish culture as early as 1948/9.

Buenos Aires YKUF publications emphatically denied any trace of antisemitism in the USSR, even though many of the writers arrested had until then been regular contributors to its press in Buenos Aires and suddenly disappeared from its pages, with no explanation from the editors.[64] At the same time, YKUF journalists focused their attacks on Zionism as a 'clerical and reactionary' ideology, deemed dissociated from the 'Jewish masses' settled in the state of Israel (including many relatives of Argentine YKUF activists)

62 Anonymous 1950a, 4. 'National' being a cipher for its Zionist affiliation, NCFRS was created with the aim of keeping 'foreign influences' (referring to communists) away from the *landsmanshaftn*, see Anonymous, undated, [478–479]. On the CUPJA, see also Mitelberg 1953/1954, 418.

63 Gitelman 1988, 233–236; Estraikh 2018; [Chorley-]Schulz 2021.

64 Lotersztain 2014, 142–143.

who represented the 'democratic and progressive' Israel.[65] Brushing off the existence of antisemitism in the socialist bloc in that way, they further reduced Jewish emigration from Eastern Europe to the state of Israel to Zionist brainwashing.[66] Zionist publications, for their part, denounced the heavy restrictions that Eastern European countries imposed on emigration, most aggressively implemented by the USSR itself. These political tensions were on clear display at the parallel commemorative events on 19 April 1950. The YKUF promoted its gathering as a 'central event' and reaffirmed its support for the state of Israel with singing of the *Ha-tiqwāh*,[67] but Turkow stressed the need to help 40,000 Jews who wanted to emigrate from Poland to Israel at the Zionist event.[68]

The parallel events, repeated on 19 April 1951, marked the consolidation of the two separate memorial blocs. To the YKUF, Zionist commemorations of the Uprising increasingly became "una simple manifestación de dolor y contrición" [a simple manifestation of grief and contrition].[69] Opposing this form of 'passive' remembrance as apolitical, they turned that year's event into a political protest against the controversial rearmament of the Federal Republic of Germany alongside progressive voices worldwide. YKUF speeches pointed to the initiative of the Ghetto fighters to form an Antifascist bloc uniting Jews and non-Jews to fight Nazism collectively.[70] To the YKUF, this would be the appropriate response also now when world peace was once again under threat. There was an urgent need for unity in the pursuit of self-defense.[71]

That year, the DAIA renewed its sponsorship of the Zionist ceremonies for the first time since 1948. "Así la recordación tendrá mayor unidad y realce,

65 Lotersztain 2014, 146.

66 Ibid., 146, 150.

67 Anonymous 1950b, 6.

68 Ibid.

69 Anonymous 1951a, back cover.

70 Anonymous 1951b, back cover. The Antifascist bloc was formed in the Warsaw Ghetto in March 1942 by Jewish activists of the Polska Partia Robotnicza [Polish Workers' Party, PPR, a recreation of the Polish Communist Party under Nazi occupation], and members of the Left Poalei Zion, with the aim of joining forces in the war against Fascism. It numbered as many as 500 fighters but was disbanded in June 1942 following the arrest of a number of PPR activists (Gutman 1982, 170–176). However, it was instrumental in the formation of the ŻOB, see Gutman 1982, 175; Dreifuss 2017, 26.

71 YKUF newspapers constantly warned of the threat to world peace posed by German rearmament and preached the possibility of 'new Majdaneks' (Lotersztain 2014, 215).

como expresión unánime de la colectividad judía del país, por intermedio de su entidad representativa" [In this way, the remembrance will have greater unity and prominence, as a unanimous expression of the Jewish community of the country, through its representative body].[72] By demarcating the 'official' position of the Argentine Jewish community, it encouraged other institutions to take sides and weaken the YKUF in this way.[73] The strategy proved successful, as evinced by the extensive list of speakers representing many institutions.[74] Moreover, a crucial figure appeared for the first time at the 1951 Zionist ceremony: Amram Blum, a Sephardic rabbi of Hungarian origin with close ties to the Peronist government. In addition to presiding over the Rabbinical Court of the Buenos Aires Jewish community, Blum had been appointed by Perón as an adviser on religious matters in 1948.[75] In the face of the Cold War intra-communal confrontation, Blum's presence suggests the implicit alignment of Peronism with the Zionist sectors of the Jewish community and, vice versa, a savvy expression of Zionist loyalty to the government without involving non-Jewish officials, thus staying clear of Argentine political disputes.[76]

Coinciding with the tightening diplomatic and commercial relations between the state of Israel and Argentina,[77] the Zionist bloc attracted more sectors of the Argentine Jewish community each year as it increasingly 'Israelized' its commemorations of the Warsaw Ghetto Uprising. From 1952 onwards, it conformed to Israel's new policies of memory regarding the adoption of the Hebrew date of the 27 Nisan as יום השואה ומרד הגטאות [*yōm ha-šǒ'ah u-mered ha-gěṭā'ōt*, Holocaust and Heroism Remembrance Day][78] and official Israeli government figures were present at all Zionist events from 1951 until the end of the period of

72 Anonymous 1951f, 7. Closer to the date of the ceremony, the DAIA demanded Jewish institutions in Buenos Aires and neighboring towns to refrain from holding similar ceremonies before or on that date (Anonymous 1952a, 5).

73 Anonymous 1951c, 4.

74 Ibid.

75 On Blum, see Rein 2015, 129–132.

76 The DAIA's general policy towards the Peronist government was to maintain cordial ties without compromising its autonomy. See Bell 2002.

77 Rein 2001, 101–138.

78 Anonymous 1952a, 5. Dates of Zionist events 22 April (1952), 12 April (1953), 20 April (1954), 19 April (1955) and 8 April (1956)) coincided with the 27 Nisan or its eve in the Hebrew calendar. On the adoption of this date of remembrance by the Israeli Knesset in 1951, see Young 1993, 269–271.

study. All artistic and liturgical components were omitted from the 1952 Zionist commemoration (with the exception of collectively singing *Ha-tiqwāh*),[79] perhaps to spotlight the ideological message of multiple speakers. The main speaker was Israel's new minister to Argentina and popular figure in Buenos Aires Zionist circles, Jacob Tsur (1906–1990).[80] Large crowds had greeted him on the day of his arrival, waving the Argentine and Israeli flags, and accompanied him to the Casa Rosada [Pink House], office of the president of Argentina, where Tsur saluted the crowd with Perón after the protocol ceremony.[81]

Tsur's 1952 speech presented the Ghetto Uprising as אַ קאַמף פֿון עלנטסטע און פֿאַרלאָזטע [a struggle of the lonely and abandoned], whom no one had helped, and with Biblical allusions he reprimanded that no people in the world had the right to say ידינו לא שפכו את הדם הזה [our hands did not shed this blood].[82] Moreover, he argued that Jews in Palestine were the only group that had tried to help the fighters, overemphasizing the episode of thirty young Jewish volunteers from Palestine who were parachuted into Nazi-occupied territories between March and September 1944 – "a mission of national, Zionist reawakening, to save the souls of the remnant of the Jewish people, rather than a mission to save [...] lives," according to Israeli historian Tom Segev – that has gained great symbolic importance within Zionist mythology. Tsur's account necessarily omitted the experience of unity of political groups in the Ghetto fighting, so celebrated by the YKUF,[83] or the immense impact of the Soviet victory in Stalingrad on the ghetto fighters for that matter.

Despite a DAIA mandate not to hold similar ceremonies, YKUF organized its own commemoration in 1952, which involved more than twenty *landsmanshaftn*[84] and peaceful coexistence within the Jewish community was undone for good.

A few months later, in July 1952, rumors reached Buenos Aires about a

79 Anonymous 1952c, 4.

80 For budgetary reasons, Israel and Argentina established diplomatic relations through representatives holding the rank of ministers, instead of ambassadors (Rein 2001, 106, n. 17). Tsur had been appointed minister in 1949, although in practice he held the post of Israel ambassador to Argentina. In turn, Pablo Manguel was the first Argentinean minister in Tel Aviv.

81 Rein 2001, 104.

82 Anonymous 1952c, 4. He referenced Deuteronomy 21:7. This had become a Zionist refrain. Mark Turkow again lashed out at „די פֿעלשערס פֿון געשיכטע" [the falsifiers of history], all those who claimed that the fighters had received outside help.

83 Segev 1993, 86–88, citation on 87.

84 Anonymous 1952b, 4.

trial in the Soviet Union of twenty-five prominent Jewish cultural figures, including several members of the JAFC.[85] Similarly, news of the November 1952 Slánský trial in Prague reached Argentina, in which eleven well-known (mostly non-Jewish) communist leaders were tried as 'apprentices of the Zionist movement' and sympathizers of Trotsky and Tito (with whom Stalin had severed ties in 1948). Eight of them were sentenced to death and three to life imprisonment.[86] The DAIA and its associated groups strongly condemned the trials as antisemitic, while the YKUF defended the Soviet verdict against 'spies and traitors.' YKUF-affiliated entities were subsequently excluded from the two central Argentine Jewish institutions, the Asociación Mutual Israelita Argentina [Israelite Argentine Mutual Association, former Jewish burial society, AMIA], and the DAIA. Following an extraordinary assembly convened by the DAIA on 4 December 1952, delegates from more than seventy institutions agreed by majority vote on a declaration protesting the Prague Trial as fabricated slander. A DAIA communiqué disseminated in the Yiddish press demanded from every Jewish institution to adhere to the assembly's resolution as a way of separating themselves from the 'elements' that 'break the unity' of the Jewish people by serving foreign interests and thereby denigrate Argentine Judaism. It concluded that only those institutions that adhered to the Declaration of 4 December could belong to the DAIA. The YKUF refused to comply, accusing the DAIA of 'unpatriotic servility' and of being in the service of 'Yankee imperialism' in turn.[87]

From Division to Zionist Monopoly, 1953–1955

Formally, the DAIA broke all ties from the YKUF in January 1953. Despite vigorous protest, YKUF was incapable of reversing what they described as *kheyrem* [excommunication] resulting in the withdrawal of 40 percent of DAIA subsidies for five YKUF schools with a total of 1,500 pupils.[88] YKUF's continued loyalty to the Soviet Union despite news about the antisemitic campaign that would later become known as the 'doctors' plot' – nine Soviet

85 Estraikh 2018, Rubenstein and Naumov 2001.

86 Gitelman 1988, 238.

87 Lotersztain 2014, 178–180.

88 Despite the difficulties, the YKUF schools continued their activities autonomously through cooperative actions, see Visacovsky 2015, 110.

doctors with Jewish names had been arrested on charges of espionage and terrorism (1951–1953) – did not help their case.[89]

President Perón stepped in and demonstrated forceful support for the central institutions of the Jewish community. At January meeting with Zionist leaders, he defined the events in socialist countries antisemitic, declared no tolerance for anti-Jewish discrimination in Argentina, and offered aid to 'threatened' Jews to emigrate to the state of Israel or other countries of the 'free world.'[90] Welcomed by the Zionists, Perón's gesture flew in the face of YKUF, all the more so since they had begun to show support for Perón's political movement Justicialismo since the onset of his second term in June 1952 following short-lived shift of the Partido Comunista Argentino [Argentine Communist Party, PCA].[91] Faced with the failure of this attempted alliance, they started to systematically denounce the government's imprisonment of a large number of communists in the first months of 1953.[92] In the wake of Eva Perón's death in July 1952, the government had taken a more authoritarian, anti-communist course implementing harsher 'Peronization' of public administration and education. On 15 April 1953, a terrorist attack shook a public rally at Plaza de Mayo, killing seven and injuring 95. Perón exhorted the crowd to take reprisals unleashing a period of persecution of dissidents and opponents.[93] These were the circumstances in which the tenth anniversary of the Warsaw Ghetto Uprising approached.

The Zionist and YKUF blocs organized events within a week of each other. The Zionist ceremony had the dual purpose of commemorating the martyrs of the Ghetto and the fighters for the state of Israel.[94] Minister Jacob Tsur drew on a bidirectional Zionist narrative of the Uprising already evoked in a former ceremony: while the Ghetto fighters were an example and source of inspiration for the young fighters in the state of Israel on how to defend Jewish honor and virtue, the Ghetto fighters themselves drew (so Tsur claimed) strength to carry out the rebellion from the words of encouragement they had received from the Zionist movement in Palestine.[95]

89 Gitelman 1988, 238–139; Ettinger 1995.

90 Lotersztain 2014, 183–185.

91 Ibid., 186–190; Jáuregui 2012.

92 Lotersztain 2014, 211.

93 Romero 2003, 126–128.

94 Anonymous 1953a, 5–6.

95 Ibid., 5; Anonymous 1953b, 5–6. Tsur also mentioned the persecution of Soviet Jews and described those who defended Soviet accusations as 'Jewish slaves.'

A week later, at the same location, the YKUF ceremony took place without speeches due to "causas imprevistas" [unforeseen circumstances].[96] A 1939 decree of Executive Power restricted use of foreign languages in public meetings as a means to prevent 'Nazi penetration' into Argentina.[97] Even though information concerning the persistence of this measure during Perón's reign is lacking, the DAIA had become the only legitimate actor to request permits from the authorities regarding the use of Yiddish in public events. This might suggest that after the exclusion of the YKUF from the DAIA, the latter might have instigated this impediment via the authorities, or simply refused to cooperate in obtaining permission. The ceremony was limited to the coordinator's comments and performances by artists of the ייִדישער פֿאָלקס־טעאַטער [*Yidisher folks-teater*, Jewish Popular Theater, known in Argentina as YIFT].[98] To the YKUF, the event was a political act with concrete relevance for the present – an

> acto de desagravio a la memoria de nuestros guerrilleros (mancillada una semana antes, en la misma sala, por quienes se han cubierto con la ignominiosa túnica de revisionistas históricos al servicio de la reacción enlodando la memoria de nuestros más auténticos héroes)…[99]
>
> atonement for the memory of our guerrilla fighters (sullied a week earlier, in the same room, by those who have covered themselves with the ignominious tunic of historical revisionists in the service of reaction, tarnishing the memory of our most authentic heroes)…

The coordinator of the ceremony and only speaker described the ghetto fighters as revolutionaries and emphasized the

> ayuda moral que significó para los combatientes la batalla de Stalingrado, cuya victoria significó el fin del poderío nazi, y el agradecimiento a quienes durante la pasada guerra salvaron de las garras nazistas a millones de judíos.
>
> moral support that the battle of Stalingrad meant for the fighters, whose victory meant the end of Nazi power, and the gratitude to those who during the last war saved millions of Jews from the Nazis' clutches.[100]

96 Anonymous 1953e, back cover.
97 Lvovich 2003, 458, 531, 534.
98 Ansaldo 2016.
99 Anonymous 1953e, back cover.
100 Ibid.

The discursive strategy resembled that of the Zionist bloc but they communicated antipodal messages: whereas Zionists naturally stressed the Jewish internal *national* unity between the ghetto fighters and Jewish settlers in Palestine, the YKUF highlighted the *internationalist* unity of the working-class and oppressed peoples and identified the source of inspiration in the Soviet victory in Stalingrad. This echoed the Soviet narrative of the Uprising, usually depicted as "an episode, even if a momentous one, in the general Soviet-led struggle against Hitlerism."[101]

The YKUF also rejected Turkow's initiative to name the AMIA assembly hall after the chairman of the *Judenrat* [Jewish Council] of the Warsaw Ghetto, Adam Czerniaków (1880–1942). Honoring him like that was an unacceptable absurdity for YKUF militants, who used the term '*Judenrat*' as a synonym for 'traitor.'[102] They read Czerniaków's suicide on 23 July 1942, a day after the first mass extermination of Jews from the Warsaw Ghetto to Treblinka began, as making "más aún en claro su sucia tarea de entregar miles y miles de judíos a los verdugos nazis" [his dirty work of handing over thousands and thousands of Jews to Nazi executioners even clearer].[103] Finally, the 1953 YKUF commemoration was a protest against negotiations with West Germany towards the payment of compensation in which the DAIA, as a member of the 1951-founded Conference on Jewish Material Claims Against Germany, had taken an active part as the only Latin American representative.[104] The YKUF weekly concluded that their event was held as much in memory of the Ghetto Uprising as it was אַ ווירדיקן ענטפֿער די מאַרק טורקאָווס און אַנדערע, וועלכע האָבן מיט זייער אַקט פֿאַראומווירדיקט דעם אָנדענק פֿון די געטאָ־קעמפֿער [an

[101] Estraikh 2021, 11. On *khurbn* memory "in the shadow of antifascism" in socialist countries and the Soviet Union, see Bohus, Hallama and Stach 2022.

[102] For example, a well-known YKUF activist wrote: "hay corazones judíos que sólo guardan un odio patológico hacia los que salvaron a la humanidad del azote hitleriano. En esos corazones no hay cabida para el odio a los que aniquilaron a seis millones de vidas judías. Los Judenrats inspiran los sentimientos de esos corazones" [there are Jewish hearts that harbor only a pathological hatred for those who saved humanity from the Hitlerian scourge. There is no room in those hearts for hatred of those who annihilated six million Jewish lives. The *Judenräte* inspire the feelings of those hearts] (Anonymous 1953c, 14).

[103] Anonymous 1953e, back cover.

[104] Founded on the initiative of the Jewish Agency of Israel, the Conference on Jewish Material Claims Against Germany (and known as the Claims Conference) partnered with Israel and signed an agreement on compensation and restitution to Jewish victims of Nazi persecution and their heirs with the Federal Republic of Germany in September 1952 in Luxembourg. On the Claims Conference, see Zweig 2001. Further, see Anonymous 1951d, 1f; Anonymous 1951e, 1.

effective response to the Mark Turkows and others, who by their acts desecrated the memory of the Ghetto fighters].[105]

By mid-1953, in the wake of the escalating anti-communist repression during Perón's second term, YKUF faced a crisis that was indeed existential. The police banned the YKUF's fifth congress and closed the premises of its weekly publication טריבונע [*Tribune*].[106] At the end of 1953, the regime shut the YIFT theater by a municipal decree; it remained closed until Perón's fall in 1955. In 1954 and in 1955, its Warsaw Ghetto Uprising memorial event was banned by the Dirección de Espectáculos Públicos de la Municipalidad [Public Entertainment Division of the Municipality].[107] That same year saw a succession of arrests of communist activists with a suspiciously high proportion of Jewish surnames. Throughout 1953/54, *Tribune* denounced the torture of Jewish students in prisons[108] and consistently pointed to their Zionist counterparts – the resurrected *'Judenrat'*, i.e., the DAIA and its allies – complicity with 'Perón's dictatorship,' where, according to them, antisemitism was merely disguised as anti-communism.[109] In 1955, *Tribune*, under increasing threat of being discontinued,[110] warned of the outbreak of an atomic war and a reinvigorated West German *Bundeswehr*.[111]

With the YKUF increasingly marginalized, the Zionist bloc finally achieved a monopoly on organizing 'unique' and 'central' events to commemorate the Warsaw Ghetto Uprising in 1954 and 1955 with the government's implicit approval. Moreover, the 1955 ceremony included the participation of representatives of a Peronist Jewish body, the Organización Israelita Argentina [Argentine Israelite Organization, OIA].[112] One of the main speakers

105 Anonymous 1953d, 1.

106 Since most of the communist press organs had either disappeared or were operating underground, *Tribune* became almost the only party publication denouncing repression; when distribution through mail was banned, a group of volunteers delivered it by hand (Lotersztain 2014, 213).

107 Anonymous 1954a, 1, 11. Many collectives of Slavic origin had been banned since 1949 because of their real or suspected communist orientation; those remaining were controlled by the state and had to apply for permits to organize public events, which were often not granted (Zourek 2014, 48).

108 Lotersztain 2014, 216.

109 Ibid., 213; Visacovsky 2015, 120–121.

110 Lotersztain 2014, 217.

111 Anonymous 1955a, 10.

112 Anonymous 1955b, 4. The OIA was established in 1947 with government support. Although for a period of time the OIA tried to compete with the DAIA for the representation of the Jewish community, the relationship between the two became cordial and cooperative. On the creation

at the Zionist ceremony those years was Arieh Kubovy (1896–1966), Tsur's replacement as Israel's minister in Buenos Aires since September 1953, who maintained good relations with Perón's government.[113] Criticizing those who looked for 'anti-Fascist fighters' alone,[114] Kubovy inaugurated his participation in the events by urging the audience to draw a personal lesson from the European Jewish catastrophe and concluded with a vision of Zionist 'redemption':

> Cada judío debe preguntarse: ¿Por qué quedé yo con vida? ¿Qué tengo yo de mejor que aquellos otros que murieron? Cada judío debe hacer su examen de conciencia. Por medio del dolor, del sufrimiento, de la muerte, nos vemos purificados. Pero debemos superarnos y ser merecedores de asistir a la etapa de la redención.[115]
>
> Every Jew must ask himself, 'Why did I stay alive? What is better about me than those who died?' Every Jew must examine his conscience. Through pain, through suffering, through death, we are purified. But we must rise above ourselves and be worthy of witnessing the moment of redemption.

Following the Zionist memorial event in honor of the Warsaw Ghetto Uprising in 1955, Argentina was shook by violent upheaval with antisemitic undertones[116] culminating in the so-called Revolución Libertadora [Liberating Revolution] – a military coup that terminated the second presidential term of Juan Perón on 16 September 1955.[117] It transformed the memorial landscape for Jewish memory entrepreneurs as well. Further research on commemorations up until 1958 are necessary to assess the impact of the 'Revo-

and development of the OIA, see Rein 2001, 87–96; Bell 2002. On the support to Perón by certain sectors of Argentine Jewry, see Rein 2015.

113 Rein 2001, 118.

114 Anonymous 1954c, 4.

115 Anonymous 1954b, 11.

116 Rein 2001, 178f. Pamphlets circulated pointing to Jews and Freemasons close to Perón as being responsible for the separation of Church and State. On Perón's confrontation with clerical forces over this goal, see Caimari 2010.

117 Galván and Osuna 2018, 13. Fear of possible antisemitic attacks spread among the Buenos Aires Jewish community. Some opponents identified Jews with the government for various reasons: rabbi Amram Blum's ties to Perón, a recent DAIA anthology of Perón's speeches, Perón's many gestures towards non-Catholic religions. However, the sustained dialogue of Jewish leaders with Catholic and nationalist circles helped reduce antisemitic propaganda, and in the end there were no attacks on Jews, see Rein 2001, 181.

lución Libertadora' on the continuing struggles for memory among Jews of Buenos Aires. Outside the frame of this chapter, a few preliminary findings must suffice.

For the YKUF, the coup d'état meant a however limited return of freedom with *Tribune* resuming a campaign to denounce all those non-YKUF community leaders who had 'collaborated' with the Peronist power.[118] In 1956, under the dictatorship of the 'Revolución Libertadora,' its commemorative event took place for the first time after years of persecution delivering messages of pacifism, criticism of the 'jeremistas' (the proponents of 'excommunication', *'jerem'* being a Spanish transcription of *kheyrem*) and a call for unity between all Argentine Jewish political parties – but achieving this was becoming increasingly improbable by the day.[119] International developments added to the hostility between the blocs. The increasing tensions in the Middle East and concerning the Soviet weapon supply to Egypt starting in September 1955 threw the YKUF leadership into turmoil and caused outrage in most of the Argentine Jewish communities, including within YKUF's own ranks.[120] And when in 1956 the rumors about the murder of Soviet Yiddish writers were finally confirmed as true by the Warsaw Yiddish newspaper פֿאָלקס־שטימע [*Folks-shtime*, People's Voice] following the leaking of Nikita Khrushchev's Secret Speech to the 20th Congress of the Communist Party of the Soviet Union, YKUF, now in ideological crisis, had to reposition itself and reconsider its dogmatic pro-Soviet stance, but their anti-Zionist stance did not waver.[121] The Zionist faction of Argentine Jewry for its part took this revelation as a vindication of their beliefs and ideological program and made sure to comment on it also during its Warsaw Ghetto Uprising memorial event.[122]

Conclusions

The Warsaw Ghetto Uprising had an indelible impact on the postwar Jewish world, including Argentine Jewry which was transnationally linked to Eastern Europe but experienced the war and *khurbn* from afar. In this chapter,

118 Lotersztain 2014, 221–224.
119 Anonymous 1956c, back cover.
120 Lotersztain 2014, 254–258.
121 Anonymous 1956b, 10.
122 Ibid.

I have traced more than a decade of institutional remembrance ceremonies as expressions of communal politics among Yiddish-speaking Jews in Buenos Aires and shown their interdependence on developments both in international Cold War theater and Argentina itself. While YKUF struggled to keep a straight face in light of the incoming news of anti-Jewish purges in the socialist bloc, the Zionist faction allied itself to Perón's anti-communist regime.

The ideologically informed and increasingly irreconciliable readings of the Ghetto Uprising point to the nexus between *khurbn* memory and contemporary geopolitics: for memory entrepreneurs on both sides, it was clear that valuable lessons could be drawn from the events remembered for the sake of the unstable present they faced.

Two issues – contemporary socialist Poland and the state of Israel – became thorny and incompatible because of subsequent geopolitical events. A stand needed to be taken and answers to this dilemma could be found in the Warsaw Ghetto Uprising. Zionists, Mark Turkow and Jacob Tsur first among them, constructed a narrative that equalized the struggle in the Ghetto and the Jewish struggle for the 'liberation' of the 'Land of Israel' and drew causal links between the two: Ghetto fighting had been made possible by the sustained moral support of the Jews of Palestine, and the Jewish fighters in Palestine had drawn inspiration and courage from the Ghetto fighters. The YKUF constructed a narrative in which every Jewish survivor, just like Europe itself, owed their life and freedom to the antifascist fight spearheaded by the Soviet Union. This was precisely "the postwar communist-antifascist interpretational framework," in which "the victory of the Red Army over Nazi Germany was interpreted not only as a military success but as a moral and ideological victory over fascism and capitalism."[123] Accordingly, the YKUF highlighted exactly the antifascist current of the Ghetto Uprising. They concluded that the only way to defeat fascism and secure a Jewish future was to unite all sections of the community with the 'free peoples' (of socialist Republics). Not interested in collecting actual historical evidence but advancing their own political agendas, both narratives contributed to the global mythologizing of the Warsaw Ghetto Uprising, deplored by survivor scholar Joseph Wulf as early as 1949.

[123] Bohus, Hallama and Stach 2022, 3. As argued by the authors, such framework "was not necessarily in competition with Holocaust remembrance" (Ibid., 17).

Archival Sources

Anonymous, undated אַנאָנים: צענטראַל־פֿאַרבאַנד פֿון פּוילישע ייִדן אין אַרגענטינע מיט אָנגעשלאָסענע לאַנדסמאַנשאַפֿטן 30. In: Archivo Histórico de la Fundación IWO, Colección Residentes, Box 22, Digitized, [478–479].

Bibliography

Albuquerque Fuschini, German, 2011: *La trinchera letrada. Intelectuales latinoamericanos y Guerra Fría*. Santiago de Chile: Ariadna.

Anonymous, 1945 אַנאָנים: דער אימפּאָזאַנטער טרויער־אַקט אין אָנדענק פֿון אויפֿשטאַנד אין וואַרשעווער געטאָ. אין: **די פּרעסע** (בוענאָס־אײַרעס), 18 אַפּריל: 4.

Anonymous, 1946 אַנאָנים: רירנדער דערמאָנונגס־אַקט פֿאַר די העלדישע קעמפֿער פֿון וואַרשעווער געטאָ. אין: **די פּרעסע** (בוענאָס־אײַרעס), 19 אַפּריל: 4.

Anonymous, 1947a אַנאָנים: אימפּאָזאַנטער דערמאָנונגס־אַקט פֿון וואַרשעווער לאַנדסלײַט־פֿאַריין. אין: **די פּרעסע** (בוענאָס־אײַרעס), 18 אַפּריל: 4.

Anonymous, 1947b אַנאָנים: אַ גראַנדיעזער און אימפּאָזאַנטער דערמאָנונגס־אַקט אינעם פֿערטן יאָרטאָג פֿונעם אויפֿשטאַנד אין וואַרשעווער געטאָ. אין: **די פּרעסע** (בוענאָס־אײַרעס), 21 אַפּריל: 4.

Anonymous, 1948b אַנאָנים: טויזנטער ייִדן זײַנען נעכטן בײַגעווען אויפֿן מאַסן־אַקט אין לונאַ־פּאַרק. אין: **די פּרעסע** (בוענאָס־אײַרעס), 19 אַפּריל: 4.

Anonymous, 1949a אַנאָנים: דער גרויסער דערמאָנונגס־אַקט צום 6טן יאָרטאָג פֿון אויפֿשטאַנד אין וואַרשעווער געטאָ. אין: **די פּרעסע** (בוענאָס־אײַרעס), 19 אַפּריל: 4.

Anonymous, 1949b אַנאָנים: די פֿאַרטרעטערשאַפֿט פֿון אַרגענטיניש־ייִדישע אינסטיטוציעס, דאַיאַ׳ דערמאָנט דעם זעקסטן אַניווערסאַר פֿון העראָיִשן אויפֿשטאַנד אין וואַרשעווער געטאָ. אין: **די פּרעסע** (בוענאָס־אײַרעס), 19 אַפּריל: 4.

Anonymous, 1949c: La resistencia del ghetto de Varsovia recuerda la DAIA. In: *Mundo Israelita* (Buenos Aires), 23 April 1949, unpaged.

Anonymous, 1950a אַנאָנים: הײַנט די טרויער־אַקטן צום 7טן יאָרטאָג פֿון אויפֿשטאַנד אין וואַרשעווער געטאָ. אין: **די פּרעסע** (בוענאָס־אײַרעס), 19 אַפּריל: 4.

Anonymous, 1950b אַנאָנים: די טרויער־אַקטן צום זיבעטן יאָרטאָג פֿונעם אויפֿשטאַנד אין וואַרשעווער געטאָ. אין: **די פּרעסע** (בוענאָס־אײַרעס), 21 אַפּריל: 6.

Anonymous, 1951a: UNIDAD: En homenaje de los héroes y por nuestra existencia. In: *Haynt* (Buenos Aires), 19 April, back cover.

Anonymous, 1951b: Dignamente fueron honrados los héroes del ghetto. In: *Haynt* (Buenos Aires), 20 April, back cover.

Anonymous, 1951c אַנאָנים: בוענאָס־אײַרעס האָט ווירדיק באַערט דעם אָנדענק פֿון אויפֿשטאַנד אין וואַרשעווער געטאָ. אין: **די פּרעסע** (בוענאָס־אײַרעס), 20 אַפּריל: 4.

Anonymous, 1951d: Apoya la DAIA el pedido de Israel al gobierno alemán sobre reparaciones. In: *D.A.I.A. Boletín de Información* 3 (12), May: 1–2.

Anonymous, 1951e: Participará la DAIA en la conferencia judía sobre Alemania a realizarse en Nueva York. In: *D.A.I.A. Boletín de Información* 3 (15), September: 1.

Anonymous, 1951f: Recordación del levantamiento del ghetto de Varsovia. In: *D.A.I.A. Boletín de Información*, 3 (16), December: 7.

Anonymous, 1952a: Con un acto único conmemorará la colectividad el 9° aniversario del levantamiento del ghetto de Varsovia, In: *Mundo Israelita* (Buenos Aires), 5 April : 5.

Anonymous, 1952b אַנאָנים: פֿעדעראַציע פֿון ייִדישע לאַנדסלײַט־פֿאַריינען. אין: **די פּרעסע** (בוענאָס־אײַרעס), 19 אַפּריל: 4.

Anonymous, 1952c אַנאָנים: פֿײַערלעך דערמאָנט דעם אויפֿשטאַנד אין וואַרשעווער געטאָ. אין: **די פּרעסע** (בוענאָס־אײַרעס), 24 אַפּריל: 4.

Anonymous, 1953a אַנאָנים: אונדזער ייִשובֿ האָט ווירדיק באַערט די העלדן פֿון וואַרשעווער געטאָ. אין: **די פּרעסע** (בוענאָס־אײַרעס), 14 אַפּריל: 5–6.

Anonymous, 1953b אַנאָנים: רעדע פֿון יעקבֿ צור, מיניסטער פֿון ישׂראל. אין: **די פּרעסע** (בוענאָס־אײַרעס), 14 אַפּריל: 5–6.

Anonymous, 1953c: El sionismo reaccionario por el sendero del Judenrat. In: *Tribune* (Buenos Aires), 16 April: 14.

Anonymous, 1953d אַנאָנים: אַן אימפּאָזאַנטע מאַניפֿעסטאַציע פֿון ייִדישער באַוווּסטזיניקער אייניקייט. אין: **טריבונע** (בוענאָס־אײַרעס), 23 אַפּריל: 1.

Anonymous, 1953e: El Broadway resultó pequeño. In: *Tribune* (Buenos Aires), 23 April, back cover.

Anonymous, 1954a: Dos prohibiciones. In: *Tribune* (Buenos Aires), 22 April: 1, 11.

Anonymous, 1954b: En memoria de los mártires del Ghetto de Varsovia, In: *D.A.I.A. Boletín de Información* 5 (31), May-June: 10–11.

Anonymous, 1954c אַנאָנים: מיר דאַרפֿן אַראָפּנעמען אַ מוסר־השׂכּל פֿון דער טראַגעדיע מיטן פּוילישן ייִדנטום. אין: **די פּרעסע** (בוענאָס־אײַרעס), 2 מאַי: 4.

Anonymous, 1955a: Honrar dignamente la memoria de los héroes del ghetto de Varsovia. In: *Tribune* (Buenos Aires), 14 April: 10.

Anonymous, 1955b אַנאָנים: מיט ייִראת־הכּבֿוד באַערט דעם אָנדענק פֿון די זעקס מיליאָן קדושים. אין: **די פּרעסע** (בוענאָס־אײַרעס), 21 אַפּריל: 4.

Anonymous, 1955c אַנאָנים: דער לאַנדסלײַט־פֿאַריין פֿון וואַרשע און אומגעגנט אין אַרגענטינע. אין: פּיניע קאַץ א״אַ, רעד., **פּנקס וואַרשע.** בוענאָס־אײַרעס: לאַנדסלײַט־פֿאַריין פֿון וואַרשע און אומגעגנט אין אַרגענטינע בײַ דער מיטאַרבעט פֿון אַרגענטינער איקוף.

Anonymous, 1956a אַנאָנים: אונדזער ייִשובֿ האָט מיט ייִראת־הכּבֿוד דערמאָנט די גיבורים און קדושים פֿון די געטאָס און קאָנצענטראַציע־לאַגערן. אין: **די פּרעסע** (בוענאָס־אײַרעס), 10 אַפּריל: 10.

Anonymous, 1956b: Esquirlas. In: *Tribune* (Buenos Aires), April 13: 10.

Anonymous, 1956c: Dignamente fue recordada la memoria de los héroes del ghetto. In: *Tribune* (Buenos Aires), 27 April, back cover.

Ansaldo, Paula, 2016: El teatro como escuela para adultos. Un recorrido por la historia del IFT en su tránsito del ídish al español (1932–1957). In: Skura, Susana and Silvia Glocer, eds., *Teatro ídish argentino (1930–1950)*. Buenos

Aires: Editorial de la Facultad de Filosofía y Letras de la Universidad de Buenos Aires, 143–160.

Avni, Haim, 1983: *Argentina y la historia de la inmigración judía 1810–1950*. Buenos Aires: Editorial Universitaria Magnes.

Baskind. Samantha, 2019: 'Propaganda in the Best and Purest Sense of the Word': Early Representations of the Warsaw Ghetto in American Culture. In: *American Jewish History* 103 (2): 125–145.

Bauer, Yehuda, 2002: *Rethinking the Holocaust*. New Haven, Conn.: Yale University Press.

Bell, Lawrence, 2002: *The Jews and Perón: Communal Politics and National Identity in Peronist Argentina, 1946–1955*. PhD dissertation, unpublished. Columbus, Ohio: The Ohio State University.

Bohus, Kata, Peter Hallama and Stephan Stach, eds., 2022: *Growing in the Shadow of Antifascism: Remembering the Holocaust in State-Socialist Eastern Europe*. Budapest a.o.: Central European University Press.

Caimari, Lila, 2010: *Perón y la Iglesia Católica. Religión, Estado y sociedad en la Argentina (1943–1955)*. Buenos Aires: Emecé.

Calandra, Benedetta and Marina Franco, eds., 2012: *La guerra fría cultural en América Latina: Desafíos y límites para una nueva mirada de las relaciones interamericanas*. Buenos Aires: Biblos.

Chinski, Malena, 2011: Un catálogo en memoria del judaísmo polaco. La colección *Dos poylishe yidntum*, Buenos Aires, 1946–1966. In: Emmanuel Kahan, Laura Schenquer, Damian Setton, and Alejandro Dujovne, eds., *Marginados y consagrados. Nuevos estudios sobre la vida judía en Argentina*. Buenos Aires: Lumiere, 213–238.

Chinski, Malena, 2017: *Memorias olvidadas: los judíos y la recordación de la Shoá en Buenos Aires, 1942–1956*. PhD dissertation, unpublished. Buenos Aires: Universidad Nacional de General Sarmiento.

Chinski, Malena and Alan Astro, eds., 2018: *Splendor, Decline, and Rediscovery of Yiddish in Latin America*. Leiden: Brill.

Chinski, Malena, 2021: A New Address for Holocaust Research: Michel Borwicz and Joseph Wulf in Paris, 1947–1951. In: Natalia Aleksiun and Hana Kubatova, eds., *Place, Spaces, and Voids in the Holocaust*. Göttingen: Wallstein Verlag, 189–217.

[Chorley-]Schulz, Miriam, 2019: From Kiddush Hashem to the Rise of Heroines in Soviet Yiddish Literature of the 1940s. In: *Yad Vashem Studies* 47 (1): 175–207.

[Chorley-]Schulz, Miriam, 2021: *Gornisht iz nit fargesn: Soviet Yiddish Antifascism and the Holocaust*. Ph.D. dissertation. Unpublished. New York, NY: Columbia University.

Dreifuss, Havi, 2017: The Leadership of the Jewish Combat Organization during the Warsaw Ghetto Uprising: A Reassessment. Translated by Itamar Haritan. In: *Holocaust and Genocide Studies* 31 (1): 24–60.

Ettinger, Yakov, 1995: The Doctors' Plot: Stalin's Solution to the Jewish Question. In: Yaacov Ro'i, ed., *Jews and Jewish Life in Russia and the Soviet Union*. Ilford: Frank Cass, 103–124.

Estraikh, Gennady, 2018: The Life, Death, and Afterlife of the Jewish Anti-Fascist Committee. In: *East European Jewish Affairs* 48 (2): 139–148.

Estraikh, Gennady, 2020: A Quest for Yiddishland: The 1937 World Yiddish Cultural Congress. In: Marion Aptroot, ed., *Thinking Europe in Yiddish. Quest. Issues in Contemporary Jewish History. Journal of the Fondazione CDEC* 17: 96–117.

Estraikh, Gennady, 2021: The Soviet Narrative of the Warsaw Ghetto Uprising. In: *Acta Poloniae Historica* 123: 289–307.

Galván, Valeria, 2017: The Impact of the Soviet Repatriation Campaign on the Eastern European Émigré Community in Argentina (1955–1963). In: *Littera Scripta* 10 (1), https://journals.vstecb.cz/the-impact-of-the-soviet-repatriation-campaign-on-the-eastern-european-emigre-community-in-argentina-1955–1963/, February 2, 2023: 22–34.

Galván, Valeria and Florencia Osuna, eds., 2018: *La "Revolución Libertadora" en el marco de la Guerra Fría. La Argentina y el mundo durante los gobiernos de Lonardi y Aramburu.* Buenos Aires: Prohistoria.

Gitelman, Zvi, 1988: *A Century of Ambivalence: The Jews of Russia and the Soviet Union, 1881 to the Present.* New York, NY: Schocken Books.

Gross, Jan, 2007: *Fear: Anti-Semitism in Poland after Auschwitz: An Essay in Historical Interpretation.* New York, NY: Random House.

Gutman, Yisrael, 1982: *The Jews of Warsaw, 1939–1943: Ghetto, Underground, Revolt.* Translated by Ina Friedman. Indianapolis, Ind.: Indiana University Press.

Gutman, Yisrael, 1994: *Resistance: The Warsaw Ghetto Uprising.* Boston, Mass.: Mariner Boobs.

Jáuregui, Aníbal, 2012: El peronismo en los debates del Partido Comunista Argentino: 1945–1953. In: *A Contracorriente: Revista de Historia Social y Literatura en América Latina* 9 (3): 22–40.

Jelin, Elizabeth, 2002: *Los trabajos de la memoria.* Buenos Aires: Siglo Veintiuno Editores.

Kałczewiak, Mariusz, 2019: *Polacos in Argentina: Polish Jews, Interwar Migration, and the Emergence of Transatlantic Jewish Culture.* Tuscaloosa, Ala.: University of Alabama Press.

Kichelewski, Audrey, 2018: *Les Survivants: Les Juifs de Pologne depuis la Shoah.* Paris: Belin.

Kowalska, Marta, 1989: La emigración judía de Polonia a la Argentina en los años 1918–1939. In: *Estudios Latinoamericanos* 12: 249–272.

Laubstein, Israel, 1997: *BUND. Historia del Movimiento Obrero Judío*. Buenos Aires: Acervo cultural Editores.

Lotersztain, Israel, April 2014: *La historia de un fracaso: la religión judeo-comunista en los tiempos de la URSS (La prensa del ICUF en Argentina entre 1946 y 1957)*. PhD dissertation, unpublished. Buenos Aires: Universidad Nacional de General Sarmiento.

Lvovich, Daniel, 2003: *Nacionalismo y antisemitismo en la Argentina*. Buenos Aires: Javier Vergara Editor.

Mirelman, Víctor, 1988: *En búsqueda de una identidad: los inmigrantes judíos en Buenos Aires 1890–1930*. Translated by Natalio Mazar. Buenos Aires: Milá.

Mitelberg, Abraham, ed., 1953/1954 מיטלבערג, אַבֿרהם, רעד.: **יאָרבוך טשי"ד פֿון דער ייִדישער קהילה אין בוענאָס־אײַרעס**. בוענאָס־אײַרעס: ייִדישע קהילה אין בוענאָס־אײַרעס.

Patt, Avinoam J., 2021: *The Jewish Heroes of Warsaw: The Afterlife of the Revolt*. Detroit, Mich.: Wayne State University Press.

Perego, Simon, 2020: *Pleurons-les: Les Juifs de Paris et la commémoration de la Shoah (1944–1967)*. Ceyzérieu: Champ Vallon.

Perego, Simon, 2017: De l'écrit à l'oral. Le recours aux oeuvres littéraires dans les commémorations de la révolte du ghetto de Varsovie (Paris, 1945–1967). In: Judith Lindenberg, ed., *Premiers savoirs de la Shoah*. Paris: Éditions du CNRS, 293–317.

Petra, Adriana, 2022: *Intellectuals and Communist Culture: Itineraries, Problems, and Debates in Post-war Argentina*. Translated by Rebecca Wolpin. London: Palgrave Macmillan.

Porada, Katarzina, 2022: La inmigración polaca en la Argentina de entreguerras. Las políticas migratorias en el país de origen y en el de destino. In: *Revista de Indias* 82 (284): 229–256.

Rapoport, Mario and Claudio Spiguel, eds., 2009: *Relaciones tumultuosas: Estados Unidos y el primer peronismo*. Buenos Aires: Emecé.

Rein, Raanan, 2001: *Argentina, Israel y los judíos. Encuentros y desencuentros, mitos y realidades*. Buenos Aires: Lumiere.

Rein, Raanan, 2011: *¿Judíos-argentinos o argentinos-judíos? Identidad, etnicidad y diáspora*. Buenos Aires: Lumiere.

Rein, Raanan, 2015: *Los muchachos peronistas judíos. Los argentinos y el apoyo al Justicialismo*. Buenos Aires: Sudamericana.

Rollansky, Samuel, 1988a ראָזשאַנסקי, שמואל, רעד.: צו דער געשיכטע פֿון לאַנדסמאַנשאַפֿטן אין אַרגענטינע. אין: **אַרגענטינער ייִוואָ־שריפֿטן** (בוענאָס־אײַרעס) 14: 97–203.

Rollansky, Samuel 1988b ראָזשאַנסקי, שמואל: אויפֿטוען, דערגרייכונגען און באַגאַנגענע פֿעלערן פֿון דער לאַנדסמאַנשאַפֿט־באַוועגונג אין אַרגענטינע. אין: **אַרגענטינער ייִוואָ־שריפֿטן** (בוענאָס־אײַרעס) 15: 65–77.

Romero, Luis Alberto, 2003: *Breve historia contemporánea de la Argentina.* Buenos Aires: Fondo de Cultura Económica.

Rouquié, Alain, 1982: *Poder militar y sociedad política en la Argentina: 1943–1973.* Vol 2. 2 Vols. Translated by Arturo Iglesias Echegaray. Buenos Aires: Emecé.

Rubenstein, Joshua and Vladimir P. Naumov, eds., 2001: *Stalin's Secret Pogrom: The Postwar Inquisition of the Jewish Anti-Fascist Committee.* New Haven, Conn.: Yale University Press, in association with the United States Holocaust Memorial Museum.

Rucker, Laurent, 2008: Israël, l'Union Soviétique et la Russie. In: Alain Diekhoff, ed., *L'État d'Israël.* Paris: Fayard, 373–385.

Rupprecht, Tobias 2015: *Soviet Internationalism After Stalin: Interaction and Exchange between the USSR and Latin America during the Cold War.* Cambridge: Cambridge University Press.

Schenkolewski-Kroll, Silvia, 1991: The Influence of the Zionist Movement on the Organization of the Argentinian Jewish Community: The Case of the DAIA 1933–1946. In: *Studies in Zionism* 12 (1): 17–28.

Schwarz, Jan, 2008: A Library of Hope and Destruction: The Yiddish Book Series 'Dos poylishe yidntum' (Polish Jewry) 1946–1966. In: *Polin. Studies in Polish Jewry* 20: 173–188.

Segev, Tom, 1993: *The Seventh Million: The Israelis and the Holocaust.* New York, NY: Hill and Wang.

Senkman, Leonardo, 1991: *Argentina, la Segunda Guerra Mundial y los refugiados indeseables, 1933–1945.* Buenos Aires: Grupo Editor Latinoamericano.

Senkman, Leonardo, 2007a: Ser judío en Argentina: las transformaciones de la identidad nacional. In: Paul Mendes-Flohr, Yom Tov Assis and Leonardo Senkman, eds., *Identidades judías, modernidad y globalización.* Buenos Aires: Lilmod, 403–454.

Senkman, Leonardo, 2007b: Los sobrevivientes de la Shoa en Argentina: su imagen y memoria en la sociedad general y judía: 1945–50. In: *Arquivo Maaravi: Revista Digital de Estudos Judaicos* 1 (1), https://periodicos.ufmg.br/index.php/maaravi/article/view/13905/11086, November 11, 2022: 1–31.

Sheinin, David, 2006: *Argentina and the United States: An Alliance Contained.* Athens, Ga: University of Georgia Press.

Sofer, Eugene, 1982: *From Pale to Pampa.* New York, NY: Holmes & Meier Publishers.

Slucki, David, 2019: 'A Struggle Unparalleled in Human History': Survivors Remember the Warsaw Ghetto Uprising. In: *American Jewish History* 103 (2): 203–225.

Tsentral-farband fun poylishe yidn in Argentine, 1945 צענטראַל־פֿאַרבאַנד פֿון פּוילישע ייִדן אין אַרגענטינע: **מעמאָריע און באַלאַנס פֿון דעם 1טן יאַנואַר 1944 ביזן 31סטן דעצעמבער 1944.** בוענאָס־אײַרעס: צענטראַל־פֿאַרבאַנד פֿון פּוילישע ייִדן אין אַרגענטינע

Visacovsky, Nerina, 2015: *Argentinos, judíos y camaradas. Tras la utopía socialista.* Buenos Aires: Biblos.

Visacovsky, Nerina, ed., 2022: *Cultura judeo-progresista en las Américas.* Buenos Aires: Ediciones ICUF, Colección Archivos–CEHTI and Imago Mundi.

Weinstein, Ana and Eliahu Toker, 2004: *La letra ídish en tierra argentina: Bio-bibliografía de sus autores literarios.* Buenos Aires: Milá.

Wolff, Frank, 2013: Revolutionary Identity and Migration: The Commemorative Transnationalism of Bundist Culture. In: *East European Jewish Affairs* 43 (3): 314–331.

Wulf, Joseph, 1949 וואָלף, יוסף: לא דובים ולא יער. אין: **פּראָבלעמען** (פּאַריז) 2, אויגוסט 6–5.

Young, James, 1993: *The Texture of Memory: Holocaust Memorials and Meaning.* New Haven, Conn: Yale University Press.

Zertal, Idith, 2010: *La nación y la muerte. La Shoá en el discurso y la política de Israel.* Translated by Marta Pino Moreno. Buenos Aires: Del Nuevo Extremo.

Zonabend, R., 1952 זאָנאַבענד, ר.: די פֿעדעראַציע טרעט אַריַין אין איר אַכטן לעבנסיאָר. אין: **לאַנדסמאַנשאַפֿטן** (בוענאָס־איַירעס) 1, 30 יולי: 2.

Zourek, Michal 2014: *Checoslovaquia y el Cono Sur 1945–1989, Relaciones políticas, económicas y culturales durante la Guerra Fría.* Praga: Universidad Karolina de Praga / Editorial Karolinum.

Zweig, Roland, 2001: *German Reparations and the Jewish World: A History of the Claims Conference.* London: Frank Cass.

Binyamin Hunyadi

Di lebedike meysim – The Walking Dead

Volf Tambur and Romanian post-1945 Yiddish Literature

וויפֿיל לעבנס, שווייסן און מיִען	How many lives, sweat and strife
האָבן דורות אין דער וויסטע צעזייט	have proliferated generations in the desert
אַז איצט זאָלן ייִדישע קינדערלעך בליִען	so that now Jewish children shall bloom again
און קייטלען מיט ווירדע די קייט?!	and link the chain with dignity?![1]

Upon receiving the ייִדישער קולטור־פֿאַרבאַנד [*Yidisher kultur-farband*, Jewish Cultural Association, YKUF] Zhenovsky prize in 1980 and the קולטור־קאָנגרעס [*Kultur-kongres*, Culture Congress] prize for his book האַרבסט מיט זון [*Harbst mit zun*, Sunny Autumn],[2] published the same year, the Romanian Yiddish prose writer, poet and translator, Volf Tambur [Wolf/ Vladimir Tambour/Tamburu] (1915–1995) became a household name in Jewish circles in both the United States of America and Israel. He was promoted to being one of the foremost representatives of Romanian Jewish literature, alongside Mozes Rosen (1912–1994), Romania's chief rabbi, and Yisroel Berkovitsh [Israil Bercovici] (1921–1988), "secretar literar" [literary specialist] of Romania's Yiddish theater. At the same time, the now newly proclaimed laureate of the Yiddish American radical left was caught in the Yiddish Cold War and its cultural fronts. Tambur was invited on a lecture tour in North America, on which he was to familiarize audiences with the realities of Romanian life, especially following the devastating Vrancea earthquake of 1977, an event which caught significant international attention. Yiddish-speaking audiences, however, were more likely to be interested in thornier aspects of Romanian life, such as the right of Romanian Jews to emigrate to Israel and the ever-present reality of antisemitism in Eastern Europe. Tambur also ac-

The writing of this article was made possible by the generous support of Beit Sholem Aleichem, Tel Aviv, Israel. I'd like to thank the editors of the volume Prof. Dr. Miriam Chorley-Schulz, Dr. Alexander Walther, and Prof. Roland Gruschka as well as Roman Levit for their valuable feedback.

1 From the poem יורדים [*Yordim*, Impoverished, ruined men, 1954] (Ayzikovitsh 1962, 130).

2 [Goldenshteyn] 1981, 188f. Itshe Goldberg's congratulatory speech held at the YKUF-ceremony was later published in: ייִדישע קולטור [*Yidishe kultur*, Yiddish Culture]. Goldberg 1981, 40–42. Tambur, who was not present at the ceremony sent an excerpt from his book *Harbst un zun* as a sign of appreciation: Tambur 1981, 42f, 58.

cepted an invitation extended by the Jewish Public Library in Montreal and held a presentation there on 9 May 1982.[3] In Montreal, Tambur was greeted by several *landslayt* [countrymen], including Leyzer [Eliezer] Bash (1918–?), a fellow writer and a friend of Tambur's prior to his immigration to Canada. Both were natives of the Subcarpatho-Rus' region spending their early years together in Sighet [Sighetu Marmației], the writer's adopted hometown and the setting of many of his short stories.

Tambur's lecture was titled ייִדישער לעבן אין דער הײַנטיקער רומעניע [*Yidisher lebn in der hayntiker Rumenye*, Yiddish / Jewish life in Contemporary Romania], though the speaker talked very little about the actualities of Jewish life in Romania and almost not at all about his supposed field of expertise, Yiddish culture and literature under socialism.[4] Tambur's lecture fit seamlessly into the cultural milieu of the Montreal Yiddish scene, since it was supposed to affirm the picture drawn by Yiddish writers who emigrated to the city shortly after the Second World War of a culture lost to history. Yiddish cultural discourse as related to Eastern Europe focused almost exclusively on the period prior to the Second World War, and news about Yiddish literature and culture in Romania rarely penetrated the wall of conspiratorial silence woven around the country, if at all. Some Yiddish literary personages, however, kept up a continuous handling of the intellectual heritage that Tambur's lecture could tap into. Amongst the lectures held (and recorded) at the Montreal Jewish Public Library we find an evening dedicated to Bash's new book, that lamented the loss of his childhood Sighet in his פֿאַרבאָרגענע פּראָפֿילן [*Farborgene profiln*, Hidden Profiles] in 1979; at another event, Mordkhe Khosed (1909–1988), a Yiddish author born in Bessarabia, active in the Romanian Yiddish scene between the world wars, evoked the voices of the generations lost forever from his Romanian Yiddish past in דורות שרײַען מיך אַריבער [*Doyres shrayen mikh ariber*, Generations Scream out Loud at Me] in 1969. A few months following Tambur's visit Montreal celebrated Khosed's new book, שטויב און אייביקייט [*Shtoyb un eybikayt*, Dust and Eternity]. Tambur's

3 Tambur 1982b.

4 A year earlier, in a lecture given at the Hebrew University of Jerusalem, Tambur's presentation focused on the literary aspect of Jews' life in communist Romania. Tambur travelled to Israel on behest of the Hebrew University of Jerusalem to give a lecture on "Yiddish Literature in Socialist Romania." Unfortunately, we do not possess a transcript of the event and/or the state sanctioned text of his lecture. Tambur's lecture was reported in the periodical of the Union of Writers in Romania: Anonymous 1981, 24. It is interesting to note that the topic of the lecture in Jerusalem was exactly that, what was dodged in front of a Yiddish-speaking audience in Montreal.

lecture also represented an enticing glimpse into the world that was mostly understood (in North America) in the context of loss and annihilation, as by the ex-communist Polish-Yiddish poet, Binem Heler (1908–1998), who was the main speaker to commemorate the lives and tragic deaths of the Soviet poets Perets Markish (1895–1952) and Leyb Kvitko (1890 [or 1893]–1952), in 1972, or by the Sighet-born Elie Wiesel (1928–2016) and the Polish-Yiddish poet Rokhl Korn (1898–1982) – *deye-zogers* [pundits] and ardent critics of the Soviet Union.[5]

Tambur prefaced his talk by remarking that he was allowed to travel to the United States and Canada only under the condition that he serve as a *meylets-yoysher* [apologist or spokesperson] for the Romanian communist regime and advocate for its progressive treatment of Jews and their culture. He also related that the speeches he had prepared had to be authorized by Romanian censors before the tour began. Immediately after this confession, Tambur slowly folded his pre-prepared State-sanctioned speech, put it back in his pocket, and launched on what probably seemed to his audience a series of digressive musings on the Romanian-Jewish situation: from Saul Bellow's (1915–2005) visit to and misperceptions of Romania (the subject of his 1982 novel, *The Dean's December*[6]) to the issue of the intermarriage of Jewish and non-Jewish Romanians and the social hardships experienced under Ceaușescu's regime (to whom Tambur ironically referred to as *melekh* [king] alluding to the dictator's well-known *folie des grandeurs*). Strikingly, Tambur's decision to deviate from the official protocol and to hold a speech unsanctioned by state authorities does not seem to have affected his status as a representative of the Romanian state on other occasions. Two years after his 1984 US tour, he visited Israel twice.[7]

5 Bash's book appeared a year earlier in 1978: Bash 1978, Bash 1979, Khosed 1969, Khosed 1969b, Khosed 1981, Khosed 1982, Heler 1972, Korn and Wiesel 1972. These are merely a few examples from the decade preceding Tambur's lecture, though they exemplify the general interest and the topics discussed pertaining to Eastern Europe at the Montreal Jewish Public Library.

6 Bellow 1982. Bellow returned once more to the topic of Romania (and Romanian characters) in his last novel, *Ravelstein*, Bellow 2000. Bellow travelled with his wife, Alexandra Ionescu-Tulcea (1935–) to Romania in December 1978. Several of the motives in *The Dean's December* were inspired by this visit. Bellow talked about his impressions of Romania and the later reactions to his novel by Romanian intellectuals in his conversations with Norman Manea: Bellow and Manea 2007, 172–175. See also Leader 2005, 189–193.

7 Volf Tambur to Sore Kohen Se-Lavan (Ida Cohen Selavan), Bucharest, 12 March 1984 (Abraham Schwadron Autograph Collection, The National Library of Israel, Jerusalem).

Despite its seeming openness, what Tambur's lecture left unsaid was nevertheless far more revealing than what it openly claimed. In this case, it was precisely the status of Yiddish and Yiddish literature in Romania in the post-1945 era that was left out. This is a curious omission but possibly speaks volumes about the predicament and surprising leeway Yiddish intellectuals from the socialist bloc faced both at home and when speaking as ambassadors to 'Western' audiences. Tambur himself, after all, played a key role in the history of Romanian Yiddish Literature after 1945, in particular in the period of Ceaușescu's 'minor cultural revolution,' a wide-reaching reform of Romania's cultural life along National Communist lines.[8] Transgression of the allegedly rigid party line was a through-line of his literary career – to a significant degree, as we will see, thanks to the relative freedom Yiddish afforded him and others.

The survival of Yiddish culture in Romania was a much-discussed topic in Romania's Yiddish press in the 1970s and 1980s, and, as part of this public discussion, Tambur worked relentlessly to establish a Romanian Yiddish literary canon, while also publishing many poems, short stories, novellas, novels, and literary translations as means of enlarging its future corpus and shaping its direction. The present chapter will try to supply what was left unsaid throughout Tambur's lecture on Yiddish literature in Romania and examine the important personal role he played in shaping and influencing the Yiddish literary corpus that flourished, at least on paper, in the highly sectarian, Byzantine and xenophobic Romania of the 1970s and 80s.

"Maior Vladimiru"[9] – The Beginnings of a Militant Literary or Literary / Military Career

Unlike other important Romanian-Jewish writers and dramatists who first rose to prominence in the 1950s and 60s, like the aforementioned Yisroel Berkovitsh, Moyshe Laks [Lax] (1887–1979), and Note Roytman

8 On the possible origins of the 'minor cultural revolution' and its impact on Romanian cultural life see Shafir 1981, 420–445.

9 In a series of articles, the author and secretary of the Jewish community, Marcel Marcian (1914–2007), relates the manipulations of the Romanian intellectual elite, in relation to his personal story. In an episode he tells how he met Volf Tambur, or as he was known in Yiddish literary circles 'maior Vladimiru' at writer and theater director Yulian Shvarts's apartment. Tambur was walking up and down in the apartment, which made it clear to Marcian that the apartment was tapped, and the people present wanted to make sure that everything discussed there was heard 'on the other side' (Marcian 1997, 15).

(1900–1966), Tambur did not start his career as a Yiddish political and literary activist. His career was elliptical, with somewhat surprising leaps between the different career paths.[10]

He was born in a small village in the vicinity of Sighet. His father was a *melamed*, a religious teacher of children who found it hard to scrape together a living in their hamlet, and so decided to relocate the family to Sighet, the closest town, though still very Jewish and traditional, with potentially more opportunities for the family. Tambur received a traditional rabbinical education, the family being among the followers of the rebbe of Vizhnits, whose court they visited when occasion permitted.[11] He grew up in the restless years of interwar Romania, when political turmoil, the emergence of extremist parties, and economic hardship forced people to adopt hitherto unexplored survival strategies and political alliances.

Concurrently, and perhaps paradoxically, the increasingly oppressive and antisemitic atmosphere of the interwar period saw the emergence of a Yiddish cultural renaissance.[12] The Yiddish cultural tradition of the vast newly gained territories (Bukovina, Bessarabia, Transylvania and Southern Dobrudja) was far richer and better-established than that of historical Romania (Wallachia and Moldova) alone. The newly integrated post-WWI Greater Romania served in those early years as a meeting ground for different groups of Yiddish writers from geographically and culturally disparate regions. In this way, a new cultural center was born, the מיזיניק [*mizinik,* the youngest child], the youngest member of the so-called Yiddishlands, the international web of Yiddish literary creativity.[13] In his adoptive hometown of Sighet, Tambur could experience firsthand these developments in Yiddish culture and creativity, and he associated with the members of the town's literary avant-garde, a group calling itself יונג־רומעניע [*Yung Rumenye*, Young Romania] and their literary periodical, אויפֿגאַנג [*Oyfgang*, Sunrise].[14]

The group clearly fashioned itself after the Yiddish literary avant-garde

10 On Yisroel Berkovitsh's role in the Yiddish cultural milieu in Romania in the 1950s and 1960s cf. Grözinger 2002, 179–202. On Laks and Roytman see Korn 1989, 294–296; Berkovitsh 1973, 32–33. See also Laks' obituary in Anonymous 1980, 189.

11 Tambur 1985, 71–76.

12 On the repercussions of the peace treaties in Romanian politics see Mușat 1982, 9–45.

13 On the invention and evolution of the concept Yiddishland, cf. Gal-Ed 2021, 141–169.

14 Keren-Kratz 2017, 184f.

group יונג־ווילנע [*Yung Vilne*, Young Vilna] that was created in Vilna and other such groups. The goal of *Yung Rumenye* was to tap into the literary circuits of Vilna, Warsaw, Łódź, Berlin, and Kiev, the centers of Yiddish literary creativity between the world wars.[15] Though they did not directly challenge the central role these places played in Yiddish culture, *Yung Rumenye* nonetheless endeavored to draw attention to the emerging and distinct voices from the periphery of Yiddish literature. They believed, as it was stated in the introduction of *Oyfgang*, that it was imperative to raise the cultural level of Yiddish in Romania, where even in some areas densely populated by Jews the language and its culture was not deemed סאַלאָנמעסיק [*salonmesik,* presentable] and was even treated as something אומריינס [*umreyns,* repelling].[16] *Oyfgang* as opposed to *Yung Vilne*, had no clear political orientation or it did not align itself with a certain political platform, though it was certainly in opposition to the prevailing ultranationalist Romanian politics and conservative literary tastes of the time, and against Jewish assimilationism.[17] In the Romanian case, the break with old traditions did not translate into a revolt against old literary practices. Rather it was intended as a renewal of the efforts to create a modern literary corpus in Yiddish that reflected upon the distinct cultural environment of Yiddish in Romania.

Tambur started to publish short stories in the Chernivtsi based Yiddish periodical דאָס יודישע וואָרט [*Dos yudishe vort*, The Jewish Word] in 1935.[18] These short stories were later included in his first two collections of short stories, בײַ דער טיר [*Bay der tir*, At the Door] and מײַן היים [*Mayn heym*, My Home].[19] These two books were prepared for print by the author himself who worked in a print shop at the time. Already in these early books one detects Tambur's leftist leanings – he became an official member of the Party during his stay in Chernivtsi – an ideology to which few of his compatriots adhered at the time. In the 1930s, the Partidul Comunist Român [Communist Party of Romania] numbered but a few hundred members throughout the country.[20]

15 On literary centers in Yiddish cf. Shmeruk 1988, 142–155; Estraikh 2000, 17–38 and Novershtern 2015, 61–76.

16 [Izrael] 1933b, 1.

17 On the political dimensions of the literary activities of the *Yung Vilne* group cf. Novershtern 1989, 383–398.

18 Tambur's first short story in *Dos yudishe vort* was published in January 1935, Tambur 1935, 2.

19 Tambur 1937, Tambur 1940.

20 Tismaneanu 2003, 37–85.

Besides his literary activities Tambur may also have participated in the printing and distribution of illegal communist literature, though it is hard to tell whether this actually happened. It might as well have been a means to help him get drafted into the Romanian army and to garner support for his Yiddish-communist cultural activities.[21] Rumor has it that the Zionist activist, journalist, and Hungarian-language prose writer Dezső Schön [David/Dovid Shen/Sheyn] (1906–2000) provided Tambur with the necessary funds for the printing of his first book.[22] Following the Hungarian occupation of Northern Transylvania, Tambur was conscripted for forced labor service in the Hungarian army, while his wife and small daughter were left behind in Sighet and later deported along with the town's remaining Jewish population of 11,000 to Auschwitz in 1944.[23] Tambur's forced labor division fell into Soviet hands during their service in the Ukraine, which probably saved his life from the cruel fate suffered by most such units.[24] Later Tambur was evacuated to Soviet Central Asia, where he was employed as a Hungarian-language writer and journalist among the Hungarian-speaking POWs.[25] At some point, Tambur switched allegiances and joined the volunteer-based Divizia Tudor Vladimirescu [Tudor Vladimirescu Romanian Foreign Legion], a force created by the Soviets in October 1943 to aid the war effort.[26] It is unclear

21 Dezső Schön knew Tambur personally from their youth in Sighet, but they met once again in 1975, on Schön's second visit to Romania during communist times: Schön 1975, 2.

22 In view of the political maneuvering in Romania it is hard for the saying or its intentions to attain full credibility. The statement was made in a Hungarian language periodical printed in Bucharest on the occasion of the appearance of Tambur's collection of short novels and stories, the first book that broke his long period of literary silence (Rót 1976, 7).

23 Braham 1983, 15.

24 Pihurik 2007, 40–66.

25 See for example Tambur 1943b, 3. *Igaz Szó*, the periodical of the Hungarian language POW's was printed in Moscow. In the article Tambur writes, "Elképzelhettem-e, hogy a Szovjetunióban a hadifoglyok igazi magyar népdalokat fognak dalolni? Elképzelhettem-e, hogy egy hadifogolytábor olyan lehet, mint valami virágos kert? – Mert ilyen nyáron a mi táborunk." [Could I have ever imagined that in the Soviet Union POW's will sing real Hungarian folksongs? Could I have ever imagined that a POW camp was like a flower garden? Because our camp is like that in the summer.] See also Tambur 1943, 4. The article quotes a note sent by the 'journalist' Tambur to the editors', in which he expresses his gratitude for the heartfelt treatment of POW's by the Soviets and expresses his wish "katonák akarunk lenni egy új magyar hadseregben. Hálásak vagyunk a Szovjetuniónak, hogy támogat bennünket az új, népi Magyarország felépítésében" [we want to be soldiers in the new Hungarian army. We are grateful to the Soviet Union for its support in the building of a new People's Republic of Hungary].

26 Gosztony 1991, 193.

whether Tambur established or tried to establish any contact with the ייִדישער אנטיפֿאשיסטישער קאָמיטעט [*Yidisher antifashistisher komitet*, Jewish Antifascist Committee, JAFC] (established in 1941 and institutionalized in 1942) or the dissident members of the Romanian Communist Party during his captivity. But given the fact that he first identified himself as a non-Jewish Hungarian and later as a Romanian journalist joining the liberating forces of the Soviet Union, it is safe to presume that he could not or felt that it was unadvised to do so.

We find an echo of the conflicted position of Jewish POWs who swore allegiance to the Soviet army in one of Tambur's short novels. In his אין געראַנגל מיט זיך [*In gerangl mit zikh*, In struggle with oneself], printed in his 1975 first major collection of post-1945 writings, מאַראַמאָרעשאַנער, דערציילונגען [*Maramoreshaner, dertseylungen*, People of Maramureş, Novellas],[27] the protagonist Leyby is tasked by the Soviets to carry out a mission in the recently liberated Budapest. He is chosen for this task thanks to his Hungarian-speaking background, having been brought up in a Hungarian Jewish cultural milieu in Transylvania. The protagonist feels foreign in the Hungarian capital and is the target of slanting glances and innuendoes not only from the local population, which makes no effort to veil its hostility towards the representatives of a foreign army, but also from his fellow party members, who poke fun at his alien (Jewish) accent. Leyby feels torn by the complexities of his identity, homesick, but has no home to go back to, as his Jewish Transylvania was destroyed in the חורבן [*khurbn,* destruction, Holocaust]; at the same time, he feels loyal to the party, yet suffers immensely from those he sees poisoning the communist ideals they seem to promote (and which he himself holds dear). Furthermore, antisemitism has merely taken on new forms under new circumstances after the victory over fascism. Unlike his protagonist, who lingered at the crossroads undecided, Tambur himself decided to return to Romania in tow of the Soviet-Romanian forces and joined the Romanian army of the new Socialist Republic, in which he was to serve for the following two decades.

27 Tambur 1975, 137–247.

Tambur's *Sunless Spring*: A Pioneer of Socialist Realism

Tambur was among the first to reflect on the life of Jews and their reactions to the Hungarian occupation and ghettoization prior to the deportations from Sighet. His first novel, פֿרילינג אָן זון [*Friling on zun*, Sunless Spring], published in Arad in 1947, was meant to be the first part of a trilogy exploring the lives of three Jewish characters immediately preceding and following the war years in the new, communist Romania.[28] Only the first part of the trilogy, however, appeared in the 1940s, while the second part was published years later after the author had reentered the Romanian Yiddish literary scene in the collection *Maramoreshaner*. The third part remained uncompleted.

The novel *Friling on zun* revolved around the life of Serl, אַ טונקל ברוינע כמעט ציגײַנעריש שוואַרצינקע מיט געקרײַזלטע האָר [וואָס] איז געווען אַ ביסל צו קליין און צאַרט פֿאַר אירע יאָרן [a dark-brown, almost Gipsy-looking black-and-curly-haired girl, who was a bit too small and fragile for her age],[29] a young woman, a communist activist, working in her aunt's sausage factory before the war. She understands the threat after the occupation of Northern Transylvania by the Hungarian forces but like the small group of underground communist activists of which she is a member, practically does nothing.[30] She observes the ghettoization of her family, friends, and fellow comrades with mournful acquiescence. As circumstances evolve, however, she finds passivity untenable. The Hungarian gendarmerie, who keep order in the ghetto, try to coerce and torture Jews to hand over their "concealed treasures," the jewelry and valuables that they have supposedly kept hidden before being forced to relocate to the ghetto. Serl comes to their attention as a well-known communist activist in town, and they take her to a warehouse where interrogations are conducted. The policemen want to force themselves upon her when a sudden change comes over Serl's whole personality. She discovers her will to stand up to violence:

> ווי פֿון אַ קעסל, אַן אויפֿגעהיצטן, וואָס האָט געפּלאַצט האָט עס געשלאָגן פֿון איר מיט
> האַס, עקל און אָפּשײַ. עס האָט געדאַכט אַז זי איז, חלילה, פֿונעם זין [אַראָפּ]. דאָס געשריי

28 Tambur 1947. An announcement at the end of the novel *Friling on zun* informed readers that the second part לייבי [*Leybi*, Leyby] was already in print, but it appeared only twenty years later (ibid.).

29 Tambur 1947, 11.

30 On the complete inertia of the underground communist cell that remained in Romania, see Levy 2001, 68–78.

> איז געווען אַ היסטערישעס, ווי פֿון איינעם, וואָס שרײַט זיך אַליין צו פֿאַרטייבן, איידער ער וויל זיך וואַרפֿן אונטער אַ באַן. דעם זשאַנדאַר איז אַ שוידער אַריבער איבערן לײַב. ער האָט דערזען, אַז אָנשטאָט אַ מיידל, אַ פֿרוי צום געניסן, האָט ער פֿאַר זיך אַן אויפֿגערייצטע חיה, וואָס איז אימשטאַנד מיט איר גיפֿט צו פֿאַרסמען אַלץ און יעדן אַרום איר. ער האָט זי אָנגעכאַפּט בײַם קאָפּ האָר און אַ שלײַדער געטון. זי איז אומגעפֿאַלן.[31]
>
> As from a boiling kettle that explodes, hatred, disgust and revulsion flamed up in her. It seemed to her as though she had lost her mind. Her screaming was hysterical, like someone screaming to deafen their own thoughts before throwing themself under a train. A shiver ran through the gendarme's spine. He realized that instead of a girl, a woman to enjoy, he had in front of him a beast coiling to strike, that could easily poison everything and everyone around it. He grabbed her by the hair and pushed her away. She fell to the floor.

Serl suddenly transforms into a completely new being, her sense of self-preservation directing her actions. Her identity and past seem to be effaced in the present situation. Her act of revolt arises as a natural reaction in an attempt to reclaim her bodily integrity.[32] She becomes untouchable, a force that the gendarmes cannot deal with, and so they release her unharmed. Though Serl's act of victory could not save her from deportation, when the time comes, she faces it with a sense of pride and belief in her own will to survive. Through her character Tambur tried to create a realistic depiction of a hero, who is not motivated by extrinsic forces and ideologies that are largely dependent on environment and circumstance, but by the awakening of her own moral compass. However, we do not see an evolution of character in the novel, the actions she undertakes rooted in her passivity.

Though Yiddish communists tended to choose a very broad interpretation of 'revolt,' Tambur's Serl nevertheless presents, at least initially, as a communist anti-hero, one who is offered a chance to rebel at every step of the way but for whom acts of rebellion continue to seem impracticable under the circumstances she finds herself in. Historical circumstances change dramatically during the novel's plot, the fall of fascist Hungary and Romania, the re-annexation of Northern Transylvania to Romania, create a seemingly

31 Tambur 1947, 60.

32 The acts that revolted one way or the other against the fascist mechanisms of annihilation were interpreted by Yiddish historians, artists, and critics alike in the communist bloc as key moments of *vidershtant* [revolt] (see Ruta 2018, 118–121; Mark 1954, 7–16).

ripe situation for "revolution" and drastic societal change. Though Serl escapes from Nazi hands, she does not serve as a catalyst for revolutionary change. Contrary to the Soviet redefinition of קידוש־השם [*kidesh-hashem,* martyrdom] in narratives that from the 1940s turned to female characters to connect to traditional sources and to utilize them for a new Soviet patriotic meta-narrative, Tambur's hero denies dying and sacrificing herself in the novel in the most unspectacular way.[33] Thus, *Friling on zun* becomes a reversed *kidesh-hashem* story, where there is no redemption, no virtue upheld and no price paid for a better future, or as in a traditional Jewish narrative, an undeservedly harsh punishment for "the numerous sins" of the community.

Tambur's first novel is unique in that it posits a communist woman as its protagonist, but it does not adhere to the conventions of other authors on the Left, in that his heroine acts the same way as everyone else around her, and her political persuasion does not make her an exception to the rule. The 'Soviet liberation' of Romania does not bring her salvation either, as she finds it hard, or nearly impossible to fit in as a Jew after the horrors of Auschwitz. Even after returning from the camps her detachment does not abate, and she finds solace in a quasi-religious belief in the deterministic historical role of the Jewish people. In the novel Tambur evokes a similar complementary relationship between Jew and antisemite as did Jean-Paul Sartre (1905–1980) around the same time:[34]

> ייִדן קאָנען נישט אַנטלויפֿן, זיך אויסבאַהאַלטן אין אַ ווינקל, און אַפֿילו אויך דעמאָלט נישט, ווען מ׳וועט דאָס ווינקל אָנרופֿן ייִדנלאַנד. אויך דאָרט וועט מען זיי אויפֿזוכן די ייִדן, זיי זענען נייטיק די שׂונאים פֿון דער ציוויליזאַציע, זיי קאָנען נישט לעבן אָן ייִדן...
> ...איז דאָך די זעלבע האַנט וואָס מאַכט פּראָפּאַגאַנדע, אַז ייִדן זאָלן פֿאָרן קיין פּאַלעס־טינע און האָבן כּלומרשט נישט וואָס צו זוכן אין אייראָפּע – די זעלבע האַנט וואַכט בײַ די טויערן פֿון פּאַלעסטינע, אַז ס׳זאָל חלילה זיך נישט אַרײַנגנבֿענען אַ ייִד...
> ...בלײַב!... דאָס לעבן איז דאָ, ווי אומעטום, דאָס זעלבע – אַ קאַמף. דאָס ייִדישע לעבן איז אַ טאָפּלטער קאַמף – אומעטום פּונקט ווי דאָ אומעטום – דאָס זעלבע...[35]

> Jews cannot escape, they cannot hide in a corner, not even if they call that corner the 'Land of the Jews.' They will seek them out, the Jews, the enemies of civilization need them, they cannot live without the Jew...

[33] On women heroes and the Soviet re-interpretation of the *kidesh-hashem* theme in Soviet Yiddish literature see [Chorley-]Schulz 2019, 175–208.

[34] *Réflexions sur la question juive* was published originally in 1945 in *Les Temps Modernes*. For an English translation see Sartre 1967.

[35] Tambur 1947, 103.

> ...the same hand that makes propaganda that Jews should go to Palestine, and that they seemingly have nothing to do in Europe – is the same that watches over the gates of Palestine, that God forbid a Jew might somehow sneak in...
>
> ...Stay!... Life, as everywhere else, is the same as here – a struggle. And the life of a Jew is a struggle on two accounts – everywhere, the same as here, everywhere – is the same...

Tambur's first novel was met, not surprisingly, with negative reviews in both the Romanian and Yiddish presses from fellow writers on the Left.[36] The bitter criticism that *Friling on zun* received was probably one of the reasons why Tambur decided to dedicate his life to military service,[37] and apart from one short story secularizing the biblical account of Moses משה: אַ מעשׂה ווי אין חומש [*Moyshe, a mayse vi in khumesh*, Moses: A Story as in the Torah, Arad, 1948], and occasional radio interviews in Yiddish,[38] he dissociated himself from any Yiddish cultural activity for decades. After the initial impetus of reorganization and attempts at reviving the vibrant literary life of the 1930s, the 1950s saw the rapid and aggressive centralization and Stalinization of Yiddish cultural activism in Romania, and Jewish cultural institutions sank into a climate of suspiciousness and rivalry, where alliances were constantly shifting due to the unpredictable party line.[39] In his 1982 Montreal lecture, Tambur stated that he was so disgusted by the machinations of the active members of the Yiddish cultural establishment at the time that this inartistic environment made him relinquish writing for two decades, and more importantly it made him "cease to be a Jew."

We do not know how exactly he imagined "ceasing to be a Jew" to look like, but Romanian Communist policies left enough space for ambiguities in the definition of "Jewishness." Romania, like the Soviet Union, set up in 1945 דער ייִדישער דעמאָקראַטישער קאָמיטעט [*Der yidisher demokratisher komitet*, the Jewish Democratic Committee], which essentially was Romania's own

36 See Grözinger 2002, 76f. Grözinger mistakenly discusses Tambur's novel under the title פֿרילינג און [!] זון [*Friling un zun,* Spring and Sun]. Tambur also mentions the polemics around his first novel: Tambur 1977, 284.

37 The critic Shloyme Bikl called Tambur אַ מיליטערישער ,שישקע׳ אין דער סאָוועטישער רומעניע [an army 'big shot' in Soviet Romania]: Bikl 1961, 308.

38 On this see Anonymous 1983, 123.

39 On the Communist takeover of Jewish institutions and tactics used for that end see Glass 2002, 212–238.

יעווסעקציע [*Yevsektsye*, Jewish Section in the Soviet Communist Party], with anti-religious and anti-Zionist propaganda that tried to reinforce a Jewish identity based on ethnic belonging and socialism.[40] Ceaușescu's ascendance to power, however, brought with it the rise of Mozes Rosen (1912–1994), chief rabbi of Romania, and the fall of the traditional Soviet-type policies towards Jews.[41] From the 1960s on, Jews were represented as a religious community, though in a certain sense, similar to other ethnicities, had their own channels of cultural self-expression: the Yiddish-language theater, book publishing, and a Yiddish-language radio program. Unlike other ethnic minorities in Romania, the Jewish community had no daily newspaper in their own minority language, but uniquely in the communist bloc they were allowed to print a periodical in the language of the "Jewish religion," i.e. Hebrew.[42] The situation seems to have been so ambiguous that even Ceaușescu himself was confused at times whether to refer to Jews as members of a religious denomination or an ethnic group with its own cultural means of expression and Yiddish as their "national language."[43] Apparently Tambur continued this tradition of ambiguity even in his lecture in Montreal.

A Minor (Yiddish) Cultural Revolution: Tambur's Return to Literature

Volf Tambur returned to the Romanian Yiddish literary scene in 1973, following the 'minor cultural revolution' and the strengthening of diplomatic ties between the state of Israel and Romania. His first new publications include short stories and articles on the history of the Jewish press in Romania. These pieces were published in the official periodical of the Jewish community in Romania, established in 1956 of which Tambur later became one of the editors: the trilingual (Romanian, Yiddish, and Hebrew) *Revista cultului mozaic din R.P.R.* [צײַטשריפֿט פֿונעם רעליגיעזן ייִדנטום פֿון דער רומענישער פֿאָלקס-רעפּובליק\כתב עת של היהדות הדתית ברפובליקה העממית הרומנית; *Tsaytshrift funem religyezn yidntum fun der rumenisher folks-republik*,

40 Glass 2002, 212–225.

41 Rosen 1990, 164–168.

42 Estraikh 2008, 14.

43 Ceaușescu on occasion referred to Yiddish as a language of a "co-inhabiting nationality" in Romania, and not as a language of a religious group: Ceaușescu 1983, 118.

Periodical of the Mosaic Religion in the Romanian People's Republic; short: *Tsaytshrift*].[44] The *Revista* was the main and only regularly appearing Yiddish periodical in the communist period in Romania after the Bucharest-based Yiddish איקוף־בלעטער [*YKUF-bleter,* YKUF-Gazette] was discontinued at the end of 1952.[45] Thus, publishing in the journal was equivalent to re-entering the Jewish community, at least in a literary-cultural sense.

Tambur won his first major recognition in the Romanian Yiddish and international literary scene for the aforementioned collection of childhood reminiscences and short novels entitled *Maramoreshaner*, that appeared two years later.[46] The stories in this volume center on the town of Sighet and its surroundings. Some are based on the author's childhood reminiscences (collected under the title מײַן ברודער פֿײַבוש [*Mayn bruder Feyvush,* My Brother Feyvush]), others depict fictionalized episodes from the period of Hungarian occupation (e.g., מיט דער געלער אַרמבאַנד [*Mit der geler armband,* In the Yellow Armband]), while a third group focuses on the failed attempts of establishing a just society within the communist bloc, free from racism (e.g., אין געראַנגל מיט זיך, *In gerangl mit zikh*). Tambur's new narrative approach was well-adapted to Romania's new nationalist literary agenda, which – somewhat similar to the Soviet cultural policies in the 1930s – focused on the folk-rootedness of the common people, their ties with their physical and national environment, and their natural moral virtues.[47] In this, Tambur was followed by those Yiddish writers who survived the Stalinized cultural milieu

44 Tambur's first articles in the *Tsaytshrift* were a study of fellow Sighet poet, Berl Shnabl, and on the editor of the 19th century Yiddish periodical היועץ [*Ha-yoyets,* The advisor]: Tambur 1972b, 10; Tambur 1972c, 11. The article on Shnabl was translated and appeared in the Romanian section of the periodical: Tambur 1972, 2.

45 Decision to close down the three Jewish periodicals in Romania in Yiddish, Hungarian, and Romanian (*YKUF-bleter, Új út* and *Viata noastra*) was made in March 1953 at a session of the Comitetul Democrat Evreesc [Jewish Democratic Committee]. However, it seems that the Yiddish periodical had already ceased circulation in 1952, as no extant copies of *YKUF-bleter* had been found in the major collections of Yiddish periodicals after that year. See Comitetul Democrat Evreesc, rola 1376, cadru 983–1005, Arhivele Naţionale Istorice Centrale, Bucharest, Romania. The author wishes to thank Dr. Corina L. Petrescu (The University of Mississippi) for drawing his attention to the files pertaining to the publication of the *YKUF-bleter* and for generously sharing their content with him.

46 Tambur 1975. Some of the short stories appearing in the volume were published earlier (beginning from 1972) under different pseudonyms in the Yiddish section of the *Revista cultului mozaic din R.P.R.* [*Tsaytshrift*] (between 1956 and 1991).

47 On the transitional period from communism to National Communism as reflected in the trilingual periodical of the Jewish community of Romania see Herşcovici 2016, 166–188.

of the 1950s and 1960s (e.g., Yulian [Julian] Svarts, 1910–1977, Leon Bertish, 1897–1980, Rely Blay [Relli Blei], 1913–2000) as well as those whose books began to appear in the 1970s (Khayim Goldensteyn [Haim Goldenshtein], 1912–?; Y. Karo [Itsik Shvarts], 1906–?).[48] In *Maramoreshaner* Tambur stylistically and thematically combined motifs from Romanian Yiddish authors such as Hersh-Leyb Gotlib (1829?–1930), also known as "Hersh-Leyb Sigeter", a famous בדחן [*batkhn,* a singer and entertainer at traditional Jewish celebrations][49] and the "Sigeter Sholem Aleykhem" Hertsl Apshan (1866–1944), in an attempt to formulate a local historical-literary continuity.[50] Tambur's collection of stories and novellas was widely, even internationally circulated, and received significant praise from critics, pro- and anti-communist alike, in Romania, Hungary, the United States, and Israel. A rare enthusiastic essay by the fervent anti-communist, Sighet-born Elie Wiesel, written in Hungarian, praises Tambur's recently discovered 'masterpiece', stating that reading *Maramoreshaner*, was an "ecstatic" experience for him. According to Wiesel, the collection encapsulates the entire Jewish Eastern European world that was destroyed in the *khurbn*. It recreates the Jewish towns and hamlets, and the hopes and dreams that vanished into thin air.[51] In contrast to other 'social-realist' literary representations, the simple Jewish characters depicted in Tambur's *Maramoreshaner* cycle were never placed in a Manichaean battle between the good and evil forces of history. Their stubbornness in maintaining their tradition helps them tackle the hardships of everyday life, despite not rescuing them from the poorest rungs of society. As the wheel of history turned and modern communist Romania was established, their disappearance seemed inevitable.

Tambur's two main novels לעבעדיקע מתים: מעשׂיות פֿונעם עולם־האמת [*Lebedike meysim: mayses funem oylem-hoemes,* The Undead: Stories from the Underworld] and שיר־המעלות: טרעפּנגעזאַנג [*Shir-hamayles: Trepngezang*, The

48 The authors mentioned here were all active in the minuscule Romanian communist underground movement before WWII.

49 Dorfzon [Harendorf] 1929, 7; Izrael 1933, 10f; Shnabl 1934, 2f.

50 The epithet was commonly used in the Sighet Jewish parlance for Apshan but became more widely used after publications by the well-known Yiddish literary critic, Shloyme Bikl (see Bikl 1961, 308f); republished in the Tel Aviv-based trilingual (Hebrew, Hungarian and Yiddish) periodical *Máramarossziget* (Bikl 1962, 1f).

51 Wiesel 1976, 9. It is not clear whether the article was translated or was penned originally in the Hungarian by the author.

Song of Ascent] are considered perhaps his greatest critical achievements at home and abroad and, indeed, central to any understanding of his artistic vision behind the Iron Curtain.[52] The two novels present a harsh critique of the social climate in communist Romania, the first in the form of a hellish allegory for bureaucratization, and the second from a socialist-realist point of view, written as part and not outside of the general Romanian discourse of the possibilities of criticism of the communist system. *Lebedike meysim* is, not by chance, a reimagining of Itsik Manger's (1901–1969) די װוּנדערלעכע לעבנס־באַשרײַבונג פֿון שמואל־אַבא אַבערוואָ (דאָס בוך פֿון גן־עדן) [*Di vunderlekhe lebensbashraybung fun Shmuel-Abe Abervo (Dos bukh fun gan-eydn),* The Amazing Life Story of Shmuel-Abe Abervo (The Book of the Garden of Eden), 1939] refigured in a communist setting. Manger's novel follows the narrative of an infant who relates his adventurous life before being born. Abe Abervo's story is a lived journey through the afterlife as imagined by the folkloric fantasy weaved around Jewish traditional lore. His adventures take place in Gan Eden where souls return and come to life anew. The story however takes place before the main protagonist's birth as opposed to the more classic imaginings of an otherworld after death, a narrative choice preferred by Tambur.

The bureaucratic and Kafkaesque *oylem-hoemes* [afterlife; literally 'World of Truth'] can only be 'a world of falsities,' an immense parody of the communist system. Tambur's 'living dead' are all awaiting their trial to be let into Paradise but what truly awaits them is more akin to the entanglements of a show-trial, where the accused have no way to free themselves from the clutches of the system. In *Lebedike meysim* he adopts the bleak language of judicial proceedings, so unlike his previous highly-praised idiomatic Sighet Yiddish.[53] In this he imitates Moyshe Altman's (1890–1980) neutralized, 'leveled' Yiddish, which he developed for his מדרש פּנחס [*Medresh Pinkhes*, Midrash According to Pinchas].[54] As opposed to his earlier novel די װינער קאַרעטע [*Di viner karete*, The Viennese Coach], and especially his later שמעטערלינגען [*Shmeterlingen*, Butterflies, 1939], replete with localisms and a close and faithful depiction and linguistic reproduction of his childhood Bessarabia, for *Medresh Pinkhes* Altman developed a landmark style, in which he abstained

52 Tambur 1976, Tambur 1982.

53 See for example Shvarts 1970, 76–84.

54 Several critics of *Medresh Pinkhes* underlined the novel's special, idiosyncratic use of Yiddish. A summary of the critical responses see Roytman 1990, 92–95. On the roots of Altman's literary style see Bikl 1955, vii–xiii.

from the use of the Slavic component in Yiddish, and probably due to the influence of the Romanian linguistic and cultural environment 'internationalized' the Yiddish used in the novel by way of using words taken from Romance languages. Tambur followed Altman's stylistic example and wrote in a 'synthetic' Yiddish, devoid of the natural, local sensibility that characterized his other writings.

In *Lebedike meysim* a disturbing world of ghosts is invoked that seems to draw upon different facets of his own past and present experience in communist Romania. These 'souls,' however, are no living spirits, as their actions seem to be dictated and 'animated' by a system which is completely devoid of a soul. Everything is topsy-turvy in this World-To-Come – not only does it exist outside the borders of physical space, but it also transcends normal life on the linguistic level, as its speech and thought appear to be caught up in the byzantine maze of 'Soviet-speak.' The *Lebedike meysim* speak of a נאַכטבוך [*nakhtbukh*, nightary] instead of a טאָגבוך [*togbukh*, diary], and they speak of things 'rare as a black raven,' as opposed to a 'white raven' (meaning 'once in a blue moon').[55] In this fictional setting, as in real communist countries, here newcomers had to acquire the new ideologized speech forms and learn through trial and error how to speak and act correctly in unfamiliar circumstances. If one assumed that justice and righteousness reign in the underworld, that it is a well-ordered and rational society, then one is quickly disabused of such notions. The souls, inactive during the day, come out at night to assist in the judicial proceedings that will eventually determine their eternal fate. While those being judged are caught up in this eternally transitional state, the בית־דין־של־מעלה [*bezdn-shel-mayle*, celestial council of justice] deliberates on their sins and merits. As it happens in life, most cases are not clearcut. The protagonist, a retired military officer, Zelikovitsh – the name itself testifies to the character's otherworldly nature (זעל, *zel* meaning 'soul' in Yiddish) – was given a military burial, not a Jewish one, since his widow hoped that by denying her husband's Jewish roots, she might increase her pension (a hope in which, we learn later, she is disappointed). Zelikovitsh as a name for the main protagonist of the novel seemed to have been a self-referential choice for the author, as Tambur at times used this name as

55 This is a rare case of idiomatic loan from Hungarian into Yiddish. "Ritka mint a fehér holló" is an idiomatic expression in Hungarian, which does not exist either in Romanian or other Yiddish dialects. Tambur seems to use the expression as a common feature of the Yiddish used in *Lebedike meysim*.

one of his own pseudonyms, which also explains the many clearly autobiographical motives in the novel.

Since Zelikovitsh appears before the court in military uniform and not in תכריכים [*takhrikhim*, Jewish burial robe], it is not even clear who should have jurisdiction over his fate, a Jewish or non-Jewish court. His liminal state as an unmoored soul grants him greater clarity and a more unbiased perspective on his surroundings. These traits allow him to befriend Monides, who fulfills a Virgil-like role for him in his descent through hell. Monides explains to Zelikovitsh the dynamics of their world, and slowly but surely initiates him into the finer details of his case. Monides is also Jewish, but he conceals his identity from every living or dead soul, though his background seems to be common knowledge among the spirits. In one of the most dramatic episodes of the novel, Monides relates a shocking episode from his past life during WWII, in which he was forced to kill a captive Jew who was concealing his Jewishness by wearing a Nazi uniform and trying to blend in with the occupying forces.[56]

Tambur's second major novel, *Shir-hamayles* curiously opens with a quotation from the 'Supreme Leader' Ceaușescu. Ceaușescu was not Tambur's first choice to introduce his new novel. In July 1980 he turned to the Yiddish literary historian and folklorist, the first chair of the Yiddish department at the Hebrew University in Jerusalem Dov Sadan (1902–1989), and asked him to pen the foreword to his novel, as he stated: צו וואָס טויג מיר אַזאַ הקדמה? מע דאַרף אַמאָל אונטערשטופּן אַ וואָגן אויך ווען ער פֿאָרט באַרג־אַראָפּ. וועט עס זיַין פֿאַר מיר אַ זכיה און אַ חיזוק [Why do I need such a foreword? One must give a push to a wagon even if it goes downhill. It would be an honor and an encouragement for me].[57] We can only speculate what Sadan's answer might have been if he cared to write back to Tambur at all. Most probably Sadan declined Tambur's offer, as he assumedly did not want to be associated with a publication printed in the socialist bloc. The fact remains that Tambur's novel appeared with an excerpt by Ceaușescu and a foreword by the author himself. The paragraph in Yiddish, in which Tambur quotes Ceaușescu, tells the reader:

מיר זענען די וואָס האָבן דעם חובֿ און די אויפֿגאַבע צו מאַכן גערעכטיקייט – לאָמיר

[56] Tambur 1976, 249–254.

[57] See Volf Tambur to Dov Sadan, 8 July 1980. Dov Sadan Collection, The National Library of Israel, Jerusalem.

זשע עס טון הײַנט ווען סע לעבן יענע וואָס קאָנען די ווירקלעכקייט און ווייסן ווי אַזוי די זאַכן זענען געשען. איבערלאָזן דאָס פֿאַר דער געשיכטע און דער צײַט וואָלט באַטײַט אפֿשר בײַצוטראָגן אויסבאַהאַלטן דעם אמת און אים פֿאַלשן.[58]

We are the ones whose duty and task it is to pursue justice – let us do so today, while those who know the present and who have known the past are still alive. To leave this to the hands of history and time would perhaps mean to hide the truth and to falsify it.

To find a quotation by Ceaușescu on the first page of a Yiddish book raises questions concerning its role in the book's narrative. One might presume that such textual elements were relatively common in Romanian literature in the 1980s, a time when Ceaușescu's cult of personality was at its height, but in fact we rarely find other epigraphs quoting the 'Supreme Leader' in either Romanian or other minority literatures in Romania. One would be inclined to think that Ceaușescu's words somehow related to the tragic history of Romanian Jews, and that perhaps he meant to make amends with regard to Romania's role in the *khurbn*, but this is not the case.

Here, as on many other occasions, Ceaușescu offers a personal interpretation of Romanian history.[59] One of the major tactics of his National Communist ideology was a wholesale rejection of the past, prior to his ascension to power in 1965, as a period of oppression and injustice, thereby disavowing the part he himself had played in that period of Romania's history.[60] As part of the refurbishing of Romanian history, all blame for the aggressive collectivization, mass imprisonments and show trials, and even for the crimes committed in Transnistria against Romanian Jews, was placed on the major minority groups living in Romania, i.e. Germans, Hungarians and Jews. For the immense suffering of the first decades of Communist rule in Romania, the Jews were primarily held accountable – as was Ana Pauker (1890–1960),

58 Tambur 1982, 2. Based on the citation in Tambur's novel, it would seem that the quotation was based on an original Yiddish translation of Ceaușescu's works. However, this was not the case. Unlike in the Soviet Union, neither Georghe Georghiu-Dej (1901–1965), nor Ceaușescu's works were translated to or serialized in Yiddish. Apparently, the translation was based on Ceaușescu's collected works in Romanian, and the excerpt was translated by Tambur himself. For the original see: Ceaușescu 1982 (II), 182.

59 For Ceaușescu's political philosophy of the history of Romanians and other minorities living in modern day Romania (the so called 'co-inhabiting nationalities') see Ceaușescu 1983, 7–35.

60 Ceaușescu was brought to the Central Committee of the Romanian Workers' Party (from 1965 Romanian Communist Party) in 1952 after Ana Pauker had been purged.

or individuals perceived as Jewish (for example, the ethnic Hungarian Vasile Luca (1898–1963) who was married to the Jewish Elisabeta Luca (née Birnbaum).[61] In this light, and especially given the subsequent plot of the novel, the epigraph reads as subversive and irreverent, and might have well appeared so to many of its contemporary readers. The illusory sense of reconciliation and appeasement implicit in the dictator's statement is subtly but clearly laid bare.

While the work outwardly takes on the sanctioned form of the socialist-realist novel, and while its epigraph appears *prima facie* in line with the cult of personality, the whole reveals a pointed critique not only of the 'official' genre to which it purportedly belongs, but also of the falsification by the Communist Party of its past actions in Romania, particularly towards Jews. The effects of such falsification were adequately described by Romanian sociologist Remus Campeanu: "Becoming is replaced by unending repetition. Eviscerated of its substance, history itself becomes atemporal. Perpetual movement gives way to perpetual immobility… [H]istory… loses the quality of duration."[62] Tambur's novel, by offering a critique of a supposedly 'historico-critical' discourse, revitalizes history and snatches it from the hands of those who would do it violence.

The protagonist of *Shir-hamayles* is a young communist activist of Roma extraction, Naon Dancsó, who becomes politically active during the most harrowing period of Romanian communism, i.e. the aggressive agrarian collectivization of the 1950s. He sees in the new communist ideology an opportunity to blend in with the majority culture, changes his name to Naum Dănciulescu, and decides to shed every identifying mark that might disclose his origins. Later, he becomes romantically involved with a Jewish comrade who shares his desire of leaving the past behind. Betty Markovici is ashamed of her Jewish petit-bourgeois background, of the intellectual capital with which she was brought up, both of which she attempts to shed through her life and activism within the party. The relationship of Markovici and Dănciulescu plays out as a mirror game of projections, each using the other for the furtherance of their identity aims. Whereas for Dănciulescu the desire to become an apparatchik brands him as a traitor to his family, for Markovici par-

61 Levy 2001, 198.

62 Campeanu 1986, 22; quoted and analysed in Verdery 1991, 249.

ty membership means an escape from her Jewish *petit bourgeois* background. In this sense, it is more of a 'marriage of convenience' than a relation of love.

Unexpectedly, Markovici becomes pregnant, which gives an extraneous and unexpected seal of permanence to their bond. Both their attempts to free themselves from their past and imprinted identity fail miserably; their child, Ovidiu, bears on his body all the physical features associated with both Jews and Roma.[63] The choice of name speaks for itself – a reference to the Roman poet Ovid, a forced exile in Tomis (today Constanța in Romania), famous for his work *Metamorphoses* – a long account of ambiguous and often pathetic changes of shape. Dănciulescu falls victim to the communist purges against 'new members' (those who joined the party the years after the Second World War), which began in 1952, and is sent to prison for a lengthy period while his wife is dying of breast cancer. Already fatally ill, her friends from her early party days try to ameliorate her situation by suggesting that she should denounce her husband and divorce him. Markovici is unwilling to follow their advice and accepts her humiliation at the hands of the committee that expels her from the party.[64] Emaciated by cancer, she decides to bequeath a story to the infant Ovidiu that would somehow explain the tragic decisions that she and the boy's father had to make during their lives. The story within the story revolves around the historic figure Josephus Flavius, who, while in Rome, is treated by his fellow Jews as a traitor to his people, and, as a final humiliation is commissioned by the emperor to commit to paper the history of the great victories of Rome in the province of Judea. Flavius has no option but to comply with the request, but side by side with his glorifying account of Rome's successful campaign he undertakes to write the history of his own people, a superior history, partaking of the eternal, standing in monumental opposition to the pyrrhic military victory of Rome.[65] Though Flavius is unable to justify his treason in the eyes of his fellow Jews, he commits himself to a task that goes beyond the narrow political and national affinities of his day. In this symbolic story Markovici tries to communicate to her son that however traitorous their actions may seem, there is a lesson to be learned from the terrible times they were forced to live through, an object lesson warning the next generation of illusions that may appear as ideals but in fact carry with them

63 Tambur 1982, 143f.

64 Ibid., 223–230.

65 Ibid., 180–217.

a fateful danger. Tambur's lesson in Jewish history and the description of the difficult moral decisions of his Josephus present similarities to such narratives as Lion Feuchtwanger's German classic *Der jüdische Krieg* [The Jewish War] (1932), and Mordkhe Tsanin's Yiddish historical opus אַרטאַפּאַנוס קומט צוריק אַהיים [*Artapanus kumt tsurik aheym*, Artapanus Comes Back Home, first part published in 1967].[66] Though *Shir-hamayles* does not lack in melodramatic scenes and primitive poetical intermezzos, it successfully draws attention to the conflicts faced by minority ethnic groups in an extremely nationalistic society and shows how these social tensions were played out on a personal level.

The Yiddish literary critic Elye Shulman (1907–1986) summed up the values of Tambur's novel:

> טאַמבורס נײַעסטער ראָמאַן [...] פֿאַרמאָגט אַלע מעלות פֿון זײַן זגאַל שרײַבן – אָבער צייכנט זיך גראָד אויס מיט דער קלאָרקייט און געוואַגטקייט. ער שרײַבט אָפֿן וועגן דעם לעבן אין רומעניע ווען אין לאַנד האָט געהערשט דער סטאַליניזם – און עס לייענט זיך ווי אַ שאַפֿונג וואָס איז געשריבן אין אַ גאַנץ פֿרײַער מדינה. די טעמע ווערט אַנטוויקלט אויף אַ נאַטירלעכן אופֿן און דער נאַראַטיוו איז גיך און ביסטרע, הגם עס זענען דאָ אָפֿט קאָמענטאַרן. בכלל איז אַ זעלטנקייט צו לייענען אַזאַ ראָמאַן וואָס איז געשריבן אין אַ מזרח־אייראָפּעיִשן לאַנד.[67]
>
> Tambur's latest novel [...] possesses all the values of all his previous writings – but outstrips them in its clearness and boldness. He writes openly about life in Romania when the country was under the thumb of Stalinism – and it reads as if it was written in an entirely free country. The theme is developed in a natural way and the narrative is fast-going and lively, though interspersed with commentary. Altogether, it is rare to come across such a novel, which was written in an Eastern European country.

It is somewhat puzzling to read such an analysis by a critic as penetrating as Shulman in the pages of (in name, at least) socialist New York פֿאָרווערטס [*Forverts*, Jewish Daily Forward] which was used to wage 'holy war' on everything that had to do with communism in the United States and amongst Jews in the Soviet bloc.[68] Cultural flag-bearers were often depicted as collaborators with evil regimes and their art denounced as nothing more than vacuous ver-

66 Feuchtwanger 1932, Tsanin 1967.

67 Shulman 1982, 39; Shulman had steadily written positive reviews on Tambur's works on the pages of the *Forverts*: Shulman 1976, 2; Shulman 1978, 2; Shulman 1979, 6, 7.

68 Estraikh 2010, 33–60.

biage in service of the politics of oppression. Apparently Tambur succeeded in deceiving not only Romanian censorship but the authoritative critic of the *Forverts* as well. Though, for obvious reasons, the novel takes place in the pre-Ceaușescu times, Stalinism never really ended in Romania.[69] The country continued to embrace Stalin's nationalist communism even in the face of attempted reforms within the Soviet Union. The problematic approach, not to say xenophobia, towards Romania's minorities reached its climax in the time of the novel's appearance which makes the latter all the more noteworthy.[70] The apparatchiks of cultural production in Romania have probably read with great satisfaction that even in a hostile journal they could create the great illusion of "an entirely free country."

Bukareshter shriftn – Illusions Regained

Tambur's greatest editorial achievement was undoubtedly the publication of the בוקאַרעשטער שריפֿטן [*Bukareshter shriftn*, Bucharest Writings] beginning in 1978.[71] In the introduction to the first issue of the periodical, the editors expounded on the periodical's ultimate goal in the following terms:

> [שטעלן] זיך פֿאָר די אָרטיקע שרייַבער־משפּחה מיטן גאַנצן הויזגעזינט. די פּען וואָס די שרייַבער האָבן דאָ אויסגעטרויט, פֿאַרבינד אונדז מיט אַנשי־שלומינו פֿון ייִדישלאַנד.[72]

> […] to represent the local family of writers, every member of the household. The pen they entrust to the public connects us with our fellows in Yiddishland.

Yiddish critics in the West did not fail to appreciate the significance of such a statement: it not only invited curious Western observers to glimpse into the intellectual and cultural life of a communist country behind the Iron Cur-

69 Tismaneanu 2003, 37–85.

70 Miklós 1985, 7–25.

71 The *Bukareshter shriftn* was edited by Volf Tambur and other long card-holding members of the Romanian Communist Party such as Khayim Goldenshteyn, Izo Shapiro (1903–1981) and Y. Karo. Goldenshteyn and Shapiro were part of the small Romanian communist contingent that had fought in the Spanish Civil War. Volf Tambur and Y. Kara fought against the Nazis in WWII. Fighting in the international corps in the Spanish Civil War and being active in the party's underground period lent a special status to activists in the post-1945 period. On this see Rotman 2005, 151.

72 Anonymous 1978, 5.

tain, but also spoke about Yiddishland – that supra-territorial, trans-political, and trans-ideological domain enabling literary encounters on the common ground of language and culture.[73] It is not by chance that the introduction mentions Jewish literary figures as inspirations for the periodical's mission and goals, such as the Jewish German poet Heinrich Heine (1797–1856), the most 'canonical' of Romanian Yiddish writers, Itsik Manger (1901–1969), and even the Hebrew poet Hayim Nahman Bialik (1873–1934). Somewhat quixotically, the editors mention the Romanian poet (and rabid antisemite) Mihai Eminescu (1850–1889) as another such inspirational figure. Each of these names represents an ideological stance that seems to embody one of the new cultural tendencies informing Romanian Yiddish literature.

The inclusion of Eminescu in such a list appears to be a gesture towards cultural revisionists in the *protochronist* vein: it tried to represent this 19th century poet historically known for his ultraconservative political views as the founder of a modern Marxist sociology, a visionary critic of bourgeois society, the first progressive class-conscious literary personality and the greatest poet of the common Romanian man.[74] Heine in Romanian Marxist literary criticism was treated as a Romantic poet, whose work was complementary to that of Eminescu, who levelled a harsh critique against the elites. In the Jewish discourse in Romania – similar to Yiddish literary criticism of Heine's works in the Soviet Union – his oeuvre represented a blend of Jewish and humanistic values.[75] Manger, along with other émigrés was banned from the Jewish cultural discourse in Romania for a long time. Leaving Romania was considered treason that made dissident intellectuals suspect and unworthy to play a formative role in communist Romania's cultural life. Under the flag of National Communism, however, he was granted special status, and together with Moyshe Altman, Eliezer Shteynbarg (1880–1932), Yankev Shternberg (1890–1973), and Yankev Groper (1890–1966) became one of the household names of the new Yiddish-Romanian canon. The recognition of his representative status reached its peak in 1979, when Romanian Yiddish writers established an Itsik Manger Circle within the Uniunea Scriitorilor din România

73 Shulman 1978, 2.

74 Verdery 1991, 156–166.

75 For the *Rezeptionsgeschichte* of Heine's works in the Soviet Union from the 1930s till the 1950s see Wachsmann 2002, 69–182. On the development of Heine-criticism in the communist period in Romanian, see Hristea 2015, 199–238.

[Union of Romanian Writers] with Tambur as secretary.[76] In 1983, the Union published an anthology of Manger's works translated by the Jewish Romanian poet Nina Cassian (1924–2014) and Yisroel Berkovitsh.[77] Bialik's projected role in the Romanian-Yiddish canon is harder to determine: his inclusion was perhaps one way to satisfy the canon organizers' ideal of holism; and a tribute to the iconic status Bialik enjoyed in the new Israeli canon, i.e. another gesture towards Israel in this era of strengthening diplomatic ties between Romania and Israel.

The *Bukareshter shriftn*, during its decade of existence, published original literature – both poetry and prose – from communist Romania, studies on the history of Yiddish in Romania, reviews of newly published books on Jewish topics and translations from Romanian and Romanian minority languages, such as German, Hungarian, and Ukrainian. Prominent contributors included such figures as Tania Lovinescu (1924–2014), Arnold Hauser (1929–1988), and József Méliusz (1909–1995). Tambur was not only one of its editors – he contributed to both the periodical's literary and the critical sections and was one of its key Yiddish literary translators, having intimate knowledge of German, Hungarian, Romanian, and Ukrainian cultures, and languages. We may surmise that like the *Revista cultului*, where articles were self-censored and then also officially censored by the journal's editor-in-chief and de facto censor Mozes Rosen,[78] a similar arrangement was put in place for the *Bukareshter shriftn*. As Tambur related in his Montreal lecture, in Romania the Romanian, Hungarian, and German daily press was scrutinized scrupulously by censorship, while Yiddish publications could enjoy a relative freedom of expression.[79]

Bukareshter shriftn thus presented a vibrant picture of cultural exchange and socialist internationalism. It was not only important to save Yiddish works from oblivion via translations into Romanian, but it was also vital to translate other co-territorial languages into Yiddish, especially if they touched upon Jewish topics. The *Bukareshter shriftn* was the last great effort by the communist Yiddish-speaking cadre active in the 1970s and 1980s to sustain

76 Anonymous 1979, 2.

77 Manger 1983.

78 Herșcovici 2016, 182–183.

79 Tambur 1982.

a (perhaps illusionary) vibrant culture, before it quickly disappeared. The periodical continued to appear until 1988, when it finally ceased operations. With Tambur's emigration to Israel in 1986 the periodical lost its chief editor and architect. When it folded, it signaled the last great intellectual effort by a generation, which was the first to embrace communism as Romanian Jews and the last to abandon it as Yiddish culture activists.

Conclusion

In his 1982 lecture Tambur used two metaphors to describe the dynamics of Romanian life. One was the metaphor of bifocal glasses, where the bespectacled person must decide which optic field to use, whether he wanted to look at something distant or to focus on a closer object. If he chooses the wrong one, all he sees are blurry images. Were we to read Tambur's own oeuvre through this metaphor, we may well argue that the mutually beneficial economic ties between Romania and Israel in those years (made closer, paradoxically, by both countries' oppressive attitude towards minorities and their common emphasis on nationalism)[80] enabled the rapidly shrinking Romanian Yiddish literary scene to remain alive, and even, to some extent, to thrive despite the regime's inherent and insurmountable irrationality and repressive policies. This scene, unlike that of Romanian literature itself or of its other minority literatures (especially German and Hungarian),[81] enjoyed a relative freedom of expression and was able to voice critique on social problems of past and even present-day Romania.[82] In the 1970s and 1980s Tambur came out with a new volume of prose almost every year, and was intensely involved in the editing of *Bukareshter shriftn* – the central organ of Romanian Yiddish literary creativity for a decade. Though assiduous in emphasizing his Romanian patriotism, Tambur was, however, unable to avoid the hardships of living under a nationalistic dictatorship. According to his correspondence with the American Jewish writer and culture activist Khaye Sore Kohen Se-Lavan (Ida Cohen Selavan), he started to prepare his family's emigration to Israel in

80 On the attitude towards minorities in the State of Israel see Dowty 1991, 41–48.

81 On Romanian state censorship and its effects on German language literature in Romania see Spiridon 2012, 444–462. About the situation of the Hungarian minority in the period see Miklós 1985.

82 On the strong and positive Israeli-Romanian diplomatic ties see Govrin 2002, 1–17.

1984, visiting the country twice. He registered his children and relatives for emigration to Israel in 1985, and they moved in September 1986. At least in the first years of their emigration, the family experienced various hardships: Tambur's son, a computer analyst, was unable to find employment; Tambur himself, now a dissident, was prohibited from working as the editor of the *Bukareshter shriftn*, and it folded two years later. He himself lived in Jerusalem in relative obscurity until his death in 1995. His passing followed, by one year, that of another emblematic and controversial figure of Romanian Jewish culture under the dictatorship, Romania's chief rabbi, Mozes Rosen.[83]

Bibliography

ANONYMOUS, 1978 אַנאָנים: פֿאַרן פֿאָרהאַנג. אין: **בוקאַרעשטער שריפֿטן** (בוקאַרעשט), 1: 5–6.

ANONYMOUS, 1979: Cenacluri literare. In: *România literară* (Bucharest), 45: 2.

ANONYMOUS, 1980 אַנאָנים: משה לאַקס. אין: **בוקאַרעשטער שריפֿטן** (בוקאַרעשט), 3: 189.

ANONYMOUS, 1981: Prezențe Româneşti: Israel. In: *România literară* (Bucharest), 40: 24.

ANONYMOUS, 1983 אַנאָנים: אַ פֿערטל יאָרהונדערט ייִדישע אוידיציעס ביַים רומענישן ראַדיאָ: אַ שמועס מיטן לאַנגיאָריקן רעדאַקטאָר פֿון די ייִדישע אוידיציעס ביַים רומענישן ראַדיאָ – שלום רובינגער. אין: **בוקאַרעשטער שריפֿטן** (בוקאַרעשט), 6: 120–126.

AYZIKOVITSH, Froym, 1962 איַיזיקאָוויטש, אפֿרים: **לידער**. תּל־אָבֿיבֿ. פּולי

BASH, Eliezer, 1978 באַש, אליעזר: **פֿאַרבאָרגענע פּראָפֿילן**. מאָנטרעאַל. ל. באַש.

BASH, Eliezer, 1979 באַש, אליעזר: **ליטעראַרישער אָוונט לכּבֿוד אליעזר באַש צום דערשיַינען פֿון זיַין בוך פֿאַרבאָרגענע פּראָפֿילן**. <https://archive.org/details/ybc-fbr-683_4682>, January 23, 2023.

BELLOW, Saul, 1982: *The Dean's December*. Harmondsworth: Penguin.

BELLOW, Saul, 2000: *Ravelstein*. London: Viking.

BELLOW, Saul and Norman MANEA, 2007: 'Before I Go': A Conversation with Norman Manea. In: *Salmagundi* (New York), 155–156: 172–175.

BERKOVITSH, Yisroel, 1973 בערקאָוויטש, ישׂראל: די אַנטשטייונג און אַנטוויקלונג פֿון דער ייִדישער ליטעראַטור אין רומעניע. אין: **ייִדישע קולטור** (ניו־יאָרק), 35: 1, 32–33.

BIKL, Shloyme, 1955 ביקל, שלמה: דער דערציילער משה אַלטמאַן: ביאָגראַפֿיש־קריטישער אַריַינפֿיר. אין: משה אַלטמאַן, **געקליבענע ווערק**. ניו־יאָרק: ציִשאָ: ז–יג.

BIKL, Shloyme, 1961 ביקל, שלמה: דער מאַרמאָראָשער דיכטער יוסף האָלדער. אין: שלמה ביקל, **רומעניע: געשיכטע, ליטעראַטור־קריטיק, זכרונות**. בוענאָס־איַירעס: קיום.

BRAHAM, Randolph L., 1983: *Genocide and Retribution: Holocaust in Hungarian Ruled Transylvania*. Boston, Mass.: Kluwer-Nijhoff Publishing.

[83] See the correspondence between Volf Tambur and Ida Cohen Selavan, 25 September 1981–March 1987. Abraham Schwadron Autograph Collection, The National Library of Israel, Jerusalem.

[Chorley-]Schulz, Miriam, 2019: From “Kiddush Hashem” to the Rise of Heroines in Soviet Yiddish Literature of the 1940s. In: *Yad Vashem Studies* 47: 175–208.

Campeanu, Pavel, 1986: *The Origins of Stalinism: From Leninist Revolution to Stalinist Society*. Armonk, NY: M. E. Sharpe.

Ceaușescu, Nicolae, 1982: *Opere alese*. Vol. 2. Bucharest: Editura Politica.

Ceaușescu, Nicolae, 1983: *The Philosophical Thinking of Romania's President Nicolae Ceausescu: The Nation and the Co-inhabiting Nationalities in the Contemporary Epoch*. Bucharest: Meridiane Publishing House.

Dorfzon, Shmuel-Yankev [Harendorf, Shmuel-Yankev], 1929 דאָרפֿזאָהן, שמואל־יעקבֿ [האַרענדאָרף, שמואל־יעקבֿ]: אַ פֿאַרגעסענער עלטער־זיידע. אין: **דער מאָמענט** (וואַרשע), 283: 7.

Dowty, Alan, 1991: Minority Rights, Jewish Political Traditions, and Zionism. In: *Shofar* 10 (1): 23–48.

Estraikh, Gennady, 2000: From Yehupets Jargonists to Kiev Modernists: The Rise of a Yiddish Literary Centre, 1880s–1914. In: *East European Jewish Affairs* 30 (1): 17–38.

Estraikh, Gennady, 2008: *Yiddish in the Cold War*. London: Legenda.

Estraikh, Gennady, 2010: Professing Leninist Yiddishkeyt: The Decline of American Yiddish Communism. In: *American Jewish History* 96 (1): 33–60.

Feuchtwanger, Lion, 1932: *Der jüdische Krieg*. 3 Vols. Amsterdam: Querido.

Gal-Ed, Efrat, 2021: Yiddishland: A Promise of Belonging. In: *Journal of Modern Jewish Studies* 20 (2): 141–169.

Glass, Hildrun, 2002: *Minderheit zwischen zwei Diktaturen: zur Geschichte der Juden in Rumänien, 1944–1949*. München: R. Oldenbourg.

Goldberg, Itshe, 1981 גאָלדבערג, איטשע: פּריז צו וואָלף טאַמבור. אין: **ייִדישע קולטור** (ניו־יאָרק), 3: 40–42.

[Goldenshteyn, Khayim], 1981 ג[אָלדענשטיין], ח[יים]: וואָלף טאַמבור – לאַורעאַט פֿון קולטור־קאָנגרעס אין איקוף־פּרעמיע. אין: **בוקאַרעשטער שריפֿטן** (בוקאַרעשט), 4: 188–189.

Govrin, Yosef, 2002: *Israel-Romanian Relations at the End of the Ceausescu Era: As Observed by Israel's Ambassador to Romania, 1985–89*. London: F. Cass.

Gosztony, Peter, 1991: *Stalins Fremde Heere: Das Schicksal der nichtsowjetischen Truppen im Rahmen der Roten Armee, 1941–1945*. Bonn: Bernard & Graefe Verlag.

Grözinger, Elvira, 2002: *Die jiddische Kultur in Schatten der Diktaturen: Israil Bercovici, Leben und Werk*. Berlin: Philo.

Heler, Binem, 1972 העלער, בינעם: **פּרץ מאַרקיש און לייב קוויטקאָ – זייער לעבן, זייער שאַפֿן, זייער טראַגישער אומקום**, <https://archive.org/details/ybc-fbr-275_4275>, January 30, 2023.

Herșcovici, Lucian-Zeev, 2016: Apologetics and the Search for Roots: The Jewish Past in Romania as Presented in *Revista Cultului Mozaic*, 1956–1976. In: *Revista de Istorie a Evreilor din România* 1 (16–17): 166–188.

Hristea, Mihaela, 2015: *Receptarea lui Heinrich Heine în literatura română*. Bucharest: University of Bucharest.

Izrael, Yisroel-Dovid, 1933a איזראַעל, ישׂראל־דוד: דער ערשטער ייִדישער פֿאָלקסדיכטער אין די קאַרפּאַטן־בערג. אין: **אויפֿגאַנג** (סיגעט), 3: 10–11.

[Izrael, Yisroel-Dovid], 1933b די רעדאַקציע [איזראַעל, ישׂראל־דוד], צו אַלע פֿרײַנט פֿון ייִדישן וואָרט! אין: **אויפֿגאַנג** (סיגעט), 1: 1–2.

Keren-Kratz, Menachem, 2017: The Social and Cultural Role of Small Jewish Literary Centres – The Case of Sighet, Romania. In: *Journal of Modern Jewish Studies* 16 (2): 184–185.

Khosed, Mordkhe, 1969a חסיד, מרדכי: **דורות שרײַען מיך אַריבער**. מאָנטרעאַל: פּחד קראני ורעדה!.

Khosed, Mordkhe, 1969b חסיד, מרדכי: **מרדכי חסיד־אָוונט לכּבֿוד זײַן בוך „דורות שרײַען מיך אַריבער"** <https://archive.org/details/ybc-fbr-209_4209>, January 23, 2023.

Khosed, Mordkhe, 1981 חסיד, מרדכי: **שטויב און אייביקייט**. מאָנטרעאַל: מ. חסיד בוך פֿאָנד קאָמיטעט – קאַנאַדער קאָונסיל גראַנט.

Khosed, Mordkhe, 1982 חסיד, מרדכי: **אַן אָוונט לכּבֿוד מרדכי חסיד צו דערשײַנען פֿון זײַן בוך פּאָעזיע „שטויב אין אייביקייט"**. <https://archive.org/details/ybc-fbr-1088_5083>, January 23, 2023.

Korn, Rokhl, and Elie Wiesel, 1972 קאָרן, רחל, וויזל, אליזער: **אָנדענק אַקאַדעמיע – געווידמעט די מיט 20 יאָר צוריק אומגעבראַכטע ייִדישע שרײַבער אין רוסלאַנד**. <https://archive.org/details/ybc-fbr-281_4281>, January 23, 2023.

Korn, Yitskhok, 1989 קאָרן, יצחק: ייִדיש אין קאָמוניסטישן רומעניע. אין: **ייִדיש אין רומעניע: עסייען**. תּל־אָבֿיבֿ: אַבֿוקה, 294–296.

Leader, Zachary, 2005: *The Life of Saul Bellow: Love and Strife, 1965–2005*. London: Jonathan Cape.

Levy, Robert, 2001: *Ana Pauker: The Rise and Fall of a Jewish Communist*. Berkeley, Calif.: University of California Press.

Manger, Itsik, 1983: *Balada Evreului care ajuns de la Cenusiu la Albastru*. Translated by Nina Cassian and Yisroel Berkovitsh. Bucharest: Kriterion.

Marcian, Marcel, 1997: Câte ceva despre rezistența obediențelor. In: *Contemporanul* (Bucharest), 8: 15.

Mark, Ber, 1954 מאַרק, בער: **אומגעקומענע שרײַבער פֿון געטאָס און לאַגערן**. וואַרשע: ייִדיש בוך.

Miklós, Tamás Gáspár, 1985: *Censorship, Ethnic Discrimination and the Culture of the Hungarians in Romania*. New York, NY: International Helsinki Federation for Human Rights.

Mușat, Mircea, and Ion Ardeleanu, 1982: *Political Life in Romania, 1918–1921*. Translated by Sanda Mihailescu. Bucharest: Editura Academiei Republicii Socialiste România.

Novershtern, Avraham, 1989: Yung Vilne: The Political Dimension of Literature. In: *The Jews of Poland between Two World Wars*. Edited by Yisrael Gutman. Hanover, NH: University Press of New England: 383–398.

Novershtern, Avraham, 2015 נוברשטרן, אברהם: **כאן גר העם היהודי: ספרות יידיש בארצות הברית.** ירושלים: מאגנס – האוניברסיטה העברית

Pihurik, Judit, 2007: Magyar katonák és zsidók a keleti hadszíntéren 1941–1943. In: *Múltunk* (Budapest), 52 (3): 40–66.

Rosen, Mozes, 1990: *Dangers, Tests and Miracles: The Remarkable Life Story of Chief Rabbi Rosen of Romania as Told to Joseph Finkelstone*. London: Weidenfeld and Nicolson.

Rotman, Liviu, 2005: *The History of Jews in Romania: The Communist Era until 1965*. Vol. 4. Translated by Karen Gold. Tel-Aviv: Tel-Aviv University.

Roytman, Leonid, 1990 רויטמאַן, לעאָניד: **משה אַלטמאַן: זײַן לעבן און שאַפֿן: מאָנאָגראַ־פֿיע.** מאַגיסטער־אַרבעט: אוניברסיטת בר־אילן

Rót, Attila, 1976: "Elsüllyest világról…". In: *A Hét* (Bucharest), 7: 7.

Ruta, Magdalena, 2017: *Without Jews? Yiddish Literature in the People's Republic of Poland on the Holocaust, Poland and Communism*. Edited by Jessica Taylor-Kucia. Kraków: Jagiellonian University Press.

Sartre, Jean-Paul, 1967: *Anti-Semite and Jew*. Translated by George J. Becker. New York: Schocken.

Schön, Dezső, 1975: Jiddis irodalom Romániában: "Örökké várni fogom…": Wolf Tambur: Máramarosiak című könyve megjelenése alkalmából. In: *Új Kelet* (Tel-Aviv), 8348: 2.

Shafir, Michael, 1981 שפיר, מיכאל: **האינטלקטואל והמפלגה: המפלגה הקומוניסטית הרומנית והאינטליגנציה הקראטיבית בתקופת צ׳אושסקו, 1965–1972.** דיסרטציה: האוני־ברסיטה העברית בירושלים.

Shmeruk, Khone, 1988: Aspects of the History of Warsaw as a Yiddish Literary Centre. In: *Polin* 3: 142–155.

Shnabl, Berl, 1934 שנאַבל, בערל: הערש־לייב סיגעטער. אין: **די וואָך** (בוקאַרעשט), 30: 3–2.

Shulman, Eliyohu, 1976 שולמאַן, אליהו: אין ייִדישער ליטעראַטור וועלט: אַ פֿראַזע בוך פֿון אַ ייִדישן שרײַבער אין רומעניע. אין: **פֿאָרווערטס** (ניו־יאָרק) 28620: 10

Shulman, Eliyohu, 1978 שולמאַן, אליהו: אַ ליטעראַרישער גרוס פֿון רומעניע. אין: **פֿאָרווערטס** (ניו־יאָרק) 29323: 2

Shulman, Eliyohu, 1979 שולמאַן, אליהו: צוויי ייִדישע שרײַבער פֿון מאַראַמאַראָש־סיגעט. אין: **פֿאָרווערטס** (ניו־יאָרק) 29455: 6, 7

Shvarts, Yulian, 1970 שוואַרץ, יוליאַן: מאַרמאַראָשער ייִדישע ווערטער בײַ וואָלף טאַמבורן. אין: **ייִדישע שפּראַך** (ניו־יאָרק) 30: 76–84

Spiridon, Olivia, 2012: Die Rumäniendeutsche Literatur nach dem Zweiten Weltkrieg: Eine Überblicksdarstellung. In: *Études Germaniques* 3: 444–462.

Tambur, Volf, 1935 טאַמבור, וואָלף: אין די ערשטע טעג. אין: **דאָס יודישע וואָרט** (טשערנאָוויץ), יאַנואַר 4: 2

Tambur, Volf, 1937 טאַמבור, וואָלף: **בײַ דער טיר: דערציילונגען.** טשערנאָוויץ: ייִדיש וואָרט

Tambur, Volf, 1940 טאַמבור, וואָלף: **מײַן היים: דערציילונגען.** סיגעט: צענטראַלאַ.

Tambur, Volf, 1943: Demokratikus Magyarországot. In: *Igaz Szó* (Moscow), 50: 4.

Tambur, Volf, 1943b: Csalódtam… In: *Igaz Szó* (Moscow) 52: 3.

Tambur, Volf, 1947 טאַמבור, וואָלף: **פֿרילינג אָן זון: ראָמאַן**. אַראַד: ייִדיש וואָרט.

Tambur, Volf, 1972: Poetul maramureșan Berl Șnabl. In: *Revista cultului mozaic din R.P.R.* (*Tsaytshrift*) (Bucharest), 287: 2.

Tambur, Volf, 1972b טאַמבור, וואָלף: דער מאַרעמורעשער ייִדישער דיכטער בערל שנאַבל. אין: **צײַטשריפֿט פֿונעם רעליגיעזן ייִדנטום פֿון דער רומענישער פֿאָלקס־רעפּובליק** (בוקאַרעשט), 287: 10.

Tambur, Volf, 1972c טאַמבור, וואָלף: ווער איז געווען דער רעדאַקטאָר פֿון „היועץ“?. אין: **צײַטשריפֿט פֿונעם רעליגיעזן ייִדנטום פֿון דער רומענישער פֿאָלקס־רעפּובליק** (בוקאַרעשט), 287: 11.

Tambur, Volf, 1975 טאַמבור, וואָלף: **מאַראַמאָרעשאַנער: דערציילונגען**. בוקאַרעשט: קריטעריאָן.

Tambur, Volf, 1976 טאַמבור, וואָלף: **לעבעדיקע מתים: מעשׂיות פֿונעם עולם־האמת**. בוקאַרעשט: קריטעריאָן.

Tambur, Volf, 1977 טאַמבור, וואָלף: **ייִדישע פּרעסע אין רומעניע: בײַטראָג צו אַ מאָנאָגראַפֿיע**. בוקאַרעשט: קריטעריאָן.

Tambur, Volf, 1981 טאַמבור, וואָלף: אַ ,ליטעראַטור־פּרײַז׳: במקום אַן ,אַקצעפּטיר־רעדע׳. אין: **ייִדישע קולטור** (ניו־יאָרק), 3: 42–43, 58.

Tambur, Volf, 1982 טאַמבור, וואָלף: שיר־המעלות: טרעפּנגעזאַנג. בוקאַרעשט: קריטעריאָן.

Tambur, Volf, 1982 טאַמבור, וואָלף: **ייִדישער לעבן אין דער הײַנטיקער רומעניע**. <https://archive.org/details/ybc-fbr-908_4907>, January 23, 2023.

Tambur, Volf, 1985 טאַמבור, וואָלף: בײַם וויזשניצער רבין. אין: **הערט אַ מעשׂה: מאַראַמאָרעש־סיגעטער ,טעג׳ און אַנדערע דערציילונגען**. בוקאַרעשט: קריטעריאָן.

Tsanin, Mordkhe, 1966 צאַנין, מרדכי: **אַרטאַפּאַנוס קומט צוריק אַהיים: ירושלים**. באַנד 1. תּל־אָבֿיבֿ: המנורה.

Tismaeanu, Vladimir, 2003: *Stalinism for All Seasons: A Political History of Romanian Communism*. Berkeley, Calif.: University of California Press.

Verdery, Katherine, 1991: *National Ideology under Socialism: Identity and Cultural Politics in Ceaușescu's Romania.* Berkeley, Calif.: University of California Press.

Wachsmann, Constanze, 2002: *Der sowjetische Heine: Die Heinrich Heine-Rezeption in den russischsprachigen Rezeptionstexten der Sowjetunion (1917–1953).* Berlin: Weissensee Verlag.

Wiesel, Elie, 1976: Wolf Tambur, a földim. In: *Új Kelet* 8518: 9.

Gennady Estraikh

From Esteem to Madness, and Back

Rive Balyasne's Life in Soviet Yiddish Literature

While Jews have often been called עם־הספר [*am-haseyfer*, the people of the book], the majority of 19th and 20th century Yiddish readers, in fact, preferred newspapers to books, especially as newspapers were much cheaper and carried a wide assortment of material, including literary works.[1] Consequently, Yiddish writers tended to cluster around newspapers, which could offer them a salaried employment and an outlet for their literary production. At the beginning of the 20th century, New York and Warsaw, the main centers of the Yiddish press, saw the largest concentrations of Yiddish literary circles. In the early post-revolutionary Soviet realm, previously served mainly by Yiddish printed matter published in Warsaw, Kiev shortly had the most significant concentration of literary talent, but the writers of that group either only recently saw their first publications or their pre-1917 works were known mainly to a niche circle of highbrow readers. Soon, however, Moscow emerged as the biggest center of Soviet Yiddish culture, relegating Kiev to second place.

In 1925, the American Yiddish poet H. Leivick (1888–1962), then in the orbit of the American communist press, visited the Soviet Union and concluded that his colleagues had huge opportunities there, but lacked established literary figures. As a result, beginner poets and prose writers dominated literary life.[2] In the meantime, government-sponsored Yiddish periodicals, publishing houses (or Yiddish departments at general publishing houses), theaters, and schools of various levels and types had appeared in Moscow, Kiev, Kharkiv, Minsk, and other places, predominantly in Ukraine and Belorussia. The growing infrastructure hungered for people able to write, review, and edit texts of various genres.

Newly established educational institutions, especially Yiddish departments at teachers-training colleges and universities, formed a pool for train-

1 See, e. g., Cohen 2008.

2 Bikl 1972, 446–448.

ing and recruiting a cadre of contributing authors and editorial staff. The "worker correspondents" movement, set in motion in 1922 as part of the emergent proletarian culture, also brought into literature people, stimulated to move from "the machine-tool" to literature, especially as ideologues of Soviet culture placed particularly high expectations on writers with a proletarian background.[3] In 1922, the Kiev קאָמוניסטישע פֿאָן [*Komunistishe fon*, Communist Banner],[4] then the most significant Soviet Yiddish daily, organized the first active group of worker correspondents.[5] Soon every Yiddish newspaper had its worker correspondents. They were active also in the *vant-tsaytungen* [wall newspapers] – self-made, one-copy, often handwritten organs of various organizations. In 1927, the reported number of Yiddish wall newspapers in Ukraine alone was over three hundred.[6] Melech Epstein (1889–1979), an American Jewish communist, wrote after visiting the Soviet Union that wall newspapers played a big role there, featuring in every factory shop, office, institution, and library.[7]

The rise of Rive (pronounced ree-ve) Balyasne (Riva Baliasna in Ukrainian, and Riva Baliasnaia in Russian) (1910–1980), one of many who entered the world of Yiddish letters in the 1920s, epitomizes the process of personal and literary maturation as well as the later travails of physical and professional survival in the Stalinist and post-Stalinist Soviet Union. Engaging with archival material made accessible in recent years in Ukraine, the following historical retelling of her life aims mainly at reconstructing the creative career of a poet, previously – undeservedly – overlooked and neglected by historians and literary scholars. This reconstruction from her first literary steps to the end of her life affords fresh insights and a woman's perspective (an unfortunate rarity) on the Soviet Yiddish literary environment, initially heedfully formed and then violently deformed by the regime. Balyasne's literary oeuvre, however, merits a separate analysis.

3 Hicks 2007.

4 A note on Yiddish used or reproduced in citations: titles of periodicals and citations in Soviet Yiddish orthography have been reproduced in the spelling of the original. Otherwise citations have been standardized according to the YIVO orthographic system. Transcription follows YIVO rules.

5 Portnoy 1962.

6 Slutski 1929, 72.

7 Epstein 1931, 72.

From the Machine-Tool to Literature

Ritalii Zaslavskii (1928–2004), a Soviet Ukrainian poet and translator who knew several Yiddish writers with roots in the proletarian literary movement, wondered whether this type of individual, shaped in the ideological and social conditions of that time, would have professionalized as a writer in a society other than the Soviet Union. His conclusion was that most likely they would not have, simply because – without a strong encouragement from pundits and ideologues – the thought of devoting themselves to such a "strange activity" would have never crossed their mind.[8] Zaslavskii shared these thoughts in his insightful memoir about Balyasne, one of the authors who made up a minority of women among Soviet (and not only Soviet) Yiddish authors.

The gender imbalance was particularly stark in early Soviet Yiddish literary circles. This fact can be illustrated by an open letter, published in the Moscow Yiddish daily דער עמעס [*Der emes*, Truth] on 15 April 1926, calling for cooperation between the Soviet and foreign Yiddish writers. Only one woman is listed among the 48 signatories who represented more or less fully the entire Soviet Yiddish literary 'guild;' the female signatory was Rokhl Brokhes (1880–1942), who lived in Minsk (she would be murdered in the Minsk ghetto sixteen years later) and whose stories began to appear in the Yiddish press in 1899.

Meanwhile, the number of women authors began to grow. In 1929, Khana Levin (1900–1969) made a short-lived sensation with her first poetic collection צושטײַער [*Tsushtayer*, Contribution].[9] Some, if not the majority, of the entrants were members of literary families (which should not be taken as undermining their talent): Shifra Kholodenko (1909–1974), a sister of Dovid Hofshteyn (1889–1952); Dina Libkes (1900–early 1990s), a sister of Itsik Kipnis (1896–1974); Dvoyra Khorol (1894–1982), a niece of Dovid Bergelson (1884–1952); Mira Khenkin's (1900–1960) husband, Nokhem Oyslender (1893–1962) was a leading Yiddish literary critic and scholar; Dora Khaikin's (1913–2006) husband, Ikhil Falikman (1911–1977), from the 1940s onward, specialized in writing prose on war; Rokhl Boymvol's (1914–2000) husband,

8 Zaslavskii 1997, 96.

9 Estraikh 2012; Lisek 2018, 604–638.

Zyame Telesin (1912–1996), was a fellow poet. Poetry, including children's poetry, tended to dominate as the genre of their literary works.

Balyasne did not belong to a literary family. She was born in 1910 in Radomyshl', a small historic town 35 miles east of Zhytomyr and 60 miles west of Kiev. A year after Balyasne's birth, her father went to Argentina and never reunited with his family, leaving it in woeful circumstances. In 1919, during the post-revolutionary wave of violence, the Jewish population of Radomyshl' had dramatically declined due to deaths and emigration.[10] Until 1925, Rive lived mainly in Radomyshl', including four years spent in a children's home, where her mother worked as a cook. Jewish orphanages, which were run by the state but received significant material support from the American Jewish Joint Distribution Committee, fostered in their wards an absolute devotion to Soviet-communist ideals.[11]

After finishing a 7-year local school, Balyasne moved to Kiev. There she received some vocational training and began to work at the First Shoe Factory. Such migration, from a shtetl to Kiev or another city, was not unusual for young people of her generation. Thus, Hershl Polyanker (1911–1998), later a well established Yiddish novelist, came to Kiev around the same time and first worked at one of the city's shoe factories before studying at the Pedagogical Institute. Yoysef (Yosl) Bukhbinder (1908–1993), also later a Kiev-based Yiddish writer, moved from his shtetl to Zhytomyr, worked there as a shoemaker, and then studied at the Odessa Jewish Pedagogical College. Itsik Kipnis, who worked at a tannery in his home shtetl of Sloveshno, settled in Kiev and made a name for himself with his 1926 book חדשים און טעג [*Khadoshim un teg*, Months and Days]. A worker who had migrated from a shtetl to Kiev appears as the protagonist in the early Soviet Yiddish novel, הערשל שאמײַ [*Hershl Shamay*] by Avrom Abtshuk (1897–1937), a leading proletarian author and theorist.

Kiev was considered the center of Ukrainian nationalism. This was how Moscow ideologues labelled the city in its role as the capital during Ukraine's short-lived independence, achieved after the decline and disintegration of the Russian Empire. Following the city's incorporation into the Soviet realm, the authorities punished it by the loss of its capital status. Although more than a few Yiddish literati had chosen to stay in Kiev, many moved to Moscow and

10 Veidlinger 2021, 199–204.

11 Estraikh 2016.

other places, including Kharkiv, which acted as the capital of Soviet Ukraine until 1934 and whose newly established periodicals and publishing houses provided openings in journalism and other writing jobs.

The year 1928 saw the appearance of the Kharkiv Yiddish journal entitled פּראָליט [*Prolit*], an abbreviation for *proletarishe literatur* [proletarian literature]. The periodical's publisher – the Всеукраїнська спілка пролетарських письменників [*Vseukraïns'ka spilka proletars'kykh mennykiv*, All-Ukrainian Association of Proletarian Writers, VUSPP] – took shape in the previous year under the perceptible patronage of Ukraine's Communist Party functionaries.[12] Among the Yiddish writers, who joined the VUSPP, the poet Itsik Fefer (1900–1952) occupied the leading position and was appointed to edit the proletarian literary journal.

In 1929, Fefer came to the First Shoe Factory to prepare a literary event and on that occasion met Balyasne, who had already made a poetic debut in the factory's wall newspapers. Fefer, who was ten years older than Balyasne and by then had authored several poetic collections, encouraged the 19-year-old poet to continue writing and invited her to take part in gatherings of the VUSPP's Yiddish section.[13] Before or after meeting Fefer, Balyasne was admitted to the Communist Party. She clearly embodied the type of *aktivistka*, an active, ideologically charged woman, who played important roles in various domains of Soviet life. At that time, women accounted for a quarter of the Party's Jewish membership, which was the largest share among all Soviet ethnic groups.[14] Balyasne served as a deputy in the Kiev city *soviet* [council] and was many times elected as a Party organizer.

One more thing happened in 1929: *Prolit* published her poem מײַן גליק [*Mayn glik*, My Happiness].[15] However, she was not invited to participate in the אלמאנאך װאופּספּ [*Almanakh VUSPP*, Almanac of the VUSPP], which came out in the same year. The editors apparently still considered the young worker in the category of callow poets, and included poems by more experienced women writers: Khane Levin, Dina Libkes, and Anita (Anyuta; Khane) Pyatigorskaya (1893–1943). The latter's first poetic publication was in 1925 in another Kharkiv Yiddish literary journal די רויטע װעלט [*Di royte velt*, Red

12 Luckyj 1990, 77.

13 Delo 149868, 25.

14 Konstatinov 2007, 239.

15 Balyasne 1929.

World], which convened predominantly those writers averse to proletarian literature. By the end of the 1920s, however, in the increasingly intolerant ideological climate, writers eager to display their ideological purity rushed to recast themselves as neophytes of proletarian literature.

Between 1930 and 1934, Balyasne studied in Kiev at the Yiddish department of the Institute of Professional Education (which in 1933 merged into the Pedagogical Institute) and then, for one academic year, at the *aspirantur*, a graduate program, of the אינסטיטוט פאר ייִדישער פּראָלעטאַרישער קולטור [*Institut far yidisher proletarisher kultur*, Institute for Jewish Proletarian Culture] – the rival of the Vilna-based ייִדישער וויסנשאַפֿטלעכער אינסטיטוט [*Yidisher visnshaftlekher institut*, Jewish Scientific Institute, YIVO] which established its own *aspirantur* around that same time.

The Vilna graduate program set itself the task of providing "intensive scholarly preparation by acquainting [students] with sources, by delving into methodology, by teaching them to do scholarly work independently and to take a scholarly approach to the problems of Jewish culture and society."[16] And while strictly speaking, any graduate program (or *аспирантура* [*aspirantura*] in Russian) in the Soviet Union was supposed to pursue the same goal,[17] the Kiev Institute, by that time the biggest center for academic work conducted in Yiddish (and to a significant degree *on* Yiddish), enrolled also writers as students, including Dora Khaikin, Nathan Zabara (1908–1975), Avrom Gontar (1908–1981), Elye Gordon (1907–1989), and even Itsik Fefer and Dovid Hofshteyn. It seems that, at least partly, their training took a form of a literary seminar led by Max Erik (Zalman Merkin) (1898–1937), a historian of Yiddish literature, who emigrated from Poland in 1929 and worked in Minsk until 1932 before moving to Kiev to become the head of the Institute's department of literary scholarship and criticism.

The year 1934 was very important in the life of 24-year-old Balyasne. First, Ukraine's Державне видавництво національних меншин [*Derzhavne vydavnytstvo natsional'nykh menshyn*, Publishing House for the National Minorities] brought out אין איבערוף [*In iberuf*, Calling the Roll], her collection of poems written between 1928 and 1931. Second, 1934 saw the establishment of the Союз советских писателей [*Soyuz sovetskikh pisateley*, Union of Soviet Writers, USW] as the only official literary organization in the country. In the

16 Kuznitz 2014, 153.

17 Cf. Tsekhovoi 2021.

same year, a Yiddish section, chaired by Fefer, had consolidated Ukraine's Yiddish writers at the republican branch of the USW and, together with similar sections in Belorussia and Moscow, had shaped the state-sponsored Yiddish literary terrain.

Balyasne's 1934 book qualified her to join the USW and its Yiddish section in 1936. This was tantamount to being recognized as a *professional* writer. However, she did not become a freelancer. In the years before the beginning of Nazi Germany's 1941 invasion of the Soviet Union, Balyasne worked as a political editor, or censor, but also as a regular literary editor at the Державне відавнітство національних меншин [*Derzhavne vydavnytstvo natsional'nykh menshyn,* Publishing House for the National Minorities]. An utterly successful product of Soviet social and professional advancement, Balyasne fitted perfectly into the role of a censor, trusted to meet the strict criteria of unconditional, vigilant loyalty to the Party and, even more importantly, to Joseph Stalin.[18]

Like the prevailing majority of other Yiddish writers in Ukraine, Balyasne herself remained unscathed by the mass repressions taking place in the second half of the 1930s. The available historical sources do not disclose any cogent reason explaining a discernible pattern of the purges: the Ukrainian secret police showed intriguing "leniency" towards Yiddish authors, whereas similar literary circles in Belorussia suffered greatly during the same period.[19] True, in 1936 the authorities closed the *Institut far yidisher proletarisher kultur* and many of its staff members, including Max Erik, became victims of the purges. A meagre, albeit academically strong, remnant of the Institute took the shape of the קאַבינעט פאַר ייִדישער קולטור [*Kabinet far yidisher kultur*, Office for Jewish Culture] at the Академія наук УРСР [*Akademia nauk URCR*, Academy of Sciences of the Ukrainian Soviet Socialist Republic].[20]

1937 and 1938 were not only years of mass arrests, but also years of public criticism and recriminations. Fefer faced accusations of committing various "Trotskyist crimes," including, most notably, praising Leon Trotsky in his poetry.[21] It seemed as if the ground had opened under his feet. Subjects of the secret police's interest easily turned into prey of their colleagues, who did

18 Stoian 2013.

19 Estraikh and Budnitskii 2020.

20 Melamed 2020.

21 Anonymous 1937, Leont'ev and Tagans'kyi 1937.

their utmost to insulate themselves by manifesting their loyalty to the regime and their righteous indignation about any activities deemed harmful to the country. Balyasne, however, bravely defended Fefer during a Party meeting and suggested issuing him a reprimand rather than expelling him from the Party.[22] Significantly, Trotsky was hailed in literary works by many writers, many of whom got off with only a fright, although Trotskyism became routinely equated with fascism.[23] Ultimately, Fefer also stayed afloat. Probably as a way of showing his appreciation, Fefer edited Balyasne's 1940 poetic volume ליכטיקע סטעזשקעס [*Likhtike stezhkes*, Light Paths], full of poetic lines expressing the author's happiness with her life, e.g.:

כ׳לעב, ווי ס׳לעבט דער צוויט אין זומער,
ווי עס לעבן רײַפֿע זאַנגען,
ווי די זאַפּט פֿון פֿרישע בלומען,
ווען די זון איז אויפֿגעגאַנגען.[24]

I live like the blossom lives in summer,
Like ripe grain ears live,
Like the nectar of fresh flowers
When the sun has risen.

But her defense of Fefer should not let us believe that Balyasne stepped into the breach for just anyone. In June 1940, she was summoned to be questioned by the secret police who were interested in gathering information on Khaym Gildin (1884–1944), her neighbor in the cooperative apartment building ROLIT [Робітник літератури, *Robitnik literatury*, Worker of Literature], purpose-built for writers in Kiev in the mid-1930s. Expelled from the Party in 1937, Gildin, a veteran of the Jewish revolutionary movement and a pioneer proletarian author, was arrested in 1940, mainly for an attempt to organize a collective protest of writers against the dramatic downsizing of the Yiddish cultural infrastructure, including the phasing out of virtually the entire system of Yiddish education. The interrogator heard from Balyasne what he wanted to hear: that some of Gildin's works were anti-Soviet, with slander concerning the Party and the working class.[25]

22 Delo 149868, 60–61.

23 Babiukh 2007, Sloin 2021.

24 Yiddish original quoted in Gotlib 1945, 34.

25 Delo 147157, 25.

While poetry remained the main genre in her creative output, Balyasne also tried her hand in writing travel impressions. Her short book בוקאָווינער פאַרצייכענונגען [*Bukoviner fartseykhenungen*, Notes from Bukovina], came out in 1941. In the summer of 1940, the Soviet Union annexed Northern Bukovina, previously part of Romania, turning it into a Soviet Ukrainian region with the central city of Chernivtsi. Balyasne was not new to this genre. Earlier, in 1938, she collaborated with Hershl Polyanker in writing documentary prose. It came out in Ukrainian as *Калініндорфські нариси* [*Kalinindorfs'ki narysy*, Notes from Kalinindorf] about the first Jewish district in the Soviet Union established in 1927. Like the four other later-established Jewish districts, comprising predominantly Jewish villages, or *colonies*, in Ukraine and Crimea (then part of the Russian republic), it was destroyed during the war that took the Soviet Union by surprise with the Nazi attack on 22 June 1941 spelling the brutal end to the experiment of settling tens of thousands of Jews on the land and thus making them "productive."[26]

The day after the Nazi attack began, Balyasne spoke at a rally organized by the USW.[27] As the German Wehrmacht closed in on Kiev, Balyasne and her family evacuated to the city of Ufa, the capital of the Bashkir Autonomous Republic, situated southwest of the Ural Mountains, where she served in various capacities before being appointed as a censor in the regional agency. Among the Ukrainian institutions and organizations relocated to the Bashkir capital were the Academy of Sciences, including the Office for Jewish Culture, and the Presidium of the republican branch of the USW. It seems that Balyasne's involvement in the Party organization of the USW made her eligible to be evacuated with the Presidium.[28] In 1942, she took part in a rally, which mirrored the establishment of the ייִדישער אַנטיפאַשיסטישער קאָמיטעט [*Yidisher antifashistisher komitet*, Jewish Antifascist Committee, JAFC], which was destined to play an unintended central role in Soviet Jewish cultural life. At the Ufa rally, she spoke alongside poet Dovid Hofshteyn, head of the Cabinet Elye Spivak (1890–1950), and prose writer Avrom Kahan (1901–1965).[29]

In 1943, a collection of her poems *Стихи, 1941–1942* [*Stikhi*, Poems, 1941–1942] was published in Russian translations under the imprint of

26 See, e.g., Dekel-Chen 2005.

27 Tsalik and Sekihei 2003.

28 Cf. Lubchenko 1999, 46.

29 Delo 149868, 149.

Ukraine's USW despite appearing in Ufa. Maksym Rylskii (1895–1964), a leading Ukrainian poet, edited the collection. The translators were well-established literati: Iakov Gorodskoi (1898–1996), Mark Shekhter (1911–1963), Rafail Skomorovskii (1899–1962), and Elena Il'ina (1901–1964). The opening poem, "Моему народу" [*Moemu narodu*, To My People], the last line of which reads "Гражданка я, еврейка я!" [*Grazhdanka ya, evreyka ya!*, I am a citizen, I am a Jewess!], echoes Fefer's probably most famous poem איך בין א ייִד [*Ikh bin a yid*, I am a Jew], which first appeared on 27 December 1942 in the JAFC's newspaper אייניקייט [*Eynikayt*, Unity] and was later frequently anthologized as a sample of Soviet Jewish patriotism.

Delayed Punishment

In 1944, Balyasne, like several other Yiddish writers, including Hofshteyn, Kahan, and Kipnis, returned to Kiev. Babyn Yar (Babi Yar in Russian), the killing site of tens of thousands of Jews, became a prominent theme in the memorialization of Nazi atrocities in the Soviet Union and Balyasne immortalized the massacre in powerful poetic lines in 1966.[30] After the Nazi occupation, Kiev's Yiddish cultural infrastructure lay in utter ruins, with little signs that the Soviet authorities had plans for its full revival to the prewar level.

Balyasne spent most of August and September 1944 in Chernivtsi and its surrounding areas that had been liberated six months prior. Comparable to her trips to Bukovina and Kalinindorf in the 1930s, the USW sponsored her trip aimed at collecting material for a poem, which would appear in book form in 1947 and translated into Ukrainian as *Дівчина з Іванкова* [*Divchyna z Ivankova*, A Girl from Ivankov]. During her trip, she encountered another Yiddish poet, Naftole Herts Kon (1910–1971). Born in Storozhynets, fifteen miles from Chernivtsi, he grew up in the then-Romanian city and later left for Warsaw, where he was arrested for his links with the Polish communist underground. In 1933, he was allowed to emigrate to the Soviet Union, where his foreign "connections," interpreted this time as a proof of alleged links with Polish spying agencies, led to another arrest in 1937. He was released from the gulag in 1941. Rehabilitated, Kon appeared in Chernivtsi as a correspondent of *Eynikayt*.

30 See, e.g., Dvuzhil'naia 2015, 116.

Both Kon and Balyasne were appalled by the attitude of the Soviet authorities toward local Jews, who faced various obstacles in their pursuits to rebuild their shattered lives. Alarming rumors about more restrictions and expulsions exacerbated the already difficult situation. The writers had a meeting with Ivan Zeleniuk (1909–1966), Party head of the region, who allowed them to convene a public gathering aimed at explaining the real situation and dampening intra-Jewish tensions. According to Kon's report, over two thousand people came to listen to him and Balyasne.[31] Significantly, an illusion of liberalization as the regime's gratitude for wartime patriotism and heroism took hold of the intelligentsia and this emboldened them to raise their voice.[32]

In 1946, Balyasne took part in another initiative. Together with Avrom Kahan she met with Konstantin Litvin (1907–1994), the functionary responsible for agitation and propaganda at the Central Committee of Ukraine's Communist Party organization (in 1953–1956, he served as Ukraine's Minister of Culture). Their suggestion was to resume the activities of the Yiddish section at the USW, and to launch a Yiddish literary publication in Kiev. They enlisted the support of Itsik Fefer, who happened to have come to Kiev from Moscow. Fefer spoke at a meeting of the leading members of the USW about the 1943 North America tour, undertaken by him, now one of the top figures in the JAFC, and Shloyme Mikhoels (1890–1948), chairman of the JAFC and director of the Московский Государственный Еврейский Театр, [*Moskovskiy gosudarstvenny Evreyskiy Teatr,* Moscow State Yiddish Theater, short: GOSET]. The Central Committee endorsed both suggestions: the Yiddish section, chaired by Hershl Polyanker, resumed its work, and the literary almanac דער שטערן [*Der shtern*, Star] began to appear in 1947.[33] An almanac entitled היימלאַנד [*Heymland*, Homeland] was launched in Moscow in the same year.

Meanwhile, a high profile scandal developed over the publication of Itsik Kipnis' story אָן חכמות, אָן חשבונות [*On khokhmes, on kheshboynes*, Without a Second Thought] in the Łódź newspaper דאָס נײַע לעבן [*Dos naye lebn*, New life] on 19 May 1947. A story about a Ukrainian woman in a Nazi-occupied Ukrainian town who risked her life by adopting two Jewish orphans in order to save them, rubbed against the early postwar party line on the eve of the an-

31 Delo 149868, 170.

32 Zubkova 1998, 88.

33 Delo 149868, 72, 73, 112.

ti-Jewish purges and was condemned as egregiously nationalistic: first, Kipnis inscribed his concerns that the adopted children would lose their sense of belonging to the Jewish nation, and second, he wanted Jews to speak Yiddish and, generally, to be openly proud of their Jewishness. In particular, he craved to see a red Star of David on the breasts of Jewish Red Army soldiers, pinned next to their medals earned in battle. Two months later, sixteen Kiev-based members of the section of Yiddish writers, including Balyasne, took part in a heated meeting, that reached the verdict to expel Kipnis from the USW. Also in July 1947, Oleksander Korniychuk (1905–1972), head of the Ukrainian Writers Union, referred to this decision in his speech at a high profile meeting in Moscow. At that same meeting, Yiddish poet and chair of the Moscow Yiddish section Leyb Kvitko (1890–1952) deplored Kipnis for staining the honor of being called a Soviet writer. For all that, Kipnis remained a member of the USW, albeit only until his arrest two years later, on 29 June 1949.[34]

By the time of Kipnis's arrest, virtually the entire infrastructure of Yiddish cultural life was in ruins. Yiddish writers had been living in a state of fear since 16 September 1948, the day of Dovid Hofshteyn's arrest. Even before that, not everyone was convinced that Mikhoels's death in January 1948 was really the tragic outcome of an ordinary traffic accident. 20 November 1948 saw the last issue of *Eynikayt*, the Moscow Yiddish newspaper. The JAFC was dissolved on the same day. Established within wartime propaganda machinery of the Soviet Information Bureau, the JAFC had de facto become the bedrock and center for Yiddish cultural life in the country. Five days after JAFC's liquidation, the Moscow Jewish publishing house *Der emes* was closed. In early February 1949, the authorities shut down the remaining two Yiddish literary periodicals, *Heymland* and *Der shtern*. Meanwhile, the USW was instructed to dissolve its Yiddish sections. Yiddish theaters, including amateur ones, disappeared one by one. Likewise, the remaining Yiddish schools and academic bodies were shut. All this happened against the backdrop of arrests of Yiddish writers and other literati in Moscow, Kiev, Minsk, Birobidzhan, Vilna, and several other cities. Among those arrested were two women: Rive Balyasne and Luba Vasserman (1905–1975), the latter of which had come to the Soviet Union from Palestine and settled in Birobidzhan.[35]

34 Altshuler 2004.

35 Kotlerman 2017, 199–206.

Before and after the war, the Stalinist repressions consumed many ambitious people daring to show initiative. The Soviet saying "any initiative is punishable" exists for good reason. According to the always amorphous 'rule book,' though, an initiative must originate from the top of the Soviet hierarchy. This might lead us to deduce that it was Balyasne's participation in the grassroots initiatives making her 'culpable' a couple of years later. The real reason for her arrest, however, was altogether different: she, like hundreds of thousands of other Jews and non-Jews, was singled out not so much for *personal* 'crimes,' but as a member of a 'harmful,' 'bourgeois-nationalist' group who were purged from society 'prophylactically.' Between 1948 and 1953, such a purge targeted Soviet Jewish intellectuals in order to divorce Soviet Jews from Yiddish culture. In sharp contrast particularly to the war-years, now in the paranoiac atmosphere of Cold War, Yiddish culture began to be seen as an energizing stimulus of 'nationalist' feelings. Its inherent transnationality – leading, at least potentially, to contacts with Jews in other countries, most notably the new state of Israel and the United States – caused particular concerns.

Balyasne, though, was taken into custody on 6 May 1952, significantly later than the majority of other arrested Yiddish writers, two days prior in fact to the start of a secret trial in Moscow against a group of fifteen members and staff of the JAFC, which culminated in the assassination of thirteen of them, including Perets Markish (1895–1952), Dovid Hofstheyn, Itsik Fefer, Leyb Kvitko, and Dovid Bergelson. Their execution on the night of 12 August 1952 decapitated Soviet Yiddish literary circles. The 'delay' in Balyasne's arrest occurred, most probably, because she was less visible in the literary landscape and, as outlined in this chapter, more convincingly loyal to the regime. Limited staff capacity of the repressive machinery might be an additional factor for why arrests took place intermittently. Inadvertently, thanks to Stalin's death in March 1953, many Yiddish writers were spared from prosecution. Balyasne was not one of them – being associated with too many 'enemies of the people' in various ways.

The secret police's narrative metamorphosed her fellow writers and friends, most notably Fefer, Kon, and Kahan, into accomplices of anti-Soviet conspiracies and nationalist pursuits. Thus, on 4 November 1948, Sergei Savchenko (1904–1966), Minister of State Security of Soviet Ukraine, informed Nikita Khrushchev (1894–1971), then head of Ukraine's Party apparatus, and other top officials of the republic about the arrest of Hofshteyn, "an active Jewish nationalist." In this memorandum, Balyasne was mentioned together with several writers, such as Kipnis and Kahan, who grouped around Hofshteyn "on the ground of nationalist views."[36]

While Yiddish literati were not, as a rule, prosecuted specifically for 'literary crimes,' investigators would pay close attention to their writings, searching for ideological 'flaws' that would make the indictment look more convincing. Pursuant to the November 1938 decree "Об арестах, прокурорском надзоре и ведении следствия" [About arrests, prosecutor supervision, and course of investigation], which effectively marked an end to the Great Terror of 1937/38, 'validation' of accusations became important. The 'validation' process included, in particular, the establishment of literary commissions for evaluating the ideological content of works by the arrested writers.

In 1940, Balyasne herself had been a member of a commission that scrutinized Khaym Gildin's oeuvre. In a note written in 1957, Ikhil Falikman, a member of the same commission, admitted that back then they did not aim at ascertaining the truth of the matter. Above all, they evaluated those of Gildin's stories and poems which allegedly contained ideologically flawed sections, but ignored entirely in their conclusion the positive side of his literary work.[37] Much the same was characteristic of the conclusion written by the literary scholars Zakhar Libman (1911–1981), Mikhail Bernshteyn (1910–2002), and Grigorii Verves (1920–2001) who made up the commission dealing with Balyasne's writings.[38] On 30 May 1952, the troika submitted their conclusion, which emphasized nationalist motifs in Balyasne's works. It seems that she admitted or rather was coerced to admit that her works, at least in part, engaged in Jewish nationalist themes. Her poem "To My People" was deemed particularly harmful.[39]

Fleeting contacts with foreigners – Paul (Peysekh) Novick (1891–1989),

36 Agenturnoe delo "Krug:" vol. 1, 102.

37 Delo 147157, 352f.

38 Delo 149868, 54f. In 1971, Libman successfully defended his doctoral dissertation on the *Disintegration of Human's Image in Modernist Literature*. The defense took place at the Taras Shevchenko Institute of Literature of the National Academy of Sciences of Ukraine, where Bernshtein, a leading specialist in Ukrainian literature, worked for over sixty years. Even more distinguished was Verves, later a member of Ukraine's Academy of Sciences and head of the department of Slavic literatures of the Institute.

39 Ibid., 129–130.

editor of the American Communist Yiddish daily מאָרגן־פֿרײַהייט [*Morgn-frayhayt*, Morning-Freedom], and Ben-Zion Goldberg (1895–1972), Sholem Aleichem's son-in-law known as a Soviet fellow traveler and enthusiast of the Birobidzhan project – 'reinforced' the indictment. The American journalists visited Kiev in 1946. Both were kept under tight surveillance and later recast as intelligence operatives. These roles, pinned on them without any evidence, helped to also accuse of espionage those tried in Moscow in 1952, including the leading Yiddish writers.[40] The fact that Balyasne's father lived abroad also put a cloud of suspicion over her, although the investigators seemingly did not know that Nokhem Balyasne, who lived in Junin, Argentina, followed his daughter's literary success from afar. On 19 November 1944, the Buenos Aires Yiddish newspaper די פּרעסע [*Di prese*, The Press] reprinted Balyasne's poem sent to the editors by her proud father.[41]

In Balyasne's case, like in the majority of other cases, there was no trial. The administrative, absentia sentencing by an Особое совещание [*Osoboe soveshchanye*, Special (Sentencing) Commission] did not give her a chance to have a legal defense with witness testimony. On 23 August 1952, the Commission rubber-stamped the verdict suggested by the investigators on her case file: ten years in a gulag, namely the special camp for political prisoners in the settlement of Inta, situated northwest of the Ural Mountains, in a remote and inhospitable area of Komi Republic. On 15 September, Balyasne was informed about the verdict. In Inta, she suffered a mental breakdown diagnosed as "reactive disorder."

In one of her appeals, she wrote:

> […] одиночка с бегающими крысами нарушали мою психику. Я поэт и в силу своей профессии воспринимаю многое острее, чем другие.
>
> Начались вызовы. Как правило только ночные. Засну – разбудят. Продержат пару часов, отправят в холодный бокс, снова вызывают и держат до утра.
>
> Следователь откуда-то достает бумаги, не спрашивая пишет и под утро очумевшую, ничего не соображающую заставляет подписывать. Крики его разносились по всему коридору, и он очень часто напоминал мне, что я еврейка.[42]

40 Rubenstein and Naumov 2001, 56.

41 Pomerantz 1962, 438f.

42 Delo 149868, 249.

> […] the solitary confinement [in the first days after the arrest], with rats running around, damaged my mental state. I am a poet and, by virtue of my profession, I react to many things more emotionally than others.
>
> The interrogations began. As a rule – only at night. I would be woken up just after falling asleep. After a couple of hours of interrogation, I would find myself confined in a cold box cell, and then brought once again [to the investigator] and kept until the morning.
>
> The investigator pulls out some papers from somewhere, writes something without asking any questions, and then, at dawn, when I feel completely dazed and unable to think straight, he forces me to sign the papers. His shouting can be heard all over the corridor. He often also reminded me that I am Jewish.

As a convicted 'enemy of the people,' Balyasne was mostly kept in psychiatric wards of hospitals, first in Inta, then in Kazan (Tataria), and finally in Pot'ma (Mordovia). She was eventually liberated in December 1955 with a full legal rehabilitation following in January 1956. Back in Kiev, she was reunited with her husband and son, who never stopped writing appeals to various state officials, and reinstated as a member of both the Communist Party in October 1956[43] and the Union of Soviet Writers, renamed that year as the Writers Union of the USSR.

Delayed Recognition

The years of confinement and torture took their toll and recuperation was slow and painful. According to Avrom Kahan's letter to Leyb Olitzky (1884–1975), a Polish Yiddish writer, who lived as a refugee in Ufa from 1942 to 1945, Balyasne was not well, but she could walk, wrote little by little, made attempts at publishing in Ukrainian.[44] Balyasne gradually regained her physical and mental health. In 1960, she wrote in her autobiography:

> В творческом отношении чувствую себя еще молодой, в самом цвету. Я обогатилась такими переживаниями, которые делают всегда человека более зрелым, более сильным… Однако нельзя не учесть, что из жизни моей были утеряны целых двенадцать лет.[45]

43 Delo 149868, 261.

44 Altshuler 1979, 420.

45 Russian original quoted from Beider 2003, 27.

> Creatively, I still feel young, in full bloom. I was enriched by such difficult experiences which inevitably makes a person more mature, toughen them… However, it is impossible to ignore the fact that twelve whole years of my life have been lost.

Ritalii Zaslavskii, the Soviet Ukrainian writer and poet I referred to at the beginning of this chapter, knew Balyasne well in the last decades of her life. He concluded that she "скорее недоумевала, как такое могло случиться, чем понимала, что же в действительности произошло" [was more puzzled about how such things could have happened, rather than understanding what had actually happened].[46] It also might be that, as part of her post-traumatic strategy, she felt compelled to hide her feelings behind the veneer of optimism. No doubt, it was more innocuous to manifest an unshaken loyalty to Soviet ideals. On 8 March 1960 – International Women's Day and also Balyasne's birthday – the Writers Union's Moscow weekly *Литературная газета* [*Literaturnaya gazeta*, Literary Newspaper] published a Russian translation of her poem "Моя Родина" [*Moya Rodina*, My Homeland] with such lines as:

> Родина! С любовью самой беззаветной
> Обращаюсь к каждой ласточке твоей.[47]
>
> Homeland! With my unquestioned love
> I speak to each of your swallows.

Whether mere lip service or heartfelt commitment, she was convincing: to foreign Jewish tourists she was chosen to perform the embodiment of a successful Soviet Yiddish writer.[48] And in 1961, Balyasne's literary accomplishments were nationally recognized through the publication of her poetic collections both in Russian (in Moscow) and in Ukrainian (in Kiev). 1961 also saw the establishment of the Moscow Yiddish literary journal סאָוועטיש היימלאַנד [*Sovetish heymland*, Soviet Homeland], which would dominate Yiddish literary, and partly cultural, life until the end of the Soviet period in 1991. In October 1964, Balyasne took part in a gala devoted to Yiddish liter-

46 Zaslavskii 1997, 92.

47 Balyasne 1960.

48 Sklokina 2021, 95.

ature, which took place at the October Palace of Culture in Kiev which was usually used as a concert stage. Arn Vergelis (1918–1999), editor of *Sovetish heymland*, announced that in 1965 the journal would double its periodicity from six to twelve issues a year. In addition, Советский писатель [*Sovetskiy pisatel'*, Soviet Writer], the Writers Union's main producer of books and publisher of *Sovetish heymland*, would start publishing Yiddish books by contemporary authors.[49]

Balyasne's turn came very late – in 1979, one year before her death. The line for poetic volumes could be particularly long in the bottleneck of the *Sovetskiy pisatel'*s Yiddish output. Shifra Kholodenko's book saw the light of day in 1974, Dora Khaikin's – in 1975. The title of Balyasne's 1979 Yiddish book, גאָלדענער בלעטערפֿאַל [*Goldener bleterfal*, Golden Leaf Fall] recycled the title of her book of Ukrainian translations, published in 1967 in Kiev: *Золотий листопад* [Golden Leaf Fall]. By that time, several other books of Balyasne's poetry had been published in Russian and Ukrainian translation.

Coming to terms with gulag experiences was a life-long process for many people in the Yiddish literary circles, including Hirsh Remenik (1905–1981), who headed the Moscow Yiddish journal's literary criticism section from 1964 to 1981. Sixteen years lay between his arrest and liberation in 1955. In the January 1965 issue of *Sovetish heymland*, he pointed to two approaches to Stalinism, which were, in his opinion, wrong: advocates of the first approach argued that there was no need to return to this topic because the Party had already fully eradicated the mistakes, whereas advocates of the second approach did not believe that the de-Stalinization campaign could last long and therefore were leery of participating in it. In contrast, Remenik insisted on a serious attitude toward de-Stalinization and welcomed the first attempts by journal contributors to write on this topic.[50] In 1965, Balyasne was one of those who made such an 'attempt' in her story נאָך דער גאָלדענער פּאַווע [*Nokh der goldener pave*, In Pursuit of the Golden Peacock], based on her own experience of facing Stalinist "justice"[51] right before this topic was rendered a strictly observed taboo.

Yekhiel Shraybman (1913–2005), a Yiddish writer who lived in Kishinev, remembered warmly his Kiev colleague. According to him, Balyasne "была

49 Anonymous 1964.

50 Remenik 1965.

51 Balyasne 1965.

тонким лирическим поэтом. В жизни экзальтированная, девически восторженная, открытая, подчас взбалмошная, подчас обескураживающая" [was a fine lyric poet. As a person, she was ecstatic, girlishly exhilarated, open, sometimes mischievous, and sometimes disconcerting].[52] Balyasne's books did not make her popular or famous. Rather, like the vast majority of Soviet Yiddish authors, she was overshadowed by better known writers and has so far been almost completely disregarded in scholarly and critical literature. Yet, her overall invisibility could all but delay and thus shorten her victimization in the grinds of late Stalinist purges. Her modest post-Stalinist recognition declined in the last decades of her life, when the Yiddish literary community and the readership kept dramatically shrinking.[53] One can only wonder about the size of the niche readership interested in Russian and Ukrainian translations of her and other Soviet Yiddish authors' poetry. I agree with Marat Grinberg, who writes:

> Many, and perhaps even most, of the editions of Soviet Yiddish literature in Russian fell into the unread category, purchased as symbolic markers of Jewishness both for their Jewish owners and at times for others, whom they let into the private space of their Soviet apartments. To reiterate, the phrase on the cover page – translated from Yiddish – carried a substantial emblematic weight. The books bearing it were sought out, brought home, and deposited in the bookcase often never to be opened.[54]

In the post-Stalinist years, Balyasne and her colleagues lived a relatively comfortable life, enjoying privileges bestowed on Writers Union's members, but it also was a life in an increasingly insular, obscure, and aging Yiddish literary milieu, centered around the *Sovetish heymland*. Yet, she found a solace in continuing to write poetry, even if she was one of its few readers:

ס׳איז דאָ דען אף דער וועלט א גרעסטער גליק,
ווי זײַן פארטאָן אין גרויסער דיכטער־וועלט...[55]

Is there really a greater joy in the world
Than to busy yourself in the great world of poetry…

[52] Shraybman 1988, 91.
[53] Estraikh 1995.
[54] Grinberg 2023, 108.
[55] Balyasne 1974.

Bibliography

Archival Sources

Агентурное дело "Круг," 1948. Галузевий державний архів Служби безпеки України [Sectoral State Archive of the Security Service of Ukraine, HAD SBU] 65–1-6974.

Дело 147157: По обвинению Гильдина Хайма Мордуховича, Центральний державний архів громадських об'єднань України [Central State Archives of Public Organizations of Ukraine, TsDAGO] 263–01–32980.

Дело 149868: По обвинению Балясной Ривы Наумовны, TsDAGO 263 – 01 – 44792.

Sources

Anonymous, 1937: Аноним: Разоблачить Авербаховщину до конца: письмо из Харькова. В: *Литературная газета*, 5 July: 6.

Anonymous, 1964 אַנאָנים: אָוונט וועגן דער ייִדישער ליטעראַטור אין קיִעוו ציט צו אַ זייער ריזיקן עולם;ווערגעליס זאָגט צו ייִדישע ביכער. אין: **פֿאָרווערטס** (ניו־יאָרק), דעם 11טן אָקטאָבער: 12.

Altshuler, Mordechai, ed., 1979 אַלטשולער, מרדכי: **בריוו פֿון ייִדישע סאָוועטישע שרײַבערס.** ירושלים: העברעיִשער אוניווערסיטעט.

Altshuler, Mordechai, 2004: Itsik Kipnis: The 'White Crow' of Soviet Yiddish Literature: The MGB File of 1949. In: *Jews in Russia and Eastern Europe* 2: 68–167.

Babiukh, Vitalii A., 2007: Бабюх, В. А.: Діяльність політичної цензури як форма ідеологічного контролю в Україні (1920 – 1930-ті рр.). В: *Історія України: маловідомі імена, події, факти* 24: 21.

Balyasne, Rive, 1929 באַליאַסנע, ריווע: מײַן גליק. אין: **פּראָליט** (כארקיוו) 5: 27.

Balyasne, Rive, 1960: Балясная, Рива: Моя Родина. В: *Литературная газета*, 8 марта: 3.

Balyasne, Rive, 1965 באַליאַסנע, ריווע: נאָך דער גאָלדענער פּאַווע. אין: **סאָוועטיש היימלאַנד** (מאָסקווע) 6: 44–82.

Balyasne, Rive, 1974 באַליאַסנע, ריווע: אין גרויסער דיכטער־וועלט. אין: **סאָוועטיש היימלאַנד** (מאָסקווע) 2: 109.

Beider, Khaim, 2003: Бейдер, Хаим: *Этюды о еврейских писателях*. Київ: Дух і Літера.

Bikl, Shloyme, ed., 1972 ביקל, שלמה: **פּנקס פֿאַר דער פֿאָרשונג פֿון דער ייִדישער ליטעראַטור און פּרעסע.** ניו־יאָרק: אַלוועלטלעכער ייִדישער קולטור־קאָנגרעס.

Cohen, Nathan, 2008: The Yiddish Press and Yiddish Literature: A Fertile but Complex Relationship. In: *Modern Judaism* 28 (2): 149–172.

Dekel-Chen, Jonathan L., 2005: *Farming the Red Land: Jewish Agricultural Colonization and Local Soviet Power, 1924–1941*. New Haven, Conn.: Yale University Press.

Dvuzhil'naia, Inessa F., 2015: Двужильная, Инесса Ф.: Память о Бабьем Яре в звуках музыки. В: *Часопис Національної Музичної Академії України імені П. І. Чайковського* 1: 106–119.

Epstein, Melekh, 1931 עפשטיין, מלך: **סאָוועטן־פֿאַרבאַנד בויט סאָציאַליזם: ווי אַזוי דער פֿינף־יאָר פּלאַן רופֿט זיך אָפּ אויף אַלע געביטן פֿון לעבן**. ניו־יאָרק: פֿאַרלאַג אינטערנאַציאָנאַלער אַרבעטער־אָרדן.

Estraikh, Gennady, 1995: The Era of *Sovetish Heymland*: Readership of the Yiddish Press in the Former Soviet Union. In: *East European Jewish Affairs* 25 (1): 17–22.

Estraikh, Gennady, 2016: Jewish Wards of the Soviet State: Fayvl Sito's These Are Us. In: Gennady Estraikh, Kerstin Hoge, and Mikhail Krutikov, eds.: *Children in Yiddish Literature: From Early Modernity to Post-Modernity*. Oxford: Legenda, 137–153.

Estraikh, Gennady, 2012: Khana Levin's Verdict to Free Love. In: Daniela Mantovan, ed., *Yiddish Poets and the Soviet Union, 1917–1948*. Heidelberg: Universitätsverlag Winter, 87–94.

Estraikh, Gennady, and Oleg Budnitskii, 2020: From the Great Terror to the Terror in 1941: The Case of Yiddish Writers in Soviet Belorussia. In: *East European Jewish Affairs* 50 (3): 292–308.

Gotlib, Noyekh Yitskhok, 1945 גאָטליב, נח יצחק: **סאָוועטישע שרײַבער**. מאָנטרעאַל: נ.י. גאָטליב בוך־קאָמיטעט.

Grinberg, Marat, 2023: *The Soviet Jewish Bookshelf: Jewish Culture and Identity between the Lines*. Waltham, Mass.: Brandeis University Press.

Hicks, Jeremy, 2007: Worker Correspondents: Between Journalism and Literature. In: *The Russian Review* 66 (4): 568–585.

Konstantinov, Viacheslav, 2007: Константинов, Вячеслав: *Еврейское население бывшего СССР в XX веке : Социально-демографический анализ*. Иерусалим: Изд-во Лира.

Luckyj, George S.N., 1990: *Literary Politics in the Soviet Ukraine, 1917–1934*. Durham, NC: Duke University Press.

Kotlerman, Ber Boris, 2017: *Broken Heart/Broken Wholeness: The Post-Holocaust Plea for Jewish Reconstruction of the Soviet Yiddish Writer Der Nister*. Brighton, Mass.: Academic Studies Press.

Kuznitz, Cecile E., 2014: *YIVO and the Making of Modern Jewish Culture: Scholarship for the Yiddish Nation*. New York, NY: Cambridge University Press.

Leont'ev, A., and Ia. Tagans'kyi, 1937: Леонтьев, А., Я. Таганський: Оздоровити еврейську секцію письменників України. In: *Вісті*, 24 листопада: 4.

LISEK, Joanna, 2018: *Kol isze - głos kobiet w poezji jidysz (od XVI w. do 1939 r.)*. Sejny: Pogranicze.

LUBCHENKO, Arkadii, 1999: Любченко, Аркадій: *Щоденник Аркадія Любченка*. Львів, Нью-Йорк: Видавництво МПКоць.

MELAMED, Efim, 2020: Меламед, Ефим: Как был уничтожен «венец еврейской культуры»: еврейские ученые Киева накануне и во время Большого террора. В: Геннадий Эстрайх и Александр Френкель, р. к., *Советская гениза: новые архивные разыскания по истории евреев в СССР. Т. 1*. Бостон: Academic Studies Press; Санкт-Петербург: БиблиоРоссика, 109 – 170.

POMERANTZ, Alexander, 1962 פּאָמעראַנץ, אַלעקסאַנדער: **די סאָוועטישע הרוגי־מלכות (צו זייער 10טן יאָרצײַט): וועגן דעם טראַגישן גורל פֿון די ייִדישע שרײַבערס און דער ייִדישער ליטעראַטור אין סאָוועטלאַנד.** בוענאָס־אײַרעס: ייִדישער וויסנשאַפֿטלעכער אינסטיטוט – ייִוואָ.

PORTNOY, Ephraim, 1962 פּאָרטנוי, אפֿרים: דער ערשטער ייִדישער אַרבעטער־קאָרעספּאָנדענטן־קרײַז. אין: **פֿאָלקס־שטימע** (וואַרשע), דעם 18טן דעצעמבער: 3 – 4.

REMENIK, Hersh, 1965 רעמעניק, הערש: נאָטיצן וועגן אונדזער פּראָזע. אין: **סאָוועטיש היימלאַנד** (מאָסקווע) 1: 146.

RUBENSTEIN, Joshua and Vladimir P. NAUMOV, 2001. *Stalin's Secret Pogrom: The Postwar Inquisition of the Jewish Anti-Fascist Committee*. New Haven, Conn.: Yale University Press.

SHRAYBMAN, Ikhil [Yekhiel], 1988: Шрайбман, Ихил: *Далее*... Москва: Советский писатель.

SKLOKINA, Iryna, 2021: International Tourism and the Making of the National Heritage Canon in Soviet Ukraine. In: Eszter Gantner, Corinne Geering, and Paul Vickers, eds., *Heritage under Socialism: Preservation in Eastern and Central Europe, 1945 – 1991*. New York, NY: Berghahn Books, 78 – 104.

SLOIN, Andrew, 2021: Слойн, Эндрю: "Кто фашист?": Евреи, нацисты и сталинский антифашизм. In: *Judaic-Slavic Journal* 2: 101 – 126.

SLUTSKI, Ber, 1929 סלוצקי, בער: **לעקסיקאָן פֿון פּאָליטישע און פֿרעמד־ווערטער**. קיִעוו: קולטור־ליגע.

STOIAN, Tatiana A., 2013: Стоян, Тетяна А.: Номенклатура политической цензуры в советской Украине 1920 – 1930-х гг.. В: М.В. Зеленов и В.В. Мамонов, р.к., *История книги и цензуры : материалы международной научной конференции, посвященной памяти Арлена Викторовича Блюма (30.03.1933 – 04.06.20): 29 – 30 мая 2012 г.* Санкт-Петербург: Ленинградский государственный университет имени А.С. Пушкина, 168 – 178.

TSALIK, Stanislav and Pylyp SELIHEI, 2003: Цалик, Станіслав і Пилип Селігей: Коли у червні почалась війна. In: *Літературна Ukraïna*, 19 червня: 7.

TSEKHOVOI, Nikolai P., 2021: Цеховой, Николай П.: Организационно-правовое оформление системы советской аспирантуры: основные этапы и особенности Organizatsionno-pravovoe oformlenie sistemy sovetskoi aspirantury: osnovnye etapy i osobennosti. В: *Вестник Томского государственного университета* 362: 111–115.

Veidlinger, Jeffrey, 2021: *In the Midst of Civilized Europe: The Pogroms of 1918–1921 and the Onset of the Holocaust*. New York: Metropolitan Books.

Zaslavskii, Ritalii, 1997: Заславский, Риталий: Другой жизни у нее не было: из воспоминаний о Риве Балясной. In: *Егупец* 3: 92–99.

Zubkova, Elena Iu., 1998: *Russia After the War: Hopes, Illusions, and Disappointments, 1945–1957*. Armonk, NY: M.E. Sharpe.

Miriam Chorley-Schulz

An Introduction to "Journeys: Poland"

In the anatomy of that modern cultural space called ייִדישלאַנד [Yiddishland], linking disparate regions around the globe through diverse, oftentimes overlapping, cultural and political practices in Yiddish, the territory making up פּוילן [*Poyln,* Poland] in its different historio-geographical demarcations has functioned as a chamber of its beating heart. It has had a complex cultural and social structure in itself and simultaneously pumped ideas and the bodies that carried them into the ever-constituting transnational Yiddish-speaking world. Pursuant to the rules of circulation, movement often comes back full circle: some who had left, came back to visit those who had stayed behind; others without living memory of the 'old country' embarked on heritage travels to Poland; and others journeyed through Poland as the imagined cradle of an 'untouched Jewish authenticity.'[1] Cultural, heritage, salvage-anthropological, or imagined travel to Poland, in other words, are modern Jewish traditions, overlapping and well-established since the 19th century.

Any dysfunctions and abnormalities of a heart vessel, however minute, may result in severe consequences, though, and the חורבן [*khurbn*, destruction, Holocaust] with its epicenter in German-occupied Poland was nothing short of a full-blown attack. For all the brutal ruptures and irreparable transformations this catastrophe caused, it did also alter Jewish travel. From 1945 onwards, for some time significantly impeded by Cold War restrictions to mobility, Jewish tourism turned necessarily 'dark.'[2] Visits to concentration and death camps, former ghettos and Jew-less *shtetlekh* became so significant over time that today's post-socialist Poland ranks second in most visited destinations for organized Jewish group travel with over 100,000 visitors

I would like to thank Binyamin Hunyadi, Roland Gruschka, my co-editor Alexander Walther, and the copy editor Jasmine Chorley-Schulz for the constructive criticism that improved the introduction immensely.

1 Samuel Spinner has recently explored the latter phenomenon, see Spinner 2021.

2 I am invoking here the paradigm of "Dark Tourism," tourism to places of atrocities and mass violence. The growing body of research cannot be reviewed here in detail, but see, for instance, Bajohr, Drecoll and Lennon 2020.

annually – only surpassed by Israel/Palestine.[3] It is probably safe to say that the majority of pre-*khurbn* visitors, those traveling to Poland in the immediate postwar period[4] as well as today's Jewish tourists mostly journey from the 'West' (including Israel/Palestine), in an Orientalist fashion, to the East: on the quest to reconnect with that part of history conceived of as heritage, people reverse their parents' or grandparents' redemptive journey westward by temporarily moving backward – certainly geographically, in a sense also in time, and, this is arguably a desired sensation, civilizationally (from alleged 'freedom' to 'unfreedom').[5] But what about intra-socialist travel from Poland's *East* during the Cold War?

The following travel notes by Ukraine-born, Birobidzhan-raised Arn Vergelis (1918–1999) explore a so far underappreciated kind of Jewish travel to Poland that coupled antifascist 'dark tourism' with cultural ethnography not limited to finding traces of a lost Jewish *past* but aiming to represent continuities in change of that past in the Polish Yiddish socialist *present*. First published in two consecutive fall issues of the Soviet Yiddish journal סאָוועטיש היימלאַנד [*Sovetish heymland*, Soviet Homeland] in 1965,[6] the Soviet Yiddish poet, novelist, and 'infamous' editor of that journal narrates his journey around Poland as part of a Soviet delegation in April 1965. Together with Afanasy Dimitrievich Goncharov, a Red Army major general who took part in the liberation of Auschwitz, Aleksander Lebedev, Auschwitz-survivor and assistant editor of *Медицинская Газета* [*Meditsinskaya Gazeta*, Journal of Medicine], as well as Ekaterina Belostotskaya, a Minsk ghetto and Auschwitz survivor, Vergelis participated in memorial events organized in conjunction with the 20th anniversary of the liberation of the Auschwitz camp complex

3 This includes institutionalized tourism like the Israeli youth tour to Poland "March of the Living," see Lehrer 2013, 58.

4 Please see Kijek's chapter in the present volume on this immediate postwar phenomenon.

5 This Orientalist dimension to heritage tourism is portrayed beautifully in the short stories by Polish Jewish writer Mikołaj Grynberg, see for English translation Grynberg 2020; for contemporary fictionalization and problematization of heritage-cum-dark tourism from an Israeli perspective, see Sarid 2020.

6 Vergelis 1965a, Vergelis 1965b. In this volume, we are reproducing the very first published version of the travel notes in 1965. Vergelis' travelogues underwent a few renditions and were republished in different forms and formats, including in English translation, see Vergelis 1971, Vergelis 1972, Vergelis 1976, Vergelis 1979. Our entirely new English translation of his travel notes to Poland, however, is based on a different version than the one used by Mariam Katz in 1971 and thus differs from it, cf. Vergelis 1971. Ours also includes an extensive commentary prepared by Miriam Chorley-Schulz.

by the Red Army; he reflects on his visits to the site of the Treblinka killing center as well as old-new Yiddish Warsaw; and, in a dreamscape, he takes his reader to the Yiddish world of interwar and German-occupied Poland and opines on its relevance for a cross-socialist Yiddishland.

When he embarked on his Poland trip in 1965, Vergelis had entered his fourth year as the editor-in-chief of the only post-Stalinist Soviet Yiddish journal, *Sovetish heymland*, and was at the dawn of his quarter-century long career as a globetrotter on the Soviet Yiddish Cold War cultural front that he was tasked to play a decisive role in until 1991.[7] Born in Lyubar, Ukraine, coming of age as a 'poetic wunderkind' in the Jewish autonomous region Birobidzhan, and graduating from Moscow's prestigious Yiddish department of the Pedagogical Institute, he crowned his membership in the Soviet Writers' Union with the publication of his first book in 1940, fought Nazi Germany in the Red Army from *Überfall* to victory, and survived the Stalinist purges of Jewish intellectuals as the head of the international Yiddish radio program, secretary of the Writers' Union's Yiddish section and a member of the editorial board of the literary almanac היימלאַנד (*Heymland*, Homeland) unscathed (to many suspiciously). This unique biographical combination – a card-carrying communist with Birobidzhan pedigree, veteran status, clean 'criminal' record, and extensive experience with the craft of editing and international contacts – explains his meteoric postwar rise to the top of the (however modestly) reinvigorating Soviet Yiddish cultural sphere. But it also, in addition to his polarizing personality, provided the fertile soil for the gradual construction of Vergelis as the arch-enemy of 'Jewish interests' – in the always already dogmatically anti-communist (Jewish) West, among the dissident faction of Soviet Jewry, and even among those who were, in theory, in the same political camp.[8] At the time of his 1965 Poland trip, for instance, the relationship between Vergelis and leading figures of the Polish Yiddish cultural milieu, such as Hersh Smolyar,[9] was, contrary to the depiction in his travel notes, far from

7 Estraikh 2020.

8 Further on the ambivalent portrayal of Arn Verglis, see Estraikh 2008, 65–82; Kupovetsky 2007; Estraikh 2018.

9 Hersh Smolyar (1905–1993) was a Polish Yiddish communist writer and editor who spent significant parts of his life and career in the Soviet Union. He studied at the Yiddish department at the Communist University for the Peoples of the West, one of the universities run by the Comintern, was dispatched to Kharkiv (then the Ukrainian capital) in the 1920s with the task of building the local Yiddish-speaking communist cadre editing the youth newspaper יונגע גוואַרדיע [*Yunge gvardye*, Young Guard] as part of it. Smolyar worked as a Comintern agent in Poland from 1928 to 1939 and

harmonious. Apart from the lack of personal friendship, Polish Yiddish intellectuals resisted, to Vergelis' chagrin, the latter's attempts to control whom and what they published in their organ פֿאָלקס־שטימע [*Folks-shtime*, Peoples' Voice].[10] Importantly, however, this should not be read as signs of dissidence to or disillusionment with socialism. Rather, it reveals rifts that opened up between those disparate socialist Yiddishlands behind the Iron Curtain.

In the Jewish West, things looked altogether different. From Yiddish writer and Nobel Laureate Isaac Bashevis Singer to Elie Wiesel, *khurbn*-survivor, writer, and figurehead of the Cold War campaign to 'rescue' Soviet Jewry, Vergelis was consistently denounced as an "enemy of the Jewish people"[11] alleged to having actively collaborated in the 1952 murders of veteran Soviet Yiddish literati in order to usurp their legacy. *Sovetish heymland* in their reading, was no more than a "wild mushroom" that sprouted "on the graves of those who destroyed others and themselves in the name of socialism."[12] An essential part of this construction was the false but persistent Cold War myth that the memory of the Nazi genocide of Jews was anathema to the Soviet antifascist memory regime of the Second World War. Vergelis, as the government's alleged propaganda mouthpiece, was said to have prevented a 'genuine' confrontation with the Nazi past and Jewish suffering in the pages of his journal by overwriting it with antifascist myths to whitewash communist crimes. This gradual dichotomizing of postwar memory regimes into 'genuine' *khurbn* memory in the West and obfuscatory and immoral antifascist memory in the East was itself an important Orientalist theater of the cultural Cold War starting at the end of the 1960s[13] – and the budding Western 'traffic in Soviet Jewry' played a decisive part in its formation. Mirroring the simplistic binary of resistance and collaboration which dominated the 'totalitarian school' of scholarship into Nazism and Stalinism, construed as

spent six years in prison. With the beginning of the Second World War, he fled to Soviet-occupied Białystok swiftly becoming the editor of the communist newspaper ביאַליסטאָקער שטערן [*Byalistoker shtern*, Białystok Star]. He was imprisoned in the Minsk Ghetto and was a leading member of the resistance and became the head of a partisan group. For his wartime memoir, see Smolyar 1946. He returned to Poland after the war where he held key positions as the president of the צענטראַלער קאָמיטעט פֿון די ייִדן אין פּוילן [*Tsentraler komitet fun di yidn in Poyln,* Central Committee of the Jews of Poland] and editor of the Yiddish newspaper פֿאָלקס־שטימע [*Folks-shtime*, People's Voice].

10 Estraikh 2008, 71–73.

11 Abrahamson 1985, 234; further Wiesel 1966, 8.

12 Singer 1962, 267–269.

13 For particularly incisive case study on this and the interventions of new antifascism studies, see Kékesi and Zombory 2022; specifically on Soviet Yiddish antifascism, see [Chorley-]Schulz 2021a.

identical,[14] Soviet Jews as a group were recast into liberal Jewish martyrs eager to leave the Soviet Union in order to practice Judaism and the right kind of *khurbn* memory now called 'Holocaust' in the safe haven of capitalism, while others, and Vergelis first among them, were deemed too revolutionary, too communist, too antifascist, and therefore relegated to the dustbin of Jewish history.[15] As I have shown elsewhere,[16] this itself is a recasting of scholarship into the early modern history of Spain, the Inquisition and the twin figures of the *'marrano'* and the *'converso'* – Jews forced to convert to Christianity who allegedly continued practicing Judaism in secret versus those who transgressed Jewishness for good, respectively.[17] Employed to demarcate certain expressions of Jewishness as 'acceptable' and others as not, this relation was reactivated in the Cold War in the struggle for civilizational superiority and decided in favor of the Western Holocaust memory paradigm arguably by the end of the 1970s.[18] The patterns and valuable insights of antifascist memory of the Second World War and Jewish suffering under Nazism were thereby rendered indecipherable and, from 1991 onwards, its important political messages deemed dangerous and obsolete – like communism itself.

14 In the words of Stephen F. Cohen, the policy-oriented Anglo-American academic field of Sovietology, that had anti-communism as a political-ideological basis, embraced "as axiomatic a set of interrelated interpretations to explain both the past and present (and sometimes the future) of the Soviet Union" between the late 1940s and early 1960s and narrated the history of Soviet society as "a monolithic, ideological, terroristic party-state, headed by Stalin, ruling omnipotently over a passive, frozen society of atomized new citizens." One part of that school was the equation of Stalin's Russia with Hitler's Germany claiming that Soviet communism was nothing more than "Red fascism," i.e. an iteration of Nazism in the 1930s. In the Jewish sphere, this was extended to include the *khurbn* as well. See: Cohen 1985, 3–37; for a *Begriffsgeschichte* of the term 'totalitarianism,' see Gleason 1995.

15 For this kind of anti-communism, see Irving Howe's statement: "It has seemed pointless to waste space by printing what Yiddish writers *had to* compose during the worst years of the Stalinist period," according to Irving Howe in his attempt to reintroduce Soviet Yiddish writings to an American public, since "there are some things [...] better to leave in the past." Howe and Greenberg 1977, 25; further Yiddish scholar Ruth R. Wisse about the editing process of a Penguin Anthology of Soviet Yiddish poetry: "[t]here was not much point in including odes to Stalin of the 1930s, or other examples of Leftist fervor [...]. The forced quality of most of these poems argued as forcefully against them as their discredited political enthusiasm." Wisse 1989, 17. They took their cue from Khone Shmeruk, chair of Yiddish Studies at the Hebrew University and editor of the Penguin volume, who had a deep-seated animosity to literature coming out of the Soviet Union. Thanks to both Joshua Price and Binyamin Hunyadi for their guidance here. On New York intellectuals like Howe and their ideological transformation, see Sinkoff 2020.

16 [Chorley-]Schulz 2021b.

17 The sway the early modern history of Spain holds over Soviet Jewish Studies can be glimpsed in Olga Litvak's review of important works of the field. She herself reproduces the unhelpful divide into 'marrano' and 'converso' that should be discarded, see Litvak 2016.

18 Kékesi and Zombory 2022.

The following reproduction of Vergelis' 1965 travel notes in the original Soviet Yiddish orthography side-by-side a new English translation and extensive commentary challenges this distorted Cold War image and adds to the growing body of revisionist research into antifascism.[19] In lieu of an academic article, Vergelis himself gets to introduce the memory regime of Soviet Yiddish antifascism he practiced by way of his reflections on Auschwitz, Treblinka, and the Warsaw Ghetto. His insights are testament to an active Soviet Yiddish memory culture that coupled a socialist critique of capitalism with the examinations of fascism and its spawns – racism and genocide – and mobilized the dialectics of primarily Jewish, but also non-Jewish, suffering and resistance to Nazism as a *political* weapon in the ongoing united revolutionary struggle of the oppressed. In 1965, the 20th anniversary of the liberation of Auschwitz offered an opportunity to underline on an international stage the progressive role of the Soviet Union in fighting fascism not only on the battlefields of the Eastern front a good twenty years prior but in this ongoing war of a different kind. In response to the emerging anti-totalitarian discourse in the West,[20] the State Museum Auschwitz-Birkenau under the aegis of the International Auschwitz Committee was in the midst of turning the concentration camp complex into a memory site of international scope and importance by reinforcing its antifascist messaging when the Soviet delegation arrived. National pavilions with exhibitions, including a Jewish one, were to be installed, a large-scale monument (to be unveiled in 1967) was drawn up, international meetings, and fundraising campaigns took place as part of that effort.[21]

While Vergelis walks us through the gruesome architecture of Auschwitz's former camp complex, to get to the death camp of Treblinka a couple of days later, he traversed the thick forest that once concealed the atrocities happening there only to enter another: a forest of stones. Officially unveiled shortly after Vergelis' visit in May 1964, Adam Haupt's and Franciszek Duszenko's memorial at Treblinka consists of massive 7-meter-tall granite blocks decorated with abstract reliefs and Jewish symbolism and is surrounded by 17,000 loosely spaced jagged stones inscribed with the names of *shtetlekh* wiped out

19 See e.g. García, Yusta, Tabet and Clímaco 2016, Seidman 2018, Braskén, Copsey and Featherstone 2020, Kaiser 2022, Bohus, Hallama and Stach 2022.

20 Lagrou 1999, 271.

21 Huener 2003, Chapter 5: The Internationalization of the Auschwitz Site.

under Nazi occupation.[22] Vergelis abstains from reenacting Treblinka's horrors, inhabits loss, and embraces mourning poetically. He implicitly calls upon his readers to reconstruct in their minds the landscape of mass murder that Thomas Houlton has so aptly described as a "ghostly realm that becomes its own above-ground underworld [...] dwarfted by indifferent trees"[23] akin to later documentary depictions most famously perhaps by Claude Lanzmann who similarly did without acting out the human-made horrors with the help of sepia daguerreotypes or newsreel footage on *Shoah* (1985).

Finally: Warsaw. Vergelis concludes his travelogue on a different note walking us in a dreamscape through the different periods of 20th century old-new Polish Yiddishland and narrating a story of ideological unity and mutual dependency between Yiddish Warsaw and Yiddish Moscow in war and peace times. Harmonious on the surface, it was exactly the overbearing manner, however, of casting Soviet *Yidishkayt* as *Poyln*'s 'big brother' that, according to Gennady Estraikh, had caused the friction I have alluded to between Vergelis and his Polish-Jewish comrades.

Bibliography

ABRAHAMSON, Irving, ed., 1985: *Against Silence: The Voice and Vision of Elie Wiesel.* New York, NY: Holocaust Library.

BAJOHR, Frank, Axel DRECOLL, and John LENNON, eds., 2020: *Dark Tourism: Reisen zu Stätten von Krieg, Massengewalt und NS-Verfolgung.* Berlin: Metropol.

BOHUS, Kata, Peter HALLAMA, and Stephan STACH, eds., 2022: *Growing in the Shadow of Antifascism: Remembering the Holocaust in State-Socialist Eastern Europe.* Vienna: Central European University Press.

BRASKÉN, Kasper, Nigel COPSEY, and David FEATHERSTONE, eds., 2020: *Anti-Fascism in a Global Perspective: Transnational Networks, Exile Communities, and Radical Internationalism.* London: Routledge.

[CHORLEY-]SCHULZ, Miriam, 2021a: *Keyner iz nit fargesn: Soviet Yiddish Antifascism and the Holocaust.* PhD Dissertation. Columbia University.

[CHORLEY-]SCHULZ, Miriam, 2021b: 'The Deepest Self Denies the Self': Polish Jewish Intellectuals and the Birth of 'Soviet Marranos.' In: Markus Nesselrodt and Katharina Friedla, eds., *Polish Jews in the Soviet Union (1939–1959): History and Memory of Deportation, Exile, and Survival.* Boston, Mass.: Academic Studies Press, 143–174.

22 See Young 1993, 186–192; Marcuse 2010, 87.

23 Houlton 2022, 244f.

Cohen, Stephen F., 1985: *Rethinking the Soviet Experience: Politics and History Since 1917*. New York, NY: Oxford University Press.

Estraikh, Gennady, 2020: Creating a Cold War Boogeyman: Aron Vergelis' Political Career. In: *Jewish Social Studies* 25:3: 103–129.

Estraikh, Gennady, 2018 Эстрайх, Геннадий: Одиночество еврейского редактора. К 100-летию со дня рождения Арона Вергелиса. В: *Народ книги в мире книг*, <http://narodknigi.ru/journals/133/odinochestvo_evreyskogo_redaktora/>, August 16, 2023.

Estraikh, Gennady, 2008: *Yiddish in the Cold War*. Oxford: Legenda.

García, Hugo, Mercedes Yusta, Xavier Tabet, and Cristina Clímaco, eds., 2016: *Rethinking Antifascism: History, Memory and Politics, 1922 to the Present*. New York, NY: Berghahn Books.

Gleason, Abbott, 1995: *Totalitarianism: The Inner History of the Cold War*. New York, NY: Oxford University Press.

Grynberg, Mikołaj, 2020: An Excerpt from *Rejwach*. Translated by Sean Gasper Bye. In: *Jewish Currents*, https://jewishcurrents.org/an-excerpt-from-rejwach, August 16, 2023.

Howe, Irving, and Eliezer Greenberg, eds., 1977: *Ashes out of Hope: Fiction by Soviet Yiddish Writers*. New York, NY: Schocken Books.

Houlton, Thomas, 2022: *Monuments as Cultural and Critical Objects: From Mesolithic to Eco-Queer*. New York, NY: Routledge.

Huener, Jonathan, 2003. *Auschwitz, Poland, and the Politics of Commemoration, 1945–1979*. Athens, Ohio: Ohio University Press.

Lagrou, Pieter, 1999: *The Legacy of Nazi Occupation: Patriotic Memory and National Recovery in Western Europe, 1945–1965*. Cambridge: Cambridge University Press.

Kaiser, Max, 2022: *Jewish Antifascism and the False Promise of Settler Colonialism*. Cham: Palgrave Macmillan.

Kékesi, Zoltán, and Máté Zombory, 2022: Antifascist memory revisited: Hungarian historical exhibitions in Oświęcim and Paris, 1965. In: *Memory Studies* 15:5: 1087–1104.

Kupovetsky, Mark, 2007: Aron Vergelis: Survivor of the Destruction of Soviet Yiddish Culture, 1949–1953. In: *Jews in Russia and Eastern Europe* 58: 40–94.

Lehrer, Erica T., 2013: *Jewish Poland Revisited: Heritage Tourism in Unquiet Places*. Bloomingon, Ind.: Indiana University Press.

Litvak, Olga, 2016: The New Marranos. In: Eli Lederhendler and Gabriel N. Finder, eds., *Studies in Contemporary Jewry: A Club of their own: Jewish Humorists and the Contemporary World*: 245–267.

Marcuse, Harold, 2010: Holocaust Memorials: The Emergence of a Genre. In: *American Historical Review* 115: 53–89.

Sarid, Yishay, 2020: *The Memory Monster*. Brooklyn, NY: Restless Books.

SEIDMAN, Michael, 2018. *Transatlantic Antifascisms from the Spanish Civil War to the End of World War II*. Cambridge: Cambridge University Press.

SINGER, Isaac Bashevis, 1962: A New Use for Yiddish: Review of Sovietish Heimland No. 1, July-August 1961. Published by Sovetsky Pisatel (Moscow). 128 pp. In: *Commentary* 33 (3): 267–269.

SINKOFF, Nancy, 2020. *From Left to Right: Lucy S. Dawidowicz, the New York intellectuals, and the Politics of Jewish History*. Detroit, Mich.: Wayne University Press.

SMOLYAR, Hersh, 1946 סמאָליאַר, הערש: **פֿון מינסקער געטאָ**. מאָסקווע: דער עמעס.

SPINNER, Samuel J., 2021: *Jewish Primitivism*. Stanford, Calif.: Stanford University Press.

VERGELIS, Arn, 1965a ווערגעליס, אַרן: רײַזעס. אין: **סאָוועטיש היימלאַנד** (מאָסקווע) נ׳ 10 (1965): 128–134.

VERGELIS, Arn, 1965b ווערגעליס, אַרן: רײַזעס. אין: **סאָוועטיש היימלאַנד** (מאָסקווע) נ׳ 11 (1965): 119–123.

VERGELIS, Arn, 1971: *On the Jewish Street: Travel Notes*. Translated from Yiddish by Mariam Katz. Moscow: Novosti Press Agency Publishing House.

VERGELIS, Arn, 1972: *Letters from Europe (January–March 1971)*. Moscow: Novosti Press Agency Publishing House.

VERGELIS, Arn, 1976 ווערגעליס, ארן: **רײַזעס**. מאָסקווע: סאָוועטסקי פּיסאטעל.

VERGELIS, Arn, 1979: Вергелис, Арон: *16 стран, вклюсая Монако*. Москва: Советский писатель.

WIESEL, Elie, 1966: *The Jews of Silence*. New York, NY: Holt, Rinehart and Winston.

WISSE, Ruth R., 1989: What Shall Live and What Shall Die: The Making of a Yiddish Anthology, Twelfth Annual Rabbi Louis Feinberg Memorial Lecture in Judaic Studies, University of Cincinnati.

YOUNG, James E., 1993: *The Texture of Memory: Holocaust Memorials and Meaning*. New Haven, Conn.: Yale University Press.

אהרון ווערגעליס

רייַזעס[1]

2. פּוילן

1

פּוילן הייבט זיך אָן אף דער מיט פון אן אייַזנבאַן־בריק גלייַך נאָך דעם, ווי דער צוג פאַרלירט פון אויג דעם סעמאַפאָר פון דער סטאַנציע ברעסט, און איידער ער דערזעט טעראַספּאָל. דאָרט צעגיסט זיך דער בוג אין א ברייטן לימאַן, אן אָנגעשפּיקעוועטן מיט אינדזעלעך, אף וועלכע עס האַלטן זיך אוף ווילדע גענדז. קיינער שיסט זיי דאָ ניט אראָפּ, די גענדז.

פּוילן הייבט זיך אָן אזוי:

עס רוקט זיך אָפּ די טיר אין קופּע, און א יונגער מיליטער־מאַן, אָנגעטאָן אין א רעקל מיט אָנגענייטע קעשענעס און אין גאָלף־הויזן, בעווייַזט זיך אף א רעגע און טוט א זאָג מיט אזא קאָל, פּונקט ווי ער וואָלט בא זיך אין שטוב געעפנט די טיר אף אַרייַנצולאָזן א לאַנג־דערוואַרטן גאַסט:

– דזיען דאָברי, פּאַן גענעראַל.

ער לייגט צו צוויי פינגער צו דער קאָנפעדעראַטקע און גיט א קלאַפּ אן אָפּצאַס אין אן אָפּצאַס. מיט „פּאַן גענעראַל" האָט ער געמיינט מייַן שאָכן, דעם גענעראַל אַפאַנאַסי דמיטריעוויטש גאָנטשאַראָוו, איניינעם מיט וועלכן איך פאָר קיין פּוילן אף די פייַערונגען פון פאָרלייגן א דענקמאָל אין צוזאַמענהאַנג מיט דעם 20־יאָריקן יובילייַ פון דער באַפרייַונג פון אָשווענטשים. גאָנטשאַראָוו איז געווען דער שעף פונעם שטאַב פון דער נייַנטער אַרמיי, וועלכע האָט זיך אַרייַנגעריסן אין טויט־לאַגער און געראַטעוועט די לעבן־געבליבענע אסירים. טאַקע פון זיי, פון די געראַטעוועטע, גייען אַרייַן אין אונדזער דעלעגאַציע אַלעקסאַנדער לעבעדיעוו, הייַנט דער פאַרטרעטער פונעם הויפּט־רעדאַקטאָר פון דער „מעדיצינסקאַיאַ גאַזעטאַ", און יעקאַטערינאַ בעלאָסטאָצקאַיאַ (אף דער מילכאָמע און אין טויט־לאַגער האָט זי געטראָגן דעם קאָנספּיראַטיוון נאָמען „נאַטאַשע"). [...]

[1] סאָוועטיש היימלאַנד 11 (1965): 119–123. We have retained the original Soviet orthography of Vergelis' article as originally printed in *Sovetish Heymland*.

Arn Vergelis

Journeys: Poland

Translated into English by
Miriam Chorley-Schulz and Binyamin Hunyadi

2. Poland

I

Poland begins right in the middle of a train-bridge, the moment you pass the semaphore and lose sight of the Brest station sign, and before you notice the city of Tiraspol. There, the Bug River rushes into the wide Liman, which is dotted throughout by tiny, wild, geese-inhabited islands. No one shoots at these geese.

This is the beginning of Poland:

The door of our compartment flies open and a young military man wearing a multi-pocketed jacket and a pair of golf trousers appears for a moment and speaks in a voice as though he is opening his front door at home to welcome a long-awaited guest.

– *Dzień dobry, panie General.*[1]

He touches his military cap with two fingers and clicks his heels together. The words "*panie General*" were addressed to my neighbor, the General Afanasy Dimitrievich Goncharov,[2] in whose company I am traveling to Poland for the inaugural ceremony of a memorial commemorating the 20th anniversary of the liberation of Oświęcim [Auschwitz]. Goncharov was the head of staff of the ninth division, which entered the death camp by force and liberated the surviving prisoners. From among them, from the rescued, there is in our delegation Aleksander Lebedev, today the assistant editor of *Медицинская Газета* [*Meditsinskaya Gazeta*, Journal of Medicine], and Ekaterina Belostotskaya (known during the war and in the death camp only under her codename "Natasha"). […]

1 Good morning, Mr. General.

2 Afanasy Dimitrievich Goncharov (1902–1974) was a Red Army major general during the Second World War.

באַ די וואַגאָן־פענצטער קומט פאָר אונדזער ערשטע באַקאַנטשאַפט מיט פוילן. בעלאָסטאָצקאַיאַ, אַ פרוי אין די פריִע פערציקער, מיט אײַנגעהיטער, ניט געקוקט אויף די שווידערלעכע ניסיוינעס, שיינקײַט, שטייט לעבן מיר אין אַ קאָפּטל אָן אַרבל. אויף איר האַנט – דער אויסגעבערנטער לאַגער־נומער 69835. [...]

אין וואַרשע, אויפן גדאַנסקער וואָקזאַל האָבן די דעלעגאַציע סאָוועטישע מילכאָמע־וועטעראַנען באַגעגנט אַ פאָר צענדליק טוער פונעם פוילישן „סבאָוויד" (פאַרבאַנד פון קעמפער פאַר פרײַהײַט און דעמאָקראַטיע) בעראָש מיטן אָנפירער פון דער וואַרשעווער אָפּטיילונג, בריגאַדע־גענעראַל יוזעק פעטשאַק.

עס האָט זיך אָנגעהויבן אונדזער ערשטער טאָג אין וואַרשע, דער פרילינגדיקער 10 אַפּרעל 1965. [...]

פאַן [זביגניעש] קוניצקי פירט אונדז אַרום איבער וואַרשע. שווער איבערטראָגן זיך אין די געדאַנקען אויף די כורוועס פונעם 1945, ווײַל אַרום אונדז שפיגלט זיך אין דער זון און קלינגט מיט בעטאָן, שטאָל, גלאָז און שטיין די וואַרשע־שטאָט פון 1965.

אונדזער באַגלייטער – ניט ער ווײַזט אונדז אָט די אויסטערלישע שטאָט, נאָר ער זינגט זי אויס. מיר שפּאַצירן איבער דער אויאַזדאָווער אַליי, און פאַן קוניצקי שרײַט אויף אַ קאָל: „איר זעט? – אויך די ביימער, פאַרשניטענע פון דער אַרטילעריע, האָבן מיר רעסטאַווירט!" „רעסאַווירט"... אין וואַרשע קאָן מען דאָס דאָזיקע וואָרט הערן קימאַט אַזוי אָפט, ווי דאָס וואָרט „וואַרשע" אַליין. מע האָט רעסטאַווירט מיט אַלע פּיטשעווקעס הונדערטער הײַזער. אַפילע די לייבן און די פייגל אויף די פראָנטאָנען. אַפילע די שטאַכעטן פון אַ ווײַטן יאָרהונדערט. אַפילע די לאָדן, די אײַזערנע דאַשעקעס איבער די טירן באַ די הײַזער אין סטאַרע מיאַסטאָ. די פאַשיסטן האָבן אופגעריסן און אַרויסגעפירט דעם דענקמאָל קאָפערניקן. אָבער אָט, טוט נאָר אַ קוק! – באַם סטאַשיץ־פאַלאַץ שטייט ווידער אויף זײַן אָרט דער בראָנזענער ניקאָלײַ קאָפערניק און קוקט פונדאַנען אויף דער פולשטענדיק אופגעשטעלטער (רעסטאַווירטער!) אַלטער היסטאָרישער גאַס קראַקאָווסקע פשעדמעסטשיע.

און ניט נאָר מיט דעם רעסטאַווירטן אָוואַר גרויסט זיך וואַרשע, ניט נאָר מיט דער קאָלאָנע פונעם קיניג זיגמונד אויפן זאַמקאָווער פלאַץ, ניט נאָר מיטן פאַלאַץ פון די מאַלאַכאָווסיס, וואָס איז אַ מוסטער פונעם ראָקאָקאָ־סטיל. וואַרשע פאַרגעסט ניט צו באַווײַזן אויך איר נײַע אַרכיטעקטור. דאָס הויז פון דער פאַרטיי, אָדער, ווי מע רופט עס, דאָס „אַלגעמיינע הויז" – אַ פונדאַמענטאַל און אײנצײַטיק עלעגאַנט געבײַ, פול מיט זון און מיט לופט – איז אופגעבויט אויף די זלאָטעס, וואָס עס האָבן צונויפגעזאַמלט די מיטגלידער פון דער פוילישער אַרבעטער־פאַרטיי. וואַרשע גרויסט

We make our first acquaintance with Poland through the carriage window. Belostotskaya, who is in her early forties and wearing a sleeveless blouse, is standing beside me. She had preserved her beauty despite the horrific ordeals she endured. On her arm she has tattooed the number 69835. [...]

In Warsaw, at the Gdańsk railway station, the delegation of Soviet war veterans was met by a few dozen activists [and war veterans] from the Polish "ZBoWiD" (Union of Fighters for Freedom and Democracy),[3] led by the head of their Warsaw department, Brigadier General Juzek Pęczak.

This is how our first day in Warsaw began, accompanied by spring weather, on 10 April 1965. [...]

Mr. [Zbigniew] Kunicki took us around Warsaw. It was hard to transport our minds to the ruins of 1945, surrounded as we were by the concrete, steel, glass, and stone city of Warsaw in 1965 sparkling in the sun and clinking in our ears.

Our chaperone did not merely show us this exceptional city, he serenaded its beauty. We were crossing Ujazdów alley and Mr. Kunicki exclaimed, "You see this? We *restored* even the trees that were uprooted by the artillery!" "Restored!"... You hear this word in Warsaw almost as often as the name "Warsaw" itself. Hundreds of houses were painstakingly restored to the tiniest detail. Even the lions and birds on the facades; even the railings of centuries past; even the window shutters, even the iron awnings above the doors of the houses in Stare Miasto [Old Town]. The fascists had the statue of Copernicus blown up and removed, but over there: look! – the brazen Nicolaus Copernicus stands firm in his old place, before Staszic Palace, looking down on the completely overhauled (restored!) old historic street, Krakówskie Przedmieście.

And not only on its restored past does Warsaw pride itself now – on the colonnade of King Sigmund in Zamkow square, or the palace of Małachowski, an exemplar of the Rococo style – no, Warsaw does not forget to exhibit its new architecture either. The party headquarters, better known as "The General House," a substantial but at the same time elegant building, full of sunshine and air, was built from the money collected by the members of

3 Formed on 2 September 1949 out of eleven pre-existing veteran unions, the Związek Bojowników o Wolność i Demokrację was the central veterans association of the People's Republic of Poland and the sole authority on certifying veterans' and soldiers' rights and privileges in Poland. It also played an important part in constructing public memory of the Second World War in Poland, see Wawrzyniak 2015.

זיך מיטן גראַנדיעזן קולטור־פּאַלאַץ – אַ מאַטאָנע פֿונעם סאָוועטנפֿאַרבאַנד, מיט דעם געבייַען־קאָמפּלעקס אויף דעם דאָמבראָווסקי־פּלאַץ, מיט דער פֿייַערלעכער און גרויס־קראַכישער, צוגעפּוצטער און שטרענגער, פֿרייַלעכער און צוריקגעהאַל־טענער מאַרשאַלקאָווסקי־גאַס. [...]

– זביגניעוו קאַזימיראָוויטש, – רופֿט זיך אָן צו קוניצקין דער גענעראַל גאָנטשאַ־ראָוו, – מיר האָבן נאָך ניט געזען די ייִדישע וואַרשע...

– פֿאָרן מיר טאַקע אין מוראַנאָווער ראַיאָן, דאָרט איז געווען די געטאָ.

אַפֿאַנאַסי דמיטריעוויטש דערציילט, אַז וועגן אופֿשטאַנד אין וואַרשעווער געטאָ זייַנען צווישן די אָנגרייַפֿנדיקע סאָוועטישע סאָלדאַטן אַרומגעגאַנגען לע־גענדעס. אַלעקסאַנדער לעבעדיעוו גיט צו:

– באַ אונדז אין אָשווענטשים פֿלעגט מען פֿון בלאָק צו בלאָק איבערגעבן די נייַעס פֿון מוראַנאָוו. שפּעטער האָט מען אָנגעהויבן ברענגען פֿון דאָרט די געפֿאַנ־גענע. יאָ, מיר האָבן זיי גערופֿן אַזוי, ווי מע רופֿט סאָלדאַטן, גענומען אויפֿן שלאַכט־פֿעלד קריגסגעפֿאַנגענע האָבן מיר זיי גערופֿן...

– די ייִדישע וואַרשע, פֿרעגט איר? – זעצט פֿאָר פּאַן קוניצקי. – פֿאַר אונדז איז עס אַ בלעטל געשיכטע פֿון דער הויפּטשטאָט. אָט נעמט, לעמאָשל, די דזשיקע גאַס, – מיר האָבן זיך אָפּגעשטעלט אויף דער אַנילעוויטש־גאַס, – ניט צופֿעליק איז די אַלטע גענשע אָנגערופֿן געוואָרן מיטן נאָמען פֿונעם קאָמענדאַנט פֿון דער ייִדישער קאַמפּס־אָרגאַניזאַציע אין געטאָ... גענשע־גאַס, נאַלעווקעס, נאָוואָליפּקי – נאָך פֿון נאַפּאָלעאָנס צייַטן איז דאָ געווען דער ייִדישער קוואַרטאַל. [...]

די מאַשין מאַכט אַ קרייַז אַרום אַנילעוויטשעס בונקער, אַרום דעם דענקמאָל די העלדן פֿון וואַרשעווער געטאָ. ס'איז שוין פֿאַרנאַכט. מיר שפּאַנען איבער די אַלטע גאַסן, אויף וועלכע צענדליקער הויכע נייַע געבייַען האָבן געגאָסן זייער שייַן. מיטאַמאָל – שטיק שטאַרטשענדיקע פֿון דער סאַמע ערד, צעשטשערבעטע, פֿאַר־צויגענע מיט גרויקייַט אין דער אָוונטיקער טונקלקייַט, וואַנט, וועלכע די בויער פֿון וואַרשע, אייַנגעליבטע אין רעסטאַווראַציע, היטן אָפּ, ווי אַ טייַערן סימען.

איך גיי צו צו דער וואַנט און אויפֿן סאָלדאַטישן אויפֿן דריק איך צו צו איר דעם שטערן.

2

באַנאַכט זייַנען מיר אָפּגעפֿאָרן קיין אָשווענטשים.

צווישן די פּאַסאַזשירן פֿון אונדזער צוג זייַנען בלויז צוויי – גאָנטשאַראָוו און איך

the Polish Workers' Party. Warsaw prides itself on its Palace of Culture, a gift from the Soviet Union, along with the building complex at Dąbrowski square, and the festive, grand, urban, and elegant, and at the same time strict, jovial, and modest Marszałkowska street. [...]

– Zbigniew Kazimierovicz – calls out the General Goncharov to Kunicki – we haven't seen Jewish Warsaw yet...

– We're going right to the Muranów neighborhood, where the ghetto used to be.

Afanasy Dimitrievich recalled that legendary tales circulated among the invading Soviet soldiers about the uprising of the Warsaw ghetto. Aleksander Lebedev added:

– In Oświęcim the news about Muranów spread from block to block. Later they started bringing in prisoners from there. Yes, we called them prisoners of war, as we do with soldiers who are taken captive on the battlefield...

– Jewish Warsaw? That's what you asked for, right? – continued Kunicki. – For us it's a page in the history of our capital. Take for example this street here – we stopped at Anielewicz[4] street – it's no wonder that the old Gęsia street was renamed after the commander of the fighting force in the ghetto... Gęsia street, Nalewki, Nowolipki – the Jewish quarter dates back to Napoleon's times [...]

The car circled around Anielewicz's bunker and the monument to the Warsaw ghetto heroes. It was already getting dark. We strolled through old streets lit by dozens of brand-new buildings. Suddenly, we stumbled across pieces of dilapidated wall growing out of the earth in front of us. It had a certain grayness to it in the evening gloom. These were pieces of the [ghetto] wall that the rebuilders of Warsaw, so enamored with restoration, left intact as a reminder.

I approached the wall, and in a soldierly fashion pressed my forehead against it.

2

At night we travelled to Oświęcim.

Among the passengers in our train only two – Goncharov and myself

[4] Mordechai Anielewicz (1919–1943) was a Zionist youth leader in interwar Poland and resistance fighter to Nazi fascism best known as the leader of the Żydowska Organizacja Bojowa [Jewish Fighting Organization, ŻOB] during the Warsaw Ghetto Uprising in April 1943. He was presumably killed on 8 May 1943 when the central bunker of the ŻOB was discovered.

– ניט געווען מיט צוואַנציק יאָר צוריק פֿאַרשפּאַרט אין טויט־לאַגער. די עטלעכע הונדערט מאַנצבלען און פֿרויען, פֿאַרזאַמלטע פֿון פּוילן, פֿראַנקרײַך, האָלאַנד, סאָוועטנפֿאַרבאַנד, ייִסראָעל, גריכנלאַנד, טשעכאָסלאָוואַקיע, אונגאַרן און אַנדערע לענדער, זײַנען דאָ פֿאַרבונדן צווישן זיך מיט יענער טראַגישער היימישקײַט, וואָס טרעפֿט, ווײַזט אויס, בלויז צווישן געוועזענע קאַצעטלער.

א גאַנצע נאַכט שלאָפֿט מען ניט.

– לאָמיר זיך צוזעצן אויף דער נאַרע... – זאָגט איינער צום אַנדערן, אָנווײַזנדיק אויפֿן געלעגער אין וואַגאָן־קופּע.

מע זעצט זיך צו, מע רעדט, מע רעדט, מע רעדט...

– היי, דו, מוזעלמאַן[2], אויב דו דערוויסט זיך, ווען מיר קומען אָן אויפֿן אָרט, האָסטו אַ טעלער בונאַזופּע[3], – רופֿט זיך אָן מיט אַ שמייכל אַלעקסאַנדער לעבעדיעוו צום איצטיקן מיניסטער פֿון שיף־פֿאַרקער פֿון דער פּוילישער פֿאָלקס־רעפּובליק יאַנוש בוראַקעוויטש.

– אַ טעלער בונאַזופּע? – פֿרעגט איבער בוראַקעוויטש, – אײַ, אײַ, מײַן הער, גיכער פֿון אַלץ באַקום איך אַ Genickschuss[4].

מע צעלאַכט זיך. הײַנט קאָן מען מיט אַזעלכע ווערטער זיך מאַכן פֿריילעך...

דער געוועזענער קאַצעטלער יאַנוש בוראַקעוויטש לאָזט אָבער ניט לעבעדיעווס פֿראַגע אָן אַן ענטפֿער. אָט ווי־אַזוי ער באַצייכנט די צײַט, ווען מיר קומען אָן קיין אָשווענטשים?

– אונדזער צוג וועט גיין ניט אין אויוון אַרײַן, נאָר אויף אַרבעט...

דאָס הייסט, אַז מיר קומען אָן קיין אָשוועטשים פֿאַרטאָג. אין טויט־לאַגער איז געווען אַזאַ סיידער: די באַנאַכטיקע עשעלאָנען פֿלעגן גלײַך אָפּגעשיקט ווערן אין קרעמאַטאָריע, די אינדערפֿרייִקע – אויף אַרבעט.

אַ גרײַז־גראָווע פֿרוי פֿון האָלאַנד זעצט זיך אויך צו אויף דער „נאַרע“ און הייבט אָן שטיל זינגען, קוקנדיק מיט דורכדרינגלעכע „נו, דערמאָן זיך“־אויגן אויף נאַטאַשע בעלאָסטאָצקאַיאַ:

> O du, mein Bubikopf,
> Im Lager Auschwitz war ich zwar
> So manchen Monat, so manches Jahr...[5]

– יאָ, ריווקע, יאָ... – זאָגט שטיל נאַטאַשע, – די עסעסאָווצעס פֿלעגן שטאַרק

[2] Muselmann – אויף דער לאַגער־זשאַרגאָן אַ קאַצעטלער אין דער לעצטער סטאַדיע פֿון הונגער־אויסגעשעפּטקײַט.

[3] Bunassuppe – אַ מין באַלאַנדע, געקאָכט אויף קאַרטאָפֿל־אָפּפֿאַלן.

[4] אַ קויל אין נאַקן.

[5] אָ, דו, מײַן פֿאַרשײַט מיידל, / אין לאַגער אָשוועטשים בין איך געווען / אַ געוויסן מאָנאַט, אַ געוויסן יאָר.

– had not been former prisoners of the death camp twenty years ago. The hundreds of men and women, gathered together from Poland, France, the Netherlands, the Soviet Union, Israel, Greece, Czechoslovakia, Hungary, and other countries, were bound together by a certain tragic familiarity which seems to have evolved only between former prisoners of concentration camps.

We couldn't sleep that night.

– Let's sit on the bunk… – someone said and pointed at the bed in our compartment.

And they sat down, and just talked, and talked, and talked…

– Hey, you *muselman*,[5] if you find out when we're going to arrive, you'll get a bowl of *bunazupe*[6] – with a smile on his face Aleksander Lebedev turned to Jonas Burakevicz, the present Minister for Naval Affairs of the Republic of Poland.

– A bowl of *bunazupe*? – replied Burakevic – ay, ay, mister, mister, I'd rather get a *Genickschuss*.[7]

And they broke out laughing. Today, even such words can make one jovial…

The former KZ prisoner Jonas Burakevicz could not leave Lebedev's question unanswered. This is what he had to say about arrival times at Oświęcim.

– Our train is not headed straight to the oven, but to work…

He meant that we arrive in Oświęcim at sunrise. The rule at the death camp was that evening transports were sent straight to the crematorium, morning transports to work.

A gray-haired woman from the Netherlands took a seat on one of the "bunks" and quietly started singing, and with penetrating eyes implying "Come on, remember!" she looked at Natasha Belostotskaya :

O du, mein Bubikopf,
Im Lager Auschwitz war ich zwar
So manchen Monat, so manches Jahr…[8]

– Yes, Rivke, yes… – said Natasha quietly – the SS-women beat us badly

5 Arn Vergelis commentary [AVC]: Muselmann – in camp jargon, a prisoner in the last stadium of dying of starvation.

6 AVC: Bunasuppe – a sort of thin, inedible soup which was cooked out of potato waste.

7 AVC: Shot in the neck.

8 Oh, you, my mischievous girl, / I've been in the camp Oświęcim / many a month, many a year…

שלאָגן, אויב עמעצער אין קאַראַנטין האָט ניט פאַרגעדענקט די ווערטער פון אָט דעם באַנאַלן דײַטשישן לידל... און אײַך, די ייִדן, פלעגט מען לערנען זינגען א צווייטע... א כויזעק־ליד...

– O du, mein Jerusalem…[6] – דערמאָנט זיך גלײַך ריווקע די האָלענדערין.

און איך, וואָס איך זיץ דאָ דערבײַ, דערזע מיטאמאָל א וואלד אין גרויסער־גרויסער ווײַטעניש, א וואלד, פארשנייט און פארשאָטן, פארוווייט און פארהוקעט, און איך זיץ מיט מײַנע אָדנאָפּאָלטשאנעס[7] ארום א פארטאָפּטשעטן שײַטער. מיר זײַנען אָנגעטאָן אין ווײַסע פּעלצלעך, מיר זײַנען הונגעריק און ניט געגאָלט. מיר וועלן באלד אטאקירן דאָס שטעטל, פיר־פינף וויאָרסט פונעם וואלד. דאָרט איז א פאשיסטישער צוואנגס־לאגער. מיר זיצן באַם פארלאָשענעם שײַטער און, קעדיי דערוואַרעמען מיט האס די הערצער, מורמלען מיר אין דער שטיל:

Вставай, страна огромная,
Вставай на смертный бой…[8]

[...] אין דרויסן איז שוין אינגאנצן ליכטיק. מיר פאָרן צו צו דער באן־שטאנציע אָשווענטשים. דאָס ערשטע, וואָס איך דערזע: א הויכער קוימען שטראָצט איינזאם אין הימל. „וואָס איז עס, א קרעמאטאָריע?“, – טו איך בא עמעצן א פרעג. „ניין, ס׳איז דער אָשווענטשימער כימישער זאוואָד, די גרעסטע אונטערנעמונג אין שטאָט...“

א שטאָט? זאוואָד? אין אָשווענטשים ווינען מענטשן? [...]

אָשווענטשים איז בײַס דער מילכאָמע ניט רויִנירט געוואָרן. עס לעבן דאָ ארום צוועלף טויזנט אײַנוווינער. מיר גייען פארבײַ א קינדערגאָרטן. באַם סאמע טויט־לאגער שטייען זאמד־קאסטנס, ארום וועלכע קינדער שפּילן זיך. און אויך עטלעכע הוידלקעס זײַנען דאָ פאראן, און דאָס קליינוואַרג ווייסט נאָך מיסטאָמע ניט, אז אף יענער זײַט הויכער וואנט, סאכאקל א צוויי־דרײַ הונדערט מעטער פון די הוידלקעס, שטייט נאָך ביז איצט א טליִע, אף וועלכער די געהאנגענע זיידעס און באָבעס האָבן, ניט דערגרייכנדיק מיט די פיס צו דער ערד, פריִער זיך א פּאָר מאָל אהער־אהין א הוידע געטאָן און שפּעטער שוין געבליבן הענגען מיט אויסגעצויגענע הענט און פיס, ווי אָט די ליאַלקעס אין קינדערגאָרטן, וואָס באָמבלען זיך אף ווײַסינקע שטריקעלעך. [...]

צום טויער פון טויט־לאגער זײַנען מיט דײַטשישער אקוראטקײַט צוגעפּעסטיקט דרײַ ווערטער, אויסגעשמידטע פון מאסיוון אײַזן: Arbeit macht frei.[9]

6 אָ, דו, מײַן ירושאָלאיִם...

7 סאָלדאטן, וואָס דינען אין איין פּאָלק.

8 שטיי אוף, מעדינע מעכטיקע, / שטיי אוף צום טויט־געפעכט... (שורעס פון א רוסישער ליד, וואָס איז געווען שטארק פּאָפּולער אין די יאָרן פון דער גרויסער פּאָטערלענדישער מילכאָמע).

9 ארבעט מאכט פרײַ.

in the quarantine when we couldn't remember the lyrics of this banal German song… and you Jews they taught you to sing another… a sardonic song…

– *O, du mein Jerusalem…*[9] – the Dutch woman Rivke recalled the words.

And I, sitting next to them, suddenly caught sight of a forest far off in the distance, completely covered in snow, buried and miserable, and I felt as if I was sitting once again with my fellow soldiers around a squashed out fire. We were wearing white fur coats, hungry and unshaven. We were about to attack the townlet, four or five versts[10] from the forest. There was a fascist forced labor camp there. We were sitting by the extinguished bonfire and to lash up hatred in our hearts we murmured quietly:

> Вставай, страна огромная,
> Вставай на смертный бой…[11]

[…] By now, the sun was shining bright outside. We were getting closer to the train station of Oświęcim. The first thing I noticed was a tall, lonely chimney protruding into the sky. "What is that, a crematorium?" – I asked someone. "No, that is the chemical factory of Oświęcim, the biggest industry in town…"

A town? A factory? Do people live in Oświęcim? […]

Oświęcim wasn't destroyed during the war. Around twelve thousand inhabitants live here. We passed a kindergarten. There were sandboxes not far from the death camp, children were playing here. There were also a couple of seesaws, and the toddlers probably did not know what was on the other side of the high wall – only about two or three hundred meters away a gallows still stands where their hanged grandparents were unable to reach the ground with their feet. Teetering back and forth several times, they were soon hanging with elongated arms and legs, just like these dolls in the kindergarten, wobbling on white threads […]

There are three words fixed with German accuracy onto the gate of the death camp, forged in massive iron: "*Arbeit macht frei.*"[12]

9 AVC: Oh you, my Jerusalem…

10 A verst is a measure of distance in (tsarist) Russia, equivalent to 0.66 mile or 1.06 km.

11 Rise up, mighty nation, / Rise up to the deadly fight… (Lyrics from a Russian song which was very popular in the years of the Great Patriotic War).

12 AVC: "Work sets you free."

דאָס איז געווען נאָך איין עסעסישער שווינדל, פּונקט ווי דאָס שפּילן פֿונעם אָרקעסטער באַם טרײַבן די אומגליקלעכע אַף צוואַנגס־אַרבעט...

– כאַווײרים, מיר געפֿינען זיך אַפֿן קייווער פֿון פֿיר מיליאָן מאַרטירער. – מיט אָט די ווערטער האָט אונדז באַגעגנט אין דער „אָפּיצערישער צוזאַמענווײנונג“, וואָס שטייט באַם סאַמע טויער פֿונעם טויט־לאַגער, דער פּרעמיער־מיניסטער פֿון פּוילן יוזעף ציראַנקעוויטש, אַ געוועזענער אָשווענטשימער געפֿאַנגענער.

אין דרויסן איז געווען אַזוי שטיל, אַז ווען מיר, אַ מענטשן צוואַנציק פֿאַרזאַמלטע אין דער „אָפּיצערישער צוזאַמענווײנונג“, זײַנען געגאַנגען צום אַרויסגאַנג, האָב איך אַ טראַכט געטאָן: געשיקט זיך, אַז מע וועט לייגן דעם שטיין פֿאַרן דענקמאָל די קאָרבאָנעס פֿון אָשווענטשים באַ אַזאַ קליינעם אוילעם? אַזוי שטיל איז געווען אין דרויסן! און ווען איך בין אַרויס דורך דער אָפֿענער טיר, האָב איך אַ ציטער געטאָן. פֿופֿציק טויזנט מענטשן זײַנען געשטאַנען מיטן פּאָנעם צו די גרויסע לאַגער־בלאָקן – די אויגן אָפֿן, די ליפּן צוגעשלאָסן...

ווען די פֿײַערלעך־טרויעריקע מאַניפֿעסטאַציע האָט זיך אָפּגעשטעלט אַף דעם געוועזענעם אָשווענטשימער אַפּעל־פּלאַץ, לעבן דעם זעקס־און־צוואַנציקסטן בלאָק, און אַף דער טריבונע איז צום מיקראָפֿאָן צוגעגאַנגען ציראַנקעוויטש, האָט זיך דערהערט אַן אַלאַרעם־רוף פֿון פֿאַבריק־סירענעס, באַגלייט מיט דעם פֿײַפֿן, וואָס האָט באַשײַטע געהאַט גערופֿן די אַרעסטאַנטן אַפֿן אַפּעל...

איצט, ווען איך דערמאָן זיך אין אָט די צוויי רופֿנדיקע, יאָמערנדיקע, ווי דינע שאַרפֿע ריטעלעך איבערגעפֿלאָכטענע קלאַנגען, טראַכט איך: דאָס איז געווען אַ געניִאַלער געדאַנק, וואָס האָט מעגלעך געמאַכט, אַז עס זאָלן אין איין אויגנבליק זיך אויסשפּרייטן צוויי פֿאַנטאַסטיש־מעכטיקע פֿליגל: אַף איינעם ווערט די אָשווענטשים־טראַגעדיע 1940 – 1945 אַראָפּגעבראַכט צו אונדז אין 1965, ווי אַ פֿײַנלעכע דערמאָנונג, און אַפֿן צווייטן פֿליגל קומט דאָס יאָר 1965 און אין קרעפֿטיק פֿאַרבײַלטע הענט נעמט עס איבער פֿון די פֿאַרשטאַרט־אויסגעשטרעקטע הענט פֿון אָשווענטשים די צוואָע: קיינמאָל זאָל אַזוינס מער ניט געשען! קיינמאָל מער!

This was one of the SS tricks, the same as the playing of the orchestra, when they were chasing the unfortunate to forced labor…

"Comrades, we're here at the graves of four million martyrs"[13] – with these words the Polish Prime Minster Józef Cyrankiewicz,[14] himself a former inmate of Oświęcim, greeted us at the "Officers' Quarters," which is located at the gates of the death camp.

It was so quiet outside that when we, the twenty people gathered at the "Officers' Quarters," were heading for the exit, a thought crossed my mind: is it right that we are going to place a stone on the memorial for the victims of Oświęcim in front of so few? It was that silent outside! But when I stepped outside through the open door a quiver ran through me. Fifty thousand people were standing there, facing the huge barrack blocks – eyes open, but lips tightly shut…

When the solemnly mourning demonstration stopped at the *Appellplatz* [roll call grounds] of Oświęcim, next to block twenty-six, and Cyrankiewicz stepped up to the microphone on the tribune, the alarm-call of the factory sirens sounded, followed by the whistle, which was the peremptory summons used to gather the prisoners at the *Appellplatz*…

Now, as I recall the two alarming, yammering sounds, like two thin, pointed and twisted twigs, I think to myself: this was really a genius idea, which made it possible for two fantastic, mighty wings to spread out simultaneously. One wing carried the tragedy of Oświęcim in the years between 1940–1945, brought back to us here in 1965 as a painful memory, and on the second came the year 1965 and with tightly clenched fists it took from the outstretched, benumbed hands of Oświęcim the guiding principle: Never again should such a thing happen! Never again!

13 This was the alleged number of victims at the time. Today it is estimated that between 1940 and 1945 at least 1.3 million people were deported to the Auschwitz camp complex, including the killing center of Auschwitz-Birkenau. Of these deportees, approximately 1.1 million people were murdered. The United States Holocaust Memorial Museum provides the following estimates subdivided by ethnicity: Jews (1,095,000 deported to Auschwitz, 960,000 murdered); Non-Jewish Poles (140,000–150,000 deported, 74,000 murdered); Sinti and Roma (23,000 deported, 21,000 murdered); Soviet prisoners of war (15,000 deported and murdered); other nationalities (25,000 deported, 10,000–15,000 murdered). See: https://encyclopedia.ushmm.org/content/en/article/auschwitz, August 15, 2023.

14 Józef Adam Zygmunt Cyrankiewicz (1911–1989) was premier of the Polish People's Republic twice, between 1947 and 1952 and between 1954 and 1970. Secretary of the Polska Partia Socjalistyczna [Polish Socialist Party, PPS] in interwar Poland since 1935, he was an active member of the Związek Walki Zbrojnej [Union of Armed Struggle], later Armia Krajowa [Home Army, AK], an arm of the Polish resistance movement, from the beginning of the Second World War in September 1939. Cyrankiewicz was captured by the Gestapo in 1941, was incarcerated in different concentration camps, including Auschwitz, and eventually liberated in Mauthausen by the US Army.

נאָך ציראַנקעוויטשעס און גאָנטשאַראָווס רעדעס קומט די רײ פון דעם אפעל לעקאָוועד די קדוישים, וועלכן עס לייענען אונטערן שרויט פון מיליטערישע פייַקלען דער רעקטאָר פונעם וואַרשעווער אוניווערסיטעט געוועזענער לאַגער־געפאַנגענער פּראָפּ. סטאַניסלאַוו טורסקי און דער גענעראַל עוגעניוש קושקאָ. דער אפעל איז שעקספּיריש לויט זייַן דראַמאַטישקייַט: די צוזאַמענשטויסן פון טויט און לעבן, פון דערהאַרגעטע און זייערע מערדער, פון גוטס און שלעכטס. „אייַך רוף איך, דערמאָרדעטע... איך רוף אייַך, אומגעבראַכטע אין די טפּיסע־קאַזעמאַטן און אַף די גאַסן פון שטעט... אייַך, דערשאָסענע בא דער טויטן־וואַנט אין אָשווענטשים און אין באַבי־יאַר הינטער קיִעוו... איך רוף אייַך, פאַרפּייַניקטע מיט שטעקנס אין וועג, בא דער אַרבעט און אַף די אפעל־פּלעצער... איך רוף אייַך, געשטאָרבענע פון אויסשעפּונג, פאַרפרוירענע אַף די וועגן, דערשאָסענע אין די ריוון. אייַך רוף איך, מאַרטירער פון לענינגראַד און פאַרמישפּעטע אַף הונגער־טויט אין די געטאָס, אייַך, אויסגעהונגערטע אין די קאַצעטס, אייַך, געפאַלענע בייס דער עוואַקואַציע פון די לאַגערן... אייַך רוף איך, קאָרבאָנעס פונעם שרעקלעכסטן פאַרברעכן. אייַך, וואָס זייַנען „אוועק דורכן קוימען“, אייַך רוף איך, פאַרסאַמטע מיט דיזעל־גאַז פון אוטאָס און מיטן גאַז ציקלאָן... איך רוף אייַך, דערמאָרדעטע, אייַך אַלעמען – צוואַנציק מיליאָן קאָרבאָנעס פונעם שרעקלעכסטן פאַרברעכן, צוואַנציק מיליאָן קאָרבאָנעס פון פאַשיזם. איך רוף אייַך אַלעמען: „קאָמוניסטן און גאַלאָכים, פּאָליאַקן און פראַנצויזן, רוסן און ייִדן, יוגאָסלאַוון און מאַדיאַרן, זקיינים און קינדער – קאָרבאָנעס פון דעם זעלבן פאַרברעכן, פאַרייניקטע דורכן טויט... איך רוף אייַך, געשטאָרבענע, קעדיי עס זאָלן הערן די לעבעדיקע...“

און גלייַך ווי באַם פּראָפעסאָר טורסקי וואָלטן שוין אויסגעגאַנגען די קויכעס און ער קאָן מער ניט פּאָרזעצן ווייַטער די קלאָג־ליד פון דער מענטשהייַט, שטעלט ער זיך אָפּ, אַ בלאַסער, אַ דערשיטערטער, און דעם אפעל זעצט פּאָר דער גענעראַל קושקאָ:

„אייַך אַלעמען, קאַמפּס־כאַווײרים – אַרעסטאַנטן, וואָס האָבן געקעמפט, ווי סאָלדאַטן, וואָס זייַנען געשטאָרבן אַלס אַרעסטאַנטן. איך רוף אייַך, די, וואָס האָבן קיינמאָל ניט שאָלעם געמאַכט מיטן פאַרברעכן. איך רוף אייַך, סאָלדאַטן

After Cyrankiewicz's and Goncharov's speeches, a special appeal in memory of the victims was read by the rector of Warsaw University, Professor Stanisław Turski,[15] himself a former camp inmate, joined by General Eugeniusz Kuszko,[16] followed by the thunder of military drums. The appeal was Shakespearean in its drama: the clash between life and death, the murdered and the murderers, good and evil. "I'm calling you, the murdered… I'm calling you the slaughtered in the prison-dungeons and on the city streets… to you, who were shot dead in Oświęcim at the Death Wall and in Babi Yar behind Kiev… I'm calling you, tormented with beatings on your marches, during your forced labor and at the *Appellplatz*… I'm calling you, who died of exhaustion, froze on death marches, were shot dead in the ditches. I'm calling you, martyrs of Leningrad, and you, who were doomed to die of starvation in the ghettos, and you, who were starved to death in the concentration camps, and you, who died during the evacuation of the camps… I'm calling you, you the victims of the most terrifying crime…You, who have 'gone through the chimneys,' and I'm calling you, you who were gassed in the gas-vans and with Zyklon gas… I'm calling you, all of you, who were murdered – twenty million victims of the most terrifying crime, twenty million victims of fascism. I'm calling you all: communists and priests, Poles and Frenchmen, Russians and Jews, Yugoslavs and Hungarians, the elderly, and the children – victims of the same crime… united in death… I'm calling you, you who have died so that the living could hear…"

And just as Professor Turski exhausted his energies and stopped, pale and shuddering, unable to continue this lamentation of humanity, General Kuszko picked up the appeal:

"All of you, comrades in arms – prisoners, who fought as soldiers but died as prisoners, I'm calling you, you who could never put up with the crime.

15 Stanisław Antoni Turski (1906–1986) was a Polish mathematician who was targeted by the Nazi operation against Polish academics of the Jagiellonian and other universities in Kraków, the so-called *Sonderaktion Krakau* [special operation Kraków], starting in October 1939 as part of a broader plan to eradicate the Polish intellectual elite and Germanify the Polish territories annexed to Nazi Germany. He was imprisoned in the Nazi concentration camps Sachsenhausen and Dachau. After the war, he joined the PPS (1945–1948) and later the Polska Zjednoczona Partia Robotnicza [Polish United Workers' Party, PZPR] (1948–1986). He became rector of the University of Gdańsk and Warsaw.

16 Eugeniusz Kuszko (1907–1984) was a Polish Army officer who was active in the Polish communist movement since his youth and twice convicted for communist activities in interwar Poland. During the Second World War, he fought in the Red Army and then transferred by his own request to the Polskie Siły Zbrojne w ZSRR [Polish Armed Forces in the USSR, also known as Berling's Army], namely Polish military units formed in the USSR, under the leadership of Polish communists, and took part in liberating Europe from Nazi occupation. After the war, he continued a career in the Polish armed forces.

פון דער ווידערשטאַנד־באַוועגונג אין אָשווענטשים און בוכענוואַלד, אײַך, אופ־שטענדלער פון טרעבלינקע, פון וואַרשעווער און ביאַליסטאָקער געטאָ... איך רוף אײַך, געפאַלענע העלדן פון דעם 1־טן אוקראַיִנישן פראָנט, סאָלדאַטן פון דער סאָוועטישער דיוויזיע, וואָס האָבן אופגעבראָכן דעם אָשווענטשימער טויער און פאַרלאָשן די קרעמאַטאָריעס... אײַך רוף איך – שטייט אוף און זאָגט איידעס: וואָס פאַר א גויראל מענטשן זאָלן ניט פאַרגרייטן פאַר מענטשן, איז אויך אין דעם מענטשנס קויעך דעם דאָזיקן גויראל צו ענדערן!"

און פּראָפעסאָר טורסקי, שוין א באַרויִקטער, א גרויזאַמער, ענדיקט דעם אַפּעל: „הערט אויס איר אַלע, וואָס איר זײַט געווען באַדראָט צו פאַרטיליקט ווערן! הערט אויס, איר, טעכטער און זין פון די געפאַלענע און אויסגעמאָרדעטע! הערט אויס איר אַלע, וואָס איר האָט האַנאָע פון דער זון, פונעם לעבן, איר, וואָס איר ליבט נאָענטע, אַף וועלכע איר וואַרט אָן האָפענונגען, אין נאָמען פון די, וועמעס קערפּערס עס זײַנען פאַרוואַנדלט געוואָרן אין אַש, אין נאָמען פון די, נאָך וועלכע עס איז אַפילע קיין נאָמען ניט פאַרבליבן – אין נאָמען פון זיי אַלעמען באַשווער איך אײַך: געדענקט און לאָזט קיינמאָל ניט פאַרגעסן! אין נאָמען פונעם גליק, דעם ברוטאַל צעשטערטן דורכן פאַשיזם, אין נאָמען פון די ניט פאַרענדיקטע אַרבעטן, ניט דערגרייכטע האָפענונגען, איבערגעריסענער צאַרטער ליבע, אין נאָמען פון דעם פאַכעד אין די אויגן פון די געשטאָרבענע – באַשווער איך אײַך, לעבעדיקע: מער קיינמאָל ניט!... ווײַל דאָס, וואָס איז געשען איין מאָל, קאָן געשען נאָכאַמאָל. אָבער אויב די גרענעצלאָזע אָנשטרענגונג האָט צו דעם איין מאָל א סאָף געמאַכט, איז אויך מעגלעך ניט צו דערלאָזן, עס זאָל זיך איבערכאַזערן אין דער צוקונפט. מער קיינמאָל ניט! מיר וועלן עס ניט דערלאָזן! רום זייער אָנדענק!"

אפן פּלאַץ עטעמען שווער פופציק טויזנט מענטשן. ווען מיר לאָזן זיך אראָפּ פון דער טריבונע, טוט מיר מיטאַמאָל באַם סאַמע ערשטן טראָט מײַנעם איבערן ברוקירטן פּלאַץ א שטאַרקן קלאַפּ איבערן האַרצן א נאָענטע כוואַליע פון אָט דעם איבערגעכאַפּטן מענטשישן אָטעם. איך הייב אוף דעם קאָפּ און דערזע לעבן דער טריבונע א דרײַ־פיר צענדליק ייִנגלעך און מיידלעך, וואָס זעען אויס פון דער זײַט, ווי איין גרויס לעבעדיק וועזן, א שטאַרק אומגליקלעכס אין אָט דער רעגע, א וועזן, וואָס וועט, מעגלעך, זײַן שרעקלעך אין זײַן צאָרן אין א רעגע אַרום.

שווער צו זאָגן פאַרוואָס, נאָר איך שטעל זיך אָפּ, ניט זײַענדיק בעקויעך אָפּצורײַסן דאָס אויג פון אָט די יונגעלײַט. צוויי מיידלעך אָרעמען אַרום א דריטע, וואָס וויינט, האַלטנדיק נידעריק אראָפּגעבויגן דעם קאָפּ, ווי זי וואָלט געטרונקען פון א פולן עמער. אַלע איבעריקע שווײַגן. די ייִנגלעך קרעכצן עטוואָס אָפּ די קעפּ – זיי האָבן, ווײַזט אויס, מוירע זיך אויך צו צעיאָמערן.

אַלעקסאַנדער לעבעדיעוו שעפּטשעט מיר אפן אויער:

– דאָס זײַנען געבוירענע אין די טויט־בלאָקן פון אָשווענטשים... אונדזערע קינדער...

I'm calling you, the soldiers of the resistance in Oświęcim and Buchenwald, you the rebels of Treblinka, of the Warsaw and Białystok ghettos… I'm calling you, the heroes fallen on the first Ukrainian front, soldiers of the Soviet Division who tore open the gates of Oświęcim and extinguished the crematoriums… I'm calling you, get up, and bear witness: Whatever kind of evil fate one man has prepared for another, it is always in the power of men to change that fate for the good!…"

And Professor Turski, calm, pitiless, ended the appeal in a chilling tone: "Listen, all of you, who were threatened with extermination! Listen, you daughters and sons of the fallen and murdered! Listen all of you, who are enjoying the sunshine, your life; you, who love relatives for whom you are waiting to return in vain; in the name of those whose bodies were turned to ash, in the names of those who left no name – I swear to you by their names: Remember, and do not forget! In the name of the happiness which was brutally destroyed by fascism, in the name of the unfinished work, unfulfilled hopes, sweet loves that were cut short, in the name of the fear in the eyes of the murdered – I swear to you, the living – never again!… For something which happened once may yet happen again. But if by ceaseless effort the thing has once already been stopped, then it is possible to stop it from ever happening again in the future. Never again! We won't let it happen again. Blessed be their memory!"

On the square, fifty thousand people breathed in heavily. As we descend from the tribune, on the very first step that I take on the paved square, the approaching wave of this held-in human breath knocks my heart hard. I raised my head and next to the tribune my eyes settled on a group of about thirty or forty young boys and girls, who, seen from the side, had the appearance of a single large living being, very unhappy at the present moment, a being that will perhaps transform into something terrifying in its anger, if moved to it, in a few moments' time.

Hard to say exactly why, but I stopped where I stood, unable to take my eyes off these youngsters. Two maidens embraced a crying girl, whose head was bent over, as if to drink water from a bucket. The others were silent. The young boys looked away – they were seemingly afraid of breaking out sobbing themselves.

Aleksander Lebedev whispered in my ear:

– They were born in the blocks of Oświęcim… They're our children…

איך גיי צו צו איינעם א שטארק קענטלעכן – שווארצע געקרײַזלטע האָר, עטוואָס פּײַכטע, ווייטעקדיק אופגעריסענע אויגן:

– ביסט א ייִד?

דאָס ייִנגל טוט זיך ניט קיין ריר, ער רעדט ארויס, קוקנדיק, ווי ביז אהער, אין א זײַט:

– איך ווייס ניט.

– קיינער פון אונדז ווייסט ניט, ווער מיר זײַנען, – זאָגט א צווייט ייִנגל, – די מאמעס האָבן אונדז געבוירן באהאלטענערהייט, שפּעטער האָט אונדז פארהיט דאָס לעבן די אונטערערדישע ווידערשטאנד־אָרגאניזאציע. די מאמעס און די טאטעס זײַנען אוועק אין דער גאז־קאמער...

איינע פון די צוויי מיידלעך, וואָס האָבן ארומגעאָרעמט די דריטע, האָט אליין זיך אויך צעיאָמערט, און זי, די דריטע, די שטארק פארוויינטע, בעט זיך בא איר, ווישנדיק מיטן שאלעכל דאָס נאסע פּאָנעם און דעם האלדז:

– הער אוף, רויזע, וואָס האָסטו זיך צעוויינט?

– און זי איז א ייִדישקע? – ווײַז איך אף רויזען.

– זי ווייסט אויך ניט... פּאָשעט, זי האָט זיך א נאָמען געגעבן נאָך א ייִדישער פרוי.

– רויזע, נאָך ווּעמען האָסטו זיך געגעבן א נאָמען?

– די מומע רויזע איז מיר געווען א פרעמדע... איך בין אלט געווען דרײַ כאדאָשים און פון הונגער בין איך שוין געווען א האלבער מעס... האָט זי עפּעס געטאָן מיט זיך, און ס'האָט זיך בא איר באוויזן מילך אין די בריסט... די מומע רויזע האָט מיך אויסגעהאָדעוועט...

– ווּוּהין איז זי דערנאָך אהינגעקומען?

– אין פיר און פערציקסטן האָט זי געטראָגן פאר די אופשטענדלער פון דער „זאָנדערקאָמאנדע" דעם דינאמיט, וועלכן ס'האָבן געגאנוועט אין „אוניאָן־ווערקע" דרײַ אנדערע מיידלעך. מיט אָט דעם דינאמיט האָט מען אין אָקטיאבער־כוידעש אופגעריסן דעם קרעמאטאָריע IV. דער אופשטאנד איז אָבער דורכגעפאלן, און אין יאנוואר פינף און פערציק האָט מען די מומע רויזע און אירע כאווערטעס אופגעהאנגען... מע זאָגט, אז זי איז דאן אלט געווען וויינִיקער, ווי איך איצט.

די שווײַגנדיקע מענטשן־מאסע גייט מיט בלומען אין די הענט צו דער שווארצער וואנט, בא וועלכער עס פלעגן פּאָרקומען די צעשיסונגען. דער וועג ליגט פּאָרבײַ דעם זיבן־און־צוואנציקסטן בלאָק. אף זײַן טיר – אן אופשריפט אף ייִדיש: „דאָ וועט געעפנט ווערן די אויסשטעלונג פון ייִדישן ווידערשטאנד און אומקום." פרעג בא לעבעדיעוו, וויפל ייִדן עס זײַנען אומגעקומען אין אָשווענטשים. „פון יעדע פיר אומגעבראכטע זײַנען דרײַ געווען ייִדן", – ענטפערט ער.

I turned to one of the boys, who looked familiar – black, curly hair, eyes somewhat watery, painfully open:

– Are you Jewish?

The young boy did not budge. As he spoke, he looked as before, turned aside:

– I have no idea.

– No one among us knows what we are, – said another youngster, – our mothers gave birth to us in secret, later the underground resistance movement took care of us, saving our lives. Our parents died in the gas chambers…

One of the two maidens who were embracing the girl broke out in bitter tears and the third one, with cried-out eyes, tried to console her, wiping her wet face and neck with a scarf:

– Stop, Rose, why are you crying?

– And is she Jewish? – I pointed to Rose.

– She also doesn't know… She simply called herself after a Jewish woman.

– Rose, whose name did you take?

– Aunt Rose wasn't my relative… I was three months old, and I was half-dead of starvation. She did something to herself, and she could breastfeed me with her milk… And she, Aunt Rose raised me.

– And what happened to her?

– She brought dynamite to the rebels of the *'Sonderkommando'*[17] in forty-four, which was stolen by three other girls from the 'Union-Werke.' That was the dynamite with which they blew up Crematorium-IV in October. The revolt failed, and in January Aunt Rose and her accomplices, forty-five in all, were hanged. I heard she was younger than I am now.[18]

With flowers in their hands, the silent mass approached the black wall where the executions took place. The way to the wall passed block twenty-seven. On the door there was a sign in Yiddish: "In preparation: An exhibition of Jewish Resistance and Death." I asked Lebedev how many Jews perished in Oświęcim. "Out of every four deaths, three were Jews," he replied.

17 Jewish *Sonderkommandos* [special command units] were groups of Jewish prisoners kept alive to perform a variety of slave labor for the functioning of concentration camps and killing centers as well as for the war effort and war economy. In Auschwitz-Birkenau specifically, *Sonderkommandos* were forced to perform a variety of duties in the gas chambers and crematoria involving prisoners and their bodies before and after their deaths. Members of *Sonderkommandos* were usually killed after a couple of months and replaced by new arrivals. There were very few survivors from this group.

18 On this uprising, see also Mark 1977.

מען קאָן אָנשרײַבן א גאַנץ בוך וועגן דעם, וויאַזוי א מענטש גייט ארום איבערן געוועזענעם אָשווענטשימער טויט־לאגער. נאָר איך שרײַב א קורצן רעפּאָרטאַזש, און דאָס, וואָס איך בין בעקוויעך דורך מײַן דערשיטערונג איצט ארויסברענגען, איז גענוג, קעדיי בלויז אָנצייכענען דעם וועג פון דעם אַפּעל־פּלאַץ ביז צום ארויסגאַנג.

ער ליגט, אָט דער וועג, דורך דעם שרעקלעכן עלפטן בלאָק, פונוואַנען קיינער פון די אסירים איז צוריק ניט געקומען. דאָרט האָט מען די אומגליקלעכע פארמר־טשעט אין די קארצערס און אין די בונקערס. אויב אָבער דער מענטש איז געווען, ווי מע זאָגט, פון אײַזן, האָט מען אים דערשאָסן בא דער „שווארצער וואַנט".

בישכיינעס מיטן עלפטן בלאָק – דער צענטער. מענגעלעס קיניגרײַך. דאָ פלעגט מען סטעריליזירן די פרויען און קאַסטרירן די מאַנצבלען. דאָ האָט דער „פּראָפעסאָר" הירט אָפּגעקליבן „לעבעדיקן מאַטעריאַל" אף צו שאפן אין סטראַס־בורג א קאָלעקציע פון 150 סקעלעטן צוליב אַנטראָפּאָלאָגישע אויסשטעלונגען אין דעם עסעס־אינסטיטוט פאר דערלערנען די ראַסע.

– אַזוי – פון בלאָק צו בלאָק, פון מאָרד צו מאָרד. אַזוי – פון שטעכיק דראָט צו שטעכיק דראָט, פון דעם ארײַנגאַנג אין לאַגער צום „ארויסגאַנג" דורכן קוימען...

3

א גרויסן דאַנק דיר, אַלטע פּוילישע מאַמע־שטאָט קראָקע, וואָס דו האָסט מיר געגעבן א געלעגער נאָך דעם, ווי כ'האָב א טאָג צײַט ארומגעוואָגלט אין אָש־ווענטשים. א דאַנק דיר פארן געלעגער, האָלעוויי וואָלסטו געקאָנט מיר שענקען אויך שלאָף... [...]

יאָ, איך בין מיד. נאָר איך וועל זיך ניט צושפּארן. אפן טיש ל לעבן מײַן עלנבויגן ליגט א הײַנטיקע צײַטונג, און ארײַנקוקנדיק אין איר מיט א ווינקל פונעם אויג, כאָ־זער איך איבער פאר זיך א שורע אף דער ערשטער זײַט: „אין מײַרעוו־דײַטשלאַנד לעבן איצט בא 40,000 ניט באַשטראָפטע מילכאָמע־פארברעכער"... [...]

One could write a whole book on the different ways in which you can traverse the Oświęcim death camp. But now I am only writing a short reportage, and, given my state of shock, the things I am able to note down are but a mere sketch of the way from the *Appellplatz* to the camp exit.

The path leads through the dreaded eleventh block, from which no prisoner ever returned. The unfortunate were tortured to death in prison cells and bunkers. And if a human being was made of steel, so to say, they shot them by the "Black Wall."

The camp's center is next to block eleven, the tenth block, and here was Mengele's[19] kingdom. Here they used to sterilize women and castrate men. Here "Professor" Hirt[20] selected "living specimens" to create a collection of 150 skeletons in Strasbourg, which he presented at an anthropological exhibition in the SS-Institute for the Study of Race.[21]

– This is how it happened – from one block to the other, from one murder to the next, from barbed wire to barbed wire, from the camp entrance to the "exit" through the chimneys…

3

I'm very grateful to you, oh old Polish mother-city of Kraków, for accommodating me after my day of wanderings in Oświęcim. I'm grateful for the accommodation; I only wish you would have granted me sleep as well… […]

Yes, I'm tired. But I don't want to spare myself. On the coffee table next to my elbow, today's paper is lying, and as I catch sight of it out of the corner of my eye, I repeat a sentence from the front page to myself: "Around 40,000 unpunished war criminals currently live in West Germany." […]

19 Josef Mengele (1911–1979), nicknamed "*Todesengel*" [Angel of Death], was an SS officer and 'physician' during the Second World War feared for both his role in selecting victims to either be murdered in the gas chambers immediately upon arrival or enslaved in forced labor and for the deadly experiments on prisoners he performed in Auschwitz II (Birkenau). After the war, with the assistance of a network of former SS members, he made it to Argentina and eluded prosecution of his many crimes until his natural death in 1979 in Bertioga, Brazil.

20 August Hirt (1898–1945) was a Swiss/German anatomist, SS-Hauptsturmführer, then SS-Sturmbannführer, and chairman at the Reichsuniversität Straßburg [Reich University in Strasbourg] – founded in 1941 after the annexation of Alsace-Lorraine by Nazi Germany. He performed mustard gas experiments on inmates in the Natzweiler-Struthof concentration camp and directed the procuration and preparation of the so-called Jewish skull collection – a failed Nazi plan to showcase the alleged racial inferiority of Jews housed at the Anatomical Institute at the Reichsuniversität. Hirt committed suicide in June 1945 and was tried in absentia for his crimes at the Military War Crimes Trial at Metz in 1953.

21 Further on this, see Nyiszli 1973.

צען אזייגער אינדערפרי האָט זיך אָנגעהויבן די סעסיע פונעם אינטערנאציאָנאלן אָשווענטשימער קאָמיטעט. גאַנטשאַראָוו און איך זײַנען בײַגעווען אלס געסט בלויז אף דער ערשטער זיצונג. איצט פאָרן מיר צוזאמען מיטן פאַן קוניצקי אף א טאָג קיין זאקאָפּאנע, צו די קארפּאטן. [...]

אינדערפרי דערציילט מיר לעבעדיעוו וועגן דער סעסיע פונעם צווישנפעלקערלעכן אָשווענטשים־קאָמיטעט. דאָרט איז געווען א טשיקאווער וויקועך ארום דעם ייִדישן בלאָק אף דער טעריטאָריע פונעם געוועזענעם טויט־לאַגער. ווען עס איז געגאנגען א רייד וועגן דעם געלט, וואָס די נאציאָנאלע אָרגאניזאציעס טראָגן ארײַן אף אופצובויען דעם אָשווענטשימער דענקמאָל, האָט דער פּאָרזיצער פּרנעם פארבאנד פון די געטאָ־קעמפער אין ייִסראָעל שאָלעם גראיעק („סטעפּאן“) געמאָלדן, אז דער דאָזיקער פארבאנד וועט זיך באשטײַערן, אויב דער ייִדישער בלאָק אין אָשווענטשים וועט הייסן ניט ייִדישער, נאָר ייִסראָעל־בלאָק.

דאָס האָט ארויסגערופן מאמעש א שטוינונג בא די דעלעגאטן. ערשטנס, צי איז עס דער פּאָסיקער פאל אף צו דינגען זיך? צווייטנס, אין די יאָרן פון דער אָשווענטשימער טראגעדיע איז ייִסראָעל נאָך אפילע אף דער וועלט ניט געווען און די דרײַ מיליאָן ייִדן זײַנען אין אָשווענטשים אומגעקומען ניט אלס ייִסראָעל־בירגער, נאָר אלס ייִדן. די פּרעטענזיעס צו רעפּרעזענטירן דאָס גאנצע ייִדישע פאָלק האָבן אזוי ווײַט פארפירט אייניקע פּאָליטיקער פון ייִסראָעל, אז זיי האָבן אפילע דעם אָנדענק פון די קדוישים א וואָרף געטאָן אף זייערע קאָניונקטור־קאָרטן.

שוין אף דער ערשטער זיצונג פון דער סעסיע איז קלאָר געוואָרן, אז קיינער פון די דעלעגאטן וועט ניט אונטערהאלטן אזעלכע פּרעטענזיע, און גראיעק איז געווען געצווונגען צו מעלדן, אז ייִסראָעל וועט זיך באשטײַערן פארן דענקמאָל און אויך צושיקן עקספּאָנאטן פאר דעם ייִדישן מוזיי־בלאָק...

די סאָוועטישע דעלעגאציע פליט ארויס קיין מאָסקווע. איך בלײַב נאָך איבער אין פּוילן. באם געזעגענען זיך פרעגן מיר איינער דעם אנדערן, צי ס׳איז טאקע אן עמעס, אז מיר האָבן זיך באגעגנט צום ערשטן מאָל אין טאָג פון אונדזער אָפּפאָרן קייןווארשע, דאָס הייסט, אז באקאנט זײַנען מיר צווישן זיך בלויז פינף טעג...

The meeting of the International Oświęcim Committee started at 10 a.m. Goncharov and myself were guests at the first meeting. Now we're going on a day trip to Zakopane in the Carpathian Mountains with Mr. Kunicki. […]

In the morning, Lebedev told me about the session of the International Oświęcim Committee. An unusual debate took place about the Jewish block on the territory of the former death camp. When talk turned to money, and the different national organizations were asked to contribute for the construction of the Oświęcim memorial, Shalom Grajek ("Stefan"),[22] the head of the Association of Ghetto Fighters in Israel, announced that his organization will contribute only on the condition that the block in Oświęcim be renamed the "Israel-block," instead of the "Jewish block."

This caused real astonishment among the delegates. First, was this really the occasion for haggling? Second, in the years of the Oświęcim tragedy the state of Israel had not existed yet, and the three million Jews who perished in Oświęcim did not die as citizens of Israel but as Jews. The claim of representing the entire Jewish people misleads some Israeli politicians to dare to play with the memory of the martyrs as with cards in a political game.

Already at the first session of the meeting it became clear that none of the delegates were willing to support such demands, and Grajek was forced to announce that Israel will contribute its share in the memorial unconditionally, and even send artifacts to the Jewish block exhibition…

The Soviet delegation is flying out to Moscow but I'm staying on in Poland. As we said our goodbyes, we kept asking whether it can be true that we only met for the first time on the day of our departure to Warsaw, that we, in other words, have only known each other for five days…

[22] Shalom Grajek (Stefan Grajek, 1915–2008) was one of the surviving Jewish fighters of the Warsaw Ghetto Uprising. Before the outbreak of the Second World War, he became one of the leaders of the Polish פועלי־ציון [*Pōley Ẓīyyōn*, Workers of Zion]. He moved to Israel / Palestine in 1949, and was a member of various social organizations, and active in initiatives for the commemoration of the fighters of the Warsaw Ghetto Uprising, and the memory of Polish Jewry. He was a member of the Executive Committee of Yad Vashem, amongst others.

2. פּוילן[10]

4

וועגן די עטלעכע טעג, וואָס איך בין נאָך געווען אין פּוילן – וועגן דער רײַזע קיין וראָצלאַוו און וואַלבזשיק, וועגן טרעבלינקע, – וועל איך איצט ניט שרײַבן קיין נאָכאַנאנדיקן רעפּאָרטאַזש. איך טראַכט, אַז בעסער וועט זײַן פאַרענדיקן די פּוילישע רײַזע־פאַרצייכענונגען מיט דרײַ פאַרבליבענע פון יענע טעג פאַרנאָטירונגען.

די ערשטע פאַרנאָטירונג. טרעבלינקע, 17 אַפּרעל 1965

אַף אָט דער קליינער באַן־סטאַנציע אין דער פּוילישער מאַזאָוויע בין איך אָנגעקומען אין אַן עסעריק־קאַלטן טאָג. ס'האָט זיך געדוכט, אַז דער פרילינג, וואָס האָט ערשט נעכטן אַזוי שפּרודלדיק געשפּילט, איז געווען ניט מער ווי אַן אויסדאַכטעניש.

איך בין דורכגעגאַנגען דעם וועג – פון דער באַן־ליניע און ביז דעם אָרט, ווו דער אייבערשטער שיכט ערד איז אַראָפּגענומען, און יעדער איינער, וואָס קוקט אַהין אַראָפּ, בריט זיך אָפּ אין די פאַרשטיינערטע קוילן פון דער קרעמאַטאָריע. אין דעם טרעבלינקע־דענקמאָל בין איך אַרײַן ווי אין אַ וואַלד. איך האָב קיין טאָעס ניט: כ'בין אַרײַן אין דענקמאָל, דער דענקמאָל איז אַ וואַלד, אַ וואַלד פון שטיינער. די לעבעדיקע האָבן זיי געבראַכט אַהער און אַוועקגעשטעלט אַלס אַ זייכער פון די דערמאָרדעטע. וויפל שטיינער שטייען דאָ – הונדערטער, טויזנטער? איך ווייס ניט. דאָס גאַנצע טרעבלינקער פעלד, ווו עס איז געווען דער טויט־לאַגער, איז פאַרפולט מיט גרויע שטיינער. קליינע און גרויסע. שפּיציקע און פאַרקײַלעכיקטע. שטיינער – זיידעס מיט אײַנגעבויגענע פּלייצעס. שטיינער – טאַלייסים, שטיינער – פּויסטן, שטיינדעלעך – מיידעלעך מיט אויסגעוואַשענע צעפּעלעך. אָט איז אַ מאַמע מיט אַ צעלאָזט שאַלכל, זי לויפט, דוכט זיך, צו פאַרדעקן איר קינד. אָט איז אַ שטיין ווי אַ שטיינהעקער: געזונט און ברייט אין די אַקסלען, נאָר די הענט געבונדן. לעבן אים שטייט טאַקע זי, זײַן באַשערטע. עס טיילט זיי אָפּ ניט מער ווי דאָס שטיינערנע שווײַגן. שטיינער מיט אָפּגעהאַקטע צוויײַגן און מיט אָפּגעהאַקטע קעפּ. מאַמעס מיט פאַרבראָכענע הענט. אַ יונג, וואָס הייבט אוף אַ שטיין. שטיינער – געהאַנגענע, שטיינער – אויסגעגאַנגענע פון הונגער. שטיינער, וואָס אַנטלויפן, און שטיינער, פאַרוווּנדעטע אין שלאַכט...

ניט געסטײַעט האָבן קיין שטיינער פאַר אַלע אַכט הונדערט טויזנט מענטשן
– קאָרבאָנעס. האָט מען אַף יעדן שטיין אויסגעהאַקט דעם נאָמען פון אַ שטעטל
דאָס איז דער טרעבלינקער דענקמאָל: אַ געדיכטער שטיינערנער וואַלד.

איך בין אַרומגעגאַנגען אין אָט דעם וואַלד און ניט געווען באַקוויעך ניט פרעגן עפּעס, ניט זאָגן עפּעס, די ליפּן האָבן געשעפּטשעט – ס'איז געווען אַ ליד. טאַקע דאָ, צווישן די שטיינער, האָב איך זי פאַרשריבן:

[10] סאָוועטיש היימלאַנד 11 (1965), 119–123.

2. Poland

4

I won't write a continuous reportage about those couple of days that I remained in Poland – about the journey to Wrocław and Wałbrzych, about Treblinka. I think it is better to conclude my Polish Travel Notes with three remaining notes from those days.

The First Note. Treblinka, 17 April 1965

On a bitingly cold day, I arrived at exactly that small train station in the Polish Mazovian Voivodeship. It seemed that the very spring that only yesterday sparkled so exuberantly was nothing more than an illusion.

I followed the path – from the train tracks to the location where the top layer of the ground was removed and everyone who looks down burns their fingers on the fossilized coals of the crematorium. I entered the Treblinka memorial like a forest. I am not mistaken: I entered the memorial, the memorial is a forest, a forest of stones. The living brought them here and placed them as a trace of the murdered. How many stones are standing here – hundreds, thousands? I don't know. The entire Treblinka field where the death camp was located is full of grey stones. Small and big ones. Pointy and round. Stones – grandfathers with bent shoulders. Stones – prayer-shawls; stones – fists; small stones – girls with washed braids. Right there is a mother with a loosened shawl, she is running, it seems, in order to hide her child. Right there is a stone like a stone-butcher: healthy with wide shoulders, only the hands are tied up. Next to him she is standing, his predestined wife. Not more than their stony silence is separating them. Stones with chopped off branches and chopped off heads. Mothers wring their hands. A young person who picks up a stone. Stones – hanged ones; stones – starved ones. Stones which are running away and stones, wounded in combat…

There weren't enough stones for all eight hundred thousand human beings – victims. So they engraved every stone with a name of a *shtetl.*

This is the Treblinka memorial: a dense, stony forest.

I walked around this forest and was incapable of not asking, not saying something, my lips murmured – it was a poem. Precisely there, amongst the stones, I wrote down:

וואלד... וואלד... וואלד...
גוואלד! גוואלד! גוואלד!

א וואלד פון שטיינער אף מענטשנס ביינער

א וואלד אָן סאָסנעס,
א וואלד אָן טאנען.
א וואלד פון כײַקעס,
א וואלד פון כאנעס.
א וואלד אָן מאָכן
און אָן קוקאוועס,
א וואלד פון פייגעס,
א וואלד פון כאוועס.
ניטאָ קיין פייגל,
ניטאָ קיין צוויטשערס –
א וואלד פון כאימס,
א וואלד פון איטשעס.
ניטאָ קיין קרוינען,
קיין אלטע דאָרנס,
א וואלד פון יוינעס,
א וואלד פון זאָרעכס,
א וואלד אָן גראָזן,
אפילע אָן סאָוועס
אונטער די שטיינער
ליגן שפינאָזעס.
א שטיין –
איינשטיין,
פון זײַן מאָרך און געביין,
א שטיין פון זײַן כיין,
פון זײַנע ציין,
פון זײַן גיין, פון זײַן שטיין,
פון זײַן יאָ, פון זײַן ניין –
א שטיין.

שטיינער, שטיינער,
וואָס טוט איר מיט זיך פארדעקן?
א שטיין – א שטעטל?

א שטיין – א שטעטל!
לוקאָוו און זשארנאָוו –
שטיין... שטיין....
ווערזשבניק און סארנאָוו –
שטיין...

Forest… Forest… Forest…
Help! Help! Help!

A forest of stones on top of human bones.

A forest without pines,
A forest without fir trees.
A forest of Khaykes,
A forest of Khanes.
A forest without moss,
A forest without cuckoos,
A forest of Feyges,
A forest of Khaves.
There are no birds around,
No twitter –
A forest of Khaims,
A forest of Itshes.
No treetops,
No old thorn bushes,
A forest of Yoynes,
A forest of Zorekhs,
A forest without grass,
Even without owls.
Beneath the stones
Spinozas are laying.
A stone –
Einstein,[23]
Mad out of his brain and bones,
A stone made from his grace,
From his teeth,
From his walk, from his standing still,
From his yes, from his no –
A stone.

Stones, stones,
What are you hiding underneath?
A stone – a shtetl?

A stone – a shtetl!
Łuków and Żarnów –
Stone… Stone…
Wierzbnik and Sarnów –
Stone…

23 This is a wordplay in the original Yiddish: a shteyn – Einstein.

עפשער געבליבן פינטשאָוו? ניין...
עפשער – א סימען פון ראדזין? ניין...
פולאוו – פארשטיינט,
ראדאָם – פארשטיינט,
לוקאָוו – פארשטיינט,
יודנריין!
געבליבן בלויז שטארצן
ניסראָפּים־קוימענדלעך.
ניטאָ, ניטאָ שוין
די מוישעלעך, שלוימעלעך.
און דאָ, אין דעם וואלד,
די שטיינער, פארוויינט,
שטייען געבויגן אף מענטשנס געביין.

וואלד, וואלד, וואלד...
גוואלד, גוואלד, גוואלד!
א וואלד שטייט פארגליווערט אף מענטשנס ביינער.
די שטיינער
אין הימל ווארפן שטיינער!

די צווייטע פארנאָטירונג

19 אפּרעל 1965

געטאָ... מע איז שוין צוגעוווינט צום וואָרט „געטאָ“. עס דוכט זיך, אז צומאָל פארגעסט מען אפילע, וואָס געטאָ איז אזוינס. מע דערלויבט זיך צו זאָגן: „צוריק אין געטאָ“...

ייִדן, די שטענדיק עקספּאנסיווע ייִדן, האָבן די ערשטע „פארכאפּט“ פאר זיך דאָס וואָרט ג ע ט אָ, כאָטש עס זייַנען דאָך געווען אויך אינדיאַנער אין די רעזער־וואציעס, די נעגער־„שטאָט“ הארלעם אין איינעם א בארעמהארציקן לאנד. ייִדן, קאָן מען מיינען, האָבן מיט זייער גוטן ווילן א ל י י ן ז י ך פארשפּארט אין די געטאָס...

ייִדישע געטאָס ביז דער צווייטער וועלט־מילכאָמע זייַנען „בלויז“, אזוי צו זאָגן, א נאציאָנאלער און סאָציאלער קאָרדאָן, א מיטל צו האלטן די ייִדן אין א זייַט פונעם לעבן. די ייִדישע געטאָס בייס דער נאצי־מעהומע – דאָס איז דער פלאץ לעבן שעכטהויז און דאָס שעכטהויז אליין.

איך טראכט וועגן ייִדישע געטאָס, שטייענדיק באם ווארשעווער געטאָ־דענק־מאָל אין א טריבן אינדערפרי, אין צוויי און צוואנציק יאָר ארום נאָך דעם, ווי די ייִדישע געטאָ איז געוואָרן א שלאכטפעלד, א טעריטאָריע פון אייביקן רום פאר די פארשפארטע און פאראורטיילטע, וועלכע האָבן זיך פארמאָסטן מיט זייערע אויסגעשעפּטע קויכעס קעגן דעם קויער פון די קוילערס.

Maybe Pińczów remained? No…
Maybe – a sign from Radzyn? No…
Puławy – fossilized,
Radom – fossilized,
Łuków – fossilized,
Judenrein!
Only chimneys remained,
jutting out from burnt-down houses from fire victims.
No more, all gone
The small Moyshes, Shloymes.
And there, in this forest,
The stones, bathed in tears,
Are standing bent on human bones.

Forest, forest, forest…
Help, help, help!
A forest is standing congealed on top of human remains.
The stones
Throwing stones into the sky!

The Second Note

19 April 1965

Ghetto… We got so used to the word "ghetto." It seems that at times one even forgets what a ghetto actually is. We allow ourselves to say: "Back into the ghetto"…

Jews, the always expanding Jews, first "appropriated" the word ghetto for themselves, even though there were Native Americans on the reservations, or that Black "city" Harlem in a merciful country. With good will, Jews, one could be of the opinion, confined *themselves* in ghettos…

Jewish ghettos until the Second World War were "only," so to say, a national and social boundary, a means to hold Jews on the margins of life. The Jewish ghettos during the Nazi stampede – those were the places next to the slaughterhouses and the slaughterhouses themselves.

I'm thinking about Jewish ghettos as I am standing at the Warsaw Ghetto Memorial on a gloomy morning, twenty-two years after the day when the Jewish ghetto turned into a battleground, a territory of eternal glory for the incarcerated and doomed who, all exhausted, pitted themselves against the force of the riflemen.

נאָך דער וואַרשעווער געטאָ טאָרן דאָך שוין אוודאי ניט זײַן קיין געטאָס אױף דער וועלט. ווען די וואַרשעווער געטאָ איז דערשטיקט געוואָרן, זײַנען די לעצטע מוירדים אירע דורך די קאַנאַליזאַציע־רערן אַרויס פֿון געטאָ אין וואַלד אַרײַן. ניט – אַרײַן אין געטאָ. אַרויס פֿון געטאָ!

איך שטיי באַם וואַרשעווער דענקמאָל און טראַכט: סאַראַ נעס עס איז געשען! ס׳איז דאָך ניט קיין דענקמאָל, אַ שטיק וואַנט איז עס אין מוראַנאָוו. עס שטעלט זיך מיר פֿאָר: די פֿאַשיסטישע הײַשעריקן קריכן ווידער צו דער געטאָ. די לעבעדיקע קעמפֿער האָבן זיך אוועקגעשטעלט צו באַגעגענען זיי מיט פֿײַער. אָט שטייען די מוירדים צוגעדריקט צו דער וואַנט אין סאַמע ברען פֿון שלאַכט; אַ שרעקלאָזער יונג מיט אַן איבערגעבונדענעם קאָפּ – די גראַנאַטע גרייט אין דער האַנט. לעבן אים, פֿון ביידע זײַטן, זײַנע שלאַכט־כאַווײרים, אינגאַנצן יונגע. אַ באַיאָרטער מענטש הייבט זיך אויף, שוין אַ פֿאַרוווּנדעטער, איבער דעם קערפּער פֿון אַ געפֿאַלענעם. הינטער זיי אַלעמען און עטוואָס העכער פֿון זיי – אַ פֿרוי אין אַ צעפֿליקטע קלייד, די האָר צעלאָזט איבער די אַקסלען. זי איז שווער פֿאַרוווּנדעט. מיט די לעצטע קויכעס דריקט זי צו צו דער ברוסט אַ קינד... [...]

איר, וואָס איר וואַרפֿט הײַנט שטיינער אין די שלאַכט־כאַווײרים פֿון די געטאָ־העלדן און, אויסרעכענענדיק, אַז פֿון אַ העכער אָרט וועט גרינגער זײַן צו טרעפֿן, באַמיט איר זיך אַפֿילו אַרומצוקריכן אויף די טרעפּ פֿונעם וואַשינגטאָנער ווײַסן הויז און פֿון דאָרט אַ וואָרף טאָן פֿון מאָל צו מאָל אַ שטיין אויך אין דער שטיינערנער וואַנט אויפֿן וואַרשעווער געטאָ־פּלאַץ, – פֿאַרוואָס זײַט איר אין דער ביטערער שאָ פֿון דער אויסראָטונג פֿון אונדזער פֿאָלק ניט געקראָכן אויף די וואַשינגטאָנער טרעפּ צו פֿאָדערן הילף פֿאַר די געטאָ־מאַרטירער?

אַזוי שטיי איך באַ דער וואַרשעווער דענקמאָל־וואַנט און טראַכט וועגן ייִדישע געטאָס און וועגן די, וועלכע רופֿן אונדז צוריק אַהין: פֿאַר די אויגן שווימט אַ טײַך פֿון מענטשן, אַ טײַך פֿון בלומען־קרענץ. הײַנט איז דער פּלאַץ פֿון די געטאָ־העלדן דער צענטראַלער אין וואַרשע. ניין, ניט נאָר ייִדן – די גאַנצע באַפֿעלקערונג פֿון דער פּוילישער הויפּטשטאָט שטראָמט הײַנט צו אָט דעם פּלאַץ.

נײַע, הויכע הײַזער שטייען אויפֿן אָרט פֿון די געטאָ־כורוועס. אַ זיכערע רויִקײַט, כאָטש זי איז דורכגעזיפּט דורך דער שרויט־פֿײַקלערײַ פֿון סאָלדאַטישע פּויקן, שפּרייט זיך אויס איבער דער געוועזענער געטאָ. און ניט געקוקט דערויף, וואָס דער מילכאָמע־אומרו איז אַזוי ווײַט פֿון אָט דער רויִקײַט, איז מיר דאָך ניט שווער זיך אומצוקערן מיט די געדאַנקען צו דער פּאַנאָראַמע פֿונעם אויפֿשטאַנד אין געטאָ.

פֿאַרנאַכט, אין פֿאַרטונקלטן זאַל פֿון דער וואַרשעווער פֿילהאַרמאָניע, אויף דער פֿײַערלעכער אָנדענק־פֿאַרזאַמלונג, וועל איך זאָגן אַזוי:

– די ייִדישע געטאָ פֿון וואַרשע, מע קאָן זי פֿאַרגלײַכן צו אַ ברענענדיקן טאַנק,

After the Warsaw Ghetto, it goes without saying, ghettos should not exist in this world anymore. When the Warsaw Ghetto was suffocated, its last insurgents exited the ghetto through the sewage system and fled into the forest. Not into – out of the ghetto!

I am standing at the Warsaw Memorial and think: What a miracle! It is not actually a memorial, it's simply a piece of the wall in Muranów. I am imagining a fascist swarm of locusts again crawling towards the Ghetto. The living fighters position themselves in such a way to meet them with fire. So the insurgents stood pressed to the wall in the heat of the battle; a fearless young man with a bandaged head – the grenade ready in his hand. Next to him, on both sides, there are comrades in arms, youngsters all of them. Already injured, an elderly man is placing himself over the body of a fallen man. Behind them everyone else and a little elevated from them – a woman in a torn dress, her hair loose over the shoulders. She is severely injured. With her last strength she is pressing a child to her chest… […]

You, you who throw stones at the comrades in arms of the Ghetto heroes, and, assessing that from a more elevated position it would have been easier to hit, you even seek to crawl around the steps of the White House in Washington and from there throw stones one after the other at the stony wall on the Warsaw Ghetto square, – why didn't you crawl on those Washington steps to demand help for the Ghetto martyrs in the bitter hour of the annihilation of our people?

So I am standing at the Warsaw Memorial wall and think about Jewish ghettos, and about those who call us back into them: in front of my eyes a river of human beings swim, a river of girdles of flowers. Today, the square of the Ghetto heroes is the central square in Warsaw. No, not only for Jews – today, the whole population of the Polish capital is pouring into precisely this square.

New, tall buildings have replaced the Ghetto ruins. A secure calmness sets in over the former Ghetto even though it is sifted through by the buckshot-drumming of military drums. But despite the fact that the war turmoil is so far away from this calmness, it is not difficult for me to turn my thoughts to the panorama of the Ghetto Uprising.

In the evening, in a darkened hall of the Warsaw philharmonic at the celebratory memorial event, I will say the following:

דערצו נאָך אַן ארומגערינגלטן פון די סאָנים, – צו א ברענענדיקן טאנק, וועמעס שלאכט־עקיפּאַזש האָט געשאָסן ביז דער לעצטער מינוט. דער מעטאַל פונעם טאנק איז שוין צעשמאָלצן, די טאנקיסטן זײַנען שוין פארקוילט, אָבער ארום דעם טאנק איז אזוי גרויס די צאָל פונעם סוינעס פּגראָרים, אז דאָס דערלויבט די לעבן־געבליבענע אופצוהייבן איבער די קעפּ פון די דאנקבארע דוירעס דעם טאנק, ווי אַן אייביקן דענקמאָל...

דריטע פארנאָטירונג

בעשאַס איך גיי ארום איבער די קולטור־אנשטאלטן פון ווארשע, – צווישן ייִדישן היסטאָרישן מוזיי און דער רעדאקציע פון דער „פאָלקס־שטימע", צווישן אידא קאמינסקאַס טעאַטער און דעם קולטור־געזעלשאפטלעכן פארבאנד, – פאלט מיר אײַן א געדאנק, אז אינעם דימיען וואָלט עפּשער קעדײַ געווען אזוי־אָ מיטן שפּאן אויסצומעסטן דעם מעהאַלעך צווישן נאָוואָגראָדזקע 5 און דעם אָרט, ווו ס׳איז פארן קריג געווען טלאָמאצקע 13.

גרויס איז דער מעהאַלעך צווישן אָט די צוויי צײַט־אָפּשניטן אין ייִדישן קול־טור־לעבן פון פּוילן. זײַענדיק איצט דאָ, טראַכט איך, אז ווען ס׳וואָלט געשען אזא נעס און איך וואָלט, לעמאָשל, שוין דעמלט, אין די דרײַסיקער יאָרן, געוווּסט דאָס, וואָס איך ווייס איצט, און געהאט אן ארײַנפּאָר־שײַן קיין פּוילן, וואָלט איך, קאָן זײַן, ארומגעגאנגען פון שטאָט צו שטאָט, ווו ייִדישע שרײַבער פון פּוילן האָבן דאן געוווינט, און צוזאמען מיט יעדן איינעם פון זיי געפּרוּווט ארײַנדרינגען אין דעם, וואָס עס וועט זײַן שפּעטער.

איך וואָלט געקומען אין ווארשע צו מוישע בראָדערזאָנען און עפראָיִם

– The Jewish Ghetto of Warsaw, we can compare it to a burning tank which is also encircled by the enemy, – to a burning tank whose battle crew shot until the last minute. The metal of the tank has melted down already, its crew already carbonized, but around the tank there is such a large number of corpses of the enemy that this allows for those who stayed alive to lift the tank over the heads of the grateful future generations like an eternal memorial…

The Third Note

As I was going from cultural institute to cultural institute in Warsaw, – between the Jewish Historical Museum and the editorial office of the "*Folks-shtime*," between Ida Kamińska's theater and the Socio-Cultural Society[24] [YKGF] – the idea strikes me that it would perhaps be worthwhile, in my imagination, to measure with the span of my steps the long journey that lies between 5 Nowogrodzka Street[25] and the location where 13 Tłomackie Street[26] was before the war.

Large is the distance between these two periods of time in Jewish cultural life of Poland. Now here, I am wondering whether, if I had miraculously known already back then, let's say in the thirties what I know now and if I'd had an entry visa for Poland, whether I perhaps would have traveled between the cities in which Yiddish writers were living at the time and tried with each one of these writers to permeate all those things bound to happen in the future.

I would have come to Warsaw to Moyshe Broderzon[27] and Froyim Ka-

24 The ייִדישער קולטור־געזעלשאַפֿטלעכער פֿאַרבאַנד פֿון די ייִדן אין פּוילן [*Yidisher kultur-gezelshaftlekher farband fun di yidn in Poyln*, Towarzystwo Społeczno Kulturalne Żydów w Polsce; Socio-Cultural Society of Jews in Poland, YKGF].

25 A memorial plaque of the 1944 Warsaw Uprising is attached to the wall of the apartment building which housed the headquarters of the AK's Sokół battalion.

26 13 Tłomackie Street is an important address in Jewish Warsaw. Headquarters of the פֿאַראיין פֿון ייִדישע ליטעראַטן און זשורנאַליסטן אין וואַרשע [*Fareyn fun yidishe literatn un zhurnalistn in Varshe*, Jewish Writers' and Journalists' Association] since 1916, it was the gathering place for Jewish intellectual, literary and artistic circles. Yiddish writer Zusman Segalovitsh preserved for future readers the spirit and atmosphere of this beating heart of intellectual life of prewar Yiddish Warsaw in Segalovitsh 1946. Destroyed during the war, today's Żydowski Instytut Historyczny [Jewish Historical Institute, ŻIH] is located nearby at 3/5 Tłomackie, prewar home of the Main Judaic Library.

27 Moscow-born, Łódź-raised Moyshe Broderzon (1890–1956) was a Yiddish avant-garde poet and playwright with stints in wartime and revolutionary Moscow (1914–1918) and interwar Łódź (1918–1939) where he affiliated with avant-garde Yiddish circles and formed several significant Yiddish literary groups, such as יונג־ייִדיש [*Yung-yidish*, Young-Yiddish]. Committed to enriching Yiddish poetry and literature with new forms in his numerous poetry collections, such as *tankas* (Japanese poetic form), he devoted his time in interwar Łódź to theater. In 1924, Broderzon was

קאגאנאָווסקין, וועלכע מיר האָבן נאָכן נײַן־און־דרײַסיקסטן שוין געהאלטן פאר אונדזעריקע, סאָוועטישע. שיין און שווער איז געווען זייער וועג. ריין און מוטיק – זייער געמיט. אויך דער אומרו זייערער און דער ווייטעק און אלץ, וואָס שפּעטער איז זיי אויסגעקומען איבערלעבן, – אלץ איז געווען באהויכט מיט דער גרויזאמער צײַט. טראכטנדיק וועגן זיי און וועגן די בעסטע, וואָס האָבן צוזאמען מיט זיי געשאפן די דעמלטיקע ייִדישע ליטעראטור אין פּוילן, פארשטיי איך, פארוואָס מאָרדכע געבירטיג, דער ווארשעווער פאָלקס־זינגער, וועמען איך האָב, לײדער, ניט געקענט, האָט מיט זײַן דערשיטערנדיקער ליד „עס ברענט" ארויסגעשריִען נאָך פארן קריג דעם פאָרגעפיל פונעם שפּעטערדיקן געטאָ־שוידער. איך וואָלט צווישן יענע, וועלכע האָבן אין דער טלאָמאצקע־דרײַצן־ווארשע געשאפן ליטע־ראטור פון פאראנטוואָרטלעכקײַט, געזען אויך אלטער קאציזנען, און נאָכאמאָל

ganovski[28] who we certainly thought of as our own Soviet Yiddish writers after 1939. Beautiful and hard was their path. Pure and brave – their mind. Their anxieties and pain, too, as well as everything they had to experience later on – everything was beclouded by the horrible times. Thinking about them and about the best who together with them created Yiddish literature in Poland back then, I understand why Mordkhe Gebirtig,[29] Warsaw's bard of the people, whom I sadly never had the privilege to have met, cried out already before the war with his harrowing poem "It is burning"[30] a foreboding of the hell of the later ghetto. Among those who were committed to create literature at Warsaw's 13 Tłomackie, I would have also seen Alter Kacyzne,[31]

the librettist for the first Yiddish opera performed in Warsaw, דוד און בת־שבֿע [*Dovid un Bassheve*, David and Bathsheba]. The founding with his acting students of the cabaret theater אַראַראַט (acronym for אַרטיסטישער רעוואָלוציאָנערער רעוויו־טעאַטער [*Artistisher revolutsyonerer revyu-teater*, Artistic Revolutionary Revue-Theater]) in Łódź in 1927 is one of his major achievements. In 1939, he fled the Nazi invasion of Poland first to Białystok and, in 1941, he was evacuated to a small town in Soviet Central Asia. In 1944, he started to teach at Moscow's drama school of the Государственный Еврейский Театр [State Jewish Theater, GOSET]. During Stalin's postwar purges of the Jewish cultural elite, Broderzon was arrested in April 1950 and convicted to ten years in a labor camp. He was rehabilitated and liberated in 1955 and returned to Poland in June 1956 where he died soon after in August of a heart attack.

28 Warsaw-born Froyim Kaganovski (1893–1958) was a Yiddish novelist who started his literary career at an early age and penned several novels. He survived the *khurbn* in the unoccupied Soviet Union, was a member of the ייִדישער אנטיפאשיסטישער קאָמיטעט [*Yidisher antifashistisher komitet*, Jewish Antifascist Committee; JAFC] and settled in Paris after the war.

29 Mordkhe Gebirtig (1877–1942) was a Kraków native and a famous Yiddish poet and songwriter. His first collection of songs, entitled פֿאָלקסטימלעך [*Folkstimlekh*, In the Folk Style], was published in 1920 and grew increasingly more famous. A second collection of songs with sheet music, entitled מײַנע לידער [*Mayne lider*, My Songs] came out in 1936. In 1938, Gebirtig wrote his famous ס'ברענט [*S'brent*, It is burning] – a call for action in the face of increasing antisemitism and pogroms in Poland. Initially mostly ignored, this song gained in importance during the *khurbn* becoming particularly popular among the Jewish youth and resistance movement under Nazi occupation. Consequently, it was erroneously assumed to have been written during the war years. Gebirtig was killed by Nazi fire in Kraków in June 1942.

30 On *S'brent* see also the interview with Jalda Rebling in the present volume.

31 Vilna-born Alter-Sholem Kacyzne (1885–1941) was a Yiddish writer, critic, and photographer. Settling in Warsaw in 1910 and opening a photography studio, he affiliated with Yiddish classical writer Y. L. Peretz, who became his literary mentor, and started to publish Yiddish works widely and across genres after the latter's death in 1915. In 1921, he was commissioned as a photographer by the American Hebrew Immigrant Aid Society [HIAS] to capture the misery of Polish Jews who hoped to immigrate to the United States. Following this, he regularly contributed photographs for פֿאָרווערטס [*Forverts*, Jewish Daily Forward] Sunday art supplement and for that purpose traveled all over Poland, to Palestine, Romania, Italy, Spain, and Morocco. Photography became a second area of creative output for him; it financed and shaped his literary work thematically in turn. After the outbreak of the Second World War, Kacyzne fled Warsaw with his wife and daughter and found refuge in Soviet-occupied Lviv, where he contributed to theater and radio programs set up by the Soviets. In the wake of the German attack on the Soviet Union in June 1941, he fled to Ternipil and was killed on 7 July 1941 in a Nazi-incited pogrom.

וואָלט איך הייַנט איבערגעלייענט, לעמאָשל, זייַן דראמע „דעם ייִדנס אָפּמאך‟ און דערזען אין איר די שילדערונג פון דער היטלער־מאגייפע דורכן טיפּאזש פון דער ווייַטער שפּאנישער אינקוויזיציע. פונדאנען זעט שוין מייַן אויג די ווערק פון די שעפער פון דער געהייליקטער געטאָ־ליטעראטור.

איך וואָלט אריינגעקומען אין די אָקופּאציע־יאָרן, אין רינגעלבלומס אונטערערדישן ארכיוו און אויסגעשריִען, ניט היטנדיק זיך פאר פּאָליצייען און עסעס־לייַט: „יאָ, זיי זייַנען דערגאנגען, די קסאָווים אייַערע! אין ווארשעווער ייִדישן היסטאָרישן אינסטיטוט, בא בער מארקן, האָב איך געזען, וויִאזוי דאָס אָפּגעקעמפטע און אופגעריכטע פוילן היט אָפּ יעדן אָס וועגן דער ייִדישער טראגעדיע, וועלכן איר האָט איבערגעלאָזט פאר דאָר־דוירעס‟.

זייַענדיק מיט די ייִדישע שרייַבער אין ווארשעווער געטאָ, וואָלט איך נאָכאמאָל איבערגעלעבט די פארלוסטן פון דער ייִדישער ליטעראטור. עס וואָלט מיר וויי געטאָן דאָס, וואָס עס זייַנען צוזאמען מיט די געטאָ־קעמפער פארשניטן געוואָרן די געטאָ־לידער פון ייִסראָעל שטערן, די פּאָעמע „ייִזקאָר‟ פון ייִצכאָק

and I would reread again, for instance, his drama "The Jew's Covenant" and notice in it a portrayal of the Hitler epidemic by way of the Spanish Inquisition. From here I can already see the works of the creators of the sanctified ghetto literature.

I would have visited briefly during the years of occupation Ringelblum's[32] underground archive and, in defiance of the police and SS henchmen, exclaimed: "Yes, your writings made it to us! In Warsaw's Jewish Historical Institute,[33] with Ber Mark,[34] I saw how the weary and resurrected Poland protects every letter about the Jewish tragedy which you bequeathed to us for posterity."

Being with the Yiddish writers in the Warsaw Ghetto, I would have lived through the losses of Yiddish literature one more time. How painful to see that together with the ghetto fighters the ghetto poems by Yisroel Shtern,[35] the

32 Emanuel Ringelblum (1900–1944) was a Polish Jewish historian, left-wing Labor Zionist political activist, community organizer before and during the war and the founder and leading figure of the Oyneg Shabes underground archive of the Warsaw Ghetto, parts of which were unearthed in 1946 and 1950 respectively. Its remains are housed in ŻIH in Warsaw. Vergelis refers to Ringelblum 1961. Ringelblum was killed by the Gestapo in March 1944.

33 ŻIH was founded in 1947 to replace the Centralna Żydowska Komisja Historyczna w Polsce [Central Jewish Historical Commission in Poland], a *khurbn*-research center founded in 1944 in Lublin. ŻIH still operates as a cultural and research institute in Warsaw with a specific focus on Polish Jewish history. On ŻIH's institutional history, see also Agnieszka Żółkiewska's chapter in the present volume.

34 Ber Mark (1908–1966) was a Polish Jewish historian, literary critic, essayist, and communist political activist. In 1928, he joined the Komunistyczna Partia Polski [Communist Party of Poland, KPP] and was editor-in-chief of the Yiddish communist newspaper דער פֿרײַנד [*Der fraynd*, The Friend] in 1934/35. He survived the *khurbn* in the Soviet Union, where he was an active member of the JAFC and the Związek Patriotów Polskich [Society of Polish Patriots], created by Polish communists in the Soviet Union in 1943. After the war, he returned to Poland, directed the ŻIH from 1949, and edited both the periodicals ביולעטין [*Biuletyn*, Bulletin] and בלעטער פֿאַר געשיכטע [*Bleter far geshikhte*, Pages for History]. He is probably most known for his depiction of the Warsaw Ghetto Uprising, which was published in Yiddish, Polish, and German, see Mark 1947, Mark 1954, Mark 1957, Mark 1963. On the German publication, see Alexander Walther's chapter in the present volume.

35 Yisroel Shtern (1894–1942) was a Yiddish poet and journalist who mostly lived and worked in Warsaw. Religiously observant throughout his life, affiliated with the Musar movement, with Lithuanian talmudic scholars, and Bratslav Hasidism, he nonetheless published in modernist publications as well as in many newspapers and periodicals in the interwar period. In October 1939, Shtern failed to enter the Soviet Union and returned to Warsaw. His ghetto poems are deemed lost. He was killed in Treblinka in September 1942.

קאַצענעלסאָנען, יעהוישוע פּערלעס געטאָ־ראָמאַן. איך וואָלט צווישן אַנדערס געזאָגט די שרײַבער־קדושים, אַז ייִצחאָק קאַצענעלסאָנס וועג צוריק פֿון דער העברעיִשער ליטעראַטור צו דער ייִדיש־„זשאַרגאָנישער" איז פֿאַרשטענדלעך און קלאָר: אױפֿן מוראַנאָווער שלאַכטפֿעלד האָט דאָס פֿאָלק גערעדט אױף פּראָסט ייִדיש. איך וואָלט זײ אויך געזאָגט, אַז יעהוישוע פּערלע האָט מיט זײַן כראָניק „כורבן־וואַרשע" געבראַכט נאָך איין באַווײַז, אַז אַפֿילו אין דער צײַט, ווען דער כאַלעף ליגט אױפֿן האַלדז פֿונעם לעבן, איז די ליטעראַטור דאָך אַ שפּיגל פֿון דעם לעבן.

פֿון וואַרשע וואָלט איך אַוועק איבער די שטעט פֿון דעמלטיקן פּוילן. געווען אַ גאַליציאַנער גרופּע ייִדישע שרײַבער. יאַנקעוו שודריך און מוישע

epic poem "Yizker" by Yitsḥak Katzenelson,[36] Yoshue Perle's[37] ghetto-novel were destroyed. Among other things, I would have told the writer-martyrs that Yitskhok Katsenelson's way back from Hebrew literature to Yiddish "jargon" is understandable and clear: on the battlefield of Muranów, the people spoke simple Yiddish. I would have also told them that Yoshue Perle provided with his chronicle *The Destruction of Warsaw* another proof that even at the time when the butcher's knife lies on the neck of life, literature is a mirror of life.

From Warsaw I would have continued my journey to other cities in the Poland of yesteryear.

There was a Galician group of Yiddish writers. Yankev Shudrikh[38] and

36 Yitsḥak Katzenelson (1885–1944) was a Zionist Hebrew and Yiddish poet, writer of children's literature and plays, and translator into Hebrew. Born in Karelitz, near Minsk, but based in Łódź since 1896, he started publishing Hebrew poetry at the age of fourteen and quickly earned a reputation as one of the most promising talents of the generation of Hebrew poets inspired by Ḥayim Naḥman Bialik. In Łódź, Katzenelson established a network of private Hebrew schools – a kindergarten, elementary, secondary school – operating under his direction between 1906 and 1939. Active in Łódź Zionist החלוץ [*He-ḥālūẓ*, The Pioneer] movement, he considered immigrating to Palestine, visited twice (in 1924 and 1934), but did not follow through. Following the German attack of Poland in September 1939, he was living in hiding in Łódź for three months before escaping to Warsaw with his family where he got involved in *He-ḥālūẓ* covert educational projects. In the Warsaw Ghetto, Katzenelson devoted himself to teaching Hebrew literature and biblical studies in the underground secondary school, published in the underground press and directed a drama group. Imprisoned, he also composed more than forty works, switching to Yiddish in most of them in order to reach as wide an audience as possible. יזכור [*Yizker*, Remember], the poem Vergelis refers to, can be found in Katzenelson 1984, 131–134, 613–14. His family was killed in Treblinka in the first major liquidation of the ghetto by Nazi Germany. He participated in the Warsaw Ghetto Uprising and escaped to the so-called Aryan side of Warsaw, obtained Honduran identity documents but was caught and sent to a Nazi detention camp in Vittel, France, and was eventually killed in Auschwitz in May 1944. In Vittel, he wrote one of his most significant works called דאָס ליד פֿון אויסגעהרגעטן ייִדישן פֿאָלק [*Dos lid fun oysgehargetn yidishn folk*, The Poem of the Murdered Jewish People].

37 Yoshue Perle (1888–1943) was a Yiddish novelist born in Radom but based in Warsaw from the age of 17. He wrote several (highbrow and lowbrow) novels, short stories, literary reportages and was awarded two prestigious literary prizes: by the Warsaw Yiddish PEN club in 1937 and by the Bund in 1938. In the wake of the German attack on Poland in September 1939, he fled to Soviet-occupied Lviv but faced difficulties in publishing his literary works due to his political 'untrustworthiness.' After the German attack on the Soviet Union, he returned to Warsaw and participated in the Yiddish underground cultural organizing in the Warsaw Ghetto. He survived the first mass deportations to Treblinka in the summer of 1942 and captured ghetto life in his חורבן־וואַרשע [*Khurbn-Varshe*, Destruction of Warsaw; on the publication and reception history, see Rose 2011], that Vergelis refers to, spiked with condemnations of the Judenrat, the Jewish Police, alongside the Nazis. He escaped the ghetto to the 'Aryan' side of Warsaw in March 1943, a month before the uprising, but was caught and killed in Auschwitz.

38 Yankev Shudrikh (1906–1943) was a Yiddish poet, born in the Galician village Hivniv, near Lviv, joined the revolutionary movement in his youth and published on the theme of class struggle

שימל זייַנען אומגעקומען מיט א שוידער־טויט. ווען, לאָמיר זאָגן, איך טרעף נאָך שודריכן באם לעבן, וואָלט איך מיט אים איניינעם זיך דערמאָנט, וויִאזוי ער האָט אין לוואָוו נאָך דער באפרייַונג באגעגנט זייַן ערשטן סאָוועטישן פרילינג און, ווענ־דנדיק זיך צו אים, האָט ער געשריבן:

איך עפן די פענצטער, – קום, גאסט מייַנער ליבער,
און רו זיך א ביסעלע אָפּ פון די וועגן.
און שפּעטער וועסט גיין אין די שכיינישע שטיבער,
אף אלטע באקאנטע און נאָענטע זיך פרעגן.

מיר האָבן דיר אלע אזויפיל צו זאָגן!
דו קאָנסט דאָך אונדז, ברודער, מיסטאם, ניט פארגעסן.
אוי, שווער איז די בענקשאפט געווען אונדז צו טראָגן,
און ס'איז שוין דער ווינטער געווען אונדז דערעסן.[11]

שודריך, שימל און אנדערע זייַנען גלייַך פונעם קורצן, ביז גאָר קורצן סאָוועטישן פרילינג ארייַנגעפאלן אין סאמע שרעקלעכסטן – אין פאשיסטישן – ווינטער. און דאָרט זייַנען זיי אומגעקומען אין דער ברוינער וויוגע...

איך וואָלט אויך געקומען צו א גרופּע ייִדישע שרייַבער, וואָס זייַנען פארבליבן אין זיכּאָרן פון דער ליטעראטור ווי „יונג־ווילנע". ס'וואָלט עפשער ניט געשאט, אז דעמלט זאָל איינער פון זיי, אווראָם סוצקעווער, אפריִער הערן זייַנע אייגענע ווער־טער, אין וועלכע עס האָט אין יאָרן ארום דערמאָנט בייס א „שמועס ארום רונדן

11 AVC: זשורנאל „פאָרפּאָסט" נומ. 4–5, ביראָבידזשאן, 1940.

Moyshe Shimel[39] died a horrible death. If, let's say, I would have met Shudrikh still alive, we would have remembered together how he encountered his first Soviet spring after the liberation of Lvov [Lviv] and, addressing this spring, he wrote:

> I am opening the windows, – come, my dear guest,
> And take a rest from your journey.
> And later you'll go into the neighboring houses,
> asking for old acquaintances and loved-ones.
>
> We all have so much to tell you!
> You cannot probably forget us, brother.
> Oy, heavy has been the longing to carry us,
> And we were already sick of the winter.[40]

Shudrikh, Shimel and others fell from a short, all too short Soviet spring into the most terrible – into the fascist – winter, and there they died in the brown blizzard…

I would have also come to a group of Yiddish writers who are remembered as *Yung-Vilne*.[41] Perhaps, it would not hurt for one of them, Avrom Sutzkever,[42] to remind him of his very own words which were recently brought up

in leftist journals in Poland and the Soviet Union. In 1932, he was the co-founder of the communist אַלגעמיינע יידישע אַרבעטער־פּאַרטיי [*Algemeyne yidishe arbeter-partey*, General Jewish Labor Party] and was arrested several times for 'communist activities.' His poems were sung at demonstrations and recited at illegal literary evenings. Under Soviet occupation between 1939 and 1941, Shudrikh's poems were published in Lviv, Kiev, and Minsk before his incarceration in the Lviv Ghetto under Nazi occupation. Before being killed, he organized resistance groups in the ghetto and connected with partisans. Further, see Mark 1954.

39 Lviv-born Moyshe Shimel (Maurycy Szymel) (1903–1942) was a poet writing first mostly in Polish, then also in Yiddish. In the 1930s, he was active in Warsaw's Jewish literary life and wrote for the Jewish press in Yiddish and Polish. In 1939, he returned to Lviv and published Yiddish works in סאָוועטיש ליטעראַטור [*Sovetish literatur*, Soviet Literature]. During the Nazi occupation, Shimel worked as a clerk for the Lviv Judenrat and died in the Janów labor camp. Further, see Mark 1954.

40 AVC: Shudrikh in פּאַרפּאָסט, no. 4–5. Birobidzhan, 1940.

41 יונג־ווילנע [*Yung-Vilne*, Young Vilna] was an important Yiddish literary group of a young generation of writers, poets, visual artists formally founded in 1929 and active throughout the 1930s in Vilna. Its principal members included poets Chaim Grade, Avrom Sutzkever, Elkhonen Vogler, and Leyzer Volf; prose writers Shmerke Kaczerginski and Moyshe Levin; artists Bentsye Mikhtom and Rokhl Sutzkever. In 1939, *Yung-Vilne* mentored an even younger generation of writers under the banner *Yungvald*, including Hirsh Glik, whom Vergelis mentions in a few sentences who composed the partisan hymn זאָג ניט קיין מאָל [*Zog nit keyn mol*, Never say] during the Nazi occupation. On "*Zog nisht keyn mol*", see the interview with Jalda Rebling in the present volume.

42 Avrom Sutzkever (1913–2010) is one of the most well-known Yiddish poets of the 20th cen-

טיש" אין רעדאקציע „סאָוועטיש היימלאנד" מייער פּאָדאָלני, דער קאָמאנדיר פונעם סאָוועטישן פּארטיזאנישן אָטריאד, וואָס האָט גראטעוועט סוצקעווערן. דער פּארטיזאנער, איצט אן אָנפירער פון א בוי־טרעסט, האָט דערציילט: „ווען מיר האָבן סוצקעווערן אריַינגעזעצט אין אן אעראָפּלאן אף אָפּפירן אים פון דער אָקופּירטער טעריטאָריע קיין מאָסקווע, האָט ער אונדז פארזיכערט: קיינמאָל, ביז מיַין לעצטן אָטעם, וועל איך ניט טאָן קיין שלעכטס דעם לאנד, וואָס האָט מיך גראטעוועט".

אומגעפער דאָס זעלבע וואָלט איך געקאָנט זאָגן א צווייטן באדיַיטנדיקן „יונג־ווילנער" – כאִים גראדען...

דער יונגער ווילנער דיכטער הירש גליק האָט געשאפן דאָס אומשטערבלעכע „זאָג ניט קיינמאָל". ווען הירש גליק וואָלט לעבן געבליבן און אפילו ווען ער וואָלט היַינט געלעבט אין די אויסלאנדס, אלציינס איז אומעגלעך זיך פאָרצושטעלן, אז זיַין פען זאָל שריַיבן אנטיסאָוועטישע לידער. איך ווייס ניט, צי עס איז טאקע געווען פארטראכט ווי א סימבאָל, נאָר פאר מיר איז עס טיף סימבאָליש און פון גרויסן באדיַיט – דאָס, וואָס „זאָג ניט קיינמאָל" איז אָנגעשריבן אפן מאָטיוו פון א סאָוועטישן ליד.

נאָך וועגן איין ווילנער פּאָעט – וועגן לייזער וואָלפן – טראכט איך. מיר זאָגן לייזער וואָלף, און עס קומען אוף אין זיקאָרן: „די בלויע שוואלב", „איַיזיק־מייער דיק און די אלמאָנע ראָם", „עס זיצט דער יעצערהאָרע מיט א ייִנגל אונטער א

at the "Round-Table Conversation" in the editorial offices of "*Sovetish heymland*" by Meyer Podolny, the commander of the Soviet partisan unit that rescued Sutzkever. The partisan who is now a leader of a construction business recalled: "When we put Sutzkever on a plane in order to bring him from the occupied territory to Moscow, he promised: 'Never, until my last breath, will I harm the country that rescued me.'"

Approximately the same I could say to a second important member of "Yung-Vilne" – Chaim Grade…[43]

The young Vilna poet Hirsh Glik [1922–1944] wrote the immortal song "*Zog nit keyn mol*" [Never say]. If Hirsh Glik would have stayed alive and even if he today lived abroad, it is unimaginable that his pen could write anti-Soviet poems. I do not know whether it was thought of as a symbol but for me it is deeply symbolic and highly important that "*Zog nit keynmol*" was written to the theme of a Soviet song.

I am thinking about one last poet from Vilna – about Leyzer Volf.[44] We say *Leyzer Volf*, and we immediately remember "The Blue Swallow," "Ayzik-Meyer Dik and the widow Romm," "The Evil Inclination sits with a boy under

tury starting out as a member of *Yung-Vilne*. During the Second World War, he was part of many resistance groups, starting in Soviet-occupied Vilna in 1940/41 as part of the קאָמיטעט צו זאַמלען מאַטעריאַלן וועגן ייִדישן חורבן אין פּוילן [*Komitet tsu zamlen materyaln vegn yidishn khurbn in Poyln*, Committee to Collect Material on the Destruction of Polish Jewry, on this committee, see [Chorley-]Schulz 2016], then as part of the פּאַפּיר־בריגאַדע [*Papir-brigade*, Paper Brigade, see Fishman 2017] rescuing rare books and manuscripts from Nazi extraction and smuggling weapons into the Vilna Ghetto until he joined a Jewish partisan group under Soviet command in the Naroch forest. His ghetto poems were smuggled to the JAFC in Moscow that organized airlifting Sutzkever out of Naroch to Moscow, where he became an active member of the JAFC and a witness-survivor to the destruction of Vilna and Polish Jewry with a host of publications. Sutzkever testified on behalf of Russian Jewry at the Nuremberg Trials. He returned to Poland in 1946, then moved to Paris and finally to Palestine in 1947. In Tel Aviv, he founded the literary quarterly די גאָלדענע קייט [*Di goldene keyt*, The Golden Chain] and remained its editor until its closing in 1995. On Sutzkever's role in creating an anti-communist Cold War memory culture after the Stalinist purges of Soviet Yiddish intellectuals to the chagrin of Vergelis, see [Chorley-]Schulz 2021.

43 Chaim Grade (1910–1982) is considered one of the most important Yiddish poet and novelist of the post-*khurbn* era. Growing up very religiously, he abandoned his studies at the age of twenty-two and embarked on a career as a secular poet, first in the ranks of *Yung-Vilne*. Grade survived the *khurbn* in Soviet Central Asia losing family who stayed in Vilna. He became active in the JAFC and published a couple of poetry collections in the Soviet Union before immigrating to the United States in 1948 where he reoriented himself politically. See further, Klingenstein and Zirkind 2021, [Chorley-]Schulz 2021.

44 Leyzer Volf (1910–1943) was a founding member of *Yung-Vilne*, experimental poet, and activist in the Jewish territorialist movement. Volf retreated across the Soviet border in October 1939 and published a volume soon after (see Volf 1940). In 1943, he died of starvation and illness in a small town in the vicinity of Samarkand. A posthumous volume of antifascist poems appeared in Moscow later that year, see Volf 1943 and fn 46.

בוים"... אין 1943 איז אין אוזבעקיסטאַן געשטאָרבן דער האָפענונגסלאָז־קראַנקער לייזער וואָלף, זיך ניט דערוואַרט ביזן זיג, אין וועלכן ער האָט אַזוי געגלייבט.

ניט לאַנג פאַרן טויט האָט דער דיכטער געשריבן:

א לויב, א לויב די רויטע רעפובליק
פון פרייַ און פריידיק מעכטיקן פאַרבאַנד!

מע קאָן זאָגן, אַז די ייִדישע ליטעראַטור אין פוילן האָט א סאָוועטישן פּעריאָד – זייער א פרוכטבאַרן. פאַר איר איז דאָס א צייַט פון שאַרפע ווענדפּונקטן; זי איז ווי מיטאַמאָל אַרויס (קאָן זייַן, ניט אינגאַנצן צוגעגרייט צו דעם) אויף א בלענדיק־שנייִיקן ראַכוועס, איבער וועלכן עס האָט אינגיכן זיך אופגעהויבן דער שטאַרקער מילכאָמע־ווייכער. אַרויס איז זי פון איר שטוב, א פאַרפּאָלגטע פון גאָרגלשנייַדער. און דאָ, אויפן שנייִיקן ראַכוועס, האָט זי סייַ זיך פאַרהאַרטעוועט, סייַ אַרייַנגעטעמט פרישע לופט אין די לונגען; זי האָט סייַ, נאַטירלעך, זיך אָפּגעהיט פון די גאָרגלשנייַדער און סייַ, זעט איר דאָך, איבערגעלאָזט א קייוור אין ווייַטן אוזבעקיסטאַן... [...]

ווען לייב דאָמב, דער פאָרזיצער פון דער פאַרוואַלטונג פונעם קולטור־געזעלשאַפטלעכן פאַרבאַנד פון די ייִדן אין פוילן, האָט מיר באַוויזן די אויסשטעלונג פון ביכער, וועלכע ס'האָט אַרויסגעגעבן דער וואַרשעווער פאַרלאַג „ייִדיש־בוך", האָב איך אויסגעשריִען א פאַרכידעשטער:

– אַזויפיל ביכער!

ניט לייב דאָמב, ניט דאָוויד ספאַרד, וואָס איז געווען דערבייַ, און אויך ניט די

a tree"…[45] In 1943, the terminally ill Leyzer Volf died in Uzbekistan[46] – not living to see the victory he so believed in.

Not long before his death the poet wrote:[47]

> A praise, a praise to the Red Republic
> Of the free and joyful powerful Union![48]

You can say that Yiddish literature in Poland has a Soviet period – a very fruitful one. It was a watershed moment for this literature; it suddenly erupted (perhaps not entirely prepared for it) into a blinding, snow-white horizon, over which soon enough the strong whirlwind of the war blew. This literature ran away from home, chased by the hangmen. And there, in this snow-covered space, it both became stronger and breathed new air into its lungs; it both hid, of course, from the hangmen and, as you can see, left a tomb in the vastness of Uzbekistan… […]

When Leyb Domb,[49] the chairman of the administration of the YKGF, showed me the exhibition of books published by the Warsaw publishing house ייִדיש־בוך [*Yidish-bukh,* Yiddish Book] I exclaimed in amazement:

– So many books!

Not Leyb Domb, nor Dovid Sfard,[50] who was present, nor any of the

45 AVC: Leyzer Volf's poems.

46 This is a lie. It is well-established that Leyzer Volf died of starvation and illness in a small town near Samarkand in 1943.

47 Again, Vergelis is 'massaging' the truth. Volf must have written the poem before its publication in 1940.

48 AVC: Leyzer Volf לייזער וואָלף, **לידער און סאטירע**. מעלוכע־פארלאג „דער עמעס", מאָסקווע, 1940.

49 Polish-born Leyb Domb, also known as Leopold Trepper, (1904–1982) was a Soviet intelligence agent and the head of the anti-German spy network known as "The Red Orchestra" which contributed decisively to Soviet strategy and tactics. In 1941, Trepper warned Moscow of Germany's imminent attack on the Soviet Union, predicting even its exact date, but was sadly ignored by Stalin. He was captured by German counter-intelligence and the Gestapo in 1942 but escaped eventually. After returning in 1945 to Moscow, he was imprisoned for ten years. In 1955, released and 'rehabilitated,' he returned to Poland and devoted himself exclusively to Jewish culture: he headed YKGF (see fn. 57) and its publishing house *Yidish-bukh*. In the wake of the antisemitic upheavals in Poland in 1968, Domb/Trepper wanted to move to the state of Israel to reunite with his family but he was denied an exit visa in 1974.

50 Dovid Sfard (1908–1981) was a Yiddish poet and cultural activist. He had a long Yiddish literary career and joined the KPP in 1933. A member of the Party's Jewish Bureau, he was a representative of its daily newspaper פֿרייַנד (*Fraynd*, Friend) in 1934/35. During the Second World War, Sfard lived in the Soviet Union, served as deputy chair of the Białystok branch of the Soviet Writers Union (1939–1941) and later settled in Central Asia and Moscow where he contributed to

איבעריקע כאַווײרים האָבן גאָרנישט ניט געזאָגט וועגן מײַנע היספּיילעס, נאָר אַפן צווייטן טאָג, ווען איך בין שפּעט אין דער נאַכט געזעסן מיט ספּארדן בא אים אין שטוב, האָט ער מיטאַמאָל א זאָג געטאָן:

– נו יאָ, ס׳איז מאַמעש צו כידעשן זיך: אין פּוילן לאָזן מיר איצט אַרויס מער ייִדישע ביכער, איידער אין דער מערהייַט טומלדיקע ייִדישע ייִשוווים אַף מײַרעוו... אָבער מע דאַרף ניט פאַרגעסן, אַז מיט גאַנצע פיר הונדערט פינף און דרײַסיק יאָר צוריק האָט שוין אין קראָקע געאַרבעט א ייִדישע דרוקערײַ, די האַליטשער דרוקאַרניע...

דאָס געפיל פונעם דורכגעגאַנגענעם היסטאָרישן וועג, וועמעס בוילעטסטער אויסדרוק עס איז דער פּערעץ־קולט אין הײַנטיקן פּוילן, ווערט בא די ייִדישע קולטור־טוער פון אַט דעם לאַנד טראַנספאָרמירט אין אַן אַכרײַעס־געפיל, און ניט נאָר די דאָרטיקע שרײַבער און זשורנאַליסטן – ניט נאָר ספּארד און סמאָליאַר, מירסקי, קאָרמאַן, שטראַוס־מאַרקאָ און אַנדערע – האָבן בעשאַס מײַן זײַן אין פּוילן אָן אויפהער אונטערגעשטראָכן די באַשטענדיקײַט פון אַט דעם געפיל. שמועסנדיק מיט רעפאָעל כוואַלעסן – א מאָלער, וועמעס פאַרוואָרצלטקײַט גיט צו גרויס אויסדרויער זײַן קונסט, – זיצנדיק אין צושויער־זאַל פון אידאַ קאַמינסקאַס טעאַטער און אין דער היים (אין וואָראָצלאַוו) בא דער טעאַטראַלער דינאַסטיע פון די ראָטבוימס (סאָרע ראָטבוים האָט איר רום פון א „פאַרדינסטפולער אַרטיסטן פון דער רוסלענדישער סאָוועטישער סאָציאַליסטישער רעפּובליק“ דערוואָרבן אין מאָסקווער גאָסעט, איצט וווינט זי און איז טעטיק אין פּוילן; יאַנקעוו ראָטבוים

other comrades said anything about my enthusiasm. Only on the second day, when I sat very late together with Sfard in his home, he suddenly said:

– Well, yes, it is really astonishing: in Poland, we are publishing more Yiddish books now than the majority of those boisterous Jewish centers in the West… but we shouldn't forget that 435 years ago there was already a Yiddish printer working in Kraków – the Helicz print-shop.[51]

The feeling of going through this historical journey, whose most striking expression is the Peretz cult in nowadays Poland, transforms itself into a feeling of responsibility among Yiddish cultural activists in this country, and, during my stay in Poland, not only the local writers and journalists – not only Sfard and Smolyar, Mirsky,[52] Korman, Shtraus-Marko[53] and others – continuously underlined the persistence of this feeling. Talking with Refoel Khvales – a painter, whose rootedness adds great perseverance to his art – sitting in the hall of Ida Kamińska's[54] theater and at home (in Wrocław) with the Rotbaum theater dynasty (Sara Rotbaum[55] earned her reputation as a "commendable artist of the Russian Soviet Federative Socialist Republic" in Moscow's GOSET, now she is living and working in Poland; Jakub Rotbaum[56]

the work of the JAFC. He returned to Poland in 1946 and became a central figure in the Polish Jewish community, particularly in its cultural institutions such as the publishing house *Yidish-bukh* and the journal יידישע שריפֿטן [*Yidishe shriftn*, Yiddish Writings]. In the wake of the anti-Jewish campaign in Poland in 1968, he moved to Israel and became active in the local Yiddish scene. See further, Nalewajko-Kulikov 2020.

51 Shemu'el, Asher, and Elyakim Helicz were the first printers with limited success of Hebrew and Yiddish books in Kraków, Kingdom of Poland (approx. 1530s–1550s).

52 Mikhl Mirsky (1902–1994), pen name of M. Tabatshnik, Yiddish writer and activist in the Jewish labor movement. He fled the Nazis to the Soviet Union and joined the Polish People's Army on the front against Nazi Germany. He returned to Poland and was involved in Jewish cultural institutions.

53 Shloyme Shtraus-Marko (Salomon Strauss-Marko) (1912–1992) wrote in Polish and Yiddish and published specifically on his wartime experiences.

54 Odessa-born Ida Kamińska (1899–1980) was a grand dame of Yiddish theater, particularly in interwar and postwar Poland. She survived the *khurbn* in different parts of the Soviet Union, where she played parts in Yiddish productions. After the war, she returned to Warsaw and reopened a Yiddish theater in 1946, which was state-financed from 1949 with Kamińska serving as the artistic director. Escaping the 1968 antisemitic campaign in Poland, she first moved to Israel / Palestine and then settled in New York.

55 Sara Rotbaum (1899–1970) is considered one of the most talented actresses of the ווילנער טרופּע [*Vilner trupe*, Vilna Troupe] and later joined the Moscow-based GOSET. She was the older sister of the actor, director and artist Jacub Rotbaum and of choreographer and opera director Lia Rotbaum.

56 Jakub Rotbaum [Yankev Rotboym] (1901–1994) was a theater director, actor, and painter. Born in Żelechów, he received a *kheder* education, attended high school, then studied at the School of Decorative Arts, the School of Fine Arts, and the School of Film in Warsaw and with Konstantin

איז איינער פון די בעסטע ייִדישע רעזשיסערן; ליִע ראָטבוים איז אלס רעזשיסער ארויס פון מאָסקווער טעאַטער־אינסטיטוט „גיטיס“), באקענענדיק זיך מיט די גרויסע פונעם ווארשעווער ייִדישן היסטאָרישן אינסטיטוט, – אומעטום האָב איך געזען, אז די טוער פון דער ייִדישער קולטור אין פאָלקס־פּוילן האָבן א ציל און האָבן א וועג, און אומאָפּהענגיק פון דעם, וואָס פאר א מעהאלעך און וואָסערע געשעענישן און ענדערונגען עס ליגן צווישן טלאָמאצקע 13 און נאָוואָגראָדזקע 5, איז קיין סאָפעק ניט, אז די הייַנטצייַטיקע נאָוואָגראָדזקע שטייט אף א באָדן, אין וועלכן דאָס ייִדישע פאָלק פון פּוילן האָט אלטע און נייַע וואָרצלען.

is one of the best Yiddish directors; Lia Rotbaum[57] graduated as a director from Moscow's theater institute GITIS[58]), getting to know the great scholars of Warsaw's Jewish Historical Institute, – I saw all around me that the activists of Yiddish culture in Peoples' Poland have a goal and a way to achieve it, and independent of the great distance and of all events and changes that lie between 13 Tłomackie and 5 Nowogrodzka, there is no doubt that today's Nowogrodzka is standing on a soil in which the Jewish people of Poland have old and new roots.

Bibliography

[Chorley-]Schulz, Miriam, 2016: *Der Beginn des Untergangs. Die Zerstörung der jüdischen Gemeinden in Polen und das Vermächtnis des Wilnaer Komitees.* Berlin: Metropol.

[Chorley-]Schulz, Miriam, 2021: 'The Deepest Self Denies the Self': Polish Jewish Intellectuals and the Birth of 'Soviet Marranos.' In: Markus Nesselrodt and Katharina Friedla, eds., *Polish Jews in the Soviet Union (1939 – 1959): History and Memory of Deportation, Exile, and Survival.* Boston, Mass.: Academic Studies Press, 143 – 174.

Fishman, David, 2017: *The Book Smugglers: Partisans, Poets, and the Race to Save Jewish Treasures from the Nazis.* Lebanon, NH: ForeEdge.

Katzenelson, Yitsḥak, 1984 קאַצענעלסאָן, יצחק: **ייִדישע געטאָ־כּתבֿים. וואַרשע 1940–1943.** אַרויסגעגעבן לויט אָפּגעראַטעוועטע כּתבֿ־ידן מיט אַרייַנפֿירן און דערקלערונגען פֿון יחיאל שיינטוך. תּל־אָבֿיבֿ: בית לוחמי הגיטאות און הוצאת הקיבוץ המאוחד.

Klingenstein, Susanne, and Yehudah Dov Ber Zirkind 2021: Chaim Grade: Facts of a Life. In: *In geveb*, <https://ingeveb.org/pedagogy/chaim-grade-facts-of-a-life>, September 4, 2023.

Stanislavsky, Vsevolod Meyerhold, and Shloyme Mikhoels in Moscow. Fascinated with Russian theater, he toured Poland upon his return with the lecture series "Theatrical Culture in the Soviet Union" in the hope to change Polish Yiddish theater from folklore to social and political issues. In 1929, Rotbaum was invited to work with the *Vilner trupe*, eventually becoming its artistic director and principal stage director. In 1940, he was invited to work at the Yiddish Art Theater in New York. Rotbaum returned to Poland in 1949 and served first as director of the Lower Silesian Yiddish Theater and after 1968 the only Yiddish theater in Poland.

57 Lia Rotbaum (1907 – 1994) was a choreographer and director of opera. Before the Second World War, she studied and danced under the direction of Tacjanna Wysocka and taught at the Weichert Acting Studio. Rotbaum worked with the *Vilner trupe*, יונג־טעאַטער [*Yung-teater*, Young Theater], and וואַרשעווער נײַער ייִדישער טעאַטער [*Varshever nayer yidisher teater*, Warsaw New Yiddish Theater]. From 1956 onwards, she lived in Wrocław where she taught at the School of Music and directed the Wroclaw Opera.

58 Российский институт театрального искусства, Russian Institute of Theater Arts.

MARK, Ber[nard], 1947 מארק, בער: **דער אופשטאנד פון ווארשעווער געטאָ**. מאָסקווע: דער עמעס.

MARK, Ber[nard], 1954: *Powstanie w getcie warszawskim – Na tle ruchu oporu w polsce Geneza i Przebieg*. Warsaw: Żydowski Instytut Historyczny.

MARK, Ber[nard], 1954 מארק, בער: **די אומגעקומענע שרײַבער אין געטאָס און לאַגערן און זייערע ווערק**. ווארשע: ייִדיש־בוך.

MARK, Ber[nard], 1957: *Der Aufstand im Warschauer Ghetto : Entstehung und Verlauf*. Berlin: Dietz.

MARK, Ber[nard], 1963 מארק, בער: **דער אויפשטאנד אין ווארשעווער געטאָ**. ווארשע: ייִדיש־בוך.

MARK, Ber[nard], 1977 מאַרק, בער: **מגילת אוישוויץ**. תל־אביב: ישׂראל־בוך.

NALEWAJKO-KULIKOV, Joanna, 2020: *A Citizen of Yiddishland: Dovid Sfard and the Jewish Communist Milieu in Poland*. Berlin: Peter Lang.

NYISZLI, Miklós, 1973: *Auschwitz: A Doctor's Eye-witness Account*. Translated by Tibere Kremer and Richard Seaver with a foreword by Bruno Bettelheim. London: Granada.

RINGELBLUM, Emanuel, 1961 רינגעלבלום, עמנואל: **כתבים פון געטאָ. טאָגבוך פון ווארשעווער געטאָ (1939 – 1942)**. ווארשע: ייִדיש־בוך.

ROSE, Sven-Erik, 2011: The Oyneg Shabes Archive and the Cold War: The Case of Yehoshue Perle's Khurbn Varshe. In: *New German Critique* 38 (1): 181–215.

SEGALOVITSH, Zusman, 1946 סעגאַלאָוויטש, זוסמאן: **טלאָמאַצקע 13: פון פארברענטן נעכטן**. בוענאָס־אײַרעס: צענטראַל־פאַרבאַנד פון פוילישע ייִדן אין אַרגענטינע.

STONE, Dan, 2014: *Goodbye to All That? The Story of Europe since 1945*. Oxford: Oxford University Press.

VOLF, Leyzer, 1940 וואָלפ, לייזער: **לידער און סאטירע**. מאָסקווע: דער עמעס.

VOLF, Leyzer, 1943 וואָלפ, לייזער: **די ברוינע בעסטיע**. מאָסקווע: דער עמעס.

WAWRZYNIAK, Joanna, 2015: *Veterans, Victims, and Memory: The Politics of the Second World War in Communist Poland*. Frankfurt / Main: Peter Lang.

Alexander Walther

Yiddish and the German Democratic Republic

Translating Culture, Experience, and Loss to a German Audience

In December 1970, the *New York Times* ran a review of a collection of poems about the חורבן [*khurbn,* destruction, Holocaust]. Under review was an "unusual publishing venture" from Germany – the German Democratic Republic [GDR], i.e. East Germany, to be precise. A year prior, East German publishing company Reclam[1] had published a limited art edition of 1,000 hand signed copies of an anthology of poems entitled *Meine jüdischen Augen* [My Jewish Eyes]. Named after the poem of the same name by Rajzel Żychlińsky (1910–2001), the edition was based on a 1966 poetry collection entitled *Der Fiedler vom Getto. Jiddische Dichtung aus Polen* [Fiddler of the Ghetto. Yiddish Poetry from Poland] and contained a selection of texts by authors such as Mordkhe Gebirtig (1877–1942), Dovid Sfard (1905–1981), Moyshe Shulstein (1911–1981), Avrom Sutzkever (1913–2010), Itzik Manger (1901–1969), Yitskhok Leybush Peretz (1852–1915), and the first partial German translation of Yitskhok Katzenelson's (1885–1944) דאָס ליד פֿונעם אויסגעהרגעטן ייִדישן פֿאָלק [*Dos lid funem oysgehargetn yidishn folk,* Song of the Murdered Jewish People].[2] While Żychlińsky, when approached by the *New York Times* journalist, expressed her gratitude towards the East German translator and editor of the book, Hubert Witt (1935–2016), for his 'remarkable' interpretations of the texts, Chaim Grade (1910–1982), another Yiddish author included in the selection, remarked that such a translation represented only a fraction "of what East Germans could have done to make amends."[3] Both reactions indicate the wide range of responses towards German translations of Yiddish texts after the *khurbn* ranging from enthusiastic support to organized boycott. While

1 Founded in Leipzig in 1928, Reclam is one of the oldest still running publishing houses in Germany. In 1950, the owner, Ernst Reclam, moved to Stuttgart and established the company's new headquarters. The Leipzig based part of Reclam continued publishing books until the end of the GDR. After 1990, the Leipzig branch was privatized and absorbed into the Reclam company based in Stuttgart. In 2006, the Leipzig branch was finally closed down. Today, the company solely resides in Ditzingen near Stuttgart.

2 Witt 1969, Witt 1966.

3 Shabad 1970.

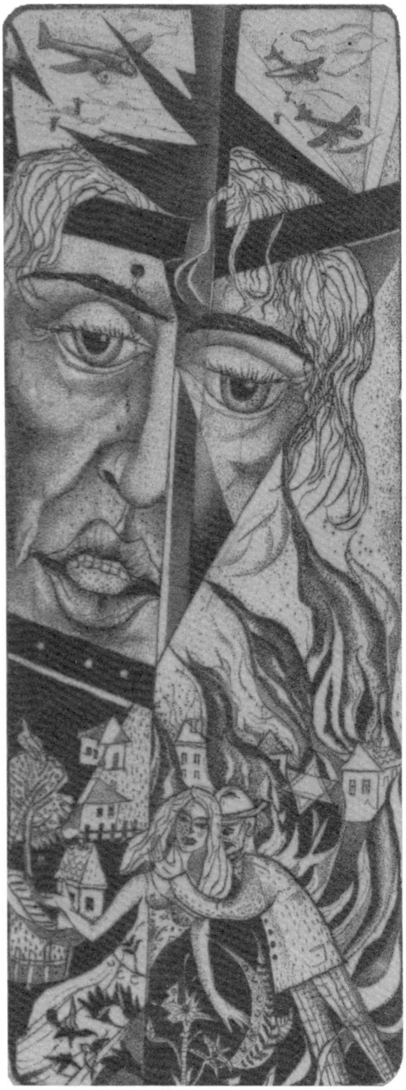

Cover Page of *Meine jüdischen Augen* (1969), illustration by Hermann Naumann, with the kind permission of Reclam Verlag.

some authors welcomed the initiative, especially by non-Jewish Germans, to translate their works for a broader public, others, like famous Yiddish writer Itzik Manger (1901–1969), explicitly refused to have their work translated into German at all.[4] His texts were only included in the anthology because Manger had been informed too late about the endeavor.

Apprehension towards German translations of Yiddish literature may also apply to West Germany, but the GDR was a special case. A socialist country, it was a part of the pledged brotherhood of other socialist states in Central Eastern and Eastern Europe and beyond. However, as it was one of three successor states of the German 'Reich,' it was also the land of the perpetrators. This inherent tension shaped how GDR politics and society coped with its National Socialist past and commemorating its victims. German-Jewish writer Jurek Becker (1937–1997), who left the GDR in 1977 for West Germany, summarized this in a speech in the early 1990s:

> Die DDR hat von ihrer ersten Stunde an mit einer Lüge gelebt. Sie erfand sich eine Geschichte, die nie stattgefunden hatte – ihre Ahnherren seien die deutschen Antifaschisten. […] Natürlich wurde über die Verbrechen der Nazis geredet, außerordentlich viel sogar, aber das waren die Verbrechen der anderen. Faschismus hatte nichts mit uns, den DDR-Menschen, zu tun. […] [D]er Schulunterricht über die Nazizeit war kein Unterricht über unsere

4 Gal-Ed 2016, 673f, 696.

jüngste Geschichte, er handelte stets von den Untaten dieser schrecklichen Aliens, die wir, die Antifaschisten, mit etwas Unterstützung durch die Rote Armee, besiegt hatten. Von den zehntausend Antifaschisten, die es in Nazi-deutschland gegeben haben mag, lebten allein acht Millionen in der DDR.[5]

[F]rom its first hour, the GDR lived with a lie. It invented a fiction that had never happened – that its ancestors were German antifascists […] The crimes of the Nazis were addressed, of course, extraordinarily much so in fact, but these were the crimes of the others. Fascism did not have anything to do with us, GDR people. […] School lessons about the Nazi past were no education about our recent history. They dealt with the atrocities of these horrible aliens, who we, the antifascists, had defeated with some help of the Red Army. Of the ten thousand antifascists who might have existed in Nazi Germany up to eight million lived in the GDR.

Most historians agreed with Becker at the time who in turn criticized, sometimes with fierce polemic, the East German state's approach to handling its Nazi past, and the history of the *khurbn* especially, claiming that the genocide was entirely ignored, concealed, or told in a distorted fashion.[6] However, in recent years, historians have shifted towards a more nuanced view, focusing more extensively on cultural and individual forms of memory practices. As British historian Bill Niven put it, "the GDR may not have been a pluralist state, but it was not without plurality."[7] The persecution of European Jewry was not denied in the GDR, and given that, at least for the first half of the state's existence, the vast majority of its population had experienced National Socialism themselves, the public certainly remembered having witnessed – or indulged in – the persecution. Yet, East German antifascist memory culture favored communist resistance fighters over other victims, and Jews usually ranged among this group of others. This was the case for state-sponsored commemorative events and the design of the major memorial sites at former concentration camps, such as Buchenwald, Sachsenhausen, and Ravensbrück. However, other aspects of public memory, from writers, editors, artists, filmmakers, journalists or members of the church engaged with the history of the *khurbn*, challenge the dominant reading of GDR memory culture that draws its evidence from state commemorative

5 Becker 2007, 266f.

6 For an overview, see: Peitsch 2015, 117–118; Herf 1997, 382.

7 Niven 2009, 207.

projects. GDR literature is an especially rich reservoir in this respect. Jurek Becker's novel *Jakob der Lügner* [Jacob the Liar] of 1969 and the eponymous movie adaption (1974) – the only GDR-produced movie ever nominated for an Oscar – are among the more known examples.[8]

So far, GDR Yiddish culture has hardly been studied, however. David Shneer's pioneering studies on Dutch-Jewish singer Lin Jaldati (1912–1988) are rare, insightful exceptions.[9] Yet, there are several traces of Yiddish cultures in the GDR, including Yiddish songs, literature, and *khurbn* testimony. In this chapter, I will discuss how Yiddish texts were translated, published, and promoted in the GDR, and analyze how translators and editors navigated a culture still shaped by the Nazi past, but structured by socialism in the present.

Yiddish as a Post-Vernacular Language and *khurbn*-Reference Trigger

After the war, Yiddish was almost absent in Germany, and the non-Jewish public showed little to no interest in Yiddish texts or Jewish culture. While the Yiddish language and culture thrived in many of the displaced persons [DP] camps, most notably in the American occupation zone, as Tamar Lewinsky has shown, it was hardly to be found in the Eastern part of Germany.[10] Soviet authorities soon closed the few DP camps that had been set-up in the immediate postwar period and thrust the vast majority of Yiddish-speaking Jews from Eastern Europe to the American occupation zone, or to other countries. The number of Yiddish speakers who remained in the Soviet zone, and later the GDR, can only be estimated, but was most likely under a hundred. At the end of the 1940s, in other words, there were hardly any native speakers of Yiddish left in East Germany, and virtually no Yiddish instruction available for non-native speakers.

This reflected the drastic changes that had occurred within Jewish communities. At a quick glance, the same diversity that had defined Jews in Germany before the *khurbn* could be found in the newly established communities after the war. Yet, since only few Jews had survived or returned – at least to the Soviet occupation zone – the population was now a collection

8 See for instance Walther 2019.

9 Shneer 2015. On the subject of Lin Jaldati, see the interview with Jalda Rebling in this volume.

10 Lewinsky 2008.

of people from vastly different and disconnected groups: liberal bourgeois, mostly secular Jews who had lived in East German cities before the war now encountered orthodox Jews from Eastern Europe who had either been liberated from the camps or had migrated from Poland in the wake of the postwar period's antisemitic pogroms. Before 1933, these two groups had mostly refrained from interacting with each other. Liberal German Jews had projected their fears onto the 'Ostjuden' [Eastern European Jews] who served "as a convenient foil for modernizing German Jews to displace characteristics labelled both negative and 'Jewish'," as Steven E. Aschheim has framed it.[11] The 'Ostjude' or 'ghetto Jew' was used by German Jewry as an opportunity to project ambitions of reframing one's own identity as well as the identity of the Other, the "same despised ghetto neighbor."[12] This also encompassed language, as Yiddish was commonly associated with and spoken by East European Jews and rejected or openly despised by bourgeois German Jewry. A minority in the communities, East European orthodox Jews did influence community life to an extent, but the communities' leadership mostly remained in the hands of the returned liberal German Jews.[13]

The few instances of Yiddish culture being performed were, therefore, meant for a broader (Jewish and non-Jewish) audience. In the late 1940s, Lin Jaldati and her husband, Eberhard Rebling (1911–2008), toured through several European countries which brought them to still united Berlin twice. In 1947, they performed at the DP camp at Berlin-Schlachtensee in Western-occupied Berlin, a year later they performed for the reconstituted Jewish community of Berlin.[14] Once the family, originally from Amsterdam, settled in the GDR in 1952, Jaldati performed more frequently. Debuting at an event organized by the Jewish community of East Berlin in memory of the November pogroms of 1938 on 9 November 1952, she became the most renowned interpreter of Yiddish songs in East Germany with *khurbn* commemorative events as annual fixtures for Jaldati and Rebling.[15]

11 Aschheim 2008, 74.

12 Ibid.

13 See Brenner 1996, Goldenbogen 2006, Niether 2004.

14 See United Nations Relief and Rehabilitation Administration (UNRRA) to Lin Jaldati, 26 April 1947, Archive of the Academy of Arts [AdK], Berlin, Lin-Jaldati-Archiv, Nr. 433; invitations in ibid., Nr. 130; CJA, 5 A 1, Nr. 183, p. 10; 5 A 1, Nr. 185. See also *Neues Deutschland*, 2 September 1948, p. 3. Cf. Shneer 2015, 211f; further, see Shneer 2021.

15 AdK, Berlin, Lin–Jaldati–Archiv, Nr. 71.

The early 1950s however, proved to be a watershed. Following antisemitic show trials in several socialist Eastern European countries, most notably against Rudolf Slánský and others in Prague, and the alleged plot of Jewish doctors in the Soviet Union, the East German government followed suit and launched a propaganda campaign against alleged Zionist and counterrevolutionary conspiracies. The campaign was mostly targeted at critical, seemingly unreliable, and treacherous Party members in higher ranks: most notably in the case of Paul Merker, a non-Jewish communist who had survived the war in exile in Mexico. Upon his return to East Germany in 1946, Merker became an advocate for Jewish issues and causes and had endorsed a law which would have enabled the restitution of formerly expropriated property to Jewish owners.[16] In its rage against alleged enemies of the party line, the government also dissolved the Vereinigung der Verfolgten des Naziregimes [Association of Those Persecuted by the Nazi Regime, VVN]. Founded in the Soviet occupation zone in 1947, the VVN was a formally non-partisan organization of survivors of Nazi persecution, but was in fact dominated by communists. Despite its mostly communist leadership, however, the VVN should be seen as an "imagined community" of survivors of different backgrounds which provided a space to express one's concerns and desires.[17] For some time, about half of its members were Jewish, and the organization became a means for Jewish socialists and communists, often also members of the Jewish community organization boards, to constitute a political force advocating for the needs of Jewish survivors.[18] This diversity, however, was looked upon with growing hostility by the government and increasingly viewed as a potential threat to its own memory politics. Accordingly, the party seized the opportunity of the antisemitic wave in 1952 to 1953 and dissolved the organization, thus gaining further control over the narrated past. Still, commemorative services continued, with Jaldati usually contributing a performance, but henceforth were mostly organized and attended exclusively by Jewish community members.

In this environment, singing in Yiddish fulfilled a specific function. Since the language was hardly ever actually spoken in East Germany, it must be

16 Geller 2005, 112–122, 169–184; Graf 2018.

17 Fulbrook 2013, 38.

18 See Walther 2019, 13.

characterized as "postvernacular," to use Jeffrey Shandler's term.[19] Less significant as an everyday language, Yiddish was primarily a symbol of a destroyed culture. Postvernacular Yiddish's "secondary, symbolic level of meaning is always privileged over its primary level," and "the very fact that something is said [or written or sung] in Yiddish [...] is at least as meaningful as the meaning of the words being uttered – if not more so."[20] Thus, when Jaldati sang Yiddish songs at events that had a clear institutional and contextual connection to the victims of National Socialism, it was more than a means of communication or expression or even cultural framing. In this case, the songs represented Yiddish culture specifically and its mostly murdered speakers as well. Regardless of whether Jewish victims were commemorated in speeches and symbols at such events, they were present in Jaldati's singing. In addition to Shandler, the specific situation of Yiddish in a German-speaking context is important to highlight. German native speakers commonly *believe* that they are capable of understanding Yiddish, and to some extent the gist of a song, as in Jaldati's case, may indeed have been decipherable to a German audience. Thus, Yiddish symbolized Jewish victims. However, it also may have fostered a tendency to alienate Jewish victims by marking them with a seemingly similar, but still different, 'exotic' language. Additionally, this association with the East projected the *khurbn* solely into the 'East' – a well-known notion denoting a space outside of one's own grasp and seemingly knowledge which was still associated with deportations, violence, and, although Germans often denied any knowledge of it: mass murder and death.

Two songs especially became Jaldati's hallmark and known in the GDR: Mordkhe Gebirtig's ס'ברענט [*S'brent*, It's burning] and Hirsh Glik's זאָג ניט קיין מאָל [*Zog nit keyn mol*, Never Say]. They assumed a metaphorical status. Regardless of whether the audience grasped the lyrics in their entirety, in parts or not at all, both songs were understood as a clear reference to the *khurbn* simply because they were sung in Yiddish in contexts which signified that Jewish suffering under and resistance to Nazi rule was addressed. Glik's song, written for the פֿאַראייניקטע פּאַרטיזאַנער אָרגאַניזאַציע [*Fareynikte partizaner organizatsye*, United Partisan Organization] in the Vilna Ghetto in 1943 and, thus, often deemed a 'Jewish Partisan Song' in the GDR, was used at the beginning of the radio feature "Sammelpunkt Shelasnastraße" [Gathering Point

19 See Shandler 2005.

20 Ibid., 22.

Shelasna Street] which told the story of the 1943 Warsaw Ghetto Uprising.[21] Konrad Wolf's movie *Sterne* [Stars] from 1959, which tells the story of a German Wehrmacht officer in charge of a concentration camp in German-occupied Bulgaria and the fate of its Greek-Jewish inmates, opens with a rendition of Gebirtig's *S'brent*. Written in response to antisemitic pogroms in 1930s Poland, Gebirtig's song assumed its wide popularity after the war also due to its semantic proximity to the later most well-known term: *Holocaust*. Long before the term 'Holocaust' became popular, though, a German audience certainly understood references to fire and burning because of the pogroms of November 1938, during which the Nazis damaged or destroyed, often by arson, more than 1,000 synagogues. These events were still vivid memories and had been addressed in commemorative services, newspaper articles, and radio announcements.[22] The metaphorical reference was also strengthened by books on the topic such as Peter Duhr's novella *Inferno* or a collection of eyewitness accounts on the *khurbn* in Poland entitled *Im Feuer vergangen. Tagebücher aus dem Ghetto* [Gone with the Fire. Diaries from the Ghetto].[23]

Additionally, the songs certainly fit the specific criteria of socialist *khurbn* memory. Both written in response to antisemitic persecution, the songs called for action and resistance. Although the history of Jewish resistance was mostly neglected in East German antifascist discourses and memory, resistance as a concept was at the center of antifascist rhetoric, imagery, and style. Thus, singing 'Jewish' resistance songs may have helped Jaldati establish an understanding of anti-Jewish persecution during National Socialism, but also to gain credibility in institutionalized antifascism that was mostly concerned with communist (whether non-Jewish or Jewish), and not specifically-Jewish resistance. By the same token, the songs were used by different singers eager to connect *khurbn* memory with a plea for socialism and resistance against new and old threats. American communist activist and artist Paul Robeson, for instance, sang Glik's *Zog nit keyn mol* in various contexts, most notably at a concert in Moscow in 1949. In the same year, Robeson and Jaldati met in Prague for a joint performance of "Songs of Two Oppressed Peoples."[24]

21 Grothe 1963, Wolf 1959.

22 See Walther 2019.

23 Duhr 1956, Im Feuer vergangen 1958. See also Stach 2022.

24 See Shneer 2021, 258, 261. For a recording of Robeson's performance in Moscow see https://soundcloud.com/yiddishkayt/zog-not-keynmol.

Yet, apart from Jaldati's acts, Yiddish played only a small part in commemorative events. These early events may be seen as a compromise at best, or an ill-advised, but usually heartfelt attempt to honor Jewish victims through a non-Jewish repertoire. Yiddish, however, was hardly featured in Jewish memory services mostly because it was not relevant to the community leaders, German-speaking Jews. Furthermore, although most events honoring Jewish victims specifically, most notably around 9 November each year, were organized by the VVN and attended by their members, the events were curated for a non-Jewish majority. In the years immediately after the catastrophe, the organizers lacked experience on how to stage a commemorative event that would cater to the needs of Jewish survivors, but also include the non-Jewish majority. These events reveal the major conflict of *khurbn* memory and commemoration of National Socialist crimes in general, in the German post-perpetrator society: the vast majority of Germans tried to evade any form of confrontation while survivors stressed the importance of confronting the crimes of the recent past.

While Yiddish songs could be superficially grasped by non-Yiddish speakers either due to context or due to an introduction by the performer, Yiddish literature, written in Hebrew script, was entirely incomprehensible even for those few who took an interest in the culture. Only a few attempts were made to translate Yiddish literature and poetry into German in the immediate postwar years. Some of Sholem Asch's works like איסט ריווער [*Ist river*, East River, 1946, German in 1947] were translated into German, but were published in Switzerland or Sweden.[25] An early example from the GDR, however, are translations of works by German writer Hedda Zinner (1905–1994).

In 1933, Zinner fled from Berlin to Vienna, Prague, and finally Moscow where she arrived in 1935. Before being evacuated to Ufa in the Bashkir Autonomous Soviet Socialist Republic after the German assault on the Soviet Union in 1941, she had travelled the Soviet Union and met numerous Soviet writers of different ethnic and national backgrounds. Likely inspired by Maxim Gorky's 1934 appeal to regard hitherto neglected areas of literature like folklore, Zinner assembled a collection of poetry from various languages spoken in the Soviet republics, among them poems by Itsik Fefer, Shmuel Halkin, Dovid Hofshteyn, and Perets Markish.[26] These efforts were part of the

25 Asch 1947.

26 Kelletat 2021.

internationalist and cosmopolitan campaign launched in the Soviet Union in the 1920s and 1930s which sought to build a proletarian world literature and establish the aesthetic representation of socialist internationalism, as well as circumvent Western, transatlantic intellectual dominance, by seeking new collaborations across Europe and Asia.[27] Born in Lviv, Zinner was certainly familiar with languages other than German, but hardly spoke them herself, including Russian. Thus, she mostly worked with others who assisted her in translating the poems. Leyb Kvitko, member of the ייִדישער אנטיפֿאַשיסטישער קאָמיטעט [*Yidisher antifashistisher komitet*, Jewish Antifascist Committee, JAFC] and co-editor of JAFC's journal אייניקייט [*Eynikayt*, Unity], translated the Yiddish poems into German for her. Zinner then published some in the German communist exile press in the Soviet Union, and finally the anthology *Freie Völker – Freie Lieder* [Free Peoples - Free Songs].[28]

The book was reissued in the GDR in 1951, merely months before Fefer, Halkin, Hofshteyn, Kvitko, and Markish were arrested and, with the exception of Halkin, murdered on 12 August 1952.[29] It is unclear *when* Zinner learned about their deaths – rumors did circulate about their demise particularly in Yiddishland, but their murder was only confirmed by Khrushchev in his secret speech in 1956.[30] In her autobiography *Selbstbefragung* [Self-Interview] (1989) several decades later, she mentions working with Kvitko, cites his poem "Verbundenheit" [Connection], and ends the brief paragraph by lamenting:

> Ich übersetzte in der Folgezeit viele Gedichte von Kvitko und von anderen jüdischen Dichtern. Echten Dichtern, großen Dichtern. Echten Sowjetbürgern. Zu denken, daß sie ermordet wurden, ist schwer zu ertragen.[31]

> Subsequently, I translated many poems by Kvitko and other Jewish poets. Real poets, great poets. Real Soviet citizens. To think that they were murdered is hard to bear.

In 1953, she published a two-volume travelogue of her trips through the Soviet Union in which she included some of the translated poems, each with a brief introduction.

27 Clark 2011, Clark 2021, [Chorley-]Schulz 2021.
28 Zinner 1939.
29 Estraikh 2018.
30 [Chorley-]Schulz 2021. See also the interview with Jalda Rebling in this volume.
31 Zinner 1989, 50.

In these metatexts, Zinner presented the poems as literature that aptly captured the process of the Soviet peoples in their journey from Tsarist backwardness to Soviet socialist progress without foregrounding the writers' Jewishness. Dovid Hofshteyn's poem "Aus einem Brief an eine Zwanzigjährige" [From a letter to a twenty year old], according to Zinner, encapsulated the feeling that "ältere Sowjetmenschen" [older Soviet people] had when observing the "Aufschwung dieser Jugend" [upswing of this youth].[32] Leyb Kvitko's poem "Verbundenheit" impressed upon her the "Bewußtsein des neuen Lebens, das neue Verhältnis zur Erde, zum Dorf" [awareness of the new life, the new relationship with the earth, with the village] which had followed the Soviet revolution.[33] What might seem today as a subversive act of honoring the murdered and recognizing their great talent in the knowledge of their demise was probably more an expression of admiration of these Yiddish poets and their poetry as representing the essence of the Russian Revolution. Inadvertently then, she did indict Stalin as the executioner of socialist visions. Since Zinner did not introduce Hofshteyn nor Kvitko as Jewish writers of Yiddish poetry, however, this particular context was lost on her readers.

Publishing Yiddish Classics

"[M]ore alien to us than a culture
that was lost centuries ago"[34]

Zinner was a pioneer and connected prewar antifascist activism and the ideals of communist internationalism with the efforts in the immediate postwar period. But apart from her, Yiddish was mostly absent from the field of literature at the time. The tradition of translating contemporary Yiddish literature into German, starting at the end of the 19th century, was only hesitantly taken up by publishers in East Germany and West Germany. The reasons are obvious: merely years after the collapse of Nazi Germany, the societies in both states were certainly organized and governed differently, but had hardly forsaken their anti-Jewish sentiments and antisemitism. Depending on book sales, German publishers catered to the wishes of their customers. More so, and by no means only a (East and West) German phenomenon, publications on the *khurbn* were scarce in general, but books on the topic

32 Zinner 1953, 27.

33 Ibid., 145.

34 Assessment by Anne Gabrisch, BArch, DR 1/2340a, 395–398.

from a victim's perspective translated from Yiddish were almost non-existent. Most publishers were simply ignorant of Yiddish publications, even though a modest Yiddish publishing industry came to existence in Germany itself – within the DP camps. A case in point for the overall ignorance vis-à-vis early Yiddish *khurbn*-literature is Helmut Eschwege (1913–1992).

Eschwege, born in 1913 in Hannover, survived the war in exile in Mandate Palestine before returning to Germany in 1948. A gardener by profession, Eschwege soon took an interest in the history of German Jewry, and the persecution of Jews in Nazi Germany especially.[35] Excluded from East German academia, he sought different avenues to pursue his interests. In 1954, he offered to translate Polish Yiddish writer Ber Mark's (1908–1966) study of the Warsaw Ghetto Uprising. A journalist, historian, and member of the Communist Party, Mark had fled from Poland in 1939 and survived in the Soviet Union. In various locations, he worked for the JAFC and assembled a first account of the Warsaw Ghetto Uprising from the scarce sources he managed to accumulate. Published in Polish in Moscow in 1944, his brochure was also included in דאָס שוואַרצע בוך [*Dos shvartse bukh*, The Black Book]. Having returned to Poland, Mark became a key figure in the reestablishment of Yiddish and Jewish cultural life in postwar Poland, and later the long serving head of the Żydowski Instytut Historyczny [Jewish Historical Institute, ŻIH].[36] In 1947, Mark published an updated and extended version of his study as דאָס בוך פֿון גבֿורה. אויפֿשטאַנד פֿון וואַרשעווער געטאָ [*Dos bukh fun gvure. Oyfstand fun varshever geto*, The Book of Valor. The Warsaw Ghetto Uprising].

The East German publisher Dietz, owned by the Socialist Unity Party, showed interest in Mark's book for which it was hard to find a translator, but the editor was confused as to why Eschwege wanted to translate the book from Yiddish.[37] The version on their radar was the Polish version from 1953, updated by Ber Mark in the wake of the antisemitic turn in Poland at the time.[38] In order to make his book partisan in character, he made a few, but significant changes such as removing all references to Zionist activities in the Ghetto or adding a critique of the Federal Republic of Germany, in order to

35 Walther 2020a, Walther 2020b.

36 See the articles by Agniezska Żółkiewska and Kamil Kijek in this volume. On Mark see Nalewajko-Kulikov 2010.

37 Helmut Eschwege to Dietz-Verlag, 18 February 1954, and the reply dated 23 February 1954 in BArch, DY 30/17290.

38 Mark 1947, Mark 1953.

secure not only the publication of the book but the continued existence of the Jewish Historical Institute.[39] Eventually, Eschwege's proposal was turned down, and a German translation of the Polish edition of Mark's book was published in 1957.[40]

Nine years later, however, an anthology of a variety of Yiddish texts written in the Warsaw Ghetto edited by Ber Mark was translated into German: צווישן לעבן און טויט [*Tsvishn lebn un toyt*, Between Life and Death].[41] The German publication was the result of a fruitful cooperation between the ŻIH and East German publishers, in this case the Union Verlag, the publisher of the Christian Democratic Party in the GDR. Its director, Hubert Faensen (1928–2019), had taken an interest in Jewish culture in the preceding years. In 1961, Faensen sought the help of German-Jewish writer Arnold Zweig (1887–1968), one of the most prominent figures in East German literary life, and inquired whether Zweig would be willing to edit an anthology of Yiddish short stories. Zweig declined due to his workload and worsening eyesight, but suggested his friend Rudolf Hirsch (1907–1998) whom he had met in exile in Mandate Palestine years before. Hirsch, the GDR's most prominent legal correspondent famous for his reports from various trials, most notably the Frankfurt Auschwitz trial (1963–65), agreed and later published twenty-five stories by several Jewish authors from Eastern Europe in the volume *Die Heimfahrt des Rabbi Chanina* [The Homeward Journey of Rabbi Chanina].[42] Seeking another project, Hirsch and Faensen contacted ŻIH and agreed with Mark on translating three books into German: Zalmen Skalov's account דער האַקנקרייץ [*Der haknkreyts*, The Swastika], Mark's *Tsvishn lebn un toyt*, and Peretz Opoczyński's רעפּאָרטאַזשן פֿון וואַרשעווער געטאָ [*Reportazhn fun varshever geto*, Reports from the Warsaw Ghetto].[43] Eventually, they dropped Opoczyński's report, but assembled Skalov's texts and Mark's edition together with Chaim [Charles] Goldstein's account זיבן אין בונקער [*Zibn in bunker*, Seven in the bunker, here published as *Leben ohne Stern* (Life without Star)] into one anthology entitled *Ghetto. Berichte aus dem Warschauer Ghetto 1939–1945* [Ghetto. Reports from the Warsaw Ghetto 1939–1945].[44]

39 Stach 2016, 200–201.

40 Mark 1957.

41 Mark 1955.

42 Hirsch 1962.

43 Skalov 1954, Opoczyński 1954. See the letters in AŻIH 310/474, 310/476, 310/484, 310/492, 310/507, 310/511.

44 Hirsch 1966.

This publication remained an exception. Other publishers mostly refrained from translating Yiddish texts with explicit reference to the *khurbn*. Instead, publishing houses such as Union Verlag, the East Berlin based leading GDR publisher of international fiction Volk und Welt [People and World], or Reclam Verlag in Leipzig turned to classic Yiddish authors – not unlike publishing ventures in socialist countries or in the 'West' at the same time. The first book in this small series was arguably the most well-known modern Yiddish classic: Sholem Aleichem's טבֿיה דער מילכיקער [*Tevye der milkhiker*, Tevye the Dairyman] which reproduced Alexander Eliasberg's (1879–1924) translation from 1921.[45] Although the publisher was unable to set a trend, other titles by Sholem Aleichem (Sholem Rabinovitsh; 1859–1916) and by other classic authors such as Yitskhok Leybush Peretz, Mendele Moykher-Sforim (Sholem Yankev Abramovitsh, 1863–1917), and Moyshe Kulbak (1896–1937) followed.[46] Yiddish contemporary writers, however, were hardly translated, with Isaac Bashevis Singer (1904–1991) as the only exception.[47]

The few translations point to a dilemma the editors faced. Not only was there little interest in Jewish culture among the German public generally, Yiddish specifically had also been the language of most of the victims of the *khurbn* – those the surviving German public was eager to ignore.[48] Yet, the editors did pursue a few Yiddish translation projects, and they did so for two reasons: first, they intended to honor these texts as part of the world literary canon and make them accessible to a German audience. In that, the publishers followed in the footsteps of the influential translator Alexander Eliasberg. Having translated Yiddish texts into German from the beginning of the 20th century onwards, Eliasberg helped to establish this tradition, on the one hand, and reinvigorated communist-led left literature canonization projects of the 1930s onwards, on the other.[49] But, secondly, the texts were also intended as a means to foster a confrontation with the *khurbn*. Although publishers had to take a possible rejection by the audience into account, they often deliberately published texts that not only addressed National Socialist

45 Aleichem 1955.

46 Aleichem 1965, Aleichem 1969, Kulbak 1973, Peretz 1969, Moykher-Sforim 1978.

47 Singer 1980.

48 For the reluctance to engage with Yiddish sources, not only in the German context, see Sneh 2017.

49 See Gruschka 2016.

crimes in general, but the *khurbn* specially. The victim's perspective that these texts exhibited may have been conducive for their success: the crimes themselves could be addressed, while the perpetrators could remain unnamed. In popular books like *Das Tagebuch der Anne Frank* [The Diary of Anne Frank], Bruno Apitz' (1900–1979) *Nackt unter Wölfen* [Naked among Wolves] or less widely read, but translated, books like Adolf Rudnicki's (Aron Hirszhorn, 1909–1990) *Żywe i martwe morze* [The Living and the Dead Sea] or Zofia Nałkowska's (1884–1954) *Medaliony* [Medaillons], German perpetrators were either a structuring absence or rendered monstrous, dehumanized fascists which hardly instilled a much-needed self-reflexivity in the German readership.[50] In some cases, publishers even decided to censor the original text in the translation. In Rudnicki's text, for instance, members of the Wehrmacht were described as "ścinaze głów, mordercy dzieci, specjaliści w wytapianiu tłuszczu z ludzi, specjaliści od krematoriów" [head cutters, child murderers, specialists in rendering fat from people, specialists in crematoria].[51] The description was omitted in the GDR edition – the only German translation of this book to this day.[52]

However, the predominant victim's perspective did not entail that the East German public would be exonerated. Instead, publisher's used Yiddish texts to stress the necessity of addressing Nazi crimes, the *khurbn*, and the culture of Eastern European Jewry that was destroyed almost in its entirety. They did this in two ways: through metatexts and via the, sometimes tedious, print approval procedure. In order to print a book, publishers had to apply to the responsible office in the Ministry of Culture for permission. This required written assessments from the responsible editor and an external expert familiar with the subject matter. The assessments summarized the content and justified the publication. Critical texts or those that appeared ambivalent in their interpretation, especially by authors deemed politically unreliable, had to be handled with particular care. In some cases, the editors consulted with the authors before a manuscript was submitted and implemented certain changes. Most of the time, the ministry only read the expert opinions because the department was not staffed to review several hundred manuscripts per year. In the case of particularly explosive topics, such as environmental pro-

50 Frank 1957, Apitz 1958, Nałkowska 1956, Rudnicki 1960.

51 Rudnicki 1959, 340.

52 See Taterka 2010, 207.

tection, the inner-German border, historical works, or whenever skepticism arose during the report-review, the censorship office consulted other experts. The longer a print approval process remained with the administration, the more problematic the processing became. The ministry and the publishers usually maintained a good relationship. Accordingly, only few book projects were rejected entirely which, however, points less to a liberal censorship practice than to a strict preselection by the publishers.[53] The editor's role in this process can hardly be overestimated. As in other areas in state socialist societies, responsibility was often outsourced from the authorities themselves to lower positions or outside institutions. The publishers, thus, were themselves responsible for the texts they submitted for approval, and it was up to them to preselect the most promising projects and convince the ministry of their worth. Another way to ensure a book's publication were prefaces or epilogues penned by the editors in which they could contextualize and address potential 'ideological shortcomings.' The editor's metatexts of Yiddish books in translation must, therefore, be read as strategies within the East German literary production scene.

Antifascism was the basis for most of the assessments submitted to the ministry. The editors stressed that antifascism would dictate the necessity for the East German public to confront Jewish life and culture before the *khurbn* in order to reflect upon the effects of its destruction. The doubled destruction of millions of human beings and an entire cultural world should be remembered and worked through in unison. Hans Marquardt (1920–2004), head of Reclam, for instance, stressed that through Sholem Aleichem's [and Isaac Bashevis Singer's] literature "erhält die mit der blutigen faschistischen ‚Neuordnung Europas' untergegangene ostjüdische Welt Gestalt und Gesicht" [the Eastern Jewish world that perished with the bloody fascist 'New Order of Europe' takes on a shape and face], and, simultaneously this literature would remind "die ältere Generation, die Zeugen der ‚schlimmen Jahre', auch an ihr Versagen vor der Geschichte" [the older generation, the witnesses of the 'terrible years,' also of their failure before history].[54] Jutta Janke (1932–2004), the responsible editor for Polish literature at Volk und Welt who also took an interest in Yiddish culture, claimed her edited volume of Jewish jokes and anecdotes would "die Erinnerung wachhalten an eine Welt, die durch das

53 See Barck, Langermann, and Lokatis 1997.

54 Sholem Aleichem 1984, 176.

scheußlichste Verbrechen der Menschheitsgeschichte fast völlig vernichtet wurde: die Welt der osteuropäischen Juden" [keep alive the memory of a world that was almost completely annihilated by the most heinous crime in human history: the world of East European Jews].[55] Questions about perpetration were rarely explicitly raised in these texts, but, as Marquardt's comments allude, haunted them.

Since culture was at the epicenter of socialist social policy, editors ensured to highlight the political significance of the submitted manuscripts and framed them as a necessary partisan addition to East German literature and the antifascist project. According to the Hebraist Heinrich Simon (1921–2010), fascism had not only been concerned with the "Tötung von Individuen, sondern um totale Vernichtung von Kulturen" [killing of individuals, but with the total destruction of cultures] which is why "die sozialistische DDR" [the socialist GDR] was obligated to keep alive "das Andenken an diese Bevölkerungsgruppe durch die Bewahrung und Pflege des kulturellen Erbes, das sie uns hinterlassen hat" [the memory of this population group by preserving and cultivating the cultural heritage they left us].[56] Another editor stressed the GDR's obligation "gegenüber einer Welt, die [...] so gut wie gänzlich vernichtet wurde, und die uns [...] fremder geworden ist als eine vor Jahrhunderten versunkene Kultur" [towards a world that [...] has been almost completely destroyed, and which has become [...] more alien to us than a culture that was lost centuries ago].[57]

Editors also seized this opportunity to express restrained criticism. An outside expert praised the memoirs of Bella Rosenfeld Chagall (1895–1944), Marc Chagall's (1887–1985) wife, and concluded: "Sollten wir über die Bräuche und Feste der Juden, die in grosser Zahl Nachbarn, Landsleute waren, nicht ein wenig mehr wissen als bisher?" [Shouldn't we know a little more than we do now about the customs and celebrations of the Jews, who in large numbers were neighbors, compatriots?] This would fill a "empfindliche Lücke – nicht nur auf dem Büchermarkt" [sensitive gap – not only in the book market].[58] His insertion clearly aimed at the lack of engagement

55 Janke 1975, 198.
56 Assessment by Heinrich Simon, 2 March 1973 & 16 October 1974, BArch, DR 1/2358, 68–71, quote 71.
57 Assessment by Anne Gabrisch, BArch, DR 1/2340a, 395–398.
58 Assessment by Hermann Schäfer, BArch, DR 1/2360a, 263–270.

with Jewish culture in the GDR. Yet, it is also obvious that Jewish culture was mostly located in the 'East.' The loss of a German-Jewish culture was rarely lamented in such terms.

Furthermore, editors and experts expressed their hope that Yiddish literature could help overcome antisemitic prejudices. Although the government kept stressing that antisemitism and 'racial hatred' had been abolished in the GDR, others insisted that it still needed to be addressed.[59] In an assessment of Sholem Aleichem's מאָטל פּייסי דעם חזנס [*Motl Peysi dem khazns*, Motl Peysi the Cantor's Son], the writer Helfried Schreiter (1935–1992) pointed out that the German public only knew about Jews in a distorted way. Especially for the younger generation Jews were "mostly known only from the descriptions of their parents or in connection with Hitler's inhuman policy of extermination."[60]

The attempt of (exclusively non-Jewish) editors to promote Yiddish literature could, however, take a turn for the worse and unintentionally reproduce stereotypes. Fritz J. Raddatz (1931–2015), then editor at Volk und Welt and later one of the most influential literary critics in West Germany, lauded an edition of Sholem Aleichem's *Tevye* by stressing the "politische Aufgabe" [political task] to show the audience that the "jüdische Prototyp weder Bankier Mendelssohn noch Tietz-Kaufhäuser-Besitzer sind, sondern – Tewje, der Milchhändler" [Jewish prototype is neither banker Mendelssohn nor Tietz department store owner, but – Tevye, the milk merchant].[61] With good intentions in mind, Raddatz merely exchanged one stereotype for another.

The endorsement of Sholem Aleichem and Tevye as *the* idealized Jewish figure enables a comparative view across bloc borders. Some ten years after Raddatz' assessment, Sholem Aleichem's story rose to become the arguably most well-known story of Eastern European Jewry. Since its premiere on Broadway in 1964, the musical *Fiddler on the Roof* has served as a means of romanticizing the shtetl and East European Jewish life. Thereby, "the shtetl past thus configured became a resource for the two related urges of affirming

59 See for instance the speech the writer Johannes Bobrowski gave at the Evangelische Akademie Berlin-Brandenburg in December 1962: "Die Beschäftigung der Literatur mit dem Antisemitismus hat diesen nicht überwunden. Er ist da" [Literature's preoccupation with antisemitism has not overcome it. It is here] (Bobrowski 1967, 29).

60 Assessment by Helfried Schreiter, 29 July 1964, BArch, DR 1/3939, 226f.

61 Assessment, dated 8 February 1954, BArch, DR 1/3266, 218f. The papers in AdK, Berlin, Verlagsarchiv Volk und Welt, No. 1380.

the Jews' Americanness as legitimate, and creating a sense of distinctiveness and difference," as Markus Krah has argued. Idealizing shtetl life via *Fiddler* and other representations of Yiddish culture also fostered a process of secularization from Judaism to Jewishness and *Yidishkayt*.[62] In the GDR, however, the same musical, staged at East Berlin's Komische Oper over 500 times until 1988, served different purposes.[63] For one, the musical was a welcomed opportunity for the East German public to engage with a widely inaccessible Western – even more: American – cultural phenomenon and to escape the boundaries of socialist cultural productions. The musical's success, however, also points to necessities and demands of the East German public after the *khurbn*. Despite the sincere approach of Walter Felsenstein (1901–1975), the artistic director of the Komische Oper and his team, *Der Fiedler auf dem Dach* [Fiddler on the Roof] did enhance a clichéd and romanticized image of the shtetl around 1900 and, thus, blended in with and shaped the (half-) knowledge of the audience about East European Jewry.

More so, a tale of concern and loss told in a light, uplifting mode, *Fiddler* hardly sparked any discussion about the gradual death of the world it depicted. On the contrary, as Monica Rüthers has argued, the success of the musical in both German states may also be explained as it "entlastete sowohl die sozialistische DDR, wie auch das westdeutsche Publikum: Das zaristische Russland hatte die Juden auf dem Gewissen" [relieved both the socialist GDR, as well as the West German public: Tsarist Russia had the Jews on its conscience].[64] Exoticizing East European Jewry fostered the image of Jews as aliens in Germany, and, thus, the audience was not forced to engage with the loss of German-Jewish culture and the murder of German Jews in the *khurbn*. This deficit was pointed out at times, but hardly affected the musical's success. In an epilogue of the 1984 edition of Sholem Aleichem's *Tevye*, Reclam head Hans Marquardt complained about the musical for having been stripped of the class conscious criticism the original text provided. Moreover, Marquardt lamented that the celebration of the East European Jewish world depicted in the musical lacked any reference to its later destruction, and quoted from a study by Leon Brandt:

62 Krah 2018, 226–227, 235. See also Roskies 1999.

63 See Coors 2019, 64; Weber 2009.

64 Rüthers 2012, 156.

> 'Anatewka' mit seinen Typen und Träumen hatte seinerzeit überall Beifallsstürme ausgelöst, wo sich doch eher Tränen bewegen müßten. Denn als diese Welt noch lebte und so war, wie man sich heute dafür begeistert, da rührte sich keine Hand, um sie vor dem Untergang zu retten
>
> 'Anatevka' with its types and dreams had caused storms of applause everywhere at that time, where tears should have fallen instead. For when that world was still alive, and was as we enthusiaste about it today, no hand moved to save it from ruin.[65]

Translators and Language

Most Yiddish literature published in the GDR were reissues of older translations by Alexander Eliasberg. Only few texts were actually translated in the GDR, mostly due to lack of Yiddish native speakers. Apart from native speakers like Mottek Weinryb who translated the aforementioned anthology *Tsvishn lebn un toyt* only few non-Jewish Germans like Jürgen Rennert (*1943), Hubert Witt or Jutta Janke took an interest in the language.[66] Without language courses or study materials, they needed to improvise and seek contact to others learners of Yiddish. Witt, for instance, long serving editor at Reclam, studied German language and literature in Leipzig in the 1950s and, despite the lack of textbooks, chose Yiddish as a further language of study. In conversation with the author, Jürgen Rennert cited Volk und Welt as an important influence since an interest in Eastern Jewish culture was palpable there. Rennert claimed he was motivated to devote himself to the language by Janke, who also showed an interest in Yiddish literature through her study of Polish literature and the *khurbn*. At Humboldt University, both learned Modern Hebrew, and later Yiddish through self-study. Reading Yiddish-language periodicals such as פֿאָלקס־שטימע [*Folks-shtime*, People's Voice], published in Poland, and the influential סאָוועטיש היימלאַנד [*Sovetish heymland*, Soviet Homeland], published in the Soviet Union, soon became important resources for study and sources of inspiration. Moreover, the Jewish community of East Berlin re-established a library in 1977 which provided access to books otherwise difficult to obtain. It became a popular learning and meeting place for those interested in Jewish culture.[67] In the 1980s, benefitting from these earlier efforts, a new generation

65 Marquardt 1984, 176. See also Brandt 1981, 12.

66 For Weinryb see conversation with Jalda Rebling in this volume.

67 Conversation with Jürgen Rennert, 2 February 2017. See also Stach 2016, Links 2010.

Jutta Janke, no date, Academy of Arts, Berlin, VuW 724.

of Yiddish literature enthusiasts emerged: Andrej Jendrusch, Peter Kelm, and Beate Petras translated Yiddish literature, Jalda Rebling, Ilona Schlott, Karsten Troyke, as well as the band *Aufwind* sang and helped re-popularize Yiddish songs. Still, the output of translated Yiddish literature in the GDR remained marginal.[68]

Concerns about prevailing prejudices and the need to convince the authorities also affected the work of these translators. Thus, Yiddish had to be framed in accordance with the presumed wishes and needs of the ministerial censors. Jürgen Rennert, for one, described Yiddish as the language of the "Unterprivilegierten und Entrechteten" [of the underprivileged and disenfranchised], in a nutshell: a language of the working class. In the same paper, he lauded that Yiddish took a clear "antifeudalistisch[e], antibourgeois[e], antikapitalistisch[e] Haltung" [anti-feudal, anti-bourgeois, anti-capitalist stance].[69] The idea of addressing socialist values and ideas to let Yiddish literature appear suited for socialist aims is evident. The assessments of these texts often read like a short history of the Yiddish language with a partisan character. The connection made between socialism and Yiddish was by no means absurd. Yiddish classics like Sholem Aleichem, Mendele Moykher-Sforim, and particularly Yitskhok Leybush Peretz, who had a radical socialist period, wrote about daily life in the Eastern European shtetl in the hope of drawing attention to the situation of the Eastern Jewish population. Also, the אַלגעמיינער ייִדישער אַרבעטער־בונד [*Algemeyner yidisher arbeterbund*, General Jewish Labor Bund, Bund], established at the end of the 19th century, tried to unite socialist ideals and Jewish life and identity.[70] The Russian Revolution only enhanced these efforts, resulting in the Soviet embrace

68 See Halpern 1989, Burg 1988, Sholem Aleichem 1990.

69 Assessment by Jürgen Rennert, 19 January 1977, BArch, DR 1/2211a, 376–380, quote 377.

70 Pickhan 2009, Wolff 2021.

of and engagement with Yiddish particularly in the 1920s and 1930s and the existence of a specific Soviet Yiddish culture until the demise of the Soviet project.[71]

Translators also had to reflect the special circumstances this literature was published in and adapt their interpretations accordingly. They needed to find a compromise on how to present this 'alien' literature to a German, mostly non-Jewish audience. Debates like the fierce criticism of German Jewish philosopher and historian of Jewish mysticism Gershom Scholem (1897–1982) regarding Alexander Eliasberg's translations in the 1910s did not bubble up in the GDR. Scholem argued that Eliasberg's adaption of Yiddish texts into a German literary culture, by translating, for instance, terms of Jewish culture and religion into German equivalents – תורה [*toyre*] into "Gelehrsamkeit" [erudition], מנין [*minyen*] into "privater Gottesdienst" [private service], מיקווה [*mikve*] into "[rituelles] Bad" [ritual bath] – would distort these terms and concepts, and should instead be "annäherungsweise umschrieben werden" [approximately paraphrased].[72] Apart from general discussions about the possibility of translating an entire cultural world into another, Eliasberg was also, in his time and later, criticized for his

> nostalgische, romantisierend-verklärende Bearbeitungen, in denen Ambiguitäten, modernistische Ideen, Satire, Sozialkritik, Ironie sowie erotisch-sexuelle Anspielungen abgemildert, abgeändert oder weggelassen wurden.[73]

> nostalgic, romanticizing, transfiguring adaptations in which ambiguities, modernist ideas, satire, social criticism, irony, and erotic-sexual allusions were toned down, changed or omitted.

There are only few traces of such considerations in the GDR, but the metatexts indicate that editors and translators did reflect on how to interpret this world for their audience. In an assessment, Jürgen Rennert noted that the translations by Eliasberg and others were mostly written for "ein noch vorhandenes, assimiliertes" [a still existing, assimilated] German Jewish audience in the early 20th century. Those texts seemed not entirely suitable for a non-Jewish audience living in the GDR decades later. Instead, he praised

71 See among others Shneer 2004, Shternshis 2006, [Chorley-]Schulz 2021.

72 Gerhard [Gershom] Scholem, 1917: Zum Problem der Uebersetzung aus dem Jidischen, cit. in Grossman 2009, 96–98.

73 Gruschka 2016, 381.

Hubert Witt's translation of Mendele Moykher-Sforim's פֿישקע דער קרומער [*Fishke der krumer*, Fishke the Lame] to be "von schöner Spröde" [of beautiful brittleness] and hoped that this language would have a ",entmythologisierenden' Effekt" ['demythologizing' effect] and undercut "konventionelle Erwartungsmuster" [conventional patterns of expectation].[74] Concerns about still-existing antisemitism always accompanied these book projects. Witt noted that he refrained to translate the poems in his anthology from both a "strengen Transkription" [strict transcription] and a "rein neuhochdeutscher Fassung" [pure new High German version] but chose a compromise according to the "Gestus des Gedichts" [nature of the poem].[75] Yet, other aspects of Yiddish classics were necessarily lost in translation. Sholem Aleichem's incomparable humor, for instance, heavily relying on puns, idioms, and wordplay strategically using the different components of the Yiddish language, were decipherable for his multilingual native readership but almost untranslatable into other languages and cultural contexts, including in East Germany.[76] In her edition of Jewish jokes, Jutta Janke hinted at the problem and provided a few examples of jokes that did not work any longer once translated into German.[77] Moreover, aspects of social criticism which lay at the heart of the Yiddish classics were addressed in the assessment, of course, but since most texts were reissues of Eliasberg's translations, who had mostly toned down these issues, those aspects had to be pointed out specifically in the metatexts.

Still, translators were eager to convey an 'authentic' impression of the Eastern European Jewish world which indeed lay at the center of Yiddish classics: a poverty-ridden world, marked by oppression and class struggle. Foregrounding the socialist core of this literature both ticked the necessary political boxes to convince the ministry of its worth and found a ready audience with shared sensibilities. Describing the world of Mendele's *Fishke der krumer*, Hubert Witt noted:

> Vieles, was aus heutiger Distanz am Fischke-Roman ins Exotische entrückt oder romantisch verklärt erscheint, war von den Zeitgenossen als krasse Realisitk empfunden worden. […] Manches, was spielerisch tändelnd daherkommt, ist sehr ernst zu nehmen: die scheinbar groteske Einlage über

74 Assessment by Jürgen Rennert, 19 February 1977, BArch, DR 1/2211a, 376–380.

75 Witt 1966, 276.

76 Gruschka 2016, 381; Schwarz 2012.

77 Janke 1976, 200–202.

Cover of Mendele's *Fishke der krumer*, 1978, Leipzig: Reclam, with the kind permission of Reclam Verlag.

> einen hausierenden Autor in Odessa z.B. ist eine sehr alltägliche Episode aus dem Leben eines damaligen jiddischen Schriftstellers.[78]

> Much of the Fishke novel, which from today's distance appears exoticized or romantically transfigured, was perceived by contemporaries as stark realism. [...] Some of what comes across as playful dalliance is to be taken very seriously: the seemingly grotesque interlude about a peddling author in Odessa, for example, is a very everyday episode from the life of a Yiddish writer of that time.

Witt wanted to ensure that his audience understood the relevance of these seemingly strange characters. Reflecting the necessity to familiarize the audience with this world, Yiddish classics were also frequently published along with drawings by the Soviet-Jewish artist Anatoli Kaplan (1902–1980). Born in the Russian Pale of Settlement, Kaplan grew up in the world of Sholem

78 Moykher-Sforim 1978, 167.

Aleichem and others. In the 1950s, he began illustrating Yiddish classics like Aleichem's *Tevye* or Mendele's *Fishke*, thus creating the tableau for a "ostjüdisches Welttheater" [Eastern Jewish world theater], as Witt put it.[79] Kaplan's drawings were similar to the works of Marc Chagall, one of the most prominent artists to have painted this world, but because they were black and white, the depicted situations often appeared melancholic and gloomy. It remains unclear whether Kaplan's drawings helped the audience familiarize themselves with the East European Jewish world. Due to the illustrations, however, the books usually had to be printed lavishly and were published in large-format editions which negatively affected the price and perhaps the audience's ability and desire to buy them. Jürgen Rennert expressed his concerns about this issue, arguing that antisemitism may be "durch die Hintertür auffällig aufwendiger Aufmachung wieder eingeschleppt wird, was die oft glanzvollen Vor- und Nachworte auszuräumen bemüht sind" [brought back in through the back door of conspicuously elaborate presentations which the often glamorous prefaces and epilogues endeavor to dispel].[80]

Networks

Translated Yiddish literature in the GDR was also a testament to the manifold transnational connections that editors, publishing houses, or translators upheld. Rennert, for instance, established friendships with Yiddish writers in socialist countries, such as Mark Rasumny (1896–1988) in Riga and Israil Bercovici (1921–1988) in Bucharest.[81] Additionally, several book projects were based on fruitful cooperations between East German publishers and institutions such as ŻIH in Warsaw. The genesis of Hubert Witt's previously mentioned anthology of poems, *Der Fiedler vom Getto*, aptly illustrates this. In the early 1960s, Witt started to gather Yiddish *khurbn*-poems by mostly Eastern European writers. In 1963, he visited ŻIH in Warsaw which, at the time, had already established itself as a pioneer in *khurbn* research, also in the GDR. With the help of ŻIH's director, Ber Mark, Witt collected more poems, and finally submitted the manuscript to the authorities in 1965. Mark con-

79 Moykher-Sforim 1978, 170.

80 Assessment by Jürgen Rennert, 19 February 1977, BArch, DR 1/2211a, 376–380, quote 378.

81 For Bercovici and the work of the Romanian Jewish State Theater see Corina Petrescu's text in this volume.

tributed a preface which provided a seemingly reliable reading but addressed controversial issues as well, such as the creation of the state of Israel. In a letter to the Ministry of Culture, Witt's publisher Reclam justified their editor's trip to Warsaw and the book project in general by stressing that such an anthology would surely provoke positive reactions from "jüdischen Kreisen des Auslands" [Jewish circles abroad].[82] Since the GDR government was constantly concerned about its reputation, it was rather cunning of the publisher to raise such a prospect.

This strategy proved successful. In 1967, only a year after Witt had published his anthology, he planned an art edition of his book, and asked an artist to provide accompanying drawings. The sculptor Hermann Naumann (*1930) was contracted to submit his work by June 1967, but by then the project was facing a serious backlash. The Third Arab-Israeli War (5 June 1967 – 10 June 1967), which had begun only days before Naumann's deadline, was accompanied by a fierce anti-Zionist-cum-antisemitic propaganda campaign in GDR newspapers and had Yiddish star singer Lin Jaldati effectively banned from performing for years to come. Other projects, like Witt's anthology, were threatened as well. The publisher, however, was clever enough to use this situation in an appeal to the ministry. They argued that the publication of a bibliophile edition of Yiddish poetry could take the wind out of any accusations of antisemitism by foreign press agencies. The permission to print was granted with only few requested changes. One such change regarded a depiction of the Star of David. In an image of the Warsaw Ghetto Uprising, two figures holding a flag with the Star of David are facing an SS soldier with heavy weaponry. According to post-1967 East German geopolitics, the Star of David was too directly associated with the 'imperialist' state of Israel and could therefore not simultaneously symbolize a righteous struggle against fascism. Naumann had to revise. The published version did include the image in question, but the Star of David was almost indiscernible.[83]

Despite such difficulties, books like Witt's anthology were positively reviewed and at times eagerly anticipated by the public. Stephan Hermlin (1915–1997), a writer of Jewish decent, was so fascinated by the edition that he wrote a page-long review.[84] When the Komische Oper in East Berlin pre-

82 Reclam-Verlag to the Ministry of Culture, 2 September 1963, Reclam Archiv Leipzig, Nr. 298.

83 Witt 1969, 113.

84 Hermlin 1966.

miered *Fiddler on the Roof* in 1971, they asked for a permission to cite poems from the volume in their program.[85] Even the *New York Times* noticed this pricey, but beautifully made edition. Reactions from East German readers are scarce, but the rare letters available indicate that these books did have an impact. A reader from Dresden, for instance, asked the publisher for more background material on the subject. He was preparing a talk on Yiddish poetry for his local cultural group.[86]

Hubert Witt, 1979, picture by Christian Kraushaar, Academy of Arts, Berlin, Foto-AdK-O 468–3.

Conclusion

Yiddish literature in translation was certainly available in the GDR, but never fully included the literary canon. Translators such as Jutta Janke, Jürgen Rennert, and Hubert Witt provided the East German public with small insights into an otherwise unknown world, but the response remained marginal. Sholem Aleichem's novel דער פֿאַרכּישופֿטער שנײַדער [*Der farkishefter shnayder*, The Bewitched Tailor] sold so poorly, for instance, that the publisher finally gave away the remaining copies.[87] An added difficulty was that Janke, Rennert, Witt, and others by no means acted as a collective united in the interest in making Yiddish culture accessible. Rather, tension and competition stifled ambitions for joining forces, though never so far as to seriously jeopardize individual book projects. Be that as it may, these titles did contribute to the rise in attention given to Jewish culture, especially since the 1970s. It was then that despite the public campaign against Israel, editors and translators even endeavored to publish Israeli writers in the GDR. Samuel Joseph Agnon (1887–1970) and the West German success Ephraim Kishon (1924–2005), were also published in the GDR since the 1960s thanks to the efforts of editors like Jutta Janke and others.

Analyzing translated Yiddish texts in the GDR can, thus, give us insight

85 See the letters in Reclam Archiv Leipzig, No. 298. However, there is no poem in the later program booklet. I am thankful to the Komische Oper for providing the material.

86 Reclam Archiv Leipzig, Nr. 298.

87 Coors 2019, 65.

into the techniques and processes of a memory culture 'from below' and its transnational entanglement within the socialist world and beyond. Instead of focusing on the state, party leadership, and censorship, we should look for efforts and opportunities that were taken to incorporate the memory of Jewish victims into the hegemonic antifascist memory culture. Intentions ranged from "making amends," as the *New York Times* suggested, to recognizing and celebrating Yiddish literature, especially for its unique political and literary value in a socialist worldmaking project.

Bibliography

Archival Sources

Archive of the Academy of Arts [AdK], Berlin

Archiwum Żydowskiego Instytutu Historycznego w Warszawie [Archive of the Jewish Historical Institute, Warsaw, AŻIH]

Bundesarchiv Berlin [BArch]

Reclam-Archive, University of Leipzig

Sources

ANONYMOUS, 1948: [Announcement of concert given by Lin Jaldati], In: *Neues Deutschland*, 2 September 1948, 3.

ANONYMOUS, 1958: *Im Feuer vergangen. Tagebücher aus dem Ghetto*. Berlin [GDR]: Rütten & Loening.

APITZ, Bruno, 1958: *Nackt unter Wölfen. Roman*. Halle: Mitteldeutscher Verlag.

ASCHHEIM, Steven E., 2008: Reflection, Projection, Distortion: The "Eastern Jew" in German-Jewish Culture. In: *Osteuropa* 58 (8–10): 61–74.

BARCK, Simone, Martina LANGERMANN and Siegfried LOKATIS, eds., 1997: *„Jedes Buch ein Abenteuer". Zensur-System und literarische Öffentlichkeiten in der DDR bis Ende der sechziger Jahre*. Berlin: Akademie-Verlag.

BECKER, Jurek, 2007: *Mein Vater, die Deutschen und ich. Aufsätze, Vorträge, Interviews*. Frankfurt a. M.: Suhrkamp.

BOBROWSKI, Johannes: Benannte Schuld – gebannte Schuld? In: Ders., *Selbstzeugnisse und Beiträge über sein Werk*. Berlin [GDR]: Union Verlag.

BRANDT, Leon, 1981: *Abschied von Tewjes Welt. Lebensbilder aus dem jiddischen Stätel*. Köln: Kiepenheuer & Witsch.

BRENNER, Michael, 1996: East European and German Jews in Postwar Germany, 1945–50. In: Michal Y. Bodemann, ed., *Jews, Germans, Memory. Reconstructions of Jewish Life in Germany*. Ann Arbor, Mich.: University of Michigan Press, 49–63.

BURG, Josef, 1988: *Ein Gesang über allen Gesängen*. Leipzig: St. Benno.

[Chorley-]Schulz, Miriam, 2021: *Keyner iz nit fargesn: Soviet Yiddish Antifascism and the Holocaust*. PhD Dissertation, Columbia University, New York, NY.

[Chorley-]Schulz, Miriam, 2021: "The Deepest Self Denies the Face": Polish Jewish Intellectuals and the Birth of the "Soviet Marrano". In: Katharina Friedla and Markus Nesselrodt, eds., *Polish Jews in the Soviet Union (1939–1959). History and Memory of Deportation, Exile, and Survival*. Boston, Mass.: Academic Studies Press, 143–174.

Clark, Katerina, 2011: *Moscow, the Fourth Rome. Stalinism, Cosmopolitanism, and the Evolution of Soviet Culture, 1931–1941*. Cambridge, Mass.: Harvard University Press.

Clark, Katerina, 2021: *Eurasia without Borders. The Dream of a Leftist Literary Commons, 1919–1943*. Cambridge, Mass.: Harvard University Press.

Coors, Maria, 2019: Tewje in Deutschland: Zu Übersetzungspraktiken von Werken eines jiddischen Autors im Kontext der deutsch-jüdischen Geschichte des 20. Jahrhunderts. In: Markus Krah, Mirjam Thulin, and Bianca Pick, eds., *Transformative Translations in Jewish History and Culture*. Potsdam: Universitätsverlag Potsdam, 57–72.

Duhr, Peter, 1956: *Inferno*. Berlin [GDR]: Rütten & Loening.

Estraikh, Gennady, 2018: The Life, Death, and Afterlife of the Jewish Anti-Fascist Committee. In: *East European Jewish Affairs* 48 (2): 139–148.

Frank, Anne, 1957: *Das Tagebuch der Anne Frank*. Berlin [GDR]: Union Verlag.

Fulbrook, Mary, 2013: East Germans in a Post-Nazi State. Communities of Experience, Connection, and Identification. In: Mary Fulbrook, and Andrew I. Port, eds., *Becoming East German. Socialist Structures and Sensibilities after Hitler*. New York, NY: Berghahn Books, 33–55.

Gal-Ed, Efrat, 2016: *Niemandssprache. Itzik Manger – ein europäischer Dichter*. Berlin: Jüdischer Verlag im Suhrkamp Verlag.

Geller, Jay Howard, 2005: *Jews in Post-Holocaust Germany, 1945–1953*. Cambridge, Mass.: Cambridge University Press.

Goldenbogen, Nora, 2006: Neu beginnen. Über die Anfänge jüdischen Lebens in Dresden und Sachsen nach 1945. In: Helga Krohn, and Gudrun Maierhof, eds., *Deutschland – trotz alledem? Jüdische Sozialarbeit nach 1945*. Frankfurt a. M.: Fachhochschul-Verlag, 97–121.

Graf, Philipp, 2018: "Dem Gesetzentwurf gibt das Zentralsekretariat seine Zustimmung" – Eine neue Sicht auf die Restitutionsfrage in der Sowjetischen Besatzungszone. In: *Jahrbuch des Simon-Dubnow-Instituts* 17: 271–298.

Grossman, Jeffrey A., 2009: Das Fortleben des Jiddischen vor und nach 1945. Übersetzungen und Transformationen. In: Eva Lezzi, and Dorothea M. Salzer, eds., *Dialog der Disziplinen. Jüdische Studien und Literaturwissenschaft*. Berlin: Metropol-Verlag, 77–106.

Grothe, Horst, 1963: Sammelpunkt Shelasnastraße. Dokumentation zum 20. Jahrestag des Aufstandes im Warschauer Ghetto. In: *Deutschlandsender*. Deutsches Rundfunkarchiv Potsdam, 2013258000.

Gruschka, Roland, 2016: Der Blick auf das ‚Ostjudentum'. Deutsche Übersetzungen jiddischer Literatur 1897–1933. In: Hans Otto Horch, ed., *Handbuch der deutsch-jüdischen Literatur*. Berlin. De Gruyter Oldenbourg, 375–387.

Halpern, Ber, 1988: *Ein Dreier zum Sabbat. Ostjüdische Geschichten*. Leipzig: St. Benno.

Herf, Jeffrey, 1997: *Divided Memory. The Nazi Past in the Two Germanys*. Cambridge, Mass.: Cambridge University Press.

Hermlin, Stephan, 1966: Gesang der Klage und der Zuversicht. Zu einer Sammlung jiddischer Dichtung. In: *Neue Zeit* 22 (212), 10 September 1966: 7.

Hirsch, Rudolf, 1962: *Die Heimfahrt des Rabbi Chanina und andere Erzählungen und Geschichten aus dem Jiddischen*. Berlin [GDR]: Union Verlag.

Hirsch, Rudolf, 1966: *Ghetto. Berichte aus dem Warschauer Ghetto: 1939–1945*. Berlin [GDR]: Union Verlag.

Janke, Jutta, ed., 1975: *Von armen Schnorrern und weisen Rabbis. Witze, Anekdoten und Sprüche*. Berlin [GDR]: Volk und Welt.

Kelletat, Andreas F., 2021: Hedda Zinner, 1905–1994. In: *Germersheimer Übersetzerlexikon UeLEX* (online), <http://uelex.de/uebersetzer/zinner-hedda/>, March 6, 2023.

Krah, Markus, 2018: *American Jewry and the Re-Invention of the East European Jewish Past*. Berlin a. o.: de Gruyter.

Kulbak, Moische, 1973: *Die Selmenianer*. Berlin [GDR]: Volk und Welt.

Lewinsky, Tamar, 2008: *Displaced Poets. Jiddische Schriftsteller im Nachkriegsdeutschland, 1945–1951*. Göttingen: Vandenhoeck & Ruprecht.

Links, Christoph, 2010: Witt, Hubert. In: Helmut Müller-Enbergs et. al., eds., *Wer war wer in der DDR*. Berlin: Christoph Links Verlag, 1434f.

Mark, Ber, 1947 מאַרק, בער: **אויפֿשטאַנד פֿון וואַרשעווער געטאָ. דאָס בוך פֿון גבֿורה.** לאָדש: פֿאַרלאַג דאָס נײַע לעבן.

Mark, Ber, 1953: *Powstanie w getcie warszawskim na tle ruchu oporu w Polsce: geneza i przebieg*. Warsaw: Żydowski Instytut Historyczny.

Mark, Ber, ed., 1955 מאַרק, בער: **צווישן לעבן און טויט.** וואַרשע: ייִדיש־בוך.

Mark, Ber, 1957: *Der Aufstand im Warschauer Ghetto. Entstehung und Verlauf*. Berlin [GDR]: Dietz.

Marquardt, Hans, 1984: Nachwort. In: Sholem Aleichem 1984, 175–179.

Moykher-Sforim, Mendele, 1978: Mendele Mojcher-Sforim: *Fischke der Lahme. Bettlerroman*. Leipzig: Reclam.

Nalewajko-Kulikov, Joanna, 2010: Three Colors: Grey. Study for a Portrait of Bernard Mark. In: *Holocaust. Studies and Materials* 2: 205–226.

Nałkowska, Zofia, 1956: *Medaillons*. Berlin [GDR]: Aufbau-Verlag.

Niether, Hendrik, 2014: *Leipziger Juden und die DDR. Eine Existenzerfahrung im Kalten Krieg*. Göttingen: Vandenhoeck & Ruprecht.

Niven, Bill, 2010: Remembering Nazi Anti-Semitism in the GDR. In: Bill Niven, and Chloe Paver, eds., *Memorialization in Germany since 1945*. Basingstoke: Palgrave Macmillan, 205–213.

Opoczyński, Perec, 1954 אָפּאָטשינסקי, פּרץ: רעפּאָרטאַזשן פֿון וואַרשעווער געטאָ. וואַרשע: ייִדיש־בוך.

Peitsch, Helmut: Antifaschistisches Verständnis der eigenen jüdischen Herkunft in Texten von DDR-SchriftstellerInnen. In: Elke-Vera Kotowski, ed., *Das Kulturerbe deutschsprachiger Juden. Eine Spurensuche in den Ursprungs-, Transit- und Emigrationsländern*. Berlin: De Gruyter Oldenbourg, 117–142.

Peretz, Yitskhok Leybush, 1969: Izchok Lejb Perez: *Baal Schem als Ehestifter und andere Erzählungen*. Berlin [GDR]: Volk und Welt.

Pickhan, Gertrud, 2009: Yiddishkayt and Class Consciousness: the Bund and Its Minority Concept. In: *East European Jewish Affairs* 39 (2): 249–263.

Roskies, David G., 1999: *The Jewish Search for a Usable Past*. Bloomington, Ind.: Indiana University Press.

Rudnicki, Adolf, 1959: *Żywe i martwe morze*. Warsaw: Ksiazka i wiedza.

Rudnicki, Adolf, 1960: *Das lebende und das tote Meer*. Erzählungen. Berlin [GDR]: Aufbau-Verlag.

Schwarz, Jan: Speaking Tevye der milkhiker in Translation: Performance, Humour, and World Literature. In: Gennady Estraikh, ed., *Translating Sholem Aleichem. History, Politics and Art*. London: Legenda, 199–214.

Shabad, Theodore, 1970: German Amends to Yiddish Poets. In: *New York Times*, 1 December 1970: 59.

Shandler, Jeffrey, 2005: *Adventures in Yiddishland. Postvernacular Language and Culture*. Berkeley, Calif.: University of California Press.

Shneer, David, 2004: *Yiddish and the Creation of Soviet Jewish Culture. 1918–1930*. Cambridge, Mass.: Cambridge University Press.

Shneer, David, 2015: Yiddish Music and East German Antifascism: Lin Jaldati, Post-Holocaust Jewish Culture and the Cold War. In: *The Leo Baeck Institute Year Book* 60: 207–234.

Shneer, David, 2021: Singing between Two Worlds: Lin Jaldati and Yiddish Music in Cold War Europe and Divided Berlin, 1945–1953. In: *Journal of Modern Jewish Studies* 20 (2): 248–273.

Sholem Aleichem [Aleykhem], 1955: Scholem Alejchem: *Die Geschichten Tewjes des Milchhändlers*. Berlin [GDR]: Volk und Welt.

Sholem Aleichem [Aleykhem], 1965: Scholem Alejchem: *Der Sohn des Kantors*. Berlin [GDR]: Volk und Welt.

Sholem Aleichem [Aleykhem], 1969: Scholem Alejchem: *Der behexte Schneider*. Berlin [GDR]: Volk und Welt.

Sholem Aleichem [Aleykhem], 1984: Scholem Alejchem: *Tewje, der Milchmann*. Leipzig: Reclam.

Sholem Aleichem [Aleykhem], 1990: Scholem Alejchem: *Der Fortschritt in Kasrilewke und andere alte Geschichten aus neuerer Zeit*. Berlin: Buchverlag Der Morgen.

Shternshis, Anna, 2006: *Soviet and Kosher. Jewish Popular Culture in the Soviet Union, 1923–1939*. Bloomington, Ind.: Indiana University Press.

Singer, Isaac Bashevis, 1980: *Satan in Goraj*. Berlin [GDR]: Volk und Welt.

Skalov, Zalmen, 1954 סקאַלאָוו, זלמן: **דער האַקנקרייץ**. וואַרשע: ייִדיש־בוך.

Sneh, Perla 2017: Khurbn Yiddish: An Absent Absence. In: Wendy Lower, and Lauren Faulkner Rossi, eds., *Lessons and Legacies XII. New Directions in Holocaust Research and Education*. Chicago, Ill.: Northwestern University Press, 215–231.

Stach, Stephan, 2016a: Sein Partisanenstückwerk war ein Meisterstück. Ins staatlich kontrollierte DDR–Verlagswesen brachte er frischen Wind. Zum Tod des Leipziger Lektors Hubert Witt. In: *Frankfurter Allgemeine Zeitung* 67 (250), 26 October 2016: 12.

Stach, Stephan, 2016b: 'The Spirit of the Time Left Its Stamp on These Works': Writing the History of the Shoah at the Jewish Historical Institute in Stalinist Poland. In: *Remembrance and Solidarity. Studies in 20th Century European History* 5: 185–212.

Stach, Stephan, 2022: "The Jewish diaries […] undergo one edition after the other." Early Polish Holocaust Documentation, East German Anti-Fascism and the Emergence of Holocaust Memory in Socialism. In: Kata Bohus, Peter Hallama, and Stephan Stach, eds., *Growing in the Shadow of Antifascism. Remembering the Holocaust in Communist Eastern Europe*. Budapest: Central European University Press, 275–301.

Taterka, Thomas, 2010: „Das kann dem deutschen Leser nicht zugemutet werden." Polnische Literatur über Konzentrationslager und Judenvernichtung in der DDR. In: Micha Brumlik, and Karol Sauerland, eds., *Umdeuten, verschweigen, erinnern. Die späte Aufarbeitung des Holocaust in Osteuropa*. Frankfurt a. M.: Campus, 203–224.

Walther, Alexander, 2019: Jewish Anti-Fascism? "Kristallnacht" Remembrance in the GDR between Propaganda and Jewish Self-Assertion. In: Wolf Gruner, and Steven J. Ross, eds., *New Perspectives on Kristallnacht. After 80 Years, the Nazi Pogrom in Global Comparison*. West Lafayette, Ind.: Purdue University Press, 259–282.

Walther, Alexander, 2020a: (Jüdische) Historiker*innen in der DDR und die Erforschung von Judentum und Shoah. In: Jörg Ganzenmüller, ed., *Jüdisches Leben in Deutschland und Europa nach der Shoah*. Köln: Böhlau, 195–218.

Walther, Alexander, 2020b: Helmut Eschwege and Jewish Life in the German Democratic Republic. In: Jay Howard Geller, and Michael Meng, eds., *Re-*

building Jewish Life in Germany. New Brunswick, NJ: Rutgers University Press, 101 – 117.
Weber, Lothar, 2009: Der fünfte Berliner Sektor. Eine Lange Nacht über die Traditionen des Milchmanns Tewje. In: *Deutschlandfunk*, 16 May 2009, <https://www.deutschlandfunk.de/der-fuenfte-berliner-sektor.704.de.html?dram:article_id=85823>, March 6, 2023.
Witt, Hubert, ed., 1966: *Der Fiedler vom Getto. Jiddische Dichtung aus Polen*. Leipzig: Reclam.
Witt, Hubert, ed., 1969: *Meine jüdischen Augen. Grafischer Zyklus. Jiddische Dichtung aus Polen*. Leipzig: Reclam.
Wolf, Konrad, 1959: *Sterne*. DEFA-Studio für Spielfilme / Studio für Spielfilme, Sofia, GDR / Bulgaria.
Wolff, Frank, 2021: *Yiddish Revolutionaries in Migration. The Transnational History of the Jewish Labour Bund*. Chicago, Ill.: Haymarket Books.
Zinner, Hedda, 1939: *Freie Völker, freie Lieder*. Kiev: Staatsverlag der Nationalen Minderheiten der USSR.
Zinner, Hedda, 1953: *Alltag eines nicht alltäglichen Landes*. Berlin [GDR]: Verlag Kultur und Fortschritt.
Zinner, Hedda, 1989: *Selbstbefragung. Erinnerungen, Aufzeichnungen in sowjetischer Emigration*. Berlin [GDR]: Buchverlag Der Morgen.

Jalda Rebling

Yiddish in East Berlin

A Concert-Lecture

*

On 22 November 2021, at Friedrich Schiller University in Jena, Germany, during the second winter of the Covid-19 pandemic, Jalda Rebling, Daniel Weltlinger, and Tobias Morgenstern gave a virtual concert-lecture as part of the POLIN Museum of the History of Polish Jews GEOP workshop "Hidden in Plain Sight: Yiddish in the Socialist Bloc and its Transnationality, 1941–1991." Rebling narrated the story of Yiddish music in East Germany [GDR] and the essential role the Jaldati-Rebling family played within it. The narration was interspersed with well-known and lesser-known Yiddish songs out of the repertoire of Lin Jaldati, famed Yiddish performer, antifascist activist in the German Democratic Republic and Rebling's mother. The concert-lecture followed by a Q&A was joined by dozens across the globe through Zoom and commenced with an early 1950s recording of Jaldati singing Yiddish poet and songwriter Mordkhe Gebirtig's (1877–1942) folksongs אַמאָל איז געווען אַ מעשׂה [*Amol iz geven a mayse*, Once upon a time there was a story] followed by the trio's performance of היי, ציגעלעך [*Hey, tsigele*, Hey, little goats]. The concert-lecture was followed by a conversation between Jalda Rebling, Miriam Chorley-Schulz, and Alexander Walther that was edited for length and clarity. The song lyrics were edited, as well.

*

Lin Jaldati, Eberhard Rebling, and their daughter Kathinka, 1946. Jalda Rebling's private collection

This picture was taken in 1946 when Lin had returned from Bergen-Belsen, and my father [Eberhard Rebling] and sister Kathinka had come out of their respective hiding places. Lin was performing Yiddish songs in Amsterdam at the Sholem Anski Yiddish Club in the middle of the 1930s. In 1936, my father came to the Netherlands. He had left Germany because he hated what was going on there. He fell in love with her. And, although he was a professor of musicology, he had never heard Yiddish songs – so she taught him.

But Yiddish in Amsterdam? How come? Lin grew up in the Nieuwe Kerkstraat in Amsterdam, a street where mostly Jews from Eastern Europe lived, so her daily language was Yiddish. When the Germans entered the Netherlands in 1940, Lin and Eberhard joined the resistance.[1] Eventually, they were betrayed. Lin and her sister went from Westerbork to Auschwitz, and later to Bergen-Belsen in the same trains that Anne and Margot Frank were in. They met the Frank sisters, and the Dutch girls took care of each other. Her parents and her brother Jakob were murdered in Auschwitz.

Shortly after Jaldati's return, she started performing again. Jaldati and Rebling went to Scandinavia, to Poland, and also to Germany where they performed in Berlin. At this time, people started telling my parents, we need you here, come here. At first, they wouldn't but as the Cold War ensued, it became more difficult for them, as communists, to find work in the Netherlands. Not to mention that my father also had an argument with the Dutch

1 For the story of Jaldati and Rebling in Amsterdam under German occupation, see van Iperen 2018 and van Iperen 2020.

Communist Party. They wanted him to turn on his friends and colleagues, which he refused. They were unemployed when Nathan Notowicz,[2] whom they knew from the resistance in the Netherlands, offered them a job in East Berlin. So finally, they went to East Berlin, the most difficult decision my mother had to make in her life.

On 14 December 1952, they gave a concert at the Haus der Deutsch-Sowjetischen Freundschaft [House of German Soviet Friendship].[3] The program announced the songs as "Kampf- und Partisanenlieder" [Fighting and Partisan Songs], but what they actually performed was a diverse mix of songs, among them several *chalutzishe* [Zionist pioneers'] songs she used to perform for Jewish communities in the Netherlands, in Scandinavia, or in displaced persons [DP] camps in Germany, such as Mordkhe Gebirtig's famous song ס׳ברענט [*S'brent*, It's Burning] of 1937.[4]

1) ס׳ברענט! ברידערלעך ס׳ברענט!	1) It's burning! Brothers it's burning!
אוי, אונדזער אָרעם שטעטל נעבעך ברענט!	Oy, our poor shtetl alas is burning!
בייזע ווינטן מיט ירגזון	Angry winds with rage
רײַסן, ברעכן און צעבלאָזן	Are tearing, smashing and blowing
שטאַרקער נאָך די ווילדע פֿלאַמען,	Higher still the wild flames,
אַלץ אַרום שוין ברענט.	All around now burns!
[…]	[…]
4) ס׳ברענט! ברידערלעך ס׳ברענט!	4) It's burning! Brothers it's burning!
די הילף איז נאָר אין אײַך אַליין געווענדט.	Help can only come from you.
אויב דאָס שטעטל איז אײַך טײַער,	If our shtetl is dear to you,
לעשט מיט אײַער אייגן בלוט,	Extinguish the fire with your very blood,
באַווײַזט אַז איר דאָס קענט.	Prove that you can do it!
שטייט ניט, ברידער, אָט אַזוי זיך	Don't just stand there, brothers,
מיט פֿאַרלייגטע הענט.	With folded hands!
שטייט ניט, ברידער. לעשט דאָס פֿײַער –	Don't stand there, brothers. Put out the fire –
אונדזער שטעטל ברענט![5]	Our shtetl is burning!

2 Nathan Notowicz (1911–1968), studied music in Düsseldorf, emigrated to Amsterdam in 1933, member of the communist resistance, returned to Germany in 1946, was appointed professor of music history in East Berlin in 1950.

3 Mass organization in the GDR promoting friendly ties with the Soviet Union.

4 Scholars agree that Mordkhe Gebirtig wrote *S'brent* in 1937 in response to the pogroms in Przytyk (1936) and Brisk (1937) in interwar Poland. During the חורבן [*khurbn,* destruction, Holocaust], it was adopted particularly by Jewish partisans as a symbol of defiance and continued to play a prominent role in postwar Yiddish song culture and *khurbn* memory. On Gebirtig, see Schneider 2000, von Seltmann 2018.

5 Gebirtig 1946, 33, 34.

HAUS DER KULTUR DER SOWJETUNION

Zentrales Haus der Gesellschaft für Deutsch-Sowjetische Freundschaft

Sonntag, den 14. Dezember 1952 19.00 Uhr, Marmorsaal

Musikabend

„Kampf- und Partisanenlieder"

PROGRAMM

Hej zigelech, Ballade	Mordechaj Gebirtik
Raisele, Liebeslied	Mordechaj Gebirtik
Schlof schojn, majn hungerik mejdele, Wiegenlied	Mordechaj Gebirtik
Zip zapekl, Spottlied	Volkslied
Drei ostjüdische Tänze für Klavier . .	Alexander Krejn
Awremele un Josele, Kinderlied . . .	Mordechaj Gebirtik
's Drimlen fajgl ojf di zwajgn, Wiegenlied	aus einem KZ
In Kamf	Kampflied 1905
Rabojssaj, Spottlied	Volkslied
Gamal gamali, Kamelenlied	Jemenitisches Volkslied
A Pintale	Volkslied
Chanele lernt loschon kojdesch . . .	Volkslied
Es brennt (1942)	Mordechaj Gebirtik
Zwei Niguniem für Klavier	Eberhard Rebling
Das Lied von Birobidschan	Volkslied
Wer der erschter wet lachn, Kinderlied	Mordechaj Gebirtik
Leierkastenlied, Bettlerlied	Volkslied
Partisanenlied (1942)	Hirsch Glik

Ausführende:

Lin Jaldati (Sopran), **Dr. Eberhard Rebling** (Klavier)

(234) Robert Fröhlich, O 34, Tilsiter Str. 22 — 4189 482575/52 AfIDDR

Program of Jaldati's concert "Kampf- und Partisanenlieder", 14 December 1952, East Berlin. Archive of the Academy of Arts, Berlin, Lin-Jaldati-Archiv, Nr. 71.

At the time, Jaldati could not have known that only months before, on 12 August 1952, the most famous Soviet Yiddish writers and intellectuals had been murdered in Moscow. When I tell people that my mother gave such a concert in December 1952, they don't believe it – staging such a concert in East Berlin and at the house German-*Soviet* friendship at that.

She gave numerous other performances of Yiddish songs in the years to follow, and people loved her. Still today, people approach me telling me about how they remember her performances. In East Germany, Jaldati had a very deep impact on people. She did what writer Anna Seghers had asked her to do at the World Peace Conference in 1949 in Paris: help clean the 'rubble' from people's heads – namely the spiritual, if not ideological rubble that Nazi Germany left behind rather than the physical one that so many other so-called *Trümmerfrauen* [rubble women] helped clear during those days in order to reconstruct German cities that lay in ruins.

In the 1960s, Jaldati met the Yiddish singer Perry Friedman from Canada. While he lived in our house for several weeks, Friedman and Jaldati began a Hootenanny: gatherings of young people who were interested in folk songs and music and sang together. In the revolutionary spirit of the 1960s, people did not only sing Yiddish songs at these hootenanny clubs, but songs from around the world, including songs of protests. It was in one of those clubs, later called Singeklubs [singing clubs], that I, for the first time, performed a Yiddish song in public.[6] The song was היי! דזשאַנקאָיע [*Hey! Dzhankoye*, Hey! Dzhankoi] – a revolutionary Soviet Yiddish song about Jewish life on a collective farm in the North Crimean Dzhankoi after the October Revolution of 1917.

אַז מען פֿאָרט קיין זעוואַסטאָפּאָל,	When you go to Sevastopol,
איז ניט ווײַט פֿון זימפֿעראָפּאָל,	Not too far from Simferopol,
דאָרטן איז אַ סטאַנציע פֿאַראַן.	There's a little depot there.
ווער דאַרף זוכן נײַע גליקן?	Why seek your luck elsewhere?
ס'איז אַ סטאַנציע אַן אַנטיקל	It's an old depot
אין דזשאַנקאָיע, דזשאַן, דזשאַן, דזשאַן.	in Dzhankoye, Dzhan, Dzhan, Dzhan.
היי דזשאַן, היי דזשאַנקאָיע	Hey, Dzhan, hey Dzhankoye,
היי דזשאַנווילי, היי דזשאַנקאָיע	Hey, Dzhanvili, hey Dzhankoye,
היי דזשאַנקאָיע, דזשאַן, דשזאַן, דשזאַן.	Hey Dzhankoye, Dzhan, Dzhan, Dzhan.

6 Bruhn 2022, Brauer 2020.

ענטפֿערט ייִדן אויף מײַן קשיא	Jews, answer my question,
וווּ׳ס מײַן ברודער, וווּ׳ס אַבראַשע?	Where's my brother Abrashe?
ס׳גייט בײַ אים דער טראַקטאָר ווי אַ באַן.	He who rides his tractor like a train.
די מומע לאה בײַ אַ קאָסילקע	Aunt Leah is at the mower,
ביילע בײַ דער מאָלאָטילקע	Bella is working the thresher,
אין דזשאַנקאָיע, דזשאַן, דזשאַן, דזשאַן.	In Dzhankoye, Dzhan, Dzhan, Dzhan.
ווער זאָגט אַז ייִדן קענען נאָר האַנדלען	Who says that Jews can only be traders
עסן פֿעטע יויך מיט מאַנדלען,	And eat fat soup with almonds
נאָר ניט זײַן קיין אַרבעטסמאַן?	But cannot be workingmen?
דאָס קאָנען זאָגן נאָר די שׂונאים.	Only our enemies can say that.
ייִדן, שפּײַט זיי אָן אין פּנים,	Jews, let's spit right in their faces,
טוט אַ קוק אויף דזשאַן, דזשאַן, דזשאַן.	Simply look at Dzhan, Dzhan, Dzhan.
אַרבעט צוזאַמען ווי ברידער,	Work together, all as brothers,
ייִדן און גויים, ווײַסע און נעגער,	Jews and Gentiles, White and Black,
פֿאַר אַ בעסערן עולם הבא.	For a better world to come.
אויף דער וועלט, אַ וועלט וואָס איז גוט,	In this world, a world that is good,
מענטשן וועלן געפֿינען ברידערשאַפֿט	Men will find brotherhood
אין דזשאַנקאָיע, דזשאַן, דזשאַן, דזשאַן.[7]	In Dzhankoye, Dzhan, Dzhan, Dzhan.

On 4 June 1967, the house of Polish-German Culture at Friedrichstraße in East Berlin held a big memorial event in honor of Mordkhe Gebirtig's twenty-fifth *yortsayt* [anniversary of his death]. Gebirtig was murdered that day in 1942 as he was forced to march from the Kraków Ghetto to the train station on the way to the Bełżec death camp. Coincidentally, it was also the beginning of the so-called Six-Day War, i.e. the Third Arab-Israeli War. The same day, the East German government asked famous (and less famous) Jews to sign a declaration condemning the aggressor: Israel. But my mother and several others refused to sign. From that moment onward she disappeared from official cultural, TV and radio programs, but she did not stop performing. During those years, she played shows in little clubs or churches, and even a concert here in Jena at the university. And she certainly continued to travel with Yiddish songs around the world.

This phase of 'blacklisting' ended in 1975 when she was suddenly invited to perform at the Berliner Festtage – a prestigious international culture festi-

7 Mlotek 2004, 227.

Lin Jaldati and Eberhard Rebling performing at the student club "Rosenkeller," Jena, 1960s. Walther Streit, Photo Archive of the Friedrich Schiller University, Jena.

val. She was asked to give a concert at the famous Deutsche Theater [German Theater] which sold out within two hours. One concert turned into three, and with that her second career took off. Until her last concert in 1987 she performed there every year.

In 1978, she was preparing a show celebrating what would have been Anne Frank's 50th birthday. Jaldati needed an actress to read from the diary, and when my father asked me: "Jalda, would you be willing to join us?" I accepted. I was an actress at the time, so I gladly agreed to reading from the diary. But when my mother asked me to sing Yiddish songs with her as well, I resisted at first! I grew up with the songs of my mother. I was singing her songs probably even before I was born. When she urged me to share the stage with her, I started to study the language. In those days, Jewish Studies did

Concert at the GDR Embassy in Washington, D.C., 1986. Archive of the Academy of Arts, Berlin, Lin-Jaldati-Archiv, Nr. 290.

not exist in the GDR, and you could not learn Yiddish at a university. But I had my teacher, Mottek Weinryb, and I read סאָוועטיש היימלאַנד [*Sovetish heymland*, Soviet Homeland] and the Polish פֿאָלקס־שטימע [*Folks-shtime*, People's Voice]. I went to the library, and I found Yiddish books. And in the end, Jaldati convinced me to sing Yiddish songs with her on the occasion of Anne Frank's 50th birthday, and the rest is history. Once my sister Kathinka joined the family ensemble in 1982, we had wonderful years performing all over the world: at Yad Vashem in Jerusalem or Hebrew Union College in New York, in Paris, Amsterdam and other places. We travelled the world as the only Yiddish theater of the German Democratic Republic.

ליד פֿון שלום[8]	**Peace Song**
שפּיל זשע מיר אַ לידעלע אין ייִדיש,	Play me a song in Yiddish
דערוועקן זאָל עס פֿרייד און ניט קיין חידוש,	It should awake pleasure and not astonishment
אָט אַלע, גרויס און קליין, זאָלן קענען דאָס פֿאַרשטיין,	So that all, young and old, can understand it
פֿון מויל צו מויל דאָס לידעלע זאָל גיין!	From mouth to mouth the song shall go!
שפּיל, שפּיל, קלעזמערל, שפּיל	Play, play, musician, play
ווייסט דאָך וואָס איך מיין און וואָס איך וויל –	You know what I mean and what I know
שפּיל, שפּיל, שפּיל אַ לידעלע פֿאַר מיר,	Play, play, play a tune for me
שפּיל אַ לידעלע מיט האַרץ און מיט געפֿיל!	Play with heart and soul!
אַ לידעלע אָן זיפֿצן און אָן טרערן	A song without sighs and tears
שפּיל אַזוי אַז אַלע זאָלן הערן,	Play so that all can hear
אַז אַלע זאָלן זען איך לעב און זינגען קען,	That all can see I'm alive and I can sing
שענער נאָך און בעסער ווי געווען.	Even more beautifully and better than it was.
שפּיל זשע מיר אַ לידל פֿון שלום!	Play me a song about peace!
זאָל שוין זײַן שלום, ניט קיין חלום!	Let there be peace already, let it not be a dream!
אַז פֿעלקער, גרויס און קליין, זאָלן קענען זיך פֿאַרשטיין,	So nations, great and small, can understand each other
אָן קריג און מילחמות זיך באַגיין.	Without engaging in battles and wars.
לאָמיר זינגען אַ לידעלע צוזאַמען,	Let's sing the little song together
ווי גוטע פֿרײַנד, ווי קינדער פֿון איין מאַמען!	Like good friends, like children of one mother!
מײַן איינציקער פֿאַרלאַנג,	My only request is that
ס'זאָל קלינגען פֿרײַ און פֿראַנק,	it rings out freely and honestly –
אין אַלעמענס געזאַנג, אויך מײַן געזאַנג![9]	In everyone's song, my song too!

After the collapse of the Berlin Wall in 1989, we were amazed to see so many Klezmer bands performing in reunited Germany, singing our songs. We had already experienced a similar hype, only ten years earlier! In the late 1970s, a renewed interest for Yiddish emerged in East Germany, parallel to the advent of the peace movement. We sang Yiddish songs against atomic weapons in the West and East. Out of this movement, the Bürgerbewegung [opposition movement in the GDR] emerged. At the time, Yiddish songs slowly took on different meanings as well. In November 1982, I performed at

8 Name used by Lin Yaldati. Conventional name: שפּיל זשע מיר אַ לידעלע אין ייִדיש [*Shpil zhe mir a lidele in yidish*, Play Me a Song in Yiddish].

9 Mlotek 2004, 240–241.

the Reglerkirche [Regler Church] in Erfurt during an event commemorating so-called *Kristallnacht* [Nazi Pogrom Night on 9 November 1938]. And the church was full.

I don't think that people filled up the church to commemorate dead Jews, at least this was not the sole reason. They came because something happened in Reglerkirche that was not part of the official cultural life of the GDR. Yiddish became a subculture – a culture of people who were starting to fight for their rights from below. And why Yiddish? Surely because of its linguistic closeness to German which makes many German-speakers believe that they intuitively understand it. But more importantly because it is the language of the powerless, as Yiddish writer Isaac Bashevis Singer said so beautifully in his Nobel Prize speech.

Interview with Jalda Rebling

By Miriam Chorley-Schulz and Alexander Walther

Alexander Walther: You mentioned that the most difficult decision in your mother's life was to go to East Germany [GDR]. When she got there, she had to make a living and started performing – not for any audience, but for the children of those responsible for her parents' and family's death. Did she ever manage to resolve this conflict?

Jalda Rebling: She never did. There were many days when she would not leave the house. She had depressive episodes, and sometimes made me stay home from school to be with her. Or she said, let's go shopping, but she simply needed someone to hold her hand. I remember my mother's hand suddenly grabbing my hand when she saw someone she mistrusted. It was difficult.

In 1985, we visited our family in Amsterdam for the first time. The entire family was together, and I asked: "Can you tell me who betrayed you in the war, who betrayed your house?" Suddenly the entire family jumped up and started shouting at each other. I was confused but I understood that I touched on a point nobody had ever talked about. Everybody was feeling somehow guilty. This lasted until 2003 when we learned the details of the betrayal, published in the book *Kopgeld* by Ad van Liempt, and that in fact not one of them had anything to do with the betrayal.[1]

My mother had a set narrative about how she spent her time in the concentration camp. Some years ago, I found a text in a book by Mirjam Pressler about Anne Frank,[2] and in it was a story that resembled the one my mother told in our Anne Frank program. I remember how difficult it was for her to utter these words, and how she was fighting with herself every time. And it was the same words. So, I asked Mirjam Pressler: "Where did you find these words?" And she replied: "It's from the archives from Otto Frank." And then I understood: right after the war, the Red Cross was collecting eyewitness

The interview includes translated transcription of the Q&A that followed the concert-lecture and of a follow-up conversation between Jalda Rebling and the editors of this volume.

1 Liempt 2002.

2 Pressler 2000.

reports, and she must have given this one to them. That was the story she stayed true to, always, but there was a lot that she never spoke about. And I think this was the biggest problem of our family.

The atmosphere in society changed after the Nazi generation died out. I always wanted to leave, but never did. I did not leave because I had to take care of my mother and my children. And when the Berlin Wall came down, one of my teenage sons said to me: "Mama, we'll stay here." And so we stayed. We experienced the fantastically creative years in the 1990s roughly until 2005, 2010. It was then that big money took over Berlin and destroyed places like the theater we created at the Hackesches Hoftheater.

Now as a *bobe* [grandmother], looking back on my life in Germany, mostly in Berlin, though I was traveling the world, it was good to be here, to sing with people, to discuss with people. And I think it's important for a Jew to raise his or her voice in this country and not to hide their Jewishness. We should be more visible in this country. People are saying: "I never met a Jew." And I always respond: "How do you know? We don't wear yellow stars anymore!" It is still very difficult. The gap the חורבן [*khurbn*, destruction, Holocaust] left us will never be filled, but we want to build a future for our children and grandchildren.

Miriam Chorley-Schulz: Jaldati also sang in the DP camp in Berlin-Schlachtensee in 1947. How did that come about?

JR: Well, Jaldati returned from Bergen-Belsen and the doctors didn't believe she would survive. But she gave her first concert in Amsterdam already in September 1945. In 1947, as soon as she could walk again, they went on tour. They were in Sweden, Finland, and Poland, and also went to Berlin. There they saw a performance by the Yiddish Theater בדרך [*Ba-derekh*, On the Way][3] organized by the cultural office in Berlin-Schlachtensee.[4] Some performers from the DP camp came together and improvised a song and cabaret program under the title שׂונאים צולהכעיס [*Soynim tselokhes*, Defying the Enemies] on a small stage. Jaldati felt at home and sang along to some of the songs. The organizer recognized her and asked her to perform on one of the next days.[5] In 1948 and 1949, they were at the World Peace Congresses in Wrocław and Prague, and that's where they met Paul Robeson.

3 Yiddish theater formed in the DP camps in Berlin.

4 Further, see Shneer 2015, Shneer 2021.

5 Jaldati, Rebling 1995, 414 f.

Lin Jaldati and Paul Robeson, Prague, 1949. Archive of the Academy of Arts, Berlin, Lin-Jaldati-Archiv, Nr. 267.

AW: I imagine your parents were quite strong characters, and it mustn't have always been easy to grow up in that household, to find your own path. But you did, nonetheless. At first, you went to acting school, then your mother asked you to perform with her on stage. You said you hesitated at first, but did you ever regret joining?

JR: No, never. It was a lot of fun. Mom had been working with dad for more than fifty years. But you know how it is. Preparing a show is not easy. Sometimes I suddenly have an idea and the musicians have to improvise and vice versa. And it was the same with my parents, just that now there were the three of us on stage. But it was more on the fun side.

The real problem ran much, much deeper. When I was a teenager, and I was a very nasty teenager, a hippie, I had to find my path. In 1967 after the war, I wore a large *magen david* [Star of David] just to provoke. In those years I was lucky. We VIP children were still protected. So I was able to study, nobody prevented me from studying and I could live my life. Several years later, times changed in East Germany.

MCS: Apart from your Jewish identity, you are also a woman and so is your mother. To what extent did that play a role?

JR: I was socialized in the GDR. When Anna [Rebling's wife] tells me – she comes from West Germany – that she wasn't allowed to open a bank account as a woman until 1974, and her mother brought her daughters solemnly to the bank to open the account, I cannot believe it. At that age I had been earning my own money for some time. For us GDR women, although we know today that not everything went well, but for us it was completely normal to stand on our own two feet. And the first time I was consciously discriminated against as a woman was when I came back from the US [as a trained cantor] and said: "Well guys, now I know it all, I'm teaching everybody." And even the wonderful Rabbi [William] Wolff[6] from Schwerin, when I said I'll come and do the Seder ceremony, he said: "You can't do that, you're a woman." So, until then, that had not really played a role in my life.

AW: Can you describe the Yiddish scene in the GDR a bit more? How did people get to know each other? Did they support each other or not?

JR: A Yiddish 'scene' is a bit of a stretch. There was no Yiddish scene in the GDR. There were a lot of Jewish artists, Jewish musicians and Jewish scientists who all knew each other, who were part of my parents' circle of friends. It is this Jewish intellectual circle I grew up in which makes me believe I grew up in a different GDR than everyone else.

There were always people who were sent to my mom, especially those who came from Poland. And there are two stories of two different Yiddish-speaking women who came from Poland, and they both told me the same story. One, Sarah Bialas, came in 1963, and the Weinryb family, they came a little later in 1968 during the antisemitic campaign that happened in Poland at the time. Both somehow ended up with my mom; somebody sent them to her, because: do you want to arrive in Germany as Jews? Not necessarily. You can't imagine it today, but all these old Nazis were still around. And you recognized them immediately. You recognized them all. I can't tell you why.

6 William Wolff (1927–2020), born in Berlin, fled to London in 1939, journalist, ordained rabbi in 1984, served in various congregations, 2002–2015 State Rabbi of Mecklenburg-Western Pomerania.

Anyway, they were sitting with my mother and both women told me that Jaldati said to them: "Get out of here, get out, take your children, get out to America or Israel, don't stay here."

My mother had different faces. On the one hand, she was the woman who studied very carefully who was trying to mess with her and whom she can trust – she had an uncanny instinct for people. On the other hand, she was the woman who allowed herself to be persuaded to go to East Germany for the sake of realizing a dream of an ideal world – '*moshiakh* [Messiah] now' – which she saw did not actually work.

There was a Jewish intellectual scene, but not a Yiddish scene. There were always people with whom Yiddish was spoken. But there was no real Yiddish scene. That didn't exist until after 1975, when a turning point took place in Germany: people suddenly began to take an interest in Yiddish and the whole Wandervogel [Wandering Bird] movement began to sing Yiddish, not knowing what they were singing.

AW: In the 1980s some people, mostly from non-Jewish contexts, started to deal with Yiddish, like the band *Aufwind* [Upswing],[7] Karsten Troyke[8] and others. Jürgen Rennert[9] started much earlier, as did others. What was that like? Was that strange, nice to observe, or did you think, what kind of people are they?

JR: Well, I was always happy to see someone dealing with Yiddish. I didn't start drawing and learning Hebrew letters basically until when I was pregnant with my second child in 1975. I didn't understand at all why. I just started to learn Hebrew and I didn't realize that all this would become so important in my life. My interest coincided with the "Klezmer Revival" and people in the US who had the same intention. That it occurred simultaneously to a gigantic comeback for Jaldati was also due to a generational change. It was then that

7 *Aufwind*, founded in East Berlin in 1984, performed concerts in and made trips to socialist states.

8 Karsten Troyke (*1960), singer, actor, has been performing since the 1980s, including Yiddish songs.

9 Jürgen Rennert (born 1943 in West Berlin) is a German writer. Having grown up with his grandmother in West Berlin, Rennert moved to East Berlin in 1953 to live with his parents. In addition to being a writer and poet in his own right, he emerged as an editor, poet, and translator of literature from Yiddish, Russian, Czech and Hungarian. Under the leadership of Jalda Rebling, he founded the "Days of Yiddish Culture" in East Berlin in 1987 together with Stefan Schreiner.

the first neo-Nazis appeared, that is, the first conscious next Nazi generation in the GDR, wearing FDJ [Freie Deutsche Jugend, Free German Youth, the GDR's youth organization] shirts. This generational change triggered something. Other grandchildren started to ask questions of their grandparents. How was the *khurbn* possible?

We suddenly found ourselves in this Yiddish boom ten years prior to the one in the Federal Republic of Germany. That had to do with the fact that GDR authorities certainly didn't want to be seen as antisemitic. They had to perform a balancing act between the position that, on the one hand, as antifascists they support all minorities and, on the other hand, they flirted with their Arab friends and talked about the "aggressor Israel" and so on. That was already a contradiction. In 1967 with the 'Six-Day War,' when Jaldati refused to sign that declaration, I was walking around with a thick Star of David around my neck. An FDJ functionary was irritated and said, take that off, that's the sign of the imperialistic aggressor. And I said: "No, those are my grandparents who were murdered in Auschwitz." He got red ears and didn't know what to say anymore.

If you held a memorial somewhere to commemorate *khurbn* victims with Yiddish songs on 9 November, nothing happened. The police might have broken up the unregistered meeting, but nobody was arrested. I only know of one story of someone who was expelled because of an alleged Zionist conspiracy, but he belonged to the Havemann circle.[10] So it was crystal clear what had actually happened. But apart from that, you could speak Yiddish, no one ever knew what to think. And that's where an alternative scene emerged, and that includes Troyke, *Aufwind*. Rennert is a bit different, I don't know how he came to Yiddish. Then there was [Andrej] Jendrusch, who did great translations.[11] But I didn't realize at the time that I was the only Jew in the group.

AW: I would be interested to know how performances were organized. Since it was the GDR, I imagine it to be very bureaucratic, but then a lot of it sounds very improvised. How did you organize things?

10 Robert Havemann (1910–1982), German chemist, resistance fighter during National Socialism, survived the war in imprisonment, came into trouble with the Socialist Party in the early 1960s and was put under house arrest in 1976 until his death.

11 Andrej Jendrusch (*1958), studied Romance languages, translator and interpreter, translated from Yiddish and Ladino.

JR: Like a sleepwalker. I just did it. How often did we have an event somewhere and someone stood there and said: "Who's taking responsibility here?" – "I am." – "But don't you have to ask your boss?" – "I don't have a boss. I'm just going to do what we've always done." That may sound a lot like sleepwalking to a historian in retrospect. In Boulder, at the University of Colorado, David Shneer asked me in his class:

"Who funded your concerts?"

"What do you mean?"

"Well, who funded your projects?"

"We had an idea and then we just implemented it. And then we wrote letters to different promoters, and they invited us."

"Yes, but who financed the concerts that you gave?"

"That went through the cultural association."

This went on until he got it out of me that the GDR financed culture. I simply didn't understand the question. For his students it was a surprise. The state GDR financed and paid for Jewish culture?! But yes, we just did it. We, my two musicians and I were invited by churches or the Kulturbund [Cultural Association, the cultural mass organization in the GDR] and other alternative places, student cellars like the Moritzbastei in Leipzig or elsewhere. I have been Lin's *sheliekh* [messenger] to go out to the little *shtetelekh* she didn't want to go anymore.

Think of the 'Days of Yiddish Culture.' In 1984, we were in Zurich with the Jaldati Rebling Ensemble at the First European Yiddish Festival – a gigantic event, and a great success for us. We met colleagues from all over Europe there. And on the way back from Zurich I said: "Okay, European Yiddish Festival, but where are the people from Bucharest? Where are the people from Warsaw?" I had already heard rumors of a group in Vilna, probably through סאָוועטיש היימלאַנד [*Sovetish heymland*, Soviet Homeland] or something. "But Berlin had actually been a Yiddish center in the 1920s so we should organize such a Yiddish festival in Berlin." – "How do you want to do that?" The first person I talked to was Eugen Gollomb in Leipzig.[12] Eugen Gollomb was in the early 1980s one of my very important teachers, who was also willing to teach a woman. Helmut Aris[13] swept me off my feet like a piece of dirt, but

12 Eugen Gollomb (1917–1988), chairman of the Jewish Religious Community of Leipzig, 1967–1988.

13 Helmut Aris (1908–1987), Chairman of the Jewish Community of Dresden, 1953–1987, President of the Association of Jewish Communities in the GDR, 1962–1987.

Gollomb was willing to teach me. I regularly went to Leipzig and sat with him and questioned him. And he had many answers as well as new questions. He said, I'd like to do that, I have some standing in the city of Leipzig, but I can't get a Yiddish festival through here. Then I went to Dresden. All my friends there said, great idea, no chance.

In East Berlin, there were "residential area clubs" – locations where residents could meet and stage little events. There was one at Czarnikauer Straße, this strange neighborhood in East Berlin: Kopenhagener Straße, Dänenstraße, which led to the station at Bornholmer Brücke, really in the middle of Prenzlauer Berg. That was a really exciting place. There were readings there, concerts, Yiddish as well. We read Der Nister there and everything we could get a hold of. And it was run by Liane Düsterhöft.[14] Then the gasometers were blown up under great protest in East Berlin. But, due to the protests and in the course of the 750-years Berlin celebration at the time and all this nonsense, suddenly old became chic again and they left these administrative gasometer buildings standing. A theater was set up there, which was to be called Theater unterm Dach [Theater under the Roof]. Liane Düsterhöft was commissioned by the SED district leadership to run this theater. She said: "I'm collecting your ideas now. What ideas do you have?" I said: "I have one. Three days of Yiddish culture." – "Oh yes, then we'll do that." So I gathered everyone from Berlin: Jürgen Rennert, Jutta Janke,[15] *Aufwind* of course, Karsten Troyke, Andrej Jendrusch, Peter Kelm, a physicist who did beautiful Yiddish translation, Beate Petras, she also translated Yiddish. Without money. No one was paid for the work, no one. Rennert made a little booklet, and that was it. I had a Yiddish typewriter, I got it in 1986 in the US from the National Yiddish Book Center in Amherst. We did a three-day program and announced it all over Berlin. We had the house. There were no fees or anything like that. And then we just did it.

MCS: And who came?

JR: On the last page of the *Berliner Zeitung* [Berlin Newspaper] theater

[14] Liane Düsterhöft (*1936), actress, studied at the Ernst Busch Drama School in East Berlin.

[15] Jutta Janke (1932–2004), studied Polish studies at Humboldt University in East Berlin, editor at Volk & Welt publishing company, initiated numerous translations from Polish and some from Yiddish to German, promoted authors like Stanisław Lem in the GDR.

Program booklet of the first 'Days of Yiddish Culture,' 1987, and the typewriter from Amherst. Jalda Rebling's private collection. Picture by Judith Kessler.

performances were announced, usually from the Staatsoper [State Opera], Deutsches Theater, and so on. And at the bottom it said one day: Three Days of Yiddish Culture, Kulturhaus im Ernst-Thälmann-Park. The event was sold out within three hours. Well, with 80 seats, what do you want, but still – something was in the air. Then the ZDF [Zweites Deutsches Fernsehen; consortium of the public-law broadcasting institutions of the Federal Republic of Germany] signed up and then those in the SED district management woke up. I needed someone to take responsibility for the 'cultural policy' as it were. I went to Weißensee to the newly founded "committee for entertainers." They tried to get us freelancers, 'entertainers,' which included me, under one roof, just like the visual artists' association and the writers' association. The managing director was Eike Sturmhöfel[16] and we knew each other. I told him I needed this piece of paper from him. "Yes, sure, go ahead. Listen, you write me

16 Eike Sturmhöfel (1941 – 1995), studied art history and German literature, director of a student theater, employed at the cultural department of the FDJ leadership, 1987 – 1989 director of festivals and competitions in the General Directorate at the Committee for Entertainment Arts, after 1990 cook and newspaper vendor.

something and I'll sign it." Then I wrote something, he reworded it a bit, put it on his letterhead and then they took over the "cultural-political responsibility." We then moved from the last page of the *Berliner Zeitung* to the first page of *Neues Deutschland* [New Germany, the SED's central newspaper] – another naïve thing. How should I have known that [GDR leader Erich] Honecker wanted to go to America and believed in the *Protocols of the Elders of Zion*? He thought, be good to the Jews and then you will get an invitation to the White House. And suddenly they started to support Jewish culture. Within a few weeks, I was part of the GDR's committee working on what the UNESCO had announced as the "World Decade for Cultural Development." And suddenly with a UNESCO sign in my hand, I was able to open doors – such as inviting people from Warsaw or Bucharest to perform in the GDR.

Then there was the dream to get the Yiddishists from East and West together. The Wall fell. Nobody was responsible for anything. So, I thought, that's it, we will not continue. And then we got an invitation from the UNESCO in Bonn. We went to Bonn and told them what we are doing and they decided to support us. In this way, we got money to continue the festival and were finally able to invite our friends from the YIVO – Institute for Jewish Research in New York and the ייִדישער וויסנשאַפֿטלעכער אינסטיטוט [*Yidisher visnshaftlekher institut*, Jewish Scientific Institute, YIVO] in Vilna. And we brought them together and decided to focus on a special local Yiddish culture every year.

This is that matter-of-factness with which we have always lived. And because I was independent – I mean, in the GDR, rent and electricity and milk and butter weren't a factor. And if you didn't pay your rent for a month, that wasn't a problem. Sure, I broke my leg in 1981, and I broke it pretty badly, and I walked with crutches for half a year. I would have starved to death with two children in the GDR if my family hadn't helped. But otherwise, the way we think about it today – how do we pay the rent, and can you still afford heating or something – that wasn't up for discussion at all.

AW: Can you say something about the reactions of the audience? There is a short text from your father in which he writes that after the concerts many young people always came and wanted to talk.[17] What did they ask? And what were they like?

17 Rebling 1988.

JR: Yes, very, very often. They in fact asked about Israel very quickly. And then I told them: "People, I need fifteen minutes to tell you about history, history that you don't know." And then I told them about the British occupation and so on. These were very common questions. Other questions went in the direction of Yiddish: what is Yiddish? Where does it come from? What does it have to do with German? My mother was often asked, how did you manage to survive? Many people also came who knew Polish and recognized Polish or Russian terms in Yiddish, so they asked how was it connected? We explained this hodgepodge of Yiddish and why there are so many different languages.

We made a recording of the Anne Frank program for GDR television in 1980 once and there was an audience in it, too. Some years ago, there was the exhibition 'Anne Frank in the GDR' at the Anne Frank Center in Berlin. There I met the camerawoman who recorded this program. And she said that we just let the camera roll, longer than expected, because the questions from the youth were getting more and more interesting. So many questions that also had a lot to do with Judaism, which they all had no idea about. How could they? Then she told us the next day that the material was gone. Someone had "cleaned up."

People were insanely curious, because our concerts were one of the rare opportunities to learn more about *Yidishkayt*. But I can also remember when this "Holocaust" series aired and everyone had seen it on West German TV – except for people in Dresden – that people addressed me saying: we didn't know all that. I remember a scene from Erfurt, in the center there was a huge bookstore, and I took the woman I was talking to, who had just said that to me, by the hand and said: "Look, there's Rybakov, *Heavy Sand*,[18] and there you have *Bilder des Zeugen Schattmann*,[19] and there you have this and that. If you wanted to know, you could have known." But it's always a question of whether you want to know.

We were messengers of *Yidishkayt*. In Leipzig, after a concert, people came up to me and said: "We have just returned from Vilna. There's even a synagogue there!" I replied: "There is also a synagogue here in Leipzig." – "What do you mean, where?" – "Yes, right here behind the train station. A beautiful synagogue and a very open community." There was no security

18 Rybakov 1981.

19 Edel 1969.

there yet, you could just walk in and ring the bell and then you found someone who answered your questions. They were completely horrified because they didn't know that. How much do you really want to find out, do you want to know?

Also, Jaldati's presence in the GDR made her hard to ignore sometimes. After 1967, she suddenly disappeared from the programs on television and radio. But recently a historian sat with me and said: "I found such a strange program in Dresden for the celebrations 9 November 1968 with the radio and a string quartet. And suddenly Lin Jaldati was in the middle of it." Well that's easy to explain: Kurt Goldstein, who was the head of the Auschwitz Committee in the GDR and a member of the International Auschwitz Committee, was also one of the heads of the Radio Committee of the GDR.[20] So of course he invited his radio people to these events. And such an event could not take place without Jaldati. She always quarreled with Kurt Goldstein, because Goldstein always exaggerated resistance in Auschwitz, and she said: "I didn't witness any resistance in Auschwitz, I didn't see any." Lin was the one who always emphasized the Jewish victims in Auschwitz. Another ongoing quarrel with Kurt Goldstein.

AW: Maybe just to pick up on your remarks about the late 1980s. The high point of *khurbn* memory, on a state level at least, in the GDR happened in 1988 on the 50th anniversary of '*Kristallnacht*.' Suddenly, there were all these exhibitions and concerts and things popping up – an "epidemic of remembrance" as a journalist phrased it.[21] Were you annoyed by that?

JR: Yes, I was annoyed. For one because they did not look at their German Jewish history. And it was for that reason that I started to look for German Jewish material myself. In 1994, we produced a CD called "Jews in Germany" for which we dug up all sorts of material. The incentive was to tell Germans: "Wait a minute, we are not strangers, we are neighbors. And we were here before the Christians came. We also had some quarrels in the

20 Kurt Goldstein (1914–2007) was a journalist and radio director. He fought in the Spanish Civil War in the International Brigades, was interned in France in 1939, was extradited to Germany in 1942, then he was deported to Auschwitz, was a forced laborer in the sub-camp Jawischowitz, was taken to Buchenwald in 1945, and liberated in April 1945. He first worked for the FDJ, from 1956 for the radio of the GDR, in 1976 became Vice President of the International Auschwitz Committee, and from 1982–1991 was Secretary of the Fédération Internationale des Résistants.

21 Genin 1994.

Klezmer scene. Suddenly, there was a strange discussion on whether non-Jewish people should be allowed to play Jewish music. I always answered: "There's good music and there's bad music. Are Jews allowed to play Johann Sebastian Bach?" What is this nonsense? It doesn't matter what kind of music you play, just be careful with it.

AW: In December 1983, you and your family took a very special trip that wasn't that easy to organize in the GDR: you went to Israel and performed there. What did you expect to find when you went to Israel?

JR: When we went to Israel, everybody said it wouldn't be a good idea to go with a Yiddish program to Israel. Nobody is interested in Yiddish in Israel. We went anyway. Jan Boeles, the cultural attaché from the Dutch embassy, had organized it for us. We were completely overwhelmed by how much interest in Yiddish there was! We were invited by the בית התפוצות [*Beit Hatefutsot*, House of the Diaspora, today the Museum of the Jewish People], but also gave a performance in Yad Vashem in memory of Anne Frank. That was the first time that German songs were performed there, a song by [German poet] Erich Fried, "Ich bezeuge" [I testify], composed by Paul Dessau, and Pablo Neruda's and Hanns Eisler's "Friedenslied" [Peace Song]. It was very moving. Then suddenly they asked us: "Could you also give us a Brecht & Eisler program?"[22] People are interested in Brecht and Eisler so we spontaneously organized another concert.

MCS: Speaking of travel, tell us the story of how you got this typewriter to the GDR?

JR: We went to the US in 1986. The Bauman family, Irma and Mordecai Bauman, had organized the tour, because they were here at some point for the Leipzig Fair making a film about Johann Sebastian Bach. And then I

[22] Bertold Brecht (1898–1956) was a German theater practitioner, playwright, poet and leading Marxist theoretician of epic theater ("dialectical theater") and the "Verfremdungseffekt" [alienation effect]. Coming of age during the Weimar Republic, he wrote *Die Dreigroschen Oper* [The Threepenny Opera] with Kurt Weill and began a life-long collaboration with the Austrian composer Hanns Eisler (1898–1962). After Hitler's rise to power, both Brecht and Eisler fled Germany, and both returned to East Berlin after the war. Brecht established the theater company Berliner Ensemble with his wife and long-time collaborator, actress Helene Weigel. Eisler is probably best known for composing the national anthem of East Germany.

The Jaldati/Rebling family in New York, 1986. Archive of the Academy of Arts, Berlin, Lin-Jaldati-Archiv, Nr. 299.1.

played with Lin Jaldati and Eberhard Rebling in Leipzig, and they were so excited and said: "You guys must come." They organized a tour there. It was quite a success. We played at Hebrew Union College, in downtown New York, and other places. *The New York Times* printed an article about us. In the picture, my sister and I look like typical American Jewish princesses [laughs].

And then we were in Amherst [at the Yiddish Book Center] and met Aaron Lansky.[23] A woman showed us around, and I was completely blown away. She said: "If you want any books, take them." And I felt like a child in a candy store, coming from East Berlin, and I started gathering books there. Then she said: "Do you want a typewriter? We're just switching to computers here." At that time, I didn't know how to spell the word 'computer,' and they put this typewriter in my hand. Then I had a bag full of books and a Yiddish typewriter. How do I get it through customs in East Berlin? But I was lucky. We took a complicated flight via Ljubljana, but the plane had to land in Dubrovnik due to a storm, where we got stranded. From there, we went

23 Aaron Lansky (*1955), founder of the National Yiddish Book Center in Amherst, Massachusetts.

not to Ljubljana, but to Belgrade where we were stranded again. The airport was full, hopeless to find anyone, any information. I sat my family down and said: "I'll take the tickets, you stay here and don't move from the spot." I started walking and suddenly I saw a person handing out tickets. He was sitting somewhere in the corner. "We want to go to East Berlin. Can we get on with you somehow?" He spoke German, an Austrian. He took our tickets and our passports and I had my boarding pass. I went back to my family. We flew on one of those mini planes to Vienna and had a connection to East Berlin. There we happily landed again, but without our suitcases. They turned up a few days later. I went to Schönefeld airport with my sister to pick them up and thought of something clever to explain everything. We went to the baggage claim area, they handed us the suitcases, we signed a sheet, took the suitcases and went home.

MCS: Was there a conceptualization of "Yiddishland," as it were, in the GDR?

JR: Yiddishland has always been there, has always existed. When people came to our house, there was always an open door, and there were always lots of people around and of course they spoke Yiddish. Yiddishland is a personal experience. I went to Kiev for the "Days of Yiddish Culture" – we're talking about the early 1990s now – and I asked my way through, from door to door, how to do it. And my colleague, Liane Düsterhöft, who was with me, asked me: "How do you do it?" – "How do I do what?" – "Well, you come in, look people in the eye and you talk and immediately start telling each other where you come from." Well, we are Jews. [laughs] That's completely normal for us, recognizing each other. I knew it from Berlin, from the Jewish contexts as quite a lonely Jewish child in an East German postwar school. As soon as I met people who somehow had a similar story or same history, there was an immediate connection. Probably we should call it "Jewishland" because not every Jew spoke מאַמע-לשון [*mame-loshn*, mother tongue; Yiddish]. But Yiddish as an international language was always natural. It's the same with Klezmer music. When I hear Klezmer 'revival,' I'm always irritated. Why do you think you need a nice title for something that has always been there?

I am also troubled, especially in the modern Yiddish circles, by this separation of Yiddish and Torah. It's nonsense. One has so much to do with the other. Just the other day I had another discussion about Jewish music. Can you separate sacred music from secular music? No, it is not possible at all. One is inconceivable without the other. And I truly believe in the diaspora we have no chance to survive as Jews without Torah. This has nothing to do with going to *shul* regularly, it's about our heritage. Too often have I met non-Jewish Yiddish singers who did not understand the context.

An anecdote comes to my mind. Some years ago, in Potsdam, when Professor Grözinger [a German scholar in Jewish Studies] gave his great archive [of Yiddish music] to the world, he really wanted us to be there. And then these guys sit there, Sasha Nemtzov[24] and Aaron Eckstaedt, now the director of the Jewish High School in Berlin. They were students at Potsdam in those days. They had found a field recording of three songs which came from an arrangement of this new school from Leningrad. One was a very corny Bundist song. יאָמער פֿון אונדזערע זאַלציקע טרערן [*Yomer fun undzere zaltsike trern*, Lament from our salty tears] was the name of the song: "Our life is so heavy and there is a whole sea of tears | but we don't need a *moshiakh* [Messiah] | we take our own lives in our hands."[25] And Eckstaedt announced the song and said a bit jokingly: "They even wanted to do away with the Messiah." And I said: "Hey, didn't you get it? Bundism, the intention of the Bundists is to have the Messiah now." That's exactly the same thing the Chabadniks are doing. We must do something now to change the world. We bring the Messiah, not wait for him to come. Some things are connected but are often only viewed from one side and not dialectally.

MCS: On the occasion of the 70th anniversary of the so-called Night of the Murdered Poets, I would be interested to know the extent of what people in the GDR knew about this and when it became known. Is this why they read Soviet Jewish writers in particular?

JR: Lin Jaldati gave a concert in November 1952 at the House of German-Soviet Friendship with Yiddish songs, and David [Shneer],[26] who com-

[24] Sasha Nemtzov (*1963), pianist, musicologist, educated in Leningrad, professor of the history of Jewish music at Franz Liszt Academy of Music in Weimar.

[25] Jaldati quoted the song from memory and paraphrased it.

[26] David Shneer (1972–2020) was a scholar of Jewish history and Yiddish Studies with a specific focus on Yiddish in the Soviet Union and the GDR. This volume is conceived as a Festschrift for Shneer. Please see Gregg Drinkwater's contribution in this volume.

pared Eberhard's programs with the officially published one, found out that she always sang *chalutzishe* [Zionist pioneers'] songs, too – only now it said Yiddish partisan songs or whatever. They just gave them completely different titles.

There were also texts by Perets Markish, which were read at another concert at the *Möwe*.[27] Yes, people knew the Soviet Yiddish poets. Why? Because left-wing people were always looking for like-minded people: Where are our origins? We knew about Yiddish in the Soviet Union. My dad had already performed works by Alexander Kren and others, of this new Soviet school, in the 1930s. And of course, they knew about the Soviet Yiddish poets. There were rumors about the gulag, of course, because people came back from them. But those who came back mostly kept quiet.

I don't know how much pressure they were put under. After the 20th Party Congress of the Communist Party of the Soviet Union and Khrushchev's speech, there was a moment of opening up. I vaguely remember considerable discussions and arguments between my parents and their friends about that, but I was too small to understand the content.

The first Yiddish song I sang in public was אַז מען פֿאָרט קיין סעוואַסטאָפּאָל / איז ניט ווײַט פֿון סימפֿעראָפּאָל / דאָרטן איז אַ סטאַנציע פֿאַראַן [When you go to Sevastopol / it is not far from Simferopol / There is a train station there]. My mom had a book with a collection of songs by Beregovsky[28] which I found and used. We kept saying, we know far too little about Yiddish in the Soviet Union. We know about Poland, of course, but we knew relatively little about the Soviet Union.

It was only in 1984 or 1985 – I was doing theater and was busy with other things until then – that I went to Bucharest and met with Israil Bercovici.[29] There we talked a lot about the Soviet Yiddish poets, because перестройка [*perestroika*, openness] was peeking around the corner. Bercovici went to his cupboard and unpacked a few things. And among other things, he showed

27 Artists' Club Die Möwe [Seagull] in East Berlin.

28 Moisei Iakovlevich Beregovsky (1892–1961), Soviet Jewish folklorist and ethnomusicologist from Ukraine. He collected, transcribed, and analyzed melodies, texts and culture of Yiddish folk song and explored the interconnectedness between East European Jewish and Ukrainian folk music.

29 Israil Bercovici (1921–1988), playwright, theater maker, content director of the Teatrul Evreiesc de Stat [Bucharest Jewish State Theater]. See the contribution by Corina Petrescu in this volume.

me this beautiful text from Hirsh Osherovitsh:[30] זיבן פֿאַרלוירענע יאָרן, זיבן געפֿונענע טעג [Seven lost years, seven found days]. And that's when we started to look very intensively at the Soviet Yiddish poets and picked up a little bit here and there, since increasingly more of their stories came to light.

Oh, wait, there is a piece missing. Helmut Eschwege.[31] It must have been at the end of the 1960s, 1968 maybe. I was in Dresden a lot then... because of love. [Laughs] Helmut Eschwege gave me all these books about the Slansky trials, and in the context of Prague 1968 I read a lot about Noel Field[32] and all those stories. I also had huge discussions with my parents. As a teenager one is very rebellious and very unfair. That was already a big topic and it remained so.

Soviet Yiddish poetry irritated a lot of Party functionaries. We sang the דזשאַנקאָיע [*Dzhankoye*] song in 1966 or 1967, i.e. before the so-called Six Day War, at Kongresshalle [Congress Hall, in Berlin] with the Oktoberklub [October Club].[33] And the topic kept us busy until the 'Days of Yiddish Culture.' If you look at the program of the first 'Days of Yiddish Culture,' Soviet Yiddish poets were everywhere. Three days before our festival, I got a call from the district leadership. He wanted to find out what we would actually be doing there – especially because the West German journalist and *ZDF* correspondent in East Berlin Peter Merseburger had registered. This voice on the phone, unknown to me, asked if Ber Halpern[34] was an American poet.

30 Hirsh Osherovitsh (1908–1994), Soviet Yiddish writer, wrote for the Jewish Antifascist Committee, including contributions to the "Black Book", was arrested in 1949 during the Committee's dissolution, released in 1956, and emigrated to Israel in 1971.

31 Helmut Eschwege (1913–1992), German-Jewish historian, emigrated via Denmark to Estonia in 1934, to Palestine in 1937, via Prague to Dresden in 1946, and produced various works for the SED, later at Technical University in Dresden. Never recognized in GDR historiography, Eschwege started working on a study about the *khurbn* in the 1950s, being among the first historians to do so in either German state. The book could not appear in the GDR, but he managed to publish a source anthology on the *khurbn* in 1966, and a volume on the history of synagogues in Germany in 1982. See Walther 2020.

32 Noel Field (1904–1970), American diplomat and spy for Soviet intelligence, head of the Unitarian Service Committee during World War II, was arrested in Prague in 1949 for alleged American espionage that ended in various show trials. He was released from prison in 1955 and died in Hungary.

33 Oktoberklub, most famous singing club in the GDR, founded in 1966 from the Hootenanny movement by folk music fans in the GDR.

34 Ber Halpern (1902–1984) was a prose writer, storyteller, journalist, and certified construction engineer, born in the town of Darsūniškis, Lithuania. After a stint in Uruguay and Paris, he returned to the Soviet Union where he was persecuted and sent to the gulag. His profession as a construction engineer saved his life. After his rehabilitation in 1956, he settled in Vilna, where he

I said: “No, he is a Soviet Yiddish poet.” The guy on the other end didn’t know what to think and was confused. The festival was saved through Soviet Yiddish poetry.

And when did I learn about 12 August 1952? That’s an interesting question. I think it must have been in the context of the long conversations with Helmut Eschwege. That actually came to me in the late 1960s, and I had huge discussions with my parents, because they suspected more than they really knew. That is unimaginable for us today. Something happens somewhere in the world, and you have it immediately on your mobile device. That didn’t exist back then. And the rumors kept coming. My sister Kathinka studied in Moscow and, of course, she was in this Russian-Jewish musician circle, her teacher was Yury Yankelevich. I think she would have known more, but she didn’t talk about it either.

MCS: Did you see Soviet Yiddish culture as a predecessor and tradition that you carried on in the GDR?

JR: Soviet Yiddish culture? Yes and no. I can talk about me and my family. The people who were involved with Yiddish in the GDR, they were a handful of people. It wasn’t known big and wide. It was clear from the 20th Party Congress that a lot of things were going wrong. And my father had a fight with the Communist Party in the Netherlands already in 1947 because of the whole story, and everybody knew that something was going wrong, but it was a bit like, it cannot be what must not be. Somehow, we suspected it, but maybe didn’t really want to know. When I came home with the books that Eschwege had given me, there were arguments with my parents again, but the quarrel was mainly between my mother and father. Eberhard always tried to defend the official line a bit, while Lin said: “No, don’t do that.” She saw it all a bit differently. We can’t do this to our own people, they are our people. What is happening here?

The problem was that we simply didn’t have the books. The first time I read Der Nister in the 1980s I was overwhelmed! That was my introduction to Hasidic literature, that was the very reason I started to deal with Jewish mysticism. Yes, he was my entry into what I do today. I have always shim-

continued working as a construction engineer. He published several books as well as in the Moscow journal *Sovetish heymland*, in Warsaw’s פֿאָלקס־שטימע [*Folks-shtime*, People's Voice], and in Paris’s נײַע פּרעסע [*Naye prese,* New Press].

mied my way forward. If I was interested in something, I just went to the library and searched or found some teachers.

MCS: You mentioned Bashevis Singer and the “language of the powerless.” How do you see the connection between Yiddish and socialist and internationalist ideas, and, for that matter, antifascism. Are there socialist ideas that are worthwhile to return to?

JR: Where do I start? I started to deal with the אַלגעמיינער ייִדישער אַרבעטער־בונד [*Algemeyner yidisher arbeter-bund*, General Jewish Labor Bund, short: Bund] probably when I was 18, 19, or 20 years old. It was at a time when you think you know how the world is to be set up and what the old people had done wrong and how to make it better in this world. That’s when I dealt with Bundism and figured out very quickly that Lenin built his party according to the Bundist principle: namely small groups, small learning groups, as it is done in the Talmud school, the one who knows something goes out and immediately teaches others what he has just learned. There was a lot of Jewish thought in the whole materialistic dialectic, that is, Karl Marx, on which my classmates cut their teeth. I stood next to them, thinking, well, what’s the problem here?

I have always thought like this. All these connections were never out of my head. Or at least I became conscious of them at some point. It’s because of my mother, of course. I inherited a deep spirituality from Lin that I’m incredibly grateful for. There is a trust in the possibility of humanity, even now, when really everything is going down the drain, rapidly, the possibility, there is always something new emerging. The forest burns, some idiot gets the idea that pine trees should be planted there again, because pine trees have always been planted there and the poor little pine trees, they wither. But then small birches and small beeches and oaks come. This possibility of the world to regenerate itself again and again, I see this crisis right now as a gigantic possibility for our world and yes, I grew up with that. Is it Jewish? Yes, it is, it’s Jewish. That’s what I grew up with.

Manés Sperber tells an adorable story about a boy named Berele.[35] They were in *kheyder* together and Berele suddenly gets the idea that when the *moshiakh* comes, the world turns upside down. The two boys started prac-

[35] Sperber 1981.

ticing headstands and walking on their hands. Years later as he gets older, he has long since left traditional Judaism and implemented revolutionary movements instead, he realizes that nothing has moved him as much as the idea of the *moshiakh*; that the world can change, that the world must change, and that it will change. This is also my credo.

Where is all of this going? We lived through '89. None of us who were there on the streets in 1989 wanted the Wall to fall, that wasn't the issue at all. The issue was a GDR where you can breathe, where you can make a simple photocopy without a Stasi uncle standing right next to you, where everyone can have a telephone, and where a passport is not a valuable thing but a matter of course for everyone. What became of the revolution has nothing whatsoever to do with what we actually wanted. But that's the way it often is with change. Today, it sometimes feels like the collapsing GDR. Nothing works anymore. Everything is getting tighter, and everyone is under more pressure. But people are starting to think about alternatives again. And that's where we'll get back to. I don't know how it all looks all around. But that basic trust, that's what my mother taught me. And that's deeply Jewish. At least for me. And whether that's a socialist idea; how you categorize it ideologically? Simply: a just world.

Bibliography

Brauer, Juliane, 2020: *Zeitgefühle – wie die DDR ihre Zukunft besang. Eine Emotionsgeschichte*. Bielefeld: Transcript.

Bruhn, Cornelia, 2022: Die FDJ-Singebewegung – eine staatliche Veranstaltung? Engagement und Entfremdungsprozesse in der Sphäre staatssozialistischer Jugendkultur in der DDR. In: Jörg Ganzenmüller, and Bertram Triebel, eds., *Gesellschaft als staatliche Veranstaltung? Orte politischer und kultureller Partizipation in der DDR*. Köln: Böhlau, 151–181.

Edel, Peter, 1969: *Die Bilder des Zeugen Schattmann. Ein Roman über deutsche Vergangenheit und Gegenwart*. Berlin (GDR): Verlag der Nation.

Gebirtig, Mordkhe, 1946 געבירטיג, מרדכי: **ס׳ברענט**. קראָקע: צענטראַלע ייִדישע היסטאָ־רישע קאָמיסיע בײַם צ.ק. פֿון פּוילישע ייִדן אָפּט.

Genin, Salomea, 1994: Erinnerungen einer Jüdin in der DDR. How the GDR turned a Jewish self-hating Communist into a Jew (Wie die DDR eine jüdisch-sich-selbst-hassende Kommunistin zur Jüdin machte) oder How I Came Back to the Fold (Wie ich in den Schoß der Familie zurückkehrte). In: *Horch und Guck* 12: 44–51.

JALDATI, Lin and Eberhard REBLING, 1995: *Sag nie, du gehst den letzten Weg. Lebenserinnerungen 1911 bis 1988.* Marburg: BdWI-Verlag.

MLOTEK, Chanah, 2004: *Songs of Generations: New Pearls of Yiddish Song.* Amherst, Mass.: Jewish Book Center of the Workmens.

PRESSLER, Mirjam, 2000: *Anne Frank. A Hidden Life.* New York, NY: Dutton Children Books.

REBLING, Eberhard, 1988: Zwischen Schmejchl un trern. Das jiddische Lied gestern und heute. In: *Musik und Gesellschaft* 38 (11): 568–572.

RYBAKOV, Anatoly, 1981: *Schwerer Sand.* Berlin (GDR): Verlag Neues Leben.

SCHNEIDER, Gertrude, 2000: *Mordechai Gebirtig: His Poetic and Musical Legacy.* Westport, Conn.: Praeger.

SHNEER, David, 2015: Yiddish Music and East German Antifascism: Lin Jaldati, Post-Holocaust Jewish Culture and the Cold War. In: *The Leo Baeck Institute Year Book* 60: 207–234.

SHNEER, David, 2021: Singing between Two Worlds: Lin Jaldati and Yiddish Music in Cold War Europe and Divided Berlin, 1945–1953. In: *Journal of Modern Jewish Studies* 20 (2): 248–273.

VAN LIEMPT, Ad, 2002: *Kopgeld. Nederlandse premiejagers op zoek naar joden, 1943.* Amsterdam: Uitg. Balans.

VAN IPEREN, Roxane, 2018: *'t Hooge Nest.* Amsterdam: Lebowski.

VAN IPEREN, Roxane, 2020: *The Sisters of Auschwitz: The True Story of Two Jewish Sisters' Resistance in the Heart of Nazi Territory.* London: Seven Dials, 2020.

VON SELTMANN, Uwe, 2018: *Es brennt: Mordechai Gebirtig, Vater des jiddischen Liedes.* Erlangen: Homunculus Verlag.

SPERBER, Manès, 1981: Berele. In: Ulf Diederichs, ed., *Dein aschenes Haar, Sulamith. Ostjüdische Geschichten.* Düsseldorf: Diederichs, 129–131.

WALTHER, Alexander, 2020: Helmut Eschwege and Jewish Life in the German Democratic Republic. In: Jay H. Geller and Michael Meng, eds., *Rebuilding Jewish Life in Germany.* New Brunswick, NJ: Rutgers University Press, 101–117.

Corina L. Petrescu

The Penetrable Iron Curtain:

The Bucharest Jewish State Theater's Tour to Israel in 1968

On the imagined map of Yiddishland, Romania never occupied a prominent place no matter its geographic configuration.[1] Although the city of Iaşi was the birthplace of professional Yiddish theater in the late 19th century, and in the interwar period of the 20th century, the country's capital, Bucharest, hosted several prolific Yiddish writers and artists of popular and high arts, transnational inquiries into Yiddish theater's history tend to ignore the events that unfolded there.[2] My research is an attempt to correct this situation.

With all its limitations and impositions, it was Romania's postbellum socialist regime that afforded the country the opportunity to become a promoter of Yiddish culture well into the 21st century. Aside from backing the revival of a Yiddish language press and literature, in 1948, the authorities sanctioned the establishment of a permanent, state-subsidized Yiddish-language theater Teatrul Evreiesc de Stat [Jewish State Theater, TES] in Bucharest.[3] While in the Soviet Union, the anti-Jewish purges claimed their first victims that year, in Romania the curtain rose on elaborate Yiddish performances, which audiences in Bucharest and in other centers of Jewish life attended eagerly.

The authorities' support for Yiddish was ideological, in compliance with the ideals of the interwar Jewish socialist movement(s) and state-sponsored

1 From the middle of the 19th century, the geographic borders of 'Romania' changed several times. At its most expansive, from 1918 to 1940, as Greater Romania, it included the following provinces: Bukovina, Bessarabia, Moldova, Dobruja, Wallachia, Transylvania, Banat, Crişana, and Maramureş. In 1940, Bessarabia, Northern Bukovina, and Southern Dobruja became part of the Soviet Union and Bulgaria, respectively, and they remained part of these countries after World War II giving Romania its present-day borders.

2 On Iaşi's role for Yiddish theater see Sandrow 1977 and Bercovici 1998; on Yiddish culture in interwar Bucharest aside from Bercovici see Crăciun 2018, 133–152 and Chiriac 2022; for important overviews about Yiddish theater that do not include anything on Romania see Berkowitz 2003, Nahshon 2009, and Berkowitz and Henry 2012. Even such books as Caplan 2018 and Quint 2019 only touch upon Romania peripherally and rely exclusively on the 1976 Yiddish edition of Bercovici's monograph, which has not aged well.

3 On the Yiddish press and literature see Binyamin Hunyadi's contribution to this volume. Originally and in keeping with the spelling norms of the time the theater was called Teatrul *Evreesc* de Stat. After the spelling reform of 1953, the name changed to Teatrul *Evreiesc* de Stat, which is still the correct spelling today and the one I use.

Soviet Yiddish culture. They proclaimed Yiddish the language of the people and, in sync with Soviet ideals, declared it the national language of Jews, ousting Hebrew as the language of Jewish backward religiosity and bourgeois nationalism, particularly Zionism. Yet, for the writers, journalists, and actors who expressed themselves in the language it was their natural creative outlet, even if the artistic language of most Jews in the country was Romanian followed by Hungarian, German, and then Yiddish.[4] In provinces such as Moldova and Maramureş, where Yiddish was widely spoken, the regime's support for the language and its culture aligned with pre-existing local practices. In Wallachia with its strongly acculturated Jewish population, Yiddish had gained artistic stature during the interwar period thanks to a vibrant press and theater activities. Hence, at least in the first decade, for participants in Yiddish culture, the state's efforts did not come across as endeavors to de-Romanize and re-ethnicize Jews but rather as attempts to rebuild a cultural milieu destroyed during the war years.

From the point of view of the regime, promoting Yiddish culture permitted the authorities to pride themselves on affording equal rights to all of Romania's inhabitants and to co-opt ethnic institutions for its propagandistic purposes. Yet, an enclave of Yiddish culture also created ethnic unity within Romanian Jewry beyond the inherent differences of praxis among its forming communities and the shifting tendencies of the official discourse. Cultural outlets such as the press, literature, or theater offered a space of alterity, within which journalists and literati could thematize specific Jewish concerns or draw attention to incongruities between the theory and the praxis of Romania's state socialism. Furthermore, by allowing Yiddish culture to be present in the official public sphere, the regime indirectly made its survival possible under the most unlikely circumstances. Throughout the years of state socialism, more than any other Jewish institution, TES embodied the dichotomy of simultaneously preserving Jewish identity behind the Iron Curtain and representing Romania's political regime. TES practiced a form of "integrated nonconformism," which led the institution to operate within the given parameters of the Romanian state but also allowed it to structure the memory discourse surrounding Yiddish theater, even if obliquely.[5] The

4 See Cajal and Kuller 2004, 422–459, and Axmann 2007.

5 Markiewicz-Lagneau 1976, 65.

fact that TES enlisted famous actors of the interwar Yiddish stage – Maurice Siegler (1879–1965), Beno Popliker (1903–1984), Dina Koenig (1906–1964), Sevilla Pastor (1906–1981), Samuel Fischler (1912–1982), or Seidy Glück (1922–1997) – gave it also, at least until the early 1970s, the touch of glamour it needed to do so with pizzazz.

I scrutinize TES's balancing act of upholding Jewishness and advertising for Romania's version of state socialism as it transpires from an extensive interview with TES's manager Franz Auerbach (1915–2002) during the theater's first international tour, which took the ensemble to Israel in 1968.[6] I examine the tour's cultural and diplomatic relevance as articulated in Auerbach's viewpoints, and I show that the Iron Curtain became remarkably permeable when state interests on both of its sides aligned. In the context of Israel's rediscovery of Eastern Europe for its cultural fabric and in the aftermath of the Arab-Israeli War of 1967, TES's tour promoted an image of Romania as a progressive socialist country with liberal minority policies. It did so not only to Israeli society but also to the democratic political West.

*

The 1960s in Romania stood under the sign of change and hope. At the country's highest political level, head of state Gheorghe Gheorghiu-Dej's (1901–1965) sudden death in March 1965 saw the unanticipated rise to power of Nicolae Ceaușescu (1918–1989). Gheorghiu-Dej had been an unapologetic Stalinist his entire life, an agile politician capable of outmaneuvering his opponents even when his situation seemed dire, and a shrewd strategist adept at the postwar political games.[7] The last years of his leadership saw important developments for Romania's position within the Eastern bloc and beyond. Gheorghiu-Dej oversaw the withdrawal of the Soviet troops from Romania in 1958, as a sign of appreciation for the role he had played in the aftermath

6 This article would not have been possible in its current form without the extraordinary assistance of Israela Becker, who translated the Hebrew texts and also made sure that my Yiddish translations were accurate, Boris Yentin, Director at The Israeli Center for the Documentation of the Performing Arts at Tel Aviv University, (henceforth ICDPA), who provided me with copies of the posters advertising for TES's shows in Israel, and Yael Dinar, Director of the Yehuda Gabay Theater Archive in Tel Aviv (henceforth GTA), who made available to me the playbill for TES's shows and several reviews. I thank them all for their support and interest in my work.

7 For pertinent analyses of the Gheorghiu-Dej era see Shafir 1985; Tismaneanu 2003, 85–186; and Cioroianu 2005, 319–391.

of the failed Hungarian Revolution of 1956. He launched Romania on a quasi-autonomous political course culminating in April 1964 with a declaration on the main issues of world communism – a move political scientist Vladimir Tismaneanu has called "a self-styled version of national communism"[8] – and, because of this divergence from the Soviet line, he initiated Romania's rapprochement with the West.

The declaration issued in April 1964 was of paramount importance for Romania's future for two reasons. First, it summed up the Romanian leadership's idea of intra-bloc relations based on national independence, sovereignty, equality, noninterference in the affairs of other parties and states, and cooperation based on mutual advantage versus the Soviet notion of socialist internationalism under Moscow's tutelage. Secondly, it afforded Gheorghiu-Dej the opportunity to isolate the Party[9] and the country from the influences of anti-Stalinism manifest in other Eastern bloc countries in the aftermath of Nikita Khrushchev's denunciation of Stalin's purges in 1956. With that, Gheorghiu-Dej established a precedent, which his successor, Ceauşescu, would replicate more than once during his rule: banking on the strong anti-Soviet sentiments of the Romanian people, both men rejected Soviet doctrines under the pretext of anti-imperialism or anti-interventionism only to strengthen national unity around the Romanian Party and ensure unflinching loyalty to its leader. Coupled with this approach was an opening up to the Western world in international politics, while maintaining a strict control on all matters domestically. It is in this complex postwar political terrain that the rise and harnessing of Yiddish in Romania must be placed and understood.

When Ceauşescu took over as General Secretary of the Party following Gheorghiu-Dej's death in 1965, he was the youngest member of the politburo at 47 years old, relatively unknown to the people, and presumably no threat to the old political guard as he had no real revolutionary biography to boast about.[10] While following Gheorghiu-Dej's course of anti-Sovietism, he drew attention to himself internationally for the first time when he proclaimed Romania's neutrality after the 1967 Arab-Israeli War, by refusing to sign the final

8 Tismaneanu 2003, 178.

9 Romania's Communist Party changed its name from Romanian Communist Party (May 1921) to Romanian Workers' Party (February 1948) and back to Romanian Communist Party (July 1965), see Tismaneanu 2003, 93 and 194. I use the term 'Party' to refer to this political association regardless of its official title at a given moment.

10 For Ceausescu's biography see Kunze 2017.

communiqué of the Warsaw Pact, which condemned Israel as an aggressor. Moreover, the Romanian Party issued a separate declaration further strengthening its diplomatic relations with the Israeli state.[11] Mozes Rosen, Romanian Jewry's uncontested leader as both chief rabbi (1948–1994) and president of the Federația Comunităților Evreiești din România [Federation of Jewish Communities in Romania, 1964–1994], claimed credit for convincing the Romanian government that "by doing good to the Jews, [...] it could obtain advantages in matters of favorable public opinion, trade relations, [and] political sympathies."[12] His calculations bore fruit and satisfied each side: the government reaped Western benefits, Romanian Jewry persevered under state socialism and did not lose its Jewishness either religiously or culturally.

Emigration to Israel and the impact of individual decisions to leave or not marked Jewish Romanian life in the 1960s. Particularly after Ceaușescu came to power, the norm became, according to historian Dennis Deletant, "to let those who so wished emigrate" and, in so doing, "facilitate the process of creating a homogeneous Romania based on the majority Romanian element."[13] By allowing Jewish emigration, Ceaușescu's regime also played at a democratic vein of Romanian state socialism in stark contrast to its Soviet or Polish versions. Moreover, it advanced its agenda of Western rapprochement, earned favors particularly with the USA, and gained hard currency through the ransom fee it charged per person. The emigration arrangements between Israel and Romania took place under the guise of humanitarian acts as migration from Romania was dubbed a matter of "family reunification." This strategy allowed the Romanian state to simulate consideration for Israel's needs, while lending a favorable ear to demands from the West not to restrict Jewish relocation from Eastern Europe. At the end of 1969, Romania and Israel began to operate according to written contracts first agreed upon for three years and, after 1972, signed every five years.[14] Steadily, yet in carefully controlled numbers, Jewish Romanians emigrated to Israel until Ceaușescu's downfall in December 1989.[15]

11 For details see Stanciu 2014, 775–795.

12 Rosen 1992, 218. According to editor Michael Riff, chief rabbi Rosen wrote the text in 1987 and asked that it be published unaltered in 1992, which suggests that his views on the matter had not changed even after the fall of the Iron Curtain.

13 Deletant 1995, 210.

14 Ioanid 2015, 92.

15 For the exact number of emigrants per year between 1958 and 1999 see Govrin 2002, 261.

Culturally, the political changes of the 1960s found their expression in the efforts to move away from the complete indebtedness to the Soviet Union in artistic matters, to increase the presence of Western artifacts in the country, and to instrumentalize national symbols. With regards to the realm of theater, the authorities decided to promote original contemporary plays by offering financial incentives to living playwrights.[16]

TES was expected to participate in the fabrication of national excitement around this cultural project. In a letter from 2 August 1967, the Comitetul de Stat pentru Cultură şi Artă – Consiliu Teatrelor [Theater Council of the State Committee for Culture and Art] instructed TES's management that "e[ra] de dorit" [it was desirable] for the theater to include local contemporary dramatic works in its repertoire.[17] TES had to prioritize its collaborations with playwrights, whose works were inspired by "lupta poporului … pentru libertate națională şi socială, pentru socialism" [the people's struggle for national and social freedom, [and] for socialism] and by "problemele omului contemporan" [the problems of the contemporary man]. In addition, it had to pay particular attention to shows that targeted the youth and the development of its spiritual profile in line with that of the state. The Council explicitly asked TES to improve its repertoire by the beginning of the new season and communicate to the Council the titles of the specific shows with which it would mark the 20th anniversary of the Romanian republic in December 1967. TES had to comply with these demands even if the community whose cultural expression it – supposedly – was, had vastly different concerns from those of the Romanian authorities.

Following chief rabbi Rosen's approach of accordance-to-endure, mentioned above, manager Auerbach and dramaturge Israil Bercovici (1921–1988), navigated the political reality with keen attention to the state's demands and TES's survival. The uncontested highlight of the institution's early history was its first ever international tour, which, in the summer of 1968, took the theater to Israel. Aside from exposure to the world beyond Romania's borders, the tour also advanced TES to a new status, namely that of an international cultural broker on behalf of the Romanian state.

An interview with Auerbach published in the *General Anzeiger* [General Gazette] from Bonn in early April 1968 indicates that at the time there were

16 Vasile 2013, 228.

17 Letter in Bercovici Collection (henceforth BC) 1417 b 1845.

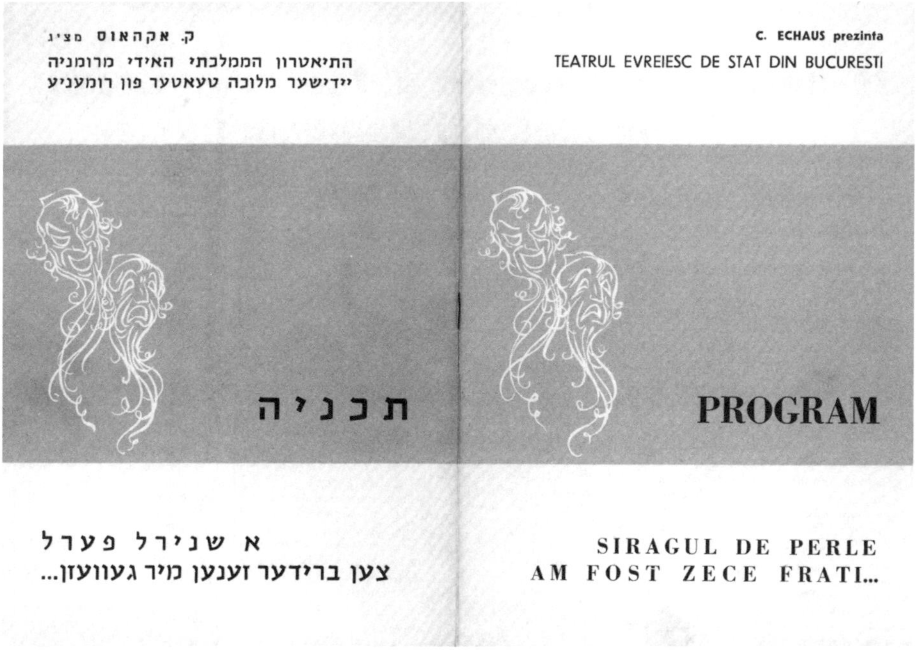

Program of TES's tour through Israel, 1968. From the collection of the Yehuda Gabay Theater Archive at the Sha'ar Zion Library-Beit Ariela, Tel Aviv, Israel.

talks underway between the Agenția Română de Impresariat Artistic [Romanian Agency for Artistic Representation and Promotion] and the West German Inter Nationes about a tour to the Federal Republic of Germany, but it never came about.[18] In June 1968, reporter Zeev Ben Chaim claimed in an article for the Romanian-language Israeli newspaper *Viața noastră* [Our life] that TES's ensemble could have gone to Canada but it had preferred to tour Israel instead.[19] Whatever the reasons and the behind-the-scenes maneuvers, between 26 June and 7 August 1968, TES showcased its art for Israeli audiences and practiced soft diplomacy in agreement with its new role as cultural ambassador for Ceaușescu's regime.[20]

In his interview with the Romanian-language, Israeli newspaper sponsored by the local Communist Party *Glasul poporului* [The People's Voice,

18 Schmidt-Mühlisch 1968, [n. p.].

19 Chaim 1968b, [n. p.].

20 For an overall analysis of the tour based on the reviews available in BC see Grözinger 2002, 304–308.

20 de ani de existență a Teatrului Evreesc de Stat din România

Ne vorbește F. I. AUERBACH, directorul T. E. S.

Turneul Teatrului Evreiesc de Stat din București în Israel, se apropie de sfîrșit. Vreme de aproape 6 săptămîni, artiștii TES., au adus în orașele țării mesajul SINGURULUI teatru din lume care, păstrează intacte și promovează cu măiestrie valorile tradiției și folclorului evreiesc.

In turneul din Israel, am văzut două spectacole din repertoriul amplu și multilateral al T.E.S.. Atît a fost însă suficient, pentru a sugera și ilustra marile sale posibilități, înaltul său nivel artistic.

In aceste zile — la 1 august — se împlinesc 20 de ani de activitate a Teatrului Evreiesc de Stat din Romnia. Ne-am adresat directorului teatrului, I. F. AUERBACH, care, cu amabilitate, a răspuns întrebărilor noastre.

„Dacă pe plan mondial se poate vorbi de un regres care se confundă aproape cu dispariția, în România, acest teatru se bucură în ultimii 20 de ani de o renaștere uimitoare. ...Stim foarte bine — a subliniat I. F. Auerbach — că entuziasmul cu care am fost primiți în Israel, se îndreaptă și către țara noastră, care ne oferă condiții optime de existență".

— Implinirea a 20 de ani de existență a Teatrului Evreiesc de Stat din România — ne declară directorul TES — ne prinde în plină activitate în turneul întreprins în Israel.

Trebuie să subliniez, că teatrul nostru este continuatorul unei vechi și strălucite tradiții de teatru evreiesc în România. Pe meleagurile noastre, la Iași, **Avram Goldfaden**, părintele teatrului evreiesc, a pus în anul 1876 piatra de temelie la „Pomul Verde", primului teatru profesionist. Această dată a intrat în istoria teatrului idiș din lumea întreagă. De atunci și pînă acum, există teatru idiș în România.

F. I. AUERBACH
— director T.E.S.

■ Cum apreciați cei 20 de ani de existență ai Teatrului Evreiesc de Stat din România?

— Dacă pe plan mondial se poate vorbi despre un regres ce se confundă aproape cu dispariția teatrului idiș, în afară de Israel, în România acest teatru se bucură in ultimii 20 de ani de o renaștere uimitoare. Această renaștere nu este întîmplătoare, deoarece ea se datorează unor factori sociali bine determinați. Acești factori sociali sunt pe deoparte existența unui număr însemnat de iubitori de teatru și literatură idiș și pe de altă parte, politica înțeleaptă pe tărîm artistic, care muncii în construirea socialismului. O confirmare a celor relatate este faptul că din cele peste 40 de scene din România, există și înfloresc 6 teatre maghiare, 2 germane și una idiș. Aceste cifre sunt corespunzătoare numărului locuitorilor aparținînd minorităților respective din țară. Ele sunt o dovadă grăitoare a liniei ascendente de dezvoltare a tuturor instituțiilor teatrale incluzînd bineînțeles și teatrul nostru.

Actorii și slujitorii teatrului se bucură de respectul și aprecierea deosebită din partea spectatorilor și autorităților. Nivelul noului spectator a crescut și implicit și exigența sa față de producția teatrală.

tic și în ultimă instanță, întregul colectiv artistic.

■ Care credeți că au fost momentele importante, pe planul creației artistice, al TES?

— Teatrul nostru a avut desigur și puncte culminante artistice în decursul celor 20 de ani de existență ca Teatru de Stat. Mi-aș permite să scot în evidență din cele peste 100 de premiere realizate în această perioadă, următoarele: **Intrigă și iubire** de Schiller, **Bolnavul închipuit** de Moliere, **Visul lui Goldfaden** de Rotbaum, **Mercadet** de Balzac, **Jurnalul Annei Frank,** laureată într-un concurs republican. **Opera de 3 parale** și **Mutter Courage** de Brecht, **Vrăjitoarea** de Goldfaden și bineînțeles, coroana literaturii idiș Tevie **Lăptarul** de Suelm Alehem dramatizată de colegul nostru **Beno Popliker.** Vreau să precizeze că această alegere, poartă pecetea subiectivității mele. Enumerarea acestor titluri nu cuprinde nici pe departe totalității succeselor artistice ale teatrului nostru.

■ Cum își desfășoară activitatea Teatrul Evreiesc de Stat din București? Care sunt proiectele de viitor?

— Teatrul nostru dispune de un personal artistic, administrativ și tehnic permanent. Realizăm anual între 6-8 premiere și pe planul de spectacole figurează cam 15 piese, diferența constituind-o reluările. Intregul proces de producție de la executarea decorurilor și costumelor pînă la finisarea artistică a spectacolelor, are loc în incinta teatrului. Deși dispunem de regizori, scenografi și dirijori, invităm din cînd în cînd și alte forțe artistice aparținînd altor scene.

Pe lîngă spectacolele serale, **teatrul nostru organizează matinee literare** care au loc aproape regulat duminică dimineață. Ele se compun dintr-o conferință susținută în majoritatea cazurilor de secretarul nostru literar **Israil Bercovici** și de o parte artistică cu participarea actorilor și orchestrei noastre, sub conducerea experimentată a ar-

în Israel. Marea epopee a glorioasei răscoale din ghetoul Varșoviei nu trebuie uitată, ea constituind una din marile acte eroice ale poporului evreu din timpurile noastre. Lupta tragică și plină de demnitate a eroilor din această piesă împotriva forțelor negre ale fascismului conțin învățăminte nepieritoare.

Publicul din Israel ne-a făcut o primire frățească. Noi știm că entuziasmul cu care ne-a primit se îndreaptă și către țara noastră, care ne oferă condiții optime de existență și ne oferă posibilitatea de a apare în fața publicului de peste hotare.

Spectatorii de aici, sunt calzi receptivi și foarte exigenți. Ne-am simțit bine, datorită ospitalității și prieteniei cu

I. BERCOVICI
secretar literar al T.E.S.

care am fost primiți pretutindeni. Intîlnirile oficiale s-au caracterizat printr-un respect deosebit față de România și față de noi.

Cele văzute în Israel ne-au impresionat. Frumoasele orașe cît și instituțiile de cultură sunt rezultatul unei munci grele și preseverente.

Sperăm că prin prezența noastră aici, să fi contribuit cu modestele noastre puteri, la adîncirea legăturilor prietenești dintre țara noastră și Israel.

Mulțumesc spectatorilor, autorităților și prietenilor care s-au bucurat de venirea noastră și au făcut ca să ne simțim bine în această frumoasă țară.

Interview with Franz Auerbach, *Glasul poporului*, 1 August 1968.
Courtesy: Periodical Collection of the National Library of Israel, Jerusalem, Israel.

short Glasul] published close to the end of TES's six-week-long tour on 1 August, Auerbach talked ardently about the theater's past and future.[21]

Auerbach opened his remarks with an homage to Israeli audiences, who, he pointed out strategically, had reacted keenly not only to TES's presence among them but had also showed their appreciation to the Romanian state, which "ofer[ea] [teatrului] condiții optime de existență" [offer[ed] [the theater] optimal conditions to exist]. What Auerbach did not spell out in his reverence to the Israeli public but also did not have to convey explicitly in the context of the time was the political reasoning, which had moved many spectators to attend TES's shows. Against the backdrop of the persisting Romanian-Israeli relations during and after the 1967 Arab-Israeli War, Israelis seemed more than willing to let bygones be bygones with respect to the vitriolic anti-Zionist and anti-emigration discourse the Romanian state had put forth only a decade earlier, at times also with TES's help.[22] The Romanian state was forgiven and its cultural emissary, TES, embraced and lauded unabashedly.

The well-disposed public sentiment surrounding TES in the summer of 1968 is apparent in the unnamed interviewer's opening statement, in which they hailed the troupe as "SINGURU[L] teatru din lume care păstr[a] intacte şi promov[a] cu măiestrie valorile tradiției şi folclorului evreiesc" [THE ONLY theater in the world that preserve[d] intact and promote[d] masterfully the values of Jewish tradition and folklore (emphasis in text)]. Considering that Państwowy Teatr Żydowski [Polish State Yiddish Theater, PTŻ] was also still in existence,[23] the exaggeration served the journalist to flatter the Romanian state for its cultural policies and political support of Israel. Auerbach himself fawned over the Romanian government's support for the theater in line with its Marxist ideology that afforded all national minorities the right to artistic expression and cultural endeavors. While Auerbach included Jews among Romania's national minorities, officially they did not enjoy that status as the state did not recognize them as a distinct nation or people but

21 "20 de ani" [Twenty Years] in BC 1417 s 1285. All subsequent quotes are from this interview.

22 TES performed two particularly anti-Zionist plays in 1951 – אין שאָטן פֿונעם פּאַלמענבוים [*In shotn funem palmenboym*, In the Shade of a Palm Tree] and ווידער אין דער היים [*Vider in der heym*, Home Again] – that also played into the Romanian state's anti-emigration discourse.

23 While the antisemitic attacks of 1968 in Poland took place in March, PTŻ manager Ida Kamińska did not leave her position and the country till 23 August 1968 (Morgan 2021). For details about her resettlement in New York City see Mancini 1968, 23.

only as a community of faith; but this was not the time or place for subtle distinctions.[24] TES thrived in Romania and that was Auerbach's message for Israeli readers. TES enjoyed, said Auerbach, popularity among a "număr însemnat de iubitori de teatru şi literatură idiş" [notable number of lovers of Yiddish theater and literature] in Romania, which allowed it to flourish while elsewhere in the world Yiddish stagecraft was dying out. These observations served Auerbach as a springboard into an effusive endorsement of socialism as the social structure capable of sustaining the equal cultural development of all its adherents. As proof for his claims, Auerbach invoked the existence of forty theaters in Romania among which six performed in Hungarian, two in German, and one in Yiddish, in keeping with the number of people belonging to each ethnic group.[25]

I read Auerbach's emphasis on the support that minority cultures received in Romania in the context of Yiddish culture's real but, more importantly, perceived status in Israel then. Rachel Rojanski has challenged the abiding view that the state of Israel "suppressed" and "rejected" Yiddish "as a direct result of the Zionist ideology of the 'negation of the Diaspora'."[26] However, the reality of the 1960s, fades to irrelevance when contrasted with the popular perception at the time both in Israel and in other centers of Jewish culture in the world, namely that the state of Israel had waged war on Yiddish upon its establishment and beyond. The Eichmann Trial (1961) had sensitized Israeli society to the plight of Eastern Europe to the point where it was ready to engage with the East European past in public discourse and to embrace it as long as it came in a "usable" form.[27] The production of a musical comedy based on Itzik Manger's די מגילה־לידער [*Di megile-lider*, Songs of the Megillah] in 1965 had helped to alter the image of Yiddish in Israeli society from the language of the diaspora to the linguistic expression of "a positive, attractive, and happy folk culture, accessible to all, at once amusing and moving."[28] That same year, Israeli audiences had applauded enthusiastically the Hebrew

24 See Decree 589 from 1 June 1949, about the status of the Mosaic cult in Andreescu, Nastasă, and Varga 2002, 423–429.

25 According to the 1966 census, there were 1,619,592 Hungarians, 382,595 Germans and 42,888 Jews in Romania.

26 Rojanski 2020, 2. For a critical reading of Yiddish's status in Mandate Palestine see Chaver 2004.

27 The phrase "usable past" belongs to Brooks 1918, 337–341.

28 Rojanski 2020, 243.

production of Joseph Stein's musical *Fiddler on the Roof* inspired by Sholem Aleichem's stories about Tevye the Dairyman, even if the show "embodied," as Rojanski shows, "the memories of Jewish life in Eastern Europe as imagined by Jews in the United States."[29] Yet none of these events had led to the appreciation, let alone the flourishing of Yiddish high culture in Israel and even less to state support for Yiddish theater.

Most likely aware of the popular perception about Yiddish's status in Israeli society if not prior to, then surely during TES's tour, Auerbach's remarks invited *Glasul*'s readers to ponder the contrasting attitudes towards Yiddish in the two states they knew: Romania, the socialist country many had left in the last two decades, and Israel, the capitalist democracy that did not offer Yiddish culture any support. In so doing, Auerbach insinuated that the country of their emigration had changed for the better, which TES's Israeli tour amply illustrated. Given *Glasul*'s own political leaning to the left, Auerbach's explicit and implicit remarks probably did not fall on deaf ears and affirmed the views of the readership.

Following this, TES's manager addressed the institution's history and outlined a vision for its future. He accented that TES carried on "[o] tradiți[e] veche și strălucită" [an old and brilliant tradition] that had begun with Avrom Goldfadn's first professional Yiddish theater worldwide in Iași at the beer garden Pomul verde [Green Tree]. He credited TES's domestic "exigent" [demanding] spectatorship with spurring the ensemble on to improve its performance style and repertoire ceaselessly. When asked about the highlights of TES's twenty years of existence, Auerbach was quick to note that the theater had premiered one hundred shows and among these he stressed: קאַבאַלע און ליבע [*Kabale un libe*, Intrigue and Love] by Friedrich Schiller, דער אײַנגערעדטער קראַנקער [*Der ayngeredter kranker*, The Imaginary Invalid] by Molière, אַ גאָלדפֿאַדן חלום [*A Goldfadn kholem*, A Goldfadn-dream] by Jakub Rotbaum, מערקאַדעט [*Merkadet*, Mercadet] by Honoré de Balzac, דאָס טאָגבוך פֿון אַנאַ פֿראַנק [*Dos togbukh fun Ana Frank*, The Diary of Anne Frank] by Frances Goodrich and Albert Hackett – whom Auerbach did not name although he remarked that the performance had earned national distinctions at its time –, די דרײַ גראָשן אָפּערע [*Di dray groshn opere*, The Threepenny Opera] and מוטער קוראַזש [*Muter kurazh*, Mother Courage] by Bertolt Brecht, די כּישוף־מאַכערין [*Di kishef-makherin*, The Sorceress] by Avrom Goldfadn,

[29] Ibid., 236.

and טביה דער מילכיקער [*Tevye der milkhiker*, Tevye the Dairyman] by Sholem Aleichem. It is remarkable that all these shows belong either to classic Yiddish or world literature and their equal footing invited *Glasul*'s readers not only to look upon them as tantamount but also to marvel at TES's cosmopolitan opening. In state socialism, Auerbach seems to suggest, Yiddish literature and drama had reached world class, and TES was evidence of this development. Auerbach omitted the autochthonous, contemporary, and ideological productions of the 1950s as well as the variety shows TES staged regularly and to great success. The decision to overlook the former is an obvious one in the political climate of the late 1960s; remaining silent about the latter was a tactical decision not to give Israeli readers any reason to bring TES in connection with interwar vaudevillian, popular, so called *shund* theater.

Asked to explain precisely how TES functioned, Auerbach asserted that the theater had a permanent artistic, administrative, and technical personnel, which worked together to premiere six to eight shows a year, while the total number of yearly performances including the reruns was fifteen. He emphasized that the entire production process from set and costume design to a show's last touches took place in-house as TES employed its own stage directors, scenographers, and conductors. Nonetheless to enhance its artistic output, TES collaborated occasionally with guest artists in those fields. Auerbach mentioned further that TES organized literary matinées to reach out to its audience beyond the realm of the regular shows. On Sunday mornings, dramaturge Israil Bercovici lectured in Romanian about topics that commended Jewish culture or built bridges between Jewish and non-Jewish Romanian culture, after which members of the ensemble performed musical or theatrical numbers that complemented the talks. There was however another aspect to these matinées, which Auerbach conveniently left unmentioned: they were meant to draw new spectators to the theater as TES's traditional followers dwindled away. Again, Auerbach's desire to share with *Glasul*'s readership details about TES's activities did not translate into divulging uncomfortable truths about it. Only positive information deserved sharing.

When talking about the future, Auerbach stressed the importance of the repertoire for TES's success which at that moment included works by Ludovic Bruckstein,[30] Sholem Aleichem, S. An-ski, Y. L. Peretz, and Avrom Goldfadn.

30 Ludovic Bruckstein (1920–1988), the only contemporary playwright under production in 1968, was the descendent of a rabbinical family from Maramureş, who had survived Auschwitz and

He also announced that the troupe was preparing for both domestic and international tours. TES's sojourn in Israel was the ensemble's first international foray and one cannot help but wonder what made Auerbach believe that it would not be the last, as his use of the simple present in the sentence entails: "Planurile de viitor se axează pe [...] pregătirea organizatorică a turneelor noastre în țară și în străinătate" [Future plans focus on [...] the organizational preparations for our tours in the country and abroad]. Was the addition of "and abroad" simply verbiage? Was Auerbach merely giving voice to the general sentiment of hope that inspired people in Romania in the late 1960s? Was he cautiously sowing seeds for future international appearances of the ensemble he led in view of TES's accomplishments in Israel? Whatever the thoughts behind his formulation might have been, Auerbach was aware of the utmost importance of TES's Israel tour and the weight his statements carried. He trod lightly and prudently, cognizant that his utterances addressed not just *Glasul*'s Israeli readership but also the Romanian authorities, who monitored his actions and the ensemble in general.

When asked to evaluate the tour, Auerbach proclaimed it a success and invoked as evidence the numerous thank-you messages received from Israeli spectators as well as the positive reviews in the local press of its two shows: אַ שנירל פערל [*A shnirl perl*, A Pearl Neckless] by Israil Bercovici and Haim Sloves's צען ברידער זענען מיר געוועזן [*Tsen brider zenen mir gevezn*, We Were Ten Brothers].[31]

Auerbach also hinted at critical responses.[32] However, he wrote them off as misunderstandings on the part of the reviewers, who expected *A shnirl perl* to be an American-type musical instead of what Auerbach deemed a "spectacol de folclor și cîntece evreiești la o ținută demnă și sobră" [dignifying and somber show of folklore and old Jewish songs].[33] He went as far as to pro-

several labor camps. In his works, he thematized the חורבן [*khurbn*, destruction, Holocaust] albeit in line with the official view of the Romanian authorities but also drew on Hasidic legends. He was TES's most productive modern-day Yiddish-language collaborator before his emigration in 1972. For biographical details, see Bruckstein 2017 and Erizanu 2019.

31 For some of these positive reviews collected in the original and in part also translated into Romanian by Bercovici, see Halaus 1968, 18; Lazăr 1968, [n. p.]; Chaim 1968, 15a; Hadas 1968, [n. p.]; Mr. 1968, 9a; Solomovici 1968, [n. p.]. Furthermore, for an empathetic reception that did not ignore TES's outdated performance style but also did not fault the theater for it, see Har-Gil 1968, [n. p.].

32 For these more critical responses to TES's performances, see Gal 1968, [n. p.]; Tshernov 1968, 5; Gras-Tsimerman 1968, 3.

33 According to the playbill, *A shnirl perl* included the following numbers, which shows that

Poster for TES' show *A shnirl perl*. From the "Yiddish Theater in Romania" Collection at the Israeli Center for the Documentation of the Performing Arts, Tel Aviv University, Israel.

Poster for TES' show *Tsen brider zenen mir gevezn*. From the "Yiddish Theater in Romania" Collection at the Israeli Center for the Documentation of the Performing Arts, Tel Aviv University, Israel.

claim that TES's first and foremost duty was to preserve said Jewish folklore in danger of disappearing, despite being an important part of Yiddish cul-

the term 'folklore' was used rather loosely: אַ גוטן אָוונט [*A gutn ovnt*, A Good Evening], text by Bercovici and music by Haim Schwartzman; פּראָלאָג [*Prolog*, Prologue], text by Bercovici and music by Schwartzman; !יאָ צי ניין [*Yo tsi neyn!*, Yes or No!], no other information provided; האָבן מיר אַ ניגונדל [*Hobn mir a nigndl*, We Have a Little Tune] by Avrom Goldfadn; קינדער־ו[!]יגן אויף דער עלטער [*Kinder-vign oyf der elter*, Cradling in One's Old Age], text by Bercovici and Mordkhe Gebirtig and music by Gebirtig; ביים שפּיגל [*Baym shpigl*, At the Mirror], text by Bercovici; שיר השירים [*Shir hashirim*, Song of Songs], text by Bercovici and music by Schwartzman; אַז נישט איצט... [*Az nisht itst...*, If not now...], no other information provided; חסידים טאַנצן [*Khsidim tantsn*, Hasidim Dance], no other information provided; ביי דער ווערבע [*Bay der verbe*, The Willow] by H. N. Bialik; אַ לידעלע אין ייִדיש [*A lidele in yidish*, A Yiddish Song] by Kotliar; אַז דער רבי אלימלך... [*Az der rebe Elimeylekh...*, When Rabbi Elimelech ...] by Moshe Nadir; מילכיקס [!] [*Milkhiks*, Dairy Delicacies] by Sholem Aleichem; שרהס וויגליד [*Sores viglid*, Sarah's Lullaby] by Goldfadn; איינזאַם [*Eynsam*, Alone] by Itzik Manger; וואַרניטשקעס [*Varnitshkes*, Dumplings], no other information provided; פּאַפּיר איז דאָך ווייַס [*Papir iz dokh vays*, Paper is White], no other information provided; צוויי שכנות [*Tsvey shkheynes*, Two Female Neighbors] by Goldfadn; אונטער די גרינינקע ביימעלעך [*Unter di grininke beymelekh*, Under the Little Green Trees] by Bialik; שדכנים פּירן אויס אַ שידוך [*Shadkhonim firn oys a shidekh*, Marriage Brokers Carry Out a Match] by Bercovici and Sholem Aleichem and music by Schwartzman; רבנו תם [*Rabeynu Tam*, Our Rabbi Tam] by Manger; ...פֿון דעם קלאַנג פֿון טרערן־פּערל [*Fun dem klang fun trern-perl...*, From the Sound of Tear Pearls...] by Bercovici. See playbill in GTA.

ture. He instructed his readers that Jewish folklore played a defining role in the development of Yiddish culture per se. He insisted that as an institution of art, TES cultivated Jewish folklore "în forma lui cea mai curată şi demnă" [in its cleanest and most dignified form] taking another stab at the American musical tradition, which had seen the phenomenal rise to acclaim on Broadway (1964) and on Jaffa's Alhambra Theater (1965) of *Fiddler on the Roof.*

Auerbach's decision not to address the critical responses to TES's understanding of folklore illustrates the conceptual difference between the Jewish Romanian and Israeli ways of engaging with timeworn East European artistic productions. To TES, genuine folklore was static, an expression frozen in the moment of its creation, which spoke truth about that time. With all its shortcomings, *Fiddler* looked upon East European traditions as evolving instances that could still appeal to contemporary audiences who had never known the realities of the Pale of Settlement. TES looked back melancholically, while *Fiddler* projected life forward. The three critical reviewers in Israel highlighted these aspects of the nostalgic discourse on TES's stage. Aharon Gal was the most critical. He disapproved of Israil Bercovici's decisions to perform Jewish folklore looking towards the past rather than help enrich it by embedding it in contemporary realities, as Haim Hefer had done for *Di megile* in 1965. He opined that the show presented a diasporic view of the Jew, which was no longer relevant or familiar to Israeli audiences. He credited TES with preserving Yiddish but decried that it did not further it. I. Tshernov found *A shnirl perl* to be pure nostalgia and stylistically disconnected from contemporary theatrical practices but valued TES's efforts in the larger context of Cold War realities. He saw its presence in Israel as a first step in tearing down the barriers between Jews in Eastern Europe and Israel. M. Gras-Tsimerman insisted that TES had come to Israel to celebrate its 20th anniversary yet, to his disappointment, what TES presented was a sentimental view of Jewish life in Eastern Europe, rendered artistically in a style customary prior to the First World War.

TES's second performance in Israel, *Tsen brider zenen mir gevezn*, commemorated the Warsaw Ghetto Uprising in April-May 1943.[34] A somber and gripping play, it urged its audiences never to forget the struggle of the Jewish people against fascism. In Auerbach's opinion, the play also contained valu-

34 For a discussion of the different politics involved in commemorating the Warsaw Ghetto Uprising in Buenos Aires, see Malena Chinski in this volume.

able lessons – he described them as "nepieritoare" [imperishable] – beyond the scope of its immediate topic as it exemplified "lupta tragică şi plină de demnitate" [the tragic and dignified struggle] of the Jewish people for survival. In the aftermath of the Arab-Israeli War of 1967, the statement lends itself to be read as a justification for and an endorsement of the war and its outcome. Auerbach's observations – though timidly – served up flattery to the Israeli state, as he followed them with a tribute to the Israeli theatergoers, who had given TES "o primire frăţească" [a brotherly welcome].

Auerbach concluded his interview by reiterating his viewpoint that Israeli society's reactions to TES were more than responses to a foreign cultural institution touring its state but also expressed people's gratitude toward the Romanian authorities and all they did for their country's Jewry. His closing words included more praise for the young Israeli state and commended it for its friendly relations with Romania. Finally, he expressed his hope that TES had played its part in furthering and deepening the Romanian-Israeli cooperation.

It is noteworthy that Auerbach gave this interview on the exact day of TES's 20th anniversary, 1 August, and that TES was marking this milestone on tour. Back in 1948, when the theater of the ייִדישער קולטור־פֿאַרבאַנד [*Yidisher kultur-farband*, Jewish Cultural Association, YKUF] had morphed into TES, it had also been on tour, albeit a domestic one. The parallel bears symbolic meaning: YKUF Theater's circuit across Romania had revealed to Jewish audiences in the country what Yiddish theater 'could be' under the new regime; TES's international tour presented to Israeli audiences – and the world over through reviews in international publications – what the ensemble 'had become' under state socialism; and the reactions were if not enthusiastic then certainly sympathetic to the theater's existence.[35]

*

In the 1960s, Romania distanced itself cautiously from the Soviet Union and embarked on a more autonomous political and cultural course compared to other countries of the Eastern bloc. Its recently appointed young leader, Nicolae Ceauşescu, went so far as to proclaim the country's neutrality in

35 For a balanced review in French see Cohen 1968, [n. p.], for enthusiastic reviews in Yiddish but for readers in the USA see Honik 1968, 7; Lipski 1968, 3; Slutska Kestin 1968, [n. p.], and for a sober view see Brandt 1968, 6. The lingering effect of TES's tour to Israel is evidenced by Blayzor 1971, 34–36.

the aftermath of the Arab-Israeli War of 1967 in a choreographed effort to win the sympathy of the Romanian people and the favors of the Western world for his regime. With respect to the latter, TES played its part in the authorities' endeavors at the time. Allowed on its first international tour in the summer of 1968, TES went to Israel, where it promoted a synthetic image of Romania as a progressive socialist country with liberal minority policies.

As I have argued, the Romanian authorities used TES in their efforts to introduce themselves to the Western world in the most positive light, which also meant projecting the superiority of their worldviews. As Auerbach's answers reveal, officially, Yiddish theater in Romania was authentic, artistic, engaged, and protected from financial insecurities or the whimsical desires of profit-oriented managers. This existence stood in stark contrast to Israel, where troupes propelled by the old star-system had short existences, and Yiddish stagecraft could attract the attention of the public and critics only sporadically. TES's activities and, even more so, its presence in Israel in 1968 also offered the Romanian authorities a chance to set themselves apart – culturally too – from the superpower within their own ideological camp, the Soviet Union, and appear in the better light.

In the passive-aggressive confrontations of the Cold War, every aspect of life was relevant both between the competing blocs and within the Eastern bloc itself. Eager to be involved in world politics, Ceaușescu directed his government to use any means at its disposal to reach this goal. Yiddish culture thus had its part to play as a poster child for Ceaușescu's regime. In the particular context of post-1967 Romanian-Israeli relations, TES's leadership did not mind the role assigned to the theater as it afforded the troupe opportunities that had seemed unattainable even half a decade earlier. The tour allowed its individual participants to visit Israel and to reconnect with friends and family members who had relocated there without having to defect or emigrate. It also put the institution on the international artistic map and gave it a chance to present itself to the world. For artists yearning for recognition of their talents outside the confinement of the Romanian theatrical circuit, this exposure was exhilarating and momentous. Most importantly, the tour made apparent that the Iron Curtain was not impenetrable and that integrated nonconformism, to return to Markiewicz-Lagneau's term, could be at times more beneficial and effective than taking a stand. For the next two decades, TES's leaders practiced this approach as they kept the theater alive under ever more precarious and uncertain domestic circumstances. Like all other culture outlets in the country, TES did not possess a license to artistic freedom but, unlike the other institutions, it stood in a relationship of inter-dependency with the authorities which – until the end of the 1970s – afforded it the chance to transgress the seemingly impassable Iron Curtain.

Bibliography

Archival Sources

Letter from the Theater Council of the State Committee for Culture and Art, August 2, 1967 [Israil Bercovici Collection. University of Potsdam] 1417 b 1845.

Playbill for TES's tour to Israel in 1968 [Yehuda Gabay Theater Archive at the Sha'ar Zion Library-Beit Ariela, Tel Aviv] TH 112–13.

Poster 1968, אַ שנירל פּערל and Poster 1968, צען ברידער זענען מיר געווען [The Israeli Center for the Documentation of the Performing Arts, Tel Aviv University] Collection "The State Yiddish Theater in Romania in 50s–60s".

Census data: Population according to ethnicity from the census data between 1930 and 2002, <https://insse.ro/cms/files/RPL2002INS/vol4/tabele/t1.pdf.>, June 26, 2022.

Sources

Andreescu, Andreea, Lucian Nastasă, and Andrea Varga, 2002: *Evreii din România. Mărturii documentare (1945–1965)*. Cluj-Napoca: Centrul de Resurse pentru Diversitate Etnoculturală, 423–429.

Anonymous, 1968: 20 de ani de existență a Teatrului Evreesc de Stat din România. Ne vorbeşte F. I. Auerbach, directorul T.E.S. In: *Glasul poporului* 31 (Tel Aviv), 1 August: [3].

Axmann, Elisabeth, 2007: *Fünf Dichter aus der Bukowina: Alfred Margul-Sperber, Alfred Kittner, Moses Rosenkranz, Rose Ausländer, Paul Celan*. Aachen: Rimbaud-Verlag.

Bercovici, Israil, 1998 [1982]: *O sută de ani de teatru evreiesc în România*. 2nd edition revised and completed by Constantin Măciucă. Bucharest: Editura Integral.

Bercovici, Israil [Yisroel Berkovitsh], 1976 בערקאָוויטש, ישׂראל: **הונדערט יאָר ייִדיש טעאַטער אין רומעניע, 1876–1976**. בוקאַרעשט: פּאַרלאַג קריטעריאָן.

Berkowitz, Joel, 2003: *Yiddish Theatre: New Approaches*. Oxford; Portland, Oreg.: Littman Library of Jewish Civilization.

Berkowitz, Joel, and Barbara J. Henry, 2012: *Inventing the Modern Yiddish Stage:*

Essays in Drama, Performance, and Show Business. Detroit, Mich.: Wayne State University Press.

Blayzor, Irene, 1971: Yiddish Theater Flourishes in Romania. In: *Hadassah Magazine* 53 (1) (New York), September: 34–36.

Brooks, Van Wyck, 1918: On Creating a Usable Past. In: *The Dial* 64 (7), 11 April: 337–341.

Brandt, Leon, 1968: Jüdisches Leben in Rumänien. In: *Allgemeine Zeitung* (West-Berlin) 23 (29), 18 October: 6.

Bruckstein, Alfred M., 2017: (Joseph-Leib, Arye) Ludovic Bruckstein July 27, 1920 – August 4, 1988. In: <https://freddy.cs.technion.ac.il/life/ludovic-bruckstein/>, June 3, 2022.

Chaim, Zeev Ben, 1968: Perle clasice veritabile. In: *Viața noastră* (Tel Aviv) 5 July: 15a.

Chaim, Zeev Ben, 1968b: T. E. S. a preferat turneul in Israel. In: *Viața noastră* (Tel Aviv) [n. d] June: [n. p.].

Cajal, Nicolae, and Harry Kuller, eds., 2004 [1996]: *Contribuția evreilor din România la cultură și civilizație*. 2nd edition. Bucharest: Hasefer, 422–459.

Caplan, Debra, 2018: *Yiddish Empire. The Vilna Troupe, Jewish Theater, and the Art of Itinerancy*. Ann Arbor, Mich.: University of Michigan Press.

Chaver, Yael, 2004: *What Must Be Forgotten: The Survival of Yiddish in Zionist Palestine*. Syracuse, NY: Syracuse University Press.

Chiriac, Alexandra, 2022: *Performing Modernism: A Jewish Avant-Garde in Bucharest*. Berlin: De Gruyter.

Cioroianu, Adrian, 2005: *Pe umerii lui Marx. O introducere în istoria comunismului românesc*. Bucharest: Curtea veche.

Cohen, B. H., 1968: Excellent formation artistique. In: *L'information d'Israël* (Tel Aviv) 12 July: [n. p.].

Crăciun, Camelia, 2018: "Virtually ex nihilo." The Emergence of Yiddish Bucharest during the Interwar Period. In: Ferenc Laczó and Joachim von Puttkamer, eds., *Catastrophe and Utopia. Jewish Intellectuals in Central and Eastern Europe in the 1930s and 1940s*. Berlin: Walter de Gruyter/Oldenbourg, 133–152.

Deletant, Dennis, 1995: *Ceausescu and the Securitate: Coercion and Dissent in Romania, 1965–1989*. London: Routledge.

Erizanu, Paula, 2019: "My father understood the human soul:" Remembering the Jewish-Romanian Author whose Holocaust Stories Continue to Inspire Compassion. In: *The Calvert Journal* 17 October 2019, <https://www.calvertjournal.com/articles/show/11408/ludovic-bruckstein-jewish-romanian-author-war-communism-holocaust-literature>, June 3, 2022.

Gal, Aharon, 1968: Eichal Hatarbut "Siragul de perle." In: *Adevărul* (Tel Aviv) 5 July: [n. p.].

Govrin, Yosef, 2002: *Israeli-Romanian Relations at the End of the Ceausescu Era as Seen by Israel's Ambassador to Romania 1985–1989*. London: Routledge.

Gros-Tsimerman, M[oyshe], 1968 גראָס־צימערמאַן, מ[שה]: בלאָנדזשענדיקע שטערן. אין: **לעצטע נײַעס** (תל־אָבֿיבֿ), 12טער יולי: 3.

Grözinger, Elvira, 2002: *Die jiddische Kultur im Schatten der Diktaturen: Israil Bercovici – Leben und Werk*. Berlin, Vienna: Philo.

Hadas, Israel, 1968: Întîlnire emoţionantă dintre Teatrul Evreiesc din Bucureşti şi spectatorul israelian. In: **יִדישע צייטונג** (Tel Aviv) 5 July: [n. p.]. (Available in Romanian translation).

Halaus, D., 1968: La Tel Aviv cu actorii oaspeți în fotoliu şi în culise. In: *Actualitatea în 7 zile* (Tel Aviv) 1(?) July: 18.

Honik, Yosef, 1968 האָניק, יוסף: [קיין טיטל]. אין: **דער טאָג־מאָרגען זשורנאַל** (ניו־יאָרק), 11טער יולי: 7.

Har-Gil, Shraga, 1968 הר־גיל, שרגא: התיאטרון מבוקרשט מגיע לאשדוד. בתוך: **מעריב** (תל אביב), 5 יולי: [n.p.].

Ioanid, Radu, 2015: *Securitatea şi vânzarea evreilor*. Iaşi: Polirom.

Kunze, Thomas, 2017 [2000]: *Nicolae Ceausescu. Eine Biographie*. 4th edition. Berlin: Christoph Links Verlag.

Lazăr, Samson, 1968: Folcklor [sic] şi creație literară în "Şiragul de perle." In: *Glasul poporului* (Tel Aviv) 4 July: [n. p.].

Lipski, Yitskhok, 1968 ליפּסקי, אי.: אידישער מלוכה טעאַטער פֿון רומעניע צוגאַסט אין ישראַל. אין: **מאָרגן פֿרײַהײַט** (ניו־יאָרק), 2טער אויגוסט: 3.

Mancini, Anthony, 1968: Woman in the News: Ida Kaminska, Yet One More Resting Place. In: *New York Post*, 7 December: 23.

Markiewicz-Lagneau, Janina, 1976: La fin de l'intelligentsia? Formation et transformation de l'intelligentsia soviétique. In: *Revue d'études comparatives Est-Ouest* 7 (4): 7–71.

Morgan, Barbara, 2021: Kaminska, Ida (1899–1980). In: *Women in World History: A Biographical Encyclopedia*, <https://www.encyclopedia.com/women/encyclopedias-almanacs-transcripts-and-maps/kaminska-ida-1899–1980>, June 10, 2021.

Mr., Mş., 1968: Însemnări teatrale: "Şiragul de perle." In: *Facla* (Tel Aviv) 10 July: 9a and 13a.

Nahshon, Edna, 2009: *Jewish Theatre: A Global View*. Leiden; Boston: Brill.

Quint, Alyssa, 2019: *The Rise of the Modern Yiddish Theater*. Bloomington, Ind.: Indiana University Press.

Rojanski, Rachel, 2020: *Yiddish in Israel. A History*. Bloomington, Ind.: Indiana University Press.

Rosen, Mozes, 1992: Epilogue – The Recipe. In: Michael Riff, ed., *The Face of Survival: Jewish Life in Eastern Europe Past and Present*. London: Vallentine Mitchell, 215–222.

Sandrow, Nahma, 1977: *Vagabond Stars. A World History of Yiddish Theater*. New York, NY: Harper & Row.

Schmidt-Mühlisch, Lothar, 1968: Kommt das Bukarester Jüdische Staatstheater nach Bonn? Ein G.-A.-Gespräch mit dem Intendanten der Bühne Franz Joseph Auerbach. In: *General Anzeiger* (Bonn) 5. April: [n. p.].

Shafir, Michael, 1985: *Romania, Politics, Economics and Society: Political Stagnation and Simulated Change*. Boulder, Colo.: Lynne Rienner Publishers.

Slutska Kestin, Khave, 1968 סלוצקאַ־קעסטין, חווה: דערהאָבנדיגע פֿאָרשטעלונגען פֿון רומעניש־אידישן טעאַטער אין ישראל. אין: **מאָרגן פֿרייַהייַט** (ניו־יאָרק), 18טער אויגוסט: 9

Solomovici, T[eşu], 1968: Succesul Teatrului Evreesc de Stat din Bucureşti în Israel. In: *Glasul poporului* (Tel Aviv) 11 July: [n. p.].

Stanciu, Cezar, 2014: Romania and the Six Day War. In: *Middle Eastern Studies* 50 (5): 775–795.

Tshernov, I., 1968 טשערנאָוו, אי.: די פּרעמיערע פֿון ייִדישן מלוכה־טעאַטער פֿון רומעניע: „אַ שנירל פּערל“. אין: **לעצטע נייַעס** (תּל־אָבֿיבֿ), 5טער יולי: 5

Tismaneanu, Vladimir, 2003: *Stalinism for All Seasons. A Political History of Romanian Communism*. Berkeley, Calif.: University of California Press.

Vasile, Cristian, 2013: *Politicile culturale comuniste în timpul regimului Gheorghiu-Dej*. Bucharest: Humanitas.

Binyamin Hunyadi

An Introduction to "A Quarter Century of Yiddish Broadcasting on Romanian Radio"

In his seminal 1964 book *Understanding Media: The Extension of Man*, philosopher Marshall McLuhan theorized about the power of radio in the following way: "Radio is not only a mighty awakener of archaic memories, forces, and animosities, but a decentralizing, pluralistic force, as is really the case with all electric power and media." Moreover, he claimed, it "contracts the world to village size, and creates insatiable village tastes for gossip, rumor, and personal malice."[1] According to McLuhan, radio has borne the primary responsibility for the revival of dead or dying languages in Ireland, Wales, Scotland, and Israel. Radio is a means of creating an imagined world, and establishing an illusion of a tightly knit, vibrant community, which the listener willingly buys into. It would be hard to find a more suitable characterization than McLuhan's for the effects and experiences created by Yiddish radio broadcasts in Romania in the post-1945 milieu. The fantasies established by Yiddish radio programs succeeded in forming coherent communal groups centered around Yiddish in Western and Eastern Europe, as well as an emerging sense of East European Yiddish cultural continuity.

Yiddish radio broadcasts in Romania shared some traits and challenges with the vastly more influential and variegated radio industry in the United States. Similar to its US counterpart, where stations with Yiddish programming in the 1950s vied for existence in a highly competitive market, Romanian Yiddish radio broadcasts were hampered by dependency on the political goodwill of Party potentates and the caprice of cultural administrators.[2] Both the US and Romanian Yiddish radio content producers had to cope with adverse circumstances, such as discriminatory regulation targeting less profitable stations and, in the name of putative 'public interest,' foreign language broadcasts in the American case and programming not falling narrowly in line with obligatory broadcasting service requirements or ideological lines

1 McLuhan 1964, 267.

2 On the history of Yiddish radio broadcasts in the United States see Kelman 2008, 109–134; Kelman 2009.

in Romania respectively. However, there were also significant differences between the social and political contexts in which Yiddish radio broadcasting existed in both countries. Whereas in the US Yiddish broadcasts catered to the mass market listener, seeking to find the lowest common linguistic and cultural denominator that would appeal to the widest variety of tastes and sensibilities, radio programming in Romania had no such concerns. Instead, its main care was to discharge the political obligations set upon it by the government, wherein most of its cultural content was dictated by formal Party-ideological considerations. At the same time, since Yiddish radio in Romania did not have to operate under the pressures of the capitalist market, it was able to produce Yiddish programming, which served as a means of refining the taste of their listeners and promote highbrow culture.

Romanian Yiddish radio broadcasting addressed a Yiddish-speaking community greatly reduced in numbers and yearning for the reinvigoration of pre-*khurbn* cultural life of which mere fragments seemed to remain. It met these nostalgic desires of its listeners while also spotlighting the evolving postwar Yiddish cultural scene: new radio plays and recordings were interspersed with interviews with contemporary journalists, cultural activists, authors, and actors. Broadcasting began on 5 March 1949 under the aegis of the ייִדישער קולטור־פֿאַרבאַנד [*Yidisher kultur-farband*, Jewish Culture Association, YKUF], which was responsible for supervising all facets of Yiddish cultural production in the country, from producing educational and propaganda materials for Jewish schools to Yiddish book publishing and the repertoire of the Yiddish-language Teatrul Evreiesc de Stat [Jewish State Theater]. For a decade, control over programming was restricted to the relevant personnel of the YKUF.

Romanian Yiddish radio broadcasting started out on a small scale: once a week for half an hour. Upon completion of the brand-new Romanian Radio building in 1952, it gradually expanded to three times a week, and then, between 1954 and 1956, to daily half hour broadcasts. This broadcasting schedule was maintained until the closing down of Yiddish radio in 1974, presumedly due to General Secretary of the Romanian Communist Party Nicolae Ceaușescu's (1918–1989) growing interest in mass media as a practical tool for propelling the cult of personality, which received greater emphasis in the 1970s, though the exact reason behind the closure remains unknown. Ceaușescu considered the transmissions of the Western Radio Free Europe in Romania with growing suspicion verging on obsession, at times implementing extreme countermeasures to balk its influence on the population.[3] In these circumstances, the access of Yiddish radio to the means of national broadcasting was considerably restricted, limiting content to mostly innocuous literary expressions. The heart of Yiddish culture in the 1970s began to take on a new shape as a literary culture far from the radio and the prying eyes of the party apparatchiks. The continued existence of a suspect radio broadcast would have undermined this process of withdrawal to the relative freedom of high-literature. Nevertheless, the achievement of Yiddish radio in Romania remains significant, as the longest existing radio broadcast service in Yiddish in Europe in the 20th century, both behind and beyond the Iron Curtain. As early as 1952, the technical equipment of the Romanian radio station allowed for transmissions not only to domestic audiences but also abroad.

The following interview was conducted with the longest serving member of the Romanian Yiddish broadcasting service, Sholem [Sulim] Rubinger (?–1988). It was published in the Bucharest-based Yiddish literary journal בוקאַרעשטער שריפֿטן [*Bukareshter shriftn*, Bucharest Writings] in 1983 – nine years after Yiddish broadcasting on Romanian state radio was terminated on 20 May 1974. It is reproduced here in standardized YIVO orthography and followed by an English translation for the first time. Footnotes and bibliography were added by the translators, Binyamin Hunyadi and Miriam Chorley-Schulz.

Interviews were rarely featured in the *Bukareshter shriftn* making this one unique: it was the only time in which one of the key figures of the Romanian Yiddish cultural milieu appeared in conversation on its pages. Rubinger, lesser-known today, was an active figure in Romanian Yiddish culture throughout the country's tumultuous postwar decades. He worked as a Yiddish translator, critic, journalist, and radio broadcaster in the communist period in Romania and his career path may be compared to that of members of the Teatrul Evreiesc de Stat, who worked relatively shielded from immediate political involvement.[4] Among Rubinger's most important translations is the translation into Yiddish (published in two editions, 1958 and 1961) of the

3 On the Romanian regime's response to the local broadcasts of Radio Free Europe and the state of Romanian domestic radio programming, see Ratesh 2010, 205–227; Nagat 2010, 229–238.

4 See Corina L. Petrescu's article on the Teatrul Evreiesc de Stat [Jewish State Theater] in the present volume.

diary of Anne Frank, which was first published in Dutch under the title *Het Achterhuis. Dagboekbrieven 14 Juni 1942–1 Augustus 1944* [The Annex: Diary Notes 14 June 1942–1 August 1944] in 1947 and in English as *Anne Frank: The Diary of a Young Girl* in 1952. Subsequently, he worked on the diary's theatrical adaptation which was a stage success when performed by the Teatrul Evreiesc de Stat in 1971.[5] As a critic, Rubinger published book reviews in the trilingual *Revista cultului mozaic din R.P.R* [Periodical of the Mosaic Religion in the Romanian People's Republic] and later in the aforementioned *Bukareshter shriftn.* He was also a longstanding staff member of the Yiddish section of the Romanian state radio.

As the interview indicates, Yiddish radio in Romania was dedicated, among other things, to showcase to its listeners the opinions and experiences of culturally important Yiddish-speaking figures visiting the country from abroad. Interviewees were generally affiliated with the non-communist left (either in Israel, Western Europe or the United States) or were dedicated communist activists from outside Romania. Among them were activists who did not shy away from expressing their dissatisfaction, from left-wing perspectives, with the policies of the Soviet Union and its treatment of Jews. The radio even seems to have embraced these critical voices so as to underline Romania's independence from Soviet policies and its own completely different handling of "the national question." Even during the 1950s, a period marked by ardent anti-Zionist agitation, Romanian Yiddish broadcasting, as opposed to non-Yiddish programming, refrained from attacks against Israel. The interview also reveals efforts by left-wing Yiddish activists to maintain a progressive and open cultural scene and, after political clampdowns on freedom of expression, to document the rich history of Yiddish cultural production in Romania.

5 As opposed to other Yiddish translations of Anne Frank's diaries, which were based on English versions, Rubinger seems to have translated directly from the Dutch original. See Frank and Rubinger 1958. The second edition was printed by request of the State Yiddish publishing company of Poland ייִדיש־בוך [*Yidish-bukh*, Yiddish Book] in 1961 and intended for circulation only in Poland. The stage version was based on a play by Frances Goodrich and Albert Hackett (*The Diary of Anne Frank*, 1955) and jointly translated from the English by Dovid Rubin (1893–1975), Alexander Shpiglblat (1927–2013), and Rubinger. The 1971 Romanian Yiddish stage version was directed by the well-known theater director George Teodorescu (1919–2000), who occasionally worked on Yiddish plays for the State Yiddish Theater.

Bibliography

Frank, Anne, and Sholem [Sulim] Rubinger (transl.) 1958 פֿראַנק, אַנאַ, און שלום רובינגער: **אַנאַ פֿראַנקס טאָגבוך**. בוקאַרעשט: מלוכה־פֿאַרלאַג פֿאַר ליטעראַטור און קונסט.

Frank, Anne, and Sholem [Sulim] Rubinger (transl.) 1961 פֿראַנק, אַנאַ, און שלום רובינגער: **אַנאַ פֿראַנקס טאָגבוך**. וואַרשע: ייִדיש־בוך.

Kelman, Ari Y., 2008: "The Worldly Sounds of Yiddish Radio." In: Shapiro, Edward S. (ed.), *Yiddish in America: Essays on Yiddish Culture in the Golden Land*. Scranton, Penn.: University of Scranton Press, 109–134.

Kelman, Ari Y., 2009: *Station Identification: A Cultural History of Yiddish Radio in the United States*. Berkeley, Calif.: University of California Press.

McLuhan, Marshall, 1964: *Understanding Media: The Extensions of Man*. New York, NY: Mentor.

Nagat, Germina, 2010: "Ceaușescu's War against our Ears." In: Johnson, Ross A., and E. Eugene Parta (eds.), *Cold War Broadcasting: Impact of the Soviet Union and Eastern Europe: A Collection of Studies and Documents*. Budapest – New York, NY: Central European University Press, 229–238.

Ratesh, Nestor, 2010: "Radio Free Europe's Impact in Romania During the Cold War." In: Johnson, Ross A., and E. Eugene Parta (eds.), *Cold War Broadcasting: Impact of the Soviet Union and Eastern Europe: A Collection of Studies and Documents*. Budapest – New York, NY: Central European University Press, 205–227.

אַ שמועס מיטן לאַנגיאָריקן רעדאַקטאָר פֿון די ייִדישע אוידיציעס בײַם רומענישן ראַדיאָ – שלום רובינגער

אַ פֿערטל יאָרהונדערט ייִדישע אוידיציעס בײַם רומענישן ראַדיאָ

פֿראַגע: פֿרײַנד שלום רובינגער, מיר וואָלטן אײַך געבעטן אונדז מיטצוטיילן איייניקע דאַטן וועגן די ייִדישע אוידיציעס בײַם רומענישן ראַדיאָ. ווען, אונטער וועלכע אומשטאַנדן און ווי אַזוי זענען געשאַפֿן געוואָרן די ייִדישע אוידיציעס בײַם רומענישן ראַדיאָ, וואָס האָבן אָנגעהאַלטן אַ פֿערטל יאָרהונדערט?

ענטפֿער: לויט אַ פֿאָרשלאַג פֿון דער קולטור־סעקציע פֿון ייִדישן דעמאָקראַטישן קאָמיטעט און איקוף, זענען דעם 5טן מאַרץ 1949 אײַנגעפֿירט געוואָרן ייִדישע ראַדיאָ־אוידיציעס בײַם רומענישן ראַדיאָ. תּחילת האָט מען טראַנסמיטירט די אוידיציעס איין מאָל אין דער וואָך – אַ האַלבע שעה צײַט – פֿרײַטיק אויף דער נאַכט. די ערשטע אוידיציע האָט אינויגורירט דער איקוף־כאָר, מיט וועלכן ס׳האָט אָנגעפֿירט דער באַקאַנטער קאָמפּאָזיטאָר און דיריגענט פֿונעם בוקאַרעשטער ייִדישן מלוכה־טעאַטער – חיים שוואַרצמאַן. די דאָזיקע אוידיציעס זענען געווען באַשטימט פֿאַרן אינלאַנד. פֿון אַלע שטעט און שטעטלעך האָבן מיר באַקומען קאָרעספּאָנדענצן פֿון די צוהערער אין וועלכע זיי האָבן פֿאָרגעשלאָגן וואָס זיי וואָלטן גערן געהערט אויפֿן געביט פֿון מוזיק, לידער, פֿאָרלעזונגען, סקעטשן. אין די מיינסטע שטעט פֿון רומעניע פֿלעגן זיך די צוהערער צונויפֿקומען אין זייערע קולטור־קלובן און קאָלעקטיוו אויסהערן די אוידיציעס. דער פֿרײַטיק אויף דער נאַכט פֿלעגט מיט אומגעדולד דערוואַרט ווערן.

An Interview with Sholem Rubinger, Long-Time Editor of Yiddish Broadcasting on Romanian Radio

A Quarter Century of Yiddish Broadcasting on Romanian Radio

Translation into English by
Miriam Chorley-Schulz and Binyamin Hunyadi

Question: Comrade Sholem Rubinger, we would like to ask you to tell us a few facts about Yiddish broadcasting on Romanian radio. When, under what circumstances, and how was the Yiddish program for Romanian radio created – a program which ran for a quarter of a century?

Answer: Following the suggestion of the Culture Section of the Jewish Democratic Committee[1] and YKUF, Yiddish broadcasting was introduced to Romanian radio on 5 March 1949. At the beginning, the program was broadcast once a week – for half an hour – on Friday evenings. The first broadcast opened with a recording of the YKUF-choir, headed by the well-known composer and conductor of the Bucharest Jewish State Theater[2] – Haim Schwartzman.[3] These early shows were intended for a *domestic* audience. We received letters from listeners from all the cities and towns in which they suggested what they wanted to listen to in terms of music, songs, talks, sketches. In most Romanian cities listeners would usually get together in

Originally published in vol. 6 (1983) of בוקאַרעשטער שריפֿטן, 120–126, see bibliography.

1 The Comitetul Democratic Evreiesc [Jewish Democratic Committee] was a left-wing Jewish political party founded in 1945 and dissolved in 1953.
2 The Teatrul Evreiesc de Stat [Jewish State Theater] in Bucharest was established on 1 August 1948 and active throughout the communist period. The theater played a central role in the cultural life of Yiddish-speaking Jews in the country and was considered one of the most significant cultural vehicles created by Romania's Yiddish scene, aimed at Jewish and non-Jewish audiences alike in Israel and other Western countries.
3 Haim Schwartzman (Khayim Shvartsman, 1897–1982) was a Jewish cultural activist and musician, long-time conductor of the orchestra of the Romanian Jewish State Theater. Schwartzman worked as a Hebrew and music teacher before the Second World War in the Bucharest-based Jewish Malbim and Cultura schools and other cultural institutions. After the *khurbn* Schwartzman started working as a composer and conductor for the orchestra of the Jewish State Theater. Though his children moved to Israel, Schwartzman decided to stay in Romania. He also served as conductor in recordings based on the pieces performed at the Romanian Jewish State Theater, such as Electrecord 1958, Electrecord 196?, and Electrecord 1974.

סוף 1952, ווען די גרויסע, מאָדערנע געבײַדע פֿונעם רומענישן ראַדיאָ איז אויסגעענדיקט און אויסגעשטאַט געוואָרן מיט דער געהעריקער אַפּאַראַטור, האָבן מיר אָנגעהויבן טראַנסמיטירן אונדזערע ייִדישע אוידיציעס, קודם דרײַ מאָל אַ וואָך און אין אַ קורצער צײַט אַרום יעדן טאָג, אויך צו אַ האַלבע שעה. צווישן 1954 און 1956 צוויי אוידיציעס אַ טאָג. די דאָזיקע אוידיציעס זענען שוין געווען באַשטימט אויך פֿאַרן אויסלאַנד, פֿאַר מערבֿ־אייראָפּע און אַמעריקע.

פֿראַגע: פֿרײַנד ש[לום] רובינגער, איר זענט דאָך געווען איינער פֿון די רעדאַקטאָרן וואָס האָבן אין משך פֿון אַ פֿערטל יאָרהונדערט מיטגעאַרבעט און אַ שטיקל צײַט טאַקע געווען דער שעף־רעדאַקטאָר פֿון די ייִדישע אוידיציעס בײַם רומענישן ראַדיאָ. וואָס קענט איר אונדז דערציילן וועגן דער סטרוקטור, צוועק און ציל פֿון די דאָזיקע אוידיציעס?

ענטפֿער: דער צוועק און ציל פֿון די אוידיציעס איז קודם־כּל געווען – ווי אַלע אוידיציעס פֿון די מיטלעבנדיקע נאַציאָנאַליטעטן פֿון דעם לאַנד, אויף מאַמע־לשון – באַקאַנט צו מאַכן די אויפֿטוען פֿון סאָציאַליסטישן רומעניע בײַם פֿאַרהיילן די וווּנדן פֿון דער מלחמה, בײַם לייגן די יסודות פֿאַר אַ סאָציאַליסטישערווירטשאַפֿט, ווי אויך וועגן די פּראָגרעסן אין קולטור־געזעלשאַפֿטלעכן לעבן.

פֿראַגע: ווער זענען געווען די מיטגלידער פֿון דער רעדאַקציע און וואָס פֿאַראַ אויפֿגאַבן האָבן זיי געהאַט?

ענטפֿער: תּחילת איז די רעדאַקציע באַשטאַנען פֿון פֿאָלגנדיקע מיטגלידער. שעף־רעדאַקטאָר מ. ליינוואַנד; רעדאַקטאָרשע־ספּיקערין, אַמאַליאַ קראָנענפֿעלד; רעדאַקטאָר־ספּיקער און רעפּאָרטער, שלום רובינגער; דאַקטילאָגראַפֿין, מלכּה האָראָוויץ; ברײַנע קליִער, גאָלדע וויגדער – איבערזעצערינס און אין 1970 איז צוגעקומען אַלס איבערזעצער, אײַזיק פֿוקס. ביז צום יאָר 1956 האָט מיט קורצע איבעררײַסן געאַרבעט אַלס רעדאַקטאָר און דאַן אַלס שעף־רעדאַקטאָר, דער שרײַבער און דיכטער ישׂראל בערקאָוויטש. אַלס דרויסנדיקער מיטאַרבעטער און קאָרעספּאָנדענט פֿון דער פּראָווינץ, באַזונדערס פֿאַר אונדזערע קולטור־פּראָגראַמען, קענען מיר נאָך צורעכענען דעם שרײַבער און היסטאָריקער, איציק קאַראַ, דעם פּובליציסט י. פֿײַערשטיין.

their culture clubs and listen to the shows collectively. Friday evenings were eagerly awaited.

At the end of 1952, when the big, modern building of the Romanian radio was completed and furnished with the necessary equipment, we began to broadcast our Yiddish shows, first three times a week and shortly after that every day, also for half an hour, and between 1954 and 1956 we aired two shows a day. These shows were already intended for home and *abroad*, for Western Europe and America.

Question: Comrade Sh[olem] Rubinger, as we know you've been one of the producers who worked on the Yiddish programming on Romanian radio for a quarter century and for some time even as its editor-in-chief. What can you tell us about the structure, purpose, and goal of these shows?

Answer: The purpose and goal of the broadcasting – like all programs of cohabitating nationalities in the country in their mother tongue – was, above all, to make known the accomplishments of socialist Romania in healing the wounds of the war, in laying the foundations for a socialist economy, and in the development of our cultural-social life.

Question:Who were the members of the editorial board and what were their tasks?

Answer: At the beginning, the editorial board was comprised of the following members: editor-in-chief M. [sic] Leynvand; editor-announcer Amalia Kronenfeld; myself, Sholem Rubinger, editor-announcer and reporter;[4] our typist, Malke Horovits; Breyne Klier and Golde Vigder – translators, and in 1970 Eyzik Fuks also joined as a translator. Until 1956, the writer and poet Yisroel Berkovitsh [Israil Bercovici] worked almost without a break as an editor and then editor-in-chief.[5] We can also mention writer and historian

4 Apart from their cooperation on Yiddish broadcasting, Kronenfeld and Rubinger translated plays from Romanian to Yiddish together (such as Kirițescu 1977 and the dialogues of other musical revues), that were staged by the Jewish State Theater. I (B. H.) was not able to locate an extant copy of the translation. The information is based on secondary sources. The translation may never have been published, and was merely available to the actors and staff of the Jewish State Theater. See for example a contemporary critique by Iosif 1977: she mentions Rubinger and Kronenfeld as the two translators of the play.

5 Israil Bercovici [Yisroel Berkovitsh] (1921–1988) was a Yiddish poet, playwright, translator, literary historian, journalist and, from 1955 to 1982, the literary director and head dramaturge of the Jewish State Theater in Bucharest. Having survived the *khurbn* in his native Moldova and liberated by the Soviet Army in 1944, he joined the Communist Party affiliated Comitetul Democratic Evreiesc and became an activist within the ייִדישער קולטור־פֿאַרבאַנד [*Yidisher kultur-farband*, Jewish Culture Association, short: YKUF] promoting Yiddish language and Jewish socialist culture that was markedly anti-Zionist. Lionizing the theater as the locus of Yiddish cultural creativity,

פֿראַגע: וועלכע באַקאַנטע פּערזענלעכקייטן, היגע און אויסלענדישע, האָבן אָפּגעגעבן דערקלערונגען אָדער אינטערוויוען אין ראַמען פֿון די ייִדישע אוידיציעס?

ענטפֿער: אַ היפּשע צאָל. אַלע געדענק איך נישט, אָבער לאָמיר פּרוּוון איבערציילן. קודם די היגע. בײַ פֿאַרשיידענע געלעגנהייטן, ווי נאָך רײַזעס אין אויסלאַנד און צו פֿאַרשיידענע היסטאָרישע דאַטעס, פֿלעגט רעדן בײַ אונדזערע מיקראָפֿאָנען דער רבֿ־הכּולל, דר. משה רוזן. אויך דערמאָן איך מיך צוויי זייער

I. Kara,[6] and columnist Y. Fayershteyn[7] as external staff and correspondents for the provinces, especially for our cultural programs.

Question: Which celebrities, local or foreign, gave statements or interviews in the framework of Yiddish broadcasting?

Answer: Quite a few. I won't remember all of them, but let's try and enumerate. Let's start with the local ones. On different occasions, like after travels abroad and on the anniversary of various historical events, chief rabbi Dr. Mozes Rosen[8] would usually talk to us. I also remember two very

he published a history of the Jewish theater in Romania in 1976 in Yiddish (see Bercovici 1976; an extended, revised version appeared in Romanian) in addition to several collections of Yiddish poetry (Bercovici 1974, Bercovici 1978, Bercovici 1984). In 1976, he was honored for his literary achievements by the Writers Union of Romania, in 1982 by the Romanian Academy, and in 1984 with the Vaysenberg Prize by the World Jewish Congress.

6 Y. Kara (Itsik Shvarts) (1906–1994) studied philology at the University of Chernivtsi. Kara had already been active in the interwar period in Yiddish literary life in Romania, having published articles in Yiddish periodicals associated with the modernist group יונג־רומעניע [*Yung Rumenye*, Young Romania] such as אויפֿגאַנג [*Oyfgang*, Sunrise] and שויבן [*Shoybn*, Windowpanes]. During the Second World War, Kara joined the Soviet armed forces and later, in Romania's communist period took part in the revitalization of Yiddish cultural life in Romania. Kara authored a Yiddish textbook for the new school system (1948) and published on Jewish-Romanian (Constantin Stere (1865–1936)) and Yiddish authors (Yankev Shternberg, Yisroel Berkovitsh, and Itsik Manger) in the Romanian and Yiddish presses. After 1976, Kara's short stories and novels started to appear in print in Romania, see Kara 1976, Kara 1980, Kara 1987.

7 Yoysef Fayershteyn (Iosif Faerstein) (1919–2010), later known as Anton Celaru, was a journalist, editor, and translator. First, he worked for the Yiddish periodical ייִקופֿ־בלעטער [*YKUF-bleter*, YKUF Gazette] and was the editor of the Romanian language Jewish periodical *Viața nouă* [New Life, Bucharest, 1951–1953]. Celaru was the only translator from Yiddish to Romanian who was a Yiddish culture activist in the communist period, but remained active even after the fall of the regime. He translated numerous books from Yiddish to Romanian in the two decades following the systemic political change. His last translation, Mendele Moykher-Sforim's מסעות בנימין השלישי [*Masoes Binyomin hashlishi*, The Travels of Binyamin III, In Romanian: Drumețiile lui Biniomin al treilea, Bucharest: Hasefer], was published posthumously in 2011.

8 Mozes Rosen (1912–1994), in effect the face and spokesperson of Romanian Jewry, was named the chief rabbi of Romania in 1948 in the most repressive Stalinist period of Romania's Communist rule and held the position until his death in 1994. He served as the president of the Federation of the Jewish Community from Romania since 1964. He was born in Moinești, Moldavia, to a rabbinical family from Galicia and studied both law at the University of Bucharest and towards rabbinical ordination in Vienna until the "Anschluss" in 1938. With the fascist rise to power of Ion Antonescu and the Iron Guard in September 1940, Rosen was imprisoned on the charge of being "Communist" in the Caracal internment camp, discharged in 1941 after Antonescu won the power struggle over the Iron Guard and entered into an alliance with Nazi Germany. Rosen was forced into hiding yet again to avoid deportation to Transnistria after the German attack on the Soviet Union, when Romania proactively enforced its very own eliminatory politics vis-à-vis its Jewish population and left political enemies. After the war, the so-called Red Rabbi succeeded in squaring the metaphorical circle, as it were, of leading Romanian Jewry under socialism put upon him by both the only legal Jewish organization – the Comitetul Democratic Evreiesc – and the Romanian political establishment while upholding, defending, and promoting Jewish religious and cultural life, even at times of overt antisemitism that targeted him personally. He established a network of Jewish schools and several kosher canteens as well as the community newspaper *Revista*

וויכטיקע דערקלערונגען וואָס ס׳האָט אָפּגעגעבן בײַ אונדזערע מיקראָפֿאָנען דער אַקאַ־דעמיע־מיטגליד, פּראָפֿעסאָר פֿאַר מאַטעמאַטיק מענדל חיימאָוויטש וועלכער האָט נישט איין מאָל פֿאַרטרעטן רומעניע אויף פֿאַרשיידענע קאָנפֿערענצן אין אויסלאַנד. מיר האָבן אויך גענומען דערקלערונגען פֿון אַרבעטער, אינזשענירן, פּראָפֿעסאָרן, דאָקטוירים וואָס האָבן געאַרבעט אויף פֿאַרשיידענע געביטן.

פֿראַגע: האָט איר אויך גענומען אינטערוויוען פֿאַר די ייִדישע אוידיציעס פֿון אויסלענ־דישע געסט וואָס האָבן באַזוכט רומעניע?

ענטפֿער: אַוודאי. אין די ייִדישע אוידיציעס האָבן גערעדט פּערזענלעכקייטן ווי: דר. נחום גאָלדמאַן, געוועזענער פּרעזידענט פֿון ייִדישן וועלט־קאָנגרעס; פּסח נאָוויק, ניו־יאָרק, שעף־רעדאַקטאָר פֿון דער ייִדישער צײַטונג „מאָרגן־פֿרײַהײַט״; בן־ציון גאָלד־בערג, ניו־יאָרק, פּובליציסט און ליטעראַטור־קריטיקער; ל. [ג.] קעניג, פּאַריז, שעף־רע־דאַקטאָר פֿון דער ייִדישער צײַטונג „נײַע פּרעסע״; נ. [פּסח] בינעצקי, ישׂראל, דיכטער; הערש סמאָליאַר, וואַרשע, שעף־רעדאַקטאָר פֿון דער צײַטונג „פֿאָלקס־שטימע״; יעקבֿ ראָטבאַום, וואַרשע, רעזשיסער וועלכער האָט אויפֿגעפֿירט אין בוקאַרעשטער ייִדישן

important statements that were made in our broadcasting by the member of the Academy of Sciences, professor of mathematics Mendel Haimovici,[9] who represented Romania at various conferences abroad more than once. We also took statements from workers, engineers, professors, and doctors who worked in different fields.

Question: Did you also conduct interviews for the Yiddish programs with foreign guests who visited Romania?

Answer: Of course. Well-known figures appeared on the Yiddish programs, such as: Dr. Nahum Goldmann, former president of the World Jewish Congress;[10] Peysekh Novik of New York, editor-in-chief of the Yiddish newspaper מאָרגן־פֿרײַהייט [*Morgn-frayhayt*, Morning Freedom];[11] Ben-Tsien Goldberg, New York, columnist and literary critic;[12] L. [G.] Kenig, Paris, editor-in-chief of the Yiddish newspaper נײַע פּרעסע [*Naye prese*, New Press];[13] N. [Peysekh] Binetsky, Israel, poet;[14] Hersh Smolyar, Warsaw, editor-in-chief of the newspaper פֿאָלקס־שטימע [*Folks-shtime*, People's Voice];[15] J[akub] Rot-

cultului mozaic din R.P.R. [Periodical of the Jewish Religion in the Romanian People's Republic] at home and, in the post-Stalinist period, initiated the reinstatement of international connections with Jewish communities abroad.

9 Mendel Haimovici (Mendl Khaymovits, 1906–1973) was a Romanian Jewish mathematician, who became a member of the Romanian Academy of Sciences in 1963.

10 Nahum Goldmann (1895–1982) was a Zionist activist and founder and president of the World Jewish Congress (1951–1978).

11 Peysekh Novik (Paul Novick) (1891–1989) was a communist activist, journalist, and editor working in the Yiddish communist press in the United States. Novik edited the first Yiddish communist daily, the פֿרײַהייט [*Frayhayt*, Freedom] established in 1922, and became the editor-in-chief of the later *Morgn-frayhayt* in 1939, continuing in this position until the paper's last issue in 1988.

12 Ben-Tsien Goldberg (1895–1972) was a psychologist who worked as a columnist in the Yiddish press. Goldberg's sympathetic approach to the Soviet Union, reflected in his reportage of his journey in 1934 (serialized in the טאָג [*Tog*, Day]) raised considerable controversy in the Yiddish press in the United States. Goldberg later continued publishing on the Soviet Union and on the situation and problems of the Jews there.

13 G. Kenig (Meylekh Gromb) (1909–1972) was a Yiddish journalist, editor, and editor-in-chief of the Paris-based Yiddish communist daily newspaper the *Naye prese* (1934–1993) between 1945–1972. Kenig gave an interview to the Romanian Yiddish radio on his visit to Romania in 1956. He documented his experiences in a series of articles published in the *Naye prese* in September and October of the same year, entitled רײַזע־אײַנדרוקן פֿון רומעניע [*Rayze ayndrukn fun Rumenye*, Travel Impressions from Romania].

14 With Binetsky, Rubinger probably speaks of Israeli Yiddish poet Peysekh Binetsky (1912–1966), who was born in Poland and joined the communist movement at a young age. Binetsky started his literary career by writing Yiddish revolutionary songs. During the Second World War, he was evacuated to Alma Ata. He moved to Israel in 1949 where he continued his Yiddish literary activities. Binetsky visited Romania in 1962.

15 Hersh Smolyar (1905–1993) was a communist journalist and newspaper editor. He edited the Warsaw-based *Folks-shtime* from 1950 to 1971 and is best known for his memoir about the Soviet Evsektsiia [Jewish Section of the Communist Party] (Smolyar 1978).

מלוכה־טעאַטער אייניקע פּיעסן; יעקבֿ שטערנבערג, דיכטער און טעאַטראַל, מאָסקווע; צלאַל בליץ, פּובליציסט און געזעלשאַפֿטלעכער טוער, אַרגענטינע; דר. קורט ווילהעלם, אויבעררראַבינער פֿון שוועדן; הרבֿ מאָווסאָוויטש, ניו־יאָרק; פּאַול הירשמאַן, פּאַריז.

זיי אַלע האָבן אָפּגעגעבן דערקלערונגען וועגן די ייִדישע אינסטיטוציעס וואָס זיי האָבן באַזוכט און באַזונדערס וועגן בוקאַרעשטער ייִדישן מלוכה־טעאַ־טער, פֿון וועלכן זיי זענען געווען אַנטציקט.

סע זענען געוויס געווען מער, אָבער דער זכּרון וויל נישט צוהעלפֿן.

פֿראַגע: וועלכע ייִדישע אינסטיטוציעס האָבן זיך אָפּט באַטייליקט אין די פּראָגראַמען פֿון די ייִדישע ראַדיאָ־אוידיציעס?

ענטפֿער: נישט נאָר באַטייליקט, נאָר טאַקע אַקטיוו מיטגעהאָלפֿן האָט אונדז דאָס בוקאַרעשטער ייִדישע מלוכה־טעאַטער, און טייל מאָל, פֿיל זעלטענער, דאָס יאַסער ייִדישע מלוכה־טעאַטער. אויב מיר רעדן פֿון הילף, מיינען מיר מאָראַ־לישע הילף, ווייַל מאַטעריאַל זענען די ייִדישע אוידיציעס לגמרי אויסגעהאַלטן געוואָרן פֿון דער מלוכה. אָט למשל האָבן מיר פֿאַרצייכנט אויף דער טאַשמע דעם גאַנצן ספּעקטאַקל „אַ גאָלדפֿאַדן־חלום“ אין דער רעזשי פֿון יעקבֿ ראָטבאַום. דער דאָזיקער ספּעקטאַקל איז איבערגעגעבן געוואָרן אין 5 (פֿינף)[1] סעריען, פֿינף שבתים נאָכאַנאַנד. ער האָט אַזוי אויסגענומען אַז פֿיל צוהערער פֿון אויסלאַנד האָבן געבעטן מיר זאָלן איבערחזרן די פּראָגראַמען. אָדער למשל פּאָרלעזונגען

1 The doubling of numbers is a reproduction of the original.

baum, Warsaw, a theatrical director who staged several plays at the Bucharest Jewish State Theater;[16] Y[ankev] Shternberg, poet and impresario, Moscow;[17] Tsalel Blits, columnist and cultural activist, Argentina;[18] Dr. Kurt Wilhelm, chief rabbi of Sweden;[19] Rabbi Mowshowitz, New York;[20] Paul Hirschman, Paris.[21]

They all gave statements about the Yiddish institutions they visited and particularly about the Bucharest Jewish State Theater, with which they were greatly impressed.

There were surely others, but my memory seems to fail me.

Question: What Yiddish institutions participated in the programs of the Yiddish radio?

Answer: The Bucharest Jewish State Theater and sometimes, but significantly less, the Iași Jewish State Theater not only participated but, indeed, actively helped us.[22] When we talk about help, we mean *moral* support, because materially the Yiddish programs were fully funded by the state. One of our collaborations with the theater was, for example, a recording of the entire play *A Goldfadn Dream* by J. Rotbaum.[23] The play was broadcast serially in five parts, five weekends in a row. It was so exceptional that many listeners from abroad asked us to repeat the program. Or, for example, performances

16 Jakub Rotbaum (1901–1994) was a Yiddish actor, theatrical director, and painter. He became known as the director of the ווילנער טרופּע [*Vilner trupe*, Vilna Troupe] in the 1930s. After the Second World War, he returned to Warsaw and together with Ida Kamińska (1899–1980) Rotbaum worked as the director of the Yiddish State Theater in Warsaw. He came to Romania in 1956 to direct his stage adaptation of Itsik Manger's works (see note 12).

17 Yankev Shternberg (1890–1973) was a Yiddish poet and theatrical director.

18 Tsalel Blits (pseudonym of Shmuel Iser Kahane, 1909–1986) was a Yiddish writer, translator and the head of YKUF in Argentina, and director of the left-wing Yiddish secular Peretz school in Buenos Aires. Blits visited Eastern Europe in July–August 1958 as a member of an YKUF committee from Argentina that traveled to Poland to pay tribute to the 15th anniversary of the Warsaw Ghetto Uprising. In August they visited Romania where they were invited by the representative of the Jewish community in 1956. He describes their journey and experiences in Blits 1961, 149–201.

19 Kurt Wilhelm (1900–1965) was a reform rabbi who was appointed as chief rabbi of Stockholm in 1948 and held the position until his death in 1965. He visited Romania in 1955.

20 Israel Mowshowitz (1914–1991) was a Conservative rabbi from the United States who was sent as a member of a delegation to investigate the condition of the Jews in the Soviet Union. Mowshowitz also travelled extensively throughout the world and visited several countries in the Eastern bloc, including Poland, Hungary, and Romania. He visited Romania in 1963 along with other prominent rabbis.

21 Paul Hirschman (dates unknown) was a French Jewish political and cultural activist.

22 A Yiddish-language Romanian Jewish State Theater was set up in Iași in 1949 and forced to close down in 1964. See Corina Petrescu's article on the subject in this volume.

23 Jakub Rotbaum worked on staging his most celebrated production אַ גאָלדפֿאַדן־חלום [*A Goldfadn-kholem*, A Goldfadn dream] – a dramatization of a selection of Itsik Manger's lyrical works – at the Jewish State Theater in Bucharest in 1956.

פֿון שוישפּילער. זייער אָפֿט האָבן שוישפּילער פֿונעם טעאַטער געהאַלטן פֿאָרלעזונגען. איך דערמאָן מיך ווי שטאַרק ס׳האָט אויסגענומען די פֿאָרלעזונג „גיטל פּורישקעוויטש״ פֿון שלום־עליכם אין דער אינטערפּרעטאַציע פֿון דער פֿאַרדינסטפֿולער קינסטלערין סעווילאַ פּאַסטאָר. צוהערער האָבן געבעטן מען זאָל נאָך אַ מאָל פּראָגראַמירן די פֿאָרלעזונג. ס׳האָבן זיך באַטייליקט אויך אַנדערע אַקטיאָרן. ווי: פֿישלער – מאַן און פֿרוי, כאַוויס, דינאַ קעניג, ליאַ קעניג־שטאָלפּער, בענאָ פּאָפּליקער, מ[אַנאָ] ריפּל, ס[יידי] גליק, ב[עבע] בערקאָוויטש, רודי ראָזנפֿעלד, קאַרל מאַרקאָוויטש, כּתבן און אַנדערע. סע מוז דאָ פֿאַרצייכנט ווערן אַז דער דירעקטאָר פֿון ייִדישן מלוכה־טעאַטער, פֿראַנץ אויערבאַך, האָט תּמיד געענטפֿערט מיט אַ האַרציקן יאָ, ווען מיר האָבן געבעטן צו העלפֿן אונדז אין אונדזער אַרבעט. ער פּערזענלעך האָט גערעדט בײַ אונדזער מיקראָפֿאָן וועגן גאַסטראָלן וואָס דאָס טעאַטער האָט געגעבן אין צפֿון־אַמעריקע, קאַנאַדע, ישׂראל און אויך אַנדערע געלעגנהייטן.

אויך אָפּיצירן האָבן גערעדט בײַ אונדזער מיקראָפֿאָן. איינער פֿון זיי, דער באַקאַנטער ייִדישער שרײַבער וואָלף טאַמבור האָט איינִיקע מאָל זיך באַטייליקט אין אונדזערע אוידיציעס. דעמאָלט האָט ער געטראָגן אַ מונדיר מיט די צייכנס פֿון אַ קאָלאָנעל, ווי אויך דער קאַפּיטאַן מאַלער, קאָמענדאַנט פֿון אַן אָפּטייל.

אַן אמתע גרויסע שטיצע אין אונדזער אַרבעט פֿאַר די אַלע 25 יאָר, שוין אַפֿילו נאָך דעם וואָס ער האָט געאַרבעט אַלס קינסטלערישער לײַטער און דראַמאַטורג פֿון ייִדישן מלוכה־טעאַטער, איז געווען דער דיכטער און שרײַבער, ישׂראל בערקאָוויטש. פּראָבלעמען בײַ אַזאַ אַרבעט יאַוּוען זיך געוויינטלעך, און ער האָט אונדז אַרויסגעהאָלפֿן לייזן די פּראָבלעמען.

by actors. Many times, actors from the theater did readings. I remember how exceptional the reading of "Gitl Purishkevitsh" by Sholem Aleichem was, interpreted for us by the talented artist Sevilla Pastor.[24] Listeners also asked for a repetition of that program. Other actors participated as well, such as: Fischler – husband and wife, Havis, Dina König, Lia Koenig-Stolper, Beno Popliker, M[ano] Rippel, S[eidy] Glück, B[ebe] Bercovici, Rudi Rosenfeld, Carol Marcovici, Cassvan, and others.[25] It needs to be said that the director of the Yiddish State Theater, Franz Auerbach, always responded with a heartfelt "Yes" whenever we asked him for support in our work. He personally appeared on air several times and discussed guest performances by the theater in North America, Canada, Israel, and other countries.[26]

Officers also spoke into our microphone. One of them, the well-known Yiddish writer Volf Tambur, gave us a few studio interviews. Back then, he would wear his uniform with the insignia of a colonel, as well as a captain Maler, a unit commander.[27]

A tremendous support in our work throughout its 25-year span was the poet, writer, artistic director, and dramaturg of the Jewish State Theater Israil Bercovici. All kinds of different problems in our line of work would pop up unexpectedly and he always helped in solving these.

24 Sevilla Pastor (1906–1982) was one of the "Pastor sisters," three Yiddish actresses who became famous while traveling with Morits Zigler's (Moyshe Belzer) (1879–1930) theater troupe, one of the first Yiddish troupes that appeared on the Romanian Yiddish theater scene in the interwar period. They performed mostly in Romania and Austria. Pastor remained an important figure in Romania's Yiddish theater during the communist period.

25 Samuel Fischler (1912–1982) and his wife Sonia Gurman (dates unknown) along with Isac Havis (1910–1991), Beno Popliker (1903–1984), Mano Rippel (1919–1980), Seidy Glück (1922–1997), and Isac Cassvan (dates unknown) were members of the theater company of the Jewish State Theater and among its first generation of actors, who were to define its artistic character. Dina König (1907–1964) was one of the most famous members of the Jewish State Theater. During the sixteen years of her acting career with the Bucharest Yiddish troupe, König played more than fifty different roles. Her daughter Lia Koenig (1929–) was also an actress in the Jewish State Theater prior to her emigration to Israel with her husband, actor Herman (Tzvi) Stolper (1922–1988), in 1961 where she became a prominent performer of the Hebrew-language stage. Rudi Rosenfeld (1941–2018) was a Yiddish and Romanian stage and film actor. He joined the Jewish State Theater in 1961 and played in over eighty plays in Yiddish. Rosenfeld, Carol Marcovici (1938–2006) and Bebe Bercovici (1937–2020) belonged to a younger generation of artists, who began their Yiddish acting careers in the communist period in Romania.

26 The company of the Romanian Jewish State Theater gave guest performances, among other places, in Israel (1968), the United States and Canada (1972), and East Germany (1977). See Corina Petrescu's article on the Israel trip in the present volume.

27 Tambur served for more than twenty-five years in the Romanian army and was discharged in 1972 in the military rank of colonel. On Tambur, see also Binyamin Hunyadi's chapter in the present volume. We were not able to obtain further information on the identity of the Yiddish speaking captain Maler.

פֿראַגע: אין וואָס איז באַשטאַנען אײַער קאָנטאַקט מיט די צוהערער? אויב איר האָט מיט זיי גערעדט בײַם מיקראָפֿאָן איז דאָס געווען אין איין ריכטונג, זיי האָבן דאָך אײַך נישט געקאָנט פֿרעגן? אָדער ענטפֿערן?

ענטפֿער: קודם־כּל איז בײַ אונדז געווען אַן אָפּטייל פֿאַר בריוו־קאָרעספּאָנדענץ פֿאַר אַלע דרײַצן (13) פֿרעמדשפּראַכיקע אוידיציעס. דורך די הענט פֿון דעם אָפּטייל זענען איבערגעגאַנגען צענער־טויזנטער בריוו אַ יאָר פֿון פֿאַרשיידענע לענדער און שפּראַכן. אַזוי ווי ייִדיש האָט נאָך ביזן הײַנטיקן טאָג נישט קיין לאַנד, פֿלעגן מיר באַקומען בריוו פֿון אַזוי גערופֿענעם „ייִדישלאַנד“, דאָס הייסט פֿון פֿאַרשיידענע לענדער ווו ייִדן וווינען. גענויער – פֿון די פֿאַראייניקטע שטאַטן פֿון אַמעריקע, ענגלאַנד, דײַטשלאַנד, ישׂראל, נאָרוועגן. אויך האָבן מיר געהאַט צוהערער אין ווײַטן מזרח פֿון ראַטנפֿאַרבאַנד.

צווישן אונדזערע קאָרעספּאָנדענטן זענען אויך געווען נישט־ייִדן. אַזוי למשל האָט אונדז געשריבן אַ סטודענט פֿון ניו־יאָרק, וועלכער האָט שטודירט די רומענישע שפּראַך און ליטעראַטור אויפֿן ניו־יאָרקער אוניווערסיטעט און איז גלײַכצײַטיק געווען פֿאַרשריבן אויף די קורסן פֿון פּראָפֿעסאָר אוריאל ווײַנרײַך, אויפֿן קאָלומביע־אוניווערסיטעט. דער סטודענט האָט בײַ אונדז געבעטן מאַטעריאַל פֿאַר אַ דאָקטאָראַט איבער דער קאָמעדיע „אַ פֿאַרלוירענער בריוו“ פֿונעם רומענישן קלאַסיקער יאָן לוקאַ קאַראַדזשיאַלע. ווי איבערראַשט זענען מיר געווען ווען ער האָט אונדז געמאָלדן אַז ער וועט אונדז פּערזענלעך באַזוכן. צו דער באַשטימטער דאַטע האָט ער אונדז טעלעפֿאָניש מודיע געווען פֿונעם האָטעל אַז ער קומט צו אונדז אין דער באַגלייטונג פֿון אַ פֿאַרטרעטער פֿונעם בלינד־אינסטיטוט. ווי שרעקלעך באַאײַנדרוקט זענען מיר אָבער געווען ווען מיר האָבן פֿעסטגעשטעלט אַז אונזער ליבער גאַסט איז פֿולשטענדיק בלינד. צו זיבן יאָר איז ער פֿאַראומגליקט געוואָרן און איז שוין צוואַנציק יאָר בלינד. און אין די באַדינגונגען האָט ער נאָך אין זין געהאַט צו קאָפּירן אויף דער טאַשמע אונדזערע ייִדישע אוידיציעס און אײַנאָרדענען הערונגען פֿאַר די סטודענטן, זײַנע קאָלעגן, כּדי זיי זאָלן זיך באַקענען מיט דעם לשון אַזוי ווי מע רעדט עס בכל־תּפֿוצות־האָרץ. שפּעטער מיט אַ צײַט האָב איך דאָס אַלץ געלייענט אין דער ספּעציעלער זײַט פֿאַר ייִדישער שפּראַך און ליטעראַטור אין ניו־יאָרקער „פֿאָרווערטס“. מיר האָבן אים באַשאָנקען מיט שיינע מתּנות, צווישן וועלכע די שענסטע פֿאַר אים איז געווען דאָס אויבנדערמאָנטע ווערק פֿונעם רומענישן קלאַסיקער „אַ פֿאַרלוירענער בריוו“ אין ברייל־שריפֿט. ער האָט גערעדט אַ שיין ייִדיש, נישט זײַענדיק קיין ייִד.

איך וועל אײַך דערציילן פֿון אַן אַנדערן סטודענט מיטן נאָמען קרעבס פֿון דאָרטמונד, מערבֿ־דײַטשלאַנד. ער האָט זייער שיין געשריבן ייִדיש. שטודירנדיק די געשיכטע פֿון ייִדישן טעאַטער, האָט ער בײַ אונדז געבעטן מאַטעריאַל פֿאַר אַ דאָקטאָראַט, דערונטער אַ דינע בראָשור פֿון דר. י[עקבֿ] שאַצקי, וואָס איז אַרויסגעגעבן

Question: How did you communicate with the listeners? When you talked to them through the microphone it was purely one-directional since they couldn't ask any questions or even answer any of yours, right?

Answer: First of all, we had a correspondence department for all thirteen (13) foreign language broadcasts. Tens of thousands of letters from different countries and in different languages were sent to the department. Since Yiddish to this very day has no land of its own, we received letters from the so-called Yiddishland, which means from all the different countries where Jews live. Or to be more precise, mainly from the United States, England, Germany, Israel, and Norway. We even had listeners from the far eastern borders of the Soviet Union.

There were also non-Jews among our correspondents. For example, a student wrote to us from New York who studied Romanian language and literature at New York University. He also signed up to Uriel Weinreich's courses at Columbia University. He asked us to provide him with materials for his doctorate on the comedy *A Lost Letter* by the classic Romanian author, Ion Luca Caragiale.[28] We were completely baffled when he announced his intention of visiting us in person. On the agreed-upon date he phoned us from the hotel and let us know that he was coming in the company of a chaperone from the institute for the blind. We were very impressed when we found out that our honored guest was completely blind. He had an accident when he was seven years old and had been blind for twenty years. And even in these circumstances he had it in himself to record our Yiddish broadcasts on tapes and to organize audio-presentations for his fellow students where they could get acquainted with the language as it is spoken in all the various places of the world. I read about all this later in a special Yiddish language and literature column in the New York paper פֿאָרווערטס [*Forverts*, Jewish Daily Forward].[29] We gave him nice presents, the most impressive of which was the above mentioned classic Romanian work: *A Lost Letter* in Braille. He spoke very beautiful Yiddish without being Jewish.

I want to tell you about another student by the name of Krebs, from Dortmund, West Germany. He wrote Yiddish very beautifully. He was studying the history of Yiddish theater and asked if we could give him materials for a dissertation, including a booklet by Dr. Y[ankev] Shatsky which was

28 The comedy *O scrisoare pierdută* (1883) by the Romanian writer Ion Luca Caragiale (1852–1912) is a parody of the political and social climate of Romania in his time.
29 Article in question could not be located.

געוואָרן נומערירט. (דר. י [עקבֿ] שאַצקי „די ערשטע געשיכטע פֿון יידישן טעאַטער". אונטערטיטל: „צו דר. יצחק שיפּערס ווערק" סעפּאַראַטער אָפּדרוק פֿון די „פּילאָלאָגישע שריפֿטן" פֿון ייִוואָ, באַנד 2 – ווילנע 1928. געדרוקט אין 50 עקזעמפּלאַרן) אין גאַנץ בוקאַרעשט איז געווען איין עקזעמפּלאַר אין דער פּרעכטיקער ביבליאָטעק פֿונעם שרײַבער י[שׂראל] בערקאָוויטש. מיר האָבן זיך אויך אין דעם פֿאַל געווענדט צו י[שׂראל] בערקאָוויטש, וועלכער האָט אונדז אויסגעבאָרגט דאָס ווערק אויף צו שיקן דעם סטודענט, וועלכער האָט עס מיט גרויס דאַנק צוריקגעשיקט נאָכן עקזאַמען.

אין אונדזער מוזיקאַלישן קאָנקורס אויף דער טעמע: „וואָס ווייסט איר וועגן אָנגעזעענסטן רומענישן קאָמפּאָזיטאָר דזש[אָרדזש] ענעסקו?" האָט אַ ייִדישע פֿרוי פֿון ענגלאַנד, אונדזערע אַ געטרײַע צוהערערין, געוווּנען דעם ערשטן פּרײַז.

פֿיל צוהערער האָבן אונדז געשיקט אָפּשאַצונגען וועגן אונדזערע אוידיציעס. באַזונדערס האָט זיי געפֿעלן אונדזער ייִדיש־לשון. זיי האָבן זייער אויסגעלויבט דאָס שיינע קול און לשון פֿון אונדזער רעדאַקטאָרשע־ספּיקערין אַמאַליאַ קראָנענפֿעלד. און מיר האָבן זיך טאַקע געבאָרעט פֿאַרן אָפּהיטן דאָס ייִדישע וואָרט, אַן עסק וואָס איז נישט געווען פֿון די גרינגע זאַכן.

פֿראַגע: ווי לאַנג האָט איר געאַרבעט בײַ די ייִדישע אוידיציעס פֿון רומענישן ראַדיאָ?

ענטפֿער: אַלע 25 יאָר. צען אַלס רעדאַקטאָר־ספּיקער און רעפּאָרטער. די אַנדערע צען יאָר אַלס שעף־רעדאַקטאָר. אין 1969 בין איך אַרויס אויף עמעריטור און געבליבן ביזן סוף אַ שטענדיקער מיטאַרבעטער פֿון די אוידיציעס.

דעם 5טן מאַרץ 1974 האָבן מיר נאָך געיום־טובֿט אַ פֿערטל יאָרהונדערט פֿון אונדזער באַשטאַנד, בײַ פֿײַן געדעקטע טישן, און שוין דעם 20סטן מײַ 1974 – שפּעטער מיט צען וואָכן – האָבן מיר איבערגעגעבן די לעצטע אוידיציע אין ייִדישער שפּראַך. מיר, אַמאַליאַ קראָנענפֿעלד און שלום רובינגער, האָבן זיך נישט מער געזעגנט פֿון אונדזערע צוהערער אַזוי ווי יעדן טאָג מיט: „אויף ווידערהערן מאָרגן אין דער זעלבער צײַט". נאָר פּשוט מיט – „אַ גוטע נאַכט".

איר קאָנט אײַך משער זײַן מיט וואָס פֿאַראַ האַרץ מיר האָבן זיך געזעגנט מיט אונדזערע פֿרײַנד־צוהערער פֿון פֿאַרשיידענע מערידיאַנען, נישט קאָנענדיק זיי זאָגן אַז זיי הערן אונדז צום לעצטן מאָל.

„אַ גוטע נאַכט" איז געווען אונדזער לעצטער גרוס.

published in a small number of numbered copies (Shatsky's first *History of Yiddish Theater*, published in fifty copies with the subtitle *In Recognition of the Works of Dr. Yitskhok Shiper*, an offprint from *Philological Writings*, YIVO, vol. 2, Vilna, 1928). In all Bucharest there was one single copy of this work, in the fantastic library of I[srail] Bercovici, the writer. In this as in many other cases, we turned to I[srail] Bercovici for assistance. He lent us the booklet to send to the student, who returned it back to us after he passed his exams.[30]

We hosted a musical contest on the subject of "How well do you know the preeminent Romanian composer, G[eorge] Enescu?,"[31] and one of our listeners, a Jewish woman from England, won the first prize.

Some listeners would write to tell us what they thought of our programs. They especially enjoyed our Yiddish style. They praised the voice and the eloquence of our editor and host Amalia Kronenfeld. And we really made an effort to preserve Yiddish, which is not an easy task to undertake.

Question: How long did you work for Yiddish broadcasting at the Romanian radio?

Answer: Throughout its twenty-five years of existence. For the first ten years as an editor, host, and reporter. The following ten as an editor-in-chief. In 1969 I retired but remained a regular contributor to the broadcasts to the very end.

On 5 March 1974, we were still able to celebrate the twenty-fifth anniversary of our program with richly laid tables, and a mere ten weeks later, on 20 May 1974, we transmitted our last broadcast in Yiddish. We, the hosts, Amalia Kronenfeld and Sholem Rubinger, didn't close with our usual: "Goodbye, until tomorrow at the same time," but only said "Have a good night."

You can imagine how we felt when we said that final goodbye to our friends and listeners from the different meridians, unable to tell them that they were hearing us for the very last time.

"Have a good night" was our only farewell.

30 Krebs' dissertation could not be located. Yankev Shatsky (1893–1956) was a historian of Polish Jewry, who published most of his studies in Yiddish. Yitskhok Shiper (Ignacy Schiper, 1884–1943), was a historian, who published a history of Yiddish theater in three volumes, see Shiper 1923–1928. A part of Israel Bercovici's library and archives constitutes the Israil Bercovici Estate (Israil Bercovici Nachlass) at the University Library of the University of Potsdam, Germany.

31 George Enescu (1881–1955) was a celebrated Romanian composer and musician. Many of his compositions were inspired by Romanian folk music motifs.

*

די רעדאַקציע דאַנקט דעם אונדז טײַערן חבֿר און מיטאַרבעטער שלום רובינגער פֿאַר דעם אינטערעסאַנטן שמועס. ס'איז פֿאַר אונדז אַ פֿאַרגעניגן פֿאָרצושטעלן דעם לייענער און איינצײַטיק פֿאַרפֿעסטיקן מיט אותיות פֿאַר אַלע די וואָס אינטערעסירן זיך מיט פֿאַרשיידענע פֿאָרמען פֿון ייִדישער קולטור־טעטיקייט, אַ פּעריאָד פֿון 25 יאָר ייִדישע אוידיציעס בײַם רומענישן ראַדיאָ. דאָס געהערט דער געשיכטע און האָט געפֿאָדערט פֿאַרצייכנט צו ווערן אין אַ פּינקס.

ס'איז אַ כּבֿוד פֿאַר אונדזערע העפֿטן צו זײַן די וועלכע טוען דאָס ווי אַן אָנגענעמען חובֿ.

ס'איז אָנגענעם אויך דערמיט ווײַל סע גיט אונדז די געלעגנהייט צו באַגריסן דעם ליבן חבֿר שלום רובינגער צו זײַן 75סטן געבורטסיאָר. מיר ווינטשן אונדזער טײַערן פֿרײַנד אַריכת־ימים און דעם נייטיקן כּוח ווײַטער צו פֿירן מיט דערפֿאָלג די קולטור־טעטיקייט מיט וועלכער ער האָט פֿאַרנומען און פֿאַרנעמט אַ בכּבֿודיקן פּלאַץ אין דער ייִדישער פּען־פֿאַמיליע פֿון רומעניע.

זאָל זײַן נאָמען נישט פֿעלן פֿון אונדזער זאַמלונג „בוקאַרעשטער שריפֿטן“, עד־מאה־ועשׂרים.

די רעדאַקציע

*

The editors thank our dear comrade and colleague Sholem Rubinger for the fascinating interview. It is a great pleasure for us to present to the reader, as well as to put on record for everyone who may be interested in the various forms of Yiddish culture activism, this overview of a period of twenty-five years of Yiddish broadcasting in Romanian national radio. This important chapter of recent history deserves to be noted in our annals.

It is an honor for our journal to be the one to fulfill this task like an enjoyable duty.

This is a particularly happy occasion, as it gives us the opportunity to congratulate our beloved Sholem Rubinger to his 75th birthday and to wish him longevity and the continued energy to carry on his cultural activism, through which he has held, and holds to this day, such an outstanding place in the Yiddish family of penmanship in Romania.

His name should not be absent from the pages of *Bucharest Writings* until his one hundred and 20th birthday.

The editors

Bibliography

Anonymous and Sholem [Sulim] Rubinger, 1983 אַנאָנים און שלום רובינגער: אַ פֿערטל יאָרהונדערט ייִדישע אוידיציעס בײַם רומענישן ראַדיאָ. אין: **בוקאַרעשטער שריפֿטן** (בוקאַרעשט) נ׳ 6: 120–126.

Bercovici, Israil [Yisroel Berkovits], 1974 בערקאָוויטש, ישׂראל: **אין די אויגן פֿון אַ שוואַרצער קאַווע: לידער**. בוקאַרעשט: פֿאַרלאַג קריטעריאָן.

Bercovici, Israil [Yisroel Berkovits], 1976 בערקאָוויטש, ישׂראל: **הונדערט יאָר ייִדיש טעאַטער אין רומעניע, 1876–1976**. בוקאַרעשט: פֿאַרלאַג קריטעריאָן.

Bercovici, Israil [Yisroel Berkovits], 1978 בערקאָוויטש, ישׂראל: **פֿונקען איבער דורות**. בוקאַרעשט: פֿאַרלאַג קריטעריאָן.

Bercovici, Israil [Yisroel Berkovits], 1984 בערקאָוויטש, ישׂראל: **פֿליִענדיקע אותיות**. בוקאַרעשט: פֿאַרלאַג קריטעריאָן.

Blits, Tsalel, 1961 בליץ, צאַלעל [שמואל־איסר כּהנא]: **אַ רײַזע צו אונדזערע ווייטיק און צו אונדזער פֿרייד**. בוענאָס־אײַרעס: איקוף.

I[osif], M[ira], 1977: Teatrul Evreiesc de Stat: Dictatorul de Al. In: *Teatrul* 7: 44.

Kara, Y. [Itsik Shvarts], 1976 קאַראַ, י. [איציק שוואַרץ]: **אַ מאָלדאַוויש ייִנגל**. בוקאַרעשט: פֿאַרלאַג קריטעריאָן.

Kara, Y. [Itsik Shvarts], 1980 קאַראַ, י. [איציק שוואַרץ]: **יונגע יאָרן... ווײניקער יונגע**. בוקאַרעשט: פֿאַרלאַג קריטעריאָן.

KARA, Y. [Itsik Shvarts], 1987 קאַראַ, י. [איציק שוואַרץ]: **יאָרן פֿון האָפֿענונג**. בוקאַרעשט: פֿאַרלאַג קריטעריאָן.

SMOLYAR, Hersh, 1978 סמאָליאַר, הערש: **פֿון אינעווייניק. זכרונות וועגן דער „יעווסעקציע"**. תּל־אָבֿיבֿ: פֿאַרלאַג י.ל. פּרץ.

Discography

SCHWARTZMAN, Haim [Khayim Shvartsman), 1958. *Musică populară evreiască.* Bukarest: Electrecord.

SCHWARTZMAN, Haim [Khayim Shvartsman), 196?. *Selecțiuni din operetele lui Goldfaden.* **לידער פֿון גאָלדפֿאַדנס אָפּערעטן**. Bukarest: Electrecord.

SCHWARTZMAN, Haim [Khayim Shvartsman), 1974. *A Nigndl: Cântece din folclorul evreiesc.* **לידער פֿון ייִדישן פֿאָלקלאָר**. Bukarest: Electrecord.

Contributors

Malena Chinski holds a PhD in Social Sciences from the National University of General Sarmiento and the Institute of Economic and Social Development (IDES) in Argentina. Her doctoral dissertation addressed *khurbn* commemoration within the Jewish community of Buenos Aires during the first postwar decade. She completed a postdoctoral stay in France at the École des Hautes Études en Sciences Sociales with support from the Fondation pour la mémoire de la Shoah. Her current research topics include the reconstruction of Yiddish culture in Paris in the immediate postwar period, the itineraries of surviving Yiddish writers and scholars from Eastern Europe, and memories of the Shoah in the communist Parisian Yiddish press. Among other publications, she has co-edited with Alan Astro the volume *Splendor, Decline, and Rediscovery of Yiddish in Latin America* (Brill, 2018). Currently, she is Yiddish instructor at the YIVO Institute for Jewish research and the Maison de la culture yiddish – Bibliothèque Medem.

Miriam Chorley-Schulz (née Schulz) is Assistant Professor and Mokin Fellow of Holocaust Studies at the University of Oregon and the co-founder of the EU-funded project *We Refugees. Digital Archive on Refugeedom, Past and Present* (https://en.we-refugees-archive.org/). She holds a PhD in Yiddish Studies from Columbia University and was the Ray D. Wolfe Postdoctoral Fellow at the Centre of Jewish Studies and the Centre of Transnational and Diaspora Studies at the University of Toronto. Among other publications, Miriam is the author of *Der Beginn des Untergangs: Die Zerstörung der jüdischen Gemeinden in Polen und das Vermächtnis des Wilnaer Komitees* (Metropol, 2016) which was awarded the Hosenfeld / Szpilman Memorial Award.

Gennady Estraikh is a professor at the Skirball Department of Hebrew and Judaic Studies, New York University. From 1988 to 1991 he worked as the Managing Editor of the Moscow Yiddish journal סאָוועטיש היימלאַנד [*Sovetish heymland*, Soviet Homeland]. His doctoral dissertation on peculiarities of Soviet Yiddish was defended at the University of Oxford in 1996. Between 1995 and 2002 he worked at the Oxford Institute for Yiddish Studies and at the School of Oriental and African Studies in London. His most recent books are *Transatlantic Russian Jewishness: Ideological Voyages of the Yiddish Daily Forverts in the First Half of the Twentieth Century* (Academic Studies Press, 2020), *Jews in the Soviet Union: A History: After Stalin, 1953–1967* (NYU Press, 2022), and *The History of Birobidzhan: Building a Soviet Jewish Homeland in Siberia* (Bloomsbury Academic, 2023).

Katharina Friedla is a Research Fellow and the Taube Family Curator for European Collections at the Hoover Institution Library & Archives at Stanford University. She has studied History, East European and Jewish Studies at the Free University in Berlin, the Hebrew University of Jerusalem, and received her PhD from the Department of History, University of Basel, Switzerland. Dr. Friedla has published several books and dozens of articles on nationalism, identity politics, and forced migration with a special focus on European Jewry. Most recently, she co-edited two volumes, including *Polish Jews in the Soviet Union (1939–1959): History and Memory of Deportation, Exile, and Survival* (Academic Studies Press, 2021).

Binyamin Hunyadi holds a PhD in Yiddish Studies from the Hebrew University of Jerusalem. Currently, he is a research assistant at the "Index to Yiddish Periodicals" project by Beit Sholem Aleichem at the National Library of Israel. He is working on a book manuscript on Yiddish anarchist press and literature in London and New York in 1890–1918.

Kamil Kijek is an Assistant Professor at the Department of Jewish Studies at the University of Wrocław, Poland. He was a Prins Foundation Postdoctoral Fellow at the Center for Jewish History in New York, Sosland Family Fellow at the Jack, Joseph and Morton Mandel Center for Advanced Holocaust Studies at the United States Holocaust Memorial Museum in Washington, D.C., held various fellowships in Israel, Germany, and the United Kingdom. He has published articles in *Jewish Social Studies*, *Polin*, *Gal-Ed* and *Journal of Modern European History*, co-edited four books on the history of Jews in Poland and Eastern Europe, most recently with Katerina Capkova *Jewish Lives Under Communism. New Perspectives* (Rutgers University Press, 2022). His *Modern and Radical. Political Consciousness, Culture and Socialization of Jewish Youth in Interwar Poland* will be published soon by Indiana University Press.

Corina L. Petrescu is Professor of German at the University of Mississippi. She is an accredited researcher with the National Council for the Study of the Securitate Archives (CNSAS) in Romania. Over the years, her research has been supported both by the Alexander von Humboldt and Fulbright foundations. Most recently, she is the co-editor with Valentina Glajar and Alison Lewis of *Cold War Spy Stories from Eastern Europe* (Potomac Books, 2019).

Alexandra Polyan is a postdoctoral researcher at the Institute of Slavistik, Department of Slavic-Jewish studies at the University of Regensburg, where she works under the supervision of Professor Dr. Sabine Koller. She is also an Associate Professor at the Institute of Asian and African Studies, Department of Jewish Studies at Moscow State University. Since 2020, she has been a member of "The Short Life of Soviet Yiddish Literature" research group. Her project is entitled "Return of the Violence: The Case of Perets Markish." Together with Sabine Koller, she published the German edition of Dovid Bergelson's writings *Die Welt möge Zeuge sein* (Suhrkamp, 2023). Polyan has authored approximately thirty-five articles and two co-authored books, including *Русско-еврейский Берлин: 1920 – 1941* [Russian-Jewish Berlin: 1920–1941] (Moscow: Новое литературное обозрение, 2013) together with Oleg Budnitskii. She is also a Yiddish instructor and translator.

Jalda Rebling is a cantor and actor. She graduated from the Hochschule für Schauspielkunst Ernst Busch in 1972 and grew up with the Yiddish songs of her mother Lin Jaldati, a *khurbn*-survivor. Between 1978 and 1988, Rebling and Jaldati performed together around the world from Jerusalem to New York. From 1987 to 1997, she organized the UNESCO-project Tage der Jiddischen Kultur [Days of Yiddish Culture] and, between 1993 and 2006, co-created Jiddisches LiedTheater [Yiddish SongTheater] at Hackesches Hoftheater in Berlin. Since the fall of the Berlin wall, Rebling has been an active member of both the Berlin Jewish artists group Meshulash and the first egalitarian synagogue in Berlin, the Synagogue Oranienburger Straße. She has produced LPs and CDs with Yiddish, Sephardic, and Jewish Medieval poetry and songs. Rebling received her *smikha* [rabbinic ordination] from Aleph Alliance for Jewish Renewal in 2007 and serves as the director of studies of the European Academy for Jewish Liturgy in London today.

Alexander Walther studied English and history to become a secondary school teacher at Friedrich Schiller University Jena. He received his doctorate from the University of Jena in 2023 with a study on the historical-cultural confrontation with the *khurbn* in the GDR. From 2021–2023, he worked as a project coordinator and research assistant at the University of Erfurt as part of the research network "Dictatorship Experience and Transformation." Since November 2023, he has been a research assistant at the State Museum of Archaeology Chemnitz and is preparing a year of Jewish culture in Saxony for 2026. His publications include: "Commemorating the Shoah in the GDR's (Post-)Perpetrator Society." In: *The Afterlife of the Shoah in Central and Eastern European Cultures. Concepts, Problems, and the Aesthetics of Postcatastrophic Narration*, eds. Anja Tippner and Anna Artwińska. London: Routledge, 2022, 173–191; "Helmut Eschwege and Jewish Life in the German Democratic Republic." In: *Rebuilding Jewish Life in Germany*, eds. Jay Geller and Michael Meng. New Brunswick, NJ: Rutgers University Press, 2020, 101–117; "Jewish Anti-Fascism? 'Kristallnacht' Remembrance in the GDR between Propaganda and Jewish Self-Assertion." In: *New Perspectives on Kristallnacht: After 80 Years, the Nazi Pogrom in Global Comparison*, eds. Wolf Gruner, and Steven J. Ross. West Lafayette, Ind.: Purdue University Press, 2019, 259–282.

Agniezska Żółkiewska holds a PhD and is a historian of literature, translator from Yiddish, and a researcher at the Emanuel Ringelblum Jewish Historical Institute in Warsaw as well as Gierowski & Shmeruk Prize laureate. Her publications include translations and commentary of Yiddish poetry from the *khurbn* (*Słowa pośród nocy. Poetyckie dokumenty Holokaustu* [Words in the Midst of Night. Poetic documents of the Holocaust], 2012) and a study of the postwar Jewish intelligentsia in Poland (*Zerwana przeszłość. Powojenne środowisko inteligencji twórczej. Pomoc materialna i organizacyjna ze strony CKŻP* [The broken past. The postwar environment of the creative intelligentsia. Material and organizational assistance from the CKŻP], 2017). She is also one of the translators and editors of the complete edition of the Ringelblum Archive in Polish. Since 2018 she has taken part in a long-term scientific project, which aims to create a virtual encyclopedia of the Warsaw Ghetto.